MARKETING STRATEGY AND UNCERTAINTY

MARKETING STRATEGY AND UNCERTAINTY

SHARAN JAGPAL

WITHDRAWN

NEW YORK • OXFORD
OXFORD UNIVERSITY PRESS
1999

Oxford University Press

Oxford   New York
Athens   Auckland   Bangkok   Bogotá   Buenos Aires   Calcutta
Cape Town   Chennai   Dar es Salaam   Delhi   Florence   Hong Kong   Istanbul
Karachi   Kuala Lumpur   Madrid   Melbourne   Mexico City   Mumbai
Nairobi   Paris   São Paulo   Singapore   Taipei   Tokyo   Toronto   Warsaw

and associated companies in
Berlin   Ibadan

Published by Oxford University Press, Inc.
198 Madison Avenue, New York, New York 10016

Oxford is a registered trademark of Oxford University Press

Library of Congress Cataloging-in-Publication Data

Jagpal, Sharan, 1947–
    Marketing strategy and uncertainty / Sharan Jagpal.
        p.   cm.
    Includes bibliographical references and index.
    ISBN 0-19-512573-8 (paper)
    1. Marketing.   2. Strategic planning.   3. Marketing—Management.
    4. Decision-making in marketing.   I. Title.
    HF5415.J33   1998
    658.8'02—dc21   98-16307
                                                          CIP

Printing (last digit): 9 8 7 6 5 4 3 2 1
Printed in the United States of America
on acid-free paper

Dedicated to my Parents

Classical microeconomics analyzes a highly stylized hypothetical firm. In the competitive theory a product, its price, and a cost function are given. In the monopolistic theory, a demand curve is added. In this context there is no question as to the design of the product, including tradeoff between cost and features, nor question about levels and methods of advertising to shift the demand curve, or the use of a direct sales force, or consumer research to estimate the likely results of product redesign and advertising, and so on. In short, most or all the interesting marketing questions are assumed away by the classical microeconomic models.

In this volume Professor Jagpal presents and analyzes models of the firm in which one or another aspect of marketing is at the forefront. In general, Professor Jagpal's approach is from the simple to the complex. For a given aspect of marketing, he will typically begin by analyzing a model that assumes certainty, then proceed to models that allow uncertainty. With respect to uncertainty, Professor Jagpal derives both an expected utility solution and a stock value maximization solution. In the former he assumes essentially that the firm belongs to a utility-maximizing entrepreneur; in the latter he assumes that corporate management seeks to maximize the value of the firm's stock in a CAPM (capital asset pricing model) world. In line with the objective of moving from simple to more complex models, an analysis assuming certainty (or expected utility maximization or stock value maximization) frequently starts with a one-period analysis, then moves to the many-period analysis; or starts by considering one aspect of marketing and later adds other aspects; or by assuming certainty of parameters in the random case, then considers the problems of estimation and measurement.

Professor Jagpal thus provides us with an extensive buffet of economic models and their solutions, all oriented towards one or more aspects of marketing decision making.

The models are presented at two levels: the text level and the note level. The text level confines itself to verbal and graphical arguments, and verbal summaries of the results derived analytically in the notes. The note level presents the formal models and their solutions.

While Professor Jagpal explores deeply and extensively in many directions, there is always more that could be done in any direction. Professor Jagpal advises us of desirable areas of future research, in the final chapter and elsewhere.

The text level of this book provides an introductory textbook on rational decision making in marketing. The note level, in addition to providing proofs and further references, may be considered as a source book for analysts with mathematical training who would like to see examples where mathematical analysis has been applied, and where further analysis might be of practical value. Such analysis seems to be more common in finance than in marketing, including the mathematical theory of investment and the theory of corporate finance. But there is no reason why there should be such an asymmetry in the treatment of the two subjects. Both corporate finance theory and marketing theory may be thought of as aspects of some detailed theory of the firm yet to be worked out. Professor Jagpal's pioneering book moves us forward towards such a detailed, integrated theory of the firm.

Harry Markowitz

This book deals with marketing strategy and uncertainty. Specifically, it develops analytical models that show the manager how to choose marketing strategy to maximize the firm's long-term performance. In order to provide a comprehensive treatment, the firm's long-term performance is measured using both the expected utility (popular in economics) and stock value (popular in finance) frameworks. From a managerial viewpoint, the book emphasizes analytical models that can be empirically operationalized.

Several themes permeate the work. Marketing theorists and practitioners must develop models that explicitly recognize that most firms are owned by stockholders who can diversify risk across firms; in contrast, the firm's employees (for example, the sales force) have limited diversification opportunities and cannot eliminate firm-specific risk. Because of these organizational realities, it is necessary to develop marketing models that use both portfolio theory developed by Markowitz (1952,1959) and capital asset pricing theory developed by Sharpe (1964), Lintner (1965), Mossin (1966), Ross (1976), and others.

In order to provide meaningful prescriptions for marketing and corporate strategy, we must develop multiproduct models that allow for economies of scope, uncertainty, dynamic effects (for example, learning over time by consumers and firms), and asymmetric information among the firm and its employees (for example, the sales force may be better informed about market conditions than the firm is).

Analytical and empirical marketing models must pay increased attention to heterogeneity among economic players (i.e., firms and consumers). In particular, new empirical methods are necessary in consumer behavior because heterogeneity is both multidimensional and unobservable.

Marketing and strategic planning at both the domestic and international levels must recognize the economic value of flexibility in decision making (for example, the economic value of being able to drop an unsuccessful new product or of being able to develop new market segments if a new product is successful in the targeted segment).

To deal with the problem of reader heterogeneity I have written the book at two levels, recognizing that there are two market segments: the general reader and the specialist. In order to appeal to the general reader, I have relied heavily on verbal reasoning, graphs, and numerical examples. In order to provide more information to the specialist or researcher, I have added detailed technical notes that can be skipped on the first reading. I have attempted throughout to emphasize intuition and readability over mathematical rigor.

Much of the material in this book is new. The following is a brief summary.

Chapters 1 and 2 focus on the firm's pricing decision. Chapter 1 examines the simultaneous effects of demand and cost dynamics (e.g., the learning or experience curve) on strategic pricing. In particular, we analyze the simultaneous impact of input and output uncertainty on the firm's dynamic pricing and investment decisions for different combinations of input and output market structures (i.e., monopolistic or competitive).

Chapter 2 focuses on pricing under heterogeneity and uncertainty. We propose analytical models for multiperiod decision making under uncertainty, develop models for measuring the effectiveness of coupons in single-period and multiperiod frameworks, and propose an empirical methodology for analyzing bundling strategies and classifying consumers according to whether their reservation prices for different products are additive, subadditive, or superadditive.

Chapters 3 and 4 focus on consumer behavior, paying particular attention to behavioral theory, the unobservability of consumers' decision processes, consumer heterogeneity along several dimensions, and measurement error (an endemic problem in survey data).

Chapter 3 extends the standard Lancasterian model of demand by explicitly incorporating (heterogeneous) consumer perceptions and develops a hybrid model that combines standard utility theory and reference pricing theory (an offshoot of Kahneman and Tversky's Prospect Theory, 1979). In addition, the chapter evaluates standard analytical models of consumer demand under uncertainty and proposes extensions.

Chapter 4 begins by evaluating the extant empirical literature on measuring consumer demand (e.g., conjoint analysis, choice models, cluster analysis, confirmatory factor analysis, and stochastic multidimensional scaling). We show that the random-coefficient methodology can be used to capture heterogeneity along several dimensions simultaneously. In particular, the random-coefficient model allows for heterogeneous and unobservable consumer information-processing strategies (e.g., conjunctive and disjunctive models), idiosyncratic and imperfect interpretations of the assigned preference scale by consumers, and general types of heterogeneity in preference. We propose a random-coefficient mixture model for capturing heterogeneity when a priori market segmentation is infeasible and consumers within a segment are heterogeneous; in particular, we show that this model generalizes previous statistical methods (e.g., cluster analysis) by simultaneously allowing for the general types of consumer heterogeneity mentioned previously.

Chapter 4 concludes by proposing an integrated preference model that includes standard methods (e.g., conjoint analysis, confirmatory factor methods, and stochastic multidimensional scaling) as special cases. In particular, we show how marketers can use the integrated model to explicate the consumer's decision process and to estimate the relationship between product design and preference while simultaneously allowing for unobservable heterogeneity and uncertain perceptions. Economists can apply the model to analyze "real-life" (i.e., nonexperimental) data and to test multiattribute theories of risk aversion when the payoffs are both subjective and stochastic. Marketers can use the methodology to improve marketing decision making by forming market segments according to whether consumers are multivariate risk-neutral, risk-averse, or risk-seeking.

Chapter 5 deals with the problem of coordinating the pricing structure in a multilevel channel of distribution (e.g., a distribution system where the product passes from the manufacturer to the consumer via a retailer). We focus on evaluating the profitability of a new product introduction in a multiproduct and multiperiod context. In particular, we emphasize the strategic role of cannibalization at both the manufacturer and retailer levels and the importance of segmenting retailers according to their cost of capital.

Chapters 6 and 7 analyze the firm's advertising decision from a theoretical and an empirical perspective. Chapter 6 focuses on the aggregate advertising decision and on co-ordinating the price–advertising decision under uncertainty. Chapter 7 takes a disaggregate perspective and examines the firm's media message and media mix decisions.

In Chapter 6 we use both the expected utility (EU) and multiperiod capital asset pricing models (CAPM) to develop normative multiperiod and multiproduct models of advertising for the monopolist facing uncertainty. We generalize the Nerlove–Arrow (1962) model to the case where demand is fully stochastic (i.e., the firm's price and advertising policies can have a differential effect on demand uncertainty over the product life cycle). We use the EU and CAPM valuation frameworks to develop a duopoly advertising model where demand is uncertain. We propose empirical methods for operationalizing a multiproduct advertising goodwill model in a stochastic and dynamic environment. We propose a simple anchoring model for extending the standard econometric methodology by incorporating asymmetric effects of increases and decreases in advertising in a fully nonlinear advertising model. In particular, we show how the firm can use this approach to determine whether a "pulsing" advertising strategy (i.e., patterns of the sort advertise in period 1, do not advertise in periods 2 and 3, advertise in period 4, etc.) is optimal.

Chapter 7 evaluates the extant literature on media planning and media message selection and proposes future research directions. In addition, we develop a simple multiperiod model using both the EU and multiperiod CAPM frameworks to explain why national television advertising rates fluctuate cyclically.

Chapter 8 examines the firm's compensation decision. We show that analytical models must be supplemented by empirical methods for measuring agents' unobserved ability and tracking changes in ability both cross-sectionally and over time. Although we present the theory in the context of the sales force compensation problem, the theory applies to the design of compensation plans for other individuals in the organization, including senior management.

We develop compensation models for the multiproduct, multiagent firm that faces uncertainty. We develop an analytical model for compensating agents in a multiproduct, multilevel firm (e.g., a hierarchically organized firm in which divisional managers supervise district managers who, in turn, supervise sales agents). In particular, we examine how uncertainty affects the firm's decision to delegate authority to change prices and sales call policies.

We develop dynamic compensation models in which the current level of personal selling has a stochastic effect on future demand. In particular, we show that firms should use measures of consumer satisfaction (an unobservable quantity) in the compensation plan even if these measures are imprecise. We propose empirical methods for obtaining accurate measures of satisfaction from survey data, even if satisfaction is multidimensional.

We develop a model for determining the optimal level of training by the firm when the effects of training are uncertain. In particular, the model distinguishes between firm-specific and portable training and specifically incorporates the effect of sales force turnover.

We develop a multiproduct, multiagent model of compensation that allows for general patterns of stochastic interdependence among the firm's products. The analytical framework uses capital asset pricing theory and is consistent with the multibeta model (Sharpe 1977) and the multifactor arbitrage pricing theory (Ross 1976).

We propose empirical models for personnel selection and measuring a sales agent's unobservable ability (skill). In particular, we develop a hybrid regression/confirmatory factor analysis model for using individual-level sales data (which are routinely collected by the firm) in the multiproduct firm to track salespersons' unobservable abilities over time. We show how the firm can use the empirical results for planning, resource allocation, and control at different levels (including the level of senior management in multidivisional firms), and for revising the agent's compensation plan over time based on new market-level information regarding that agent's productivity.

Chapter 9 analyzes several popular managerial propositions in domestic and international strategy. We examine whether the firm should choose a diversified product line in order to be less susceptible to such industry-wide shocks in the future as the unanticipated arrival of a new technology or an unexpected decline in demand. We present new empirical evidence on whether mergers, acquisitions, strategic alliances, and new product announcements or preannouncements add value to the firm. We review the economic theory of whether firms should market high-quality products to maximize performance and present new empirical evidence. We analyze the likely impact of the information superhighway on market structure and marketing policy. We show that, given the speed with which markets are changing (on both the technology and the demand sides), current stock prices are an imperfect guide to the firm's long-run performance. Specifically, because of informational asymmetry (recall that for competitive reasons senior managers cannot inform the stock market about all the firm's strategic options), it is essential for firms to use a deferred compensation plan for senior management to encourage them to maximize the firm's long-term performance.

We analyze whether multinational firms should pursue global marketing strategies and discuss the special problems that multinationals face in designing compensation plans for country managers and measuring their performance. We argue that the multinational firm should not follow a uniform compensation plan for its country managers. In particular, we propose that the multinational should follow a customized compensation policy for country managers and show how this policy should vary across countries depending on market risk, the economic value of the multinational's strategic options in different countries, and whether the multinational delegates the debt decision of the subsidiary to the country manager in order to take advantage of imperfections in the international capital market.

Chapter 10 discusses areas in which future research is necessary.

ACKNOWLEDGMENTS

I would like to thank my former teachers, Professors Ed Mishan (formerly of the London School of Economics) and Donald G. Morrison of UCLA, for teaching me academic values and for encouraging me to become a "doubting Thomas." I owe special thanks to Harry Markowitz for his advice and for encouraging me over the past 15 years to attempt to develop an integrated approach to marketing decision making.

The staff at Oxford University Press were extremely helpful. In particular, I wish to thank Kenneth MacLeod for his thoughtful comments and enthusiastic support. I also gratefully acknowledge the invaluable help of Karen Shapiro, Jacki Hartt, and Roger Duthie.

I would like to acknowledge the following reviewers: Pete Nye, Donald G. Morrison, Jehoshua Eliashberg, Poondi Varadarajan, and Naufel J. Vilcassim.

I deeply thank my family for their continuing encouragement throughout this project, for their indulgence, and for tolerating my numerous social lapses. My daughter, Shireen, and my sister, Ravindar Jagpal M.D., proofread the manuscript and provided useful suggestions. I owe a special debt to my wife, Mohini Jagpal, for her painstaking effort in typing and proofreading the entire manuscript. (I now understand firsthand why the standard measures of Gross Domestic Product understate social welfare.)

Caveats and Disclaimers

In order to minimize distractions to the reader, I refer to comprehensive review articles wherever possible and only provide a limited set of references. If I have failed to give credit to previous scholars the omission is purely accidental. The usual caveat applies: I am solely responsible for all errors.

Strategic Pricing in a Dynamic Environment

Pricing is a fundamental marketing tool. The firm's current price can affect future demand; for example, a low introductory price for a nondurable consumer product can stimulate future demand by encouraging repeat purchase. Similarly, the firm's pricing strategy for a new durable product is likely to affect future demand by influencing word-of-mouth activity, the future market potential, or both. The firm's cost structure also evolves over time when learning effects exist (i.e., the firm's future cost structure depends on the firm's current pricing policy). In a dynamic environment both cost and demand are uncertain over time and are subject to industry-specific and macroeconomic shocks. Consequently the firm must coordinate its investment and input purchase decisions with its marketing policy.

This chapter analyzes the firm's strategic pricing decision in a dynamic environment for different scenarios of cost and demand interdependence, distinguishing the deterministic and stochastic cases. To focus on essentials we shall assume that price is the only controllable marketing variable.

1.1 BASIC PRICING CONCEPTS

The pricing decision depends on the nature of the product, whether or not there is strategic interdependence among competitors, and the firm's planning period. Suppose the firm has already chosen the product design and the market is competitive. Now there is only one market price (say $10 per unit) because all firms' product offerings are undifferentiated. Thus if the firm charges a price higher than $10 per unit, its sales will be zero. If the firm charges a price lower than $10 per unit, other firms will be forced to match the price cut or lose all their business. Thus the firm cannot choose prices that deviate from the market equilibrium price.

> ***Key Point*** *Price is not a marketing tool when the firm operates in an industry with undifferentiated products. This result, however, does not imply that marketing is irrelevant. On the contrary, the demand for a particular firm's product will depend heavily on such firm-specific marketing features as prompt delivery and good service.*

Suppose the firm has not chosen the product design and the industry is competitive. Competitive equilibrium implies that the law of one price holds: There is one price for each product design. The firm's decision on product design is now straightforward: Examine the cost structure for each feasible product design and choose that design and associated market price which maximizes profit. Note that the firm cannot choose the product design and price independently; the law of one price prevents the firm from using price as a strategic tool.

> ***Key Point*** *The law of one price prevails in a competitive market. The firm chooses product design on the basis of the cost structure of producing different qualities and the prevailing market prices for products with different attributes. As in the case of undifferentiated products, price is not a strategic tool.*

We now consider the case of a firm selling a differentiated product. For convenience we make the following assumptions: (1) There is no strategic interdependence (i.e., the firm behaves as a monopolist and ignores competitive reaction); (2) product design is fixed; (3) the firm has a one-period planning horizon, and (4) there is no uncertainty. Now, in contrast to our previous examples, price is a strategic tool.

Suppose the firm's demand curve is DD (see Figure 1.1a). Note that DD is downward sloping: The firm must reduce price in order to sell more units.

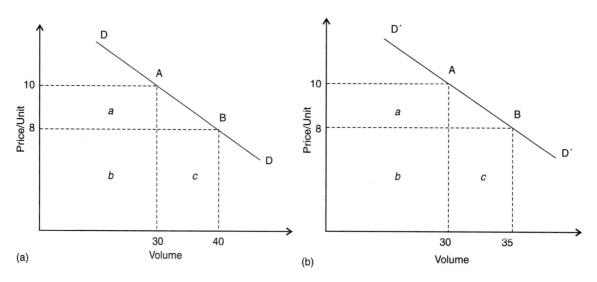

Figure 1.1a, b The price–volume relationship: Two scenarios.

Suppose the firm charges a price of $10 per unit. Then the firm sells 30 units and receives a revenue of $300 (Area *a* + Area *b*). If the firm reduces price to $8 per unit, the volume sold will be 40 units and the revenue will be $320 (Area *b* + Area *c*). In this case a price cut increases revenue: We say that the market is price-sensitive. Note that price-cutting is a double-edged sword: The firm loses Area *a* but gains Area *c*. In our example, Area *a* is $60 and represents a bonus to those consumers who were willing to pay $10 per unit for 30 units but now pay only $8 per unit as a result of the price cut. We say that the price cut provides a consumer surplus of $60 to existing consumers. Area *c* ($80) represents the firm's gain in revenue from new customers or increased purchase volume by existing customers. Hence the net effect of the price reduction is to increase revenue by $20 (Area *c* minus Area *a*). We say that the marginal revenue resulting from the price cut is $20.

Suppose the firm faces the demand curve shown in Figure 1.1b. Now the effect of the price cut from $10 to $8 per unit is to reduce revenue from $300 to $280; that is, the marginal revenue resulting from the price cut is −$20. Note that revenue falls because the revenue generated from new business (Area *c*) is less than the consumer surplus returned to existing customers at the higher price (Area *a*). We say that demand is not price-sensitive.

> **Key Point**   *The effect of a price cut consists of two opposite effects: (1) consumer surplus returned to consumers who are willing to buy at the higher price; and (2) additional revenue generated from new business. If (1) exceeds (2), marginal revenue is negative; that is, the market is not price-sensitive.*

We can now analyze those conditions when a price cut is feasible. In Figure 1.1b the marginal revenue corresponding to a price cut from $10 to $8 is −$20. Recall that total cost necessarily increases when volume increases (i.e., price is cut). Hence profits fall because of two effects: reduced revenue and increased cost. In Figure 1.1a the marginal revenue for the price cut from $10 to $8 is $20, which is positive. Hence the price reduction will increase profit provided the marginal cost of the increase in volume is less than $20.

> **Key Point**   *The firm cannot operate at a point on the demand curve where demand is price-insensitive (i.e., marginal revenue is negative).*

In order to determine the profit-maximizing price, we need to know the precise form of the demand function and the cost structure. Suppose demand is given by $q = 20 - p/4$, where q denotes volume and p the unit price, the fixed cost is $100, and the variable cost is $16 per unit. Table 1.1 shows the volumes, revenues, costs, and profits for different pricing decisions. Suppose we start from a price of $52 per unit and reduce price to $50 per unit. Profit increases from $152 to $155, a net increase of $3 ($\Delta\pi$). Note that the change in profit is the sum of two effects: a gain in revenue of $11 (revenue increases from $364 to $375) and a loss of $8 (cost increases from $212 to $220). Thus profit increases as a result of the price cut because marginal revenue exceeds marginal cost. Note that the marginal cost is the difference between two total cost figures and is therefore independent of fixed cost. Proceeding similarly, we see that profit increases to $156 if price is reduced to $48 per unit. If, however, price is further reduced to $46 per unit, profit falls to $155. The reason is that

Table 1-1 Choosing the Optimal Pricing Plan

Unit Price (p) (In Dollars)	Quantity (q)	Revenue (R) (In Dollars)	Total Cost (C) (In Dollars)	Profit ($\pi = R - C$) (In Dollars)
52	7.0	364	212	152
50	7.5	375	220	155
48*	8.0	384	228	156*
46	8.5	391	236	155
44	9.0	396	244	152
42	9.5	399	252	147
40	10.0	400	260	140
38	10.5	399	268	131
36	11.0	396	276	120

Note: * denotes the optimal policy.

marginal revenue ($391 − $384 = 7) is smaller than marginal cost ($236 − $228 = 8). Hence the profit-maximizing price is $48 per unit.

Key Point   *Profit-maximizing requires the firm to set marginal revenue equal to marginal cost. If marginal revenue exceeds marginal cost, price should be lowered. If marginal cost exceeds marginal revenue, price should be raised. Fixed costs do not affect marginal costs and are therefore irrelevant for pricing decisions.*[1]

1.2 MARKET SHARE AND STRATEGIC PRICING

Suppose management maximizes market share (see Table 1.1). Then the optimal policy is to charge a price of $40 per unit in order to maximize sales revenue and hence market share. Note that maximizing share and maximizing profit are mutually incompatible: The former policy requires setting price so that marginal revenue is zero, whereas the latter policy requires equating marginal revenue and marginal cost (a positive quantity). Thus marginal revenue is necessarily positive when the firm maximizes profit. Consequently a price reduction will always increase market share.

Key Point   *Maximizing profit and maximizing market share are inconsistent objectives. Market-share maximization always leads to a lower price than profit maximization.*

This conclusion appears to conflict with common business practice and strategic planning models that place heavy emphasis on market share. This problem can be approached from two angles: empirical and theoretical. Let us consider the empirical arguments first.

There is strong empirical evidence that market share and profitability are positively related. Furthermore, changes in market share are positively related to changes in profitability.

On the surface these findings appear to provide strong support for using market share as a proxy for profitability. There are, however, several flaws in the argument. First, we need to recognize that the sample data are censored; that is, we do not observe the history of unsuccessful (inefficient) firms. Unless success is random (a conclusion we must reject if we believe that marketing is a meaningful activity!), the observed market data cannot be representative of all firms in the industry. Consequently the measured relationship between market share and profitability is tautological; successful firms are profitable "because" they have high market share! Second, it may be incorrect to assert that market share causes profitability. If good firms segment their markets carefully, both market share and profitability will be high. Thus market share and profitability are *both* caused by good market planning; in particular, market share does not cause profitability.

Let us now consider some theoretical arguments in favor of building market share. One popular argument is that market share is a good criterion provided the market is growing rapidly. Given no other conditions (discussed later), this argument is incorrect. Consider the following simple example. A regional firm produces roof shingles. Suppose demand is growing (e.g., there is a net influx of population into the region). For simplicity, suppose that the firm has a two-period planning horizon. Thus the firm chooses prices in periods 1 and 2 to maximize the net present value of profits defined by $V = \pi_1/(1+\delta) + \pi_2/(1+\delta)^2$, where π_1 and π_2, respectively, denote profits in periods 1 and 2 and δ denotes the firm's cost of capital. Now the demand for shingles in any period depends on the price for shingles in that period and the population in that period. Because population is increasing over time, the market is growing. Given these conditions, the demand (and hence profit) in period 2 does not depend on the price charged in period 1. Consequently maximizing net present value V is equivalent to maximizing each short-term profit (π_1 and π_2) separately. In particular, maximizing market share in period 1 is suboptimal.

Key Point *Growth per se does not justify a market-share-building strategy. The optimal long-term strategy is to maximize each short-term profit stream separately, provided there is no strategic interdependence in demand over time (i.e., past prices have no effect on current demand).*

Note that if demand shifts are exogenous (i.e., outside the control of the firm), the price in period 1 does not affect profits in period 2. As a result the long-run pricing problem is equivalent to a series of short-run decisions: Strategic pricing had no role even though the market is growing.

Under what conditions does strategic pricing become relevant? Three scenarios are possible.

First, suppose there is a learning effect in production (i.e., the cost of production in any period depends on accumulated production or "experience"). Suppose the firm charges a price in period 1 to maximize short-term profit. This pricing plan—known as *myopic pricing*—may be inferior to charging a lower price in the first period in order to lower future costs and hence increase future profits. We shall refer to this experience-curve scenario as *cost dynamics*. Note that the pricing problem is now strategic because the price in the current period affects future profitability.

Second, suppose the demand in period 2 depends on the price in period 1. For example, consider the introduction of a new, frequently purchased product. If the introductory (i.e., period 1) price is low, the trial rate (i.e., the proportion of the market that tries the product) will be high. Some of these triers will repurchase the product in period 2 depending on their product usage experience and the price in period 2. In addition, some new consumers will try the product in period 2 depending on the price in period 2. Consequently the demand in period 2 increases when price is lowered in period 1. Alternatively, consider the case of a durable product. In this case there are two opposing effects: (1) A lower price in the first period reduces the future market potential (i.e., the firm "borrows" sales from the future); we say that there is a negative diffusion effect; and (2) a lower price in the first period leads to higher demand in the future because of a positive word-of-mouth effect or an increase in the firm's reputation over time. We say that there is a positive diffusion effect. Thus the net diffusion effect can be either positive or negative depending on the type of product and the phase of the product life cycle (for example, word-of-mouth effects are likely to be stronger when the product is in the introductory phase). We refer to these types of demand interdependence as *demand dynamics*.

Third, the firm could be simultaneously faced with cost dynamics and demand dynamics. For example, the product may be new to the marketplace and, in addition, the production technology is new to the firm.

1.3 COST DYNAMICS

Consider the cost dynamics scenario first. Suppose a new production technology has become available. If the firm introduces the new technology, it will learn with experience (i.e., the average cost of production depends on the accumulated production volume). For convenience, consider a two-period planning horizon and assume that the demand is stable over time.[2] Intuitively we expect that the optimal policy might require the firm to overshoot the optimal "myopic" production volume (i.e., to build market share in volume terms) by accelerating the learning process, reducing period 2 costs, and hence increasing period 2 profits. That is, it may be desirable to trade off immediate profits for future profits. We now examine whether this intuition is correct.

Figure 1.2 shows the demand curve DD in period 1 and the associated marginal revenue curve MR. Note that DD is downward sloping and that MR always lies below DD; that is, price always exceeds marginal revenue.[3]

Let p_1^m and p_2^m, respectively, denote the myopic prices (i.e., the prices that maximize profit in period 1 and then maximize profit in period 2). Let p_1^* and p_2^* denote the strategically correct prices that maximize performance (i.e., net present value) by recognizing the cost dynamics of the experience curve.

Myopic pricing fails to recognize the future benefits from accelerated learning in period 1. Hence the myopic price p_1^m is higher than the strategic price p_1^*. See Appendix A for a formal proof. Because the myopic price in period 1 is too high, the myopic output q_1^m in period 1 is too low. See Figure 1.2.

In order to compare the myopic and strategic prices in period 2, it is necessary to examine the cost structure in period 2. Let AC_2^m denote the average cost in period 2 given the myopic pricing plan (see Figure 1.3). Note that AC_2^m is downward sloping because of the experience effect and becomes flatter as experience increases (i.e., the gains from additional experience fall as experience is accumulated). Let AC_2^* denote the average cost in period 2 given the strategic pricing plan. Recalling that myopic pricing leads to insufficient learning,

Figure 1.2 Myopic and strategic pricing plans in period 1. Note: (1) G and E denote myopic policy and H and F denote strategic policy. (2) $OG = p_1^m$, $OE = q_1^m$; $OH = p_1^*$, $OF = q_1^*$.

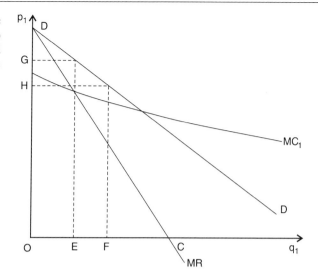

we know that AC_2^* is always below AC_2^m. The only remaining issue is to determine what these results imply about marginal costs in period 2.

Let MC_2^m and MC_2^*, respectively, denote the marginal cost curves corresponding to AC_2^m (myopic pricing) and AC_2^* (strategic pricing). Because AC_2^m and AC_2^* are downward sloping, MC_2^m and MC_2^* are also downward sloping. Furthermore, MC_2^m is always above MC_2^* (see Figure 1.4 and Appendix A).

We can now compare the myopic and strategic prices in period 2. Myopic pricing requires setting price in period 2 (p_2^m) such that marginal revenue MR equals marginal cost MC_2^m; see point A in Figure 1.4. Strategic pricing chooses price (p_2^*) to equate marginal revenue MR and marginal cost MC_2^*; see point B in Figure 1.4. Hence the strategic price in period 2 is less than the myopic price. Thus the strategic price is always lower than

Figure 1.3 Average cost in period 2 given myopic and strategic pricing. Note: m denotes myopic pricing and * denotes strategic pricing.

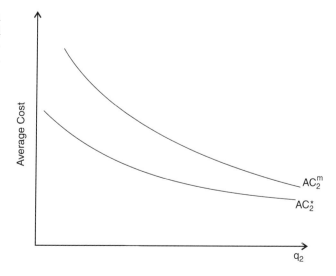

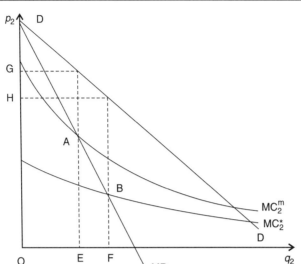

Figure 1.4 Myopic and strategic pricing in period 2. Notes: (1) m denotes myopic pricing and * denotes strategic pricing. (2) OG = p_2^m; OE = q_2^m; OH = p_2^*; OF = q_2^*.

the myopic price. This result generalizes to the multiperiod case (see Clarke, Darrough, and Heinike 1982, and Kalish 1983, Theorem 1) and the case where demand shifts are exogenous (i.e., outside the firm's control).

An interesting question is what strategic pricing implies about market share. Because the myopic prices are too high in both periods, the market share measured in volume terms will be too low in each period. The result for market share in revenue terms is more interesting. Comparing points A and B in Figure 1.4, we see that optimal pricing *always* leads to a higher revenue-based market share in period 2 than myopic pricing. (Recall that marginal revenue is positive at B.) In period 1, however, marginal revenue is less than marginal cost when the firm uses strategic pricing; the firm sacrifices profits in period 1 in order to increase its profits in period 2 via accelerated learning (see Figure 1.2).

Two cases are possible. Suppose marginal revenue in period 1 is positive when the firm uses strategic pricing (see Figure 1.2). Then strategic pricing leads to higher market share in revenue terms in period 1 than myopic pricing. Suppose, however, that learning effects are significant and require setting price in period 1 such that marginal revenue is negative (i.e., the output in period 1 exceeds OC in Figure 1.2). In this case strategic pricing could lead to a lower market share in revenue terms than myopic pricing in period 1.

These results show that revenue-based market share can be a poor proxy for long-term profitability. The obvious question is why firms continue to emphasize strategies to build market share. One possible explanation lies in the separation between ownership and control typically found in the modern corporation. In particular, although the firm's total revenue and cost are public knowledge (contained in the firm's annual reports), the owners (i.e., the stockholders) do not know the revenues and costs for individual product lines in a multiproduct firm. Consequently one could argue that the stock market uses current revenue-based market share as a proxy for long-term profitability. (Recall also that market share is an "objective" measure and, unlike profit, is not subject to manipulation by managers.)

Our analysis shows that if this scenario is true, a firm in an industry with strong learning effects could be undervalued by the stock market. Because of the informational asymmetry (i.e., managers know the experience curves for different product lines but the stock market does not), this situation cannot be an equilibrium. In such cases managers can purchase the undervalued stock ("insider trading") or convey their superior information about costs (i.e., the magnitude of the gains from the experience effect) to the stock market via announcements. The latter approach may, however, be strategically suboptimal unless the production technology is protected by a patent or the investment in the new technology has already occurred (i.e., the investment is sunk).

Key Point *Suppose the firm's demand curve is either stable over time or demand shifts are exogenous (i.e., the firm's current and past prices do not affect future demand). In the presence of learning effects period-by-period "myopic" pricing is suboptimal regardless of the length of the firm's (finite) planning period. Strategic pricing requires the firm to invest in future cost savings by setting lower prices in each period than myopic pricing. Consequently in any given period strategic pricing always leads to higher volume-based market shares than myopic pricing. In a two-period model strategic pricing leads to a higher revenue-based market share in the second period. The effect on the revenue-based market share in period 1, however, is ambiguous. In particular, revenue-based market share in the first period is a poor proxy for future profitability.*

An interesting issue is how the strategic pricing plan varies with market conditions. Two important parameters are the gains from learning and the firm's cost of capital. Intuitively one might expect that as the experience curve becomes steeper (i.e., the gains from learning are more significant), the firm should increase its volume-based market share in period 1 (i.e., charge a lower price) in order to accelerate learning. This policy lowers the marginal cost curve in period 2 and consequently requires the firm to charge a lower price in period 2. Hence we expect that the more significant the learning effects are, the greater the price reductions in both periods. This intuition is correct. (See Appendix A for formal derivations.)

Suppose the opportunity cost of capital increases. The gain from future profit is now reduced. As a result the future advantages from building up experience in period 1 are reduced. Thus we expect that the firm will seek higher immediate profit and charge a higher price in period 1. This price increase leads to lowered production in period 1 and hence raises the marginal cost curve in period 2 (see Figure 1.4). The firm must, therefore, increase price in period 2. (See Appendix A for technical details.) These results show that the effects of an increase in learning are analogous to those of a decrease in the firm's opportunity cost of capital.

We now consider some practical applications. Suppose large firms have lower costs of capital than small firms. Then the model implies that given identical demand and cost conditions large firms will charge lower prices in each period than small firms.

Assume, as some authors do, that for any given industry the cost of capital for Japanese firms is lower than that for American firms; in particular, Japanese firms are able to reduce their cost of capital by using a complex system of cross-ownership whereby firms own significant holdings in each other's stock[4] (the *keiretsu* system). Given that Japanese firms focus on industries where learning effects are significant, the theory implies that Japanese firms will charge lower prices in each period than American firms that face the same cost and demand conditions. Consequently, in any given period Japanese firms will have a higher volume-based market share than American firms. In a two-period model Japanese firms will have a higher revenue-based market share than American firms in the second period; however, American firms could have a higher revenue-based market share than Japanese firms in the first period if the learning curve is sufficiently steep.

> **Key Point** *In the presence of cost dynamics the effect of a decrease in the firm's cost of capital is analogous to that of an increase in the learning rate. For both scenarios the firm reduces prices in each period.*

1.4 DEMAND DYNAMICS

We now consider the case of pure demand dynamics. That is, the price in period 1 affects the demand in period 2. There is, however, no learning effect in production (i.e., cost dynamics). We shall examine the case where a low price in period 1 increases demand in period 2. Thus our results apply for nondurables and for durables for which the net diffusion effect is positive. The interested reader can use the methodology to examine the case of durables for which the net diffusion effect is negative (i.e., the market-saturating effect of a low price in period 1 swamps the market-expanding effect of positive word of mouth).

Given our assumptions, myopic pricing fails to consider the increase in future profits that would result from charging a low price in period 1. Thus the myopic price in period 1 is higher than the strategic price in period 1, regardless of the cost structure. (See Appendix B for a formal proof.) Consequently, as in the cost dynamics case, strategic pricing leads to a higher volume-based market share than myopic pricing in period 1. Furthermore, it is not necessary that marginal revenue in period 1 be positive. The intuition here is that it may be desirable for the firm to expand the immediate customer base even if marginal revenue is negative, provided future profits can be increased by stimulating word of mouth (for durables) and generating repeat purchases (for nondurables). Thus, as in the cost-dynamics case, the impact of strategic pricing on the revenue-based market share in period 1 is ambiguous.

> **Key Point** *If a lower price in the current period increases future demand, the strategic price in the current period is always lower than the myopic price, regardless of the cost structure.*

The effect of strategic pricing on the price in period 2 depends crucially on two factors: (1) The effect of the price in period 1 on the marginal revenue in period 2 (recall that profit-maximizing behavior requires the firm to equate marginal revenue and marginal cost), and (2) the cost structure. In order to focus on "pure" demand effects, we begin with the case of constant marginal cost. This assumption is reasonable for many frequently purchased consumer products (e.g., toothpaste, soap, and detergents).

Constant Marginal Costs

In Figure 1.5a, $D^m D^m$ is the demand curve in period 2 given that the firm has priced myopically in period 1. Let $R^m R^m$ denote the marginal revenue curve corresponding $D^m D^m$. Then myopic pricing requires the firm to equate marginal revenue $R^m R^m$ and marginal cost MC. Hence the firm charges a price of OP_2^m in period 2 and sells a volume of OQ_2^m.

Now we know that the strategic price in period 1 (p_1^*) is lower than the myopic price. Let $D^* D^*$ denote the demand in period 2 given the strategic price p_1^*. Because myopic pricing in period 1 fails to consider the market-expanding effect of a low price, $D^m D^m$ is always below $D^* D^*$.

We begin with the case where $D^* D^*$ is flatter than $D^m D^m$; in particular, the market expands proportionately at all prices in period 2 when the price in period 1 is lowered. (See Appendix B for details.) Then at any given price the marginal revenues for both demand schedules are equal. Consider the myopic price OP_2^m. At this price the marginal revenues for both myopic and strategic pricing equal marginal cost. Consequently the myopic and strategic prices in period 2 are identical. These results imply that strategic pricing leads to a higher volume-based or revenue-based market share in period 2 than myopic pricing.

Suppose now that a lower price in period 1 makes the market less price sensitive at any price in period 2. For example, the number of triers of a nondurable product in period 1 is large and these triers are highly satisfied with the new product. Consider the myopic price OP_2^m. At this price the marginal revenue corresponding to the appropriate $D^* D^*$ (not shown in Figure 1.5a) will be less than the marginal cost. Consequently the strategic price must be raised from OP_2^m to equate marginal revenue and marginal cost. That is, the strategic price in period 2 is higher than the myopic price. Similarly suppose that a lower price in period 1 makes the market more price sensitive in period 2. For example, the triers of a nondurable product in period 1 increase their search effort in period 2 to discover the "best" product. Now the marginal revenue corresponding to OP_2^m exceeds the marginal cost. Hence the strategic price in period 2 is lower than the myopic price.

What do these results imply about the impact of strategic pricing on market share when the price in period 1 affects the price sensitivity of the market in period 2? Unfortunately, not much. Recalling that the myopic and strategic pricing plans require the firm to choose price–volume combinations on $D^m D^m$ and $D^* D^*$, respectively, it is straightforward to show

Figure 1.5a Myopic and strategic pricing plans in period 2: constant marginal cost. Note: The myopic and strategic prices are equal ($OP_2^m = OP_2^*$).

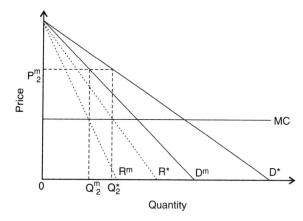

that the effects of strategic pricing on volume-based and revenue-based market share are ambiguous.

Key Point   *The effects of demand dynamics on future price and market share (volume- or revenue-based) depend crucially on the cost structure and the precise manner in which the price in the current period affects price sensitivity in the future.*

Increasing Marginal Cost

Suppose marginal cost increases with volume. Consider the case where the price in period 1 has no effect on price sensitivity in period 2 (see Figure 1.5b). The myopic price OP_2^m is chosen so that the marginal revenue at this price equals marginal cost. Now at a price OP_2^m the marginal revenue corresponding to D*D* equals the marginal revenue corresponding to D^mD^m. For a price OP_2^m the demand given strategic pricing exceeds the demand given myopic pricing (D*D* is always above D^mD^m); furthermore, marginal cost increases with volume. Hence the marginal revenue for D*D* at a price of OP_2^m is less than the marginal cost. Consequently, in period 2 the strategic price is higher than the myopic price.

Suppose a low price in period 1 reduces price sensitivity in period 2. Then the marginal revenue for the strategic demand curve D*D* at a price of OP_2^m is reduced. Hence it is necessary to raise the strategic price in period 2 even further than in the case where the price in period 1 does not affect price sensitivity in the future.

Suppose a low price in period 1 increases price sensitivity in period 2. Now the marginal revenue at a price of OP_2^m could be higher than the marginal cost. Hence the strategic price in period 2 could be lower than the myopic price.

Key Point   *In the presence of demand dynamics and increasing marginal costs, the strategic price in period 2 will in general exceed the myopic price. For the strategic price in period 2 to be equal to or lower than the myopic price, it is necessary that a low price in period 1 sufficiently increases price sensitivity in period 2.*

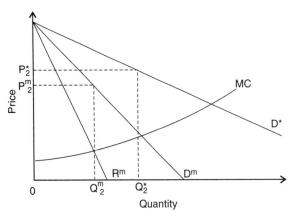

Figure 1.5b Myopic and strategic pricing plans in period 2: increasing marginal cost. Note: m denotes myopic pricing and * strategic pricing.

Decreasing Marginal Cost

Following the previous argument, we can show that, in general, the strategic price in period 2 is lower than the myopic price. A necessary condition for the strategic price to be equal to or greater than the myopic price is that a low price in period 1 reduces the price sensitivity in period 2 sufficiently.

Effect of an Increase in the Cost of Capital

An interesting question is the effect of an increase in the firm's cost of capital on strategic pricing. Recall that because of demand dynamics, the firm sacrifices profits in period 1 (i.e., charges a lower price than under myopic pricing) in order to increase profits in period 2. When the firm's cost of capital increases, incremental profits in period 2 become less attractive. Consequently the firm will raise the price in period 1 to increase profit in that period (i.e., the gap between the myopic and strategic prices in period 1 is reduced). See Appendix B for a formal proof.

As expected, the effect on the price in period 2 depends on the cost structure and the effect of the period 1 price on price sensitivity in period 2. When the price in period 1 increases, demand in period 2 is reduced. The interested reader can develop the argument graphically using Figure 1.5a and treating D^*D^* and D^mD^m, respectively, as the demand curves in period 2 when the cost of capital is low and high. Table 1.2 summarizes the main results.

> ***Key Point*** *When the cost of capital increases, the incremental value of future profit is reduced. Hence the strategic price in period 1 is increased regardless of the particular forms of the cost and demand functions. The strategic price in period 2 could remain unchanged, increase, or decrease depending upon how marginal costs change with volume and the impact of the price in period 1 on the price sensitivity in period 2. Because of the price increase in period 1, the firm's volume-based market share falls in period 1.*

Table 1-2 Effects of An Increase in the Cost of Capital On the Strategic Price in Period 2

	Scenarios		
	(a)	**(b)**	**(c)**
Constant marginal cost	0	−	+
Increasing marginal cost	−	−	?
Decreasing marginal cost	+	?	+

(a): Price in period 1 has no effect on price sensitivity in period 2.
(b): A high price in period 1 increases price sensitivity in period 2.
(c): A high price in period 1 reduces price sensitivity in period 2.

1.5 COST AND DEMAND DYNAMICS

We can now use the previous results to examine the case where there are cost dynamics (i.e., a learning effect) and demand dynamics. As in the pure demand dynamics case, consider the case where a low price in period 1 increases demand in period 2. Recall that the myopic price in period 1 is too high given cost dynamics or demand dynamics (see previous sections). Not surprisingly, this result holds when cost dynamics and demand dynamics coexist. (See Appendix C for a formal proof.) Recall that because of cost dynamics, the marginal cost curve in period 2 conditional on any given volume in period 1 is downward sloping. Furthermore, if the volume in period 1 increases, the marginal cost curve in period 2 is lowered. Note that, in contrast to the pure demand dynamics case, it is not necessary to consider different cost scenarios because both average and marginal costs are always decreasing because of the experience effect. (See Appendix B.) Hence the effect of strategic pricing on the price in period 2 depends only on the effect of the price in period 1 on price sensitivity in period 2.

Suppose the price in period 1 has no effect on price sensitivity in period 2. (See Figure 1.6.) Recalling that the myopic price in period 1 exceeds the strategic price, let $D^m D^m$ and $D^* D^*$, respectively, denote the demand curves in period 2 given the myopic price (p_1^m) and the strategic price (p_1^*). Let $G^m G^m$ and $G^* G^*$, respectively, denote the marginal cost curves in period 2 corresponding to the myopic and strategic prices in period 1. The myopic policy (price OP_2^m, volume OQ_2^m) is given by the intersection of the marginal revenue curve corresponding to $D^m D^m$ and the marginal cost curve $G^m G^m$. Now for a price OP_2^m the marginal revenues for the demand curves $D^* D^*$ and $D^m D^m$ are equal. Learning, however, implies that $G^m G^m$ and $G^* G^*$ are downward sloping and $G^* G^*$ is always below $G^m G^m$ (see Appendix C). Consequently the marginal revenue for strategic pricing given the price OP_2^m exceeds marginal cost. Hence in period 2 the strategic price is lower than the myopic price. This effect is reinforced if a low price in period 1 increases price sensitivity in period 2. If, however, a low price in period 1 significantly reduces the price sensitivity in period 2, it is possible that the strategic price in period 2 will equal or even exceed the myopic price.

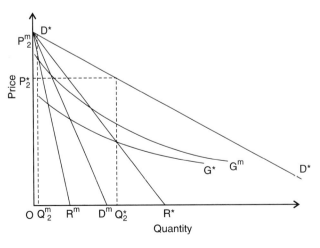

Figure 1.6 Myopic and strategic pricing plans in period 2: demand and cost dynamics. Note: m denotes myopic pricing and ∗ denotes strategic pricing.

> **Key Point**   *If there are cost and demand dynamics, the strategic price in period 1 is always lower than the myopic price. In general the strategic price in period 2 is also lower than the myopic price. Thus strategic pricing leads to higher volume-based market shares in periods 1 and 2. However, the effects on the revenue-based market shares are ambiguous.*

Effect of an Increase in the Cost of Capital

When the cost of capital increases, the firm finds it less attractive to trade off profits in period 1 for increased profits in period 2. Consequently the firm will raise the strategic price in period 1, regardless of the precise form of the demand dynamics and the magnitude of the learning effect. (See Appendix C for a formal proof.) As we expect, the effect on the strategic price in period 2 will depend on exactly how the price in period 1 affects price sensitivity in period 2.

Suppose the price in period 1 has no effect on price sensitivity in period 2. In Figure 1.6 assume that D^mD^m and D^*D^*, respectively, represent the demand curves in period 2 when the cost of capital is high and low. Then the marginal revenue at the old price OP_2^* is unchanged when the cost of capital increases. Recall that the new marginal cost curve G^mG^m is above the old marginal cost curve G^*G^* because volume in period 1 is reduced when the cost of capital increases. Hence the strategic price in period 2 increases when the cost of capital increases.

Suppose price sensitivity decreases when the demand curve moves inward to D^mD^m. Then the marginal revenue at the old price OP_2^* falls; furthermore, because of the experience effect, marginal cost is higher (recall that the new marginal cost curve G^mG^m is above the old marginal cost curve G^*G^*). Both effects reinforce each other and cause the strategic price in period 2 to increase when the cost of capital increases. If, however, price sensitivity increases when the demand curve moves to D^mD^m, the marginal revenue at the old price OP_2^* increases. Hence there is a tradeoff between the learning effect (which tends to increase price) and the effect of increased price sensitivity (which tends to decrease price). Thus the effect of an increase in the cost of capital on the strategic price in period 2 is ambiguous.

> **Key Point**   *When the cost of capital increases, the firm always increases the strategic price in period 1 when cost and demand dynamics are present. In general the firm increases the strategic price in period 2 unless a higher price in period 1 increases the price sensitivity in period 2 substantially.*

Accelerated Learning

Suppose the learning rate increases. Now, because of the simultaneous effect of cost and demand dynamics, the effect on the strategic prices is inherently ambiguous (see Appendix C). Note in particular that, in contrast to the pure cost-dynamics case, the effect of an increase in the rate of learning is not analogous to the effect of a decrease in the cost of capital.

1.6 MODEL EXTENSIONS

The previous analysis made two simplifying assumptions: The firm operates in a deterministic environment and knows the parameters of demand dynamics and the experience curve with certainty. We now relax these assumptions.[5]

First, consider the case in which the firm knows the parameters of demand dynamics with certainty; however, the gains from accumulated experience are uncertain. Suppose that the firm is risk-neutral. That is, the firm chooses prices in periods 1 and 2 to maximize the net present value of the expected profits over the two periods.

Consider any arbitrary price (and hence output) in the first period. For this output level let BCD in Figure 1.7 denote the average cost in period 1 as a function of the learning parameter α. Note that BCD is downward sloping and becomes flatter when the learning parameter increases. Let $\bar{\alpha}$ (OF in Figure 1.7) denote the learning parameter under certainty and EG the range of possible values of the learning parameter. For convenience suppose that there is a 50 percent probability that the learning parameter is OE and a 50 percent probability that the learning parameter is OG.[6] (This assumption is made purely for expository convenience.) Recall that the revenue for any given price level is fixed; hence the analysis can focus on the expected costs. Then the expected cost per unit under uncertainty is FH (the average of BE and GD), which is greater than FC. Hence in period 1 the firm's expected profit under uncertainty is lower than the profit under certainty. Thus the firm is worse off when the learning effect is uncertain.

Consider any arbitrary price in period 2 conditional on the price chosen in period 1. By repeating the same analysis we can show that the firm is worse off in period 2 as well when the learning effect is uncertain. This result can be extended to the multiperiod case.[7]

What happens if the uncertainty in the learning parameter is small (for example, the firm is familiar with the new production technology)? Then points B and D are very close to point C; consequently the dotted line BD becomes indistinguishable from the tangent

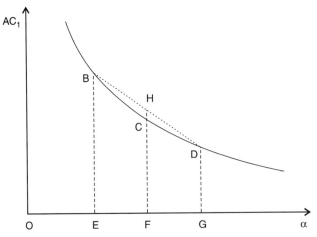

Figure 1.7 The effect of uncertainty in learning on average cost. Note: AC_1 is the average cost in period 1 given price p_1; α, the learning parameter.

to the average cost curve at C.[8] Thus the risk-neutral firm is not affected by uncertainty in learning and the certainty results discussed previously apply. Because uncertainty is small and demand is deterministic, the previous results hold when the firm is risk-averse.[9]

> **Key Point** *Suppose the monopolist introduces a cost-reducing technology in which the gains from learning are uncertain. If uncertainty is large, the risk-neutral and risk-averse firms are worse off if demand is deterministic, regardless of whether there are dynamic demand effects. If uncertainty is small, the risk-neutral and risk-averse firms will choose the same policies as they do in the case where the experience curve is known with certainty.*

Second, consider the case where demand in both periods is uncertain and there are dynamic demand effects; however, the experience curve is known with certainty. Suppose the firm is risk-neutral and the demand uncertainty is small. Now, in contrast to the previous scenario, uncertainty in demand is transmitted to cost; in particular, both output and average cost are uncertain and depend on the firm's pricing policy. Because of this interdependence we obtain an interesting result: The risk-neutral firm is better off when demand is uncertain. The intuition is that for any given pricing plan the expected revenue in each period is unchanged. The expected cost in each period, however, declines because fluctuations in demand and average cost are negatively correlated and the expected average demand and the expected average cost are constant. This result generalizes to the multiperiod case.[10]

Third, suppose both demand and the gain from learning are uncertain in both periods. Then if the uncertainties in demand and learning are small, we obtain the same result as in the previous scenario; in a multiperiod context the risk-neutral firm is better off under uncertainty than in the deterministic case.[11] This result is not surprising. Recall that because all uncertainties are small, the effects of demand and cost uncertainty on expected profits in any given period are approximately additive; furthermore, we know that uncertainty in learning has no effect on expected profits.

How should pricing policy be modified when demand and learning are uncertain? Recall that in the certainty case the firm charges a low price in the first period in order to lower future costs (i.e., the firm "invests" in experience). This conclusion does not hold in the stochastic case; without precise knowledge of the demand and experience curve functions, the results are inherently indeterminate for all the scenarios discussed.[12]

> **Key Point** *Suppose demand uncertainty is small and the experience curve is known with certainty. Then the risk-neutral firm is better off than in the deterministic case. This result holds if the experience effect is also uncertain provided the uncertainty in learning is small. In contrast to the deterministic case the risk-neutral firm may prefer not to charge a low price in the first period in order to build up experience. If uncertainty is large, the results are inherently indeterminate.*[13]

Our analysis so far has made an important assumption: The firm should choose policy to maximize net present value. This approach is correct when the cash flows are deterministic; when demand and cost are uncertain, however, the standard net present value approach will lead to suboptimal decisions. The problem is that the standard approach does not consider the sequential aspect of decision making. Consider a two-period model where demand is deterministic; the learning effect, however, is uncertain. Should the firm reject a new technology for which the net present value after choosing the "optimal" pricing strategy is negative? Not necessarily.

For simplicity suppose that the firm can determine the learning parameter with certainty at the end of the first period. Suppose the firm introduces the new technology and chooses the policy (p_1^*, p_2^*) that maximizes the net present value of expected profits.[14] At the end of period 1 the firm discovers that the learning effect is small; in particular, the optimal decision is to abandon the new technology. The standard net present value approach, however, assumes that the firm will continue to use the new production technology in period 2 and charge a price of p_2^* *regardless of whether the learning effect is small or large.* By failing to consider the economic value of flexibility, the standard net present value formula understates the economic value of the new technology.[15] Thus the optimal policy for the firm may be to introduce the new cost-reducing technology even if the standard net present value is negative; in particular, the firm can increase the value of the project by holding an option to sell the project at the end of the first period for the net scrap value.[16]

> **Key Point**   *The standard net present value approach leads to suboptimal decision making because it does not consider the economic value of flexibility.*

Our discussion so far has implicitly assumed that the sole source of cost uncertainty is technological (i.e., the randomness of the learning parameter in the experience curve). In a multiperiod context, however, randomness in input prices can have a significant effect on the firm's cost structure. For simplicity assume that demand is uncertain but there is no experience-curve effect; that is, the firm's production function (and hence cost structure) in any given period depends on the quantities of the inputs available in that period but not on accumulated production.[17] Then the firm can pursue several behavioral modes depending on the competitive structures of the input and output markets (i.e., whether the output market is monopolistic or competitive and the input market is monopsonistic or competitive).

Jagpal (1984) develops a two-period model that compares the policies of risk-neutral and value-maximizing firms for different behavioral modes and combinations of market structure (e.g., a monopolistic output market and a monopsonistic input market). In particular, the model distinguishes price- and quantity-setting behavior for different market structures and examines when the firm is willing to pay a premium to avoid uncertainty in future input prices. We outline the basic modeling approach and present several scenarios for the price-setting monopolist.[18]

Consider a two-period model in which the monopolist uses two inputs (capital and labor) to produce a given product. Both the input and output markets are uncertain; in particular, fluctuations in input and output prices can be correlated (e.g., both markets are subject to the same economy-wide shocks). The market for capital goods is competitive; however, the input market can be either competitive or monopsonistic. At the beginning of the period the price-setting monopolist chooses both price and the level of capital ex ante. The demand for the product during period 1 is uncertain and is conditional on the firm's price policy; in particular, price affects the volatility of demand nonmonotonically, and fluctuations in demand depend on two factors: Firm-specific and systematic risk. (Recall that stockholders can eliminate firm-specific fluctuations in the firm's cash flows by holding a diversified portfolio. Thus, if systematic risk is absent, the value-maximizing firm is risk-neutral.) Once demand uncertainty is resolved at the end of period 1, the firm purchases labor at the prevailing spot market price. Other input purchase policies are possible. For example, the firm can use a pure hedging strategy by entering into a long-term contract for the purchase of labor in the future at a guaranteed price. Alternatively, the firm can use a mixed hedging strategy by precommitting to purchase a fixed amount of labor in the future at a guaranteed price and additional labor if necessary at the prevailing spot price once demand uncertainty is resolved.

For the model described the main result is that the monopolist's policy depends on the types of uncertainty (i.e., firm-specific and systematic) in the input and output markets, the structure of the input market (i.e., competitive or monopsonistic), and whether the monopolist is risk-neutral or maximizes stock value. For example, suppose both the input and output markets are subject to firm-specific and systematic risk. Then if the input market is competitive, the risk-neutral monopolist will always be worse off when uncertainty is simultaneously introduced into the output and input markets provided these uncertainties are small and the wage rate and the demand are positively correlated (see Jagpal 1984, Proposition 4).[19] Thus the risk-neutral monopolist is willing to pay a premium in a long-term contract for the purchase of labor in the future. Suppose the labor market is monopsonistic and cyclical (i.e., systematic risk has a significant effect on wage rates); however, all fluctuations in the output market are firm-specific. Then the value-maximizing firm prefers the simultaneous introduction of uncertainty into the input and output markets provided the wage rate is positively correlated to the return on the market portfolio (Jagpal 1984, Proposition 8). Thus, in contrast to the previous scenario, the value-maximizing monopolist will not pay a premium to avoid uncertainty in future labor prices.

1.7 CONCLUDING REMARKS

This chapter examines the role of strategic pricing in a dynamic environment in which there are cost interdependencies over time because of learning ("experience") and demand interdependencies because of a diffusion effect (for durables) and repeat purchase (for nondurables). We show that market share is, in general, a poor proxy for long-term profitability; hence the marketing manager should exercise great caution in applying strategic planning models that emphasize the rapid buildup of market share to establish competitive advantage. Furthermore, in a dynamic stochastic environment the firm can be better off under uncertainty, especially when fluctuations in demand and cost are interdependent (a likely scenario because the input and output markets are subject to the same macroeconomic shocks). Research is necessary to extend the model to oligopolistic markets, explicitly recognizing that both cost and demand are stochastic and that cost and demand dynamics coexist.

Finally we have focused on market-level behavior and, in particular, not dealt with the important issue of pricing when consumers are heterogeneous. This fundamental marketing problem is examined in Chapter 2.

NOTES

1. Our analysis assumes certainty. Leland (1972) shows that under uncertainty the expected utility–maximizing monopolist changes price when fixed costs change.

2. Our analysis does not depend on the assumption of demand stability over time. The key assumption is that dynamic demand shifts occur purely because of exogenous shocks; in particular, current demand does not depend on past prices. See Appendix A for details.

3. Let p denote price, q quantity, and $p = f(q)$ the inverse demand function, where $\partial f/\partial q < 0$. Then the revenue for any price p is $R = qf(q)$. Differentiating with respect to q we obtain marginal revenue as $\partial R/\partial q = f(q) + q\, \partial f/\partial q$. Hence $\partial R/\partial q - p < 0$. Thus the marginal revenue curve is below the demand curve (see Figure 1.2).

4. This theory implicitly assumes that the international capital market is imperfect. If the international capital market were perfect, arbitragers would equalize rates of return across countries for any given industry. That is, the scenario described could not occur in equilibrium.

5. These extensions do not appear to have been considered in the previous literature. Majd and Pindyck (1989) and Dixit and Pindyck (1994, pp. 339–45) consider the special case where dynamic price fluctuations are uncertain (i.e., the output market is competitive and the firm does not control price) and the experience curve is known with certainty.

6. This assumption is made purely for expository convenience. As shown in note 7, the result depends on the fact that the average cost is convex in the learning parameter.

7. Consider a two-period model. Let p_1 and p_2, respectively, denote the prices in periods 1 and 2 and $q_1 = f_1(p_1)$ and $q_2 = f_2(p_1, p_2)$ the appropriate demand levels where $\partial^2 q_2/\partial p_1\, \partial p_2$ has unrestricted sign. Let $c_1 = \theta e^{-\alpha f_1(p_1)}$ denote the average cost in period 1 where the learning parameter α is random and $c_2 = \theta e^{-\alpha[f_1(p_1)+f_2(p_1,p_2)]}$ the average cost in period 2, where $[f_1(p_1)+f_2(p_1, p_2)]$ is the accumulated experience. Let δ denote the discount rate. Consider any policy (p_1, p_2). Given certainty the firm's net present value is $Z = (p_1 - \theta e^{-E(\alpha)f_1(p_1)})f_1(p_1) + (1+\delta)^{-1}(p_2 - \theta e^{-E(\alpha)[f_1(p_1)+f_2(p_1,p_2)]})f_2(p_1, p_2)$. Given uncertainty in learning, the net present value for the risk-neutral firm is $Z^* = E[(p_1 - \theta e^{-\alpha f_1(p_1)})f_1(p_1)] + (1 + \delta)^{-1}E[(p_2 - \theta e^{-\alpha[f_1(p_1)+f_2(p_1,p_2)]})f_2(p_1, p_2)]$. Subtracting, we have $Z - Z^* = -\theta f_1(p_1)(e^{-E(\alpha)f_1(p_1)} - Ee^{-\alpha f_1(p_1)}) - (1+\delta)^{-1}\theta f_2(p_1, p_2)(e^{-E(\alpha)[f_1(p_1)+f_2(p_1,p_2)]} - Ee^{-\alpha[f_1(p_1)+f_2(p_1,p_2)]})$. Now $e^{-\alpha[f_1(p_1)]}$ and $e^{-\alpha[f_1(p_1)+f_2(p_1,p_2)]}$ and convex in α. Hence using Jensen's inequality, we have $(e^{-E(\alpha)f_1(p_1)} - Ee^{-\alpha f_1(p_1)}) < 0$ and $(e^{-E(\alpha)[f_1(p_1)+f_2(p_1,p_2)]} - Ee^{-\alpha[f_1(p_1)+f_2(p_1,p_2)]}) < 0$. Thus $Z - Z^* > 0$ for any policy (p_1, p_2). This result is easily generalized to the multiperiod case.

8. Consider the model in note 7. If uncertainty in learning is small, $e^{-\alpha[f_1(p_1)]} \cong e^{-E(\alpha)f_1(p_1)} + h_1(p_1, E(\alpha))[\alpha - E(\alpha)]$, where h_1 is a deterministic function. Similarly, $e^{-\alpha[(f_1(p_1)+f_2(p_1,p_2)]} \cong e^{-E(\alpha)[f_1(p_1)+f_2(p_1,p_2)]} + h_2(p_1, p_2, E(\alpha))[\alpha - E(\alpha)]$, where h_2 is deterministic. Then the expected profit in period 1 is $(p_1 - \theta e^{-E(\alpha)f_1(p_1)})f_1(p_1)$, and the expected profit in period 2 is $(p_2 - \theta e^{-E(\alpha)[f_1(p_1)+f_2(p_1,p_2)]})f_2(p_1, p_2)$. Consequently the risk-neutral firm's policy is unaffected when uncertainty in learning is small. This result holds for the multiperiod case.

9. Consider the model in note 8. Suppose the firm is risk-averse and has a time-additive utility function. Then the firm chooses policy to maximize $Z^* = EU(\pi_1^*) + (1+\delta)^{-1}EU(\pi_2^*)$, where π_i^* denotes the random profit in period i and $U(\cdot)$ is concave in profits. For small uncertainty in learning $\pi_1^* \cong \pi_1 + h_1(p_1, E(\alpha))\theta f_1(p_1)[\alpha - E(\alpha)]$, where π_1 denotes the profit under certainty in

period 1. Hence $EU(\pi_1^*) = U(\pi_1)$. Similarly $\pi_2^* \cong \pi_2 + h_2(p_1, p_2, E(\alpha))\theta f_2(p_1, p_2)[\alpha - E(\alpha)]$, where π_2 denotes the profit under certainty in period 2. Hence $EU(\pi_2^*) = U(\pi_2)$. Thus the risk-averse firm does not change its policy when the uncertainty in learning is small. Suppose the uncertainty in learning is large. Differentiating $U(\pi_i^*)$ with respect to the learning parameter α, we have $\partial^2 U(\pi_i^*)/\partial\alpha^2 = U''(\pi_i^*)(\partial\pi_i^*/\partial\alpha)^2 + (\partial^2\pi_i^*/\partial\alpha^2)U'(\pi_i^*)$ for $i = 1, 2$, where U' and U'', respectively, denote the first and second derivatives. For all i, π_i^* is concave in α and $U''(\pi_i^*) < 0$ by risk aversion; that is, $U(\pi_i^*)$ is strictly concave in α. Hence $EU(\pi_i^*) < U(\pi_i(\overline{\alpha}))$ for all i using Jensen's inequality. Consequently the risk-averse firm is worse off when the learning effect is uncertain. These results generalize to the multiperiod case.

10. Consider a two-period model. Let $q_1 = f_1(p_1, u_1)$ and $q_2 = f_2(p_1, p_2, u_2)$, respectively, denote the demands in periods 1 and 2, where u_1 and u_2 are independent stochastic disturbances. For small uncertainty $q_1 \cong f_1(p_1, \overline{u}_1) + g_1(p_1, \overline{u}_1)(u_1 - \overline{u}_1)$, where $E(u_1) = \overline{u}_1$. For simplicity write $q_1 = f_1(p_1) + g_1(p_1)v_1$, where $v_1 = u_1 - \overline{u}_1$. Similarly $q_2 = f_2(p_1, p_2) + g_2(p_1, p_2)v_2$, where $v_2 = u_2 - \overline{u}_2$. Let $\hat{\theta}$ and $\hat{\alpha}$ denote the known parameters of the experience curve. Then the average costs for periods 1 and 2, respectively, are the stochastic quantities $c_1 = \hat{\theta}e^{-\hat{\alpha}[f_1(p_1) + g_1(p_1)v_1]}$ and $c_2 = \hat{\theta}e^{-\hat{\alpha}[f_2(p_1, p_2) + g_2(p_1, p_2)v_2]}$. Because the demand uncertainties are small $e^{-\hat{\alpha}g_1(p_1)v_1} \cong 1 - \hat{\alpha}g_1(p_1)v_1$ and $e^{-\hat{\alpha}g_2(p_1, p_2)v_2} \cong 1 - \hat{\alpha}g_2(p_1, p_2)v_2$. Thus the random profits in periods 1 and 2, respectively, are $\pi_1^* = p_1[f_1(p_1) + g_1(p_1)v_1] - [f_1(p_1) + g_1(p_1)v_1]\hat{\theta}e^{-\hat{\alpha}f_1(p_1)}[1 - \hat{\alpha}g_1(p_1)v_1]$ and $\pi_2^* = p_2[f_2(p_1, p_2) + g_2(p_1, p_2)v_2] - [f_2(p_1, p_2) + g_2(p_1, p_2)v_2]\hat{\theta}e^{-\hat{\alpha}f_2(p_1, p_2)}[1 - \hat{\alpha}g_2(p_1, p_2)v_2]$. Let Z denote the net present value of profits under certainty and Z^* the net present value of expected profits under uncertainty. After simplification we get $Z^* - Z = \hat{\alpha}\hat{\theta}e^{-\hat{\alpha}f_1(p_1)}[g_1(p_1)]^2\sigma^2(v_1) + (1 + \delta)^{-1}\hat{\alpha}\hat{\theta}e^{-\hat{\alpha}[f_1(p_1) + f_2(p_1, p_2)]}[g_2(p_1, p_2)]^2\sigma^2(v_2) > 0$, where σ^2 denotes the variance operator. Hence the risk-neutral firm is better off when demand uncertainty is introduced. This result generalizes to the multiperiod case in a straightforward manner.

11. Suppose both demand and the learning effect are uncertain; furthermore, all uncertainties are small. Then $q_1 \cong f_1(p_1) + g_1(p_1)v_1$ and $q_2 \cong f_2(p_1, p_2) + g_2(p_1, p_2)v_2$, where the vs are stochastic and $E(v_i) = 0$. See note 10. Let $E(\alpha) = \overline{\alpha}$, where α denotes the random learning effect. Then the average cost in period 1 is $c_1 \cong \theta e^{-\overline{\alpha}f_1(p_1)}\{1 - [(\alpha - \overline{\alpha})f_1(p_1) + (\alpha - \overline{\alpha})g_1(p_1)v_1 + \overline{\alpha}g_1(p_1)v_1]\}$ and the average cost in period 2 is $c_2 \cong \theta e^{-\overline{\alpha}[f_1(p_1) + f_2(p_1, p_2)]}\{1 - [\overline{\alpha}g_1(p_1)v_1 + \overline{\alpha}g_2(p_1, p_2)v_2 + (\alpha - \overline{\alpha})f_1(p_1) + (\alpha - \overline{\alpha})g_1(p_1)v_1 + (\alpha - \overline{\alpha})f_2(p_1, p_2) + (\alpha - \overline{\alpha})g_2(p_1, p_2)v_2]\}$.

Assume that the learning effect is independent of the demand uncertainties. Let Z denote the net present value of the certainty profits and Z^* the net present value of the expected profits in each period under uncertainty. After making the appropriate substitutions and simplifying, we get $Z^* = Z + \overline{\alpha}\theta e^{-\overline{\alpha}f_1(p_1)}[g_1(p_1)]^2\sigma^2(v_1) + (1 + \delta)^{-1}\overline{\alpha}\theta e^{-\overline{\alpha}[f_1(p_1) + f_2(p_1, p_2)]}[g_2(p_1, p_2)]^2\sigma^2(v_2) > 0$, where σ^2 denotes the variance operator. This result generalizes to the multiperiod case. Thus the risk-neutral firm is better off when uncertainty is simultaneously introduced into the learning effect and demand.

12. Consider the case where demand is deterministic but uncertainty in learning is large. Specifically $e^{-\alpha f_1(p_1)} = e^{-\overline{\alpha}f_1(p_1)} - f_1(p_1)e^{-\overline{\alpha}f_1(p_1)}(\alpha - \overline{\alpha}) + 1/2[f_1(p_1)]^2e^{-\overline{\alpha}f_1(p_1)}(\alpha - \overline{\alpha})^2 + R_1$, where $R_1 \cong 0$ and $E(\alpha) = \overline{\alpha}$. Similarly, $e^{-\alpha[f_1(p_1) + f_2(p_1, p_2)]} = e^{-\overline{\alpha}(f_1 + f_2)} - f_2(p_1, p_2)e^{-\overline{\alpha}(f_1 + f_2)}(\alpha - \overline{\alpha}) + 1/2[f_1(p_1) + f_2(p_1, p_2)]^2e^{-\overline{\alpha}(f_1 + f_2)}(\alpha - \overline{\alpha})^2 + R_2$, where $R_2 \cong 0$. Let Z^* denote the net present value of expected profits under uncertainty and Z the net present value of profits under certainty. After simplification we get $Z^* = Z - (\theta/2)\sigma^2(\alpha)[f_1(p_1)]^3e^{-\overline{\alpha}f_1(p_1)} - (1 + \delta)^{-1}(\theta/2)\sigma^2(\alpha)f_2(p_1, p_2)[f_1(p_1) + f_2(p_1, p_2)]^2e^{-\overline{\alpha}[f_1(p_1) + f_2(p_1, p_2)]}$.

Differentiating, we get $\partial Z^*/\partial p_1 = \partial Z/\partial p_1 - (\theta/2)\,\sigma^2(\alpha)(A+B) + \cdots$, where $A = 3[f_1(p_1)]^2(\partial f_1/\partial p_1)e^{-\bar{\alpha}f_1(p_1)} < 0$ and $B = -\bar{\alpha}(\partial f_1/\partial p_1)e^{-\bar{\alpha}f_1(p_1)}[f_1(p_1)]^3 > 0$. Hence we cannot determine the effect of uncertainty in learning on the firm's pricing policy.

13. Suppose demand is stochastic but the learning parameter $\hat{\alpha}$ is known. Consider the case $q_1 = f_1(p_1) + u_1$ and $q_2 = f_2(p_1, p_2) + u_2$, where the us are independent stochastic disturbances such that $E(u_i) = 0$ for all i. Let π_i^* denote the random profit in period i $(i = 1, 2)$. Then $\pi_1^* = p_1[f_1(p_1) + u_1] - \theta e^{-\hat{\alpha}f_1(p_1)}e^{-\hat{\alpha}u_1}[f_1(p_1) + u_1]$. Now $e^{-\hat{\alpha}u_1}$ is convex in u_1. Hence by Jensen's inequality $E(e^{-\hat{\alpha}u_1}) > e^{-\hat{\alpha}E(u_1)} = 1$. Let $E(e^{-\hat{\alpha}u_1}) = 1 + \Delta_1$, where $\Delta_1 > 0$. Using Taylor's expansion, $u_1 e^{-\hat{\alpha}u_1} = u_1[1 - \hat{\alpha}u_1 + (\hat{\alpha}u_1)^2/2! - (\hat{\alpha}u_1)^3/3! + \cdots]$. Hence $E\{e^{-\hat{\alpha}u_1}[f_1(p_1) + u_1]\} = f_1(p_1)(1 + \Delta_1) + \Delta_2$, where $\Delta_2 = E(e^{-\hat{\alpha}u_1}u_1) = E[u_1 - \hat{\alpha}u_1^2 + (\hat{\alpha})^3 u_1^3/2! - (\hat{\alpha})^3 u_1^4/3! + \cdots]$. Suppose u_1 is normally distributed. Then $\Delta_2 < 0$. Let π_1 denote the certainty profit. Then $E(\pi_1^*) - \pi_1 = -\theta e^{-\hat{\alpha}f_1(p_1)}[\Delta_1 f_1(p_1) + \Delta_2]$, which is indeterminate. Similarly we can show that $E(\pi_2^*) - \pi_2$ is indeterminate. Thus for large demand uncertainty we cannot determine if the risk-neutral firm is better off than under certainty.

14. Valuing uncertain cash flows in a multiperiod model poses significant technical problems that have not been resolved in the literature (see Machina 1984 and Quiggin 1993, pp. 121–24 for a succinct discussion). We shall make the simplifying assumption that the utility function is time-additive. Let π_i denote the cash flow in period i and $U(\pi_i)$ the utility in period i. Then the decision maker chooses policy to maximize $Q = \Sigma_{i=1}^{I} EU(\pi_i)/(1+\delta)^i$, where δ denotes the appropriate discount rate and I the planning period. The risk-neutral firm maximizes $Q_n = \Sigma_{i=1}^{I} E(\pi_i)/(1+\delta)^i$, where δ denotes the risk-free interest rate. Thus Q_n and Q can be interpreted as net present values.

15. Consider a two-period model in which demand is deterministic but the learning effect is random. Suppose the firm is risk-neutral. Using the standard net present value approach, the firm chooses the pricing policy (p_1^*, p_2^*), which maximizes $Z^* E[p_1^* f_1(p_1^*) - \theta e^{-\alpha f_1(p_1^*)} f_1(p_1^*)] + (1+\delta)^{-1} E[p_2^* f_2(p_1^*, p_2^*) - \theta e^{-\alpha[f_1(p_1^*)+f_2(p_1^*, p_2^*)]} f_2(p_1^*, p_2^*)]$, where the learning coefficient α is random. We shall refer to the pricing plan (p_1^*, p_2^*) as Policy A. Suppose uncertainty regarding α is resolved at the end of period 1. Let $\hat{\alpha}(p_1^*, p_2^*)$ denote the value of α for which $\pi_2^* = p_2^* f_2(p_1^*, p_2^*) - \theta e^{-\alpha[f_1(p_1^*)+f_2(p_1^*, p_2^*)]} f_2(p_1^*, p_2^*) = 0$. Consider Policy B, in which the firm chooses a price of p_1^* in period 1, abandons the project in period 2 if $\alpha < \hat{\alpha}$, and charges a price of p_2^* if $\alpha > \hat{\alpha}$. For simplicity assume that the abandonment value is zero [i.e., $\pi_2 = 0$ if $\alpha < \hat{\alpha}$]. Then the net present value of Policy B is $Z^{**} = E[p_1^* f_1(p_1^*) - \theta e^{-\alpha f_1(p_1^*)} f_1(p_1^*)] + (1+\delta)^{-1} \int_{\hat{\alpha}(p_1^*, p_2^*)}^{\alpha_u} [p_2^* f_2(p_1^*, p_2^*) - \theta e^{-\alpha[f_1(p_1^*)+f_2(p_1^*, p_2^*)]} f_2(p_1^*, p_2^*)]\varphi(\alpha)\,d\alpha$ where $\varphi(\alpha)$ denotes the density function of α and α_u the upper bound of α. Subtracting, we get $Z^{**} - Z^* = -(1+\delta)^{-1} \int_{\alpha_l}^{\hat{\alpha}(p_1^*, p_2^*)} [p_2^* f_2(p_1^*, p_2^*) - \theta e^{-\alpha[f_1(p_1^*)+f_2(p_1^*, p_2^*)]} f_2(p_1^*, p_2^*)]\varphi(\alpha)\,d\alpha$ where α_l denotes the lower bound of α. Now the expression in square brackets equals zero when $\alpha = \hat{\alpha}(p_1^*, p_2^*)$ and is strictly increasing in α. Hence $Z^{**} - Z^* > 0$. Thus the standard net present value understates the economic value of the project.

16. For the model in note 15 we assumed an abandonment value of zero. If the firm can exercise an option to sell the project at the end of period 1 for a positive scrap value, the economic value of introducing the cost-saving technology will increase. We refer the reader to the review paper by Pindyck (1991) and the book by Dixit and Pindyck (1994) for an extensive treatment of the valuation of "real" options. In Chapter 9 (Propositions 8 and 15) we shall discuss the relevance of real options theory to the design of managerial compensation plans.

17. Pindyck (1993) develops an interesting model that considers both input cost and technological uncertainty, which is measured by the time taken to complete a project. The model, however, does

not include price as a control variable. Our focus here is on coordinating price and investment policy in different market structures when both input prices and demand are uncertain.

18. Let $q = f(x_1, x_2)$ denote the production function, where q denotes production, x_1 is the amount of capital, and x_2 the amount of labor. Assuming that the production function is invertible, we can write the labor requirement function as $x_2 = \varphi(x_1, q)$, where $\partial\varphi/\partial x_1 < 0$ and $\partial\varphi/\partial q > 0$. Let the monopolist's demand function be $q = \alpha(p, R_m) + \beta(p)\varepsilon_1$, where p denotes price, R_m is the random return on the market portfolio, α and β are deterministic functions, and ε_1 is a stochastic term that measures firm-specific risk [i.e., $\text{Cov}(\varepsilon_1, R_m) = 0$]. To allow for different market structures in the labor market let the wage rate be $w_2 = \Omega[\varphi(x_1, q), R_m] + \delta[\varphi(x_1, q)]\varepsilon_2$, where Ω and δ are functions and ε_2 denotes firm-specific risk in the labor market [i.e., $\text{Cov}(\varepsilon_2, R_m) = 0$]. Note that, in contrast to the quantity-setting mode, uncertainty is transmitted from the output market to the labor market because the firm's future use of labor is uncertain. Now the risk-neutral firm chooses price (p) and capital (x_1) ex ante to maximize expected profit defined by $E(\pi) = p[E(\alpha) + \beta E(\varepsilon_1)] - w_1 x_1 - E\{\varphi(x_1, \alpha + \beta\varepsilon_1)[\Omega(\varphi(x_1, \alpha + \beta\varepsilon_1), R_m) + \delta(\varphi(x_1, \alpha + \beta\varepsilon_1))\varepsilon_2]\}$, where w_1 denotes the price per unit of capital. Suppose the capital asset pricing model holds. Then the value-maximizing firm chooses price and capital ex ante to maximize $V = \frac{E(\pi) - a_m p\ \text{Cov}(\alpha, R_m) + a_m\ \text{Cov}\{\varphi[\Omega(\varphi, R_m) + \delta\varepsilon_2], R_m\}}{1 + r_f}$, where r_f denotes the risk-free interest rate and a_m the market price of risk.

Note that the model implicitly assumes a "putty-putty" technology because the capital input chosen ex ante can be flexibly combined with labor when production actually occurs. See Kon (1983) for a model of the competitive firm facing uncertainty in a "putty-putty" world with technological fixedness. Furthermore, in contrast to most dynamic investment models under uncertainty (see Dixit and Pindyck 1994 and the review papers by Pindyck 1991 and Abel 1990), our model does not assume that the input and output markets are competitive. Future research is necessary—particularly from a marketer's viewpoint—to develop investment models under uncertainty when markets are oligopolistic and firms are price setters. See Dixit and Pindyck (1994, pp. 314–15) for a survey of the sparse literature in this area.

19. The proof is obtained by expanding the appropriate terms in $E(\pi)$ and V (see previous note) using the Taylor expansion.

Appendix A

Comparison of Strategic and Myopic Pricing Plans in the Presence of Experience Effects

Consider a two-period model where p_1 and p_2 denote the prices in periods 1 and 2, respectively. Let the demand in period i be $q_i = f(p_i)$, where $\partial q_i/\partial p_i < 0$. Let the average cost be $AC = \theta e^{-\alpha q}$, where θ is the average cost per unit when the technology is first introduced, α is a learning parameter, and q denotes accumulated volume.

A.1 COMPARISON OF STRATEGIC AND MYOPIC PRICING

The firm's profit in period 1 is defined by

$$\pi_1 = \left(p_1 - \theta e^{-\alpha f(p_1)}\right) f(p_1) \tag{A.1}$$

and the profit in period 2 is

$$\pi_2 = \left(p_2 - \theta e^{-\alpha[f(p_1)+f(p_2)]}\right) f(p_2) \tag{A.2}$$

Under myopic pricing, the firm chooses price in period 1 (p_1^m) to maximize π_1. In period 2, the firm chooses price (p_2^m) to maximize π_2 given p_1^m. Under strategic pricing, the firm simultaneously chooses p_1^* and p_2^* to maximize the net present value of profits defined by $V = \pi_1 + \pi_2/(1+\delta)$, where δ denotes the opportunity cost of capital.

Differentiating V with respect to p_1 and p_2, respectively, we get

$$V_1 = \frac{\partial V}{\partial p_1} = \frac{\partial \pi_1}{\partial p_1} + (1+\delta)^{-1} f(p_2)\left[\theta\alpha\left(\frac{\partial f}{\partial p_1}\right)e^{-\alpha[f(p_1)+f(p_2)]}\right] \tag{A.3}$$

$$V_2 = \frac{\partial V}{\partial p_2} = (1+\delta)^{-1}\left\{\left[1 + \theta\alpha\left(\frac{\partial f}{\partial p_2}\right)e^{-\alpha[f(p_1)+f(p_2)]}\right]\right.$$
$$\left. f(p_2) + \frac{\partial f}{\partial p_2}(p_2 - \theta e^{-\alpha[f(p_1)+f(p_2)]})\right\} \tag{A.4}$$

Now $\partial \pi_i/\partial p_1 = 0$ when $p_1 = p_1^m$. Evaluating V_1 at p_1^m, we obtain

$$V_1|_{p_1=p_1^m} = (1+\delta)^{-1} f(p_2)\theta\alpha(\partial f/\partial p_1)e^{-\alpha[f(p_1)+f(p_2)]} < 0$$

Hence $p_1^* < p_1^m$ by the concavity of V_1. That is, the strategic output in period 1 (q_1^*) is greater than the output in period 1 under myopic pricing (q_1^m).

In order to compare p_2^* and p_2^m, it is necessary to examine the marginal costs in period 2 for myopic and strategic pricing.

Let the total cost in period 2 for the myopic policy be $C_2^m = q_2\theta e^{-\alpha(\hat{q}_1+q_2)}$. Then the marginal cost in period 2 using myopic pricing is $\partial C_2^m/\partial q_2 = MC_2^m = \theta e^{-\alpha\hat{q}_1}e^{-\alpha q_2}(1 - \alpha q_2)$. Let the total cost in period 2 for the strategic pricing policy be $C_2^* = q_2\theta e^{-\alpha(q_1^*+q_2)}$. Then the marginal cost in period 2 using strategic pricing is $\partial C_2^*/\partial q_2 = MC_2^* = \theta e^{-\alpha q_1^*}e^{-\alpha q_2}(1-\alpha q_2)$. Hence $(\partial C_2^m/\partial q_2)-(\partial C^*/\partial q_2) = \theta e^{-\alpha q_2}(1-\alpha q_2)(e^{-\alpha\hat{q}_1}-e^{-\alpha q_1^*}) > 0$. Thus MC_2^m is always above MC_2^*. (See Figure 1.4.) Hence $p_2^* < p_2^m$. This result generalizes to the multiperiod case (i.e., $p_i^* < p_i^m$ for any i). See Clarke et al. (1982) and Kalish (1983, Theorem 1).

Let AC_2^m, and AC_2^*, respectively, denote the average costs in period 2 given the myopic and strategic pricing plans, where $AC_2^m = \theta e^{-\alpha(\hat{q}_1+q_2)}$ and $AC_2^* = \theta e^{-\alpha(q_1^*+q_2)}$. Differentiating, we obtain $(\partial AC_2^m/\partial q_2) - (\partial AC_2^*/\partial q_2) = \theta\alpha e^{-\alpha q_2}(e^{-\alpha q_1^*} - e^{-\alpha\hat{q}_1}) < 0$, recalling that $q_1^* > q_1^m$. (See Figure 1.3.) Similarly $(\partial MC_2^m/\partial q_2) - (\partial MC_2^*/\partial q_2) = -\alpha\theta e^{-\alpha q_2}[1 + (1 - \alpha q_2)](e^{-\alpha\hat{q}_1} - e^{-\alpha q_1^*}) < 0$ recalling that $(1 - \alpha q_2) > 0$. Hence, MC_2^m is steeper than MC_2^* for any q_2 as shown in Figure 1.4.

A.2 EFFECT OF PARAMETER SHIFTS

In order to determine the effect of parameter shifts on strategic pricing, it is necessary to determine the sign of $\partial^2 V / \partial p_1 \, \partial p_2$. Differentiating Eq. (A.3), we have

$$\frac{\partial^2 V}{\partial p_1 \, \partial p_2} = (1 + \delta)^{-1} \theta \alpha e^{-\alpha[f(p_1) + f(p_2)]} \left(\frac{\partial f}{\partial p_1} \right) \left(\frac{\partial f}{\partial p_2} \right) [1 - \alpha f(p_2)] > 0 \quad \text{(A.5)}$$

Suppose the firm's opportunity cost of capital (δ) increases. The impact on the strategic pricing plan is given by $\partial p_1^* / \partial \delta$ and $\partial p_2^* / \partial \delta$. Using the comparative statics method (see Silberberg 1990, Chapter 6), we have

$$\frac{\partial p_1^*}{\partial \delta} = \left[\left(\frac{-\partial^2 V}{\partial p_1 \, \partial \delta} \right) \left(\frac{\partial^2 V}{\partial p_2^2} \right) + \left(\frac{\partial^2 V}{\partial p_2 \, \partial \delta} \right) \left(\frac{\partial^2 V}{\partial p_1 \, \partial p_2} \right) \right] D^{-1} \quad \text{(A.6)}$$

where $D = [(\partial^2 V / \partial p_1^2)(\partial^2 V / \partial p_2^2) - (\partial^2 V / \partial p_1 \, \partial p_2)^2] > 0$ by the second-order conditions. Now $\partial^2 V / \partial p_2 \, \partial \delta = 0$ using the first-order conditions. Furthermore

$$\frac{\partial^2 V}{\partial p_1 \, \partial \delta} = -(1 + \delta)^{-2} \theta \alpha \left(\frac{\partial f}{\partial p_1} \right) f(p_2) e^{-\alpha[f(p_1) + f(p_2)]} > 0$$

Substituting these results in Eq. (A.6), we have $\partial p_1^* / \partial \delta > 0$. Similarly we can show that $\partial p_2^* / \partial \delta > 0$, recalling that $\partial^2 V / \partial p_1 \, \partial p_2 > 0$. Hence the firm increases prices in both periods when the opportunity cost of capital increases.

Suppose learning is accelerated (i.e., α increases). Let $C_1 = f(p_1) e^{-\alpha f(p_1)}$ denote the total cost of production in period 1 and $C = [f(p_1) + f(p_2)] e^{-\alpha[f(p_1) + f(p_2)]}$ denote the total cost of producing the accumulated output (i.e., the sum of the outputs in periods 1 and 2). Proceeding as before we have

$$\frac{\partial p_1^*}{\partial \alpha} = \left[\left(\frac{-\partial^2 V}{\partial p_1 \, \partial \alpha} \right) \left(\frac{\partial^2 V}{\partial p_1^2} \right) + \left(\frac{\partial^2 V}{\partial p_2 \, \partial \alpha} \right) \left(\partial^2 V / \partial p_1 \, \partial p_2 \right) \right] D^{-1} \quad \text{(A.7)}$$

On simplification, we obtain

$$\frac{\partial^2 V}{\partial p_1 \, \partial \alpha} = \theta \left(\frac{\partial f}{\partial p_1} \right) \left[C_1 + \left(\frac{\partial C_1}{\partial q_1} \right) f(p_1) + \left(\frac{\partial C}{\partial q_1} \right) f(p_2)(1 + \delta)^{-1} \right] < 0$$

recalling that marginal cost is strictly positive. Similarly we have

$$\frac{\partial^2 V}{\partial p_2 \, \partial \alpha} = \theta \left(\frac{\partial f}{\partial p_2} \right) \left[\left(\frac{\partial C}{\partial q_2} \right) f(p_2) + C \right] (1 + \delta)^{-1} < 0$$

Substituting these results into Eq. (A.7), we have $\partial p_1^* / \partial \alpha < 0$. Similarly we can show that $\partial p_2^* / \partial \alpha < 0$. Hence if learning is accelerated, the firm will charge lower prices in both periods. Thus the effect of an increase in learning is analogous to that of a decrease in the opportunity cost of capital.

B

Comparison of Strategic and Myopic Pricing Plans in the Presence of Demand Dynamics

Consider a two-period model where p_1 and p_2 denote the prices in periods 1 and 2, respectively. Let the demand in period 1 be $q_i = f(p_1)$, where $\partial q_1/\partial p_1 < 0$ and the demand in period 2 be $q_2 = g(p_1, p_2)$, where $\partial q_2/\partial p_2 < 0$ and $\partial q_2/\partial p_1 < 0$ (i.e., a low price in period 1 increases demand in period 2). The reader can use the methodology to examine the case where a low price in period 1 "borrows" demand from period 2 [i.e., $\partial q_2/\partial p_1 > 0$].

Let the cost in period 1 be $C_1 = \phi_1(q_1)$, where $\partial C_1/\partial q_1 > 0$ and the cost in period 2 be $C_2 = \phi_2(q_2)$, where $\partial C_2/\partial q_2 > 0$. Note that because of demand dynamics the price in period 1 affects q_2 and hence the cost in period 2.

B.1 COMPARISON OF STRATEGIC AND MYOPIC PRICING

The firm's profit in period 1 is $\pi_1 = p_1 f(p_1) - \phi_1(f(p_1))$ and the profit in period 2 is $\pi_2 = p_2 g(p_1, p_2) - \phi_2(g(p_1, p_2))$. Under myopic pricing, the firm chooses price in period 1 (p_1^m) to maximize π_1. In period 2, the firm chooses price p_2^m to maximize π_2 given p_1^m. Under strategic pricing, the firm simultaneously chooses p_1^* and p_2^* to maximize the net present value of profits defined by $V = \pi_1 + \pi_2/(1 + \delta)$, where δ denotes the opportunity cost of capital.

Differentiating V with respect to p_1 and p_2, respectively, we have

$$\frac{\partial V}{\partial p_1} = \frac{\partial \pi_1}{\partial p_1} + (1 + \delta)^{-1} \frac{\partial g}{\partial p_1} \left(p_2 - \frac{\partial \phi_2}{\partial q_2} \right) \tag{B.1}$$

$$\frac{\partial V}{\partial p_2} = (1 + \delta)^{-1} \left[g + \left(p_2 - \frac{\partial \phi_2}{\partial q_2} \right) \frac{\partial g}{\partial p_2} \right] \tag{B.2}$$

recalling that $\partial \pi_1/\partial p_2 = 0$. Now Eq. (B.2) implies that $(p_2 - \partial \phi_2/\partial q_2) > 0$ when $p_1 = p_1^*$ and $p_2 = p_2^*$. Hence Eq. (B.1) implies that $\partial \pi_1/\partial p_1 > 0$ when $p_1 = p_1^*$ and $p_2 = p_2^*$. However, π_1 is concave in p_1. Hence $p_1^m > p_1^*$. Thus the strategic price in period 1 is lower than the myopic price.

As discussed in the text, the effect of strategic pricing on the price in period 2 depends crucially on the effect of the price in period 1 on price sensitivity in period 2 and the cost structure. We consider two formulations of the demand function in period 2: multiplicative and additively separable.

Case 1: Multiplicative Separability

Suppose the demand in period 2 is $g(p_1, p_2) = \alpha_1(p_1)\alpha_2(p_2)$, where $\partial \alpha_1/\partial p_1 < 0$ and $\partial \alpha_2/\partial p_2 < 0$. This specification implies that the price in period 1 has no effect on price sensitivity[1] in period 2. Equivalently, a price reduction in period 1 leads to a proportionate expansion in demand in period 2 at all prices. Equation (B.2) now reduces to

$$\frac{\partial V}{\partial p_2} = (1+\delta)^{-1}\alpha_1(p_1)\left[\alpha_2(p_2) + \left(p_2 - \frac{\partial\phi_2}{\partial q_2}\right)\left(\frac{\partial\alpha_2}{\partial p_2}\right)\right] \qquad \text{(B.3)}$$

Suppose marginal cost (i.e., $\partial\phi_2/\partial q_2$) is constant. Then the expression in square brackets does not depend on p_1. Hence the price in period 2 does not depend on the price in period 1. Consequently the myopic and strategic pricing plans will lead to the same price in period 2.

Suppose marginal cost is not constant. Let $p_2 = \mu(p_1)$ solve Eq. (B.3). Setting the total differential of Eq. (B.3) to zero and solving, we have

$$\frac{dp_2}{dp_1} = -\left(\frac{\partial^2 V}{\partial p_1\,\partial p_2}\right)\bigg/\left(\frac{\partial^2 V}{\partial p_2^2}\right)$$

where $\partial^2 V/\partial p_2^2 < 0$ by concavity. Hence sgn $(dp_2/dp_1) = $ sgn $(\partial^2 V/\partial p_1\,\partial p_2)$.

Differentiating Eq. (B.3) with respect to p_2, we have

$$\frac{\partial^2 V}{\partial p_1\,\partial p_2} = (1+\delta)^{-1}\left\{\left(\frac{\partial\alpha_1}{\partial p_1}\right)\left[\alpha_2(p_2) + \left(p_2 - \frac{\partial\phi_2}{\partial q_2}\right)\left(\frac{\partial\alpha_2}{\partial p_2}\right)\right]\right.$$

$$\left. - \alpha_1(p_1)\left(\frac{\partial^2\phi_2}{\partial q_2^2}\right)\left(\frac{\partial q_2}{\partial p_1}\right)\left(\frac{\partial\alpha_2}{\partial p_2}\right)\right\} \qquad \text{(B.4)}$$

Now the term in square brackets equals zero by the first-order conditions. Hence sgn $(dp_2/dp_1) = $ sgn $(\partial^2 V/\partial p_1\,\partial p_2) = -$sgn $(\partial^2\phi_2/\partial q_2^2)$. Recall that the strategic price is always lower than the myopic price in period 1. Hence the strategic price is higher (lower) than the myopic price in period 2 depending on whether marginal cost is increasing (decreasing).

Case 2: Additive Separability

Suppose the demand in period 2 is additively separable and has the form $g(p_1,\ p_2) = \alpha_1(p_1) + \alpha_2(p_2)$, where $\partial\alpha_1/\partial p_1 < 0$ and $\partial\alpha_2/\partial p_2 < 0$. This specification implies that a lower price in period 1 makes the market less price sensitive[2] in period 2. Now $\partial^2 V/\partial p_1\,\partial p_2 = (1+\delta)^{-1}(\partial\alpha_1/\partial p_1)[1 - (\partial^2\phi_2/\partial q_2^2)(\partial\alpha_2/\partial p_1)] < 0$ provided $\partial^2\phi_2/\partial q_2^2 \geq 0$. Hence, in contrast to the case where demand is multiplicatively separable, we can only compare the strategic and myopic prices in period 2 if marginal cost is constant or increasing. Following the previous approach, it is easy to show that in these cases the strategic price exceeds the myopic price in period 2.

B.2 EFFECT OF PARAMETER SHIFTS

Suppose the opportunity cost of capital δ increases. We are interested in the impact on the strategic prices (i.e., $\partial p_1^*/\partial\delta$ and $\partial p_2^*/\partial\delta$). Solving for $\partial p_1^*/\partial\delta$, we have

$$\frac{\partial p_1^*}{\partial \delta} = \left[\left(\frac{-\partial^2 V}{\partial p_1\, \partial \delta}\right)\left(\frac{\partial^2 V}{\partial p_2^2}\right) - \left(\frac{\partial^2 V}{\partial p_1\, \partial p_2}\right)\left(\frac{-\partial^2 V}{\partial p_2\, \partial \delta}\right)\right]E^{-1} \tag{B.5}$$

where $E = [(\partial^2 V/\partial p_1^2)(\partial^2 V/\partial p_2^2) - (\partial^2 V/\partial p_1\, \partial p_2)^2] > 0$ by the second-order conditions. Now $\partial^2 V/\partial p_1\, \partial \delta = -(1+\delta)^{-2}(\partial g/\partial p_1)(p_2 - \partial \phi_2/\partial q_2) > 0$ using Eq. (B.1). Similarly, $\partial^2 V/\partial p_2\, \partial \delta = 0$ using Eq. (B.2). Hence $\partial p_1^*/\partial \delta > 0$, recalling that V is concave in p_2. Thus the firm will always increase the price in period 1 when the opportunity cost of capital increases.

The sign of $\partial p_2^*/\partial \delta$ depends crucially on the effect of the price in period 1 on price sensitivity in period 2 and on the precise form of the cost structure. Specifically

$$\frac{\partial p_2^*}{\partial \delta} = \left[\left(\frac{-\partial^2 V}{\partial p_2\, \partial \delta}\right)\left(\frac{\partial^2 V}{\partial p_1^2}\right) - \left(\frac{-\partial^2 V}{\partial p_1\, \partial \delta}\right)\left(\frac{\partial^2 V}{\partial p_1\, \partial p_2}\right)\right]E^{-1} \tag{B.6}$$

Hence $\operatorname{sgn}(\partial p_2^*/\partial \delta) = \operatorname{sgn}(\partial^2 V/\partial p_1\, \partial p_2)$.

Case 1: Multiplicative Separability

Suppose marginal cost is constant. Then $\partial^2 V/\partial p_1\, \partial p_2 = 0$ and $\partial p_2^*/\partial \delta = 0$. Suppose marginal cost depends on volume. We have already shown that $\operatorname{sgn}(\partial^2 V/\partial p_1\, \partial p_2) = -\operatorname{sgn}(\partial^2 \phi_2/\partial q_2^2)$. Hence, $\operatorname{sgn}(\partial p_2^*/\partial \delta) = -\operatorname{sgn}(\partial^2 \phi^2/\partial q_2^2)$. Thus if the opportunity cost of capital increases, the strategic price in period 2 is decreased (increased) according as marginal cost increases (decreases) with volume.

Case 2: Additive Separability

We have shown that $\partial^2 V/\partial p_1\, \partial p_2 < 0$ provided marginal cost is constant or increases with volume. In these cases, $\partial p_2^*/\partial \delta < 0$. Note that, in contrast to the multiplicatively separable model, the sign of $\partial p_2^*/\partial \delta$ is inherently indeterminate if marginal cost decreases with volume.

NOTES

1. Let ε_2 denote the price elasticity of demand in period 2. Then $\varepsilon_2 = -(\partial g/\partial p_2)(p_2/g)$. Substituting $\partial g/\partial p_2 = \alpha_1(p_1)[\partial \alpha_2(p_2)/\partial p_2]$, we have $\varepsilon_2 = -[\partial \alpha_2(p_2)/\partial p_2](p_2/\alpha_2)$, which does not depend on p_1. Recall that marginal revenue = price (1 + 1/price elasticity). Hence the marginal revenue at any price p_2 does not depend on p_1.

2. The absolute value of the price elasticity in period 2 is $|\varepsilon_2| = -(\partial g/\partial p_2)(p_2/g) = -(\partial \alpha_2/\partial p_2)$ $\{p_2/[\alpha_1(p_1) + \alpha_2(p_2)]\}$. Differentiating with respect to p_1, we have $\partial |\varepsilon_2|/\partial p_1 = p_2(\partial \alpha_2/\partial p_2)$ $(\partial \alpha_1/\partial p_1)(\alpha_1 + \alpha_2)^{-2} > 0$.

Comparison of Strategic and Myopic Pricing Plans: Cost Dynamics and Demand Dynamics

Consider a two-period model where p_1 and p_2 denote the prices in periods 1 and 2 respectively. Let the demand in period 1 be $q_1 = f(p_1)$ where $\partial q_1/\partial p_1 < 0$ and the demand in period 2 be $q_2 = g(p_1, p_2)$ where $\partial q_2/\partial p_1 < 0$ and $\partial q_2/\partial p_2 < 0$. Let the average cost in period 1 be $c_1 = \theta e^{-\alpha q_1}$ and the average cost in period 2 be $c_2 = \theta e^{-\alpha(q_1+q_2)}$ where α denotes the learning parameter.

C.1 COMPARISON OF STRATEGIC AND MYOPIC PRICING

The firm's profit in period 1 is $\pi_1 = [p_1 - \theta e^{-\alpha f(p_1)}]f(p_1)$ and the profit in period 2 is $\pi_2 = [p_2 - \theta e^{-\alpha(f(p_1)+g(p_1,p_2))}]g(p_1, p_2)$. Under myopic pricing, the firm chooses price in period 1 (p_1^m) to maximize π_1. In period 2, the firm chooses price (p_2^m) to maximize π_2 given p_1^m. Under strategic pricing, the firm simultaneously chooses p_1^* and p_2^* to maximize the net present value of profits defined by $V = \pi_1 + \pi_2/(1 + \delta)$ where δ denotes the opportunity cost of capital.

Differentiating V with respect to p_1 and p_2 respectively, we have

$$\frac{\partial V}{\partial p_1} = \frac{\partial \pi_1}{\partial p_1} + (1+\delta)^{-1}\left[\left(\frac{\partial g}{\partial p_1}\right)(p_2 - c_2) + \theta g\alpha\left(\frac{\partial f}{\partial p_1} + \frac{\partial g}{\partial p_1}\right)e^{-\alpha(f+g)}\right] \quad \text{(C.1)}$$

$$\frac{\partial V}{\partial p_2} = (1+\delta)^{-1}\left\{\left(\frac{\partial g}{\partial p_2}\right)(p_2 - c_2) + g\left[1 + \theta\alpha\left(\frac{\partial g}{\partial p_2}\right)e^{-\alpha(f+g)}\right]\right\} \quad \text{(C.2)}$$

Evaluating Eq. (C.1) at (p_1^*, p_2^*), we have $\partial\pi_1/\partial p_1|_{p_1^*} > 0$, recalling that p_2 does not affect π_1. But π_1 is concave in p_1. Hence $p_1^* < p_1^m$. That is, the strategic price is lower than the myopic price in period 1.

For a comparison of the myopic and strategic prices in period 2, see the discussion in the text.

C.2 EFFECT OF PARAMETER SHIFTS

In order to determine the effects of parameter shifts on the strategic pricing plan, it is necessary to determine the sign of $\partial^2 V/\partial p_1 \partial p_2$. Differentiating Eq. (C.1) with respect to p_2, we have

$$\frac{\partial^2 V}{\partial p_1 \partial p_2} = (1+\delta)^{-1}\left\{\left(\frac{\partial^2 g}{\partial p_1 \partial p_2}\right)(p_2 - c_2) + \left(1 - \frac{\partial c_2}{\partial p_2}\right)\frac{\partial g}{\partial p_1}\right.$$

$$\left. - \left[\left(\frac{\partial^2 c_2}{\partial p_1 \partial p_2}\right)g + \left(\frac{\partial g}{\partial p_2}\right)\left(\frac{\partial c_2}{\partial p_1}\right)\right]\right\} \quad \text{(C.3)}$$

Now $(1 - \partial c_2/\partial p_2) > 0$ using the first-order condition $\partial V/\partial p_2 = 0$. Hence $(1 - \partial c_2/\partial p_2)\partial g/\partial p_1 < 0$. However, $-(\partial g/\partial p_2)(\partial c_2/\partial p_1) = \theta\alpha(\partial g/\partial p_2)(\partial f/\partial p_1 + \partial g/\partial p_1)e^{-\alpha(f+g)} > 0$. Hence $\partial^2 V/\partial p_1\,\partial p_2$ is inherently indeterminate.[1]

C.3 CHANGE IN THE COST OF CAPITAL

Suppose the cost of capital δ increases. The effect on the strategic price p_1^* is given by

$$\frac{\partial p_1^*}{\partial \delta} = \left[\left(\frac{-\partial^2 V}{\partial p_1\,\partial \delta}\right)\left(\frac{\partial^2 V}{\partial p_2^2}\right) + \left(\frac{\partial^2 V}{\partial p_1\,\partial p_2}\right)\left(\frac{\partial^2 V}{\partial p_1\,\partial \delta}\right)\right]^{-1} F \tag{C.4}$$

where $F = [(\partial^2 V/\partial p_1^2)(\partial^2 V/\partial p_2^2) - (\partial^2 V/\partial p_1\,\partial p_2)^2] > 0$ by the second-order conditions. Differentiating Eq. (C.1), we have

$$\frac{\partial^2 V}{\partial p_1\,\partial \delta} = -(1 + \delta)^{-2}\left[\left(\frac{\partial g}{\partial p_1}\right)(p_2 - c_2) + \theta\alpha g\left(\frac{\partial f}{\partial p_1} + \frac{\partial g}{\partial p_1}\right)e^{-\alpha(f+g)}\right] > 0$$

Differentiating Eq. (C.2) we obtain $\partial^2 V/\partial p_2\,\partial \delta = 0$ using the first-order condition. Hence $\partial p_1^*/\partial \delta > 0$ using the concavity of V. Thus, if the cost of capital increases, the firm raises the strategic price in period 1. For a discussion of the sign of $\partial p_2^*/\partial \delta$, see the text.

C.4 CHANGE IN THE LEARNING RATE

Suppose the learning rate (α) increases. Now $\partial^2 V/\partial p_1\,\partial\alpha \neq 0$ and $\partial^2 V/\partial p_2\,\partial\alpha \neq 0$. Recalling that $\partial^2 V/\partial p_1\,\partial p_2$ cannot be signed, we see that $\partial p_1^*/\partial\alpha$ and $\partial p_2^*/\partial\alpha$ are ambiguous. Note that, in contrast to the pure cost-dynamics case, the effect of an increase in the rate of learning is not analogous to the effect of a decrease in the cost of capital.

NOTES

1. No useful simplifications are obtained by making g separable in its arguments. Suppose $g(p_1,\,p_2) = \alpha_1(p_1) + \alpha_2(p_2)$. Now $\partial^2 V/\partial p_1\,\partial p_2 = (1+\delta)^{-1}[(1 - \partial c_2/\partial p_2)\,\partial g/\partial p_1 - g(\partial^2 c_2/\partial p_1\,\partial p_2) - (\partial g/\partial p_2)(\partial c_2/\partial p_1)]$ where $(\partial^2 c_2/\partial p_1\,\partial p_2) = \alpha^2\theta(\partial g/\partial p_2)(\partial f/\partial p_1 + \partial g/\partial p_1)e^{-\alpha(f+g)} > 0$ and $\partial c_2/\partial p_1 = -\theta\alpha(\partial f/\partial p_1 + \partial g/\partial p_1)e^{-\alpha(f+g)} > 0$. Hence the sign of $\partial^2 V/\partial p_1\,\partial p_2$ is ambiguous. Suppose $g(p_1,\,p_2) = \alpha_1(p_1)\alpha_2(p_2)$. Now $\partial^2 g/\partial p_1\,\partial p_2 = (\partial\alpha_1/\partial p_1)(\partial\alpha_2/\partial p_2) > 0$. However $\partial^2 c_2/\partial p_1\,\partial p_2 = -\alpha\theta e^{-\alpha(f+g)}[\partial^2 g/\partial p_1\,\partial p_2 - (\alpha\,\partial g/\partial p_2)(\partial f/\partial p_1 + \partial g/\partial p_1)]$, which is inherently ambiguous. Hence, as in the additive separability case, we cannot determine the sign of $\partial^2 V/\partial p_1\,\partial p_2$.

Pricing Under Uncertainty and Heterogeneity

This chapter focuses on pricing under uncertainty and pricing in markets that are characterized by heterogeneity. We shall examine both single- and multiperiod models. In our discussion of new product pricing policies we shall consider both the expected utility and stock market paradigms. In our discussion of consumer heterogeneity we distinguish nondurables and durables and explicitly consider the role of consumers' risk attitudes.

2.1 PRICING UNDER UNCERTAINTY: BREAK-EVEN PRICING

Suppose a firm is planning to introduce a new coffee-making machine in the marketplace. The firm must determine whether the new product is financially attractive and, if so, what the price should be. The crux of the problem is that demand is unknown. That is, the firm does not know precisely how many coffee-making machines consumers will purchase at any given price. We assume initially that the firm knows all costs. Specifically the fixed costs are $50,000 per period and the variable cost per coffee-making machine is $10.

One pricing approach is to begin by determining how many machines the firm must sell at any given price in order to recoup total costs (i.e., the sum of fixed and variable costs). Consider a price of $15 per machine. The firm's gross profit margin per machine is $5. Recalling that fixed costs are $50,000, we see that the firm must sell at least 10,000 units in order to make a profit. We say that the break-even volume at a price of $15 is 10,000 units. Proceeding similarly, we can determine the break-even volumes at different prices. For example:

Price per Unit	Break-Even Volume (Number of Units)
$12	25,000
$15	10,000
$20	5,000

The firm now chooses that pricing plan that maximizes the subjective probability of earning a positive profit. Note that this criterion is equivalent to minimizing the probability of bankruptcy.[1] Furthermore, it is straightforward to recast the break-even criterion in terms of other managerial objectives (for example, market share).

Suppose the "best" price is $20 per unit and implies a subjective bankruptcy probability of 10 percent. The only remaining question is whether the firm should continue with its existing product line or introduce the new product. Clearly the firm will not introduce the product if a 10 percent probability of bankruptcy is too high. If a 10 percent probability of bankruptcy is acceptable, the firm will introduce the new product at a price of $20 per unit.[2]

This pricing method for new products—break-even pricing—attempts to simplify decision-making under uncertainty. Specifically, the firm does not need to estimate the feasible demand levels for a new product at different prices (e.g., minimum, maximum, and most likely). Note, however, that the firm does not escape the problem of demand estimation because break-even pricing implicitly requires the firm to estimate the probability of bankruptcy at each price level. Furthermore, as the example illustrates, break-even pricing tends to lead to high prices because the break-even volume falls faster than price increases.[3] For example, if the price increases from $12 to $15 (a 25 percent increase), the break-even volume falls from 25,000 to 10,000 units (a 60 percent decrease). In addition, break-even pricing requires the firm to focus on accounting profits and downside risk (i.e., the probability of bankruptcy) rather than upside gains. This orientation may be reasonable for a small firm with limited resources or a firm for which the investment in the new product is strategic (i.e., the product accounts for a significant fraction of the firm's investment). In general, however, the firm that uses break-even pricing is likely to make excessively conservative decisions. That is, by emphasizing downside risk, the firm will pass up potentially lucrative new product opportunities. Furthermore, even if the firm accepts these new product opportunities, it is likely to suboptimize by charging an excessively high price.

Key Point *Break-even pricing is an heuristic for new product pricing under uncertainty. Although the firm does not require explicit demand estimates for different pricing plans, the firm must nonetheless estimate the subjective probability of bankruptcy for each pricing plan. In general, the firm will charge an excessively high price and may even forego potentially lucrative new product opportunities.*

The previous analysis assumed that costs are known. We now extend the break-even pricing method to the more general new-product situation where both demand and cost are uncertain. Suppose the firm expects the variable cost per coffee-making machine to range from $9 to $11 per unit but is not certain what the precise cost will be. We consider three variable cost scenarios: $9, $10, and $11 per unit. Following the previous approach, we can compute the break-even volumes at different prices for each cost scenario. The results are shown in Table 2.1. Note that if the price is high (say $20 per unit), the break-even volume does not change very much when the variable cost goes up from $9 to $11 per unit. In contrast, if the price is low (say $12 per unit), the break-even volume changes dramatically as variable costs vary. For example, when variable costs change from $10 to $11 per unit (a 10 percent increase), the break-even volume goes up from 25,000 units to 50,000 units

Table 2-1 Break-Even Volumes (In Units) for Different Cost Scenarios

	Variable Cost per Unit		
Unit Price	**$9**	**$10**	**$11**
$12	16,667	25,000	50,000
$15	8,333	10,000	12,500
$20	4,545	5,000	5,556

(a 100 percent increase). Consequently, break-even pricing pushes the firm even further towards the safe strategy of charging a high price.

> **Key Point**   *When both cost and demand are uncertain, the firm that uses break-even pricing will be more likely to charge a high price.*

The previous analyses focused on one element of the marketing mix: price. In practice the firm that introduces a new product will often find it necessary to advertise. Consequently, the firm needs to coordinate its pricing and advertising decisions. We now extend the basic break-even pricing model to deal with this scenario. In order to focus on essentials, we assume that the variable cost per unit is known to be $10 per unit. The reader should use our approach to examine the case where both cost and demand are uncertain.

Suppose the firm is considering three prices ($12, $15, and $20 per unit) and four levels of advertising spending ($0, $10,000, $20,000, and $30,000). Thus the firm must choose one of 12 price–advertising combinations. Proceeding as before, we can compute the break-even volumes for each of the 12 marketing plans. The results are shown in Table 2.2. Note that the break-even volumes are relatively stable as advertising is increased, provided the price is high (say $20 per unit). In contrast, when the price is low (implying a low unit profit margin), the break-even volume is quite sensitive to advertising. Thus the firm is likely to choose a high-price, high-advertising strategy.

> **Key Point**   *Under break-even pricing, the firm is likely to choose a high-price, high-advertising policy. The high price increases unit profit margins; consequently the break-even volume is less sensitive to incremental advertising.*

Table 2-2 Break-Even Volumes (In Units) for Different Price–Advertising Scenarios

	Advertising			
Unit Price	**$0**	**$10,000**	**$20,000**	**$30,000**
$12	25,000	30,000	35,000	40,000
$15	10,000	12,000	14,000	16,000
$20	5,000	6,000	7,000	8,000

2.2 PRICING UNDER UNCERTAINTY: SOME REFINEMENTS

Expected Profit

As discussed, break-even pricing does not require the firm to make explicit demand estimates at different prices. Furthermore, by emphasizing downside risk, break-even pricing leads to excessively conservative decision making. Suppose, in contrast to break-even pricing, the firm chooses an explicit objective function and makes specific demand estimates for different prices. Assume initially that the firm seeks to maximize expected profits and that the variable cost per unit is constant ($10). Suppose the firm expects the following demand levels and probabilities at a price of $15 per coffee-making machine:

Demand	Probability
15,000	0.2
20,000	0.6
25,000	0.2

These probabilities can be determined in several ways. One approach is for the product manager to compute objective probabilities based on the history of "similar" new products. Alternatively, the product manager can assign these probabilities subjectively. If several decision makers are involved, consensus probabilities can be used. If the probability estimates of different managers diverge, the firm can iterate several times to arrive at a set of consensus estimates (for example, by using the Delphi method).

Given these beliefs and demand estimates, we can estimate the expected demand by weighting each demand level by its probability. Thus the expected demand is 20,000 units. Recalling that the profit margin is $5 per unit, we see that the expected profit is $100,000. Proceeding similarly, the firm can determine the expected profits for prices of $12 and $20 per unit. Suppose these expected profits are $120,000 and $80,000, respectively. Thus the firm will charge a price of $12 per unit.

Note that in order for the firm to use the expected profit criterion, it must specify all possible demand levels at a given price. Furthermore, the firm can ignore the volatility of demand in computing expected profit. Specifically, all that is necessary is to compute expected demand and determine the profit corresponding to this demand level.

The previous approach, despite its intuitive appeal, is not general and works only when the gross profit margin per unit is constant at all feasible demand levels (i.e., variable cost per unit is constant). Suppose the variable cost per unit decreases with volume. Specifically assume that:

Volume (in units)	Variable Cost per Unit (in $)
15,000	10
20,000	8
25,000	6

As before, the expected demand given a price of $15 is 20,000 units. The profit corresponding to this level of demand is $140,000. The expected profit, however, is $144,000. Thus the firm cannot ignore the volatility of demand by using the expected demand to compute expected profit. Note that the reason for the discrepancy in the two figures above is that the gross profit margin depends on volume (e.g., the gross profit margin per unit is $5 if demand is 15,000 units and $9 per unit if demand is 25,000 units).

Key Point   When demand is uncertain, the firm can simplify its analysis of expected profit by focusing on the expected (average) demand at different prices provided the variable cost per unit is constant over feasible demand levels. This method is inappropriate if the variable cost per unit varies with demand (e.g., there are economies of scale). In such cases the firm must explicitly consider the volatility of demand because the gross profit margin varies with volume.

Risk Aversion

According to the expected profit criterion, the firm should ignore the volatility of profit. For example, the firm should be indifferent between a product opportunity that promises a guaranteed profit of $100,000 (e.g., a cost-plus contract) and a new product opportunity that has a 50 percent chance of losing $50,000 and a 50 percent chance of earning $150,000. Most firms, however, are risk-averse and will choose the safer investment to avoid volatility.

For any given scenario should the risk-averse firm charge a lower price than the risk-neutral firm? Although intuition might suggest that the risk-averse firm should always charge a higher price than the risk-neutral firm, the answer is not so straightforward. We assume initially that the firm is owned by one individual; alternatively, the owners of the firm agree on a group utility function that represents their collective preferences. Thus the firm chooses pricing policy to maximize expected utility. For simplicity we shall consider a one-period model in which demand is uncertain and average cost is constant.

Several scenarios are possible.[4] Suppose the variability of demand does not depend on the firm's pricing policy (i.e., all demand shocks are exogenous to the firm). Then the risk-averse firm charges a lower price than the risk-neutral firm. The intuition is that by reducing price the firm reduces the volatility of profit; hence it is beneficial to trade off a reduction in expected profit for reduced volatility in profit. Suppose uncertainty affects demand multiplicatively [i.e., $q = f(p)u$, where q denotes demand, p price, and $u > 0$ is a stochastic disturbance term]. Then the ratio of expected demand to the standard deviation of demand is constant regardless of the firm's pricing policy. Consequently, the risk-averse and risk-neutral firms charge the same price. Suppose demand is more predictable at high prices than at low prices. Then the variability of profit could increase at low prices. Consequently the risk-averse firm charges a higher price than the risk-neutral firm.

Key Point   The effect of risk aversion on prices depends on the precise manner in which price affects the volatility of demand.

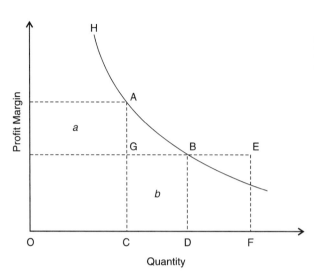

Figure 2.1 Risk aversion and the effectiveness of a price cut. Note: Profit margin = price − average cost.

Suppose the firm is already producing a product and is contemplating a price reduction. How does risk aversion affect price policy? To focus on essentials assume that average cost is constant over feasible demand levels. In Figure 2.1 suppose the firm is operating at point A and is planning a price reduction. (Note that the vertical axis measures the unit profit margin and not price.) The problem is that the firm is uncertain about the effect of the price cut on demand. Suppose B corresponds to the expected demand when the price is reduced; in particular, Area a equals Area b. Will the firm be indifferent between the two pricing plans?

The loss (Area a) is guaranteed, whereas the gain is uncertain with expected value given by Area b. Because the firm is risk-averse, it will only reduce price if the expected gain exceeds the guaranteed loss. Hence Area b must exceed Area a. That is, the demand curve must be more elastic than under certainty (i.e., the expected demand OF must exceed OD). The more risk-averse the firm is, the farther out point E is.

> ***Key Point*** *The more risk-averse a firm is, the more price sensitive the market must be for a price reduction to be effective. This result holds even if competitors do not react to the firm's price reduction.*

Capital Market Risk

The previous analysis implicitly assumed that the firm is owned by one individual; alternatively, if the firm is owned by several individuals, decisions are made according to a group utility function. Suppose instead that the firm is owned by a diverse group of shareholders who can diversify across all firms in the economy. The crucial difference from the case where the firm is individually owned is that stockholders are not concerned about the variability of the firm's profits per se. Stockholders are only concerned with the residual risk remaining after the firm has introduced the new product and stockholders have diversified their portfolios across firms. This residual risk—known as *systematic risk*—and the firm's expected profits jointly determine the firm's market value.

To illustrate, suppose the firm announces that the new coffeemaker will be introduced at a price of $15 per unit. The stock market implicitly forms its expectations about expected profit; say this figure is $100,000. Because stockholders are collectively risk-averse, the stock market will reduce the expected profit by a risk premium corresponding to the systematic risk of the new product. Suppose the stock market views a price of $15 per unit as a premium-pricing strategy and expects the demand of the premium segment to be volatile over the business cycle. That is, the systematic risk of this pricing plan is high. Suppose the risk premium is $30,000. Then the stock market values the new product at $70,000, the certainty equivalent of profits. Suppose instead that the new product is introduced at a price of $12 per unit, the stock market perceives that the expected profit is $110,000, and the risk premium is $20,000 (i.e., the stock market perceives this "mass-pricing" strategy to have lower systematic risk than the "premium-pricing" strategy). Hence the stock market values the new product at its certainty equivalent of profit, $90,000. Thus the firm should choose the low-price strategy.

> **Key Point**   *If the firm is owned by a diverse group of shareholders, the risk premium depends on the systematic risk of the new product at different prices. This systematic risk does not depend on the variability of profits per se.[5] In particular, systematic risk is the residual risk that remains after shareholders have diversified their portfolios. Thus the firm should price the product to maximize stock value (i.e., the certainty equivalent of profits).*

There is a fundamental distinction between the definitions of risk in the expected utility and capital market models. In the expected utility model the owner cannot diversify; consequently the volatility of profit has a crucial effect on pricing policy. In contrast, the risk premium in a capital market model is defined by $R = \rho[a_m \sigma(\Pi)\sigma(R_m)]$, where a_m denotes the market price of risk (i.e., a measure of the collective risk attitudes of investors in the economy), $\sigma(\Pi)$ the standard deviation of the firm's profits, $\sigma(R_m)$ the random return on the market portfolio (i.e., the value-weighted average return an investor could obtain by holding a fully diversified portfolio of assets in the economy), and ρ the correlation between $\sigma(\Pi)$ and $\sigma(R_m)$.

Note that the risk premium depends crucially on the correlation (ρ) between the firm's cash flows and the return on the market portfolio. Suppose $\rho = 0$. That is, all fluctuations in the firm's profits are idiosyncratic. Then by diversifying stockholders can eliminate risk completely. Consequently the value-maximizing firm behaves as if it is risk-neutral; in particular, the volatility of profit has no effect on the pricing decision.

This result has important implications for managerial compensation contracts. For example, a manager whose compensation is tied to profits is likely to choose a pricing policy that provides "safe" profits. However, the firm might be better off by targeting a market segment where profits are more volatile but ρ is small.

> **Key Point**   In a stock market model the correlation between the firm's profit and the return on the market portfolio has a crucial effect on the firm's stock value. The firm may prefer a price and segmentation policy that increases the volatility of profit provided this policy reduces cyclical fluctuations in profit (i.e., ρ is small).

Competitive and Dynamic Effects

The previous analyses implicitly assumed that the firm is a monopolist (i.e., competitive entry is not possible) and that the firm has a single-period horizon. We now relax these assumptions. Let us first consider competitive entry. Suppose the firm charges a "high" price for the new product. In a world of asymmetric information, potential entrants are likely to use the high price as a proxy for high industry profitability. Consequently the pioneering firm may find it prudent to price sufficiently below the monopoly price (i.e., the optimal price ignoring competition or potential competition) to preclude entry. This strategy is known as *limit pricing* and involves a tradeoff between lost current profits and increased future profits.

Let us now consider multiperiod effects, explicitly recognizing that demand is unknown. Suppose the firm introduces the new product at a low price but finds that demand is considerably below its prior expectations. If the firm raises price in the next period, consumers may use the first-period price as a reference point and further reduce purchases, making the firm worse off. Consequently the firm may prefer to charge a "high" introductory price for the new product and lower the price subsequently if demand is low.

> **Key Point**   In a world of asymmetric information, the firm has an incentive to charge a lower price than the monopoly level in order to preempt competitive entry and safeguard future profits. In contrast, if future consumer price expectations are important, the firm has an incentive to charge a high introductory price to safeguard future profits if demand in the introductory period is significantly below the forecasted level.

2.3 PRICING UNDER UNCERTAINTY: THE MULTIPERIOD CASE

Consider a firm that is planning to introduce a new product in a frequently purchased product category (e.g., shampoo). The firm must now use a multiperiod horizon because product trials alone cannot lead to financial success; repeat purchases are necessary. Suppose the market potential (i.e., the maximum number of potential buyers) is 1,000,000 consumers. The firm seeks to compare two pricing plans: a low price of $3 per unit and a high price of $5 per unit. Assume that the variable cost per unit is $1. Management expects one of two scenarios to occur if the price is $3 per unit: a low trial rate of 5 percent with a probability of 30 percent and a high trial rate of 10 percent with a probability of 70 percent. If the trial rate is low (5 percent), the product appeals to a niche market. Consequently, the repeat rate

Figure 2.2 A two-period pricing model assuming a price of $3 per unit. Expected number of trials = $1,000,000[(0.05 \times 0.3) + (0.10 \times 0.7)] = 15,000 + 70,000 = 85,000$; expected number of repeat purchases = $(15,000 \times 0.9) + (70,000 \times 0.6) = 55,500$.

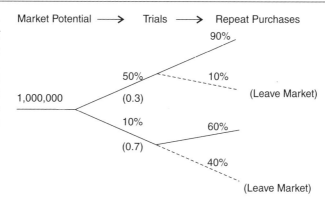

will be high (90 percent). If the trial rate is high (10 percent), the product has wider initial appeal; consequently the repeat rate is lower[6] (60 percent). Figure 2.2—known as a decision tree—summarizes this information. We shall assume in our analysis that consumers only purchase one unit at a time. As shown in Figure 2.2, the expected number of trials in the introduction period is 85,000 units and the expected gross contribution is $170,000. During the next period the expected number of repeat purchases is 55,500 units and the expected gross contribution is $111,000.

Suppose the firm performs a similar analysis for the $5 per unit scenario (details omitted) and obtains the following results:

Expected Profit

Price per Unit	Period 1	Period 2
$3	$170,000	$111,000
$5	$140,000	$150,000

Assume initially that the firm is risk-neutral and the risk-free interest rate is 10 percent per period. Then the net present values for the pricing plans are:

Price per Unit	Net Present Value (at 10%)
$3	$270,909
$5	$276,364

Hence the risk-neutral firm will charge $5 per unit.

We can now extend the analysis to deal with uncertain costs. Suppose the firm believes that the variable cost per unit could range from $0.80 to $1.20 and that the expected variable cost per unit is $1.00. Then the previous results are unchanged because fluctuations in cost do not affect the expected profit provided the expected variable cost per unit is constant.

Suppose the firm cannot specify the expected variable cost per unit. Then we can use sensitivity analysis to help decision making. Suppose the variable cost per unit is c, which is uncertain. Then the unit profit margins for the $3 and $5 prices, respectively, are $(3 - c)$ and $(5 - c)$. We can now determine the "break-even" value of c such that the firm is indifferent between the two pricing plans.[7] Solving, we find that the risk-neutral firm prefers the $3 price provided $c < 0.92$. Management can use this result subjectively to choose the price of the new product.

Suppose the firm is owned by risk-averse stockholders who can diversify.[8] As in the risk-neutral case, the firm chooses policy to maximize the net present value of profit. However, the discount rate is higher and reflects the risk premium which stockholders require to bear the systematic risk of the new product. Suppose the discount rate is 15 percent per period. Then the net present values for the pricing plans are:

Price per Unit	Net Present Value (at 15%)
$3	$266,522
$5	$270,435

Hence the risk-averse firm will charge $5 per unit.

The previous analysis is somewhat oversimplified because we used the same risk-adjusted discount rates for both pricing plans. In reality the two prices we considered—$3 and $5 per unit—are strategically different because they imply targeting distinct market segments with different sensitivities to general market conditions. Consequently the risk-adjusted discount rate will differ across pricing plans. To illustrate, suppose the risk-adjusted discount rate for the high-price policy is 20 percent and that for the low-price policy is 15 percent (i.e., the high-price policy leads to higher systematic risk than the low-price policy). Then the appropriate net present values are:

Price per Unit	Net Present Value
$3	$266,522
$5	$265,000

Hence, in contrast to the risk-neutral case, the low-price strategy maximizes the value of the firm.[9]

Key Point   *In a multiperiod setting, the firm must be careful in estimating cash flows because future outcomes (e.g., repeat purchase rates) depend crucially on previous events (e.g., trial rates). Different pricing plans often imply distinct market segmentation strategies, each of which exposes the firm to a different degree of market risk. Consequently, the value-maximizing firm should use a different discount rate to evaluate each pricing plan.*

2.4 BUNDLING

The previous models focused on uncertainty at the market level. In the remainder of this chapter we shall focus on consumer heterogeneity and consider uncertainty at a disaggregate level.

Suppose there are two firms A and B, each operating in unrelated industries. For convenience assume that there are three types of consumers in each industry (labeled Segments 1, 2, and 3, respectively) and that each segment is of equal size. Without loss of generality assume that each segment is of size one. In order to focus on demand effects, suppose the unit cost of production for each firm is $5 and that the reservation prices (i.e., the maximum prices a segment is willing to pay) are as shown in Table 2.3. Note that for any segment the reservation price of the bundle (A + B) is the sum of the reservation prices for A and B, respectively. We say that products A and B are independent. (This assumption will be relaxed.)

If firms make pricing decisions independently, each firm makes a profit of $30 and charges a price of $20 per unit. Note that Segment 1 is willing to pay $30 per unit for firm A's product but pays $20 per unit. Thus Segment 1 obtains a consumer surplus of $10. Similarly Segment 2 obtains a consumer surplus of $10.

Should firms A and B coordinate their pricing plans even though they are in unrelated industries? The answer is yes because both firms share a common customer base. Consider Segment 1. Because the products are independent, Segment 1's reservation price for the bundle (A + B) is $40, which is the sum of Segment 1's reservation prices for A and B, respectively. Similarly the reservation prices for the bundle for Segments 2 and 3 are also $40. Hence if firms A and B coordinate their pricing policies, the optimal plan is to sell the bundle (A + B) for $40 and discontinue the separate sale of A and B. Given this policy the firms earn a joint profit of $90, which exceeds the joint profit of $60 if the firms act independently. This policy of selling only an assortment of products is known as *pure bundling*. Note that in our example each segment pays its reservation price for the bundle and obtains zero consumer surplus.

Key Point   *Firms in unrelated industries can gain by using a pure bundling strategy provided the industries share a common customer base and the reservation prices for segments are negatively correlated across industries. This result does not depend on a cost-reduction argument.*

The previous result is stylized because all segments share a common reservation price for the bundle. In reality we expect these bundle reservation prices to vary across segments. Furthermore, these reservation prices need not be negatively related. Consider the scenario in Table 2.4. For convenience, assume that the previous cost conditions hold. Note that the rankings of reservation prices differ by segment. For example, Segment 1 has the highest reservation price for A (rank 1) and the second-highest reservation price for B (rank 2).

Suppose firms A and B act independently. Then A charges a price of $20 per unit and earns a profit of $30. B charges a price of $16 per unit and earns a profit of $33. Hence the joint profit earned by A and B is $63. Segment 1 earns a consumer surplus of $10 from A

Table 2-3 Analysis of Bundling Strategies

Segment	Reservation Prices		
	A	**B**	**Bundle (A + B)**
1	$30	$10	$40
2	$10	$30	$40
3	$20	$20	$40

Table 2-4 Analysis of Bundling Strategies

		Reservation Prices	
Segment	**A**	**B**	**Bundle (A + B)**
1	$30	$20	$50
2	$10	$16	$26
3	$20	$25	$45

and a consumer surplus of $4 from B. Segment 3 earns a consumer surplus of $9 from B. Hence the aggregate consumer surplus in the marketplace is $23.

Suppose firms A and B seek to enhance their performance by coordinating their pricing plans. One possibility is to sell the bundle (A + B) for $50. Under these conditions Segment 1 will buy the bundle and obtain zero consumer surplus. We must now focus on Segments 2 and 3 and determine a pricing plan that maximizes profitability for these segments. One possibility is to charge a price of $25 per unit for B. Given this price, Segment 3 will buy B. The firm, however, must drop A from the market. The net result of this pricing decision is that Segment 1 buys the bundle at $50, Segment 3 buys B for $25, and the joint profit for the firms is $60. Note that this policy of *mixed bundling* (i.e., selling a pure bundle and separately selling individual components) reduces joint profits compared to the case where each firm acts independently.

Another possibility is to price the bundle at $45 and sell to Segments 1 and 3. Given this plan and the cost structure, the firms must sell B at $16 per unit (Segment 2 will buy) and drop A from the market. The joint profit from this mixed bundling plan is $81, which is $18 more than the joint profit if both firms act independently. Note that under this pricing plan Segment 1 has a consumer surplus of $5, Segment 2 has zero consumer surplus, and Segment 3 has zero consumer surplus. Hence the aggregate consumer surplus in the marketplace is $5. Recalling that the aggregate consumer surplus was $23 when the firms priced independently, we see that the net reduction in consumer surplus ($18) equals the net increase in joint profits. The reader should verify that the mixed bundling plan discussed above is optimal and can examine alternative scenarios by changing the reservation prices in Table 2.4.

This analysis leads to several conclusions. If products A and B are made by the same firm, price coordination across products can increase performance if the customer bases overlap. The implementation of this strategy can be risky (see the first mixed bundling plan above) and requires detailed knowledge of reservation prices for products A, B, and the bundle of A and B. Hence market research is necessary. If two firms produce one product each (A and B, respectively), a merger will add value even if there are no cost savings. If the two firms produce multiple products, the effect of a merger will be small unless A and B represent significant fractions of the firms. In such cases, the two firms may find it attractive to form strategic alliances where the emphasis is on joint pricing plans that focus on pricing bundles to common consumers. Note that strategic alliances can reduce joint profits even if each firm knows the exact distribution of reservation prices for each segment that buys its product. Improved performance requires precise knowledge of the joint distribution of reservation prices for all segments across products.

> **Key Point** *A mixed bundling plan can increase joint profits provided there is a significant overlap of consumers across these industries; without precise knowledge of the joint distribution of reservation prices for all segments, a coordinated pricing policy can reduce performance.*

The previous analysis assumed that the products are independent (i.e., for any segment the reservation price of a bundle is the sum of the separate reservation prices for each product in the bundle). Suppose the reservation prices are *superadditive*. Then the reservation price of the bundle exceeds the sum of the reservation prices of each product in the bundle. Consequently the gains from bundling (pure or mixed) will increase. If the reservation prices are *subadditive*, the reservation price of the bundle is less than the sum of the reservation prices of each product in the bundle. Consequently the gains from bundling are reduced. Bundling may, however, still enhance joint profits. (For example, replace each value in the last column in Table 2.3 by $38 and compute the joint profit using a pure bundling plan.)

> **Key Point** *Bundling may be profitable even if the reservation prices are subadditive.*

The above analysis shows that the key empirical issue in operationalizing bundling policies is to determine the joint distribution of reservation prices of all segments for different products and bundles, distinguishing segments for which the products are superadditive, independent, or subadditive. In practice, it is difficult to form these segments a priori; consequently a mixture methodology is necessary. Jagpal, Jedidi, and Krishna (1996) have developed a probit mixture algorithm to estimate the joint distribution of reservation prices for the unobserved segments using a choice experiment. They have conducted simulation and real-life studies and plan to report their results shortly.

2.5 PRICING USING COUPONS: A ONE-PERIOD MODEL

Suppose a cereal manufacturer faces two heterogeneous consumer Segments A and B with demand schedules as shown in Table 2.5. To focus on essentials suppose the segments are of equal size (unity), the unit cost of production per box of cereal is constant ($0.50), and the cereal is perishable. (The reasons for the last assumption will become clear shortly.) If the firm follows a uniform pricing policy, the market price is $0.90 per box and the firm's maximum profit is $1.20. Given this scenario, Segment B buys one unit at $0.90 but is willing to pay $1.00. Hence Segment B obtains a consumer surplus of $0.10. Segment A buys two units for $1.80 but is willing to pay $1.90. (Why?) Hence Segment B obtains a consumer surplus of $0.10.

How can the firm extract these consumer surpluses from Segments A and B? One possibility is to market two sizes: a regular box priced at $1.00 and a double-sized "economy" box priced at $1.90. (Strictly the firm has to charge a price slightly below $1.90 for the double pack in order to induce Segment A to buy the double pack.)

Table 2-5 Profitability Analysis in Cereal Example Assuming Uniform Pricing

Price	Segment A	Segment B	Market	Profit
$1	1	1	2	$2(1 - 0.5) = \$1.00$
$0.90*	2	1	3	$3(0.9 - 0.5) = \$1.20*$

* denotes optimal values.

Assume that there are no economies or diseconomies of scale in producing the double pack. Then the firm's profit is $1.40 and Segments A and B are forced to pay their reservation prices (i.e., their consumer surpluses are zero). Note that the firm's profit under segmented pricing equals the firm's profit under uniform pricing ($1.20) plus the consumer surpluses obtained by Segments A and B under uniform pricing ($0.10 for each segment).

Alternatively, the firm could include a coupon worth 10 cents in the regular cereal box, which it sells at a price of $1.00; in particular, the coupon must expire at the end of the period. (Strictly the coupon amount must be marginally above 10 cents to induce Segment A to use the coupon.) Note that the firm's profit will be identical to that under the previous pricing plan. This example illustrates an important result: Several marketing policies can generate equivalent results. We say that there are multiple equilibria in this market.

> **Key Point**   *When reservation prices across consumers are heterogeneous, the firm will find it desirable to segment the market and apply different marketing policies to each segment. Several marketing policies may generate equivalent results (e.g., couponing or selling the product in different sizes).*

It is important to note that the firm does not need to know the identities of the consumers in each segment. Once the firm has introduced its differentiated marketing policy, consumers will automatically sort themselves into segments. If the firm needs to advertise to inform consumers about the new policies (e.g., couponing), the firm will find it advantageous to know the identities of consumers in Segment A to eliminate waste in advertising.

The previous analysis assumes that the firm knows the reservation prices and sizes of each segment. In general, the firm is likely to have limited information regarding these data. Consequently the firm may find it desirable to test the coupon policy using a "limited-period offer" or a small-scale test market. Because the production of the larger pack may require incremental setup costs and changes in the production process, the firm may find it desirable to simulate the introduction of the larger pack. One possibility is to offer consumers two options in a test market: a regular box priced at $1 and a double pack (i.e., two regular boxes attached to each other) priced at $1.90 with the label "limited-time offer: ten cents off regular price" or a description to this effect.

> **Key Point**   *In the real world the firm may not know the reservation prices of all segments. Furthermore, there are incremental costs associated with any segmented pricing plan. Consequently the firm should consider performing a limited test before changing the national pricing policy. The test should emphasize that the double-packed product or coupon is a limited-time offer. This policy will reduce the likelihood that consumers will lower their future reservation prices (e.g., by expecting future prices to be lower), hence reducing the firm's future profits if the firm decides not to implement the segmented pricing plan on a national basis.*

2.6 PRICING USING COUPONS: A MULTIPERIOD MODEL

The single-period model implicitly made several assumptions. First, the coupon must expire at the end of the period. Otherwise the price-insensitive Segment B will use the coupon in the next period and obtain a consumer surplus of 10 cents per purchase. Second, the consumer cannot make forward purchases and hoard the cereal. This condition requires that the cereal be perishable (e.g., it contains no preservatives) or that consumers incur very high (strictly infinite) storage costs. These storage costs can be financial or implicit (e.g., storage space is scarce). We now relax these assumptions.

   To distinguish the analysis from the single-period case, we shall refer to the segments as C and D, respectively. In order to focus on essentials, we shall assume that (1) unit production costs are constant over time (e.g., there is no inflation or the planning period is sufficiently short); (2) double packing does not entail any economies or diseconomies of scale; (3) Segments C and D are of equal size (unity), (4) both segments have a common planning horizon (two periods), and (5) the firm seeks to maximize long-term profit (i.e., net present value). We shall distinguish two scenarios. First, consumers have homogeneous reservation prices but heterogeneous storage costs. Second, consumers have heterogeneous reservation prices and heterogeneous storage costs.

Homogeneous Preferences, Heterogeneous Holding Costs

Suppose Segments C and D each have reservation prices of $1 per regular-sized box of cereal and consume the cereal at the same rate over time. If the firm uses uniform pricing, it will charge a price of $1 per regular box and make a profit of $1 every period. Neither segment will hoard provided the market price of $1 is expected to be stable. Now suppose Segment C has very high storage costs (e.g., space is at a premium or the opportunity cost of money is high). Segment D, however, has low storage costs and is willing to accelerate its purchases provided a double pack is available at a price of $1.90 or lower. Thus Segment D's implicit opportunity cost of money is 11.1 percent per period [i.e., $1.90 = 1 + 1/(1 + r_D)$, where r_D is Segment D's opportunity cost of money].

   Suppose the firm employs a double-pronged strategy: Market the regular size at $1 per box and a double-sized pack at $1.90 per box. Segment C will buy the regular-sized box at $1 per box in each period. In contrast, Segment D will buy the double pack in period 1, make no purchase in period 2, buy the double pack in period 3, make no purchase in period

4, and so on. Because Segment C's purchase behavior is the same as it was under uniform pricing, we need only consider Segment D's behavior.

Under the double-packing strategy, the firm's profit from Segment D will oscillate over time: $0.90 in period 1, zero profits in period 2, $0.90 in period 3 and so on. Under uniform pricing, Segment D provides a profit of $0.50 in each period. Thus the firm prefers double-packing provided the firm's cost of capital exceeds 25 percent per period[10] [i.e., $0.90 > 0.50 + 0.50/(1 + r_f)$, where r_f denotes the firm's cost of capital]. Note that for double packing to work, the firm's cost of capital must exceed Segment D's cost of capital so that Segment D benefits by performing a warehousing (inventory) function.[11] Furthermore, this condition is necessary but not sufficient (e.g., the firm loses by double packing if the firm's cost of capital is 20 percent per period). The reason is that the consumer compares the net present values of *prices*, whereas the firm compares the net present values of *profits* that are obviously smaller than the associated prices. As in the one-period model, the firm could achieve the same result by a coupon policy (i.e., including a coupon for 10 cents in the regular box and not offering a double pack) where the coupon expires at the end of period 1.

An interesting question is whether a national brand has a greater incentive to use coupons than a store brand does (e.g., a brand sold under the name of a supermarket chain). Recall that the profit margin per unit for a national brand typically exceeds the unit profit margin for a store brand; in addition, the demand for national brands is likely to be more cyclical than the demand for store brands (i.e., national brands have a higher cost of capital). Both effects reinforce each other; consequently national brands are more likely to use coupons than store brands.

These results have several managerial implications. First, short-term measures of the profitability of couponing are inappropriate because profits will oscillate over time. Consequently the firm should measure a brand manager's performance over a sufficiently long period of time. Second, the firm should segment consumers according to holding costs. For example, geographical segmentation may be appropriate because suburban consumers have more space than city dwellers (the former have lower implicit storage costs). Thus *even if consumers have homogeneous reservation prices for the product*, the firm will find it profitable to pursue a coupon policy in the suburbs but not in the city.

> ***Key Point*** *Segmentation via couponing can increase the firm's profitability even if consumers have homogeneous preferences, provided holding costs differ across consumer segments. The firm's cost of capital must be sufficiently larger than that of a consumer segment to induce that segment to perform an inventory function (i.e., hoard). National brands will typically gain more from a couponing policy than store brands.*

Heterogeneous Preferences, Heterogeneous Holding Costs

In order to analyze the effects of heterogeneous preferences and heterogeneous holding costs, we return to the example in Table 2.5. Assume that the price-inelastic Segment B has very high storage costs. The price-elastic Segment A, however, has low storage costs.

Specifically, if the regular-sized box is priced at $1, Segment B will purchase and consume one box per period. If the double-sized box is sold at $1.90 (or equivalently the regular-sized box is sold at $1 and includes a 10-cent coupon good towards future purchase), Segment A purchases and consumes one double-sized box per period. Neither segment holds any inventory, and the firm's profit is $1.40 per period. We shall refer to this as the *base policy*.

Suppose Segment A can be induced to purchase two double-sized boxes for $3.70 on a given purchase occasion, and to consume one double-sized box in each of periods 1 and 2. Then Segment A's implicit cost of capital is 5.6 percent per period [i.e., $3.70 = 1.90 + 1.90/(1 + r_A)$, where r_A is Segment A's cost of capital]. Because of Segment A's accelerated buying under this policy, the firm's immediate profit will increase by $0.80 compared to the base policy, decrease by $0.90 in the next period, and the cycle of gains and losses will repeat itself. Hence the firm will find the new policy profitable if the firm's cost of capital exceeds 12.5 percent per period. Note that, as in the one-period model, this policy can be achieved using different marketing policies (e.g., "Buy X units and get one free"). Hence multiple equilibria are possible.

Suppose that the price-elastic Segment A has very high storage costs but Segment B has low storage costs; in particular, Segment B is willing to pay $1.85 for the double pack. In this event Segment B will consume the equivalent of one regular-sized box every period and perform an inventory function. Suppose the firm charges a price of $1.85 for the double-pack. Then Segment B will hoard the product; however, by reducing the price of the double-pack to $1.85, the firm returns a consumer surplus of $0.05 to Segment A every period. Consequently by adopting this policy, the firm increases profit in period 1 to $1.70 from $1.40 using the base policy. Hence the incremental profit in period 1 using the new policy is $0.30. The firm, however, incurs a marginal loss of $0.55 in period 2 because it is forced to return consumer surplus to Segment A every period. Thus the firm will gain from the new policy only if the firm's cost of capital exceeds 83.3 percent per period [i.e., $0.30 > 0.55/(1 + r_f)$, where r_f is the firm's cost of capital].

Key Point   *If the more price-sensitive Segment A has lower storage costs than the less price-sensitive Segment B, the firm has a strong incentive to induce Segment A to hoard. The firm's gains from making consumers hold inventories are substantially reduced if the more price-sensitive Segment A has higher storage costs than the less price-sensitive Segment B.*

The previous analyses assumed that each segment has the same number of customers. Suppose the segments are of unequal size, have heterogeneous reservation prices, and incur unequal holding costs. Then the gains to the firm from inducing accelerated buying are increased if the more price-sensitive segment is larger and has lower storage costs than the less price-sensitive segment. These gains are reduced and may even be eliminated if the more price-sensitive segment is larger and has higher storage costs.

These results suggest that the firm should classify consumers into segments on the basis of their reservation prices and holding costs. As in the homogeneous reservation price case, national brands have a greater incentive to encourage accelerated buying than store brands do because national brands have higher unit profit margins and higher costs of capital.

> **Key Point**   *The firm should form segments by simultaneously analyzing the distribu-tions of consumers' reservation prices and holding costs. The gains from couponing are increased to the extent that a segment can be found which is sufficiently large, is highly price-sensitive, and has low holding costs. In general, national brands will gain more from couponing than store brands.*

2.7 PRICE SKIMMING

Our analysis of heterogeneity has focused on nondurables. We now consider the case of durable products.

The Basic Model

Suppose a firm has produced a new computer that will help the user to reduce payroll-processing costs. Assume that there are three business Segments A, B, and C of equal size (unity) with reservation prices, respectively, of $10,000, $8,000, and $6,000 per computer. The manufacturing cost per computer is $3,000. For simplicity assume that no segment will purchase more than one computer. If the firm chooses uniform pricing, it will set a price of $8,000 per computer, sell two units, and make an immediate profit of $10,000 (see Table 2.6).

Thus in the introduction period Segment B pays a price equal to its reservation price of $8,000. Segment A obtains a consumer surplus of $2,000, the amount by which Segment A's reservation price exceeds the market price. Segment C does not purchase the computer. During the next period, only Segment C is left in the market. Consequently the firm reduces the price to $6,000 and earns a profit of $3,000. Thus if the firm uses this uniform pricing policy, the immediate profit is $10,000 and the next period's profit is $3,000. Note that Segment C's consumer surplus is zero.

How can the firm capture Segment A's consumer surplus? Suppose the firm charges an introductory price of $10,000 at time 0 (Segment A will buy), reduces the price to $8,000 in time 1 (Segment B will buy), and further reduces the price to $6,000 in time 2 (Segment C will buy). Each segment pays a price equal to its reservation price (i.e., all consumer surpluses are zero). This policy of price discrimination over time is often referred to as *price skimming*. Note, in particular, that the price-skimming strategy is based purely on the

Table 2-6 Uniform Pricing Policy for a Computer

Price	Demand	Revenue	Cost	Profit
$10,000	1	$10,000	$3,000	$ 7,000
$ 8,000*	2	$16,000	$6,000	$10,000*
$ 6,000	3	$18,000	$9,000	$ 9,000

* denotes optimal values.

Table 2-7 Comparison of Uniform Pricing and Price Skimming

Profits	$t = 0$	$t = 1$	$t = 2$
Uniform pricing	$10,000	$3,000	—
Price skimming	$ 7,000	$5,000	$3,000
Incremental profit from price skimming	−$ 3,000	$2,000	$3,000

heterogeneity of different segments' reservation prices and has nothing to do with economies of scale or learning effects in production. (We assumed that unit costs are constant.)

Will the firm choose the price-skimming policy discussed above? Clearly the firm cannot earn a larger total profit than it does by price skimming. However, this analysis is incomplete because it does not consider the time value of money. Specifically, by using price skimming the firm loses $3,000 at time zero, gains $2,000 at time 1, and gains $3,000 at time 2 (see Table 2.7). Consequently price skimming is only profitable if the firm's incremental net present value is positive (i.e., the opportunity cost of capital is less than 38.7 percent per period).[12]

> **Key Point** *Price skimming is a policy of price discrimination over time and increases the firm's total profit by capturing consumer surplus. This policy enhances profitability unless the firm's cost of capital is very high.*

The Effect of Competition

The previous analysis assumes that the pioneering computer manufacturer behaves as a monopolist and can ignore competitive reaction or entry (e.g., the computer technology is covered by a patent). In general the firm cannot ignore competitive entry by new entrants. Suppose the computer manufacturer is "first to the market" and chooses a price-skimming strategy (i.e., an introductory price of $10,000 per computer). In a world of asymmetric information, potential entrants could take this price as a signal of industry profitability. Suppose Segment A buys the computer at the introductory price of $10,000 and a new competitor enters the market in the next period. Assuming that the computers offered by both manufacturers are similar, both firms will share the market equally in the next period. Hence the pioneer will sell one computer in the next period for a profit of $3,000. Because the computers are similar, either Segment B or Segment C will buy at random from the pioneer. Thus, as a result of competitive entry, the pioneering computer manufacturer will make an immediate profit of $7,000 and a profit of $3,000 next period if it adopts a price-skimming policy. As discussed earlier, the pioneer makes an immediate profit of $10,000 by using a uniform pricing strategy. Thus the uniform pricing strategy is superior, assuming that the cost of capital is positive.

> **Key Point** *The gains from a price-skimming strategy are reduced and can even be eliminated if the introductory skimming price induces competitive entry.*

Consumers' Expectations

Our previous analysis of consumer decision making is incomplete because we did not consider price expectations. Specifically we did not allow the consumer to postpone purchase hoping that future prices will fall (i.e., the consumer expects the firm to play a price-skimming game). Suppose the firm chooses an introductory price of $10,000 and Segment A expects the firm to reduce the price to $8,000 next period. Now if Segment A postpones purchase, it loses the benefit from the computer for one period but expects to pay $2,000 less next period. Suppose the net present value of the lost stream of benefits by delaying purchase (i.e., reductions in payroll-processing costs) is $3,000. Then Segment A will purchase the computer immediately for $10,000. Suppose instead that the net present value of the savings from delaying purchase is $1,500. Then Segment A will delay purchase if Segment A's cost of capital is less than 33.3 percent per period, and purchase the computer for $10,000 otherwise. In general, we expect that a given segment's reservation price (i.e., the net present value of all future benefits from the computer) is positively related to the net present value of the lost benefits from delaying purchase. Thus price skimming will be a viable strategy unless the segments have highly asymmetric price expectations.

> **Key Point**   *Consumers do not necessarily purchase a durable if the price is less than or equal to their reservation price for the durable. They will postpone purchase if the marginal benefits from waiting exceed the marginal losses from having reduced usage of the durable.*

Consumer Uncertainty

Our analysis so far has not considered consumer uncertainty. Suppose an industrial firm is planning to introduce a new cost-saving product into the marketplace. However, consumers are uncertain about the magnitude of the cost reduction they can achieve by using the product. Assume that there are two segments with homogeneous expectations; in particular, each segment believes that by using the product the expected cost savings will be $5,000 per period. Suppose both segments are risk-averse; in particular, Segment A is less risk-averse than Segment B. Assume that both segments are of equal size (unity). Then the reservation price for each segment is less than $5,000 and Segment A has a higher reservation price than Segment B. Suppose the reservation prices for Segments A and B are $4,000 and $3,000 (these values are the certainty equivalents of the cost savings to Segments A and B, respectively).

One approach for the firm is to use a price-skimming strategy. Alternatively, the firm can attempt to increase the reservation prices of each segment by disseminating objective information quantifying the cost savings from using the new product. Suppose the new product leads to a cost reduction of $5,000 with certainty. Then, if the firm is successful in its strategy, the reservation price for each segment will increase to $5,000 (i.e., consumers will become homogeneous) and the firm will be able to maximize profit by pursuing an undifferentiated pricing policy. Note that this strategy outperforms the price-skimming approach. (In practice the firm will incur advertising or selling costs. Consequently the gain in profit must be balanced against the cost of implementing the market education strategy.)

> **Key Point**   *The firm should form market segments for new products based on consumers' risk aversions. When consumers are uncertain in their evaluations of a new product, a price-skimming strategy can outperform an undifferentiated pricing strategy even if consumers have homogeneous perceptions. However, a price-skimming strategy may be suboptimal. In particular, the firm may be able to increase profits further by combining several marketing instruments (e.g., advertising and price) and pursuing an undifferentiated pricing strategy.*

2.8 CONCLUDING REMARKS

This chapter has focused on pricing under uncertainty and pricing in markets that are characterized by consumer heterogeneity. In particular, we have shown the relevance of capital markets for the firm's pricing decision under uncertainty in single- and multiperiod frameworks. We have also examined how asymmetries in the cost of capital among consumers and firms lead to mutually beneficial exchange opportunities (e.g., the firm can use a couponing strategy to encourage consumers to perform a warehousing function). For simplicity we have assumed that manufacturers deal directly with consumers. In many cases, however, wholesalers or distributors are interposed between manufacturers and consumers (i.e., there are several levels in the channel of distribution). Hence it is necessary to extend the theory. Chapter 5 discusses pricing under heterogeneity and uncertainty in markets where there are several levels in the distribution channel.

NOTES

1. An interesting question is the relationship between maximizing expected utility and minimizing the probability of bankruptcy. It can be shown that although the two criteria are compatible (i.e., maximizing some utility functions reduces to minimizing the probability of bankruptcy), they are not equivalent.

2. In extreme cases, the break-even criterion can lead to the rejection of all new product opportunities because such opportunities often involve nontrivial probabilities of bankruptcy. The firm can now attempt to salvage the break-even criterion by trading off expected profits with the probability of bankruptcy using the *safety-first* criterion. However, the safety-first criterion eliminates the major advantage of break-even pricing: the lack of a need to specify the demand levels at any given price.

3. Let $x = F/(p - c)$ denote the break-even volume, where F denotes fixed cost, p price, and c the unit cost of production (assumed constant). Differentiating with respect to p and multiplying by $(-p/x)$, we get $\varepsilon = p/(p - c) > 1$, where $\varepsilon = -(\partial x/\partial p)(p/x)$ denotes the absolute value of the elasticity of the break-even volume with respect to price. Hence the break-even volume falls faster than price increases.

4. Suppose demand shocks are exogenous to the firm. Let $q = f(p) + u$ denote demand, where p is price and u is a disturbance term such that $E(u) = 0$. Let $\pi = (p - c)[f(p) + u]$ denote profit, where c is the constant unit cost. Let $U(\pi)$ denote the firm's utility function, where $U' > 0$, $U'' < 0$ by risk aversion, and the primes denote derivatives. Let p_n denote

the price that maximizes the expected profit defined by $W = E(\pi) = (p - c)f(p)$ and p_r the price that maximizes expected utility defined by $Z = EU(\pi)$. Differentiating Z, we obtain $\partial Z/\partial p = [f(p) + (p - c)(\partial f/\partial p)]E(U') + E(U'u)$. Evaluating $\partial Z/\partial p$ at p_n, we get $\partial Z/\partial p|_{p_n} = E(U'u) = \text{Cov}(U', u) < 0$ by risk aversion. But Z is concave in p. Hence $p_r < p_n$. That is, the risk-averse firm will price lower than the risk-neutral firm. Suppose uncertainty is multiplicative $[q = g(p)u$, where $\partial g/\partial p < 0$ and $u > 0]$. Then $\partial Z/\partial p = \partial W/\partial p$ using the first-order conditions. Hence the risk-neutral and the risk-averse firms will choose the same price. Consider the general case where $q = f(p) + g(p)u$, where p denotes price, f and g are functions, u is a disturbance term, and the sign of $\partial g/\partial p$ is arbitrary. Proceeding as before, we get $\partial Z/\partial p|_{p_n} = [g + (\partial g/\partial p)(p - c)]\,\text{Cov}(U', u)$, where Cov denotes the covariance operator and $\text{Cov}(U', u) < 0$ by risk aversion. Suppose $g + \partial g/\partial p(p - c) < 0$ (i.e., the variance of profit decreases when price increases). Then $\partial Z/\partial p|_{p_n} > 0$. But Z is concave in p. Hence $p_r > p_n$. That is, the risk-averse firm charges a higher price than the risk-neutral firm. If $[g + (\partial g/\partial p)(p - c)] > 0$, $p_r < p_n$.

5. Suppose the capital asset pricing model holds. Let $V = [E(\Pi) - R](1 + r_f)^{-1}$ denote the value of the firm's stock, where Π denotes the firm's random profit, R is the risk premium, and r_f is the risk-free interest rate. Then $R = a_m \rho \sigma(\Pi)\sigma(R_m)$, where a_m denotes the market price of risk, $\sigma(\Pi)$ the standard deviation of the firm's profits, R_m is the return on the market portfolio (i.e., the value-weighted average return an investor could obtain by holding a fully diversified portfolio of all assets in the economy), $\sigma(R_m)$ is the standard deviation of R_m, and ρ the correlation between Π and R_m. Differentiating V with respect to price, we get $\partial V/\partial p = \{\partial E(\Pi)/\partial p - a_m \rho \sigma(R_m)[\partial \sigma(\Pi)/\partial p]\}(1 + r_f)^{-1}$. Hence the stock market model implies the same directional results as the expected utility model. (See previous note.) For example, in the generalized uncertainty case, evaluating $\partial V/\partial p$ at the risk-neutral price, we have $\partial V/\partial p < (>)0$ if $\partial \sigma(\Pi)/\partial p > (<) 0$ provided $\rho > 0$.

   Suppose the firm introduces a new product that is distinct from its existing product line (i.e., there are no cost or demand synergies). Let π_1 and π_2, respectively, denote the incremental profits if the firm chooses prices of $\$15$ and $\$12$ per unit for the new product. Then $\text{Cov}(\pi_1, R_m)/\text{Cov}(\pi_2, R_m) = \rho_1 \sigma(\pi_1)/\rho_2 \sigma(\pi_2)$ for $\rho_2 \neq 0$, where Cov denotes the covariance operator. Note that the variabilities of profits $[\sigma(\pi_1)$ and $\sigma(\pi_2)]$ affect systematic risk. However, there is a correction factor based on ρ_1/ρ_2. Thus the systematic risk for a price of $\$15$ per unit could be lower than the systematic risk for a price of $\$12$ per unit even if $\sigma(\pi_1) > \sigma(\pi_2)$ provided ρ_1 is sufficiently small. Consequently, in contrast to the expected utility model, the risk premium for a price plan that increases the variability of profit could actually decrease. The intuition is that when ρ_1 is small the fluctuations in the firm's profits are primarily random (i.e., the systematic risk component is small and is not related to general economic conditions). Hence stockholders can eliminate most of the risk by diversifying, even if the firm's profits are highly volatile.

6. The repeat purchase rate depends on the degree of heterogeneity among the consumers who try the product. When the trial rate is high, we expect the group of triers to be more heterogeneous and to include a larger fraction of experimenters. Consequently, the repeat rate is lower when the trial rate is high.

7. Let Q_1 and Q_2, respectively, denote the net present values for unit prices of $\$3$ and $\$5$. Then $Q_1 = (3 - c)(85000 + 55500/1.10)$ and $Q_2 = (5 - c)(35000 + 37500/1.10)$. Hence $Q_1 > Q_2$ if $c < 0.92$.

8. Suppose the firm maximizes expected utility (i.e., the owner cannot diversify). For any price policy i let $\pi_1^{(i)}$ and $\pi_2^{(i)}$, respectively, denote the profits in periods 1 and 2. Assume that the utility function is time-additive and the risk-free discount rate is d. Then the firm chooses policy to maximize $Z = EU(\pi_1^{(i)})/(1+d) + EU(\pi_2^{(i)})/(1+d)^2$, where $U(\cdot)$ denotes the appropriate utility.

9. This analysis can be extended to include the economic value of flexibility (i.e., the option of abandoning the project at the end of the first period if demand is poor). See Chapter 1, Section 1.9, for a discussion of real options.

10. The analysis in the text assumes that the firm has a two-period planning horizon. The results are unchanged if the firm has an infinite horizon. The incremental net present value by implementing the double-pack strategy now becomes

$$\Delta\text{NPV} = 0.40 - \frac{0.50}{(1+r_f)} + \frac{0.40}{(1+r_f)^2} - \frac{0.50}{(1+r_f)^3} + - \cdots \infty$$

$$= \left(0.40 - \frac{0.50}{(1+r_f)}\right) Q$$

where

$$Q = 1 + \frac{1}{(1+r_f)^2} + \frac{1}{(1+r_f)^4} + \cdots$$

But $Q > 0$. Hence $\Delta\text{NPV} > 0$ if $0.40 - 0.50/(1+r_f) > 0$, which is the same condition as in the two-period planning horizon case.

11. For Segment D let p denote the reservation price of one unit and r_c the cost of capital. Suppose Segment D can be induced to hoard the double pack at a price of $2p - \alpha$, where $\alpha > 0$. Then $(p-\alpha) - p/(1+r_c) = 0$. Let c and $2c$, respectively, denote the unit production costs of a single and a double pack and r_f the firm's cost of capital. Then the incremental net present value to the firm of inducing Segment D to hoard the double pack is $Z = [(p-\alpha) - p/(1+r_f)] - c[1 - 1/(1+r_f)]$.

Suppose the firm and Segment D have the same cost of capital. Then $Z < 0$. Hence the firm will not induce Segment D to hoard the double pack. Note that $r_f > r_c$ is a necessary condition for $Z > 0$.

Rewriting Z, we have $Z = m[1 - 1/(1+r_f)] - \alpha$, where $m = p - c$ denotes the unit profit margin. Differentiating Z, we have $\partial Z/\partial m > 0$ and $\partial Z/\partial r_f > 0$. Thus the firm's gain from inducing Segment D to hoard the double pack increases with the gross margin and the firm's cost of capital.

12. Let r denote the firm's cost of capital. Then the net present value of the incremental profits from price skimming is $z = -3000 + 2000/(1+r) + 3000/(1+r)^2$. For $z > 0$ we require that $r < 0.387$.

Consumer Behavior: A Theoretical Perspective

This chapter examines several paradigms of consumer behavior and discusses their relevance to the marketing manager. We begin with the deterministic case and examine the standard Lancasterian (1966) model of demand, which examines the relationship between product attributes and consumer preference. We then propose an extended Lancasterian model that explicitly incorporates consumers' perceptions and show how this model helps the manager in choosing marketing strategy (i.e., coordinating the marketing mix, understanding market structure, and determining the impact of new products). We discuss prospect theory (see Kahneman and Tversky 1979) and examine the implications of reference prices for dynamic pricing policy. In particular, we propose a hybrid model that combines the concept of consumer surplus (standard in microeconomic models) and the value function in prospect theory (i.e., the value that consumers place on gains and losses when market prices deviate from consumers' reference prices) and show that this model leads to different predictions about market behavior than conventional economic models. Finally, we examine consumer choice under uncertainty (e.g., the consumer's perceptions about a product's benefits are unclear) and show how the manager can use choice models to improve decision making.

In our discussion we shall pay special attention to consumer heterogeneity and market segmentation. Although we shall touch on empirical issues, our primary focus is theoretical. Chapter 4 examines empirical estimation in detail and proposes new methods for explicating the "black box" that intervenes between product attributes and preference or choice while simultaneously allowing for different types of heterogeneity (e.g., consumers can follow different information-processing strategies and have heterogeneous perceptions).

3.1 A LANCASTERIAN MODEL: HOMOGENEOUS PERCEPTIONS

We begin with a simple model where all consumers are well informed; that is, consumers' perceptions are deterministic and homogeneous (see Lancaster 1966). A consumer's preference for any given brand depends on the brand's attributes; the consumer behaves as if (s)he thinks in *attribute space*. (Some authors use the phrase *characteristics space* because they refer to the brand's attributes as characteristics.) For simplicity we shall assume that each brand has two attributes X and Y, each of which is fully divisible (i.e., the consumer can purchase fractional units). In addition, the consumer can create a hybrid product by mixing brands in any desired proportion. While the latter assumptions are not descriptively accurate in most cases, they can be easily relaxed at some price in complexity.

Suppose the consumer faces the following market opportunities:

	Brand 1	Brand 2	Brand 3
Units of X	7	2.5	5.0
Units of Y	9	5.0	1.5
Price per package	$10	$5	$5

Because all brands are fully divisible, we can conduct the analysis using an arbitrary level of spending on the product category, say $10. The consumer's opportunities are now:

	Brand 1	Brand 2	Brand 3
Units of X	7 units	5 units	10 units
Units of Y	9 units	10 units	3 units
Amount spent	$10	$10	$10

In Figure 3.1, A, B, and C correspond to the combinations of X and Y that the consumer can obtain by spending $10 on Brands 1, 2, and 3, respectively. Because of product divisibility, the consumer can attain any combination of X and Y shown on the line segment BA by allocating the $10 between Brands 1 and 2. For example, the consumer can attain point E (the midpoint of BA) by spending $5 on Brand 1 and the remaining $5 on Brand 2. Similarly, the consumer can choose any point on AC by combining Brands 1

Figure 3.1 Determination of the efficient set.

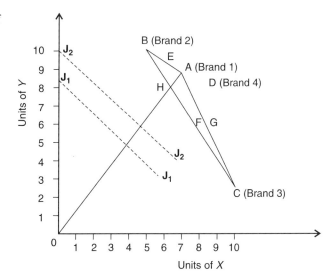

and 3 and any point on BC by combining Brands 2 and 3. What happens if the consumer combines all three brands? These combinations correspond to points in the triangle ABC. Consequently the consumer can attain any point on the edges of triangle ABC (i.e., AB, BC, and AC) or within the triangle.

Suppose both attributes X and Y are desirable to the consumer (i.e., more is better). Now the consumer will never purchase all three brands, *regardless of the precise form of the consumer's preferences*. Consider any point in triangle ABC, say F. Moving horizontally to point G on AC gives the consumer more of X without reducing the amount of Y, while holding spending constant. Consequently all consumers will prefer G to F regardless of their precise preferences. Similarly the consumer will never choose a point on BC where he combines Brands 1 and 3. Consequently the consumer will only choose points on the broken line segment BAC (the efficient set) and purchase at most two brands. This result is general: The maximum number of brands the consumer can choose equals the number of attributes.

> **Key Point**   If consumers have homogeneous and deterministic perceptions, all consumers will choose from a common set of brands known as the efficient set, *regardless of their precise preferences. The maximum number of brands that the consumer will buy is the number of relevant attributes.*

Knowledge of the efficient set (the broken line BAC in Figure 3.1) is very useful to product managers. Suppose the price of Brand 1 is increased from $10 per package. Point A in Figure 3.1 now moves inward toward the origin. H represents the combination of X and Y that Brand 1 provides when its price is raised to $11.06. (Show this.) Consequently Brand 1 is no longer efficient when its price is raised above $11.06 per package. Thus Brand 1 will disappear from the market if its price is increased beyond $11.06 per package. *This result is independent of the precise distribution of consumer preferences.* Suppose a new entrant introduces Brand 4, which provides the combination of X and Y shown by point D in Figure 3.1 for an outlay of $10. Now Brand 2 will be eliminated from the market.

> **Key Point**   The efficient set depends on market prices. Incumbent firms can determine the maximum prices that their rivals can charge. Potential entrants can determine who their rivals will be if they introduce a new product with a given attribute configuration. Because consumers' perceptions are deterministic and homogeneous, the manager does not require knowledge of the precise structure of consumer preferences in order to perform this analysis.

In reality firms need to know what market shares and profits to expect at different prices. The answer depends crucially on the precise forms of consumers' preference functions and the distribution of income in the population. Assume initially that each consumer spends $10 on the product category. (This assumption will be dropped later.) We shall assume that all consumers follow the same preference structure. Consumers, however, are heterogeneous because they value attributes X and Y differently. For convenience we shall assume that consumer i's preferences can be represented[1] by the linear structure $U_i = a_i x + b_i y$, where

a_i and b_i are importance weights, x denotes the amount of attribute X, y the amount of attribute Y, and U_i is an index of preference. Note that the importance weights vary across consumers; that is, consumers have heterogeneous preferences. To illustrate, consider a consumer whose preferences are given by $U_i = 0.4x + 0.6y$. Let us arbitrarily set $U_i = 5$. Now all combinations of X and Y that satisfy $5 = 0.4x + 0.6y$ are equally preferred by this consumer. In Figure 3.1, the straight line J_1J_1 gives all the combinations of x and y that yield a utility of 5. We say that J_1J_1 is the indifference curve corresponding to $U_i = 5$. Consider another value for U_i, say, $U_i = 6$ (a more preferred situation than $U_i = 5$). Proceeding as before, we can show that the new indifference curve J_2J_2 is parallel to J_1J_1 and above it. The consumer seeks to get onto the highest possible indifference curve. The only constraint is that the consumer must choose a point on the efficient set (the broken line segment BAC). As Figure 3.1 shows, the slope of this consumer's indifference curves lies between the slopes of BA and AC. Consequently this consumer will choose Brand 1. Now consider a consumer whose indifference curves are steeper than AC (i.e., X is very important). This consumer will choose Brand 3. Similarly a consumer whose indifference curves are flatter than BA (i.e., Y is very important) will purchase Brand 2. Using the slopes of AB and AC (see Figure 3.1), we have the following results[2]:

Slope of Consumer's Indifference Curves	Brand Chosen
0.0 to −0.5	Brand 2
−0.5 to −2.0	Brand 1
less than −2.0	Brand 3

We can now relax the unrealistic assumption that each consumer spends $10 on this product category. Suppose a consumer spends $20 instead. The efficient frontier BAC now moves outwards "parallel" to itself (i.e., there is a pure rescaling effect). Because the slopes of the consumer's indifference curves are unchanged, the consumer's brand choices will remain unaffected.[3] Thus consumers' brand choices are independent of how much they spend on the product category. Two remaining issues must be resolved to operationalize the theory. First the firm must form the three segments where segment membership is based on the slopes of the indifference curves. (Empirical methods for doing this will be discussed in Chapter 4.) Second the firm must determine how much each segment spends on the product category in question.[4] This information is sufficient to determine the volume-based and revenue-based market shares of each brand.

> ***Key Point*** *If consumers have homogeneous and deterministic perceptions, we can analyze consumer behavior in two steps. First determine the efficient set and then determine brand choices by examining the preference structures of consumers. Given knowledge of the preferences and product category spending levels for consumers, we can determine the market shares of all brands in the market. If a new product provides a different combination of existing product attributes and does not change consumers' preference structures (i.e., importance weights), we can predict the impact of the new product on the volume-based and revenue-based market shares of all products in the market.*

3.2 THE LANCASTERIAN MODEL: SOME REFINEMENTS

The standard Lancasterian model made two simplifying assumptions. First, consumers think in terms of physical attributes. Alternatively, we can study consumer behavior using a paramorphic stimulus–response approach, where the brand attributes are the stimuli and preference is the response. In other words, there is no need to explicate the consumer's information-processing strategy. Second, the number of attributes is fixed. We now relax these assumptions.

Suppose consumers analyze product attribute information in two steps. In the first step they determine what benefits these attributes provide. For example, a consumer who plans to purchase a new car may begin by determining how safe, economical, and reliable a particular brand is. The perceived benefits are "safety," "economy," and "reliability." In the second step consumers form their preferences on the basis of these perceived benefits. For the moment, we assume that consumers have homogeneous perceptions (i.e., all consumers agree on the combination of benefits that any given brand offers).

Following our approach in the previous section, suppose that the consumer can purchase any combination of Brands 1, 2, or 3. Each brand provides three attributes: X, Y, and Z. All brands are fully divisible. The market opportunities available to the consumer for $10 (an arbitrarily chosen value) are:

	Brand 1	Brand 2	Brand 3
Units of X	8	9	6
Units of Y	8	5	12
Units of Z	4	6	2
Amount spent	$10	$10	$10

Consumer decision making proceeds in two steps. First, consumers transform product attribute information into product benefit information according to the following transformation:

	X	Y	Z
Units of B_1	5	3	4
Units of B_2	3	6	4

where B_1 and B_2 denote product benefits. (Chapter 4 proposes empirical methods for determining this transformation.) For example, one unit of X provides 5 units of B_1 and 3 units of B_2. Second, consumers form their preferences on the basis of these benefits. These data imply the following relations among brands and product benefits:

	Brand 1	Brand 2	Brand 3
Units of B_1	80	84	74
Units of B_2	88	81	98
Amount spent	$10	$10	$10

Figure 3.2 shows the combinations of product benefits available to the consumer for an outlay of $10.[5] Recall that the consumer always prefers more of a benefit to less. Following

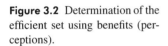

Figure 3.2 Determination of the efficient set using benefits (perceptions).

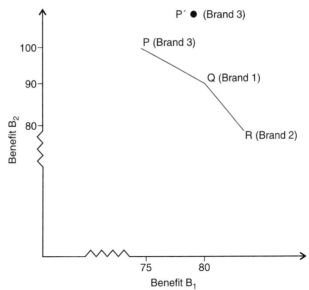

the approach in the basic Lancaster model, we see that the efficient set is the broken line segment PQR. Hence the consumer will purchase at most two brands even though each brand has three attributes. This example illustrates an important general result: *If consumers make evaluative judgments in terms of product benefits, the maximum number of brands the consumer will purchase is the number of benefit dimensions and not the number of attributes.* In most cases, the number of benefits is significantly smaller than the number of attributes. Consequently the results obtained by using the standard Lancasterian approach (i.e., measuring the direct links from attributes to preference) are not general.

This refinement of the basic Lancasterian model provides two important managerial advantages. First, by defining the market in terms of consumer benefits rather than physical attributes (an engineering approach), the manager obtains improved understanding of competitive structure and potential competition. Consider a brand manager of a national brand of orange juice. Using the standard Lancasterian model, the manager will incorrectly define the industry as all brands of orange juice. This definition of the market could be a strategic mistake because orange juice brands are vulnerable to competition from carbonated soft drinks that provide similar consumer benefits (say "thirst quenching" and "refreshing") but contain different physical attributes.

Second, the revised model provides insight into the impact of new products in cases where the basic model provides no guidance. Our previous analysis showed that, *if no new attributes are introduced*, the marketing manager can use the basic Lancasterian model to predict the impact of a new brand on competitive structure and performance. Suppose the new brand introduces a new physical attribute. Then the standard Lancaster model offers no predictions about the impact of the new product. Recall that, before the new product is introduced, consumers' preferences are defined in terms of the old attributes. In our example, the preference of the ith consumer was defined as $U_i = a_i x + b_i y$, where a_i and b_i are importance weights and x and y denote the amounts of the old attributes. After the new product introduction, the standard model requires us to redefine U_i in terms of all attributes, including the new attribute [i.e., $U_i = f(x, y, z)$, where f denotes a deterministic function and z denotes the amount of the new attribute]. Consequently the old importance weights of product attributes and indifference curves are meaningless. That is, unless the manager conducts additional research to determine consumers' new preference functions, the manager cannot determine the impact of the new product. Using the revised approach, there is no need to re-estimate preference functions provided the new product does not introduce a new benefit dimension (as is often the case). The only step necessary is to determine the relationship between the new set of attributes and the benefits. Given this information, the manager can analyze different new product scenarios and determine the impact of these products on the marketplace.

Key Point *The efficient set of brands can be too large if we use the standard Lancaster model and measure the direct relationship between product attributes and preferences. By defining products in terms of product benefits instead of product attributes, we can correctly define the competitive structure of the market. Furthermore, we can predict the impact of new products that introduce new attributes into the marketplace provided no new product benefits are introduced.*

The previous analysis assumed that consumers have deterministic and homogeneous perceptions (i.e., all consumers share the same beliefs about the bundle of benefits provided by a given brand). In Figure 3.2, all consumers agree that P, Q, and R, respectively, represent the benefits provided by Brands 3, 1, and 2. Given this scenario, the efficient set of brands is common for all consumers.

Suppose there are two consumer segments with heterogeneous perceptions. Both segments perceive Brand 1 to be located at Q and Brand 2 to be located at R (see Figure 3.2). The first segment, however, perceives Brand 3 to be located at P and the second segment perceives Brand 3 at P'. As discussed earlier, the following pairs of brands can be efficient for the first segment: Brands 1 and 2 (the line segment QR) and Brands 1 and 3 (the line segment PQ). For the second segment, Brand 1 is dominated: the efficient set consists of Brands 2 and 3 only.

This example illustrates that the efficient set of brands can vary across consumers if perceptions are heterogeneous. The managerial and empirical implications are fundamental.

First, the marketing manager cannot ignore the consumer's information-processing strategy and simply investigate the reduced-form relationship between a product's physical attributes and consumer preferences. Even if such an approach is statistically correct (this issue is discussed in Chapter 4, Section 4.4), the results will be seriously misleading if perceptions are heterogeneous. Specifically the manager will fail to recognize that different brands compete in different segments and is therefore likely to commit strategic mistakes.

Second, by explicitly investigating perceptual heterogeneity, the manager can coordinate price and advertising message policy. For example, the manager of Brand 1 can use a comparative advertising strategy aimed at Brand 3. This advertising strategy should be aimed at the second segment and, in particular, should attempt to move P′ (see Figure 3.2) toward P. If this strategy is successful, the efficient sets for both segments will include Brand 1.[6] Obviously the efficacy of this policy will be increased if the firm can target members of the second segment in a focused way. Chapter 4, Sections 4.3 and 4.6, discuss empirical methods for market segmentation.

Third, the perceived benefits (i.e., B_1 and B_2 in Figure 3.2) to a consumer can vary depending on the context of produce use. For example, a consumer might evaluate a cracker along the dimensions "crunchiness" and "robustness" when deciding whether to consume the cracker as a snack. (In this example B_1 denotes "crunchiness" and B_2 "robustness.") In contrast, the same consumer could evaluate the cracker along the dimensions "blandness" and "thinness" when deciding whether to consume the cracker with a dip. (B_1' now denotes "blandness" and B_2' "thinness.") *Consequently the efficient set will vary depending on the context in which the product is used.* A manager who fails to recognize this fact will misunderstand the market structure and nature of competition in the industry. Additionally, the number of salient benefits could vary across product-use occasions. For example, two dimensions—B_1 and B_2—are salient for the snack context. Three dimensions, however— B_1', B_2', and B_3'—could be relevant when the cracker is used in the dip context. In this case the efficient set (and consequently consumer behavior) could vary depending on the product-usage context; the consumer will purchase at most two brands for a snack occasion and at most three brands for use with a dip.

> **Key Point**   *The manager should explicitly analyze consumer perceptions instead of using the simpler stimulus–response methodology to establish the links between a product's physical attributes and consumers' choice. By understanding consumer perceptions, the manager can coordinate price and advertising policy, obtain improved understanding of market structure, form segments based on perceptual heterogeneity, and improve the firm's performance.*

The previous analyses implicitly make several strong behavioral assumptions. First, no harm is done if we assume that consumers behave as if they compare all brands. (See the discussion on the determination of efficient sets.) From a descriptive viewpoint this assumption is obviously incorrect at the individual level. The moot point, however, is whether the assumption creates problems at the aggregate level. (This question will be discussed in detail in Chapter 4.) Second, the consumer is always willing to trade off attributes regardless of the levels of the attributes. See the indifference curves in Figure 3.1. In reality, because of the onerous informational demands of "rational" behavior, consumers often resort to a variety of simplifying heuristics. For example, a consumer could proceed in two steps. Choose a cut point, say, $x = 4$, $y = 3$ and eliminate all brands for which $x \leq 4$, $y \leq 3$ (see Figure 3.1). This information-processing approach—known as a conjunctive decision rule—implies that for any brand with $x \leq 4$, no amount of Y will induce the consumer to even consider the brand. In the next step compare all brands in the *consideration set* (i.e., brands for which $x > 4$ and $y > 3$) using a tradeoff approach. As one expects, the managerial and empirical implications of such an information-processing strategy are significant. Chapter 4 discusses these issues in detail and examines other information-processing heuristics.

> ***Key Point*** *Suppose consumers follow different information-processing heuristics. Then the "separation theorem," which allows us to analyze separately the efficient set and consumer preferences, does not hold. In particular, the alternatives from which consumers choose (i.e., the consideration set) can vary across consumers even if perceptions are homogeneous and nonstochastic.*

3.3 PROSPECT THEORY AND A HYBRID MODEL OF CONSUMER BEHAVIOR

The previous analysis assumed that prices act as constraints on consumer choice and that perceptions and preferences are deterministic. Several behavioral theorists have argued that, even if prices are deterministic, price has an additional role.[7] Prospect theory (Kahneman and Tversky 1979) argues that individuals evaluate gains and losses separately in terms of departures from a reference point.[8] In the context of pricing, the reference point is a reference price.

Consider a consumer whose reference point for a 6-ounce bar of Dove soap is $1.50 (see Figure 3.3a). Then if the consumer pays $1.20, there is a gain of $0.30. The "value" of this gain is AB. Note that the "value" function gets flatter in the gain dimension as gains increase. We say that the consumer is risk-averse in the domain of gains. Suppose instead that the consumer pays $1.80 for the 6-ounce bar of Dove soap. The loss in value is CD. Note that the value function is very steep in the domain of losses near the reference point and flattens out as losses increase. We say that the consumer is risk-seeking in the loss domain.

The shape of the value function (i.e., concave in gains and convex in losses) leads to some interesting conclusions when combined with a key behavioral assumption: Prospect theory argues that individuals evaluate *each* gain and *each* loss separately. This assumption contrasts sharply with that made in traditional utility theory, which argues that gains and losses are combined before being evaluated—an assumption known as asset integration.

Prospect theory has several important managerial implications (see Thaler 1985). Because the value function becomes flatter when gains increase (i.e., the value function

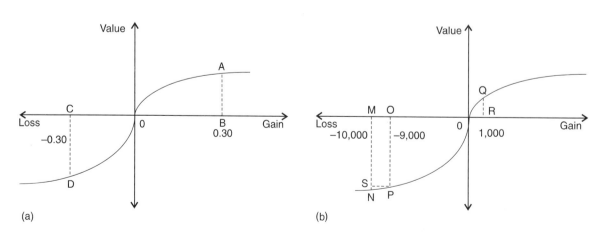

(a)   (b)

Figure 3.3a, b Value functions in prospect theory.

is concave in the gain domain), firms should choose policies that separate gains. Similarly, because the value function becomes flatter when losses increase (i.e., the value function is convex in the loss domain), the firm should choose policies that combine losses. The case of mixed gains and losses is more interesting. In Figure 3.3b consider two pricing policies for an automobile. Using the first pricing plan, the firm charges a price of $9,000. The loss in value to the consumer is OP. Using the second plan, the firm charges a price of $10,000 and offers the consumer a cash-back rebate of $1,000 after purchase. In this case the loss in value to the consumer is MN and the gain is QR. Recalling that the consumer evaluates gains and losses separately, we see that the consumer prefers the rebate plan. (Recall that the value function is relatively flat in the vicinity of a loss of $10,000.) Note that according to traditional theory the consumers would be indifferent between the two pricing plans: In fact, allowing for the time value of money (i.e., the delay in obtaining the rebate), the consumer would prefer the cash price of $9,000 over the rebate plan!

The manager, however, faces several important empirical and theoretical problems in applying prospect theory to pricing policy (see Chandrashekaran and Jagpal 1995a,b). A consumer's reference price is unobservable to the researcher; furthermore, reference prices are likely to vary across the population (i.e., consumers are heterogeneous). Reference price need not be unidimensional; for example, consumers may use internal reference prices (IRPs), external reference prices (ERPs), or both. The literature suggests several ways to measure IRP including fair price (x_1), price last paid (x_2), and a weighted average of prices paid on the last y occasions (x_3), where the researchers specifies y a priori. Because each measure is only a proxy for IRP, no single measure may be appropriate. Similar difficulties occur in operationalizing the construct of external reference price (e.g., a brand's list price is an imperfect measure of ERP because consumers vary in the extent to which they discount this information). Another issue is how consumers combine different pricing cues. For convenience consider internal reference price. Then the *unitization* theory implies that the measures of IRP are formative (i.e., IRP is a weighted index of the separate measures). (See Figure 3.4a.) Alternatively, the *nonunitization* theory implies that the measures of IRP are reflective. (See Figure 3.4b.)

Chandrashekaran and Jagpal (1995a,b) addressed these issues using the structural equation methodology.[9] (Chapter 4, Section 4.6, discusses this methodology. For the moment the reader should note that this methodology allows us to estimate systems of equations,

Figure 3.4 Alternate models of internal reference price (IRP). Note: x_i are indicators of IRP $(i = 1, 2, 3)$; ζ, structural error; and δ_i, measurement errors $(i = 1, 2, 3)$.

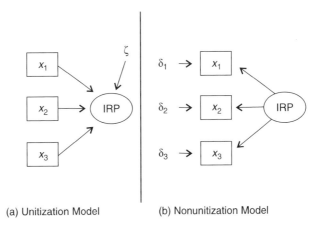

(a) Unitization Model   (b) Nonunitization Model

distinguishing among structural and measurement errors.) They conducted an experiment in which consumers were given different types of reference pricing information for several durables. The results showed that single measures of IRP are inappropriate. Furthermore, different segments use different information-processing strategies (i.e., unitization and nonunitization); in particular, the results depend on the product, the context (e.g., gift giving and personal use), and the degree of task involvement.

> **Key Point** *Prospect theory provides different predictions about market behavior than standard economic theory. Managers can use the structural equation methodology to form market segments based on consumers' IRPs and ERPs. The appropriate model structure (e.g., whether consumers use unitization or nonunitization strategies) is likely to vary across products and depend on the product usage context.*

We can refine the approach by developing hybrid models that combine the standard economic approach and prospect theory. In particular, we can use a conjoint analysis procedure (see Kohli and Mahajan 1991) to estimate the distribution of reservation prices for a given brand in the population (reservation prices measure the maximum amounts consumers are willing to pay for the brand) and the Chandrashekaran and Jagpal (1995a,b) approach to estimate IRPs and ERPs. In this way the firm can form segments based on consumers' reservation prices and reference prices.

To see how this information can be used to form market segments, consider Figure 3.5. Suppose the current price of a given brand is $10. Recall that consumer surplus is the difference between a consumer's reservation price and the price paid (e.g., a consumer whose reservation price is $12 and who pays $10 for the product obtains a consumer surplus of $2). Then the four segments of interest are A, B, C, and D. Each consumer in Segment A obtains a positive total benefit: consumer surplus (referred to as *acquisition utility* by some authors) is positive and so is the value function (referred to as *transaction utility*). Consequently segment A will buy the product.[10] For consumers in Segment B, acquisition utility is negative and the transaction utility positive. Thus the firm can appeal to nonusers in Segment B by increasing the reference price. One way is to persuade the consumer that the

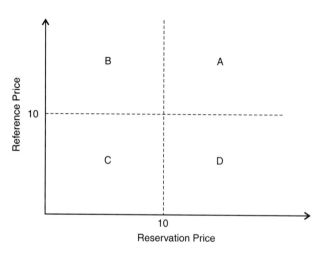

Figure 3.5 Market segmentation using reference prices and reservation prices.

fair price should be higher because the brand is expensive to make. The effectiveness of this policy depends on the extent to which such nonusers can be selectively targeted. Segment C is problematic because both acquisition utility and transaction utility are negative. Nonusers in Segment D have positive acquisition utilities and negative transaction utilities. They can be reached in the same way as nonusers in Segment B. We cannot, however, determine a priori if nonusers in Segment B are more attractive than nonusers in Segment D.

> **Key Point**   *The manager should determine the distribution of internal reference prices and form segments. This method can be improved if conjoint analysis is also used to estimate the distribution of reservation prices. Nonusers in two segments should be targeted: those with high reference prices and low reservation prices and those with low reference prices and high reservation prices. Precise knowledge of value functions is necessary to choose among these segments.*

One refinement should be added. Our discussion has focused on internal reference price. As discussed, consumers can be influenced by external reference price as well (e.g., a manufacturer's suggested retail price). Consequently the consumer has two reference points. Strictly, standard prospect theory does not apply: That theory was developed for single-valued outcomes. One approach to deal with multiple reference points is to assume additive separability.[11] (Thus total consumer benefit = consumer surplus $+w_1 V_1 + w_2 V_2$, where V_1 and V_2 are the value functions corresponding to internal reference price and external reference price, respectively, and w_1 and w_2 are weights to be estimated. Recall that these weights are necessary because consumer surplus is measured in monetary terms and the Vs are not.) In particular, the manager can form segments based on consumer surplus (i.e., preference heterogeneity), consumers' valuation of gains and losses in the domain of internal reference price, and consumers' valuation of gains and losses in the domain of external reference price. The empirical methods proposed in Chapter 4 can be used.

> **Key Point**   *Consumers may use several reference prices (e.g., internal and external reference prices). Standard prospect theory is not strictly applicable because gains and losses are coded in two dimensions. One procedure that combines standard economic theory and prospect theory is to assume additive separability and form segments based on a simultaneous analysis of preferences (i.e., reservation prices) and value functions.*

The previous discussion focused on the use of reference price as a strategic tool. We now analyze the implications of prospect theory for market behavior. In order to focus on essentials, we shall assume that the firm cannot affect a consumer's reservation prices and that the consumer's reference price is a scalar (which varies across consumers). Furthermore, the consumer cannot stockpile the product. Suppose the manager reduces price by a small amount, say from $10 to $9.50. This price cut will increase sales volume in the current period if the price cut is larger than some consumers' perceptual thresholds.[12] Consumers' reference prices, however, may be unaffected because the stimulus (i.e., price cut) is relatively small. We say that the new price is not assimilated. What is the impact of the price cut on future demand? None. The reason is that the distribution of reservation prices and reference prices is unchanged (see Figure 3.5). The managerial implication is that standard price theory applies. In particular, the manager need not consider dynamic effects when deciding on a price cut.

What happens if the price cut is "large" (e.g., from $10 to $6)? As expected, current demand increases (i.e., there is a movement down the demand curve). Interestingly, future demand is unaffected because reference prices are unchanged! The reason is that the stimulus (i.e., price cut) is large and is therefore contrasted (i.e., not internalized). Consequently, as in the previous scenario, the manager can analyze the effect of a price cut using the standard static (i.e., one-period) approach.

What happens if the price cut is moderate (e.g., from $10 to $8)? In this case, current demand increases as before. Consumers' reference prices, however, fall because consumers assimilate (i.e., internalize) the price reduction. This assimilation effect causes the firm's future demand curve to move inward (see Figures 3.6a and 3.6b). *Hence the manager must take a dynamic perspective and recognize that a moderate price cut is likely to borrow profits from the future.*

Two cases are possible. First, suppose that when the demand curve shifts inward the market becomes more price sensitive at any given price. A simple example is shown in Figure 3.6a, where AB denotes the demand curve in period 2 corresponding to the old reference prices in period 1 and DE the new demand curve in period 2 resulting from the lowered reference prices. MC denotes the marginal cost of production and is assumed to be constant for simplicity. Let p_2 denote the optimal price in period 2 assuming no price reduction in period 1. Then, because the market has become more price sensitive, the new marginal revenue $(\widehat{MR})$ exceeds marginal cost when the price is p_2. Consequently the new price $\hat{p}_2$ is lower than p_2. The lower price, however, now leads to a further reduction in reference prices and moves the demand curve inward from DE. Let $\hat{p}_3$ denote the price in period 3. Then using the previous argument we see that $\hat{p}_3 < \hat{p}_2$ and so on. *Thus a moderate reduction in price can lead to a continuous downward spiraling of prices if reference price effects are strong.*

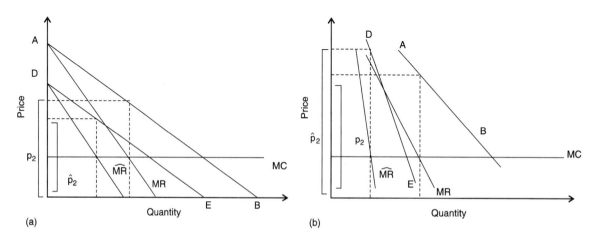

Figure 3.6a, b The dynamic effect of a shift in reference prices.

Second, suppose the market becomes less price sensitive when demand falls because of the reduction in reference prices (see Figure 3.6b). Now $\hat{p}_2 > p_2$. Thus reference prices increase in period 3, causing the demand curve to shift from DE toward AB. Hence $\hat{p}_3 < \hat{p}_2$. Similarly, $\hat{p}_4 < \hat{p}_3$ and so on. *Consequently after the price reduction in period 1, prices will oscillate in future periods.*

Key Point   *Managers can analyze small and large price changes using standard economic theory. If price changes are moderately large, reference prices will change because consumers assimilate the price stimulus. Consequently the manager must use a multiperiod framework to evaluate moderate price changes.*

The previous analysis suggests that changing consumers' reference prices is potentially risky. In fact, the firm can incur significant losses if price changes are moderate. What steps can the firm take to ensure that price changes do not have a deleterious effect on reference prices? One approach is to sell the product in an unusual size. For example, shampoo and soap manufacturers often sell their products using the slogan "Limited-time-offer. Twenty-five percent more at regular prices." Reference price theory suggests that firms should use this mode instead of a straightforward price cut in order to prevent reference prices from falling and reducing future demand and profitability.

Key Point   *Firms may find large price cuts to be dysfunctional even if the market is highly price sensitive and competitors do not react. In a dynamic framework the optimal policy for the firm may be to introduce moderate price cuts while taking steps to prevent the brand's reference prices from falling and hence reducing future profits.*

Our previous discussion has used the words small, moderate, and large imprecisely. In order to operationalize the theory, we need to construct dynamic experiments and determine how sensitive reference prices are to price changes. The methodology is straightforward and easy to implement (see Chandrashekaran and Jagpal 1995a,b). We expect the results to vary by product and usage context.[13] To illustrate, "fair price" may be the primary determinant of internal reference price for a given product. The firm can use this knowledge to introduce moderate price cuts without lowering internal reference prices. Thus a shoe retailer might use the slogan: "We just got an excellent deal on a manufacturer's overrun of shoes and are passing the savings along to you."

In general the firm should form segments on the basis of the distribution of reference prices in the population and selectively target segments. Suppose a moderate price cut has a minimal effect on Segment 1's internal reference prices. Then the manager can target Segment 1 using the price cut, realizing that current profits can be increased without sacrificing future profits. In contrast, suppose a moderate price cut lowers Segment 2's internal reference prices significantly. Then the manager should be cautious about targeting Segment 2 because future profits from this segment are likely to be reduced.

> **Key Point**   *For any given product, empirical analysis is necessary to distinguish whether consumers regard a given price change as small, moderate, or large. Consumers are likely to have heterogeneous perceptions regarding the magnitude of a given price change. Managers should form segments based on the degree of heterogeneity in reference prices and reservation prices in the population and selectively target segments.*

Our analysis has focused on price paid and internal reference price. Recall that the firm can also change the external reference price (e.g., by changing the manufacturer's suggested retail price). The previous approach can be applied to this more realistic scenario in a straightforward manner though the details will be more complicated. Some guidance is available. Experimental evidence shows that consumers tend to discount extreme external reference prices. ("This car has a list price of $15,000. I will, however, sell it to you for $4,000.") Thus the value function for ERP cannot be strictly monotonic throughout the gain domain. Finally, although we focused on the monopolistic firm (i.e., we did not consider the effect of competitive reaction), reference price theory has important policy implications for oligopolistic markets.

> **Key Point**   *Theory should be developed to analyze the simultaneous effects of prices, Internal Reference Prices, and External Reference Prices on market equilibrium in oligopolistic markets.*

3.4 THE EFFECT OF UNCERTAINTY

The previous analyses assumed that consumers' perceptions are deterministic. What happens if perceptions are uncertain? As one might expect, perceptual uncertainty can lead to inconsistent choices. For example, when asked to choose between Brands A and B, a consumer may choose A on one occasion and B on another even though the consumer's preferences have not changed. We say that the consumer is intransitive.

Luce (1959) developed a simple theory to explain intransitivity *without invoking perceptual uncertainty*. Suppose a Lucean consumer assigns utilities of 10 and 20 to Brands A and B, respectively. Then the consumer will choose A one-third of the time and B two-thirds of the time [$\frac{2}{3} = 20/(10 + 20)$]; that is, the consumer is intransitive.

From a behavioral viewpoint, Luce's theory is restrictive because, even though choice is probabilistic, utility is deterministic. (The Luce model leads to additional technical difficulties that will be discussed shortly.) Behavioral scholars inspired by Thurstone have emphasized that individuals perceive the same stimulus differently because of perceptual errors (e.g., biases in judgment) and other idiosyncratic differences. This viewpoint leads naturally to the conclusion that utility must be random (contrast the Luce model); consequently the consumer's choices are intransitive.

Suppose a consumer is asked to choose among three brands of a product: A, B, and C. Let the random utilities for A, B, and C, respectively, be $U_A = \ln 10 + \varepsilon_A$, $U_B = \ln 20 + \varepsilon_B$, and $U_C = \ln 30 + \varepsilon_C$ where the εs are random variables with zero means. Assume that the εs are independent across brands and follow identical Gumbel distributions. (The reason for these assumptions will become clear momentarily.) Now the logit Model Applies[14]: In particular, we obtain the following intuitive results: Probability (A) $= \frac{1}{6}$ [i.e., $10/(10 + 20 + 30)$], probability (B) $= \frac{1}{3}$, and probability (C) $= \frac{1}{2}$. Note that the forms of the logit and Luce models are very similar. There is, however, an important difference. The Luce model requires ratio-scaled utilities (i.e., the zero point is unique). In contrast, logit is very general because the Model Allows any monotonic increasing transform of the utility function, much in the spirit of deterministic classical utility theory.[15]

> **Key Point**   *The intuitively appealing Lucean results can be obtained without imposing the stringent assumptions of ratio-scaling and deterministic utilities. The logit model leads to a Luce-type representation while allowing utility to be random; in particular, the logit utility function is invariant to monotone increasing transforms.*

Suppose now that a new Brand D is introduced and that this brand is identical to Brand B. That is, $U_D = \ln 20 + \varepsilon_D$. What does the logit model imply about the consumer's new choice probabilities? Following the previous approach, we see that probability (A) $= \frac{1}{8}$, probability (B) $= \frac{1}{4}$, probability (C) $= \frac{3}{8}$, and probability (D) $= \frac{1}{4}$. Note that the relative probabilities of any pair of brands in the old choice set (A, B, C) are unaffected by the introduction of Brand D. For example, the relative probabilities of A and B remain in the ratio 1:2. This property—known as the independence of irrelevant alternatives (IIA)—leads to a paradoxical conclusion.[16] Suppose n clones of Brand B are introduced into the market. Then probability (A) $= 1/(2n + 6)$ and probability (C) $= 3/(2n + 6)$. If n is large, Brands A and C will each have probabilities approaching zero. This implication is problematic: We do not expect inferior brands (Brand B and its clones) to drive out the superior Brand C! (The Luce model leads to the same difficulty.)

Fortunately, several diagnostic tests of the IIA property[17] and appropriate statistical treatments are available. Before discussing these methods, however, we examine the relationship between IIA and market segmentation. In particular, we demonstrate that the logit model only implies that IIA holds at the segment level. IIA does not hold at the aggregate market level (see Ben-Akiva and Lerman 1985, p. 110, for a lucid example).

Suppose the market consists of two segments. For simplicity assume that the members of each segment are homogeneous and that initially there are two Brands A and B. Suppose Segment 1's utilities are $U_A = \ln 90 + \varepsilon_A$ and $U_B = \ln 10 + \varepsilon_B$. Segment 2's utilities, however, are $U_A = \ln 10 + \varepsilon_A$ and $U_B = \ln 90 + \varepsilon_B$. (For notational simplicity we do not use subscripts or superscripts to denote segments.) Assume that both segments are of equal size. Suppose Brand C—a clone of Brand B—is introduced into the market.

What is the impact on market shares at the segment and aggregate levels? The results are shown in Table 3.1. Note that IIA holds at the segment level. Specifically, in Segment 1 the relative market shares of Brand A and B are in the ratio 9:1 before and after Brand C is introduced. In Segment 2 the relative market shares of Brands A and B are also unaffected by the new product introduction and remain in the ratio 1:9. Thus IIA implies that *within each segment* the new Brand C draws market share from the incumbent brands in proportion to their old market shares. These properties (IIA and proportional draw), however, do not hold at the aggregate market level. Specifically, the new ratio of relative market shares for A and B after the new product introduction (43.54:28.23) differs considerably from

Table 3-1 Market Shares for Heterogeneous Segments

	Brand A	Brand B	Brand C
Before:			
Segment 1	90%	10%	
Segment 2	10%	90%	
Population share	50%	50%	
After:			
Segment 1	81.82%	9.09%	9.09%
Segment 2	5.26%	47.37%	47.37%
Population share	43.54%	28.23%	28.23%

the prior ratio (50:50). Note in particular that Brand C draws proportionately more from Brand B than from Brand A even though Brands A and B have equal shares prior to the new product entry.

Key Point   *The logit model makes the strong assumption of the independence of irrelevant alternatives. Consequently logit can yield paradoxical results for market behavior. Researchers should estimate logit models at the segment rather than the aggregate level and perform specification tests to detect departures from IIA. Market-level data may not satisfy IIA even though individual market segments do.*

Before we discuss procedures for estimating market behavior when IIA does not hold, it is useful to examine the meaning of a departure from IIA. The fact that the error terms are correlated for at least some alternatives implies that something systematic has been omitted from the model. To make matters concrete consider a simple example. Suppose two brands of soap are available in the market: a national brand and a store brand. Both brands are available in each of two package sizes that need not be equal: small and large. Thus the consumer's choice set consists of four alternatives.

Let B index brands and S index package size. Then a general representation is $U_{BS} = V_{BS} + \varepsilon_{BS}$, where U_{BS} is the random utility corresponding to a given brand–package-size combination,[18] V_{BS} is the deterministic component of utility and ε_{BS} is the random error term; in particular, $\varepsilon_{BS} = \alpha_B + \beta_S + \gamma_{BS}$, where α_B denotes the error due to evaluating the brand, β_S the error due to evaluating package size, and γ_{BS} is the residual error, which is purely random (i.e., the residual error is uncorrelated across all brand–package-size combinations).

Suppose $\alpha_B = \beta_S = 0$ (i.e., ε_{BS} is purely random). Then IIA holds, and we can analyze all the brand–package-size combinations simultaneously using the joint logit model (see Ben-Akiva and Lerman 1985, pp. 278–80).

Now suppose the consumer is uncertain in evaluating brands and package sizes (i.e., $\alpha_B \neq 0$ and $\beta_S \neq 0$). Consider two alternatives: national brand and small package size (Alternative a) and national brand and large package size (Alternative b). Then ε_{BS} will be correlated for alternatives a and b because both alternatives share the same feature: national brand. Hence IIA does not hold.

The simplest solution when IIA does not hold is to impose some behavioral structure and to assume that either $\alpha_B = 0$ for all brands or $\beta_S = 0$ for all package sizes. That is, either the consumer has no uncertainty in evaluating brands or the consumer has no uncertainty in evaluating package sizes. (These assumptions are obviously restrictive and will be relaxed.)

Suppose we fix $\beta_S = 0$. Then the model simplifies considerably; in particular, under appropriate statistical conditions[19] we can use the nested logit model. (See Ben-Akiva and Lerman 1985, Chapter 10, and Anderson, de Palma, and Thisse 1992, pp. 46–48, for technical discussions.) Consider Model A in Figure 3.7. Given our assumptions, the consumer behaves as if he follows a sequential decision strategy. In the first step he decides whether to buy the national or store brand; conditional on this choice the consumer decides which package size to purchase.[20]

Suppose we fix $\alpha_B = 0$. Then the consumer follows Model B in Figure 3.7. In the first step the consumer decides which package size to buy; conditional on this choice the consumer decides which brand to purchase.

Suppose the nested logit formulations are theoretically justifiable. What are the managerial implications? Consider the manager of a store brand who is planning to add a large package size to the store-brand product line. Then if consumers follow Model A, the large package size will have a strong cannibalization effect because alternatives that fall in the same section of the tree are highly similar. (See Figure 3.7.) If consumers follow Model B, however, the net sales of the store brand are likely to increase. Given knowledge of which model is correct, parameter estimates of the appropriate utility function, and the profit margins for different brand–package-size combinations, the store manager can determine the overall product-line effect of the new product introduction. The analysis can be further refined if the manager can identify segments a priori and determine segment sizes; in this case the manager should perform separate analyses for each segment and aggregate the results across segments to determine market behavior.

One important question needs to be answered: How can the manager determine if a group of consumers follows Model A, B, or the joint logit Model C, which assumes that $\alpha_B = \beta_S = 0$? Model C is a special case of Model A; we say that Model C is nested in Model A. Similarly Model C is a special case of Model B. Consequently we can compare

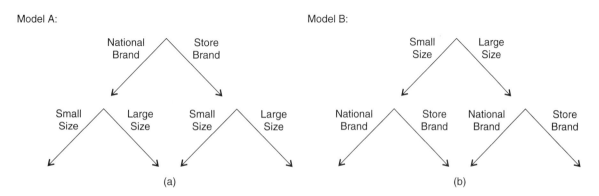

Model A:

Model B:

(a)

(b)

Figure 3.7a, b Alternative models of consumer choice.

Model A with Model C and Model B with Model C in a straightforward manner using standard tests for nested models. Models A and B, however, are not nested. To perform this comparison we must use a more elaborate test for non-nested models. (See Ben-Akiva and Lerman 1985, pp. 311–19, for a detailed example.)

What are the limitations of the nested logit model? As discussed, the assumption that either α_B or β_S is identically zero is difficult to justify a priori on behavioral grounds. Although the nested logit model is more general than the joint logit model, the nested logit framework does not allow for general patterns of substitution across alternatives. The assumption of equal variability for all brand (package-size) effects may not be appropriate. For example, consumers are likely to be more uncertain in evaluating a new or unfamiliar brand than in evaluating an established brand. The brand and package-size errors for a given individual are likely to be correlated because of judgment heuristics and perceptual biases. The number of nested logit models (assuming that such representations are reasonable) can be large if the dimensionality of the choice set increases. For example, suppose that consumer choice involves three dimensions: store, brand, and package size. Then the consumer can choose one of six sequential decision-making strategies. Although the researcher can sometimes eliminate some sequential strategies a priori, the remaining set of nested logit models can still be large.

The general probit model provides a flexible statistical framework for addressing these difficulties (see Ben-Akiva and Lerman 1985, pp. 299–300, and Daganzo 1979, Chapter 3, for a detailed discussion). In particular, the general probit Model Can simultaneously incorporate all three errors in the utility function ($\alpha_B \neq 0$, $\beta_S \neq 0$, and $\gamma_{BS} \neq 0$), allow for unequal variances for each brand or package-size error, and allow for general patterns of correlation among the error terms (e.g., correlations between α_B and β_S). Perhaps most important from a marketing manager's viewpoint, the general probit Model Allows one easily to incorporate consumer heterogeneity.[21]

One additional marketing issue deserves attention. We know that consumers can follow different decision processes. Suppose Segment 1 follows Model A (consumers choose brand first and then package size), whereas Segment 2 follows Model B (consumers choose package size first and then brand). Alternatively, suppose that some consumers are informed whereas others are uninformed (e.g., one segment does not face uncertainty in making brand comparisons and the second segment does). If the marketer can form segments a priori, he can use the nested logit modeling approach discussed above. The problem is that it is necessary to form segments based on unobservable consumer decision processes; hence the manager may be unable to form the segments a priori.

To deal with this problem (known as *post hoc segmentation*), it is necessary to estimate a *finite mixture probit model* that simultaneously forms market segments and estimates model parameters.[22]

Key Point   *The general probit model provides a rich framework for analyzing consumer choice when the consumer's choice decision involves several dimensions (e.g., for a frequently-purchased product the dimensions could be the type of brand and the package size). Specifically the probit model allows for general forms of substitution among alternatives by explicitly allowing for consumer error along each choice dimension; in particular these errors can be correlated. Consequently the probit model can allow for a wide variety of judgment heuristics and perceptual biases.*

3.5 CONCLUDING REMARKS

This chapter shows that standard microeconomic demand theory should be supplemented by behavioral theory. For example, the marketing manager can gain considerable insight by explicitly measuring the consumer's perceptions and recognizing that consumers are heterogeneous and have uncertain perceptions. In particular, such knowledge allows the manager to coordinate the marketing mix, selectively target different market segments, and understand the market structure. Prospect theory, in particular reference pricing theory, is also highly relevant for strategic pricing and should be used in a hybrid model that incorporates the basic economic concept of consumer surplus. Standard choice models (logit and probit) and preference models (such as conjoint analysis) are reduced-form methods that consider the mappings from objective product attributes to choice and preference, respectively; they do not Model Consumer perceptions.

In order to implement these theories and to extend standard preference and choice models, we need to address several important empirical issues: Consumers' perceptions are unobservable and uncertain, consumers can idiosyncratically interpret scales assigned by the researcher, and consumers use different information-processing heuristics. Chapter 4 examines these issues in detail and proposes new empirical methods.

NOTES

1. We remind the reader that this representation is purely paramorphic; the consumer behaves "as if" (s)he follows the postulated structure. In later sections, we shall examine the implications of using a theory that ignores the actual process which consumers use in forming judgments and making choices.

2. Suppose a consumer's indifference curves have exactly the same slope (-0.5) as AB in Figure 3.1. Now the consumer's purchase decision is ambiguous because all combinations of Brands 1 and 2 on BA are equally acceptable. We do not expect this ambiguity to be serious in practice because there is a continuum of consumers with different importance weights.

3. This result does not depend on the linearity of the indifference curves; all that is necessary is that the indifference curves are "parallel" to each other (i.e., the utility function is homothetic). See Silberberg (1990, p. 97) for a discussion of homothetic functions.

4. The approach described is slightly oversimplified. The first step—determining brand choice—is correct. The second step, however, could lead to aggregation bias if there is significant intra-segment variability in expenditure on the product category. In such cases individual-level estimates should be constructed and summed to obtain segment-level responses.

5. For convenience our analysis assumes that we can measure benefits on a per-dollar basis. For this approach to be valid, we require that benefits are measured on a ratio scale (i.e., the zero point is unique). As discussed in Chapter 4, it is not necessary to assume ratio scaling in a perceptual model; in fact, most statistical models only require interval scaling. This assumption of ratio scaling, however, allows us to separate the discussions on consumer efficiency and consumer choice.

6. In reality, comparative advertising will change the perceived locations of Brand 3 *and* Brand 1. Furthermore, because segments are not watertight, comparative advertising can affect both segments' perceptions of Brands 3 and 1. An additional factor is that comparative advertising gives Brand 3 free publicity (i.e., consumer awareness of Brand 3 is enhanced). Finally, comparative

advertising is likely to change the consumer's reference point (i.e., benchmark against which brands are compared). These refinements are important; however, they simply underscore the need to understand the consumer's decision process and highlight the limitations of the more straightforward stimulus–response approach of measuring the links between product attributes and preference or choice.

7. Economists have generally accepted that in the framework of conspicuous consumption the consumer's utility increases with price. Alternatively, price can act as a signal of quality to uninformed consumers. In this case, the efficient set will vary across segments because perceptions are heterogeneous.

8. Prospect theory is subject to several technical difficulties (see Quiggin 1993, pp. 50–52, for a succinct discussion). Prospect theory is subject to violations of dominance. In addition, prospect theory requires that the number of states is finite; different means of approximating a given continuous probability distribution by discrete prospects can lead to very different evaluations. Recent research has attempted to deal with these shortcomings (see Wakker and Tversky 1991, Gul 1991, and Quiggin 1993, pp. 157–58).

9. Assume that consumers follow a nonunitized information-processing strategy (see Figure 3.4b). Suppose there are three measures of internal reference price: x_1, x_2, and x_3. Consider the confirmatory factor model

$$x_1 = \alpha_1 + \lambda_1(\text{IRP}) + \delta_1$$
$$x_2 = \alpha_2 + \lambda_2(\text{IRP}) + \delta_3$$
$$x_3 = \alpha_3 + \lambda_3(\text{IRP}) + \delta_4$$

where the αs and γs are parameters, the δs denote measurement errors, $\text{Cov}(\delta_i, \delta_j) = 0$ for $i \neq j$, and $\text{Cov}(\text{IRP}, \delta_j) = 0$ for all j. This model is exactly identified and can be estimated using a standard confirmatory factor approach. See Chapter 4.

Alternatively, suppose consumers follow a unitized information-processing strategy. Let $\text{IRP} = \gamma_1 x_1 + \gamma_2 x_2 + \gamma_3 x_3 + \zeta_1$, where the γs denote parameters and ζ_1 structural error (e.g., the effect of omitted variables). Let $\eta = \beta\text{IRP} + \zeta_2$ denote an unobserved response variable (say, behavioral intention). Let $y = \eta + \varepsilon$, where y denotes a measure of η and ε measurement error. This MIMIC Model Can be estimated using standard structural equation methods (see Jöreskog and Sörbom 1993). Note that the unitized and nonunitized models are not nested; consequently we can compare these models using the RMSEA and ECVI statistics (see Browne and Cudeck 1993).

Future research should proceed in two directions. First, one should develop a more stringent test by developing additional measures of IRP so that the model is overidentified. Second, one can test the model using $\ln x_i$ and $\ln(\text{IRP})$. This formulation is more consistent with adaptation theory (Helson 1964). Conceivably, the model structure (i.e., linear or log-linear) could vary across products. In comparing results for the linear and log-linear models, the researcher should not use the standard goodness-of-fit statistics because the scales vary across models (e.g., the indicators are x_i and $\ln x_i$). In particular, the ECVI and RMSEA statistics should be used to make these Model Comparisons.

10. For simplicity, we abstract from competitive conditions. In a multibrand situation the consumer will choose that brand which provides the largest total benefit.

11. Consider any given consumer. For any Brand i let p_i^R, p_i^1, and p_i^2, respectively, denote the consumer's reservation price, internal reference price, and external reference price. Let Q_i denote the consumer's total benefit and p_i the price of the brand. Then $Q_i = (p_i^R - p_i) + \varphi V(p_i : p_i^1, p_i^2)$, where V denotes the value function and φ is a scaling constant. Assuming additive separability, we have $Q_i = (p_i^R - p_i) + \beta_1 V_1(p_i : p_i^1) + \beta_2 V_2(p_i : p_i^2)$, where β_1 and β_2 are parameters and V_1 and V_2 denote the appropriate value functions. Because Q_i is unobservable, we need a proxy. One possibility is an interval or ratio-scaled measure of behavioral intention $I_i = \theta_1 + \theta_2 Q_i + v_i$, where the θs denote the individual's idiosyncratic scaling parameters and v_i denotes measurement error. The estimated regression equation for the individual is $I_i = \alpha + \gamma (p_i^R - p_i) + \varphi_1 V_1(p_i : p_i^1) + \varphi_2 V_2(p_i : p_i^2) + \varepsilon_i$, where $E(\varepsilon_i) = 0$, $\mathrm{Cov}(p_i^R, \varepsilon_i) = 0$, $\mathrm{Cov}(p_i, \varepsilon_i) = 0$, $\mathrm{Cov}(V_1, \varepsilon_i) = 0$, and $\mathrm{Cov}(V_2, \varepsilon_i) = 0$. In practice, the scaling parameters vary across individuals because consumers idiosyncratically interpret the assigned scale. Chapter 4 examines in detail how to estimate models of this type, allowing for general patterns of heterogeneity (i.e., all parameters including the scaling coefficients vary across individuals).

12. A perceptual threshold is sometimes referred to as the "just noticeable difference." According to the Weber–Fechner law, perceptual thresholds vary proportionally with the strength of the stimulus. In a pricing context, for example, a consumer is more likely to notice a price cut of $2 if the initial price is $4 rather than $40. In general, we expect some heterogeneity in perceptual thresholds because purchase frequency and product information vary among consumers.

13. One interesting issue is whether the assumption of reflective indicators in the confirmatory factor model (see note 9) is appropriate. An alternative "unitization" theory argues that the indicators of internal reference price are formative (see Figures 3.4a and 3.4b). Preliminary evidence in Chandrashekaran and Jagpal (1995a,b) suggests that both theories are correct depending on the product and usage context. These results imply that serious statistical error will be introduced if unitization theory holds, the researcher excludes relevant xs, and IRP is an independent variable in a behavioral equation. If, however, the confirmatory factor model is correct, omitting relevant xs simply reduces statistical efficiency.

14. The logit assumption of independent and identically distributed Gumbel errors leads to the closed-form result that probability $(i) = e^{\mu V_i} (e^{\mu V_A} + e^{\mu V_B} + e^{\mu V_C})$, where V_i denotes the deterministic component of utility for brand i, and μ is a scaling factor. By convention, we set $\mu = 1$ for identification because μ cannot be distinguished from the parameters in the Vs (see Ben-Akiva and Lerman, p. 68, for a proof). Note that the logit representation does not require Gumbel-distributed errors. Yellott (1977) and Anderson, de Palma, and Thisse (1992, pp. 39–43) discuss alternative random error models that lead to the logit form.

15. Suppose $U_A > U_B$. Then if F is a monotone-increasing transform of U, $F(U_A) > F(U_B)$ trivially. Thus, as in the classical deterministic theory, we cannot use the signs of cross-derivatives of the sort U_{xy}, where x and y denote the arguments of U to determine if x and y are substitutes or complements.

16. The logit and Luce models are special cases of the class of simple scalable models. This class of models implies IIA (see Tversky 1972a,b).

17. See Hausman and McFadden (1984) and McFadden (1987).

18. Suppose brand and package size do not share perceptual attributes (e.g., package size denotes economy and brand denotes quality). Then the additively separable form $V_{BS} = \varphi(B) + \theta(S)$ may be appropriate, where φ and θ denote functions. Suppose brand and package size share

perceptual attributes (e.g., both package size and store brand denote economy). Then we may require the form $V_{BS} = \varphi(B) + \theta(S) + \eta(B, S)$. Behavioral theory should be used in choosing the functional form of V_{BS}. Suppose $\alpha_B = 0$ and $\beta_S = 0$. Then the general model reduces to $U_{BS} = \varphi(B) + \theta(S) + \eta(B, S) + \gamma_{BS}$. Assume that the γ_{BS} are identically and independently distributed Gumbel variables. This model is known as the *joint logit form*.

19. The necessary assumptions are: (1) α_B is independent of γ_{BS} for all store and package size combinations; (2) the γ_{BS} are independently and identically distributed with a common scale parameter μ_S; and (3) α_B is distributed so that the maximum value of U_{BS} has a Gumbel distribution with scale parameter μ_B. For economically meaningful results $\mu_B \leq \mu_S$ (see McFadden 1978, pp. 86–87). It can be shown that only the ratio μ_B/μ_S is identified. Hence it is necessary to "set the scale" of the utility measure by normalizing the Model And setting either μ_B or μ_S to equal one (see Ben-Akiva and Lerman 1985, p. 287).

20. It can be shown that the IIA property holds at the first stage (brand choice) and at the second stage (package size choice conditional on brand choice). See Ben-Akiva and Lerman (1985, pp. 286–90) for details. The latter result is intuitive because the brand effect (i.e., the sum of the deterministic component and the stochastic error due to the brand chosen in the first stage) is equal for all package sizes and is therefore irrelevant. See Ben-Akiva and Lerman (1985, p. 290) for a more precise algebraic statement. Note that the IIA property does not hold for arbitrary pairs of alternatives (for example, the choice between a national brand with a small package size and a store brand with a small package size).

21. We illustrate the general probit approach using a simple model. Let i index alternatives and n index consumers. Consider the linear-in-parameters random utility model $U_{in} = \beta_{in}x_{1i} + \beta_{2n}x_{2i} + \varepsilon_{in}$, where the xs denote product attributes and β_{1n}, β_{2n}, and ε_{in} are random. Let $\beta_{1n} = \overline{\beta}_1 + \psi_{1n}$ and $\beta_{2n} = \overline{\beta}_2 + \psi_{2n}$, where $\overline{\beta}_1$ and $\overline{\beta}_2$ denote the appropriate average parameter values for the population, $E(\psi_{1n}) = E(\psi_{2n}) = 0$ by construction, and $\mathrm{Cov}(\psi_{1n}, \psi_{2n}) \neq 0$ in general where Cov denotes the covariance operator.

Then we can write $U_{in} = \overline{\beta}_1 x_{1i} + \overline{\beta}_2 x_{2i} + \varepsilon'_{in}$, where $\varepsilon'_{in} = \varepsilon_{in} + \psi_{1n}x_{1i} + \psi_{2n}x_{2i}$. Suppose the random vector $(\varepsilon_{in}, \psi_{1n}, \psi_{2n})$ has a multivariate normal distribution. Then we can use the general probit model to capture the heterogeneity in the population [i.e., we can estimate $\overline{\beta}_1, \overline{\beta}_2, \sigma^2(\psi_{1n}), \sigma^2(\psi_{2n})$, and $\mathrm{Cov}(\psi_{1n}, \psi_{2n})$] because the vector of errors ε'_{in} has a multivariate normal distribution with mean vector zero. See Daganzo (1979, pp. 85–87) for a detailed discussion.

We argue that the probit methodology should be used in marketing studies where a priori market segmentation is infeasible or intrasegment variability is high. In the past probit was computationally burdensome; recent work (McFadden 1989) has made probit estimation computationally less demanding.

Some researchers have argued that in most cases logit should be used because the logit and probit estimates are similar. We caution against this conclusion. Consider the following extreme scenario. Suppose the utility of Brand A is $U_A = \ln 10 + \varepsilon_A$ and the utility of Brand B is $U_B = \ln 30 + \varepsilon_B$. Suppose ε_A and ε_B have independent normal distributions such that the variance of ε_A is small (approximately zero) and the variance of ε_B is 0.3. Then the logit model implies that probability (A) $= \frac{1}{4}$. In reality, probability (A) $\cong 0$. Clearly logit and probit will give different results.

22. There are two standard approaches for handling unobservable heterogeneity in choice models. First, if theory suggests that the number of segments is finite, one can use the mixture logit model

(see Kamakura and Russell 1989). Second, if heterogeneity is continuous, one can estimate random-coefficient logit or probit models (see Ben-Akiva and Lerman 1985, pp. 124–25, and Daganzo 1979, Chapter 3). These methods, however, implicitly assume that all consumers follow the same decision process. In contrast, a finite mixture probit Model Can simultaneously capture heterogeneous consumer decision processes [e.g., $\alpha_B = 0$ for Segment 1, whereas $\beta_S = 0$ for Segment 2] and heterogeneity in parameters for consumers in a given segment. Jedidi, Jagpal, and Krishna (1996) have developed an algorithm to estimate a finite mixture probit model with a scalar error term and fixed parameters for each segment. It should be possible to extend their finite mixture model to capture heterogeneity in consumer decision making by including several error terms as in the standard multinomial probit model.

Consumer Behavior: An Empirical Perspective

So far our analysis of consumer behavior has been theoretical and somewhat abstract. Our main conclusions were that the manager must explicitly recognize that consumers are likely to have heterogeneous perceptions and preferences and even follow different information-processing strategies. This chapter evaluates available empirical methods for analyzing consumer preference and develops new methods for simultaneously treating different forms of heterogeneity (e.g., consumer information-processing strategies and model parameters). In addition, we develop an integrated consumer decision process model that explicates the role of perception in consumer decision making and allows one to measure perceptual error. Our focus throughout is managerial; that is, we are particularly interested in developing preference models the manager can use to predict market behavior, develop new products, and coordinate marketing policy. We begin with the case where the manager has limited information and proceed to cases where the manager has more detailed knowledge of the consumer.

4.1 LIMITED INFORMATION

Suppose the manager is seeking new product opportunities; in particular, the manager does not know which product attributes, benefits, or product functions are important to the consumer. One approach is to begin by identifying a key market segment or segments. For example, a cereal manufacturer may choose a target segment comprising married women in the 30- to 40-year age group with children under 10 years of age. The next step is to choose a small sample—typically 8 to 12—from that segment and conduct qualitative research. For reasons to be discussed shortly, the firm does not choose this sample according to a statistically controlled plan: We say that the sample is a convenience sample.

Why does the firm not choose a statistical sampling plan (e.g., a random sample from the target segment)? After all, statistical sampling plans provide the important benefit of allowing the manager to quantify the results and make probabilistic statements. (The reader has no doubt seen the results of political surveys that are of the sort, "Based on a random sample of size 400, the poll shows that, subject to an error of ± 2 percent, politician X is preferred by 54 percent of the population.") Although this argument has merit, the reasons for not choosing a statistical sampling plan are practical. At this stage of the analysis the firm is primarily interested in obtaining qualitative information and does not know what to quantify. Furthermore, statistical sampling is expensive. Hence the firm chooses a convenience sample from the target segment.

Having chosen the sample—known as a focus group—the firm determines the scope of the product-related issues to be discussed by the group and appoints a moderator to supervise the discussion. This discussion is unstructured; in particular, the moderator does not solicit quantitative information from the members of the focus group. We say that the focus group is exploratory.

What are the advantages of the exploratory focus group methodology? First, the firm can use the results to identify those product benefits the target segment is seeking. In particular, the firm can use the results to identify market opportunities and obtain valuable information regarding consumer heterogeneity. For example, by conducting separate focus group sessions on the East and West Coasts, a coffee manufacturer may find that heavy ground-coffee drinkers on the East Coast are satisfied with existing brands; in contrast, heavy ground-coffee drinkers on the West Coast do not find the flavor of existing brands to be sufficiently robust. The firm can also use the focus group results to screen out certain changes in product design or product function without wasting significant resources in time and money to develop and test new products that are likely to fail in the marketplace. Second, the firm can conduct focus group sessions quickly (typical sessions last anywhere from one to two hours) and inexpensively. Third, because of the availability of modern audio–video technology, top management can observe the focus group sessions firsthand. As a result, top management can play a meaningful role early in the product development process and does not need to depend solely on the inferences drawn by lower-level managers.

The previous discussion assumed that the firm uses the focus group method purely for exploratory research. The firm can, however, also use focus groups to perform quasiexploratory research if additional information is available. For example, suppose that the firm has already developed a product concept or product prototype and seeks to predict the trial rate for the target segment.[1] One approach for the firm is to conduct a focus group session to obtain qualitative information from consumers (as in the exploratory case); in addition, the firm collects quantitative information on the purchase intentions of consumers using a 5-point scale (say), where 1 denotes "definitely will not purchase" and 5 denotes "will definitely purchase" the new product. In such cases the firm should always inform the focus group about the price of the new product so that the consumers' stated intentions data are meaningful.

The quasiexploratory focus group method can be extended in several ways. For example, the firm can measure both the trial and the repeat purchase probabilities for frequently purchased products provided the product is available in physical form. The firm can collect these data for different product usage contexts. To illustrate, a potato chip manufacturer can ask consumers to state their intentions to purchase potato chips for two product usage contexts: "snack" or "meal accompaniment." For simplicity we shall assume that there is one product usage context and that the firm only collects intention data.

Suppose the firm conducts a focus group session with twelve consumers and includes price in the product description. In particular, four consumers state that they will "definitely" or "almost definitely" buy the new product (i.e., these consumers assign scores of 4 or 5 to the five-point intentions question). Is it reasonable to conclude that the expected trial rate for the target segment is 33.3 percent (i.e., $\frac{4}{12}$) and to compute a confidence interval for this estimate?

This approach is problematic because the sample is not statistically controlled; furthermore, the experimental design requires members of the focus group to interact with each other and the moderator. Consequently the responses of the individuals in the sample are not independent (e.g., the purchase probabilities for a given individual can change over the course of the session). Thus we cannot determine the accuracy of the estimated trial rate even if we combine intentions data across several focus groups from the same segment in order to increase the sample size.

Because of these statistical difficulties, firms use industry-specific heuristics to compute point estimates of the trial rate from focus group data. The conventional wisdom is that the "top box" approach (i.e., the fraction of consumers who choose the highest score on the intentions question) typically underestimates the trial rate and the "top two box" approach (i.e., the fraction of consumers who choose the highest or the second highest score on the intentions question) overestimates the trial rate. As discussed, it is meaningless to use focus group data to compute a confidence interval for the trial rate or to make probabilistic statements.

> ***Key Point*** *Focus group sessions are a useful vehicle for identifying new product opportunities and eliminating bad product ideas. Focus groups can also be used to diagnose deficiencies in the marketing mix (e.g., the advertising message). Their primary purpose is to generate qualitative information and to help the firm make sequential decisions. The manager should be cautious in interpreting quantitative data from a focus group study. Other qualitative research methods can be a useful supplement to focus group studies. These methods include brainstorming within the firm and obtaining feedback from distributors and the sales force.*

4.2 CONJOINT ANALYSIS: BASIC METHODOLOGY

Suppose the manager has used the focus group or some other methodology to identify the product design attributes that influence consumer preference. For example, consider a computer manufacturer who has determined that the consumer's preference for a computer depends on two product attributes: computer speed (X_1) and computer data storage capability (X_2). In this section for simplicity we do not consider an important product attribute: price.

In general we expect consumers to have heterogeneous preferences; for example, some consumers value computer speed highly, where as others put more emphasis on data storage. We say that the importance weights of the attributes vary across consumers. Three key managerial issues are: Can we determine the importance weights of given product attributes for different consumers? If so, can we meaningfully group consumers into segments based on these importance weights? Given these results, can we predict the likely effect of introducing a new product with particular attributes or levels of attributes on the market share, sales, and profit of the firm's product line?

Conjoint analysis is a widely used technique to address these issues.[2] In essence, conjoint analysis attempts to measure the product attribute → preference relationship. In this section we shall describe the mechanics of the basic conjoint methodology using a simple example. In later sections we shall discuss refinements of the conjoint methodology and the effect of different consumer information-processing strategies on the results from conjoint experiments.

Estimating an Individual-Level Conjoint Model

As discussed above, the first step in conjoint analysis is to determine the relevant product attributes; in our example the computer manufacturer has determined that the salient product attributes are computer speed and data storage capability. In practice the manager can determine the relevant product dimensions using a variety of methods ranging from subjective market knowledge and focus group sessions to statistical methods such as exploratory factor analysis and multidimensional scaling. (We shall discuss confirmatory factor analysis and multidimensional scaling later in this chapter.) The next step is to choose the levels of the attributes in the conjoint experiment. This step requires managerial judgment. Suppose the computer manufacturer has chosen the following nine combinations of attributes ("profiles"):

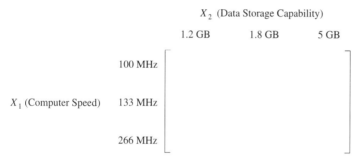

Note that for the range of values considered this conjoint experiment includes all possible combinations of computer speed and data storage. We say that the firm is using a "full-profile" experimental design.

Having chosen the profiles, we must choose a method to measure consumer preferences. Two methods are available. First, we can ask a consumer to rank the nine different profiles. Recall that in our example the consumer always prefers more of a given attribute (say computer speed) provided the level of the other attribute (data storage capacity) is held constant. Thus we expect all consumers to rank the 100 MHz, 1.2 GB profile the lowest (i.e., all consumers will assign a rank of 9 to this profile) and the 266 MHz, 5 GB profile the highest (i.e., all consumers will assign a rank of 1 to this profile). However, consumers can differ in their rankings of the remaining seven profiles depending on the importance weights they assign to computer speed and data storage capability. Second, we can ask the consumer to assign a scaled score to each profile (say from 1 to 10, where 1 denotes the lowest and 10 the highest score). This information—a rank or scale score for each profile—is sufficient to allow us to estimate the product attribute → preference relationship. We shall focus on the second approach, which is known as *metric conjoint analysis*, because this method is simpler, has desirable statistical properties, and is widely used in practice.[3]

Before estimating the conjoint model, we need to specify the form of the preference function. The crucial issue is whether the effect on preference of changing one product attribute at a time (e.g., increasing computer speed from 100 to 133 MHz) depends on the fixed levels of the other attributes (in this case, data storage capability). Suppose the answer is "no." Then each product attribute has its own independent effect on preference. We say that the preference model has main effects only. If the answer is "yes," the effect on preference of changing computer speed depends on data storage capability and vice versa. We say that the preference model includes interaction effects. Assume initially that a main effects model is appropriate.

The first step is to designate one combination of product attributes (say a computer speed of 100 MHz and a data storage capability of 1.2 GB) as the base profile. This choice is purely arbitrary.[4] In the next step, we estimate the main effects of the product attributes using a straightforward dummy variable regression approach.[5] Recall that the conjoint experiment includes three levels of computer speed and three levels of data storage capacity. Hence the regression model includes two main effects for each product attribute (one fewer than the number of categories in each case).

Suppose the results for a given consumer are as shown in Figure 4.1. In our discussion we shall use the words "utility" and "preference" interchangeably because the former is conventional in the literature.

Recall that we arbitrarily designated the 100 MHz–1.2 GB profile as the base case. Hence the value of the intercept in the regression model corresponds to the utility of a computer with this combination of product attributes. Figure 4.1 shows that the *incremental* utility in going from a computer speed of 100 to 133 MHz is 2. We say that the *part worth* of 133 MHz is 2. Note that the part worths are relative and not absolute quantities.[6] Similarly, the part worth of a computer with a speed of 266 MHz is 3. From a managerial viewpoint, we see that the consumer perceives a large gain in moving from a computer speed of 100 to 133 MHz (a part worth of 2) but a relatively small gain in going from a computer speed of 133 to 266 MHz (an increase in part worth of 1). Furthermore, the consumer's preference for a given computer depends heavily on its data storage capability (see Figure 4.1).

Not surprisingly, main-effects conjoint models are appealing to managers. The results can be easily understood graphically. In addition, the manager can analyze one attribute at a

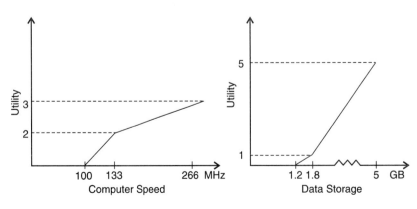

Figure 4.1 Hypothetical results from a main-effects conjoint model.

time and make tentative product decisions after evaluating preferences and manufacturing costs. To illustrate, for our hypothetical consumer (see Figure 4.1) the incremental utility of a 133 MHz,1.8 GB computer over the base computer (100 MHz, 1.2 GB) is 3, which is simply the sum of the separate part worths of a computer with speed 133 MHz and data storage capacity 1.8 GB.

Market Segmentation Using Conjoint Analysis

The previous discussion suggests that a firm can use conjoint analysis to measure a consumer's preference structure and match a product offering to the consumer's needs. In reality, there are many potential consumers, and it is generally not profitable for the firm to customize a product offering for each consumer. Therefore, the key issues are to determine whether there is one population or several subpopulations (segments) and to measure the degree of heterogeneity within each segment. Following standard marketing practice assume that the number of subpopulations (segments) exceeds one. We shall deal with the important case of one population with heterogeneous consumers in the next section.

The firm can use two methods for market segmentation depending on the information available. First, the firm can form segments a priori if it has sufficient market knowledge. In our example, the computer manufacturer may have decided before conducting the conjoint study that there are three distinct segments: large businesses, small businesses (e.g., individual-owned enterprises or partnerships), and homeusers. Thus the firm knows both the number of segments and the segment membership of any given consumer. This approach is known as *a priori segmentation*. Second, if the firm does not have sufficient knowledge to form segments a priori, it must use the conjoint results to identify the segments and to determine the segment to which a given consumer belongs. This approach is known as *post hoc segmentation*. Two scenarios are possible: (1) The firm knows the number of segments before conducting the conjoint experiment, and (2) the firm cannot specify the number of segments in advance. We say that Scenario (1) is confirmatory and Scenario (2) is exploratory. Most post hoc segmentation studies assume Scenario (2).

We shall consider the exploratory form of post hoc segmentation; that is, before conducting the conjoint experiment the firm does not know the number of segments or any given consumer's segment membership. The confirmatory form of post hoc segmentation is considerably simpler because the number of segments is known a priori. The firm can now use a sequential data analysis strategy. In the first step the firm performs individual-level conjoint analysis to determine the part worths of each attribute for all consumers in the sample. In the next step the firm pools these individual-level part-worth data and uses a clustering method to determine the number of segments and any given consumer's segment membership. (We shall discuss clustering methods in detail in the next section.) The firm then chooses a target segment(s) and searches for socioeconomic and demographic variables that are correlated to segment membership. Having identified such variables, the firm chooses an optimal marketing policy (e.g., product design and media message strategy) to reach the target segment(s).

To illustrate this approach, consider our computer example. For simplicity assume that a main-effects conjoint model is appropriate for all consumers and that the firm uses a full-profile approach with the following treatments: two levels of computer speed (100 and 133 MHz) and two levels of data storage capability (1.2 and 1.8 GB). Suppose the base profile is the 100 MHz, 1.2 GB computer. Then there are two part-worth coefficients for each consumer (one for a speed of 133 MHz and the other for a data storage capability of 1.8 GB).

Before forming the segments, however, we must deal with a subtle point. The consumer's true preferences are unobservable; the only data we have are *estimated* preferences, which we obtain by forcing all respondents to use a *common* preference scale. Recall that in our example we required all consumers to respond on the same scale with end points 1 and 10. Suppose all consumers use the assigned preference scale in the same way (e.g., a score of 4 means the same thing to all consumers). Then it is correct to cluster consumers based on the part worths obtained from individual-level analysis. If, however, consumers use the preference scale idiosyncratically, *clustering based on the raw part worths will be misleading*. The intuition is that for any given consumer these raw part worths reflect the combined effect of the true weights (which are unobservable) and that consumer's particular interpretation of the common scale assigned to all consumers by the researcher.

How can one resolve this difficulty? One approach is to "standardize" the individual-level coefficients (part worths in our example) prior to clustering. However, the theoretical literature on standardization in clustering models is sparse and provides limited guidance on choosing an appropriate standardization method (see Milligan 1996, pp. 352–54, for a review). More important, we can show that commonly used standardization methods are inappropriate for conjoint studies because they are not model-based and perform standardization by variable rather than by individual. A theoretically correct method is to standardize the conjoint coefficients separately for each individual, ignore the intercepts, and perform cluster analysis using these transformed data.[7] (In the next section we shall propose more general methods for handling heterogeneity.)

In our example suppose the standardized part worths have been estimated for each individual and are as shown in Figure 4.2a. Each point represents the standardized part worths for a 133 MHz, 1.8 GB computer for a given consumer.

As Figure 4.2a shows, there are three well-separated segments (i.e., the "between-group" variation is large) and the degree of heterogeneity in a segment is low (i.e., the

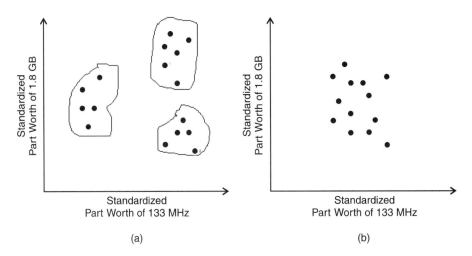

(a)   (b)

Figure 4.2 Forming market segments using standardized part worths.

"within-group" variation is small). Obviously, the manager will be pleased with these results. Suppose the standardized part worths are as shown in Figure 4.2b. Then the segments are not well defined. Hence the firm will find it difficult to develop separate marketing policies for each segment.

Suppose the manager can define the market segments a priori. Then, in contrast to the post hoc segmentation case, the manager does not need to pursue a sequential data analysis strategy because clustering is unnecessary (segment membership is known). In particular, the manager can directly analyze the individual-level conjoint results for each segment to predict that segment's response to the introduction of a new product with a specified profile. Furthermore, as discussed below, it is correct to analyze market behavior using the raw part-worth estimates for each individual, regardless of whether consumers idiosyncratically interpret the preference scale.

Conjoint Analysis and Market Behavior

Recall that the manager is not interested in analyzing consumers' preferences per se but rather in understanding and predicting market behavior.

In our example suppose that the firm has conducted a conjoint experiment and estimated the part worths of each product attribute for each consumer in the sample. Then we can use two approaches to determine the sales and market shares of different products at the segment and market levels. Both methods are based on the raw (unstandardized) individual-level part worths regardless of whether the firm has performed a priori or post hoc segmentation. (Note that we are assuming a part-worth model only for convenience; the methodology applies to more general conjoint models that include interactions.)

The first method is known as the *first-choice* method and assumes that the consumer always chooses that product that provides him with the highest expected preference. Thus the first-choice method is consistent with expected utility theory. Of course, the consumer's true preference (and hence the expected preference) for any given product is unobserved. It is, however, straightforward to show that we can operationalize the first-choice method in a conjoint experiment by assuming that the consumer chooses that product that provides the highest estimated preference score using the assigned interval scale.[8]

Second, in contrast to the first-choice method, we can argue that the consumer's choices are uncertain and attempt to determine the consumer's choice probabilities for different products based on the conjoint results. This approach is known as the *share-of-preference* method and is philosophically similar to the random utility model used in choice models. To illustrate this method, consider a simple example where the consumer has the choice of buying a 100 MHz, 1.8 GB or a 133 MHz, 1.2 GB computer. Suppose the estimated utilities are 6 and 8, respectively.[9] Then the estimated probability of choice for the 100 MHz, 1.8 GB computer is $6/(6+8) = \frac{3}{7}$, and the estimated probability of choice for the 133 MHz, 1.2 GB computer is $\frac{4}{7}$.

The problem is that the typical measure of preference is interval-scaled and does not have a unique zero point. Thus in our example we could equivalently have labeled the end points 2 and 11 instead of 1 and 10. If we had chosen these alternative end points, the estimated preferences for each computer would simply have increased by 1. (Some authors would say that we have translated the preference scale by shifting the origin by 1 unit.) Consequently, the estimated probability of choosing the 100 MHz, 1.8 GB computer would be $7/(7 + 9) = \frac{7}{16} \neq \frac{3}{7}$. Clearly, there is a serious problem if arbitrary scale changes affect the probabilities of choice! Thus the manager should not use the share-of-preference method if the preference measure is interval-scaled.

Are there any conditions when it is correct to use the share-of-preference method? The answer is "yes" provided preference is measured on a ratio scale, the true unobserved preference is a deterministic function of the product attributes (i.e., the error term in the conjoint model occurs purely because of measurement error and not omitted variables), and Luce's choice axiom holds. These conditions are stringent.[10]

Key Point *Conjoint analysis is a useful method for determining the product attribute → preference relationship. If the manager can define market segments a priori before conducting the conjoint study, the manager can use the raw estimates of the individual-level conjoint parameters to predict market behavior. If the manager cannot determine a given consumer's segment membership before conducting the conjoint study, one approach is to first standardize each consumer's estimated conjoint parameters and then perform cluster analysis to determine the number of segments and a consumer's segment membership. For both scenarios (a priori and post hoc segmentation) the manager can analyze the product attribute → choice relationship and estimate how product design changes will affect sales, market shares, and profits. Thus the manager can eliminate potentially unsuccessful new products and answer "what if" questions based on different assumptions about competitive behavior (e.g., a new product introduction by a competitor). The first-choice method is theoretically superior; the manager can also use the share-of-preference model provided he uses a ratio-scaled measure of preference and is confident that the conjoint model is well specified (i.e., the functional form is correct and there are no omitted variables).*

4.3 CONJOINT ANALYSIS: A REVIEW AND SOME REFINEMENTS

Let us begin with a review of the conjoint methodology. We shall assume that consumers behave "as if" they think in terms of physical attributes. This assumption will be relaxed in Section 4.4, where we examine the effect of different consumer information-processing strategies on the results of a conjoint experiment.

Individual-Level Conjoint Analysis

Consider first the design of a conjoint experiment. In the previous section we discussed an individual-level experiment with two product attributes (computer speed and data storage capability each having three levels). In the example each consumer was asked to evaluate all nine combinations of the attributes. We say that the experiment used a full factorial "3 × 3" design. Full factorial designs provide an important advantage: They allow us to estimate all main effects *and interactions*. As discussed in the previous section, a main-effects model can be restrictive (e.g., in our computer example the effect on preference of changing computer speed can depend on the data storage capability of the computer).

What happens if we estimate a main-effects model in a full-factorial conjoint experiment but interactions are important determinants of preference? The main-effects estimates will be correct on average.[11] However, the omission of interaction effects will lead to increased error in the model and hence provide unstable estimates of the main effects. More important, failure to include interaction effects will lead us to mismeasure the effect of changing the effect of product design on preference. For example, we may erroneously conclude that certain product design changes are unimportant (e.g., the incremental gain to the consumer of changing the computer speed from 133 to 266 MHz is not significant). One implication is that the firm could miss attractive market opportunities.

> **Key Point**   *The manager should carefully examine if part-worth conjoint analysis is meaningful. Failure to allow for interactions can lead to serious managerial error.*

In the previous section we examined a simple conjoint model with two attributes and three levels of each. In most practical applications several attributes are likely to be salient. Suppose four attributes are salient and the manager seeks to examine three levels of each. (Many conjoint experiments include more than four attributes.) A full factorial design would require the consumer to evaluate $3^4 = 81$ profiles. This task is formidable, and the results (assuming that the consumer can be persuaded to perform such a task!) are likely to be unreliable.

Several alternatives are available. First, we can choose a subset of the 81 profiles such that these profiles are uncorrelated to each other (there are many such subsets) and ask the consumer to evaluate only this subset of profiles (known as an orthogonal array). What are the implicit assumptions of this methodology? We must now assume that the consumer's preferences can be described using a main-effects (i.e., part-worth) model.[12] As discussed above this assumption may be incorrect. Second, in order to simplify the consumer's task, we can ask the consumer to evaluate pairs of attributes instead of full profiles (a procedure known as *tradeoff analysis*). The problem here is that the consumer is likely to impute values to the excluded attributes. Consequently even if a main-effects model is appropriate, we can obtain biased estimates of the part worths.

Given these difficulties and the need to obtain preference data using several attributes, what should the manager do? One approach is to ask each consumer to evaluate a limited number of profiles, pool the data across individuals, and fit a sufficiently general preference model that includes interaction effects. As discussed in the next section, analyzing such data is not straightforward. For the moment we continue our focus on individual-level analysis.

The consumer's preferences are unobserved and can only be inferred. In particular, the consumer's stated preference (e.g., a score on a 10-point scale) is only an indicator of the consumer's true preference and is subject to measurement error. What is the implication of using consumers' stated preferences in conjoint studies? Recall that the dependent variable in the conjoint model contains measurement error; however, the independent variables (i.e., the profiles) are fixed by experimental design and are therefore error-free. Hence if the conjoint model is well specified, the conjoint parameters will be correctly measured on average (i.e., the parameters will be unbiased). However, the measurement error in preference will make these estimates unstable. Consequently, if the error in measuring preference is large, the manager is likely to conclude that salient attributes are not significant[13] and hence miss market opportunities.

> ***Key Point***   *When a conjoint experiment requires the consumer to evaluate several attributes, a full-factorial experiment is often infeasible. Researchers can use an orthogonal design or a tradeoff approach to finesse the problem. However, these methods are not a panacea. The effect of using consumers' stated preferences in a conjoint experiment is to introduce measurement error. As a result, the conjoint estimates are correct on average but unstable. The managerial implication is that conjoint analysis may not be useful in analyzing product categories with which the consumer (or more generally the target market segment) is not familiar.*

Another issue is the degree of precision with which consumers evaluate the profiles. We expect that consumers will evaluate some profiles more confidently than others. What is the implication for conjoint analysis? The problem is that the conjoint model now suffers from heteroscedasticity (i.e., the variability of the error term differs from profile to profile). We know from standard econometric theory that the conjoint estimates will be unbiased but the usual significance tests are erroneous. In addition, the bias in these tests can go in either direction.[14] Thus the manager could include irrelevant attributes or exclude salient attributes. (As discussed, heteroscedasticity in individual-level conjoint models can lead to the selection of the wrong set of attributes. In such cases we face the "masking variable" problem. Specifically, if we use individual-level results as inputs to a clustering program to form market segments, the results can be meaningless even if only one or two irrelevant parameters are included. See Milligan 1996, pp. 348–52 for a review of the sparse statistical literature on the effect of masking variables on the accuracy of clustering algorithms.)

> ***Key Point***   *The results from a conjoint experiment can be distorted if the magnitude of error in consumers' stated preferences varies across profiles. Statistical methods are available for the diagnosis and treatment of this problem (known as heteroscedasticity). From the standpoint of experimental design, the manager should attempt to minimize the problem by choosing product profiles with which the consumer is reasonably familiar.*

Another issue is that of product credibility. If a product profile is implausible, the consumer's stated preferences can be seriously biased. The obvious solution is to eliminate implausible product profiles from the conjoint experiment. This approach, however, can adversely affect the experimental design. For example, orthogonal designs may become infeasible because plausible product profiles necessarily have correlated features (e.g., the consumer expects the horsepower and gas mileage of an automobile to be negatively related). Despite this problem—known as multicollinearity—the standard conjoint estimates will be unbiased. However, these estimates may be unstable. If multicollinearity is severe, the manager can use a Stein-type "shrinkage" estimator to obtain more accurate estimates of the parameters. (See any standard text in econometrics.) One problem is that shrinkage estimators are biased; consequently, although the manager can predict the effect of a given product design change on preference, he cannot perform significance tests on the individual conjoint coefficients. Hence, although predictive accuracy may not be adversely affected, it may not be possible to optimize product design.

> **Key Point**   *Conjoint studies should not include implausible product profiles even if the statistical design of the experiment is adversely affected. If necessary the researcher should statistically treat the multicollinearity problem resulting from correlated profiles.*

Another potential problem (generally ignored in the literature) is consumer fatigue. At the very least we expect the responses of consumers to be more accurate early in an experiment. When the consumer evaluates a moderately large number of profiles (say 30), the consumer's responses are likely to include more "guessing" as the experiment proceeds. How does fatigue affect the conjoint estimates?

Suppose the consumer's responses are correct on average; however, as a result of consumer fatigue the consumer's responses contain more measurement error as the experiment proceeds. Recall that we encountered this problem—heteroscedasticity—earlier when we discussed the effect of product familiarity on the accuracy of a consumer's responses. Thus fatigue does not lead to biased estimates of the conjoint parameters; however, the significance tests will be biased (i.e., the manager is likely to make incorrect inferences about the effect of a change in product design). What happens if as the experiment proceeds, fatigue leads the consumer to guess at random? Now the conjoint estimates will be meaningless.[15]

How can a manager deal with the problem of consumer fatigue? One approach is to reduce the number of profiles the consumer is required to evaluate. Alternatively the manager can use statistical methods to address the problems. He can test for heteroscedasticity in the conjoint model and attempt to treat the problem statistically using the fact that the variability of the error term depends on the order in which the consumer evaluates the profiles. Alternatively, the manager can search for influential data using standard statistical procedures, recognizing that the consumer's response is atypical when the consumer is fatigued. If the manager detects influential data, he should re-estimate the model after eliminating these observations or use a statistical procedure that reduces the weights given to these observations.

Another problem (not generally addressed in the conjoint literature) is that the consumer's memory of a previous judgment can affect the consumer's current judgment. For example, if the consumer suspects that he has overrated a particular profile, he may compensate by underrating the current one. We say that the error terms in the preference model are serially correlated (negatively in our example). We know from standard econometric theory that the effect of serial correlation is analogous to that of heteroscedasticity. Thus the conjoint parameters will be unbiased; however, significance tests will be distorted. The manager should therefore use standard econometric methods to detect and treat serial correlation.

> **Key Point**   *Conjoint studies should test for and treat the effects of consumer fatigue and consumer memory. Standard statistical methods can be used to provide correct statistical tests of significance and to develop robust estimates of the parameters.*

Suppose the researcher fails to include a salient attribute. What does this omission do to the conjoint results? The consumer will impute a value to the missing attribute. If we are lucky, this imputed value will be uncorrelated to the profiles in the conjoint experiment. In this case the only effect is that the stated preferences will contain more measurement error. Consequently the conjoint estimates will be unbiased but unstable.

What happens if the imputed value for the missing attribute is correlated to the product profiles in the study? For example, suppose that in a preference study for automobiles the researcher inadvertently excludes the attribute "miles per gallon" but includes the weight of the automobile. The consumer is likely to assume that a heavy automobile provides low gas mileage (i.e., the missing attribute is negatively correlated to the included attribute). In this case the conjoint model is misspecified, and the conjoint results will be meaningless.

> **Key Point** A conjoint experiment should include all salient attributes. The manage-rial implication is that good qualitative research (e.g., focus group studies) and man-agerial judgment or knowledge of the marketplace are crucial prerequisites for conjoint analysis.

So far we have ignored a key marketing variable: price. Conjoint experiments frequently include price as a product attribute. Is this approach consistent with economic theory? Consider a consumer with an income of $\$y$. Suppose the consumer is asked to evaluate a product profile "x" that has a price of $\$p$. Let $U(x)$ denote the consumer's utility (preference) for the product. Then for a "two-good" world the consumer's utility if he purchases this product is $U' = U(x)+(y-p)$, where $(y-p)$ represents the consumer's residual disposable income. In particular, $(y - p)$ is a proxy (numeraire) for the maximum utility the consumer can obtain after allocating resources across all other available products in the market.

Note that in the two-good model the coefficient of p is -1. Is it therefore necessary to constrain the price parameter to -1 in a conjoint model that includes price as an attribute? The answer is "no." Recall that we typically measure preference on an interval scale where the numerical values assigned to the end points are arbitrary (except that we must assign a higher value to the upper end point). Consequently, the measured coefficient for price depends on the particular preference scale chosen and need not be constrained. The only theoretical requirement is that the price coefficient in a conjoint model must be negative.

Two other points should be noted. First, unless price is a signal of quality, the two-good model implies that price can only have a main effect in a conjoint study. (Why?) Second, unless the analysis is conducted at the individual level, conjoint studies that use price must explicitly include income as an explanatory variable *even if $U(x)$ is common for all members in the group.*[16]

> **Key Point** Including price as an attribute in conjoint studies is consistent with economic theory. Unless individual-level conjoint analysis is conducted, conjoint models that use price should explicitly include income, particularly when analyzing consumer durables.

Conjoint studies often include "brand" as an attribute in the product profile. (Witness the attention given in the managerial and academic literatures to measuring the effect of *brand equity*.) This approach is not possible in individual-level conjoint studies because the preference model becomes tautological (the number of profiles trivially equals the number of brands). Consequently we must analyze pooled data across individuals using one of the methods discussed below.

The Heterogeneity Problem

So far we have focused on individual-level conjoint analysis. We now address the fundamental problem of consumer heterogeneity. We continue with our computer example and assume for convenience that the consumer's preferences can be defined by a linear main-effects model of the form $P^i = w_0^i + w_1^i x_1 + w_2^i x_2 +$ error, where i indexes consumers, P denotes the unobserved preference, the ws denote importance weights, x_1 computer speed, and x_2 computer data storage capability.

Suppose we know a priori that there is one population of heterogeneous consumers (see area A in Figure 4.3a). For the population the point Z denotes the weighted average of the importance weights for computer speed and data storage. We say that Z is the centroid. The problem is that we do not know area A or point Z. Assume that a conjoint experiment has been conducted using a random sample of 300 consumers. Then the analysis can proceed in three ways.

First, we can perform individual-level analysis to estimate the importance weights for each individual in the sample. As discussed in the previous section, this approach is straightforward, allows consumers to interpret the preference scale idiosyncratically, and provides unbiased estimates of the conjoint parameters for all individuals (i.e., these estimates are correct on average if the conjoint model is well specified). Individual-level analysis allows us to determine which attributes are significant for a given consumer and to predict individual and market behavior. In addition, if the firm can measure the relationship between these individual-level weights and observable consumer characteristics (such

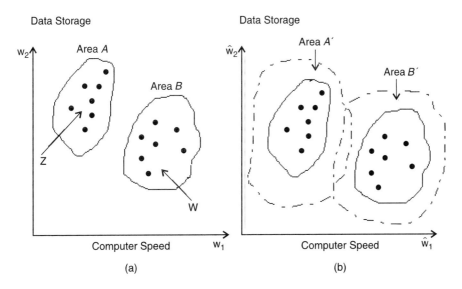

Figure 4.3 Importance weights in a two-segment example.

as income), it can target a particular group (segment) in the population to maximize performance.[17]

In spite of these advantages, individual-level conjoint analysis leads to several difficulties. Even if we analyze a large number of consumers we will always obtain an area such as area A' which is larger than area A. (Why?) See Figure 4.3b. Consequently, although we will correctly estimate the average importance weights for the population (point Z), the population will appear to be more heterogeneous than it is.[18] Individual-level analysis is not feasible when the number of profiles is large; important, even if the number of profiles a consumer evaluates is small, we must estimate a large number of parameters. In our simple two-attribute example we need to estimate 1,200 parameters (four parameters for each individual)! Furthermore, unless each consumer evaluates a large number of profiles, the individual-level conjoint parameters will be unstable. Thus individual-level analysis is likely to lead to imprecise estimates of market behavior.

Second, we can pool the data across the sample and fit one conjoint model with fixed coefficients. This approach considerably simplifies the experimental design by requiring the consumer to only evaluate a limited number of profiles; in particular, we can estimate interaction effects without using a full-profile approach, which may be infeasible or impractical. In addition, the fixed-coefficient method leads to a substantial reduction in the number of parameters to be estimated (in our example it is only necessary to estimate 4 parameters instead of 1,200). Thus the parameter estimates are likely to be more stable than those obtained from individual-level analysis. We must, however, make stringent assumptions in order to justify the fixed-coefficient method.

Suppose all consumers interpret the preference scale identically. Then the fixed-coefficient method will correctly estimate the centroid (point Z in Figure 4.3a) even if the sample is moderate.[19] However, the firm will be unable to determine the degree of heterogeneity in the population. For example, we cannot distinguish whether all consumers are identical (i.e., the importance weights for every consumer in the population are given by point Z) or whether the population is heterogeneous (see area A in Figure 4.3a). We say that there is an identification problem.[20] Furthermore, unless the conjoint model includes individual-specific variables (such as income), the first-choice model implies that all consumers behave identically. This property is problematic (point Z is not equivalent to area A).

Suppose consumers interpret the preference scale idiosyncratically. Then we face additional difficulties because the error term in the fixed-coefficient conjoint model will capture the joint effects of heterogeneity in the true importance weights and of consumers' idiosyncratic interpretation of the assigned preference scale. Hence the identification problem is compounded.[21]

How can we deal with these difficulties? One possibility is to use a third approach (not generally used in practice) that treats heterogeneity by allowing the conjoint coefficients to vary randomly across the population. This approach includes the fixed-effects model as a special case and can be implemented using a random-coefficient regression model (see Swamy 1970 and Judge, Hill, Griffiths, Lutkepohl, and Lee 1982, pp. 503–7). The appropriate data-analysis strategy depends on the shape of area A (see Figure 4.3) and whether consumers idiosyncratically interpret the preference scale.

Suppose all consumers interpret the preference scale in the same way and the true conjoint weights in the population follow a multivariate normal distribution (i.e., area A in Figure 4.3 is elliptical). Then considerable parsimony can be achieved. In particular, we can capture the model structure using a random-coefficient regression model with only 10 parameters (the means and variances of the weights, the covariances of these weights, and the variance of the error term in the conjoint model) and use a straightforward maximum likelihood approach to estimate the parameters. In contrast to individual-level modeling, if the conjoint model is correctly specified and the sample is sufficiently large, this approach will correctly determine the degree of heterogeneity in the population (area *A*).[22] Having estimated the parameters of the random-coefficient conjoint model, we can predict market behavior, preferably using a holdout sample. (A similar strategy can be used to analyze choice models when the model parameters have a multivariate normal distribution. See Daganzo 1979, pp. 92–93, for a theoretical discussion of the random-coefficient probit model and Elrod and Keane 1995 for a recent marketing application.)

Suppose we do not know the precise form of heterogeneity (i.e., the shape of area *A* in Figure 4.3) or consumers idiosyncratically interpret the preference scale. Then we cannot use the procedure discussed in the previous paragraph. For example, suppose that the true conjoint weights in the population have a multivariate normal distribution but consumers idiosyncratically interpret the preference scale. Then the parameters in the measured preference model cannot have a multivariate normal distribution.[23] Furthermore, it may be difficult to justify standard parametric representations theoretically because the individual-level conjoint weights are products of random variables. In such cases we should pool the data and estimate the random-coefficient conjoint model directly in one step using a general (preferably nonparametric) empirical Bayes procedure and then use the results to predict market behavior.

Note that the random-coefficient conjoint model is a theoretically valid way of analyzing pooled data. The method is highly parsimonious compared to individual-level analysis and includes the fixed-effect conjoint model as a special case (set the variances of all regression parameters and covariances for all pairs of parameters to zero). Furthermore the random-coefficient model preserves two important advantages provided by the individual-level model. The results do not depend on idiosyncratic differences among consumers in interpreting the assigned preference scale. In addition, the random-coefficient approach is consistent with expected utility theory.[24]

Key Point *If there is one population, the researcher should analyze the pooled data for the conjoint experiment using a parametric or nonparametric (as appropriate) random-coefficient model. From a parameter estimation viewpoint the random-coefficient model is a compromise between conducting individual-level analysis and estimating a fixed-coefficient model by pooling data across all individuals. The random-coefficient approach is theoretically attractive because it correctly measures the degree of heterogeneity in the population and allows consumers to interpret the preference scale idiosyncratically. Simulation and empirical studies are necessary to compare the robustness of the three methods for treating heterogeneity (i.e., using pooled data to estimate fixed-coefficient and random-coefficient models or conducting individual-level analysis). In particular, these studies should distinguish* both *heterogeneity in importance weights and in consumers' interpretation of the preference scale.*

In practice we are often unable to assert a priori that there is only one population; in fact many marketers believe that the market contains multiple populations (segments) and that each segment is heterogeneous. We first consider the simple case where the firm knows the number of segments a priori and the size of each segment. Suppose the firm knows that there are two segments, each of which is heterogeneous (see areas A and B in Figure 4.3b); furthermore, the firm knows consumers' group membership a priori. As in the single-population case, the firm does not know the degree of heterogeneity in each segment (areas A and B) or the segment centroids.

Suppose the firm conducts a conjoint experiment using random samples from each segment.[25] (We say that the firm is using a stratified sampling plan.) Because consumers' group membership is known a priori, we can analyze the pooled data for each segment separately using the random-coefficient conjoint approach described above. As in the single-population case, the random-coefficient method allows for general types of heterogeneity (i.e., shapes of areas A and B) and allows all consumers to interpret the preference scale idiosyncratically, regardless of segment membership.

In many cases, however, the firm cannot form market segments a priori. Suppose as before that there are two segments with importance weights shown by areas A and B, respectively, in Figure 4.3b. However, the firm does not know the number of segments, the size of the segments, or the group memberships of consumers. Consequently the firm cannot use a stratified sampling plan. Assume that the firm obtains a random sample from the unknown superpopulation, which consists of the unknown segments. Then we need to choose a statistical procedure for determining the number of groups (clusters), the size of each segment, the degree of heterogeneity within each group, and the segment to which a given consumer belongs.

Given this scenario, we can use two philosophically different probabilistic clustering approaches to form the segments: fixed-partition and random-partition models (see Bock 1996 for a detailed review and, in particular, pp. 386–406). Fixed-partition models (also known as "discrete classification models") are generally used in practice; these methods include a wide class of statistical models that use different statistical criteria (e.g., maximum likelihood, Bayesian loss functions, and the variance criterion) to form partitions. All fixed-partition models have one common feature: They do not explicitly include the probabilities of group membership as parameters. Random-partition models (also known as "mixture" models), in contrast, are theoretically more appealing because they assume that the subpopulations (segments) are generated by a specified statistical process in which the probabilities of group membership (i.e., the segment sizes) are explicit parameters.

Consider the fixed-partition approach for market segmentation. Assume initially that all consumers interpret the preference scale in the same way. Recall that we do not know the true importance weights for any given individual and only have estimates for these parameters. Furthermore, in our example there are two unknown segments. Then, as discussed in the single-population case, we will observe data in the dotted areas A' and B' instead of areas A and B even if the samples are large. Note that areas A' and B' overlap, whereas areas A and B do not. Consequently our ability to form segments is impaired regardless of the size of the sample.

Despite its importance, this issue—the efficiency of clustering in the presence of measurement error—has received very little attention in the marketing and statistical literature. Although empirical evidence is scant, simulation studies suggest that the problem is serious. Milligan (1980) found that, even if the number of groups is known a priori (an unlikely scenario) and the correct variables are used for clustering, fixed-partition clustering algorithms performed poorly when the data contain errors. Milligan and Cooper (1988) considered the more general case where the number of clusters is not known. Not surprisingly, their results show that the performance of fixed-partition algorithms deteriorates when the number of clusters is unknown.

Given these limitations of fixed-partition clustering methods, how can we perform market segmentation in conjoint studies when the consumer's group membership is unknown? One straightforward solution is to eliminate the source of the problem: individual-level estimation. In particular, use the mixture model and directly analyze the pooled data using a random-coefficient specification for each segment. Before we can use the mixture approach, however, it is necessary to show that the model is identifiable (i.e., the model parameters are unique).

Suppose the importance weights for each segment follow a multivariate normal distribution (i.e., the areas A and B in Figure 4.3 are ellipses) and all consumers in a given segment interpret the preference scale in the same way. Then the mixture model is identified.[26] That is, it is theoretically possible to determine the number of segments (two in our example), the degree of heterogeneity in each segment (areas A and B in our example), and the size of each segment (i.e., the probability that a given consumer belongs to a particular segment). Because the distributional form for the data is known, we can use the maximum likelihood approach to estimate the mixture model parameters and determine the segment membership of each consumer in the sample. Having assigned consumers to segments, we can proceed as in the known group case and use a Bayesian approach to estimate segment- and market-level market behavior.

Suppose the importance weights for each segment follow arbitrary multivariate distributions (i.e., areas A and B in Figure 4.3b have unknown shapes) or consumers idiosyncratically interpret the preference scale. Then the conjoint parameters cannot have a multivariate normal distribution; consequently the mixture model may not be identified.[27] Given the absence of a well-developed theory establishing mixture identifiability for arbitrary distributions, simulation studies should be conducted to test the robustness of the random-coefficient mixture model, which incorrectly assumes multivariate normality.

The reader should note that even when mixture models are identifiable, the statistical theory for determining the number of clusters is not fully developed. The root of the problem is that the regularity conditions do not hold. (For example, a three-cluster solution is not a special case of a four-cluster solution except in the trivial sense that the fourth cluster exists with probability zero!) Hence it is not theoretically valid to use likelihood ratio tests or difference statistics to determine the number of clusters. Although a number of heuristic criteria have been proposed to determine the number of clusters in a mixture model (these include the Akaike 1974 Information Criterion, the Schwarz 1978 Bayesian Information Criterion, Bozdogan's 1987 Consistent Akaike Information Criterion, and Bozdogan's 1994 Information Complexity Criterion), the empirical evidence on their relative performance is limited. See Bock (1996, pp. 423–29) for a succinct review. Furthermore, limited evidence is available regarding the relative performance of fixed-partition and mixture models (see Bock 1996, pp. 404–5 for a review). Thus simulation and empirical studies are necessary to examine the robustness of the conjoint methodologies we propose when the data belong to unknown segments and multivariate normality does not hold for each segment (e.g., consumers interpret the preference scale idiosyncratically and the true conjoint weights have a skewed distribution).

> ***Key Point*** *Mixture models with random coefficients provide a general method of detecting unobservable heterogeneity among consumers in conjoint studies. This modeling strategy is optimal if the true preference weights for each segment have a multivariate normal distribution and all consumers interpret the assigned preference scale in the same way. If consumers in each segment have heterogeneous preferences and interpret the preference scale idiosyncratically, mixture identifiability is not guaranteed. Simulation and empirical studies are necessary to test the robustness of the multivariate normal mixture model under distributional misspecification; studies are also necessary to compare the efficiency of fixed-partition and mixture conjoint models for different scenarios.*

4.4 CONJOINT ANALYSIS: A BEHAVIORAL PERSPECTIVE

As discussed in Section 4.2, conjoint studies seek to measure the relationship between product attributes and preference. On the surface this modeling strategy appears to require stringent behavioral assumptions; in particular, consumers evaluate all products, simultaneously process all information regarding a given product, and are always willing to trade off one product attribute for another. We know that these assumptions are often descriptively false. For example, some consumers evaluate a product in terms of "benefits" and not in terms of physical attributes. Others use heuristics to eliminate certain products from consideration in order to simplify decision making. Given that the conjoint framework may be descriptively unrealistic, how broad is the class of information-processing models that conjoint analysis can paramorphically represent?

Consider a simple model where the consumer examines all attributes for each product simultaneously but thinks in terms of product benefits rather than product attributes. We say that the consumer thinks in terms of *perceptual space* and not in terms of *attribute space*. In our computer example suppose that the product attributes are computer speed (X_1), data storage capability (X_2), and the duration of the manufacturer's product warranty (X_3); in addition, the product benefits are performance (P_1) and reliability (P_2). Suppose the consumer uses the following information-processing strategy in evaluating a given computer profile. In the first step transform the product information for the profile into perceptions of performance (P_1) and reliability (P_2). These perceptions are uncertain; in particular, the perceptual errors can be correlated, especially for new products. In the next step evaluate these perceived benefits. Note that the consumer's true preference (P) depends on the product benefits $(P_1$ and $P_2)$; furthermore, all these values are unobservable to the researcher. Recall that in a conjoint study we measure P on a scale that is subject to measurement error (i.e., $P_m \neq P$, where P_m denotes measured preference). What are the consequences of ignoring the consumer's information-processing strategy and directly measuring the relationship between the product attributes and P_m using conjoint analysis? We refer to this estimation strategy using observable quantities as a stimulus–response methodology.

Consider individual-level analysis. Suppose the relationship between perceptions and preference is linear; a reasonable assumption in our computer example because "more is better." In general, we expect the mapping from attributes to perceptions to be nonlinear and uncertain. For example, successive increases of 1 GB in data storage lead to diminishing returns in performance. Given this scenario, the reduced-form conjoint estimates will be unbiased, and statistical testing will be correct *regardless of the magnitude of the measurement error in preference or whether the perceptual errors are correlated to each other.*[28]

A more interesting case occurs if the relationship between perceptions and preference is nonlinear. Consider a soft drink conjoint study. Suppose the relevant perceptions are "sweetness" and "fizziness." We expect that for any consumer there are optimal levels of sweetness (P_1^*) and fizziness (P_2^*); that is, (P_1^*, P_2^*) is the consumer's ideal point. As in the computer example, assume that the relationship between the physical attributes and perceptions is nonlinear and stochastic. What are the implications of using conjoint analysis to estimate directly the relationship between attributes and measured preference? The variability of the error term now differs across profiles: Heteroscedasticity is inherent in the model.[29] Hence the conjoint model will provide unbiased estimates of the effect of product attributes on preference; however, the significance tests will be incorrect. From a policy viewpoint the manager may include or exclude relevant product attributes.

Key Point *In an attribute → perception → preference model, standard conjoint estimates and statistical tests will be correct if the mapping from perception to preference is linear, regardless of whether the attributes → perceptions mapping is nonlinear and uncertain. If, however, the perception → preference relationship is nonlinear (e.g., as in an ideal-point model), the conjoint estimates can lead to erroneous managerial decisions because of the inherent heteroscedasticity in the model. When estimating ideal-point conjoint models in which consumers process information in perceptual space, the researcher should test for and treat heteroscedasticity.*

Given that conjoint analysis can parsimoniously represent the consumer's decision-making strategy, are there any disadvantages to using this stimulus–response methodology? Consider an individual-level conjoint experiment. Suppose the unexplained variance in the model is 40 percent. The problem is that we cannot distinguish whether this unexplained variance is due to perceptual error or omitted variables in the model. For example, the following two scenarios will lead to the same result: (1) There are no omitted variables but perceptual error is large, or (2) the effect of omitted variables is large but perceptual error is zero. Thus there is an identification problem.

Key Point *Conjoint analysis does not allow the manager to distinguish whether a lack of fit in the model occurs because the consumer has uncertain perceptions or the model has excluded relevant attributes. In order to optimize marketing policy, the manager needs a methodology that allows him to distinguish these scenarios. For example, advertising is strategically important when a consumer has uncertain perceptions. Furthermore, if the perceptual errors are correlated, advertising may be effective even if the advertising message focuses on only one perceptual dimension. Hence brief advertisements (e.g., 15-second TV commercials) may be optimal.*

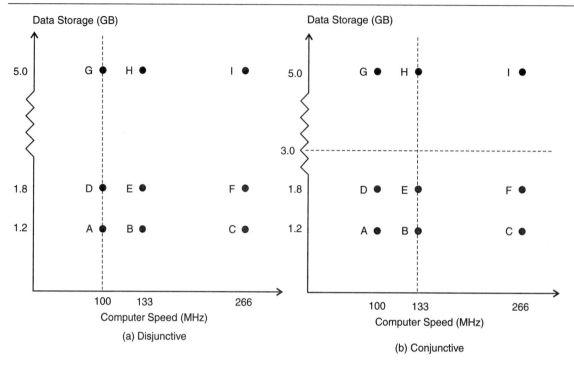

Figure 4.4 Disjunctive and conjunctive rules in a conjoint experiment.

The previous analysis assumed that consumers evaluate all the profiles; however, they process information in *perceptual space* and not in terms of *attribute space*. What happens if the consumer processes information by attribute and not by profile as assumed so far? Consider the simple computer conjoint experiment discussed earlier (see Figure 4.1). Assume that we ask the consumer to evaluate the nine profiles shown in Figures 4.4a and 4.4b. Suppose the consumer uses the following rule: Consider only computers that provide a speed of 133 MHz or higher. This heuristic is an example of a disjunctive rule; a rule where the consumer specifies minimum thresholds for some (one in our case) but not all attributes.

In Figure 4.4a, the disjunctive rule implies that the consumer eliminates profiles A, D, and G. We say that the remaining profiles (B, C, E, F, H, and I) constitute the consideration set. What does this information-processing strategy imply for individual-level conjoint analysis? The only restriction on the model is that all the main effects for computer storage must be zero; in particular, general patterns of interaction are allowed between computer speed and data storage. (Why?)[30]

Consider a different rule where the consumer specifies minimum thresholds for all attributes (i.e., a conjunctive rule). In our example, suppose the consumer will only consider computers with a minimum speed of 133 MHz and a minimum data storage capability of 3 GB (see Figure 4.4b). Thus the consumer will only consider profiles H and I. Then it is straightforward to show that all main effects are zero and that the consumer's preference can be parsimoniously described using two interaction terms.[31]

> **Key Point**   *Properly specified conjoint models can provide a paramorphic representation of conjunctive and disjunctive information-processing rules without being descriptively correct.*

Our previous discussion focused on individual-level analysis. The manager, however, is primarily interested in market behavior. Suppose consumers follow either conjunctive or disjunctive rules, use different cutoff values for each attribute, and have heterogeneous preferences. How can the manager predict market behavior?

One approach is to recognize that the true conjoint weights vary randomly across the population and analyze the pooled data across all individuals (in general interaction effects will be necessary).

Suppose that there is one population. (Note that it is not necessary to assume that there are several populations when consumers use different information-processing strategies.) Then we can estimate the model using the random-coefficient approach described previously by distinguishing two cases. In the first scenario assume that all consumers use the preference scale in the same way. Then we can use a parametric approach if we know the distribution of the conjoint weights in the population (say multivariate normal). If the sample is sufficiently large, we shall be able correctly to determine the degree of heterogeneity in the population and separate out the effect of omitted variables in the conjoint model.[32] In the second scenario assume that we do not know the pattern of heterogeneity in the data (i.e., we cannot specify the distribution of the conjoint parameters in the true preference model) or consumers use the preference scale idiosyncratically. Then we can analyze the pooled data using a nonparametric empirical Bayes method. As discussed previously, these methods are consistent with the hypothesis that consumers maximize expected utility.

Suppose there are several unknown populations. Then we can use the random-coefficient mixture approach discussed previously.

> **Key Point**   *Suppose that consumers have heterogeneous preferences and use conjunctive or disjunctive information-processing strategies. Then we can pool the data across individuals and estimate a parametric or nonparametric (as appropriate) random-coefficient conjoint model. No new methodology is required beyond that discussed in the case where consumers evaluate all profiles.*

Are there any information-processing rules that conjoint analysis cannot paramorphically represent? Consider a consumer who follows a lexicographic rule. Using this method, the consumer pursues the following sequential information-processing strategy: Order salient attributes by importance, choose the most important attribute, and determine the best alternative using that attribute. If a tie occurs, use the second-most-important attribute to evaluate those alternatives that were tied in the first step. Continue this procedure until only one alternative remains. Then it may not be feasible to represent the consumer's preferences using only one number (an assumption that is necessary in conjoint analysis).

Another attribute-based decision rule is *elimination by aspects* (see Tversky 1972b). Using this rule, the consumer selects an attribute with a probability that is proportional to that attribute's importance. In our computer example, suppose the consumer selects computer speed with a probability of 70 percent. In the next step, the consumer eliminates all unsatisfactory profiles (e.g., those that do not exceed a threshold requirement for speed). In our example, suppose the consumer uses a threshold of 133 MHz. Then 70 percent of the time the consideration set is C, F, and I. In 30 percent of the cases, however, the consumer will evaluate the profiles along the attribute of data storage. Suppose the threshold level for data storage is 1.8 GB. Then 30 percent of the time the consideration set will be G, H, and I. We know from our discussion of conjunctive and disjunctive models that the conjoint model can accurately depict the consumer's preferences for any *given* consideration set. The problem now is that there is more than one consideration set (two in our simple example). Thus, contrary to the assumption of the conjoint model, we need several numbers to represent the consumer's preference, one for each consideration set.

Key Point   *The conjoint representation of preferences can be used to represent a consumer's preference structure paramorphically provided we can measure preference using a single value. This approach is not feasible if the consumer follows an elimination by aspects information-processing strategy and may not be feasible if the consumer follows a lexicographic model.*

Can we capture the spirit of the elimination by aspects model (i.e., the fact that consideration sets can be stochastic) in the conjoint framework? Jedidi, Kohli, and DeSarbo (1996) propose a model in which preference is a single-valued function; on any choice occasion, however, consumers only consider those alternatives whose utilities exceed a fixed but unobserved threshold value. (The threshold values are assumed to be fixed across alternatives for a given individual but are allowed to vary across individuals or segments.) Thus consideration sets are stochastic.

Jedidi et al. develop an algorithm for estimating the threshold model at different levels of aggregation (individual or segment); their algorithm also allows the researcher to estimate a fixed-coefficient mixture model in which segment membership and the number of segments is unknown a priori. Jedidi et al. propose the following empirical procedure. Ask individuals in a conjoint experiment to proceed in two steps. First, sort the profiles into two groups (acceptable and unacceptable) and then evaluate only the subset of alternatives in the acceptable group using an assigned preference scale. Having obtained these data, use a tobit model to estimate the threshold values and conjoint parameters at the appropriate level of aggregation.

Although the Jedidi et al. method is quite general and allows for stochastic consideration sets in preference studies (an important contribution), it does not fully consider heterogeneity; for example, the fixed-coefficient mixture model does not allow us to determine the degree of heterogeneity within a given segment or explicitly allow for consumers to interpret the assigned preference scale idiosyncratically. One approach to deal with these issues is to combine the random-coefficient modeling approach described earlier with the Jedidi et al. method.

> **Key Point**   *Conjoint models with threshold values can allow for stochastic consideration sets provided it is correct to use a single-valued function to represent the consumer's preference. To allow for stochastic consideration sets, general forms of heterogeneity in preference, and idiosyncratic interpretations of the preference scale, we can use a tobit model combined with a random-coefficient conjoint model specification. (See Amemiya 1985, pp. 360–411, for a discussion of the tobit model.) This general framework includes the standard disjunctive and conjunctive models with fixed consideration sets as special cases.*

4.5 THE MEASUREMENT OF PERCEPTIONS

Our discussion so far has focused on the stimulus–response methodology to measure preferences. Marketers and psychologists, however, are extremely interested in behavioral processes and, in particular, in understanding human perceptions. Consider the following simple example. Two brands of analgesic (a store brand and a national brand) provide identical physical attributes. However, consumers perceive these brands to be different. Suppose the manager believes that the salient perceptual dimensions are "gentleness" and "effectiveness." That is, the manager knows the number and meaning of the dimensions a priori. Then the manager should analyze perceptions using a confirmatory approach. We discuss two such methods: confirmatory factor analysis and confirmatory multidimensional scaling.

In order to use confirmatory factor analysis, it is necessary to collect ratings data (using a scale from 1 to 7, say) from a large sample of consumers; in particular, we need to use at least two measures for each perceptual dimension. This condition is required so that the model is identified.[33] Let us denote gentleness and effectiveness, respectively, by F_1 and F_2. We seek to determine the degree of perceptual heterogeneity for the store and national brands and whether consumers' perceptions are correlated (for example, whether consumers believe that a gentle analgesic is likely to be less effective than a stronger analgesic). Let $F_1^{(1)}$ and $F_2^{(1)}$, respectively, denote the perceptions of gentleness and effectiveness for the store brand and $F_1^{(2)}$ and $F_2^{(2)}$ the corresponding perceptions for the national brand. The problem is that these perceptions are unobservable; furthermore, the observables (i.e., the consumer's responses) contain measurement error. See Figure 4.5.

Assume that all consumers interpret the scales in the same way. Then for sufficiently large samples we can use the standard multisample confirmatory factor analysis model to estimate the model parameters. (See Jöreskog 1971.) (The optimal estimator depends on

Figure 4.5 A confirmatory factor model for analgesics. Note: Gentleness and effectiveness, respectivity, have K and M indicators ($K \geq 2$, $M \geq 2$).

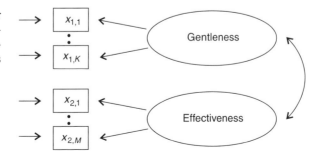

whether we can specify the distribution of perceptions a priori. For example, maximum likelihood will be efficient if perceptions have a multivariate normal distribution; if we cannot specify the distribution a priori, a preferable strategy may be to use the generalized least squares or the asymptotic distribution free estimator.) Consequently we can determine the degree of perceptual heterogeneity among consumers for each brand and test whether the mean perceptions of gentleness and effectiveness for the store and national brands differ.[34]

The confirmatory factor model provides an important advantage: It explicitly considers measurement error in the scales and allows detailed hypothesis testing (for example, the manager can compare the unrestricted model with a model in which the degree of perceptual heterogeneity is the same for both brands). However, the confirmatory factor model is managerially limited; the methodology does not allow us to measure perceptual error or whether these perceptual errors are correlated.[35] Consequently the manager cannot distinguish between "informed" and "uninformed" consumers or coordinate advertising strategy with the other elements in the marketing mix. In addition, if consumers idiosyncratically interpret the scales, the standard approach for estimating confirmatory factor models using covariances leads to an identification problem (except for the trivial case of unidimensional perceptions).[36]

An alternative approach for examining perceptions is confirmatory multidimensional scaling (see, for example, Ramsay 1982a,b). In contrast to confirmatory factor analysis, the researcher does not collect rating data on particular perceptual dimensions; instead, the researcher asks consumers to compare pairs of brands and indicate their degree of similarity on only one scale (from 1 to 7, say, where "1" indicates highly dissimilar and "7" indicates highly similar). This methodology suffers from the same difficulties as confirmatory factor analysis; in particular, one cannot distinguish perceptual and measurement errors.[37]

Key Point   *Confirmatory factor analysis and confirmatory multidimensional scaling are statistical tools for examining perceptions. These methods are superior to exploratory factor analysis and exploratory multidimensional scaling because they allow the manager to test explicit theories of perceptions and incorporate measurement error. However, they do not allow the manager to distinguish between information-processing (i.e., perceptual) errors by consumers and measurement errors in the scales. Consequently the manager cannot use the results to segment consumers according to their degree of product knowledge or coordinate advertising and marketing mix decisions (e.g., price).*

4.6 AN INTEGRATED PREFERENCE MODEL

In this section we propose an integrated methodology that addresses the problems that face standard conjoint analysis, confirmatory factor analysis, and confirmatory multidimensional scaling models (see Jagpal 1986, 1988). Before discussing the general preference model, we briefly discuss the rationale for estimating consumer decision-process models rather than reduced-form methodologies that paramorphically represent consumer decision processes.

As discussed previously, conjoint analysis provides a parsimonious method for representing different information-processing rules (e.g., the conjunctive and disjunctive models). Furthermore, we can use a random-coefficient conjoint method to analyze general types of heterogeneity in the data while allowing each consumer to interpret the assigned preference scale idiosyncratically. One important managerial limitation of the conjoint method (including the general random-coefficient specification) is that the model cannot separate the effects of perceptual error and those of omitted variables in the model. Thus, even if the conjoint model predicts behavior accurately, the conjoint results do not allow the manager to coordinate advertising decision making with decisions regarding product design and price. In particular, the manager cannot distinguish "informed" and "uninformed" consumers to whom advertising should be targeted. Because the conjoint model is a reduced-form specification, we cannot test whether price is a signal of quality or simply a constraint on choice. Furthermore, as will be discussed, although the conjoint model is consistent with expected utility theory, the conjoint specification does not allow the manager to distinguish consumers according to their multivariate risk attitude.

As discussed in the previous section, standard methods for analyzing perceptions (including confirmatory factor and multidimensional scaling models) do not allow us to measure perceptual errors. Consequently the manager cannot form market segments based on whether consumers are informed or not; in addition, he cannot coordinate advertising and marketing mix strategy.

We now propose a general model that addresses these limitations (see Jagpal 1988). Consider the analgesic example discussed in the previous section. Suppose that the manager has determined that the relevant perceptual dimensions are gentleness and effectiveness (see Figure 4.6); in addition, the relevant product attributes are x_1, x_2, and x_3. Let the unobserved variable η_1 denote perceived gentleness and the unobserved variable η_2 perceived effectiveness. As in the standard confirmatory factor analysis model, we need at least two measures for each perceptual dimension to ensure identifiability. For each product profile (these profiles may be hypothetical or real) the consumer provides rating data on each perceptual dimension; in addition, the consumer provides a preference rating on an assigned scale

Figure 4.6 An integrated preference model for analgesics. Note: x_1, x_2, x_3 are product attributes; x_4, the covariate; η_1, gentleness; η_2, effectiveness; P, preference; y_1, y_2, y_3, y_4, perceptual measures; y_5, a measure of preference; u, structural error; $\varepsilon_1, \varepsilon_2, \varepsilon_3, \varepsilon_4, \varepsilon_5$, measurement errors; and ζ_1, ζ_2, perceptual errors.

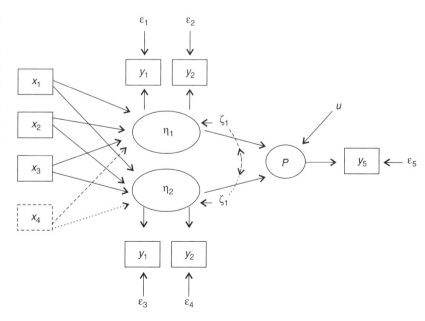

(from 1 to 7, say) as in a standard conjoint experiment. In our example the scales y_1 and y_2 measure perceived gentleness, y_3 and y_4 measure perceived effectiveness, and y_5 measures the unobserved preference. Note that the consumer first transforms attribute information into uncertain perceptual information and then forms his preferences; in particular, the perceptual errors ζ_1 and ζ_2 are correlated. Note that the model allows for systematic biases in information processing (the perceptual errors can be correlated) and explicitly recognizes that all the measures (y_1 through y_5) contain measurement error.

Suppose initially that the mapping from perceptions to preference is linear ("more is better"); the mapping from product attributes to perceptions, however, can be nonlinear. For example, effectiveness increases at a decreasing rate as the amount of pain killer (a physical attribute) in the analgesic is increased.

Individual-Level Analysis

Suppose we ask any given individual to evaluate a sufficiently large number of profiles. Then, except for one parameter, we can estimate the model using the standard structural equation methodology (see, for example, Jöreskog and Sörbom 1993). The exception is that we cannot separate the effect of omitted variables (u) on the consumer's true preference and the effect of measurement error (ε_5) in the preference scale.[38] (See Figure 4.6.) Once we have estimated the model parameters, we can determine the consumer's estimated preference for each brand and use the results to predict individual-level behavior as in the conjoint model. It is straightforward to show that this approach is consistent with the theory that the consumer maximizes expected utility.[39]

The problem with individual-level analysis is that the parameter estimates are likely to be unstable given the large number of parameters in the model (18 in our simple example, assuming that the relationship between product attributes and perceptions is linear). Hence we need a methodology that allows us to pool data across individuals.

The Heterogeneity Problem

Suppose all individuals interpret the perceptual and preference scales identically. Assume initially that the manager knows that there is one population.

One approach is to include covariates that account for heterogeneity in perceptions; for example, we may hypothesize that those who are familiar with a given brand have different perceptions from those who are not. (Let x_4 in Figure 4.6 denote familiarity.) Then we can pool the data across individuals and brands and estimate a fixed-coefficient structural equation model (Model A). Note that Model A allows for heterogeneous and stochastic perceptions; in addition, the perceptual errors can be correlated.

We can extend this model in several ways. Suppose price is a signal of quality. Then price affects preferences in two ways. First, price affects perceptions and hence preference (that is, price has an indirect effect); second, price has a direct effect on preference by acting as a constraint on behavior as in the usual conjoint model (Model B). Now we can compare Models A and B in a straightforward manner, recalling that Model A is a special case of Model B. (In Model B set all parameters involving price to zero.) Similarly we can estimate a model in which both brand and product attributes affect perceptions (Model C) and compare

Models C and A to determine if any "brand-equity" effects exist in the marketplace.[40] We can estimate other behavioral models similarly.[41] The model can also be extended to allow for brand-specific effects on perceptual error (i.e., heteroscedastic disturbances).

Suppose that there are several heterogeneous populations and that the manager can perform a priori segmentation. Then we can use the standard multisample structural equation methodology (using appropriate covariates in each group to allow for heterogeneity in perceptions) to analyze data simultaneously from a random sample of consumers drawn from these populations (see Sörbom 1974). We can use the results to distinguish informed and uninformed consumer segments (for any given perceptual dimension compare the variances of the perceptual errors across groups), predict the effect of given product design changes on the behavior of each segment, and coordinate marketing policy (i.e., price, product design, and advertising message strategy). For example, if Segment 1 has uncorrelated perceptual errors whereas Segment 2 has correlated errors, the advertising message for Segment 1 may need to focus simultaneously on both perceptual dimensions; in contrast, the advertising message for Segment 2 may be effective even if it focuses on only one perceptual dimension. Thus 15-second TV spot may be effective for Segment 2 but not for Segment 1.

Suppose the marketer believes that there are several heterogeneous populations but cannot determine the number of populations a priori or consumers' group memberships. Then, as in the conjoint case, we need to perform post hoc segmentation.

One approach is to use a sequential data analysis strategy. First, pool the data and perform cluster analysis on the observables to form the groups. Then apply the standard multisample structural equation methodology to estimate the model parameters. This approach is inefficient. We know that the observables contain measurement error; furthermore, clustering methods perform poorly in such cases (see Milligan 1980). An additional problem with the sequential data-analysis strategy is that the clustering is based on the levels of the variables and not on the hypothesized model structure (i.e., the true perceptual and importance weights).

A second approach is to analyze the pooled data directly in one step using a mixture specification in which the probabilities of group membership and the parameters for each group are unknown. This approach does not suffer from the difficulties of the sequential method because the clustering is based on the model structure and the parameter values of the hypothesized consumer decision-process model, not the levels of variables that are measured with error. Suppose that for any given group all the errors and covariates have a multivariate normal distribution (the perceptual errors can be correlated); furthermore the number of groups is finite (a reasonable assumption). Then the mixture model is identified (see Jedidi, Jagpal, and DeSarbo 1997b, Appendix).[42] Consequently we can use the general mixture structural equation methodology developed by Jedidi, Jagpal, and DeSarbo (1997a,b). Specifically, we can simultaneously determine the number of clusters and the model parameters for each group while explicitly allowing for measurement error and the hypothesized structure of the consumer decision problem. Extensive simulations (see Jedidi, Jagpal, and DeSarbo 1997b) show that the mixture model significantly outperforms the sequential data analysis strategy. Furthermore, the algorithm is robust provided the distribution of the errors does not depart significantly from multivariate normality (in particular, kurtosis is mild) and we use the Consistent Akaike Information Criterion (see Bozdogan 1987) or the Bayesian Information Criterion (see Schwarz 1978) to determine the number of clusters.

The reader should note that, although Jedidi, Jagpal, and DeSarbo (1997a,b) have used the mixture approach to estimate large structural equation models (including models with feedback among the endogenous latent variables) using both "real-life" and simulated data, the mixture model has yet to be applied to test the general preference model using market data. Jagpal (1986) has performed simulation experiments to test the general preference model discussed above for the known group membership case. His results suggest that the standard maximum-likelihood structural equation methodology (and associated test statistics) is robust provided the sample is reasonably large and the data are not highly kurtotic.

Model Extensions

We first discuss managerial applications and then statistical issues.

An important advantage of the structural equation methodology is that we can practically implement the theory of multiattribute risk aversion developed by Richard (1975), Miyamoto (1988), and others. Before discussing the statistical procedure, we need to distinguish three scenarios for multivariate risk: risk-neutrality, risk-aversion, and risk-seeking. These scenarios are quite different from their analogs in the univariate case. For concreteness we shall define these scenarios in the context of our example in which the relevant "attributes" are unobservable and stochastic perceptions (gentleness and effectiveness).

Suppose each perceptual dimension has two levels: low and high. Consider the case where the consumer is asked to choose between "lotteries" A and B, where each lottery corresponds to the purchase of a different analgesic brand. For simplicity assume that the price of each brand is equal; in addition, each brand offers the same number of tablets or capsules and requires the same dosage. Lottery A offers the consumer an even chance of obtaining a combination of low effectiveness and high gentleness or a combination of high effectiveness and low gentleness. Lottery B offers even odds of obtaining a combination of low effectiveness and low gentleness or a combination of high effectiveness and high gentleness. Then the consumer who chooses lottery A is multivariate risk-averse, the consumer who chooses lottery B is multivariate risk-seeking, and the consumer who is indifferent to both lotteries is multivariate risk-neutral (i.e., each brand has an equal probability of purchase). The intuition for these definitions is straightforward; for example, the consumer is multivariate risk-averse if he prefers even odds of getting some of the "best" and some of the "worst" over even odds of getting all of the "best" or all of the "worst."

These definitions lead to the following restrictions on the preference ("utility") function in our example. (See Richard 1975 for proofs.) The consumer is multivariate risk-neutral if the preference equation is additively separable in perceptions. Note that this specification does not imply that the consumer is risk-averse in a unidimensional sense; for example, the effect of increasing effectiveness on preference while holding gentleness constant can be decreasing (this corresponds to the familiar case of risk-aversion in the single-attribute case) or increasing (the case of risk-seeking in the single-attribute case). If the consumer is multivariate risk-averse (risk-seeking), the preference equation cannot be additively separable in the perceptual dimensions; in particular, the interaction effect between the perceptual dimensions is negative (positive).

Standard experimental methods for estimating multivariate risk-aversion models (see Miyamoto 1988) are not meaningful in marketing applications because the attributes are perceptual (and hence cannot be fixed by the researcher) and the distributions of these perceptions are subjective (and hence are unobservable to the researcher). Furthermore, and important, the manager needs to determine consumers' multivariate risk attitudes in a real-life (nonexperimental) setting.

We now show that structural equation modeling provides a straightforward method to test if the consumer is multivariate risk-averse, neutral, or risk-seeking. Consider any arbitrary nonlinear mapping from product attributes to perceptions; however, for simplicity assume that the mapping from perceptions to preference is not of the ideal-point type. Consider two models. In the first case the mapping from perceptions to preference is linearly separable (Model A); that is, the consumer is multivariate risk-neutral. For simplicity assume that $P = \varphi_1 P_1 + \varphi_2 P_2 + u$, where P denotes the true unobservable preference, P_1 and P_2 the uncertain perceptions, the φs are parameters, and u the effect of omitted variables. In the second case, the consumer is either multivariate risk-seeking or risk-averse (Model B). Specifically $P = \varphi_1 P_1 + \varphi_2 P_2 + \varphi_{12} P_1 P_2 + v$, where v is stochastic and $\varphi_{12} > (<) 0$ if the consumer is multivariate risk-seeking (risk-averse). Then Model A is nested in Model B [set $\varphi_{12} = 0$]. Consequently we can estimate both models using the nonlinear structural equation methodology and apply standard test statistics to determine the consumer's multivariate risk attitude.[43] Note that the approach can be used to test for multivariate risk aversion using more general functional forms provided the nonlinear structural equation model is linear in parameters.

The conjoint methodology, in contrast, is a stimulus–response methodology that measures the reduced-form relationship between preference and product design. Consequently conjoint analysis cannot be used to determine the consumer's multivariate risk attitude. In particular, the presence of interactions between the physical product attributes does not provide any evidence about the consumer's multivariate risk attitude.[44]

Another important area in which the methodology can be applied is the estimation of "ideal-point" perceptual models (e.g., when evaluating soft drinks, the consumer compares the perceived levels of "sweetness" and "fizziness" of available brands to optimal levels for these dimensions). As discussed below, we can use a nonlinear structural equation model to estimate the model parameters; in contrast, it is not possible to use the reduced-form conjoint methodology to determine the ideal point.[45]

We now discuss the statistical conditions that are necessary to estimate nonlinear structural equation preference models.

Suppose there is either one population or several known populations and that in each case we can use covariates to capture heterogeneity. Then the nonlinear structural equation model is identified provided the covariates and the error terms have a multivariate normal distribution.[46] Hence we can estimate the model (including the ideal point) using the generalized least-squares procedure developed by McDonald and implemented in the COSAN program (Fraser 1980).

If we cannot specify the populations a priori, the data are generated by a mixture model. The problem now is that because of the nonlinearity in the structural model, the observables cannot have a multivariate normal distribution. Consequently the mixture may not be identified. One heuristic approach is to extend the Jedidi, Jagpal, and DeSarbo methodology (1997a,b) to the nonlinear structural equation model and perform simulations to test the robustness of the model distinguishing cases where the number of groups is known or unknown.

Limitations and Future Research

Our analysis assumed that all consumers use the perceptual and preference scales in the same way; furthermore, covariates capture heterogeneity in a population(s). Suppose these conditions are not satisfied; that is, all consumers idiosyncratically interpret the assigned scales and the measurement and structural parameters are distributed randomly across the population. (In Figure 4.6 the links from the product attributes to perceptions and from perceptions to preference are random.) Can the methodology be extended to deal with these cases?

We can proceed in two ways. First, we can ignore the structure of the problem and estimate the implicit reduced-form conjoint model that links the product attributes to preference. In this case idiosyncratic differences among consumers in interpreting the perception scales have no effect on the reduced-form parameters; only idiosyncratic differences among individuals in interpreting the preference scale matter. Furthermore, in general the reduced-form coefficients will not be normally distributed.[47] Consequently we can analyze the pooled data using a nonparametric random-coefficient regression specification. As discussed in Section 4.3, this approach is consistent with expected utility theory and allows us to predict market behavior.

Although this procedure is parsimonious and allows us to estimate the reduced-form weights for each individual, the managerial usefulness is limited. Because the method estimates the reduced-form mapping from product attributes to preference, there is a fundamental identification problem; for example, the method cannot distinguish two consumers who have the same reduced-form weights but have different perceptions.[48] Thus the conjoint methodology only allows us to "optimize" a subset of marketing variables: product design and price. However, because the conjoint methodology does not measure perceptions, we cannot choose an optimal marketing strategy by coordinating the price and product design decisions with advertising policy.

Second, we can estimate both the structural and measurement models using a random-coefficient structural equation framework in which all the model parameters are random. (Recall that perceptions are endogenous variables in the model and consumers idiosyncratically interpret the perceptual scales.) To my knowledge no algorithm is currently available for estimating random-coefficient structural equation models. Jagpal, Jedidi, and Ansari are attempting to develop an empirical Bayes procedure to estimate this class of structural equation model (which includes the general preference model as a special case).

In our analysis the final outcome of the decision-process model is preference (see Figure 4.6); in particular, we showed that our statistical procedure is consistent with the theory that the consumer maximizes expected utility. Choice theory, in contrast, argues that consumer behavior is inherently random. (See Ben-Akiva and Lerman 1985 for an excellent discussion of the logit choice model and Daganzo 1979 for a succinct presentation of the probit choice model.) An interesting area for future research is to extend the general structural equation modeling approach to choice theory. New algorithms will be necessary for simultaneously estimating the full system of equations, especially when the relationship between perceptions and preference ("utility" in choice models) is nonlinear. Meanwhile we can proceed with the following limited-information data analysis strategy in the special case where all consumers interpret the perceptual scales in the same way. (Recall that when estimating choice models we do not collect preference data.)

In the first step, use the structural equation approach discussed above to estimate perceptions while allowing for perceptual error.[49] In particular, if segments can be defined a priori, use the standard multisample structural equation methodology with covariates to allow for heterogeneity (Sörbom 1974). Alternatively, if the number of segments (based on perceptions only) is unknown a priori, we can use the mixture structural equation model developed by Jedidi, Jagpal, and DeSarbo (1997a,b). In the second step, use the estimates of the perceptual dimensions as regressors in a choice model. In order to incorporate heterogeneity in the importance weights of the perceptual dimensions (that is, to perform *benefit segmentation*), we can use a random coefficient (see Daganzo 1979, pp. 92–93, for a discussion of the probit model and Ben-Akiva and Lerman 1985, pp. 124–25, for a discussion of the logit model) or a finite-mixture choice model (see Kamakura and Russell 1989).

4.7 CONCLUDING REMARKS

This chapter shows that the random-coefficient conjoint model is consistent with expected utility theory, allows consumers to interpret the preference scale idiosyncratically, paramorphically represents different forms of heterogeneity in parameters and in information-processing rules (e.g., the conjunctive and disjunctive rules), and provides a parsimonious tool to predict market behavior. Furthermore, mixture modeling combined with a random-coefficient conjoint formulation provides a general method for performing post hoc market segmentation that does not suffer from the limitations of sequential data analysis strategies (i.e., first estimating conjoint models and then performing clustering). Standard statistical tools for analyzing perceptions (confirmatory factor analysis and stochastic multidimensional scaling) cannot distinguish perceptual error. Consequently the firm cannot use the results to group consumers by risk attitude or to integrate advertising strategy with the other elements of the marketing mix.

We propose a general structural equation model that explicates the relationship among product attributes, perceptions, and preference, allows for both perceptual and preference heterogeneity, and measures perceptual error. In particular, the methodology can be used to test nonlinear preference models with perceptual errors; consequently, the marketing manager can use the methodology to segment consumers according to their risk-seeking attitudes and to estimate unobserved "ideal points" in perceptual space.

From the standpoint of economic theory the proposed methodology addresses a fundamental problem in experimental economics: Both the payoffs and probabilities can be subjective; furthermore, the payoffs can be multidimensional. (The problems of testing expected utility theory using experimental data even in a univariate setting are well known. See Quiggin 1993, pp. 127–30, for a succinct summary of the technical difficulties. See Machina 1983b and Quiggin, Chapter 4, for a detailed discussion.) Consequently we can use the structural equation methodology to determine whether expected utility theory is robust in a real-life (market) setting; in particular, we can test multivariate theories of risk aversion.

In closing, we should note that several important theoretical alternatives to the standard expected utility model have been recently developed. This class of extensions is known as "generalized expected utility" models. (See Quiggin 1993 for an extensive discussion.) Machina (1982) suggests that we dispense with the troublesome independence axiom in standard utility theory (which implies a strict separation between a consumer's evaluation of different states and consequently excludes such concepts as regret). Machina shows that if preferences are smooth, a "local" utility function can approximate preference in the neighborhood of a given cumulative distribution function; in particular, the local utility function itself changes when the individual's wealth does. Other authors have suggested that the independence axiom should be weakened but not eliminated. For example, probabilities should be replaced by a weighting function that depends on the cumulative probability distribution of the states (see the rank-dependent expected utility models developed independently by Quiggin 1982, Gilboa 1987, Allais 1988, Schmeidler 1989, and others). More drastically, separate weighting functions should be applied to both the probabilities and the utilities before computing the expected utility. (See the ordinally independent utility models proposed by Green and Jullien 1988, Quiggin 1989, and Segal 1989, the cumulative prospect theory model axiomatized by Wakker and Tversky 1991, and Gul's disappointment-aversion model 1991).

At present empirical methods for operationalizing generalized utility models using market-level data appear to be unavailable; furthermore, these theories have yet to be extended to the multivariate case (see, however, Grant, Kajii, and Pollak 1992). An interesting area for future research is to develop empirical tests that can allow for heterogeneity and use market-level data to distinguish generalized expected utility models from standard expected utility theory (which can be operationalized using the random-coefficient conjoint and nonlinear structural equation models discussed above).

NOTES

1. The manager can use alternative quasiexploratory methods. For example, he can use exploratory multidimensional scaling to identify gaps in the market. (Multidimensional scaling is a statistical technique that is used to measure perceptions using similarity data. We shall discuss confirmatory multidimensional scaling in a later section.)

2. Although mathematical psychologists have dealt with conjoint measurement for many years, Luce and Tukey (1964) are generally acknowledged as the pioneers of the field. See Green and Srinivasan (1978, 1990) for reviews of the conjoint literature in marketing.

3. Let P_m denote the measure of preference. Metric conjoint analysis assumes that the preference scale is at least interval-scaled. That is, all transforms of the sort $P'_m = \theta_1 + \theta_2 P_m$, where $\theta_2 > 0$, are permissible. For example, using 1 and 10 as end points for the preference scale is equivalent to using 2 and 11 as end points. Consequently standard least-squares regression procedures that minimize the unexplained variance in the dependent variable (measured preference) are meaningful. When the preference measures are ranks, the preference scale is ordinal; hence the concept of variance is ill-defined and standard metric regression procedures are inappropriate. One approach for handling rank-ordered preference data in a conjoint experiment is to use a nonmetric conjoint method (e.g., MONANOVA). These methods are more complex than metric methods, cannot easily handle such statistical problems as heteroscedasticity and serial correlation, and do not lead to straightforward significance tests for the model parameters. (We can use jackknifing or bootstrapping to construct approximate confidence intervals for the regression coefficients in

a nonmetric conjoint model. These procedures, however, are tedious.) Empirical evidence also suggests that the predictive accuracy of conjoint models is not significantly affected if rank-ordered (nonmetric) data are analyzed using the standard metric regression approach. Hence the only advantage for using rank-ordered preference data is if this data collection method leads to lower measurement error than collecting interval-scaled preference data. Empirical evidence is limited.

4. For simplicity consider a conjoint experiment in which there is only one treatment variable (say computer speed) with K categories. Then in the standard dummy variable regression model with an intercept term we need $(K - 1)$ dummy variables to distinguish the K categories. That is, we must designate one of the categories as the base case. This procedure is easily generalized to the case where the conjoint experiment includes several treatment variables (see note 5 for an example).

5. In our example each product attribute has three levels. Hence it is necessary to use two dummy variables for each product attribute (one fewer than the number of categories in each case). Let D_1 and D_2 represent the dummy variables for computer speed and D_3 and D_4 the dummies for data storage capability. Several equivalent operationalizations can be used. For example, choose the 100 MHz, 1.2 GB profile as the base case and define

$$D_1 = 1 \text{ for 133 MHz and 0 otherwise;}$$

$$D_2 = 1 \text{ for 266 MHz and 0 otherwise;}$$

$$D_3 = 1 \text{ for 1.8 GB and 0 otherwise;}$$

$$D_4 = 1 \text{ for 5 GB and 0 otherwise.}$$

Let P denote the true but unobserved preference. Assume that P is at least interval-scaled. Then the true main-effects regression model is $P = a_0 + a_1 D_1 + a_2 D_2 + a_3 D_3 + a_4 D_4 + \zeta$, where the a's are fixed coefficients and ζ denotes the effect of omitted variables. Let $P_m = \theta_1 + \theta_2 P + \varepsilon$ denote the observed measure of preference, where θ_1 and θ_2 are parameters, $\theta_2 > 0$, and ε is a stochastic term that reflects measurement error. Then the measured regression model is $P_m = (a_0 + \theta_1) + \theta_2 (a_1 D_1 + a_2 D_2 + a_3 D_3 + a_4 D_4) + \theta_2 \zeta + \varepsilon$. The coefficients $a_1 \theta_2$ and $a_2 \theta_2$, respectively, denote the "part worths" of computer speed, and $a_3 \theta_2$ and $a_4 \theta_2$ denote the "part worths" of data storage capability. Note that the estimated part worths depend on the preference scale used (i.e., the value of θ_2); however, the ratio of any pair of estimated part worths yields the ratio of the part worths in the true but unobserved preference model. The distinction between P and P_m is unimportant for individual-level conjoint analysis; however, as will be discussed later, it is crucial to distinguish between P and P_m in market segmentation studies.

6. See notes 4 and 5.

7. Surprisingly the psychometric literature has paid very little theoretical and empirical attention to the effects of variable standardization on clustering models (see Milligan 1996, pp. 352–54, for a review). Fixed-partition clustering algorithms are known to be sensitive to differences in variance among the variables being clustered. Consequently researchers often use a variety of methods to standardize the data by variable prior to performing cluster analysis (see Milligan 1996, pp. 352–53, for examples). This approach is ad hoc because it does not explicitly recognize the model structure that generates the data or the fact that individuals may interpret psychological scales idiosyncratically.

We now show that cluster analysis based on the results of a conjoint experiment must standardize the regression parameters by individual and not by variable. Let i index consumers, P^i denote consumer i's true but unobserved preference, and P^i_m denote the consumer's measured preference on a given scale (from 1 to 10 in our example). Then the true but unobserved preference model is $P^i = \alpha^i_0 + \alpha^i_1 D_1 + \alpha^i_2 D_2 + \zeta^i$, where $D_1 = 1$ if computer speed is 133 MHz and 0 otherwise and $D_2 = 1$ if data storage capability is 1.8 GB and 0 otherwise.

Let $P^i_m = \theta^i_1 + \theta^i_2 P^i + \varepsilon^i$, where θ^i_1 and θ^i_2 are deterministic, $\theta^i_2 > 0$ (i.e., consumers use the assigned preference scale idiosyncratically), and ε^i denotes measurement error. Then the measured model for the ith consumer is $P^i_m = (\alpha^i_0 + \theta^i_1) + \theta^i_2 \alpha^i_1 D_1 + \theta^i_2 \alpha^i_2 D_2 + \theta^i_2 \zeta^i + \varepsilon^i$. For the ith consumer let $\hat{\beta}^i_0$, $\hat{\beta}^i_1$, and $\hat{\beta}^i_2$, respectively, denote the regression estimates of $\alpha^i_0 + \theta^i_1$, $\theta^i_2 \alpha^i_1$, and $\theta^i_2 \alpha^i_2$. Let $\hat{q}^i = \sqrt{(\hat{\beta}^i_1)^2 + (\hat{\beta}^i_2)^2}$ and define $\hat{\varphi}^i_1 = \hat{\beta}^i_1 / \hat{q}^i$ and $\hat{\varphi}^i_2 = \hat{\beta}^i_2 / \hat{q}^i$. Then the "standardized" part worths $\hat{\varphi}^i_1$ and $\hat{\varphi}^i_2$ for consumer i depend on the true part worths (α^i_1 and α^i_2) and are independent of consumer i's interpretation of the preference scale (i.e., the values of θ^i_1 and θ^i_2).

Note that unless all consumers interpret the preference scale identically, we cannot form clusters based on the values of the αs. Furthermore the individual-level intercept terms are scale-dependent and should therefore be excluded from the cluster analysis. It is straightforward to show that standardization by variable is meaningless given the model structure. In addition, even if (ζ^i, ε^i) has a bivariate normal distribution and the number of profiles is large (i.e., the $\hat{\beta}$s are approximately normally distributed), $\hat{\varphi}^i_1$ and $\hat{\varphi}^i_2$ will not be normally distributed. Hence it is incorrect to use clustering methods that assume that the variables being clustered are normally distributed.

8. Let i index consumers, P^i denote the consumer's true preference, and Z^i the consumer's measured preference. Following the approach in note 7, we obtain the conjoint model $Z^i = (\theta^i_1 + \theta^i_2 \alpha^i_0) + \theta^i_2 \alpha^i_1 D_1 + \theta^i_2 \alpha^i_2 D_2 + (\theta^i_2 \zeta^i + \varepsilon^i)$. Recall that for all i, $Z^i = \theta^i_1 + \theta^i_2 P^i + \varepsilon^i$, where $\theta^i_2 > 0$ and $\theta^i_2 \neq \theta^j_2$ ($i \neq j$). Hence maximizing expected utility, $E(P^i)$, is equivalent to maximizing $E(Z^i)$. If the conjoint model is correctly specified, the individual-level estimates $\hat{Z}^i$ are unbiased for all profiles, regardless of the number of profiles. Hence the first-choice method is consistent with expected utility theory.

9. The estimated preference for a 100 MHz, 1.8 GB computer is $\hat{P} = \hat{a}_0 + \hat{a}_3$, and the estimated preference for a 133 MHz, 1.2 GB computer is $\hat{P} = \hat{a}_0 + \hat{a}_1$, where the carets denote the parameter estimates obtained from conjoint analysis.

10. Let the true preference model for the ith consumer be $P^i = \alpha^i_0 + \alpha^i_1 D_1 + \alpha^i_2 D_2 + \zeta^i$, where $\zeta^i \equiv 0$ for all i (i.e., there are no omitted variables). Let P^i_j denote the ith individual's preference for the jth profile. Assume that Luce's choice axiom holds. Then the true probability that consumer i chooses profile j is $\mu^i_j = P^i_j / (P^i_1 + \ldots + P^i_J)$, where J denotes the number of profiles. Suppose the measured preference Z^i_j is ratio-scaled; in particular, $Z^i_j = \theta^i_1 + \theta^i_2 P^i_j + \varepsilon^i_j$, where $\theta^i_1 \equiv 0$ for all i and ε^i_j is stochastic. Let $\hat{Z}^i_j$ denote the estimated preference using conjoint analysis. Then the share-of-preference method uses the estimated probabilities $\hat{\mu}^i_j = \hat{Z}^i_j / (\hat{Z}^i_1 + \ldots + \hat{Z}^i_J)$ to predict market behavior. It is straightforward to show that the $\hat{\mu}^i_j$ estimates are biased but consistent. Given that consumers evaluate a limited number of profiles, the share-of-preference method can lead to poor estimates of the true choice probabilities even if the (stringent) assumptions of the model hold.

11. Consider any given individual indexed by i. Suppose the data are in mean-differenced form. Let $\tilde{P}_i = (P_{i1}, \ldots, P_{iJ})'$ denote the vector of the individual's true preferences, where J denotes

the number of profiles evaluated. Let X_i and Z_i, respectively, correspond to the design matrices for the main effects and interactions. Then the true preference model is $\tilde{P}_i = X_i \tilde{\beta}_i + Z_i \tilde{\mu}_i + \tilde{\zeta}_i$, where $\tilde{\beta}_i$ and $\tilde{\mu}_i$ are vectors of unknown regression weights and $\tilde{\zeta}_i = (\zeta_{i1}, \ldots, \zeta_{iJ})'$ denotes a vector of structural disturbances. Let $\tilde{P}_i^m = \theta_{2i} \tilde{P}_i + \tilde{\varepsilon}_i$ denote the mean-differenced measured preferences, where $\theta_{2i} > 0$ and $\tilde{\varepsilon}_i = (\varepsilon_{i1}, \ldots, \varepsilon_{iJ})'$ is a vector of measurement errors. Then the true model is $\tilde{P}_i^m = X_i(\theta_{2i} \tilde{\beta}_i) + Z_i(\theta_{2i} \tilde{\mu}_i) + (\theta_{2i} \tilde{\zeta}_i + \tilde{\varepsilon}_i)$.

Suppose we erroneously estimate a main-effects model. Let $\text{est}(\theta_{2i} \tilde{\beta}_i)$ denote the least-squares estimator of $\theta_{2i} \tilde{\beta}_i$ in the misspecified model. Then $\text{est}(\theta_{2i} \tilde{\beta}_i) = \theta_{2i} \beta_i + (X_i'X_i)^{-1}X_i'(Z_i\theta_{2i}\tilde{\mu}_i + \theta_{2i}\tilde{\zeta}_i + \tilde{\varepsilon}_i)$.

Suppose the profiles are orthogonal. Then $(X_i'X_i)^{-1}X_i'Z_i \equiv 0$. Hence $E[\text{est}(\theta_{2i}\tilde{\beta}_i)] - \theta_{2i}\tilde{\beta} = \tilde{0}$, the null vector. Thus we obtain unbiased estimates of the main effects. Let $\hat{\Sigma}$ denote the covariance matrix of $\text{est}(\theta_{2i}\tilde{\beta}_i)$. Then the presence of $Z_i\theta_{2i}\tilde{\mu}_i$ in $\text{est}(\theta_{2i}\tilde{\beta}_i)$ makes the model heteroscedastic and inflates the diagonal elements of $\hat{\Sigma}$ even in large samples. Thus the absolute values of the t-statistics for the estimated main effects are driven to zero.

If the design is not orthogonal, then $(X_i'X_i)^{-1}X_i'Z_i \neq 0$. Hence $E[\text{est}(\theta_{2i}\tilde{\beta}_i)] - \theta_{2i}\tilde{\beta}_i \neq \tilde{0}$, the null vector. That is, the estimates of the main effects are biased.

12. In practice we can use more complex approaches and estimate a limited number of interactions in the conjoint experiment. See any standard text on experimental design (for example, Kirk 1982).

13. In a regression model, measurement error in the dependent variable is captured in the stochastic disturbance term. Consequently the t-statistics for all parameter estimates shrink towards zero when the measured preferences contain error.

14. Least-squares estimates weight each disturbance term in the sample equally. This approach is incorrect when the disturbances are heteroscedastic. For example, if the consumer is unfamiliar with a given profile, his or her response is likely to be more variable. Consequently, the absolute magnitude of the error is likely to be large. A reasonable procedure is therefore to reduce the weight attached to this observation by using a weighted least-squares procedure.

15. Consider any given individual indexed by i. Suppose the data are in mean-differenced form. Let $\tilde{P}_i = (P_{i1}, \ldots, P_{iJ})'$ denote the individual's true preferences, where J denotes the number of profiles evaluated, X_i the matrix of design variables in the conjoint experiment, and $\tilde{\zeta}_i = (\zeta_{i1}, \ldots, \zeta_{iJ})'$ a vector of structural disturbances. Then the true preference model is $\tilde{P}_i X_i \tilde{\beta}_i + \tilde{\zeta}_i$, where $\tilde{\beta}_i$ is a vector of regression weights. Let $\tilde{P}_i^m = \theta_{2i} \tilde{P}_i + \tilde{\varepsilon}_i$ denote the mean-differenced measured preferences, where $\theta_{2i} > 0$ and $\tilde{\varepsilon}_i = (\varepsilon_{i1}, \ldots, \varepsilon_{iJ})'$ is a vector of measurement errors. Let $\text{est}(\theta_{2i}\tilde{\beta}_i)$ denote the least-squares estimator in the conjoint model using $\tilde{P}_i^m$. Then $\text{est}(\theta_{2i}\tilde{\beta}_i) = \theta_{2i}\tilde{\beta}_i + (X_i'X_i)^{-1}X_i'(\theta_{2i}\tilde{\zeta}_i + \tilde{\varepsilon}_i)$. Suppose $E(\varepsilon_{iJ}) \neq 0$ because of fatigue (e.g., the consumer evaluates profile J last). Let β_{ik} denote the kth element of $\tilde{\beta}_i$. Then $E[\text{est}(\theta_{2i}\beta_{ik})] - \theta_{2i}\beta_{ik} = \alpha_{kJ}^{(i)} E(\varepsilon_{iJ}) \neq 0$ for all k, where $\alpha_{kJ}^{(i)}$ is the (k, J)th element of $(X_i'X_i)^{-1}X_i'$. Hence all the parameter estimates are biased.

16. The problem is mitigated if the researcher performs a priori segmentation based on income. Failure to address the problem is likely to have serious consequences, particularly for consumer durables.

17. Note that the individual-level weights are scale-dependent if consumers interpret the preference scale idiosyncratically (see note 5). In such cases we should standardize the weights by individual prior to performing this analysis. For the example discussed in note 7 let the estimated weights for D_1 and D_2, respectively, for the ith individual be $\text{est}(\theta_2^i \alpha_1^i)$ and $\text{est}(\theta_2^i \alpha_2^i)$. Let $q^i =$

$\sqrt{\text{est}^2(\theta_2^i \alpha_1^i) + \text{est}^2(\theta_2^i \alpha_2^i)}$. Then the standardized weights for individual i are $\text{est}(\theta_2^i \alpha_1^i)/q^i$ and $\text{est}(\theta_2^i \alpha_2^i)/q^i$, which do not depend on the scale parameter θ_2^i.

18. Suppose all consumers interpret the preference scale identically and evaluate the same set of J profiles. Let i index consumers and without loss of generality assume that $\theta_2^i = 1$ for all i.

    Suppose the data are mean-differenced. Let the vector of measured preferences for individual i be $\tilde{P}_i^m = X\tilde{\beta}_i + \tilde{u}_i$, where X denotes the design matrix (not necessarily orthogonal), $\tilde{\beta}_i$ is a vector of regression weights, $\tilde{u}_i$ is a vector of disturbances such that $E(\tilde{u}_i) = \tilde{0}$ and $E(\tilde{u}_i\tilde{u}_i') = \sigma^2 I$, where $\tilde{0}$ denotes the null column vector and I the identity matrix.

    Then the conjoint estimator is $\text{est}(\tilde{\beta}_i) = \tilde{\beta}_i + (X'X)^{-1}X'\tilde{u}_i$. Taking expectations, we get $E(\text{est}(\tilde{\beta})) = E(\tilde{\beta})$. That is, the population mean of $\text{est}(\tilde{\beta}_i)$ equals the true centroid of regression weights in the population. Let $\hat{\Sigma}_{\tilde{\beta}\tilde{\beta}}$ and $\Sigma_{\tilde{\beta}\tilde{\beta}}$, respectively, denote the population covariance matrices of the estimated weights and the true weights. Assume that $\tilde{\beta}$ and $\tilde{u}$ are independent. Then $\hat{\Sigma}_{\tilde{\beta}\tilde{\beta}} = \Sigma_{\tilde{\beta}\tilde{\beta}} + E[(X'X)^{-1}X'\tilde{u}\tilde{u}'X(X'X)^{-1}] = \Sigma_{\tilde{\beta}\tilde{\beta}} + (X'X)^{-1}\sigma^2$. Let a_{kk}, b_{kk}, and c_{kk}, respectively, denote the kth diagonal elements of $\hat{\Sigma}_{\tilde{\beta}\tilde{\beta}}$, $\Sigma_{\tilde{\beta}\tilde{\beta}}$, and $(X'X)^{-1}\sigma^2$. Then $a_{kk} - b_{kk} = c_{kk} > 0$. That is, $\hat{\Sigma}_{\tilde{\beta}\tilde{\beta}}$ overstates the heterogeneity in the population.

19. Let the true preference for individual i be $P^i = w_0^i + w_1^i x_1 + w_2^i x_2 + \zeta_i$. Suppose all consumers interpret the assigned preference scale in the same way. Then the measured preferences for individual i are given by $P_m^i = \theta_1 + \theta_2 P^i + \varepsilon^i$, where $\theta_1 = \theta_1^i$ and $\theta_2 = \theta_2^i$ for all i and ε^i denotes measurement error. Let $E(w_j^i) = \overline{w}_j$ for all j. Then $P_m^i = (\theta_1 + \theta_2 \overline{w}_0) + \theta_2 \overline{w}_1 x_1 + \theta_2 \overline{w}_2 x_2 + u^i$, where $u^i = \theta_2[(w_0^i - \overline{w}_0) + (w_1^i - \overline{w}_1)x_1 + (w_2^i - \overline{w}_2)x_2] + (\theta_2\zeta^i + \varepsilon^i) = A + B$. Let σ^2 denote the variance operator. Then $E(u^i) = 0$ and $\sigma^2(u^i) = \sigma^2(A) + \sigma^2(B)$, where $\sigma^2(B) = \theta_2^2\sigma^2(\zeta^i) + \sigma^2(\varepsilon^i)$. Thus, except for the scale factor θ_2 the fixed-coefficient conjoint model for the pooled data provides an unbiased estimate of the population centroid $(\overline{w}_1, \overline{w}_2)$. However, the usual t-statistics are biased because the disturbance is heteroscedastic.

20. For the model in note 19 the error term combines the effects of heterogeneity $[\sigma^2(A)]$, omitted variables $[\sigma^2(\zeta^i)]$, and measurement error $[\sigma^2(\varepsilon^i)]$. Hence there is an identification problem. Thus a poor fit can imply that the population is heterogeneous $[\sigma^2(A)$ is large], omitted product attributes have a significant effect $[\sigma^2(\zeta^i)$ is large], the preference scale is poor $[\sigma^2(\varepsilon^i)$ is large], or some combination of the above.

21. Suppose consumers idiosyncratically interpret the preference scale. Then the true preference model for individual i is $P^i = w_0^i + w_1^i x_1 + w_2^i x_2 + \zeta^i$ and the measured preference model is $P_m^i = \theta_1^i + \theta_2^i P + \varepsilon^i$, where the θs are random in the population. Let $E(\theta_j) = \overline{\theta}_j$ for all j and drop the superscript i. Assume that the scaling factor θ_2 is independent of the ws and the error terms ζ^i and ε^i. Then $P_m = (\overline{\theta}_1 + \overline{\theta}_2\overline{w}_0) + \overline{\theta}_2\overline{w}_1 x_1 + \overline{\theta}_2\overline{w}_2 x_2 + \varepsilon''$, where $\varepsilon'' = (\theta_1 - \overline{\theta}_1) + (\theta_2 w_0 - \overline{\theta}_2\overline{w}_0) + (\theta_2 w_1 - \overline{\theta}_2\overline{w}_1)x_1 + (\theta_2 w_2 - \overline{\theta}_2\overline{w}_2)x_2 + (\theta_2\zeta + \varepsilon)$. Note that $E(\varepsilon'') = 0$ and that $\sigma^2(\varepsilon'')$ depends on both preference heterogeneity (i.e., the distribution of the ws) and individuals' idiosyncratic interpretation of the preference scale (i.e., the distribution of the θs).

22. Suppose all consumers interpret the preference scale identically but have heterogeneous preferences. Let $\hat{\theta}_1$ and $\hat{\theta}_2$ denote the common scaling parameters, which are deterministic. Then $P_m^i = (\hat{\theta}_1 + \hat{\theta}_2 w_0^i) + \hat{\theta}_2 w_1^i x_1 + \hat{\theta}_2 w_2^i x_2 + \varepsilon^i$. Let $\varphi = (\hat{\theta}_1 + \hat{\theta}_2 w_0, \hat{\theta}_2 w_1, \hat{\theta}_2 w_2)$ and assume that (w_0, w_1, w_2) has a multivariate normal distribution. Recall that $\hat{\theta}_1$ and $\hat{\theta}_2$ are nonstochastic. Hence φ has a multivariate normal distribution. Let μ and Σ, respectively, denote the expected value and the covariance matrix of φ. Then we can use the standard maximum likelihood approach

in the random-coefficient model to obtain consistent and efficient estimates of μ and Σ. Note that except for the scale parameter $\hat{\varphi}_2$ we will capture the heterogeneity in the true importance weights. Having estimated the parameters of the random-coefficient model, we can predict market behavior.

23. Suppose consumers idiosyncratically interpret the preference scale. Then $P_m^i = \theta_1^i + \theta_2^i P^i$, where θ_1^i and $\theta_2^i > 0$ are individual-specific parameters. Thus in general we have $P_m = (\theta_1 + \theta_2 w_0) + \theta_2 w_1 x_1 + \theta_2 w_2 x_2 + \varepsilon$, where the θs and ws are random. Let $\alpha_0 = \theta_1 + \theta_2 w_0$, $\alpha_1 = \theta_2 w_1$, and $\alpha_2 = \theta_2 w_2$. Suppose the random vectors $\tilde{\theta} = (\theta_1\ \theta_2)'$ and $\tilde{w} = (w_0\ w_1\ w_2)'$ are independent, i.e., consumers' idiosyncratic interpretations of the preference scale are independent of the true preference weights. In particular, $\tilde{\theta}$ and $\tilde{w}$ have independent normal distributions. Then $\tilde{\alpha} = (\alpha_0\ \alpha_1\ \alpha_2)'$ cannot be multivariate normally distributed.

24. Recall that expected utility theory requires each individual i to maximize $E(P^i) = w_0^i + w_1^i x_1 + w_2^i x_2$, where P^i denotes the unobserved true preference. However, maximizing $E(P^i)$ is equivalent to maximizing $E(P_m^i) = (\theta_1^i + \theta_2^i w_0^i) + \theta_2^i w_1^i x_1 + \theta_2^i w_2^i x_2$, where P_m^i denotes measured preference and $\theta_2^i > 0$ for all i. If the total number of profiles in the experiment is large, we can obtain consistent estimates of $\theta_1^i + \theta_2^i w_0^i$, $\theta_2^i w_1^i$, and $\theta_2^i w_2^i$. (Note that the θs and ws are not identifiable.) Hence the empirical Bayes procedure is consistent with expected utility theory.

25. Because group membership is known a priori, the researcher should use a stratified sampling plan. In particular the sample size for a given segment should increase with that segment's importance and with the researcher's a priori estimates of the degree of heterogeneity in that segment.

26. For all individuals let θ_1 and θ_2 denote the common scaling parameters for measured preference. Let g index group membership ($g = 1, \ldots, G$, where G is finite). Then for all g the measured preference model is $P_m^{(g)} = (\theta_1 + \theta_2 w_0^{(g)}) + \theta_2 w_1^{(g)} x_1^{(g)} + \theta_2 w_2^{(g)} x_2^{(g)} + \varepsilon^{(g)}$, where the vector $\tilde{q}^{(g)} = (w_0^{(g)}, w_1^{(g)}, w_2^{(g)}, \varepsilon^{(g)})'$ has a multivariate normal distribution. Recall that in a conjoint experiment the xs are fixed design variables. Hence $P_m^{(g)}$ has a conditional multivariate normal distribution. However, finite mixtures of conditional multivariate normal distributions are identified (see Yakowitz and Spragins 1968). Let $P^{(g)}$ denote the mixing proportions ($P^{(1)} + \ldots + P^{(G)} = 1$), $\tilde{\mu}^{(g)} = E(\tilde{q}^{(g)})$ and $\Sigma^{(g)}$ the covariance matrix of $\tilde{q}^{(g)}$. Then there is a unique value G such that the parameters $P^{(g)}$, $\tilde{\mu}^{(g)}$, and $\Sigma^{(g)}$ are unique. That is, for sufficiently large samples we can determine the correct numbers of segments and the degree of heterogeneity within each segment.

27. Suppose the scaling parameters $\theta_1^{(g)}$ and $\theta_2^{(g)}$ are random within a given segment g. Then $P_m^{(g)} = (\theta_1^{(g)} + \theta_2^{(g)} w_0^{(g)}) + \theta_2^{(g)} w_1^{(g)} x_1^{(g)} + \theta_2^{(g)} w_2^{(g)} x_2^{(g)} + \varepsilon^{(g)}$ will not have a conditional multivariate normal distribution. Hence the mixture model may not be identified. The same ambiguity occurs if θ_1 and θ_2 are parameters, but $\tilde{q}^{(g)} = (w_0^{(g)}, w_1^{(g)}, w_2^{(g)}, \varepsilon^{(g)})'$ does not have a multivariate normal distribution.

28. Let i index the consumer's unobservable perceptions ($i = 1, 2$). For each i let the true perception be $P_i = f_i(x_1, x_2, x_3) + \zeta_i$, where f_i is deterministic, ζ_i is a stochastic term that measures perceptual error [$\text{Cov}(\zeta_1, \zeta_2) \neq 0$], and $\partial^2 f_i / \partial x_j\, \partial x_k \neq 0$ in general for all (j, k) pairs. Let P denote the consumer's unobservable preference, where $P = \beta_0 + \beta_1 P_1 + \beta_2 P_2 + \zeta_3$, the βs are parameters, and ζ_3 is a stochastic term that captures the effect of omitted variables on preference. Let $P_m = \theta_1 + \theta_2 P + \varepsilon$ denote the consumer's measured preference, where the θs are individual-specific scaling parameters and ε is a stochastic term that captures measurement error. (For notational simplicity we do not use an index for the consumer. As discussed previously, θ_1 and θ_2 will vary across consumers if consumers idiosyncratically interpret the assigned preference scale.) Then conjoint analysis estimates the model $P_m = (\theta_1 + \theta_2 \beta_0) + \theta_2 \beta_1 f_1(x_1, x_2, x_3) +$

$\theta_2\beta_2 f_2(x_1, x_2, x_3) + \varepsilon'$, where $\varepsilon' = \theta_2(\beta_1\zeta_1 + \beta_2\zeta_2 + \zeta_3) + \varepsilon$. Hence $E(\varepsilon') = 0$ and ε' is homoscedastic even if $\text{Cov}(\zeta_1, \zeta_2) \neq 0$ (i.e., the perceptual errors are correlated).

29. Consider the general nonlinear perceptual model in note 28. For any given consumer let (P_1^*, P_2^*) denote the ideal point, $P = \beta_0 + \beta_1(P_1 - P_1^*)^2 + \beta_2(P_2 - P_2^*)^2 + \zeta_3$ the unobserved preference, and $P_m = \theta_1 + \theta_2 P + \varepsilon$ the measured preference. Then $P_m = (\theta_1 + \beta_0\theta_2) + A + \varepsilon'$, where

$$A = \beta_1\theta_2\{[f_1(x_1, x_2, x_3)]^2 + (P_1^*)^2 - 2f_1 P_1^*\} + \beta_2\theta_2\{[f_2(x_1, x_2, x_3)]^2 + (P_2^*)^2 - 2f_2 P_2^*\}$$

and

$$\varepsilon' = \beta_1\theta_2[\zeta_1^2 + 2f_1(x_1, x_2, x_3)\zeta_1 - 2\zeta_1 P_1^*] + \beta_2\theta_2[\zeta_2^2 + 2f_2(x_1, x_2, x_3)\zeta_2 - 2\zeta_2 P_2^*]$$
$$+ \theta_2\zeta_3 + \varepsilon$$

Now $E(\varepsilon')$ is constant for all profiles but ε' is heteroscedastic. Hence standard conjoint analysis provides unbiased estimates of the parameters in A but leads to incorrect significance tests (i.e., the t-statistics are biased). Furthermore ε' is not normally distributed even if (ζ_1, ζ_2) has a bivariate normal distribution. Note that the ideal point (P_1^*, P_2^*) is not identified even in the simple case where the mapping from attributes to perceptions (i.e., the f_is) is linear.

30. In our example, the disjunctive decision-making rule can be represented perfectly by the conjoint model $P = \alpha_0 + \alpha_3 D_3 + \alpha_4 D_4 + \alpha_{13}(D_1 D_3) + \alpha_{14}(D_1 D_4) + \alpha_{23}(D_2 D_3) + \alpha_{24}(D_2 D_4)$, where $D_1 = 1$ if 133 MHz and 0 otherwise, $D_2 = 1$ if 266 MHz and 0 otherwise, $D_3 = 1$ if 1.8 GB and 0 otherwise, and $D_4 = 1$ if 5 GB and 0 otherwise. Note that the main effects for speed (α_1 and α_2) are 0.

31. In the conjunctive model, $P = \alpha_{14}(D_1 D_4) + \alpha_{24}(D_2 D_4)$. See note 30 for definitions of D_1, D_2, and D_4.

32. The reader should verify that the random-coefficient conjoint approach allows for different cutoff (i.e., threshold) values for individuals who follow conjunctive or disjunctive information-processing strategies. Furthermore, the random-coefficient model does not introduce heteroscedasticity.

33. Let $i = 1$ and 2, respectively, index the store and national brands. By assumption all consumers interpret the scales identically. Let x_1^i and x_2^i denote the measures of gentleness (F_1^i) and effectiveness (F_2^i). Then the confirmatory factor analysis model is

$$x_1^{(i)} = \nu_1 + \lambda_1 F_1^{(i)} + \delta_1^{(i)}$$
$$x_2^{(i)} = \nu_2 + \lambda_2 F_1^{(i)} + \delta_2^{(i)}$$
$$x_3^{(i)} = \nu_3 + \lambda_3 F_2^{(i)} + \delta_3^{(i)}$$
$$x_4^{(i)} = \nu_4 + \lambda_4 F_2^{(i)} + \delta_4^{(i)}$$

where the νs and λs are parameters and $\delta_j^{(i)}(j = 1, \ldots, 4)$ denotes measurement error. Let $\tilde{x}^{(i)} = (x_1^{(i)}, x_2^{(i)}, x_3^{(i)}, x_4^{(i)})'$, $\tilde{\mu}^{(i)} = E(\tilde{x}^{(i)})$ and $\Sigma^{(i)}$ denote the covariance matrix of $\tilde{x}^{(i)}$.

Let $\Sigma(\tilde{\theta}^{(i)})$ denote the covariance matrix of the observables in group i expressed as a function of the parameters $\tilde{\theta}^{(i)}$ for group i where $\tilde{\theta}^{(i)}$ is a vector. For identifiability the $\tilde{\theta}^{(i)}$ must be unique for given $\tilde{\mu}^{(i)}$ and $\Sigma^{(i)}$.

Set $\lambda_1 = 1$ for identification (i.e., assume that F_1 is measured on the same scale as x_1; note that there is no loss in generality). Similarly set $\lambda_3 = 1$. Let $\text{Cov}(x_j^{(i)}, x_k^{(i)}) = \sigma_{jk}^{(i)}$ for all j, k. Then $\sigma_{13}^{(i)} = \text{Cov}(F_1^{(i)}, F_2^{(i)})$. Similarly $\lambda_2 = \sigma_{23}^{(i)}/\sigma_{13}^{(i)}, \lambda_4 = \sigma_{14}^{(i)}/\sigma_{13}^{(i)}, \sigma^2(F_1^{(i)}) = \sigma_{12}^{(i)}\sigma_{13}^{(i)}/\sigma_{23}^{(i)}$, and $\sigma^2(F_2^{(i)}) = \sigma_{34}^{(i)}\sigma_{13}^{(i)}/\sigma_{14}^{(i)}$ for all i. Note that the parameters $\sigma^2(F_1^{(1)})$ and $\sigma^2(F_1^{(2)})$, respectively, capture the heterogeneity in perceived gentleness for the store brand and national brands. Similarly $\text{Cov}(F_1^{(1)}, F_2^{(1)})$ and $\text{Cov}(F_1^{(2)}, F_2^{(2)})$, respectively, capture the degree to which gentleness and effectiveness are correlated for the store and national brands. In general, the parameters $\sigma^2(F_1^{(i)}), \sigma^2(F_2^{(i)})$, and $\text{Cov}(F_1^{(i)}, F_2^{(i)})$ describe the perceptual heterogeneity for brand i. Note that these parameters can be estimated by analyzing each data set separately; however, a multisample approach is more efficient.

34. For the model in note 33 consider the appropriate elements of $\tilde{\mu}^{(1)}$ and $\tilde{\mu}^{(2)}$. Taking expectations, we get $E(x_1^{(1)}) - E(x_1^{(2)}) = [E(F_1^{(1)})] - [E(F_1^{(2)})]$ and $E(x_3^{(1)}) - E(x_3^{(2)}) = [E(F_2^{(1)})] - E[(F_2^{(2)})]$. That is, we can identify mean differences in perceptions for gentleness and effectiveness for the store and national brands. Standard multisample analysis can be used to test whether the mean differences are significant (see Sörbom 1974).

35. Consider the one-group case. Let j index individuals. Suppose the confirmatory factor model is

$$x_{1j} = v_1 + \lambda_1(G_{1j} + u_{1j}) + \delta_{1j}$$
$$x_{2j} = v_2 + \lambda_2(G_{1j} + u_{1j}) + \delta_{2j}$$
$$x_{3j} = v_3 + \lambda_3(G_{2j} + u_{2j}) + \delta_{3j}$$
$$x_{4j} = v_4 + \lambda_4(G_{2j} + u_{2j}) + \delta_{4j}$$

where $F_{1j} = G_{1j} + u_{1j}$ denotes individual j's perception of gentleness, G_{1j} denotes individual j's mean perception of gentleness, and u_{1j} is a stochastic term that measures individual i's perceptual error. Define $F_{2j} = G_{2j} + u_{2j}$ similarly. Set $\lambda_1 = 1$ and $\lambda_3 = 1$ for identification. Then $\sigma^2(F_1), \sigma^2(F_2)$, and $\text{Cov}(F_1, F_2)$ are identified. However, $\sigma^2(F_1) = \sigma^2(G_1) + \sigma^2(u_1), \sigma^2(F_2) = \sigma^2(G_2) + \sigma^2(u_2)$, and $\text{Cov}(F_1, F_2) = \text{Cov}(G_1, G_2) + \text{Cov}(u_1, u_2)$. Hence the perceptual errors [i.e., $\sigma^2(u_1), \sigma^2(u_2)$, and $\text{Cov}(u_1, u_2)$] are not identified.

36. Without loss of generality consider the one-group case. If individuals idiosyncratically interpret the perception scales, the confirmatory factor analysis model is

$$\tilde{x}_1 = \tilde{v}_1 + \tilde{\lambda}_1 \tilde{F}_1 + \tilde{\delta}_1$$
$$\tilde{x}_2 = \tilde{v}_2 + \tilde{\lambda}_2 \tilde{F}_1 + \tilde{\delta}_2$$
$$\tilde{x}_3 = \tilde{v}_3 + \tilde{\lambda}_3 \tilde{F}_2 + \tilde{\delta}_3$$
$$\tilde{x}_4 = \tilde{v}_4 + \tilde{\lambda}_4 \tilde{F}_2 + \tilde{\delta}_4$$

where the tilde notation is used to indicate that the relevant variable is random. Then we can write

$$\tilde{x}_1 = \bar{v}_1 + \bar{\lambda}_1 \tilde{F}_1 + \tilde{\delta}_1'$$
$$\tilde{x}_2 = \bar{v}_2 + \bar{\lambda}_2 \tilde{F}_1 + \tilde{\delta}_2'$$

$$\tilde{x}_3 = \bar{\nu}_3 + \bar{\lambda}_3 \tilde{F}_2 + \tilde{\delta}'_3$$
$$\tilde{x}_4 = \bar{\nu}_4 + \bar{\lambda}_4 \tilde{F}_2 + \tilde{\delta}'_4$$

where the bars denote expectations and $\tilde{\delta}'_i = [(\tilde{\lambda}_i - \bar{\lambda}_i)\tilde{F}_1 + (\tilde{\nu}_i - \bar{\nu}_i) + \tilde{\delta}_i]$ for all i. In general $\mathrm{Cov}(\tilde{\delta}'_i, \tilde{\delta}'_j) \neq 0$ for $i \neq j$ because $\tilde{F}_1$ and $\tilde{F}_2$ are not independent. Hence the model cannot be identified using the covariance matrix of observables. Suppose the λ_is are nonstochastic. Then $\tilde{\delta}'_i = (\tilde{\nu}_i - \bar{\nu}_i) + \tilde{\delta}_i$ and $\mathrm{Cov}(\delta'_i, \delta'_j) = 0$ for $i \neq j$. Set $\bar{\lambda}_1$ and $\bar{\lambda}_3 = 1$ for identification. Then $\sigma^2(\tilde{F}_1), \sigma^2(\tilde{F}_2), \mathrm{Cov}(\tilde{F}_1, \tilde{F}_2)$, and $\sigma^2(\tilde{\delta}'_i)$ are identified if $\mathrm{Cov}(\tilde{\nu}_i, \tilde{\nu}_j) = 0$ for all $i \neq j$. Note that the heterogeneity in the consumers' use of scales is absorbed into the error terms [i.e., $\sigma^2(\tilde{\delta}'_i) = \sigma^2(\tilde{\delta}_i) + \sigma^2(\tilde{\nu}_i - \bar{\nu}_i)$].

37. Let i and j index brands and k index individuals. Let d_{ijk} represent the nonstochastic distance between brands i and j for individual k. Let ε_{ijk} denote a random disturbance and δ_{ijk} the measured dissimilarity between brands i and j for individual k. Then stochastic multidimensional scaling models assume that $\delta_{ijk} = g(d_{ijk}) + \varepsilon_{ijk}$ (Model 1) or $\delta_{ijk} = g(d_{ijk} + \varepsilon_{ijk})$ (Model 2), where g is a monotone-increasing function. See Winsberg and Carroll (1989, pp. 218–19) for a discussion of these models and Ramsay (1982a,b) for an extensive treatment of the maximum-likelihood approach for estimating Model 2 under general conditions (e.g., serial correlation and heteroscedasticity).

Consider Model 1 first. One interpretation is that $g(d_{ijk})$ denotes the "true" nonstochastic distance (recall that the function g is necessary to transform from the scale of d_{ijk} to the scale for δ_{ijk}; for example, δ_{ijk} could be measured on a 10-point scale, where "1" denotes "highly similar" and "10" denotes "highly dissimilar") and ε_{ijk} denotes measurement error and the effect of omitted dimensions in computing d_{ijk}. Thus perceptions are deterministic.

A second interpretation is that perceptions are stochastic but the measured dissimilarity can be written as the sum of a deterministic component $g(d_{ijk})$ and a stochastic component ε_{ijk}. For simplicity consider the two-way model $\delta_{ij} = g(d_{ij}) + \varepsilon_{ij}$ and assume that g is linear. Let A and B index brands and assume that the Euclidean distance measure is appropriate. Suppose the perceptual coordinates for brands A and B, respectively, are $(x_{1A} + \varepsilon_{1A}, x_{2A} + \varepsilon_{2A})$ and $(x_{1B} + \varepsilon_{1B}, x_{2B} + \varepsilon_{2B})$, where the xs are deterministic and the εs denote perceptual errors. Then the true distance between brands A and B is the stochastic quantity

$$\hat{d}_{AB} = [(x_{1A} - x_{1B}) + (\varepsilon_{1A} - \varepsilon_{1B})]^2 + [(x_{2A} - x_{2B}) + (\varepsilon_{2A} - \varepsilon_{2B})]^2$$

Suppose $g = \alpha + \beta \hat{d}_{AB}$, where we assume without loss of generality that $\alpha = 0$ and $\beta = 1$. Then the observed dissimilarity is $\delta_{AB} = Q_{AB} + R_{AB}$, where

$$Q_{AB} = (x_{1A} - x_{1B})^2 + (x_{2A} - x_{2B})^2$$
$$R_{AB} = (\varepsilon_{1A} - \varepsilon_{1B})^2 + (\varepsilon_{2A} - \varepsilon_{2B})^2 + 2(x_{1A} - x_{1B})((\varepsilon_{1A} - \varepsilon_{1B})$$
$$+ 2(x_{2A} - x_{2B})(\varepsilon_{2A} - \varepsilon_{2B}) + \nu$$

where ν denotes measurement error in the dissimilarity scale.

Note that Q_{AB} is deterministic and R_{AB} is a stochastic term such that $E(R_{AB})$ is a constant; however, R_{AB} is heteroscedastic. Hence standard applications of Model 1, which assume that the error terms (ε_{ij} in two-way and ε_{ijk} in three-way models) are homoscedastic, are inappropriate when there is perceptual error. The error terms in Model 1 are serially correlated (terms of the sort R_{AB} and R_{AC}, where C denotes a third brand, contain the common error terms ε_{1A} and ε_{2A}). In addition, there is an identification problem: We cannot separate measurement and perceptual errors even in the simplest cases where g is linear.

Consider Model 2. In the trivial case where g is linear, Models 1 and 2 are equivalent; consequently Model 2 is subject to the limitations discussed above for Model 1. For general monotonic transforms Model 2 implicitly assumes that measurement error is zero. Thus, as in confirmatory factor analysis, there is a fundamental identification problem: We cannot separate measurement and perceptual errors regardless of which multidimensional scaling model is used.

38. For any single-group structural equation model let x and y, respectively, denote the vectors of observables for the exogenous and endogenous constructs. Let $\Sigma = \begin{pmatrix} \Sigma_{xx} & \vdots & \Sigma_{xy'} \\ \cdots\cdots & \vdots & \cdots\cdots \\ \Sigma_{yx'} & \vdots & \Sigma_{yy} \end{pmatrix}$

denote the covariance matrix of observables, where Σ_{xx} and Σ_{yy}, respectively, denote the covariance matrices of x and y and $\Sigma_{xy'}$ and $\Sigma_{yx'}$ the appropriate covariance matrices between x and y. Let $\Sigma(\tilde{\theta})$ denote the covariance matrix Σ, where the elements are written as explicit functions of $\tilde{\theta}$, the vector of parameters in the structural equation model. Then the model is identified if $\tilde{\theta}$ is unique for a particular choice of Σ.

We illustrate the identification methodology using our simple example with three product attributes (x_1, x_2, x_3), and one covariate (x_4), and two perceptual dimensions each with two measures. To demonstrate the general problem structure we shall depart slightly from the usual structural equation notation and denote the true preference by P rather than by "eta."

The structural model consists of two parts: the perception and preference equations. Let $\eta = \Gamma x + \zeta$ denote the vector of true perceptions, where Γ is a matrix of perceptual weights (which can be nonlinear), $x = (x_1, x_2, x_3, x_4)'$ and ζ is a vector of perceptual errors such that $E(\zeta\zeta') = \Psi = \begin{pmatrix} \psi_{11} & \psi_{12} \\ & \psi_{22} \end{pmatrix}$. Note that ψ_{11} and ψ_{22}, respectively, denote the variances of the perceptual errors in gentleness and effectiveness and ψ_{12} denotes the covariance of these perceptual errors. The preference model is $P = \beta'\eta + u$, where $\beta' = (\beta_1, \beta_2)$ and u is a scalar disturbance term.

For simplicity we shall use only one subscript to refer to the observables. The measurement model is $y_1 = \lambda_1\eta_1 + \varepsilon_1, y_2 = \lambda_2\eta_1 + \varepsilon_2, y_3 = \lambda_3\eta_2 + \varepsilon_3, y_4 = \lambda_4\eta_2 + \varepsilon_4$, and $y_5 = \lambda_5 P + \varepsilon_5$, where $\varepsilon = (\varepsilon_1, \ldots, \varepsilon_5)'$ is a vector of measurement errors such that $E(\varepsilon\varepsilon')$ is a diagonal matrix and the λs are loadings. Note that y_1 and y_2 measure gentleness (η_1), y_3 and y_4 measure effectiveness (η_2), and y_5 measures preference (P). Following the usual approach for identification, set one lambda for each unobservable to unity. Let $\lambda_1 = 1, \lambda_3 = 1$, and $\lambda_5 = 1$. Comparing Σ and $\Sigma(\tilde{\theta})$ we see that Σ_{xx} maps trivially onto itself. Hence the only equations available for identification are $\Sigma_{xy'}$ and Σ_{yy}.

Our first step is to identify the perceptual weights Γ. Let γ_i' denote the ith row of Γ. Then $\text{Cov}(x, y_1) = \Sigma_{xx}\gamma_1$ or $\gamma_1 = \Sigma_{xx}^{-1}\text{Cov}(x, y_1)$. Hence γ_1 is identified. (Note that the right-hand side consists of known quantities.) To solve for γ_2 we consider $\text{Cov}(x, y_3)$ because y_3 is an indicator of η_2. Hence $\gamma_2 = \Sigma_{xx}^{-1}\text{Cov}(x, y_3)$. Thus Γ is identified.

The next step is to identify the measurement model $(\lambda_2$ and $\lambda_4)$. Proceeding as before, we get $\text{Cov}(x, y_2) = \lambda_2\Sigma_{xx}\gamma_1$ and $\text{Cov}(x, y_4) = \lambda_4\Sigma_{xx}\gamma_2$. Hence λ_2 and λ_4 are identified.

To identify ψ_{ii} consider the covariance between any two measures of η_1. Thus $\mathrm{Cov}(y_1, y_2) = \gamma_1' \Sigma_{xx} \gamma_i + \psi_{11}$ and $\mathrm{Cov}(y_3, y_4) = \gamma_2' \Sigma_{xx} \gamma_2 + \psi_{22}$. To identify $\psi_{ij} (i \neq j)$ consider the covariance between any measure of η_i and any measure of η_j. For example, $\mathrm{Cov}(y_1, y_3) = \gamma_1' \Sigma_{xx} \gamma_2 + \psi_{12}$. Hence Ψ is identified.

To identify the measurement errors in the perceptual scales evaluate $\sigma^2(y_i)$ for $y = 1, 4$. Then we get

$$\sigma^2(y_1) = \gamma_1' \Sigma_{xx} \gamma_1 + \sigma^2(\varepsilon_1), \qquad \sigma^2(y_2) = \lambda_2^2 \gamma_1' \Sigma_{xx} \gamma_1 + \sigma^2(\varepsilon_2)$$
$$\sigma^2(y_3) = \gamma_2' \Sigma_{xx} \gamma_2 + \sigma^2(\varepsilon_3), \qquad \sigma^2(y_4) = \lambda_4^2 \gamma_2' \Sigma_{xx} \gamma_2 + \sigma^2(\varepsilon_4)$$

Hence all the measurement errors in perception are identified.

To identify the βs consider any two elements in x (say x_1 and x_2) and compute $\mathrm{Cov}(x_1, y_5)$ and $\mathrm{Cov}(x_2, y_5)$. Then $\alpha = \binom{\mathrm{Cov}(x_1, y_5)}{\mathrm{Cov}(x_2, y_5)} = W\beta$, where $W = \binom{\sigma_1}{\sigma_2}\Gamma'$ and σ_i denote the ith row of Σ_{xx} and is known. Hence $\beta = W^{-1}\alpha$ and is identified.

To identify the measurement error in preference, we compute $\sigma^2(y_5) = \beta' \Gamma \Sigma_{xx} \Gamma' \beta + \beta' \Psi \beta + \sigma^2(u + \varepsilon_5)$. Hence only $\sigma^2(u + \varepsilon_5) = \sigma^2(u) + \sigma^2(\varepsilon_5)$ is identified. Thus we cannot separate the structural and measurement errors in the preference equation.

Note that $\Sigma_{xy'}$ contains 20 equations (x and y have four and five elements, respectively) and Σ_{yy} contains 15 equations ignoring redundancies. However, we used 20 equations to identify the 20 model parameters. Hence the model has 15 degrees of freedom ($20 + 15 - 20$).

In general we can use this approach to show that the attribute → perception → preference model is identified for any finite number of perceptual dimensions (with correlated perceptual errors) provided there are at least two measures for each perceptual dimension. In particular, the model is identified even if price affects perceptions (as a signal of quality) and simultaneously affects preference directly, acting as a constraint on choice.

39. Consider the general model $\eta = \Gamma x + \zeta$ and $P = \beta' \eta + u$, where P denotes the true unobserved preference (see note 38). Then expected utility theory requires that the consumer maximizes $E(P) = \beta' \Gamma x$. The consumer's measured preference is $P_m = \theta_1 + \theta_2 P$, where $\theta_2 > 0$ and the θs are unknown. Note that maximizing $E(P_m)$ leads to the same decision rule as maximizing $E(P)$ regardless of the values of θ_1 and θ_2. Thus the usual scaling assumption in structural equation modeling [$\theta_2 = 1$] is innocuous regardless of whether the structural equation model is nonlinear.

40. One can estimate brand-equity effects in conjoint models using pooled data across subjects and dummy variables for the brands. In this framework brand equity is equivalent to a missing product attribute ("brand"). However, no insight is available regarding the mechanism by which brand affects preference.

An alternative approach for measuring brand-equity effects is to use an extended spatial multidimensional scaling model (see Winsberg and Carroll 1989, p. 218, for a discussion). For present purposes it is sufficient to consider the two-way extended spatial model $d_{ij} = [\sum_{r=1}^R (x_{ir} - x_{jr})^2 + s_i + s_j]^{1/2}$, where i and j denote brands, R is the number of dimensions in the common space shared by all brands, and s_i and s_j, respectively, are the squares of the coordinates of the ith and jth brands in the dimensions specific to those brands. Note that s_i and s_j measure the effects of missing brand-specific perceptual dimensions. The problem is that if s_i (say) is large, we cannot conclude that brand i has high brand equity. (Recall that s_i and s_j are *squared* quantities.) Furthermore, even if s_i is large, s_i's effect on preference could be negative, implying that brand i has negative equity.

The proposed structural equation method allows one to estimate a general brand-equity model using brands as covariates. In particular, one can decompose brand equity into two parts: (1) an indirect effect of brand on preference via perceptions (for any brand, this effect can be positive or negative), and (2) a direct effect on preference. Effect (2) is analogous to the effect of a missing attribute in standard conjoint models and also has unrestricted sign.

41. We can compare nested structural equation models using the standard likelihood approach. Suppose, however, we seek to compare non-nested models, for example, attributes → perceptions → preference (Model A) and attributes → preference → perceptions (Model B). Then we can compare Models A and B using the RMSEA and ECVI statistics (see Browne and Cudeck 1993 for a technical discussion). These statistics are routinely available in standard computer programs for estimating structural equation models (see, for example, LISREL 8, Jöreskog and Sörbom 1993).

When comparing models it is necessary to distinguish among the class of "observationally equivalent" models. (This important problem is ignored in most practical applications.) Consider any set of observable variables x with covariance matrix Σ. Suppose a particular measurement and structural model has parameters Θ. This model is identified if a unique Θ satisfies Σ. Now consider two distinct (possibly nested) models with parameters Θ_1 and Θ_2. In particular, the dimensionality of Θ_1 need not equal the dimensionality of Θ_2 (e.g., the two models imply different "causal" paths). The two models are observationally equivalent if a unique Θ_1 and a unique Θ_2 satisfy Σ. That is, both "causal" models fit the data perfectly. For example, in the attribute → perception → preference model, one cannot in general distinguish a model where both perceptual dimensions impact preference (Model C) and a model in which one perceptual dimension causes another (Model D). This problem of observational equivalence can be resolved by imposing additional structure on the problem. In our example Model C and Model D can be distinguished by imposing restrictions on the Γ matrix (e.g., by allowing a covariate to affect several but not all perceptual dimensions).

42. Suppose the data belong to a finite mixture with G groups. Let g index group membership and tildes denote vectors. Suppose the perceptual model for any group g is $\tilde{\eta}^{(g)} = \tilde{\tau}^{(g)} + \Gamma^{(g)}\tilde{x}^{(g)} + \tilde{\zeta}^{(g)}$, where the mapping $\Gamma^{(g)}$ can be nonlinear in the product attributes (recall that $\tilde{x}^{(g)}$ also includes covariates) and $\tilde{\tau}^{(g)}$ is a vector of intercepts. Let the measurement model for perceptions for any group g be $\tilde{y}^{(g)} = \tilde{\nu}^{(g)} + \Lambda^{(g)}\tilde{\eta}^{(g)} + \tilde{\varepsilon}^{(g)}$, where $\Lambda^{(g)}$ is a matrix of factor loadings. Let the true preference be $P^{(g)} = \alpha^{(g)} + \tilde{\beta}'^{(g)}\tilde{\eta}^{(g)} + u^{(g)}$, where $\alpha^{(g)}$ is a scalar intercept and $u^{(g)}$ is a scalar disturbance term. Let the measured preference be $P_m^{(g)} = P^{(g)} + v^{(g)}$, where $v^{(g)}$ is a scalar disturbance. (This formulation is equivalent to the model $P_m^{(g)} = \theta_1 + \theta_2 P^{(g)} + v^{(g)}$, where $\theta_2 > 0$ and θ_1 and θ_2 are invariant across groups.)

Let $\tilde{\mu}^{(g)} = \begin{bmatrix} E(\tilde{x}^{(g)}) \\ E(\tilde{y}^{(g)}) \end{bmatrix}$ denote the mean vector of observables, $\Sigma^{(g)}$ the covariance matrix of observables, and $p^{(g)}$ the mixing proportions for group g (i.e., $p^{(1)} + \ldots + p^{(G)} = 1$). For any group g suppose the covariates and the random disturbances have a multivariate normal distribution. Then the vector of observables $\begin{pmatrix} \tilde{x}^{(g)} \\ \tilde{y}^{(g)} \end{pmatrix}$ has a conditional multivariate normal distribution. (Recall that the product attributes are nonstochastic.) Hence the structural equation mixture model is identified (see Yakowitz and Spragins 1968 and the proof in the Appendix in Jedidi, Jagpal, and DeSarbo 1997b). Consequently, for large samples we can use the maximum-likelihood algorithm of Jedidi, Jagpal, and DeSarbo to determine G (the number of segments), the probabilities of group membership for any given individual, and the structural and measurement models for each group g.

Simulation evidence suggests that the mixture algorithm is robust if the distributional form (multivariate normality) is correctly specified. It is important that the algorithm appears to be robust to distributional misspecification provided the data are not excessively kurtotic (see Jedidi, Jagpal, and DeSarbo 1997b).

43. Using the approach in note 38 and the results in Kenny and Judd (1984, Appendix), we can show that nonlinear structural equation models are identified provided the model is linear in the parameters and the measurement and structural errors have a multivariate normal distribution. For example, consider the nonlinear model $P = \Sigma_{i,j}\alpha_{ij}\eta_i\eta_j + \Sigma_i\varphi_i\eta_i + u$, where P denotes true preference, the αs and φs are parameters, the ηs denote the stochastic perceptions, and u the effect of omitted variables. Then we can distinguish multivariate risk-neutral ($\alpha_{ij} = 0$ for $i \neq j$), risk-averse ($\alpha_{ij} < 0$ for $i \neq j$), and risk-seeking behavior ($\alpha_{ij} > 0$ for $i \neq j$).

44. Consider a simple model with three attributes (x_1, x_2, x_3) and two perceptual dimensions (η_1 and η_2).

In Model A the mapping from attributes to perceptions is nonlinear and the mapping from perceptions to preference (P) is linear, i.e., $P = \beta_1\eta_1 + \beta_2\eta_2 + u$, where β_1 and β_2 are importance weights and η_1, η_2, and u are stochastic. Thus the consumer is multivariate risk-neutral. Suppose $\eta_1 = \gamma_{11}x_1 + \gamma_{12}x_2 + \gamma_{13}x_3 + \mu_{12}(x_1x_2) + \mu_{13}(x_1x_3) + \mu_{23}(x_2x_3) + \zeta_1$ and $\eta_2 = \gamma_{21}x_1 + \gamma_{22}x_2 + \gamma_{23}x_3 + \varphi_{12}(x_1x_2) + \varphi_{13}(x_1x_3) + \varphi_{23}(x_2x_3) + \zeta_2$, where the φs, γs, and μs are parameters and ζ_1 and ζ_2 denote perceptual errors. Without loss of generality, assume that measured preference $P_m \equiv P$. Thus Model A implies that $P_m = \alpha_1x_1 + \alpha_2x_2 + \alpha_3x_3 + \Sigma_{i,j}\alpha_{ij}(x_ix_j) + \varepsilon_A$, where the αs are parameters and ε_A is an error term.

Now consider Model B, in which the mapping from attributes to perceptions is linear but the mapping from perceptions to preference is nonlinear. Let $\eta_i = \gamma_{i1}x_1 + \gamma_{i2}x_2 + \gamma_{i3}x_3 + \zeta_i$ for all i and $P = \beta_1\eta_1 + \beta_2\eta_2 + \beta_{12}\eta_1\eta_2 + u$, where $\beta_{12} > (<)0$ if the consumer is multivariate risk-seeking (risk-averse). Then Model B implies that $P_m = \pi_1x_1 + \pi_2x_2 + \pi_3x_3 + \Sigma_{i,j}\pi_{ij}(x_ix_j) + \varepsilon_B$, where the πs are parameters and ε_B is a disturbance. Hence Models A and B (in reduced form) cannot distinguish consumers according to multivariate risk attitude.

45. Consider a model with two perceptual dimensions. Let η_1 and η_2 denote the perceptual scores and (η_1^*, η_2^*) the ideal point. Let the true preference be $P = \beta_1(\eta_1 - \eta_1^*)^2 + \beta_2(\eta_2 - \eta_2^*)^2 + v$, where the βs are importance weights and v is stochastic. Suppose the perceptual model is $\eta = \Gamma x + \zeta$, where Γ denotes the matrix of perceptual weights and η, x, and ζ are vectors. Then (η_1^*, η_2^*) cannot be identified using the conjoint model (see note 29 for an example).

46. Consider the model in note 45. Suppose we have at least two measures for each perception. For simplicity suppose y_1 and y_2 are measures of η_1, y_3 and y_4 measures of η_2, and y_5 the measure of preference. Let ε_i denote the respective measurement errors. Let $\tilde{\alpha} = (\varepsilon_1, \ldots \varepsilon_4, \varepsilon_5 + v; \zeta_1, \zeta_2)'$. Suppose $\tilde{\alpha}$ is multivariate normal with mean vector $\tilde{0}$ and all pairwise covariances except $\text{Cov}(\zeta_1, \zeta_2)$ are zeroes.

Then we can use the approach in note 38 and the results in Kenny and Judd (1984, Appendix) to show that the nonlinear structural equation model including (η_1^*, η_2^*) is identified. The proof is omitted. Note that, in contrast to the model in which perceptions have a linear effect on preference, distributional assumptions are necessary to establish identifiability. In particular, observables of the sort $y_i^2 (i = 1, 4)$, which are necessary for identifiability, cannot be normally distributed.

Hence a generalized least-squares estimation procedure (see, for example, the COSAN program described in Fraser 1980) is necessary to estimate the nonlinear structural equation model.

In general we can show that ideal-point perceptual models are identifiable provided the number of perceptual dimensions is finite, each perceptual dimension has at least two measures, and the error terms have a multivariate normal distribution.

47. Let η denote a vector of perceptions and x a vector of exogenous variables (i.e., product attributes, covariates, and price). Then the true perceptions are $\eta = \Gamma x + \zeta$, where Γ is a matrix and ζ is a vector of perceptual errors. Let $P = \beta'\eta + u$ denote the true preference, where β is a vector of importance weights and u is a scalar disturbance term. Let the measured preference be $P_m = \theta_1 + \theta_2 P + v$, where the θs are scaling parameters and v denotes measurement error. Without loss of generality assume that $\theta_1 = 0$ and $\theta_2 = 1$. Then the reduced-form conjoint model is $P_m = \beta'\Gamma x + (\beta'\zeta + u + v)$, where $E(\beta'\zeta + u + v) = 0$. Note that conjoint analysis will give unbiased estimates of $\beta'\Gamma$ in finite samples; however, the perceptual and importance weights (β and Γ, respectively) cannot be identified. Using the structural equation methodology, we have additional information (i.e., the scores on the perceptual scales). Consequently we can obtain consistent estimates of β and Γ.

48. Suppose the perceptual and importance weights vary randomly in the population; in addition consumers idiosyncratically interpret the assigned preference scale. Let θ_1 and θ_2 denote the preference scaling parameters, P_m measured preference, β a vector of perceptual importance weights, Γ a matrix of perceptual weights, x a vector of product attributes and covariates, ζ a vector of perceptual errors, u structural error in the true preference model, and v measurement error in preference. Then the reduced-form preference model is $P_m = \theta_1 + \theta_2 \beta'\Gamma x + w$, where $w = \theta_2(\beta'\zeta + u) + v$, $E(w) = 0$, and w is homoscedastic. Note that all the right-hand-side variables are random except for the product design variables in x. In particular the reduced-form weights $\theta_2\beta'\Gamma$ will not have a multivariate normal distribution. Hence a flexible distributional form should be used to estimate the random-coefficient conjoint model.

49. As shown in note 38, we can identify terms of the sort $\sigma^2(\zeta_i)$ and $\text{Cov}(\zeta_i, \zeta_j)$ for $i \neq j$ (i.e., the perceptual errors) even if preference data are not available.

Coordinating the Channel Structure

In the previous chapters we implicitly assumed that the manufacturer sells directly to the consumer. For many products the channel of distribution interposes several levels between the manufacturer and the consumer (e.g., wholesalers, jobbers, and retailers). This chapter deals with the problem of coordinating prices in a multilevel channel of distribution. In our analysis we shall pay special attention to heterogeneity at different levels (e.g., wholesaler and consumer), multiperiod effects, new products, and uncertainty.

5.1 THE MANUFACTURER–DISTRIBUTOR CHANNEL

Suppose a manufacturer sells through an exclusive distributor (i.e., the distributor does not carry competing brands). The market demand is as shown in Table 5.1. Assume that the variable manufacturing cost per unit is $15 and the variable distribution cost per unit (e.g., providing consumer service) is $5 per unit. The distributor's fixed costs per period are $10,000, and the manufacturer's fixed costs including relevant overhead chargeable to the product are $4,500 per period.

Assume initially that the manufacturer has all the power (i.e., the manufacturer can choose from a large number of potential distributors). As shown in Table 5.1, the total channel profit is maximized if the distributor charges a price of $42.50 per unit. Specifically the gross channel profit before deducting fixed costs is $20,250. The manufacturer must now choose an appropriate price to charge the distributor so that the manufacturer can maximize its share of the total profit. The only constraint is that the distributor must be allowed to make a gross profit of $10,000 to cover its fixed costs. (Note that these fixed costs include the distributor's opportunity cost of tying up capital.)

One strategy is for the manufacturer to sell the product to the distributor at a price equal to the unit variable manufacturing cost of $15. The distributor now determines the price to charge the consumer so that the distributor's gross margin is maximized. Note that

Table 5-1 Channel Gross Profits at Different Market Prices

Price (in $)	Quantity	Gross Profit per Unit[a] (in $)	Gross Profit (in $)
25	1,600	5	8,000
30	1,400	10	14,000
35	1,200	15	18,000
40	1,000	20	20,000
42.50	900	22.50	20,250
45	800	25	20,000
50	600	30	18,000

[a] Gross profit per unit = price − (variable distribution cost per unit + variable manufacturing cost per unit).

the gross channel profits in Table 5.1 are unchanged: the only difference is that the entire gross channel profit goes to the distributor. Consequently the distributor will charge the "right" price of $42.50. However, the distributor earns all the profit! This problem is easily resolved. The manufacturer simply charges the distributor an entry fee (franchise fee) of $10,250—the difference between the maximum gross channel profit of $20,250 and the distributor's fixed cost of $10,000. As a result the manufacturer obtains all the profit in the channel and the distributor earns zero economic profit.[1]

The manufacturer can achieve the same result by offering the distributor an appropriately chosen quantity–discount schedule. The first step for the manufacturer is to determine what price to charge the distributor for 900 units—the "correct" volume. Let this price per unit be p_{900}. Suppose the distributor charges the end user a price of $42.50. Then the distributor's gross margin per unit is $(42.50 - p_{900} - 5)$. Recall that the variable distribution cost per unit is $5. Consequently the distributor's gross margin is $900(42.50 - p_{900} - 5)$.

Setting this gross margin equal to the distributor's fixed cost of $10,000, we obtain $p_{900} = \$26.39$. Thus if the manufacturer charges the distributor $26.39 per unit for an order of 900 units and the distributor charges a price of $42.50 per unit, the distributor earns zero economic profit and the manufacturer's profit is maximized. Of course, there is no guarantee that this outcome will occur. Consequently, the manufacturer's next step is to offer the distributor a price–quantity schedule such that the distributor maximizes profit only when the distributor buys 900 units at a unit price of $26.39.

Suppose the manufacturer offers the distributor a unit price of $26.39 for all purchases equal to or greater than 900 units. If the distributor orders 1,000 units, the distributor's gross margin is $1,000(40 - 5 - 26.39) = \$8,610$, which is lower than the gross margin ($10,000) for 900 units. Similarly, we can show that the distributor is always worse off whenever it orders more than 900 units. The remaining issue for the manufacturer is to price smaller orders than 900 units such that the distributor is always worse off than by ordering 900 units. Let the unit price for an order of 800 units be p_{800}. The distributor's unit gross margin is $(45 - p_{800} - 5)$. Consequently the manufacturer must set p_{800} such that the distributor's gross margin $800(45 - p_{800} - 5)$ is less than the distributor's fixed cost ($10,000). That is $p_{800} > \$27.50$. Proceeding similarly we have $p_{600} > \$28.33$. Thus any quantity–discount schedule that satisfies these inequalities and $p_{900} = \$26.39$ will lead to zero profits for the distributor.

Note that the manufacturer does not use a quantity–discount schedule to "pass along" cost savings (the unit variable manufacturing cost is constant). Furthermore, many quantity–discount schedules will accomplish the same result. One such schedule is shown in Figure 5.1. The reader should use the methodology described to show that the optimal quantity–discount schedule can be smooth and not kinked as shown in Figure 5.1. In addition, the reader should show how different combinations of entry fee and price–quantity schedules can be found such that the distributor earns zero profit (i.e., there are multiple equilibria).

Key Point *In a manufacturer–distributor relationship, the manufacturer can obtain all the channel profits by charging the distributor an entry fee, offering a quantity–discount schedule, or some combination thereof. Consequently the manufacturer has no incentive to vertically integrate forward into the distribution channel if the distribution industry is competitive.*

The previous analysis assumed that the manufacturer has all the power. In certain cases the distributor has all the power (e.g., large retailers who buy from a fragmented group of suppliers). We can use the previous method to examine how the distributor can ensure that the manufacturer's profit is eliminated. One strategy is for the distributor to charge the manufacturer an entry fee (known as a slotting fee in the retail industry, where manufacturers pay a fee to get shelf space) and purchase from the manufacturer according to a suitably chosen quantity–discount schedule.

Suppose the slotting fee is \$1,000 (an arbitrary value). The first step for the distributor is to determine what price to offer the manufacturer for the "correct" volume of 900 units. Let the unit price for this volume be p_{900}. Then the manufacturer's gross profit margin is $900(p_{900} - 15)$ because the manufacturer's unit variable cost is \$15. Recall that the manufacturer's fixed cost is now \$5,500 (i.e., \$4,500 plus the entry fee of \$1,000). Solving for the zero-profit condition, we have $900(p_{900} - 15) = 5500$ or $p_{900} = \$21.110$.

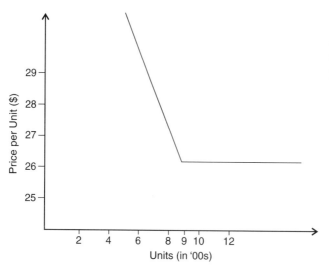

Figure 5.1 A quantity–discount schedule that maximizes the manufacturer's profit.

The remaining step for the distributor is to ensure that the manufacturer will choose this price–quantity plan. Let p_{800} denote the unit price to the manufacturer for an order of 800 units. Then p_{800} must be chosen so that the manufacturer's gross margin $800(p_{800} - 15)$ is less than the manufacturer's fixed cost of $5,500. Hence $p_{800} < \$21.875$. Proceeding similarly, we can show that $p_{600} < \$24.166$, $p_{800} < \$21.875$, $p_{1000} < \$20.500$, and $p_{1200} < \$19.583$. These boundary conditions are shown in Figure 5.2: Any price–quantity schedule below AB will drive the manufacturer's profit to zero provided $p_{900} = \$21.110$.

> ***Key Point*** *When the manufacturing industry is competitive, the monopolistic distributor can force manufacturers to earn zero profits by imposing slotting fees, offering a quantity–discount schedule, or some combination thereof. The distributor has no incentive to vertically integrate backward into a competitive manufacturing industry.*

The previous approach can be extended in a straightforward manner to analyze cooperative advertising (i.e., advertising where both the manufacturer and the distributor share the advertising cost). Suppose there is no advertising. As discussed (see Table 5.1), the maximum gross channel profit is $20,250. Suppose demand is responsive to advertising. In particular, the manufacturer has determined that the optimal level of channel advertising is $8,000 and increases the gross channel profit to $30,250 before deducting advertising costs (see Table 5.2). That is, the total channel profit increases by $2,000 when the optimal channel advertising is used. The problem is to ensure that the retailer chooses the "correct" retail price of $47.50 and does not earn economic profit.

The manufacturer can now use several strategies to garner the incremental profit. One strategy is for the manufacturer to incur the advertising expense and choose an appropriate quantity–discount schedule such that the distributor pays a unit price of $33.41 for an order of 1,100 units. An alternative strategy is for the manufacturer to offer the distributor a

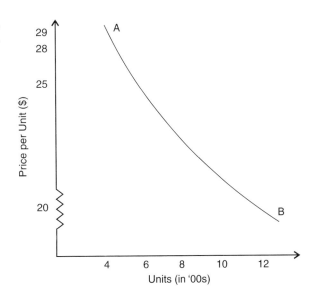

Figure 5.2 The boundary of quantity–discount schedules that maximize the distributor's profit.

Table 5-2 Channel Gross Profits when Optimal Advertising is Used

Price (in $)	Quantity	Gross Profit per Unit[a] (in $)	Gross Profit before Deducting Advertising (in $)
25	2,000	5	10,000
30	1,800	10	18,000
35	1,600	15	24,000
40	1,400	20	28,000
45	1,200	25	30,000
47.50	1,100	27.50	30,250
50	1,000	30	30,000
55	800	35	28,000

[a] Gross profit per unit = price − (variable distribution cost per unit + variable manufacturing cost per unit).

cooperative arrangement where the manufacturer spends $5,900 on advertising and the distributor $2,100. This strategy requires the manufacturer to determine an appropriate quantity–discount schedule such that the distributor pays a (lower) unit price of $31.50 for an order of 1,100 units. The reader should verify these results, determine a viable quantity–discount schedule, and show that other equivalent strategies can be used. The reader will also find it useful to solve the problem assuming that the distributor has all the power (i.e., the manufacturer makes zero profit).

Key Point   When advertising is effective, the party with economic power (i.e., the manufacturer or distributor) can use a combination of cooperative advertising and an appropriate quantity–discount schedule to ensure that the other party makes zero profit.

5.2 CHANNEL HETEROGENEITY

The previous analysis has considered aggregate market behavior. We now consider the effect of consumer and distributor heterogeneity.

Suppose a regional manufacturer sells a hammer for home use through distributors. At present the manufacturer charges distributors $10 per hammer. Suppose the manufacturer's current sales are 45,000 hammers per year and the manufacturer's variable cost per hammer is $6 per hammer (i.e., the manufacturer's gross margin is $4 per hammer). Thus the manufacturer's gross margin is $180,000. The manufacturer now wants to know whether it is profitable to reduce the price to the distributor to $9 per hammer. This policy reduces the manufacturer's margin from $4 to $3 per unit (a 25 percent reduction) and reduces the price charged to the distributor by 10 percent. Let x denote the break-even number of hammers; that is, x denotes the minimum volume such that the manufacturer is better off by reducing price. Solving for x, we find that the break-even volume is 60,000 hammers (a 33.3 percent increase). Equivalently we can say that the *break-even elasticity*[2] is 3.33 (i.e., volume must increase by at least 3.33 percent for a 1 percent reduction in the manufacturer's price). Note that the required increase in volume (33.3 percent) exceeds the reduction in the manufacturer's gross margin per unit (25 percent). The reason is that the distributor obtains a windfall (i.e., surplus) on hammers he would have bought anyway at the higher price. Management can now make a decision after subjectively evaluating the price sensitivity of the market and the likelihood of competitive price reaction.

The previous analysis focuses on aggregate market behavior and does not distinguish among types of distributor. Specifically some distributors are exclusive and carry only the manufacturer's brand of hammer. Other distributors are nonexclusive and offer consumers a choice of several brands of hammer including the manufacturer's. Suppose market research or company records reveal the sales breakdown shown in Table 5.3, where the entries in boxes denote sales through exclusive distributorships.

These data show that nonexclusive distributors account for $175,000 of manufacturer sales and a gross manufacturer margin of $70,000. Exclusive distributors account for $275,000 of manufacturer sales and a gross manufacturer margin of $110,000.

Suppose a typical nonexclusive distributorship carries two or three brands of hammer. Given this scenario, we expect other manufacturers to match the price cut. Consequently it is highly probable that, if the manufacturer introduces the price cut, it will sell the same number of hammers as before through the nonexclusive dealers, but at a reduced margin. Thus the manufacturer loses $17,500 in profit from the nonexclusive distributors.

Let y denote the break-even number of hammers sold through the exclusive distributors when the manufacturer reduces the price charged to the distributor to $9. Then the new gross contribution from the exclusive outlets $(3y)$ must exceed $127,500 (i.e., the sum of the old gross margin of $110,000 and the incremental loss of $17,500 from the nonexclusive distributors). Hence the break-even volume is 42,500 hammers. That is, the number of hammers sold through exclusive distributors must increase by at least 142.9 percent (from 17,500 to 42,500 hammers) when the manufacturer reduces the price to distributors by 10 percent (from $10 to $9 per hammer). Equivalently the break-even elasticity is 14.29. Note that a price reduction is much riskier than aggregate analysis suggests (the break-even elasticity for the market demand is 3.33).

Key Point   *When assessing the effects of a price change, the manufacturer should perform a disaggregate analysis distinguishing among exclusive and nonexclusive distributors. Aggregate analysis can be seriously misleading.*

Table 5-3 Dollar Sales by Type of Distribution Outlet

Annual Sales of Distributor (in $)	Region	
	Urban (in $)	Rural (in $)
< 50,000	100,000	100,000
50,001–100,000	80,000	75,000
> 100,000	45,000	50,000
Total	225,000	225,000

5.3 NEW PRODUCT INTRODUCTION: A SINGLE-PERIOD MODEL

Suppose the manufacturer of a hair-care product is planning to introduce a new packaging form. At present there are two competitors in the marketplace: the manufacturer and a rival. Both competitors market eight-ounce tubes. The new packaging form is an eight-ounce can. Because of the uncertainty of new product introduction, the manufacturer has conducted a consumer experiment using the planned retail prices. The results show that one out of five current users of the manufacturer's product will switch from the tube to the can. One out of ten users of the rival's product will switch to the can. In our analysis, we shall make the reasonable assumption that the introduction of the new product form does not affect primary demand (i.e., the total number of users of this hair-care product). For simplicity we consider a two-level channel consisting of the manufacturer, the retailer, and the consumer; in addition, we do not consider competitive retaliation. Assume that, for institutional reasons, retailers earn a gross profit margin of 40 percent on retail sales of all brands and that manufacturers determine the retail prices of their brands.

Because primary demand is fixed, we can conduct the analysis in terms of the volume-based market shares. The relevant cost and price information for the manufacturer's products are shown in Table 5.4. Suppose initially that the rival brand is sold at a retail price of $5.00 and provides the distributor a margin of $2.00. (These data are not shown in Table 5.4.)

We begin with the manufacturer, recalling that the manufacturer seeks to maximize the product-line profit (i.e., profit net of cannibalization). Let s and $(1 - s)$, respectively, denote the manufacturer's and rival's volume-based market shares. Using the brand-switching data from the consumer study, we see that the manufacturer's profit after the new product introduction has three components:

(a) profit from old users of the tube who do not switch to the can $\left(\frac{4}{5} \times 1.1 \times s\right)$;

(b) profit from old users of the tube who switch to the can $\left(\frac{1}{5} \times 1.20 \times s\right)$; and

(c) profit from previous users of the rival's tube who switch to the can $\left[\frac{1}{10} \times 1.20 \times (1 - s)\right]$.

Table 5-4 Price, Cost, and Margin Data for Different Product Forms

	Rival's 8-Ounce Tube	Manufacturer's 8-Ounce Tube	Manufacturer's 8-Ounce Can	Manufacturer's 16-Ounce Can
Retail price	$2.75	$3.50	$4.00	$7.00
Distributor's margin (40 %)	1.10	1.40	1.60	2.80
	1.65	2.10	2.40	4.20
Less variable manufacturing cost per unit	Unknown	1.00	1.20	2.10
Contribution margin	Unknown	1.10	1.20	2.10

The benchmark profit is the manufacturer's profit before the new product introduction (1.1s). Solving for s, we see that, regardless of the manufacturer's current market share, the manufacturer will always increase profit by introducing the can.[3]

Let us now look at the problem from the distributor's perspective. Recall that the distributor, like the manufacturer, seeks to maximize product-line profit net of cannibalization effects. Then the distributor will only carry the new product if the manufacturer's volume-based share exceeds 50 percent.[4] Thus the channel pricing structure in Table 5.4 can lead to conflict among the manufacturer and its distributors unless the manufacturer is the market leader in volume terms.

The previous analysis focused on market-level demand. In practice, the manufacturer's market share prior to the new product introduction is likely to vary across distribution outlets because of geographical differences in consumers' incomes and competitive structure. Consequently, the manufacturer should perform the profitability analysis for the new product distinguishing among different distribution segments (i.e., those in which the manufacturer's product has low and high market shares). In our example the crucial "break-even" volume-based market share is 50 percent.

Key Point   *When a new product is introduced, the channel pricing structure must be coordinated so that the manufacturer and the distributors are able to increase their respective product-line profits net of cannibalization. A channel pricing structure that is optimal for a manufacturer with a high market share can lead to serious problems if applied by a firm with a low market share. When evaluating the profitability of a new product introduction, the manufacturer should perform disaggregate analysis after segmenting distribution outlets according to the current market share of its existing products.*

Consider a different scenario. Suppose the manufacturer has the option to introduce a large 16-ounce can. See Table 5.4 for price, cost, and margin information on the manufacturer and the rival. A consumer experiment has shown that, if the 16-ounce can is available at a price of $7, one out of four of the manufacturer's present users will switch to the can (i.e., present users are price sensitive). However, only one in fifteen of the rival's customers will switch to the can, a smaller fraction than when the smaller can was offered.

Then the manufacturer will gain from the new product introduction if the manufacturer's volume-based market share is less than 84.85 percent.[5] The distributor, however, will always prefer the new product introduction regardless of the current pattern of market shares in the distributorship.

Key Point   *Manufacturers and distributors seek to maximize product-line performance. The manufacturer can substantially reduce the risk of new product introduction by cooperating with distributors. In particular, the manufacturer can choose an appropriate channel pricing structure after conducting realistic consumer experiments to determine the rates of new product acceptance and cannibalization of existing products.*

5.4 NEW PRODUCT INTRODUCTION: A MULTIPERIOD MODEL

Suppose a manufacturer has developed a new patented chemical additive that almost indefinitely extends the life of gear oil used in heavy industrial manufacturing equipment. A typical piece of industrial equipment uses 20 gallons of gear oil. At present, because of heat and friction when the equipment is used, users must replace the gear oil every two months. Government rules require users to dispose of used gear oil according to regulatory laws. The cost of disposal is $5 per gallon. At present gear oil costs the user $4 per gallon and distributors make a gross profit of $0.50 per gallon (i.e., the distributor's profit margin is 12.5 percent of the selling price). For simplicity we shall assume that there are no quantity discounts in the purchase or disposal of gear oil. In addition, because of cost constraints, the manufacturer must sell through existing distributors (e.g., developing an independent sales force is prohibitively expensive).

The problem facing the manufacturer is what price and margin structure to choose. The first step is to determine the users' reservation prices for the chemical additive. (Some authors use the phrase "value price" instead of reservation price.) Because the chemical additive provides no direct functional benefits to the user, the reservation price to the user simply equals the net cost savings from using the product. Suppose the manufacturer expects users to be conservative. Users will not use the gear oil indefinitely, even though regular use of the chemical additive allows this. Instead, users are likely to reduce the frequency with which they change gear oil from once every two months to once every four months.

In choosing its pricing policy the manufacturer should begin by determining consumers' reservation prices for the chemical additive. At present users purchase gear oil six times a year at a cost of $480 per machine. They dispose of used gear oil six times a year at a cost of $600 per machine. Hence total costs per machine are $1,080 per year. If the chemical additive is used regularly, users will purchase and replace gear oil three times a year for a total cost of $540 per year. Hence the net cost savings per machine from using the chemical additive are $540 per year. The user must, however, purchase the chemical additive three times a year to achieve these savings. Hence the user's reservation price is $180 per application. Note that because the cost savings depend purely on the gallonage used in the industrial equipment, all users have homogeneous reservation prices. Hence the price that the manufacturer should charge the end user is $180 per application. (Strictly this price will be marginally below $180 so that the end user obtains a net advantage by using the chemical additive.)

The next step for the manufacturer is to determine the distributors' margin. The key problem is to make sure that the distributor's profits (net of cannibalization) are not reduced. We shall consider two scenarios. First, assume that distributors agree with the manufacturer that users of the chemical additive will replace gear oil every four months instead of every two months. At present, distributors sell gear oil six times annually to each user and make a gross profit of $60 per user. If the chemical additive is introduced, users will only buy gear oil three times a year, providing the distributor a reduced gross annual profit of only $30. Recalling that the additive is used three times a year, we see that the manufacturer must give the distributor a margin exceeding $10 per application to eliminate the effects of cannibalized sales (i.e., an annual reduction in gross margin of $30 per user).

Second, assume that the distributor is convinced that users will never replace gear oil once the chemical additive is introduced. Now it is necessary to analyze the problem using a multiperiod framework. Consider a new user. Given the present scenario, the user will make six purchases of gear oil every year, providing the distributor an annual gross margin of $60. If the chemical additive is introduced in the market, the user will purchase gear oil only once and purchase the chemical additive three times a year. Consequently the distributor must make a tradeoff between current and future profits. Suppose the distributor's cost of capital is 10 percent per year. Then the manufacturer must provide the distributor a margin greater than $19.67 per application.[6]

Similarly we obtain the following results for different costs of capital:

Distributor's Cost of Capital (%)	*Minimum Gross Margin*
10%	$19.67
15%	$19.50
20%	$19.44

The manufacturer can now decide what price to charge the distributor. Under the first scenario where the manufacturer and distributor have common expectations the manufacturer charges the distributor a price just below $170 (the difference between the users' common reservation price of $180 and the gross margin of $10 per application necessary to compensate the distributor for cannibalized sales). Under the second scenario the manufacturer and distributor have divergent expectations about the frequency of purchase by the end users. Consequently the distributors' decisions depend heavily on the distributors' costs of capital. In particular we expect these costs of capital to vary across distribution outlets. For example, a small individually owned distributorship might have a lower cost of capital than a large distributorship. If these costs of capital range from 10 percent to 20 percent, the manufacturer may want to set a distributor margin of $19.67 per application to ensure maximum penetration of the market. (This strategy provides a windfall to distributors whose costs of capital exceed 10 percent. In the example, however, these windfalls are not significant.) Alternatively, the manufacturer can seek to lower the distributors' margins below $19.67 per application by convincing distributors that users will in fact replace the gear oil every four months.

Key Point *Before introducing a new product the manufacturer should first determine the reservation prices (i.e., "value" prices) of end users. In the next step the manufacturer should determine what margin to provide the distributor in order to compensate the distributor for profits lost through cannibalization. Multiperiod analysis may be necessary if the new product introduction changes the frequency of product usage. The optimal distributor margin will depend on the precise pattern of heterogeneity in the cost of capital for distributors.*

The previous analyses were based on objective data regarding the cost savings from using the new chemical additive. In practice, however, users are not likely to know this information. Suppose the manufacturer conducts a large-scale survey of end users to determine their perceptions of the cost of disposing used gear oil. The results show that a significant fraction of the market is misinformed. Estimates of disposal costs range from $2 per gallon to $8 per gallon. (In our example the actual cost is $5 per gallon.)

Following the previous approach, we find that for users who believe that the disposal cost is $2 per gallon the implicit reservation price is $120 per application. The reservation price for those who expect the disposal cost to be $8 per gallon is $240 per application. Note that the reservation prices of end users are heterogeneous because of differences in subjective beliefs: in reality, the cost savings to all users of the new product are identical.

Suppose the survey data are as follows:

Perceived Disposal Cost per Gallon	Fraction of End Users	Implicit Reservation Price
$2	0.3	$120
$5	0.5	$180
$8	0.2	$210

Now, in contrast to the homogeneous reservation price case, the manufacturer must explicitly consider manufacturing costs. Suppose the variable manufacturing cost per application is $15. Because primary demand is unchanged, we can conduct the analysis in terms of the fraction of end users. We shall assume that the manufacturer and distributors share the common expectation that end users who switch to the new product will replace the gear oil every four months. The interested reader can rework the example for the case where distributors expect all end users who switch to the new product to cease replacing the gear oil.

The survey results show that the manufacturer will capture 20 percent of the end-user market if the price to the end user is $210 per application. If the manufacturer drops the end-user price to $180 per application, the manufacturer will get 70 percent of the market. If the manufacturer further reduces the price to $120 per application, it will capture 100 percent of the market. Then the minimum margin that the manufacturer must offer to the distributor is $10 per application regardless of which end-user price is chosen.[7] Consequently the manufacturer can choose the channel pricing structure using the following table:

End-User Price	Fraction of Market Captured	Manufacturer's Gross Margin per Application	Profitability Index
$210	0.2	$185	37
$180	0.7	$155	108.5
$120	1.0	$ 95	95

Hence the optimal policy for the manufacturer is to set an end-user price of $180 per application and give the distributor a margin of $10 per application. (Strictly the margin is infinitesimally higher.)

The previous analysis assumes that the end-users' reservation prices are fixed; furthermore, the only marketing variable that the manufacturer can choose is price. In order to increase profits the manufacturer should consider using other elements in the marketing mix (for example, personal selling and advertising) to provide end users with objective information about the reduction in cost that they can achieve by using the new product. In this way the manufacturer can increase end-users' reservation prices and charge higher prices. If the end users are not geographically dispersed, personal selling can be effective. If the end users are dispersed, advertising through industry or trade journals can improve profits. Finally, if end users rely on the advice of distributors, the optimal strategy for the manufacturer might be to increase margins to distributors to stimulate word-of-mouth activity and hence the rate of product acceptance.

> **Key Point**   *Reservation prices can vary across end users because end users have heterogeneous beliefs about the effectiveness of a new product. The manufacturer can improve policy significantly by conducting market research to determine the distribution of reservation prices across end users. Contrary to the case of homogeneous reservation prices, the optimal pricing structure depends crucially on the manufacturer's costs. When consumers are uninformed the firm should consider using additional marketing instruments (e.g., personal selling and advertising) to increase performance.*

5.5 CONCLUDING REMARKS

This chapter examines the problem of choosing an optimal pricing policy in a channel structure with several levels. We show that quantity discounts (slotting fees) are powerful methods for manufacturers (distributors) to increase their respective profits. When contemplating a price change, the manufacturer must explicitly consider heterogeneity in the channel structure and perform disaggregate analysis; market-level analysis can be seriously misleading. When introducing a new product the manufacturer must choose pricing policy after explicitly recognizing that the distributor seeks to maximize product-line performance (just as the manufacturer does). Heterogeneity occurs both at the consumer and the distributor levels; hence the manufacturer should use both dimensions (consumer and distributor) to perform disaggregate analysis. When analyzing new products the firm should use a multiperiod approach, particularly if the new product is likely to change the frequency of use of the product. In this analysis, the firm should explicitly recognize that distributors have heterogeneous costs of capital.

The firm is likely to choose suboptimal policies in a channel context by focusing on price alone. For example, if consumers are uninformed, the optimal policy for the firm may be to use other marketing mix instruments (e.g., advertising and personal selling) in addition to price. The next three chapters examine the firm's advertising and personal selling decisions; in particular, we shall focus heavily on how to coordinate the elements in the marketing mix (e.g., price, advertising, and personal selling).

NOTES

1. This result can be easily extended to the multiperiod case. Suppose the manufacturer's opportunity cost of capital is 20 percent per year. Ignoring changes in fixed cost over time and assuming an infinite horizon for simplicity, the manufacturer should charge an entry fee of $51,250 (= $10,250/0.20).

2. Strictly, this elasticity is an average elasticity (i.e., arc elasticity) because the price reduction is not infinitesimal. However, this distinction is not important.

3. Note that the switching rates obtained from the consumer study are, by definition, only estimates. That is, the left-hand side of the inequality is random. Our approach is therefore strictly correct for the risk-neutral firm. If the sample is random and sufficiently large, the distinction is not practically important.

4. Let x denote the current volume-based market share for the manufacturer's tube in the distributorship. Then the distributor's benchmark profit is $1.40x + 2(1 - x)$. After the new product introduction, the distributor's profit net of cannibalization is $\left[\left(\frac{4}{5}\right)(1.40) + \left(\frac{1}{5}\right)(1.60)\right]x + \left[\left(\frac{1}{10}\right)(1.60) + \left(\frac{9}{10}\right)(2)\right](1 - x)$. Hence the distributor gains if the new product is introduced provided $x > 0.5$.

5. Let x denote the manufacturer's volume-based share. Then the manufacturer will gain by introducing the 16-ounce can if its product-line profits increase. Specifically $(3/4)(1.1)x + (1/4)(1.05)x + (1/15)(1.05)(1 - x) > 1.1x$, which implies that $x < 0.848$. The distributor will favor the new product introduction if its product line profits increase. Recall that the retailer's gross margin on a 16-ounce can is equivalent to a gross margin of \$1.40 on an 8-ounce equivalent. Hence the distributor will favor the new product introduction if $[(3/4)(1.4x) + (14/15)(1.1)(1 - x) + (1/4)(1.4x) + (1/15)(1.4)(1 - x)] > 1.4x + 1.1(1 - x)$, which implies that $x < 1$. But this condition is always satisfied.

6. Let r denote the distributor's cost of capital. Under the present scenario, the distributor's present value of gross profits from a user is $\Pi_1 = 60/(1 + r) + 60/(1 + r)^2 + \cdots$ to $\infty = 60/r$. If the chemical additive is introduced, the distributor's net present value of gross profits from a user who switches is

$$\Pi_2 = \frac{10 + 3q}{(1 + r)} + \left(\frac{3q}{(1 + r)^2} + \frac{3q}{(1 + r)^3} + \cdots \text{ to } \infty\right) = \frac{10}{(1 + r)} + \frac{3q}{r}$$

where q denotes the distributor's profit margin per application. Hence $\Pi_2 > \Pi_1$ if $q > (50r + 60)/[3(r + 1)]$. Suppose the distributor's cost of capital is 10 percent (i.e., $r = 0.1$). Then $q > 19.67$. Similarly, one can determine q for different values of r.

7. Let q denote the distributor's margin when the price to the end user is \$210 per application. Given that 20 percent of the end users will switch when the new product is introduced, the manufacturer must set q such that the distributor gains from the new product introduction. That is, $(60 \times 0.8) + 0.2(30 + 3q) \geq 60$, which implies that $q \geq 10$. Similarly, we can show that $q \geq 10$ for the other two end-user prices of \$120 and \$180 per application.

Advertising Budgeting in a Competitive and Uncertain Environment

This chapter analyzes the firm's advertising budgeting policy. We shall focus on the coordination of the pricing and advertising decisions under uncertainty in a multiperiod framework, competitive behavior in an uncertain environment, and empirical measurement. We shall analyze both the expected utility paradigm (popular in economics) and the stock market value model (popular in finance). In particular, we shall propose multiproduct models of advertising and empirical methods for operationalizing the theory. Chapter 7 will examine the firm's media message and media allocation decisions in detail.

6.1 CHOOSING ADVERTISING BUDGETS UNDER CERTAINTY

Choosing the advertising budget is a key managerial decision. If consumers consider all brands of a product to be perfect substitutes, the optimal advertising budget for any given brand is zero. The one exception is the case where all firms in the industry advertise collectively to increase industry demand. For example, the milk industry could advertise to increase milk consumption. We say that the milk industry is advertising to increase primary demand. In most cases of interest the brand manager advertises to increase the demand for his or her brand by differentiating that brand from other brands. We say that the purpose of advertising is to increase secondary demand. Henceforth we focus on this case.[1]

Let us assume initially that the pricing decision has already been made and that advertising does not have any dynamic effects. Furthermore, the firm is a monopolist. The immediate question is: What is the relationship between advertising and sales?

Suppose advertising is low. One can argue that this advertising policy will not be very effective, especially for low-involvement products (i.e., products that are relatively unimportant to consumers). Recall that much advertising belongs to this category (e.g., advertising for soap and toothpaste). Given that consumers have a low task involvement, there is a threshold effect: Unless a consumer is exposed to an advertising message with a minimum frequency, the message does not get stored in the consumer's long-term memory and advertising is virtually useless.[2]

What happens if advertising exceeds the threshold level? Advertising becomes productive and marginal returns to advertising may increase (i.e., each additional dollar of advertising adds more to sales volume than the previous dollar). As advertising increases beyond some point, diminishing marginal returns will set in because the firm has already efficiently targeted the most desirable segments. In particular, the firm is forced to target less attractive segments or prospects. As advertising continues to expand, the marginal returns to advertising start to approach zero. Recall that the firm's market potential—the maximum number of potential buyers—is finite. Furthermore, reaching the same consumers with increasing frequency has little or no marginal effect on sales. Hence there is a saturation effect. Finally, at extremely high levels of advertising, sales may actually diminish because of an annoyance or wearout effect: In the extreme case consumers may even stop purchasing the brand if they are subjected to excessive advertising!

Key Point *Although individual firms in a competitive industry will not find it profitable to advertise, the industry as a whole may find it attractive to advertise to increase primary demand. Most firms advertise to differentiate their brands from competing brands and focus on building secondary demand. The advertising–sales relationship is highly nonlinear because of threshold effects and varying marginal returns to advertising (which may even be negative) depending on the level of advertising spending.*

How should the firm determine the optimal advertising budget given certainty? The first step is to measure the advertising–sales relationship. We shall discuss empirical methods later. For the moment assume that the advertising–sales relationship is known and has the shape shown in Figure 6.1. The sales curve is relatively flat in the section AB where advertising is low (i.e., there is a threshold effect). The section BC displays increasing marginal returns to advertising. The section CD shows diminishing returns to advertising and flattens out considerably at high levels of advertising.[3]

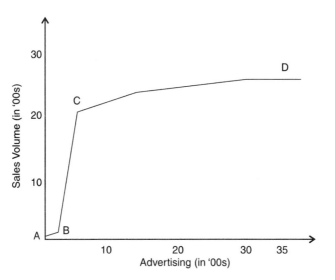

Figure 6.1 The advertising–sales volume relationship.

Table 6-1 Choosing the Optimal Advertising Budget

Advertising $	Unit Volume	Gross Revenue $	Variable Manufac- turing Cost $	Gross Contribution Margin of Advertising $	Incremental Contribution Margin of Advertising $	Net Profit $
200	102.24	1,533.67	511.22	1,022.45		−9,177.55
300	541.34	8,120.10	2,706.68	5,413.42	4,390.97	−4,886.58
400	1,245.60	18,683.95	6,227.98	12,455.97	7,042.55	2,055.97
500	2,053.65	30,804.78	10,628.26	20,536.52	8,080.55	10,036.52
1,000	2,226.94	33,404.08	11,134.69	22,269.39	1,732.87	11,269.39
1,500	2,328.31	34,924.58	11,641.53	23,283.05	1,013.66	11,783.05
2,000	2,400.23	36,003.38	12,001.13	24,002.25	719.20	12,002.25
2,500*	2,456.01	36,840.17	12,280.06	24,560.11	557.86	12,060.11*
3,000	2,501.59	37,523.88	12,507.96	25,015.92	455.81	12,015.92
3,500	2,540.13	38,101.94	12,700.65	25,401.29	385.37	11,901.29

* Denotes optimal policy

Suppose the price of the brand is $15 per unit, fixed costs are $10,000 per period, and the variable manufacturing cost per unit is $5. Table 6.1 shows the financial results for different advertising budgets. Consider a low level of advertising spending, say $200. The firm makes a net loss of $9177.55. If advertising increases to $300, performance increases and the net loss is reduced to $4886.58. When advertising increases further from $300 to $400, the incremental cost of advertising is $100. However, the incremental contribution margin of advertising is $7042.55. Clearly the increase in advertising is warranted. Proceeding similarly using this incremental approach, we see that the optimal advertising budget is $2,500 and the incremental net profit is $12,060.11.

> **Key Point** *Determining the optimal advertising budget is straightforward if we know the advertising–sales relationship and the cost structure and price are given. The advertising budget cannot be chosen without explicitly analyzing production costs. To the extent that the threshold level for advertising is high, advertising can be a barrier to entry. Advertising should be increased to the point where the incremental contribution margin from advertising equals the incremental cost of advertising. The firm will always advertise at a level where the marginal return to advertising is decreasing provided the variable manufacturing cost per unit is constant.[4]*

6.2 CHOOSING PRICE AND ADVERTISING UNDER CERTAINTY

Optimal Policy

The previous discussion assumed that the brand's price is given. This assumption is descriptively realistic because many firms separate the pricing and advertising budget decisions for strategic or organizational efficiency reasons. As we shall demonstrate, such hierarchical or sequential decision approaches can lead to serious errors. Intuitively we know that price cuts and increases in advertising are alternative methods to increase sales volume. However, there is a fundamental difference between these policies. Recall that a price cut always returns consumer surplus to those consumers who were willing to pay the higher price. In contrast, when advertising increases, there is a net increase in demand and consumer surplus is not returned to any consumer. Consequently firms must coordinate their price and advertising decisions to maximize performance.

Suppose the demand for a brand is given by $q = 100 - 10p + 10 \ln A$, where p denotes price per unit, A advertising, and q the sales volume. This specification implies that for any given advertising budget the price–quantity relationship is linear. For any given price, marginal returns to advertising diminish continuously as advertising increases.[5] Suppose fixed costs are $10 and the variable manufacturing cost per unit is $5.

Table 6.2 shows the net profitabilities for different price–advertising combinations. The optimal policy is a price of $9.39 per unit and an advertising budget of $43.9. The net profit from this policy is $138.91. Suppose the pricing manager chooses a price of $6. Then the advertising manager will choose an advertising budget of $10 and the net profits will be only $53.03: a mere 38.18 percent of the optimal profit! Similar comparisons can be made for different sequential decisions (e.g., setting a price of $7 in the first step leads to an advertising budget of $20 and a net profit of $89.91, which is only 64.73 percent of the maximum profit).

> **Key Point**   *Price and advertising decisions should be coordinated. Sequential or hierarchical decision making can be highly dysfunctional.*

The Dorfman–Steiner Theorem: Managerial Implications

Suppose price and advertising decisions are chosen optimally. Then the Dorfman–Steiner Theorem states that the following relationship holds:[6] advertising/sales revenue $= \varepsilon_A / |\varepsilon_p|$,

Table 6-2 Net Profitabilities for Different Price-Advertising Combinations

		\multicolumn{6}{c}{*PRICE*}					
A D V		**$6**	**$7**	**$8**	**$9**	**$9.39****	**$10**
E	$5	$41.09	$77.19	$93.28	$89.38	$82.43	$65.47
R	10	53.03*	86.05	109.08	112.10	107.86	95.13
T	20	39.96	89.91*	119.87	129.83	128.29	119.79
I	30	34.01	88.02	122.04*	136.04	136.09	130.06
S	40	26.89	83.78	120.67	137.56*	138.72	134.44
I	43.9**	23.92	81.74	119.56	137.38	138.91**	135.20
N	50	19.12	78.24	117.36	136.48	138.52	135.60*
G	60	10.94	71.89	112.83	133.77	136.52	134.72

Note: * Denotes conditional optimal policy given price
    ** Denotes optimal policy

where ε_A denotes the advertising elasticity and $|\varepsilon_p|$ the absolute value of the price elasticity. These elasticity concepts have straightforward meanings. Suppose $\varepsilon_A = 2$ for a given price–advertising combination. This value means that the sales volume will increase by 2 percent if advertising increases by 1 percent, provided price does not change from its initial level. Suppose $|\varepsilon_p| = 3$ for a given price–advertising combination. Then the sales volume will increase by 3 percent if price is cut by 1 percent, holding advertising fixed.

Note that because both price and advertising affect demand, each elasticity depends on the levels of both price and advertising. Thus price sensitivity depends on advertising, and advertising sensitivity depends on price. For example, if increased advertising is aimed at nonusers of the brand, the price sensitivity of the market could increase. Alternatively, if increased advertising educates current buyers about new uses of the brand, the reservation prices of current buyers will increase. Consequently price sensitivity could fall when advertising increases.

What does the Dorfman–Steiner Theorem imply for marketing policy? The first implication is that the advertising–sales ratio is positively related to the advertising elasticity. This result is intuitive: The advertising budget should be larger when advertising is more productive. The second implication is more interesting: The advertising–sales ratio is inversely related to price elasticity. To understand this result recall that when the market is price inelastic the markup over marginal cost is high. Consequently the marginal profitability of advertising is enhanced, making it worthwhile to increase advertising.

The Dorfman–Steiner Theorem has interesting dynamic policy implications. For a new product we expect price sensitivity to be low to the extent that the product or brand is differentiated (i.e., $|\varepsilon_p|$ is small). When the product is introduced, the market is likely to be responsive to advertising because consumers are not yet informed about the product (i.e., ε_A is large). Both effects reinforce each other and lead to a high advertising–sales ratio. As the product or brand progresses through its life cycle, the market becomes saturated and hence less sensitive to advertising (i.e., ε_A falls). In addition, the entry of new competitors and the increasing availability of substitutes over time implies that price sensitivity increases (i.e., $|\varepsilon_p|$ goes up). Both effects reinforce each other. Consequently we expect the advertising–sales ratio to fall over the brand or product life cycle.

Key Point *The Dorfman–Steiner Theorem implies that a brand's advertising–sales ratio is positively related to the brand's advertising elasticity and negatively related to the brand's price elasticity. In general, the advertising–sales ratio declines continuously over the brand or product life cycle.*

The Dorfman–Steiner Theorem may appear to lead to counterintuitive results when we make interindustry comparisons. For example, casual empiricism shows that the automobile and personal computer industries advertise heavily but have relatively low advertising–sales ratios. These results, however, are not surprising. Both industries are very competitive because of the large numbers of competing substitutes. Thus the price elasticity for any given brand in either industry is high. Consequently, even though advertising may be effective in differentiating a given brand from its competitors (i.e., the advertising elasticity is high), the advertising–sales ratio for that brand is low.

> ***Key Point*** *The Dorfman–Steiner Theorem implies that the advertising–sales ratio will vary across industries. However, the theorem pertains to advertising–sales ratios and not to absolute levels of advertising.*

The Effect of Changes in Market Conditions

How should the firm coordinate its price and advertising decisions when market conditions change? The answer depends crucially on the precise form of the manufacturing cost structure and the directional effect of a change in advertising on the price elasticity.[7]

Suppose advertising becomes more productive (e.g., the advertising message is improved). Then the advertising budget increases regardless of the manufacturing cost structure.[8] This result is intuitive. The effect on price, not surprisingly, depends on the manufacturing cost structure. Suppose marginal cost is constant: a reasonable assumption for many frequently purchased products. Then the effect on price depends crucially on how an increase in advertising affects the price elasticity.[9]

Suppose increased advertising makes the market less price elastic at the old price. See Figure 6.2a for a simple example. AB and CD denote the old and new demand curves and MC denotes the constant marginal cost. Note that the marginal revenue at the old price is lower than MC. Consequently the firm raises price to maximize profits. The intuition is that, because the market is less price sensitive, an increase in the profit margin augments the dollar value of an increase in sales volume resulting from advertising. If increased advertising makes the market more price elastic at the old price, the marginal revenue at the old price is higher than MC. Hence the firm reduces price to augment the increase in sales volume from the increased productivity of advertising.

The case of variable manufacturing costs is more interesting. Suppose marginal costs are increasing (e.g., the plant is working close to capacity). See Figure 6.2b. Then price

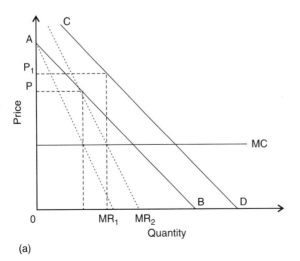

Figure 6.2a The effect on price when advertising becomes more productive: constant marginal cost.

(a)

Figure 6.2b The effect on price when advertising becomes more productive: increasing marginal cost.

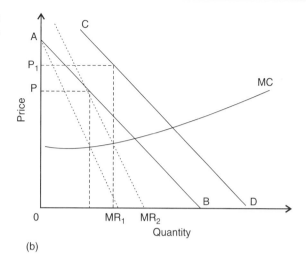

(b)

increases if increased advertising makes the market less price elastic.[10] The reason is that at the old price marginal cost has increased (marginal cost increases with volume) and marginal revenue has decreased. If, however, increased advertising makes the market more price elastic, the effect on price is ambiguous. The reason is that there are two effects that work in opposite directions; at the old price marginal revenue has increased but marginal cost has also increased.

Our discussion focused on the effect of an increase in advertising productivity. Other market changes (e.g., a change in the price of advertising) can be analyzed similarly.

Key Point *The firm must revise both its price and advertising decisions when market conditions change. If marginal production costs are constant, the policy revisions depend only on how advertising affects price elasticity. If marginal costs vary, the firm needs precise knowledge of the cost and demand structures to even determine the directions in which price and advertising should be revised.*

The important question is: What does empirical evidence show about the impact of advertising on price elasticity? Not unexpectedly the results—even those from controlled experiments—are equivocal (see Eskin and Baron 1977). As discussed, the firm's market segmentation policy has a crucial effect on the demand curve. If increased advertising is aimed at nonusers of the brand, price elasticity will probably increase. This effect will be reinforced if advertising encourages consumers to make price comparisons or search for the lowest price. Alternatively, if advertising focuses on product differentiation (i.e., raising consumers' reservation prices), increased advertising will probably reduce price elasticity. In practice both effects may be present because consumers are heterogeneous.

> **Key Point**   *The effect of advertising on price elasticity varies by segment and depends crucially on the firm's segmentation policy. Empirical results are ambiguous. The manager should first decide on an appropriate segmentation strategy and evaluate segment-level demand curves for the brand using judgment or, where possible, empirical methods. In the next step, the manager can aggregate the segment-level demand curves to determine market demand and coordinate the price and advertising decisions.*

6.3 CHOOSING PRICE AND ADVERTISING UNDER UNCERTAINTY: THE SINGLE-PERIOD CASE

The previous analyses assumed a deterministic environment. We now relax this assumption.

Current-Effects Monopoly Model

We begin with a current-effects monopoly model in which demand is uncertain and price and advertising are the decision variables. In this case analytical results can be obtained only if marginal production costs are constant.[11] This assumption is reasonable for many frequently purchased packaged products (e.g., toothpaste and soap) and some industrial products (e.g., paint and electroplating). However, the assumption of constant marginal costs will not hold for industries in which production-scale economies or experience-curve effects are significant. Henceforth we shall assume that the marginal production cost is constant.

The fundamental issue is: How do price and advertising influence the variability of sales volume? In the simplest scenario, price and advertising affect average sales only but not the volatility of sales. We refer to this case as *exogenous uncertainty*. In general, both price and advertising will have an impact on sales fluctuations. Furthermore, these effects will vary over the product life cycle.

A General Stochastic Specification of Demand

Consider advertising. During the early part of the product life cycle, the main focus of advertising is to increase product awareness in the target segment. Consequently advertising increases both average sales volume and sales variability.[12] For convenience we refer to this case as *aggressive advertising*. During the maturity phase of the product life cycle, firms often focus on customer retention (i.e., increasing the probabilities of purchase of existing customers). Hence advertising can reduce sales variability. We refer to this case as *defensive advertising*.

Consider price. Suppose the firm believes that potential competitors view a high price as a proxy for profitability. Then high prices increase demand uncertainty. Alternatively, one can argue that a low-price policy is only effective when the firm targets new segments. Hence lower prices increase demand uncertainty. The main point is that both advertising and price affect demand uncertainty depending on the firm's segmentation policies and the stage of the product life cycle. In particular, these effects need not be monotonic or symmetric. For example, either lowering price or increasing advertising may reduce demand uncertainty.

We now present a general sales function that deals with these effects. Let q denote sales volume, p price, A advertising, and u a disturbance term. Brick and Jagpal (1981) use the specification $q = f(p, A) + g(p, A)u$, where f and g are deterministic functions. If $g(p, A) \equiv 1, q = f(p, A) + u$. Hence the variability of sales volume is independent of price and advertising (i.e., the exogenous case). If $f(p, A) = 0$, the model reduces to the multiplicative form $q = g(p, A)u$. Hence the variability of sales volume increases with advertising and decreases with price; in particular, the ratio of the expected demand and the standard deviation of demand (a measure of volatility) is constant for all prices. In general, price and advertising can have nonmonotonic and asymmetric effects on demand uncertainty.[13]

Objective Function under Uncertainty

Now that we have specified the sales function, the next question is: What is the firm's objective function? The simplest assumption is that the firm chooses policy to maximize expected profits (i.e., the firm is risk-neutral). This assumption is implausible except for the limiting case where uncertainty is small.[14] In general, the firm or marketing manager is risk-averse. We can therefore specify two competing objective functions when uncertainty is large.

First, in the economic tradition, we can assume that the firm chooses policies to maximize expected utility. This formulation implies that the firm is owned by the marketing manager (an unlikely scenario in most cases) or that the manager's compensation is tied to the profitability of the product.[15] Second, we can argue that the firm chooses price–advertising policy to maximize stock value.[16] Jagpal (1982b) uses the first approach and Brick and Jagpal (1981) the second. Jagpal and Brick (1982) extend the stock market model to deal with the more general case in which the marketing mix (i.e., price, advertising, and personal selling) is optimized. Their main argument is that advertising and personal selling have asymmetric informational roles in the marketplace. For example, advertising can inform consumers about prices, hence increasing price sensitivity. However, personal selling may reduce the consumer's uncertainty about quality and hence lower price sensitivity.

Expected Utility Model. The two key managerial issues are: How should the firm choose policy when demand is uncertain? In addition, what is the impact of risk aversion on policy? To focus on essentials we shall focus on the price–advertising model. We refer the interested reader to Jagpal and Brick (1982) for a discussion of the more general problem where the firm simultaneously chooses price, advertising, and personal selling.

Exogenous Uncertainty. Consider the expected utility model where uncertainty is exogenous. Let π denote the firm's random profit given any price–advertising policy (p, A). Let $\bar{\pi}$ denote the corresponding profit in the certainty case.[17] Let Z denote the expected utility of profits π, (p^*, A^*) the optimal price–advertising policy under certainty, and (p^{**}, A^{**}) the optimal price–advertising policy under uncertainty. We seek to compare p^* and p^{**} and A^* and A^{**}.

Consider the variability of profit. Because uncertainty is exogenous, the variability of sales volume does not depend on price or advertising. Let c denote the constant marginal production cost. Then the unit profit margin $(p - c)$ decreases with price. Hence for any given advertising policy, a price cut reduces the variability of profit. In contrast, advertising has no effect on the variability of profit because demand uncertainty is exogenous.

How should the firm react to uncertainty? Recall that the firm is risk-averse. We therefore expect the firm to cut price in order to reduce the volatility of profit. How should the firm revise its advertising policy? As discussed in the previous section, the key issue is how advertising affects price sensitivity. Suppose higher advertising increases price elasticity. Recall that we expect the firm to cut prices in order to reduce the variability of profit. An increase in advertising reinforces this effect. Hence the firm should increase advertising. If higher advertising reduces price elasticity, the firm reduces advertising to reinforce the effect of the price reduction. We now show that these intuitive results are correct.

Figures 6.3a and 6.3b show the effect of uncertainty graphically. Figure 6.3a corresponds to the case where an increase in advertising increases price elasticity and Figure 6.3b to the case where higher advertising lowers price elasticity.[18]

Consider Figure 6.3a first. The $\bar{\pi}_p = 0$ curve shows the optimal price under certainty for any given advertising policy. Note that $\bar{\pi}_p = 0$ is downward sloping. This result

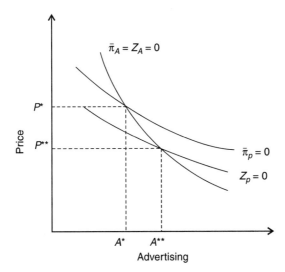

Figure 6.3a The effect of uncertainty in the expected utility model: exogenous uncertainty. Price elasticity increases when advertising increases.

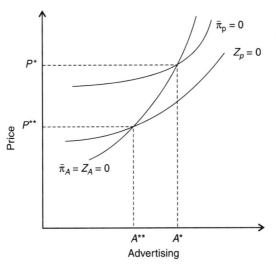

Figure 6.3b The effect of uncertainty in the expected utility model: exogenous uncertainty. Price elasticity decreases when advertising increases.

reflects the fact that the market becomes more price sensitive when advertising increases. Consequently the firm reduces price when advertising increases. Similarly the $\bar{\pi}_A = 0$ curve is also downward sloping. Note that the $\bar{\pi}_A = 0$ curve is steeper than the $\bar{\pi}_p = 0$ curve because of the maximization conditions.[19] The firm's optimal price–advertising policy (p^*, A^*) under certainty is given by the point where the $\bar{\pi}_p = 0$ and $\bar{\pi}_A = 0$ curves intersect.

Similarly, the $Z_A = 0$ curve (see Figure 6.3a) shows the optimal advertising policy under uncertainty for any given price. Note that the $Z_A = 0$ and $\bar{\pi}_A = 0$ curves coincide because advertising does not affect the variability of profits.[20] The $Z_p = 0$ curve is below $\bar{\pi}_p = 0$, reflecting our intuitive argument. Hence uncertainty causes the firm to reduce price and increase advertising if higher advertising makes the market more price sensitive (i.e., $p^{**} < p^*$ and $A^{**} > A^*$).

Proceeding similarly (see Figure 6.3b), we can show that $p^{**} < p^*$ and $A^{**} < A^*$ if higher advertising makes the market less price sensitive.

> **Key Point** *The firm's price and advertising depend crucially on uncertainty. In general, demand uncertainty depends on the phase of the product life cycle and the firm's segmentation policy. Suppose demand uncertainty does not depend on price or advertising. Then the expected utility model implies that the firm always reduces price. However, the firm reduces (increases) advertising depending on whether higher advertising makes the market less (more) price sensitive.*

Multiplicative Uncertainty. The previous analysis made the simplifying assumption that neither price nor advertising affect the volatility of sales volume. The simplest model where both price and advertising affect the variability of sales is $q = f(p, A)u$, where $u > 0$. (Sales must be positive.) In this case advertising is "aggressive" in the sense defined earlier: Higher advertising increases the variance of sales volume. However, higher prices reduce the variance of sales volume. As discussed earlier, the multiplicative uncertainty specification is a reasonable formulation of the sales function for products in the early phase of the life cycle.

How should the firm modify its price–advertising policy when uncertainty is introduced? Intuitively, we expect the risk-averse manager to lower advertising in order to reduce the variability in sales volume and hence the variability in profit. How should the firm adjust price? Suppose lower advertising reduces price elasticity (e.g., an increase in advertising encourages consumer search or price-comparison behavior). Then the firm increases price to increase the unit profit margin and hence profitability. Suppose lower advertising increases price elasticity (e.g., advertising focuses on increasing the degree of product differentiation). In this case, the firm reduces price in order to stimulate demand and offset the reduction in demand caused by the cut in advertising. These intuitive results are correct.

Figures 6.4a and 6.4b present a formal analysis. Figure 6.4a shows the case where higher advertising increases price elasticity. Note that the $Z_A = 0$ and $\bar{\pi}_A = 0$ curves are both downward sloping, reflecting the fact that higher advertising reinforces the effect of a price cut regardless of whether uncertainty is present. Furthermore, the $Z_A = 0$ curve is below the $\bar{\pi}_A = 0$ curve, reflecting the intuitive argument described in the previous paragraph.[21] As in

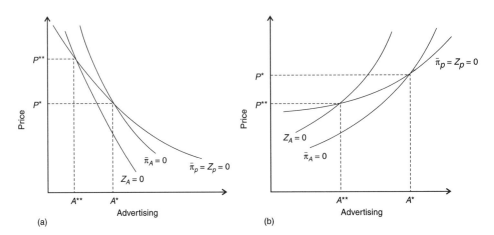

Figure 6.4 The effect of uncertainty in the expected utility model: multiplicative uncertainty. (a) Price elasticity increases when advertising increases. (b) Price elasticity decreases when advertising increases.

the exogenous uncertainty case, the $\bar{\pi}_p = 0$ curve is flatter than the $\bar{\pi}_A = 0$ curve because of the second-order conditions. Interestingly, the $\bar{\pi}_p = 0$ and $Z_p = 0$ curves coincide. That is, for any given advertising level, the firm chooses the same price regardless of whether sales are uncertain. (We discuss the rationale for this result shortly.) Hence the firm chooses a lower advertising policy and charges a higher price when sales are uncertain (i.e., $A^{**} < A^*$ and $p^{**} > p^*$).

Figure 6.4b shows the case where higher advertising reduces price elasticity. In this case the firm advertises less but charges a lower price under uncertainty ($A^{**} < A^*$ and $p^{**} < p^*$).

Why do the $\bar{\pi}_p = 0$ and $Z_p = 0$ curves coincide? The crux of the matter is that the multiplicative uncertainty formulation imposes considerable structure on the sales function. Let $\bar{q}$ denote the average sales for any given price–advertising policy. Let $\sigma(q)$ denote the standard deviation of sales. (Standard deviation measures the degree of uncertainty.) Then $\bar{q}$ and $\sigma(q)$ have a fixed ratio *regardless of the firm's price–advertising policy.*[22]

Generalized Uncertainty. Clearly the exogenous and multiplicative uncertainty specifications are special cases. More general scenarios are feasible. One possibility mentioned earlier is defensive advertising (i.e., higher advertising reduces the uncertainty in sales). This formulation may be appropriate for a product in the maturity phase of the life cycle. Similarly, in contrast to the multiplicative uncertainty model, higher prices could increase demand uncertainty (e.g., potential entrants use the current price as a proxy for long-term profits). These types of scenario can be analyzed using the general model $q = f(p, A) + g(p, A)u$. See Jagpal (1982b) for details.

> **Key Point** *The firm's reaction to uncertainty depends crucially on the precise manner in which price and advertising affect the riskiness of sales. The multiplicative uncertainty formulation is realistic for products in the early stages of the life cycle. Given this scenario, the firm will always reduce advertising under uncertainty. However, the firm will increase (lower) price if an increase in advertising makes the market more (less) price elastic. In general, the effect of uncertainty on price–advertising policy depends on the precise manner in which price affects demand uncertainty and whether advertising is defensive or aggressive.*

Changes in Market Conditions. The previous analysis focused on the effect of demand uncertainty on the risk-averse firm. We now ask: How does the degree of risk aversion affect price–advertising policy? Consider a small startup firm and a large firm facing identical market conditions. Assume in particular that both firms have identical beliefs. [That is, both firms know f and g in the sales function $q = f(p, A) + g(p, A)u$.] In general the small firm is likely to be more risk-averse than the large firm.[23] Intuitively we might expect that the small firm will choose a high price, low advertising policy. This policy is not necessarily correct.

Jagpal (1982b) shows that the effect of an increase in risk aversion is analogous to that of the introduction of demand uncertainty. In particular, this result holds regardless of the firms' tradeoffs of risk and return (i.e., the precise forms of the small and large firms' utility functions) or *the precise form of variability of sales volume*. The latter condition is particularly important for new products, which typically provide highly skewed distributions of sales (i.e., high probabilities of low and negative returns and low probabilities of large returns).

> **Key Point** *The effect of an increase in risk aversion is analogous to that of the introduction of demand uncertainty. Contrary to intuition, the optimal policy for a small firm may not be to charge a higher price and advertise less than a large firm facing the same market conditions. The exact answer depends on the firm's segmentation policy and the stage of the product life cycle.*

Uncertainty and the Advertising–Sales Ratio. An interesting question is: What is the effect of demand uncertainty on the firm's optimal advertising–sales ratio? Because demand is uncertain, the advertising–sales ratio is random. In order to avoid ambiguity, we examine the ratio of advertising to expected sales revenue (a deterministic quantity). Consider the exogenous uncertainty specification. Recall that the firm charges a lower price under uncertainty. However, advertising is higher (lower) depending on whether an increase in advertising makes the market more (less) price elastic.

Intuitively we might expect the risk-averse firm to choose a lower ratio of advertising to expected revenue under uncertainty. However, risk aversion alone is insufficient for this conclusion to hold.[24] The result depends crucially on the precise form of uncertainty (i.e., the stage of the product life cycle) and the effect of the price–advertising policy on the price and advertising elasticities. Suppose these elasticities are constant. (To avoid ambiguity we define the price and advertising elasticities using the expected demand levels.) Then the proposition holds: The firm chooses a lower ratio of advertising to expected revenue under uncertainty.[25] This result also holds for the multiplicative uncertainty case.

An interesting question is: Does the Dorfman–Steiner Theorem hold under uncertainty? The answer is yes, provided demand is defined using an appropriate risk correction.[26]

Key Point *A firm that follows the industry norm for setting advertising budgets is likely to choose suboptimal policies. Except for special cases, we cannot conclude that the risk-averse firm will choose a lower ratio of advertising to expected revenue under uncertainty. A modified Dorfman–Steiner Theorem holds for the expected utility model regardless of the particular form of uncertainty or the shape of the sales function.*

Value-Maximizing Model. So far we have focused on the expected utility model. The analysis did not make specific assumptions about the precise distributions of either demand or cash flow. Furthermore, apart from making the mild assumption of risk aversion, we did not restrict the decision maker's particular tradeoff of risk and return (i.e., the shape of the utility function).

Measuring Risk. Suppose, in contrast, that the decision maker chooses price and advertising to maximize the firm's stock price. Note that there is a fundamental difference between the treatments of uncertainty in the expected utility model and the stock market model. The latter explicitly incorporates two key aspects of institutional reality. First, the firm is not an anthropomorphic entity with a single utility function. Many stockholders own the firm and each stockholder has a different tradeoff between risk and return (i.e., utility function). Second, stockholders typically diversify their holdings across many firms. In particular, stockholders are primarily interested in the risks and returns of their investment portfolios and not the volatility of any given firm's earnings per se.

Consider the current-effects price–advertising model and assume that the objective is to maximize the firm's stock value. Suppose the firm chooses a particular price–advertising policy; in particular, the average sales volume for this policy is 100 units. (We assume for simplicity that the firm and the stock market have common beliefs. In other words, information is symmetric.) How will the stock market value this uncertain demand? Recall that the stock market is risk-averse.

How will the stock market value the firm? Let us compare two demand scenarios conditional on the firm's chosen price–advertising policy. Consider gamble A, which provides the firm with an expected demand of 100 units, and gamble B, which provides the firm with a guaranteed demand of 100 units. Because investors are risk-averse, the stock market will always prefer B. (Recall that price is fixed.) Suppose the stock market is indifferent between gamble C, which provides the firm with a guaranteed demand of 90 units, and gamble A, which is uncertain and provides an expected demand of 100 units. We say that the *certainty-equivalent demand* is 90 units. Given this risk adjustment, valuing the firm is straightforward. We can simply proceed as in the certainty case using the certainty-equivalent demand (90 units) instead of the average demand (100 units) for the given price–advertising policy.

Note that the effect of the risk adjustment in demand on the firm's stock value *always* depends on the firm's marketing policies. The key question is: What factors determine the risk adjustment? We expect that the risk adjustment will be larger if the stock market becomes more risk-averse. If the economy as a whole becomes more uncertain, stockholders' portfolio risks will be high even after stockholders diversify their holdings. If other factors are held constant, the risk adjustment for a firm that faces higher demand uncertainty will be higher than that for a firm that faces less demand uncertainty. Finally, the risk adjustment will be larger for firms in cyclical industries. As shown later, these intuitive arguments are correct.

One-Period Capital Asset Pricing Model. Consider the one-period capital asset pricing model (CAPM).[27] Let $\bar{\pi}$ denote the firm's expected profit for a given price–advertising policy and $\bar{\pi}_c = \bar{\pi} - R$ the expected profit corresponding to the certainty-equivalent demand, where R is the implicit risk premium by which the stock market reduces the firm's expected profit. Then stockholders at time 0 behave as if they expect the firm to earn a risk-free profit of $\bar{\pi}_c$ at the end of time 1. Let r denote the one-period risk-free interest rate. Hence the firm's value at time 0 is simply the net present value of the risk-free profit $\bar{\pi}_c$ [i.e., $V = \bar{\pi}_c/(1+r)$, where V denotes stock value].

Measuring the Risk Premium. We now provide a more formal analysis of the factors that determine the risk premium R, which is known as systematic risk. Let a denote the market price of risk. Roughly speaking, a measures the degree of risk aversion in the stock market.[28] a goes up when the market is more risk-averse. Let $\sigma(\pi)$ denote the standard deviation of the firm's profit for a given price–advertising policy. In our model we assumed that costs are constant; consequently $\sigma(\pi)$ depends primarily on the firm's marketing policy and the pattern of demand uncertainty.[29] Let $\sigma(R_m)$ denote the standard deviation of the return on the market portfolio. Roughly speaking, $\sigma(R_m)$ reflects the volatility of a diversified portfolio that includes all assets in the economy. Let ρ denote the correlation between π and R_m. Then ρ measures the degree of cyclicality in the firm's earnings. The firm's systematic risk R is defined by the simple multiplicative relationship $R = a\rho\sigma(\pi)\sigma(R_m)$, which confirms our intuitive arguments.

Firm-Specific (Idiosyncratic) Risk. What happens if demand (and hence profit) fluctuations are purely random? In this case $\rho = 0$ and $R = 0$. Thus the stock market values the firm solely on the basis of the firm's expected future profit. Note that the market does not apply a risk-adjustment correction, regardless of the volatility of the firm's demand [i.e., the value of $\sigma(\pi)$]. This result appears counterintuitive. However, there is a simple explanation. In this case ($\rho = 0$) the firm's cash flows do not fluctuate with the economy as a whole. Thus stockholders can completely eliminate the firm's risk by holding a diversified portfolio. Contrast the standard expected utility model in which the firm does not have any opportunity to diversify and reduce risk.

Note that the definition of risk is fundamentally different in the expected utility and stock market models and has important marketing policy implications. In the stock market model, an increase in the volatility of the firm's cash flow [$\sigma(\pi)$] has no effect on the firm's price–advertising policy if $\rho = 0$. In the expected utility model, the firm always changes policy when the volatility of cash flow increases.

> ***Key Point*** *The stock market and expected utility models define risk differently. The stock market model explicitly recognizes that the firm has many owners who have diversification opportunities outside the firm. Consequently, if demand fluctuations for the firm's product are random ($\rho = 0$), stockholders can eliminate uncertainty by diversifying. The stock market model implies that both the degree of cyclicality in demand and the volatility of the firm's cash flow are relevant for decision making. The expected utility model, in contrast, defines risk purely in terms of the variability of the firm's cash flow.*

Market Risk. Consider the effects of uncertainty and risk aversion in the one-period capital asset pricing model where the firm's controllable variables are price and advertising. Jagpal (1982b) shows that, as in the expected utility model, the effect of introducing uncertainty is analogous to the effect of an increase in risk aversion. In many cases, the effects of changes in market conditions on price–advertising policy are similar for both the expected utility and stock market models. However, the stock market model leads to more interpretable results in the generalized uncertainty case.[30]

> ***Key Point*** *Both the expected utility and stock market models lead to similar implications for price–advertising policy when uncertainty is exogenous or multiplicative. However, only the stock market model provides well-defined results for the generalized uncertainty specification.*

6.4 CHOOSING PRICE AND ADVERTISING UNDER UNCERTAINTY: THE MULTIPERIOD CASE

The previous section focused on single-period advertising models where demand is uncertain. In many cases, however, advertising can have carryover effects because of the goodwill created (e.g., advertising stimulates habitual buying). In a classic paper, Nerlove and Arrow (1962) developed a deterministic dynamic model in which the decision maker chooses price–advertising policy to maximize the net present value of the firm's profits. We shall briefly describe the Nerlove–Arrow model and its extensions. We shall then propose a general multiperiod model that allows for general patterns of demand uncertainty; in particular, we shall use both the expected utility and the multiperiod capital asset pricing valuation frameworks.

The Nerlove–Arrow Model (1962)

Let G denote the advertising goodwill at time t, p price, and A advertising. For notational convenience we do not use a subscript for time. Let the demand at time t be $D = \phi(G, p)$ and G_0 denote the advertising goodwill at time 0. Assume that demand increases with goodwill and that returns to goodwill are strictly diminishing.

Now the advertising goodwill depreciates over time because of consumer forgetting and other effects. See Zielske (1959) for experimental evidence and Vidale and Wolfe (1957) for a controlled market study. Hence the rate of change of goodwill ($\dot{G}$) is the sum of two effects: a gain because of current advertising and a loss caused by the decay in goodwill. Nerlove and Arrow (1962) use the simple model $\dot{G} = A - \delta G$, where δ is the constant proportional rate at which goodwill depreciates over time. Note that even though advertising has a linear effect on goodwill, returns to goodwill are strictly diminishing.

Let the firm's profit at time t be $\pi = p\phi(G, p) - C(q) - A$, where q denotes the sales volume and C is the cost function. Then the firm chooses price–advertising policy dynamically to maximize the net present value of the profit stream π over an infinite planning period.

The Nerlove–Arrow model provides two important insights. First, the Dorfman–Steiner Theorem holds in a dynamic setting (see Nerlove and Arrow 1962, p. 134, for details). Second, and important from a managerial viewpoint, the firm always chooses advertising to reach the optimal goodwill level as rapidly as possible.

Suppose the current stock of goodwill is too low (i.e., $G_0 < G^*$, where G^* denotes the optimal goodwill). Then the optimal policy is to advertise as much as possible (strictly, an infinite amount).[31] See Nerlove and Arrow (1962, Theorem 1). Suppose the current stock of goodwill is too high (i.e., $G_0 > G^*$). Then the firm does not advertise at all and allows goodwill to depreciate until the optimal goodwill is reached. In both cases, once the optimal goodwill is reached, the firm advertises just enough to offset the loss from the decay in goodwill (i.e., $A = \delta G^*$). (See Nerlove and Arrow 1962, Theorem 2.)

Key Point *The Dorfman–Steiner Theorem holds under certainty even if advertising has a dynamic carryover effect. If goodwill is too low, the firm increases advertising as rapidly as possible to attain the optimum level. If advertising goodwill is too high, the firm advertises as little as possible until the optimum goodwill is reached. In the special case of a new product ($G_0 = 0$), the Nerlove–Arrow model implies that advertising should be very high during the introductory phase of the product life cycle. Once the optimal goodwill is reached, only maintenance advertising is necessary.*

A General Goodwill Model of Uncertainty

The Nerlove–Arrow (1962) paper has spawned considerable research on the dynamics of advertising. Most of this literature focuses on the deterministic case. Stochastic models typically assume that price is fixed and that the firm is risk-neutral. Sethi (1977), Little (1979), and Jagpal (1982b) provide detailed reviews of this literature.

We now present a model that focuses on the effects of risk aversion and uncertainty in a dynamic market where both price and advertising are control variables (see Jagpal 1982b).

Using the previous notation, let the demand function be $q = f(G, p, A) + g(G, p, A)u$, where u is stochastic. In contrast to the Nerlove–Arrow model, the firm's current advertising affects the firm's current demand. This specification adds realism even in the deterministic case where $u \equiv 0$ (see Dehez and Jacquemin 1975). The firm's advertising policy now affects the customer retention rate (e.g., by providing reinforcement), the rate of influx of new customers, and the price elasticity of demand.[32] From a managerial viewpoint, the model is realistic because the firm must follow a gradual path in order to reach the optimal goodwill level.[33]

Dehez and Jacquemin (1975) consider a stochastic model where the firm's marketing mix does not affect the variability of demand (i.e., $g \equiv 1$). We shall focus on the general case where the variability of demand depends on price, advertising, and goodwill (see Jagpal 1982). As discussed previously, the form of demand uncertainty varies over the product life cycle and depends on the firm's segmentation policies. For analytical tractability, assume that the unit production cost c is constant. Then the firm's profit at time t is $\pi(t) = (p-c)(f+gu) - A - F$, where F denotes fixed costs. Assume as in Nerlove–Arrow (1962) that the planning period is infinite.[34]

What is the objective of the risk-averse firm facing uncertainty in a multiperiod setting? The firm can choose dynamic price–advertising policies to maximize the net present value of the stream of expected utilities from future profits.[35] Alternatively, the firm can maximize its stock value. In this case, the firm maximizes the net present value of the stream of certainty equivalents from future profits using the risk-free interest rate. In our analysis we shall consider both the expected utility and the stock market models; in particular, we shall assume that the multiperiod capital asset pricing model is the correct stock market valuation model[36] (see Constantinides 1978 for details).

The Expected Utility Model

Exogenous Uncertainty. Begin with the expected utility model and the exogenous uncertainty case; that is, advertising does not affect the variability of demand or profit. Consequently the long-run advertising elasticity is unaffected by the degree of risk aversion.[37] Although price does not affect the variability of demand, high prices increase the variability of profit. The risk-averse firm therefore tends to reduce prices. Consequently the ratio of advertising to expected revenue (henceforth *advertising–sales ratio*) falls. Thus, given identical market conditions, a small (i.e., more risk-averse) firm should choose a lower advertising–sales ratio than a large firm. These results show that a firm should not follow the industry norm for setting the advertising budget, especially if the firms in the industry are of highly unequal size.

Similarly, because goodwill does not affect the variability of profit, the goodwill elasticity is unaffected by the firm's risk aversion. Hence the ratio of optimal goodwill to expected revenue (henceforth *goodwill–sales ratio*) decreases when demand is uncertain.[38] Thus, given identical market conditions, a small (i.e., more risk-averse) firm will invest less in building goodwill than a large firm.

Multiplicative Uncertainty. Consider the multiplicative uncertainty case. This specification implies that higher prices reduce the variability of demand but higher advertising makes demand more uncertain (e.g., the product is new). Furthermore, for any set of marketing policies, *the ratio of expected demand to the standard deviation of demand is fixed*. Consequently, the advertising and goodwill elasticities do not depend on the firm's risk aversion. Thus we get the same results as in the exogenous uncertainty case.[39]

Generalized Uncertainty. The generalized uncertainty case is more interesting. The effects of risk aversion on the advertising–sales ratio and the goodwill–sales ratio depend on the precise manner in which price, advertising, and goodwill affect demand variability.[40] In particular, all elasticities (i.e., price, advertising, and goodwill) are stochastic and depend on the degree of risk aversion. Several interesting scenarios can be constructed and examined on a case-by-case basis.

Suppose that, in contrast to the exogenous uncertainty case, high prices reduce the variability of profit. Then the risk-averse firm increases price. Consequently, both the advertising–sales ratio and the goodwill–sales ratio tend to increase. Suppose higher advertising decreases the variability of demand (e.g., the firm uses a defensive advertising strategy for a product in the maturity phase of the life cycle). Then the long-run advertising elasticity and the advertising–sales ratio tend to increase. Similarly, if the variability of demand decreases with goodwill, the goodwill–sales ratio tends to increase. Note that, depending on the firm's segmentation policies and the precise way in which the firm's marketing mix affects the variability of demand, demand uncertainty can increase the firm's advertising–sales and goodwill–sales ratios.[41] Finally, regardless of the precise form of uncertainty, the Dorfman–Steiner Theorem holds. In particular, the advertising–sales ratio = (risk-adjusted long-run advertising elasticity)/(risk-adjusted price elasticity). Furthermore, the goodwill–sales ratio = (risk-adjusted goodwill elasticity)/(risk-adjusted price elasticity).[42]

Suppose the goodwill depreciation rate δ increases (e.g., a larger fraction of the firm's customers switches to competitors' brands). The firm's marginal opportunity cost of investment in goodwill increases.[43] Consequently the firm's optimal goodwill–sales ratio falls regardless of the type of uncertainty. However, neither the risk-adjusted long-run advertising elasticity nor the risk-adjusted price elasticity change. Hence the advertising–sales ratio remains unchanged as in the certainty model.

Multiperiod Capital Asset Pricing Model

Consider the multiperiod capital asset pricing model. The results are analogous to those in the expected utility model, with one important difference.[44] The cyclicality of cash flows is the key determinant of risk in the CAPM; in the expected utility model only the variability of cash flow determines risk. Suppose Firms 1 and 2 operate in the same industry and face identical market conditions (i.e., for any given marketing mix, both firms have identical cash flow distributions). Then the expected utility model implies that Firms 1 and 2 will choose identical advertising–sales and goodwill–sales ratios provided they have the same utility functions. Suppose, however, that Firm 1 targets a more cyclical segment than Firm 2 does. Then the CAPM implies that Firm 1 has a higher marginal cost of investing in advertising or goodwill. Hence Firm 1 chooses a lower advertising–sales ratio and a lower goodwill–sales ratio than Firm 2.

Key Point *The Dorfman–Steiner Theorem holds for multiperiod advertising models regardless of the form of uncertainty or the choice of valuation framework (i.e., the multiperiod expected utility model or the multiperiod capital asset pricing model). Firms should not choose their advertising budgets on the basis of the average advertising–sales ratio for firms in the industry. For the additive and multiplicative uncertainty specifications, risk aversion does not affect the goodwill elasticity. Consequently, the effects of uncertainty on the advertising–sales ratio and the goodwill–sales ratio are similar. For the generalized uncertainty case (which may be particularly appropriate for products in the maturity phase of the life cycle), the advertising–sales ratio and the goodwill–sales ratio depend on the precise form with which the firm's marketing mix affects demand uncertainty.*

Managerial Implications

Consider a new product introduction ($G_0 = 0$) or more generally the case where the goodwill at time 0 is less than the optimal level ($G_0 < G^*$). Suppose the decision maker is myopic and chooses policy to maximize short-run performance. For example, in the expected utility model, the manager chooses policy to maximize the expected utility of current profits. We expect the manager to underadvertise regardless of the particular form of demand uncertainty. The reason is that the manager ignores the future goodwill effect of advertising. The effect of myopic decision making on pricing is more interesting. Suppose lower advertising makes the market less price elastic. Then the myopic decision maker will charge a higher price than the optimal in order to increase current performance. Thus the myopic price is too high. If lower advertising makes the market more price sensitive, we expect the myopic price to be too low.

The first part of the argument is correct for both the expected utility and CAPM models: The myopic decision maker always underadvertises regardless of how the marketing mix affects demand uncertainty.[45] The second part of the argument applies to the CAPM model for all scenarios. All that is necessary is to replace the ambiguous phrase "elasticity of demand" (recall that demand is random) by "elasticity of the certainty-equivalent demand." In contrast, the second part of the argument applies conditionally in the expected utility model. Suppose uncertainty is multiplicative (e.g., the product is in the early stages of the life cycle). Then the elasticity of demand is nonstochastic.[46] Assume that the product is highly differentiated from competitive products (i.e., higher advertising decreases price elasticity). The myopic manager will overprice as predicted.[47] These results—underadvertising and overpricing—imply that the firm's expected volume-based market share will be too low, and provide some justification for the use of market share as a measure of performance. If the new product is a "me-too" product or advertising encourages comparative shopping, higher advertising could increase price elasticity. In this case, the myopic manager underprices and underadvertises. Consequently, the effect on the expected market share is ambiguous.

Suppose uncertainty is exogenous. Then the price elasticity of demand is random. Consequently we can only conclude that the myopic firm underprices if higher advertising reduces the price elasticity of expected demand.[48] Note that, in contrast to the multiplicative uncertainty case, the effect of myopic decision making on the firm's volume-based expected market share is ambiguous in the expected utility model.

We now show these arguments graphically (see Figures 6.5a and 6.5b). The superscript "m" denotes the myopic firm and "O" denotes the optimizing firm. For convenience we present the results for the multiperiod CAPM. The $W_p = 0$ curve shows the optimal prices for different fixed advertising levels in the myopic model. The $H_p = 0$ curve is defined similarly for the optimal model. Note that the $W_p = 0$ and $H_p = 0$ curves coincide. This result occurs because price does not have dynamic effects. The $W_A = 0$ curve shows the optimal advertising levels for given prices in the myopic model. As discussed in the one-period model, the $W_A = 0$ curve is steeper than the $W_p = 0$ curve. The $H_A = 0$ curve shows the optimal advertising levels for given prices in the optimal model. Note that the $H_A = 0$ curve is always to the right of $W_A = 0$, reflecting the fact that the myopic manager does not consider the future profit that accrues from building goodwill. Thus the myopic firm underadvertises ($A^m < A^O$). However, the myopic firm sets price too low (high)

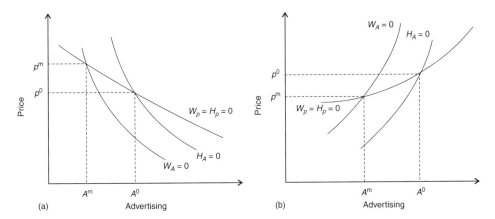

Figure 6.5 Myopic and optimal price–advertising policy in a multiperiod CAPM. (a) Higher advertising increases the price elasticity of the certainty-equivalent demand. (b) Higher advertising reduces price elasticity of the certainty-equivalent demand. Note: The superscript m denotes myopic policy and the superscript O denotes optimal policy.

depending on whether the price elasticity of the certainty-equivalent demand decreases (increases) when advertising is increased.

> ***Key Point*** *The myopic firm always underadvertises when goodwill has a carryover effect and demand is uncertain. The effect of myopic pricing is well defined in the multiperiod CAPM regardless of the precise form of uncertainty. In contrast, the effect of myopic pricing in the expected utility model is only well defined if uncertainty is exogenous or multiplicative. In general, myopic decision making can lead to excessively high market shares during a new product's introductory phase.*

Model Extensions

The previous analysis made several highly simplifying assumptions. We treated goodwill as a capital stock that strictly depreciates over time. Although this assumption may be reasonable for a mature product, advertising often stimulates word-of-mouth activity for a new product and hence increases goodwill. Thus a new product model should incorporate two effects: the loss through goodwill depreciation and the gain through the diffusion effect of advertising. Ozga (1960), Gould (1970), and Glaister (1974) develop such models under certainty. Our methodology can be extended to make these models stochastic. We did not consider the effects of changes in exogenous factors (e.g., income and interest rates) on demand. This extension is straightforward: The main effect of incorporating dynamic exogenous factors in the model is that the optimal advertising–sales ratio and the optimal goodwill–sales ratio now vary over time.[49] Our model does not allow price to have a dynamic carryover effect. This assumption is unrealistic for new products (e.g., the trial rate during a given period affects repeat purchase behavior in the future). Furthermore, even for established products, consumers use previous prices to form reference prices for current purchases.

A General Dynamic Representation. Although the generalized uncertainty model allows the firm's marketing mix to affect demand volatility, the representation of uncertainty is not complete from a dynamic viewpoint. In the multiperiod utility model, we assumed that the stochastic disturbance term has a stationary distribution (i.e., the disturbances are essentially random drawings from a common distribution). In the multiperiod CAPM we made the further assumption that the joint distribution of the stochastic disturbance term in demand (u_t) and the return on the market portfolio (R_t) is stable over time. These assumptions do not allow for general stochastic patterns over the product life cycle or general stochastic macroeconomic effects. Incorporating such nonstationarities adds considerably to model complexity.

Managerial Performance and Incentive Systems. The previous analysis simply compared the *initial* price and advertising policies chosen by the myopic and optimizing decision makers, respectively. From a managerial viewpoint, the key issue is to compare the *dynamic* price and advertising decisions chosen. For example, will the myopic brand manager of a new product continue to underadvertise over the product life cycle? What long-run pricing policy will the myopic brand manager choose? The answers to these questions are extremely relevant to the firm for designing appropriate performance measures and incentive systems. We now propose a general model to address these issues.

In order to answer these questions, we need more specific information. Intuitively we expect the particular form of uncertainty and the shape of the demand function to be crucial. This is indeed the case. Suppose neither advertising nor price affects the customer retention rate. However, the marginal productivity of advertising depends on price. Furthermore, uncertainty is exogenous [i.e., $D = \phi_1(p, A) + \phi_2(G) + u$, where u is the stochastic disturbance term].

Begin with the multiperiod CAPM. Suppose an increase in advertising reduces price elasticity. Recall that the price elasticity is defined using the certainty equivalent of demand. Then the myopic decision maker always underprices and underadvertises over the product life cycle.[50] Thus the myopic market share (volume-based or revenue-based) at any time is a poor proxy for long-term profitability.

What is the intuition behind these results? For analytical convenience we shall analyze the problem using (infinitesimal) discrete time periods, where t_0 refers to the starting point. Let the goodwill at time 0 be $\bar{G}$, "m" index myopic decisions, and "O" optimal decisions. Let p_1^m denote the myopic price in period 1, A_2^O the optimal advertising in period 2, and so on. We have already shown that when uncertainty is exogenous the myopic firm underprices and underadvertises in period 1 (i.e., $p_1^m < p_1^O$ and $A_1^m < A_1^O$). Furthermore, these results hold regardless of the form of the demand function [i.e., the shape of $\phi(p, A, G)$].

Consider decision making in period 2. We know that the myopic decision maker underadvertises in period 1. Hence the myopic goodwill at the beginning of period 2 is too low ($G_1^m < G_1^O$). Our assumption of additive separability is now crucial: In particular, the tradeoff between price and advertising in period 2 does not depend on the initial goodwill (G_1). Consequently, the myopic firm underprices and underadvertises[51] in period 2 (i.e.,

$p_2^m < p_2^O$ and $A_2^m < A_2^O$). These results ensure that the goodwill at the beginning of period 3 is too low ($G_2^m < G_2^O$). Hence the cycle continues (i.e., $p_t^m < p_t^O$ and $A_t^m < A_t^O$ for all t).

What happens if uncertainty is multiplicative? (That is, $D = [\phi_1(p, A) + \phi_2(G)]u$, where u is stochastic.) This specification is more realistic for new products—see our discussion of the single-period model. Following the same approach as in the exogenous uncertainty case, we can show that the myopic manager always underprices and underadvertises over the product life cycle.[52]

The previous uncertainty specifications impose considerable structure on demand. In particular, the exogenous uncertainty model assumes that goodwill does not affect the variability of demand. The multiplicative uncertainty model assumes that both expected demand and the variability of demand increase with goodwill. We know that an increase in goodwill stimulates expected future demand. However, depending on the focus of corporate strategy and the stage in the product life cycle, an increase in goodwill can stabilize future demand (i.e., reduce demand uncertainty). The generalized uncertainty model allows for this scenario and other stochastic demand specifications.

Using the previous approach, we can show that the multiperiod CAPM implies that the myopic firm underprices and underadvertises regardless of how the marketing mix affects the variability of demand.[53] In contrast, the results for the expected utility model are less well defined. Consider the exogenous uncertainty specification of the multiperiod expected utility model. Assume that the firm's willingness to take risks increases with the firm's wealth level. More precisely, the Arrow–Pratt coefficient of absolute risk aversion decreases with wealth.[54] Then the myopic firm underadvertises and underprices over time.[55] If uncertainty is multiplicative or generalized, the tradeoff between price and advertising in a given period depends upon the initial goodwill at the beginning of the period. Hence the results are inherently indeterminate.

> ***Key Point*** *The effect of demand uncertainty on myopic decision making depends on the precise form of uncertainty, the shape of the demand function, and the multiperiod valuation model. Suppose the demand function is additively separable in goodwill and higher advertising reduces price elasticity. If uncertainty is exogenous, the myopic decision maker underprices and underadvertises over time, regardless of whether the multiperiod CAPM or the multiperiod expected utility models hold. If uncertainty is multiplicative or generalized (e.g., an increase in goodwill stabilizes future demand), only the multiperiod CAPM results are well defined. In particular, the myopic decision maker underprices and underadvertises over time.*

Limitations. Our model assumes that the goodwill depreciation rate is constant over time. In practice this decay rate is probabilistic and depends on competitors' marketing policies, the quality of the firm's advertising message (which is likely to vary over time), and the product's stage in the life cycle. Our model also assumes that goodwill is nonstochastic. Incorporating these types of stochasticity in the model leads to considerable analytical difficulty and intractability in the general risk-aversion case (see Tapiero 1978 and Sethi 1979). Finally, our model is strictly appropriate for a monopolistic firm. Future research should develop stochastic game-theoretic oligopoly models allowing for risk aversion. Albright and Winston (1979) deal with the risk-neutral case.

6.5 CHOOSING ADVERTISING POLICY UNDER UNCERTAINTY: THE MULTIPRODUCT CASE

We now turn to a key issue: the multiproduct firm's choice of advertising policy under uncertainty. The literature in this area is sparse. Following is a brief discussion of the model in Jagpal (1982a).

We shall refer to the products as brands recognizing that the brands can be complements or substitutes. The firm's problem is to set the advertising budget for each brand to maximize product-line performance, while explicitly recognizing that the advertising for any given brand stochastically affects the demand for other brands in the product line. For example, advertising for Brand 1 can affect both the expected demand and the variability of demand for Brand 2; in particular, the directions of these effects need not be symmetric.

A General Stochastic Specification

For analytical tractability consider a current-effects model, and assume that the firm markets two brands labeled 1 and 2, respectively. Let the demand for Brand 1 be $s_1 = \alpha_1(A_1, A_2) + \beta_1(A_1, A_2)u_1$, where A_1 denotes Brand 1's advertising, A_2 Brand 2's advertising, s_1 is demand for Brand 1, u_1 is a stochastic term, and α_1 and β_1 are deterministic functions. Similarly define the demand for Brand 2 as $s_2 = \alpha_2(A_1, A_2) + \beta_2(A_1, A_2)u_2$. Note in particular that u_1 and u_2 are correlated. (Recall that Brands 1 and 2 need not belong to the same product class.)

This specification allows for general stochastic patterns of substitution and complementarity across the firm's product line. For example, if Brands 1 and 2 are different brands of toothpaste, the two brands are substitutes.[56] Alternatively, if Brand 1 is a brand of toothpaste, Brand 2 is a brand of soap, and both brands are sold under the corporate logo, the two brands are likely to be complementary.[57]

More important, our specification allows for general stochastic cross-product advertising effects. If uncertainty is exogenous ($\beta_1 = \beta_2 = 1$), the firm's advertising policies do not affect the variabilities of demand for either product. If uncertainty is multiplicative ($\alpha_1 = \alpha_2 = 0$), the stochastic cross-product effects depend purely on whether the products are substitutes or complements. Thus, if the brands are complements, an increase in advertising by Brand 1 increases the variability of demand for both brands. Similarly, if the brands are substitutes, an increase in advertising by Brand 1 increases the variability of demand for Brand 1 but stabilizes the demand for Brand 2. More general scenarios are possible (see Jagpal 1982a).

Two additional assumptions are necessary for analytical tractability.[58] Assume as in the single-product analysis that the marginal costs of production (c_1 and c_2, respectively) are constant. However, in contrast to the previous single-product models, assume that the prices of both brands (p_1 and p_2, respectively) are predetermined.

A Stock Market Model

Begin with the stock market valuation model. Proceeding as in the one-product case, let $\hat{s}_1$ and $\hat{s}_2$, respectively, denote the certainty-equivalent demands for Brands 1 and

2 corresponding to any particular policy. Then the certainty-equivalent gross profits for Brands 1 and 2, respectively, are $\hat{\pi}_1 = (p_1 - c_1)\hat{s}_1 - A_1$ and $\hat{\pi}_2 = (p_2 - c_2)\hat{s}_2 - A_2$. Suppose the fixed costs for the product line are F. Then the firm's certainty-equivalent profit for the product line is $\hat{\pi} = [(p_1 - c_1)\hat{s}_1 - A_1] + [(p_2 - c_2)\hat{s}_2 - A_2] - F$. That is, the stock market behaves as if it expects the firm to earn a guaranteed profit of $\hat{\pi}$ at the end of the period. Consequently, the firm's stock value at the beginning of the period is simply the net present value of the *certainty* profit $\hat{\pi}$ discounted at the risk-free interest rate[59] [i.e., $V = \hat{\pi}/(1 + r)$, where V denotes stock price and r is the risk-free interest rate].

Before we discuss the impacts of uncertainty and risk aversion on the firm's advertising policies, let us reexamine the meanings of $\hat{s}_1$ and $\hat{s}_2$. Let $\bar{s}_1$ and $\bar{s}_2$, respectively, denote the expected demands for Brands 1 and 2. Then, as in the one-product model, the certainty-equivalent demand for a given product is less than the expected demand for that product because the stock market is risk-averse (i.e., $\hat{s}_i < \bar{s}_i$). However, the risk adjustment ($\bar{s}_i - \hat{s}_i$) for any product i is based purely on the covariance between that product's demand and the return on the market. *In particular, the degree of correlatedness between the demands for the two brands (product lines) has no effect on the firm's stock value.*

At first glance this result appears counterintuitive. However, the anomaly is easy to resolve. Recall that stockholders hold diversified portfolios and can diversify more cheaply than the firm. Consequently diversification per se does not add to a firm's value or subtract from it. Therefore, the firm's stock value is simply the sum of the net present values of the two brands, a principle known as value additivity (see Brealey and Myers 1988, pp. 140–41 for a discussion of the value-additivity principle).

Global Effect of Uncertainty

Suppose the two brands are in the early stages of their respective life cycles. In particular, the multiplicative uncertainty model holds for both brands. What is the effect of simultaneously introducing uncertainty into both demand equations? We refer to this effect as the *global effect of uncertainty*. The answer depends on whether the brands are complements or substitutes.

Consider the case of complements. The multiplicative uncertainty specification implies that an increase in advertising by any given brand increases the variability of demand for both brands, provided advertising for the other brand is held fixed. This implication suggests that the firm should reduce advertising for both brands (and hence product-line advertising) when uncertainty is introduced. However, this conclusion is premature: We need to recognize that optimal decision making requires the firm to adjust the advertising policies simultaneously for both brands.[60] Suppose a decrease in advertising by brand j reinforces the risk-reducing effect of a decrease in advertising by brand i (i.e., the advertising interaction effects are positive). In this case, the intuition holds.

If the two brands are substitutes, an increase in advertising by any given brand increases the variability of demand for that brand but reduces the variability of demand for the other brand. Hence we expect the results to be ambiguous. This intuitive argument is correct. We can only conclude that both brands cannot increase their respective advertising budgets when uncertainty is introduced. One interesting implication is that product-line advertising for substitutes (e.g., two brands of a new product) can increase when uncertainty is globally introduced.

Marginal Effect of Uncertainty

How should advertising policy be modified if the demand for a given brand (say Brand 1) becomes more uncertain?[61] We refer to this effect as the *marginal effect of uncertainty*. Suppose the two brands are complementary. Then, as in the global uncertainty case, we expect the advertising for both brands to decrease if the advertising interaction effect is positive. Suppose the brands are substitutes and the interaction effect is negative. Now an increase in demand uncertainty for Brand 1 should lead to a reduction in advertising for that brand. However, advertising for the substitute brand should increase in order to further reduce the variability of demand for Brand 1. These intuitive results hold.[62]

> ***Key Point***   *Suppose the firm launches complementary products simultaneously (i.e., uncertainty is multiplicative) and that the advertising interaction effects are positive. Then the stock market model implies that the firm reduces advertising for each brand when demand is uncertain. If the firm launches competing brands simultaneously, the firm may need to increase product-line advertising because of uncertainty. In general, the firm must revise advertising policy for the entire product line even if demand uncertainty changes for one brand only. Paradoxically, an increase in demand uncertainty for a given brand can lead the firm to increase advertising for that brand in order to maximize product-line performance.*

More General Scenarios

The previous analysis assumed that both brands were in the introductory phases of their respective life cycles. More general scenarios can occur. For example, suppose that Brand 1 is in the introductory phase of the life cycle (i.e., demand uncertainty is multiplicative). However, Brand 2 is in the maturity phase and gears its advertising towards increasing the customer retention rate rather than expanding the market (i.e., demand uncertainty is generalized). Scenarios of this sort can be analyzed using a more general framework (see Jagpal 1982a). We can also conduct additional comparative statics experiments to determine the effects of other parameter shifts (e.g., an increase in advertising productivity for Brand 1) on product-line advertising policy.

The Expected Utility Model

Consider the expected utility model. Let π_1 and π_2, respectively, denote the random profits for Brands 1 and 2 given any product-line advertising policy. Then the firm chooses advertising policy to maximize the expected utility of the product-line profit $\pi_1 + \pi_2$. Now, in contrast to investors in the stock market, the decision maker does not hold a diversified portfolio of assets. Consequently the firm cannot value each brand separately using the value-additivity principle. *Note that, in contrast to the stock market model, correlatedness of demand for different products per se has a strategic effect on risk for the expected utility–maximizer.*

How will the expected utility–maximizer change advertising when uncertainty is introduced globally or changes marginally for a given product? Unfortunately, because the firm cannot evaluate the riskiness of each product separately (contrast the asset pricing model), the results are indeterminate even for simple classes of utility function.[63]

Key Point *The expected utility model does not allow the owners of the firm or the brand manager to diversify outside the firm. Hence the firm cannot value each brand separately as in the value maximization model. Consequently, the effect of demand uncertainty on product-line advertising is ambiguous.*

6.6 A DUOPOLY MODEL OF ADVERTISING UNDER UNCERTAINTY

So far we have implicitly assumed that the firm is a monopolist; in particular, we have not allowed for competitive reaction. We now discuss a simple one-period duopoly advertising model under uncertainty (see Jagpal 1994). Because of space constraints, we consider the stock market model and focus on the multiplicative uncertainty specification (e.g., both brands are new to the market). Jagpal (1994) examines more general uncertainty specifications and compares the stock market and expected utility models.

Suppose Firm 1 produces Brand 1 and Firm 2 produces Brand 2. For analytical tractability, assume that unit production costs (c_1 and c_2, respectively) are constant and that product prices (p_1 and p_2, respectively) are predetermined. Costs and prices need not be symmetric across firms. In our analysis we shall assume a game-theoretic framework; in particular, we assume that the competitors make advertising decisions simultaneously and do not collude.[64]

Let the demand for brand i be $d_i = g_i(A_1, A_2)u_i$, where A_1 and A_2, respectively, denote the advertising policies of Brands 1 and 2 and the u_i are stochastic disturbance terms. Let the unit contribution margins be $m_i = p_i - c_i$. Then firm i chooses its advertising policy A_i to maximize its stock price V^i.

Reaction Functions

Consider Firm 1's advertising decision. We approach the problem in the following descriptively unrealistic way[65] (see Figure 6.6). Suppose Firm 2 chooses a given advertising policy (say $1,000). Then Firm 1 chooses that advertising policy that maximizes Firm 1's value given that Firm 2's advertising is $1,000. Proceeding similarly, Firm 1 can determine the set of optimal advertising policies corresponding to different levels of advertising spending by Firm 2. Let the $V_1^1 = 0$ curves in Figures 6.6a and 6.6b describe these results. The $V_1^1 = 0$ curve is known as Firm 1's *reaction function* and simply describes Firm 1's optimal advertising decisions given particular choices of advertising policy by Firm 2. (We shall discuss the shape of the $V_1^1 = 0$ curve shortly.)

Firm 2 performs a similar analysis. Let $V_2^2 = 0$ denote Firm 2's reaction function. Now it is reasonable to argue that the noncooperative game has a solution at the point where the two reaction curves $V_1^1 = 0$ and $V_2^2 = 0$ intersect. This point is known as the Nash equilibrium.[66]

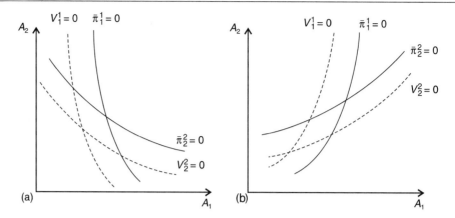

Figure 6.6 The Nash equilibrium solution in a duopoly advertising model under uncertainty. (a) Strategic substitutes. (b) Strategic complements.

Note that both reaction functions are downward sloping in Figure 6.6a and both reaction functions are upward sloping in Figure 6.6b. Furthermore, in both figures the $V_1^1 = 0$ curve is steeper than the $V_2^2 = 0$ curve. These configurations are necessary for the Nash equilibrium to be stable.[67] Figure 6.6a depicts the case where the firms' actions are strategic substitutes[68] (see Tirole 1989, p. 208, and Bulow, Geanakoplos, and Klemperer 1985, who introduced this terminology) and Figure 6.6b describes the case of strategic complements.

Global Effect of Uncertainty

What is the global effect of uncertainty?[69] Let the $\bar{\pi}_1^1 = 0$ and $\bar{\pi}_2^2 = 0$ curves, respectively, denote Firm 1's reaction function and Firm 2's reaction function under certainty. When uncertainty is globally introduced, we expect Firm 1 to reduce its advertising for any given advertising spending by firm 2. Thus $V_1^1 = 0$ is to the left of $\bar{\pi}_1^1 = 0$. Similarly, when uncertainty is introduced, Firm 2 will reduce its advertising for any given advertising spending by Firm 1. Thus $V_2^2 = 0$ is below $\bar{\pi}_2^2 = 0$. Suppose the brands are strategic complements. Then both brands reduce advertising when uncertainty is introduced (see Figure 6.6b). If the brands are strategic substitutes, we obtain the weak result that both brands cannot simultaneously increase their respective advertising outlays when uncertainty is globally introduced (see Figure 6.6a).

What is the effect of global uncertainty on stock prices? Interestingly, both firms' stock prices could increase! There is a simple explanation for this result. The global effect of uncertainty depends on both the firm's actions and the competitor's actions.[70] Hence the results are inherently ambiguous. An interesting managerial implication is that comparative advertising which increases demand uncertainty for both brands can increase both firms' stock values.[71]

Marginal Effect of Uncertainty

What is the effect of a marginal increase in demand uncertainty for Brand 1? For any given level of advertising by Brand 2, Brand 1 advertises less. That is, Firm 1's reaction function moves to the left (see Figures 6.6a and 6.6b). Firm 2, however, chooses the same advertising policy as before conditional on a given advertising policy chosen by brand 1.

Hence Firm 2's reaction function does not change. These results imply that Brand 1 always reduces advertising when the demand for Brand 1 becomes more uncertain. Brand 2 reduces its advertising if the brands are strategic complements and increases its advertising if the brands are strategic substitutes.

What is the effect of an increase in demand uncertainty for Brand 1 on stock prices? The stock price of Firm 2 always increases.[72] This result follows from the first-order conditions. The effect on Firm 1's stock price consists of two parts: (1) an effect due to competitive reaction, and (2) the standard effect in the monopoly model (which assumes no reaction). The second effect is always negative; the first effect depends on whether the products are strategic complements or strategic substitutes. In particular, the first effect is positive (negative) when the products are strategic complements (strategic substitutes). Hence, unlike the monopoly model, Firm 1's stock price could increase when Firm 1's demand becomes more uncertain. The effect on market shares is also interesting. In particular, because of competitive retaliation, Firm 1's market share (volume-based or revenue-based) could increase when the products are strategic complements. These results show that a firm's stock price can fall even though the stock market expects the firm to gain market share: In particular, it may be dysfunctional for the firm to measure managerial performance using market share as a proxy for long-run profitability.

Model Extensions

As discussed earlier, the stochastic structure of demand depends on the firm's strategic positioning and the product's phase in the life cycle. We refer the reader to Jagpal (1994) for a discussion of more general stochastic structures of demand which capture these effects.

Key Point *The global effect of uncertainty in an oligopolistic market depends on the precise forms of uncertainty in the marketplace, and whether the brands are strategic substitutes or strategic complements. Expected market share can be a poor proxy for performance in an oligopolistic industry. In contrast to the monopolistic firm, an oligopolist may be better off when demand uncertainty increases for the oligopolist's brand. Paradoxically, comparative advertising, which increases demand uncertainty for firms' products, can make all firms better off.*

6.7 DETERMINING ADVERTISING PRODUCTIVITY: EMPIRICAL ISSUES

So far our discussion has been theoretical. We now focus on the empirical issue of measuring the productivity of advertising.

Measurement Issues

Measuring Sales

Let us begin with the measurement of sales. The term *sales* is ambiguous because measurement depends on the firm's accounting practices. Some firms use a cash basis for accounting and others an accrual basis. Cash accounting requires that sales are recorded when payments are received for goods. In contrast, accrual accounting defines sales as occurring when orders are received or goods delivered. Thus ambiguity arises because sales can mean factory orders, factory deliveries, or cash payments for goods.

Suppose we use factory sales as our measure. Now even if advertising affects consumer purchases only in the immediate period when advertising occurs (a "current-effects" model), empirical analysis will show that advertising has dynamic effects! The reason is that there is a lag effect. Retailers send in orders only when their inventories are sufficiently depleted. There are further delays as the manufacturer processes the order and ships the product. Note that trade credit practices vary across industries. Hence the use of factory sales in advertising studies will lead to spurious interindustry differences in the dynamic effects of advertising.

Suppose we define sales as occurring when orders are received at the factory. Then the lag effect is shortened. Suppose we use retail sales as our measure of sales. Naturally the firm cannot realistically measure the total retail sales of its brand unless the number of retail outlets is small. In practice, firms purchase sales and market share information from commercial firms known as syndicated research agencies. These agencies use a variety of methods including store audits to construct sales and market share estimates (i.e., they collect sales data from a representative sample of retailers). The difficulty is that these methods only provide estimates.

What is the effect of using estimated rather than actual retail sales? Fortunately, the problem is not fatal because the imprecision only occurs in the dependent variable: sales.[73] As a result, if the sample is representative, the regression estimates of advertising productivity will be correct on average (i.e., unbiased). However, these estimates will be less precise than those that would have been obtained using a census measure of retail sales. The deleterious effects of sampling will be mitigated to the extent that the sample is sufficiently large or sales of the brand are homogeneous across retail stores.

> ***Key Point***   *The precise definition of sales is important. Retail sales is a better measure than factory orders or factory sales because retail sales do not introduce spurious dynamic effects of advertising. Furthermore, the retail sales measure does not depend on accounting conventions (e.g., accrual accounting or cash accounting) that define the point when a sale occurs. Because the firm relies on estimates of retail sales, the manager should scrutinize the store-level sampling plans used by syndicated agencies to collect sales data.*

Measuring Advertising

We now consider the measurement of advertising. Suppose an advertising campaign is run in June of a particular year but is paid for at a different time. Then the use of accounting data will be misleading. For example, if advertising is paid for in April and a current-effects model is correct, empirical analysis will show that advertising has a dynamic effect of two months! Advertising should therefore be defined as occurring in the period when the advertising campaign was run and not in the period when the advertising was paid for.

The Effect of Inflation

Another problem is inflation. Consider a manager who wants to estimate the advertising–sales relationship for his or her brand using monthly data for the period January 1989 through December 1994 inclusive. Suppose the advertising expenditures in both June 1989 and October 1994 are $10,000. These dollar figures are not comparable: The real advertising in October 1994 is less than the real advertising in June 1989 because of inflation. How can we address the problem? Clearly we must adjust the monthly data using an appropriate inflation index.

One possibility is to use publicly available indices such as the Consumer Price Index (CPI) compiled by the Bureau of Labor Statistics or the gross national product deflator published by the U.S. Department of Commerce. The problem is that these indices are based on data that are aggregated across many industries and are therefore likely to be misleading. We need an inflation index that is specific to the advertising sector. The more specific this index is, the better. In particular, the advertising index should be based on differential inflation rates across media and regions. There is no a priori reason why these differential inflation rates should be perfectly correlated. Recall that the media industry is heterogeneous and media prices fluctuate based on idiosyncratic variations in the supply and demand for different media. Some advertising agencies have developed such detailed microindices—however, this information is proprietary.

> **Key Point**   *Advertising should be defined as occurring in the period when an advertising campaign is run and not in the period when the advertising is paid for. In making cross-sectional regional comparisons, the manager must adjust the advertising data to correct for regional differences in the prices of different media. In making temporal comparisons, the manager should use appropriate microindices for different media to correct for differential inflation rates across media. Nominal advertising dollars should not be used.*

Statistical Issues: Single-Period Models

Choice of Functional Form

Assume initially that price is given and advertising does not have any dynamic effects. The simplest specification of the advertising–sales model is linear. We have argued earlier that linear models are theoretically inappropriate (see Section 6.1). To reinforce the point consider a linear current-effects model. Suppose the estimated sales relationship is $S_t = 50 + 2A_t$, where S_t denotes the sales volume in period t and A_t the real advertising in that period. Assume that marginal cost is constant and the firm's unit contribution margin is $5. Consider any arbitrary level of advertising spending. Then if advertising increases by $1, the sales volume increases by 2 units and the incremental gross contribution margin is $10. Consequently every $1 increase in advertising adds $9 to the firm's net profit. Clearly advertising appears to be extremely productive; in fact, the optimal advertising expenditure is infinite! (Check what happens if $S_t = 50 + 0.2A_t$.)

> **Key Point**   *Linear advertising models lead to meaningless results when marginal costs are constant. Linear models should not be used for setting advertising policy.*[74]

Temporal Data Aggregation

Consider the effect of temporal data aggregation (i.e., the length of the data reporting period). Suppose the current-effects model is correct and, in particular, advertising affects sales only in the week during which an advertising campaign is run. However, the firm reports monthly sales and advertising figures. What is the effect of this temporal data aggregation? (Some researchers use the misleading term *data intervalling bias*. As we shall show, temporal data aggregation does not necessarily lead to bias.)

Linear Models. First, consider a linear model. Let the true model be $S_t = \alpha + \beta A_t + u_t$, where S_t denotes the sales volume in week t, A_t advertising in week t, α and β are parameters, and u_t is the random error. Then if we use monthly data, the estimate of the marginal productivity of advertising β will be correct on average (i.e., unbiased). However, the effect of temporal aggregation on the precision of estimation depends on the patterns of variability in the monthly and weekly advertising data.[75] In particular, temporal aggregation can lead to reduced or increased model fit.

Nonlinear Models. We now consider a nonlinear current-effects model. Suppose the weekly sales volumes are defined by $S_t = 1 + \ln A_t$. Note that the marginal returns to advertising decrease as advertising increases. Suppose the unit price is \$100 and marginal cost is \$60 regardless of volume. Consider the advertising policies and associated sales data shown in Table 6.3. The monthly data for the first month show that if advertising is \$100, the sales revenue is \$655.54. In the second month, advertising is \$200 and sales are \$766.44.

Suppose the manager uses these temporally aggregated data to estimate the correct sales volume model $S_t = a + b \ln A_t$. The estimated sales volume model is $\hat{S}_t =$

Table 6-3 The Effect of Temporal Aggregation

Week	Sales Revenue \$	Advertising \$	Monthly Sales \$	Monthly Advertising \$
1	132.10	10		
2	159.83	20		
3	176.05	30		
4	187.56	40		
			655.54	100
5	159.83	20		
6	203.77	60		
7	215.28	80		
8	187.56	40		
			766.44	200

$-81.29 + 160 \ln A_t$ and seriously overstates the productivity of advertising ($160 >> 1$). What are the budgeting implications of temporal data aggregation? If the manager uses weekly data, he will obtain the correct model $S_t = 1 + \ln A_t$. In this event, the manager will choose the optimal policy: Set a weekly advertising budget of $40 to obtain a weekly profit of $147.56. Because of data aggregation the manager will obtain the wrong estimates *even if the functional form is correct*. In particular, the manager will choose a monthly advertising budget of $6,400 and hope to earn a monthly gross profit[76] of $169,464. In reality, the gross monthly "profit" will be a loss of $5,059.60! As one expects, the severity of the mismeasurement decreases to the extent that the firm's weekly advertising expenditures are close to the optimal weekly budgets.

> **Key Point**   *The advertising–sales relationship is likely to be highly nonlinear. Conse-quently temporal data aggregation can lead to serious errors in measuring advertising productivity even in a current-effects model. The manager should therefore use disag-gregate data where sales and advertising are properly matched.*

Other Data Aggregation Issues

Consider another form of aggregation: combining advertising dollars across media. Suppose the current-effects model is correct and the curve ABC denotes the maximum sales volumes corresponding to different levels of aggregate advertising (see Figure 6.7). For example, if advertising is OD the maximum sales volume is AD and so on. Suppose the firm misallocates resources across media. In particular sales are A′D and not AD. Assume that when advertising is OE the media policy is optimal and the sales volume is BE. When advertising is OF sales are C′F and not CF. Thus the firm observes the points A′, B, and C′ instead of A, B, and C. What is the effect of fitting a curve to A′, B, and C′? Clearly the firm will not recover the optimal sales–advertising curve. In particular, if advertising budgeting is based on the estimated sales curve, the firm will repeat its previous mistakes!

How can we address the problem? One approach is to fit a nonlinear model of the form sales $= f(\text{advertising}) + u + v$, where u and v are random errors such that $u \leq 0$,

Figure 6.7 The effect of suboptimal media plans.

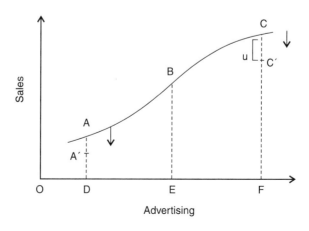

and sales and advertising are measured in real terms. The error term u (see Figure 6.7) measures the degree of inefficiency in the firm's advertising policies (e.g., the choice of the wrong media mix or the wrong advertising message). Note that u cannot be positive because the frontier ABC denotes the maximum expected sales volumes for different advertising budgets. The term v denotes the usual regression disturbance and can be negative or positive. In order to test whether previous advertising has been efficient, we can test the models sales $= f(\text{advertising}) + u + v$ and sales $= f(\text{advertising}) + v$ in a straightforward manner because these models are nested.[77]

Key Point *Data aggregation across media is problematic unless the firm distinguishes errors due to inefficiency in media planning and media message strategy from other sources of error. One approach is to estimate advertising–sales models by applying the stochastic frontier methodology commonly used in estimating production functions.*

The Omitted Variable Problem

Uncorrelated Variables. Consider the impact of estimating a current-effects model that ignores price. Suppose initially that price changes (obtained by using an appropriate deflator) are random: That is, when advertising policy varies, there is no systematic tendency for prices to go up or down. Furthermore, the degree of variability in price is the same regardless of the advertising budget.[78]

In Figure 6.8a, the average sales volume for an advertising budget of OA_1 is A_1A; conditional on this advertising policy sales vary from A_1D to A_1E. Similarly for an advertising budget of OA_2 the average sales volume is A_2B and sales can vary from A_2F to A_2G. Note that because the variability of price is unrelated to the advertising budget, the ranges DE, FG, and HJ have equal lengths.

What is the effect of estimating the sales curve by ignoring price? On average, we will recover the sales curve ABC (i.e., the estimates are unbiased). To the extent that prices vary over time, the parameters will be unstable (i.e., increasing the lengths of DE, FG, and HJ leads to less precision).

Correlated Variables. What happens in the more realistic case where price and advertising are correlated? Firms often reduce prices and increase advertising simultaneously. For example, auto manufacturers reduce the prices of unsold cars at the end of the model year and increase advertising at the same time. Similarly, firms increase both price and advertising simultaneously when the primary purpose of advertising is product differentiation and raising consumers' reservation prices for the firm's product. Thus advertising and price can be positively or negatively correlated.

Consider the case where price and advertising are perfectly negatively correlated.[79] For simplicity assume that there is no uncertainty. In Figure 6.8b, S_1S_1 is the advertising–sales curve corresponding to a particular price say $10 per unit. The firm chooses an advertising level of OA_1 when price is $10 and obtains a sales volume of A_1D. When the firm increases advertising to OA_2, it reduces price from $10 to $8 (say). Consequently the new sales curve is S_2S_2 and the sales volume is A_2E. Thus the firm observes points D and E and not D and

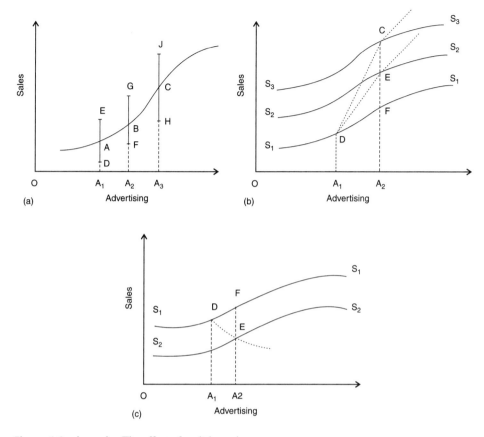

Figure 6.8a, b, and c The effect of omitting price.

F. Clearly, omitting price biases upward the productivity of advertising. Hence the firm will overadvertise.

Suppose price and advertising are positively correlated (see Figure 6.8c). In contrast to the previous case, the new sales curve $S_2 S_2$ is below the old curve $S_1 S_1$. The firm observes points D and E and not D and F. Thus omitting price biases the productivity of advertising downward. In Figure 6.8c, we obtain the paradoxical result that increases in advertising continuously lead to reductions in sales volume!

> **Key Point**   *In some oligopolistic industries price is not a strategic tool (i.e., price changes are exogenous). Consequently omitting price in advertising studies has minimal effect. In general, omitting price in advertising studies is a serious problem because the firm's advertising and price policies are correlated. Consequently the firm mismeasures advertising productivity and chooses suboptimal advertising policies.*

Measuring Dynamic Effects: Issues and Evidence

So far we have focused on the current-effects advertising model. Many researchers, however, theorize that advertising has dynamic carryover effects. To illustrate, for frequently purchased products, one might expect that advertising in a given period increases the trial rate of the product and hence current sales. Furthermore, some new triers will become repeat purchasers, hence enhancing future sales. The managerial question is whether advertising has a long lag effect; if so, advertising is an investment and not a cost.

Empirical Methodology and Evidence

What empirical evidence is available? Most previous studies focus on linear models (see Berndt 1991, pp. 384–93, and Clarke 1976 for reviews). The consensus is that the lag effect of advertising is short and certainly less than one year.

 We have argued earlier that linear models are problematic, even in a current-effects model. What nonlinear models can we use to measure the dynamic carryover effects of advertising? Jagpal, Sudit, and Vinod (1982) is one of the few studies that examines this problem. Those authors propose the translog specification for the dynamic sales model. This model is the second-order Taylor approximation (in logarithms) to any continuous function. Consequently, the translog model allows for very general patterns of carryover effect and returns to scale in advertising (i.e., marginal productivities and elasticities).[80]

 Jagpal et al. reanalyzed the well-known Lydia Pinkham monthly advertising–sales data (see Palda 1964). They found that advertising had a two-month lag effect. In addition, the standard least-squares estimates of the translog model were implausible because of multicollinearity (i.e., the regressors were highly correlated). However, the ridge estimator led to highly stable results.

 The estimates of marginal sales productivities are shown in Table 6.4. Note that at high levels of spending, the estimated marginal productivities are low regardless of the pattern of spending. For example, in March 1954 when advertising was $98,200, an extra dollar of advertising would have increased March sales by $0.0551. Similarly, when advertising is low, the marginal productivity of advertising is high. For example, an extra dollar of advertising in June 1954 would have increased sales by $ 0.5325. These results strongly support the theory of diminishing returns to advertising but do not support the theory of threshold effects.[81]

 What do the results show about dynamic effects? First, the productivity of advertising depends on the pattern of advertising spending. For example, we cannot determine the carryover effect of advertising in March 1954 without specifying the levels of spending in April and May that year. (Recall that advertising has a two-month lag effect.) Table 6.4 provides estimates of productivities given the pattern of spending actually used by Lydia Pinkham. This table is to be read diagonally. For example, the carryover effect of a marginal dollar of advertising in March 1954 is $0.0939 in April 1954 [see $MP_1(t)$ column] and $0.0194 in May 1954 [see $MP_2(t)$ column]. These results imply that, given the advertising spending levels in March, April, and May 1954, the cumulative effect of a marginal dollar of advertising in March 1954 is $0.1684 [see first row of $S_c^{(t)}$ column]. Second, note that the marginal carryover effects for a lag of one month substantially exceed the marginal current effects of advertising. This result is not surprising because the sales data represent factory sales and not retail sales. Third, previous studies that used linear

Table 6-4 Marginal Sales Productivities, MP(t), and Total Marginal Yield, S_c^t of Advertising for the Two-Period Model Using $m = 6$ Ridge Estimates

Time Period	Sales (in 100's)	Advertising (in 100's)	$MP_0(t)$	$MP_1(t)$	$MP_2(t)$	S_c^t
1954:						
March	1,728	982	.0551	.0781	.0215	.1684
April	1,539	919	.0509	.0939	.0174	.1405
May	1,324	87	.3860	.0747	.0194	1.0188
June	1,264	39	.5325	.5711	.0149	1.7110*
July	1,169	72	.2445	1.0341	.0617	1.2794
August	1,479	467	.0656	.8573	.1444	.2958
September	1,631	1,170	.0396	.1864	.1776	.1363
October	1,546	917	.0520	.0781	.0438	.1616
November	1,459	701	.0616	.0932	.0185	.1604
December	1,087	128	.2149	.0804	.0164	.7902
1955:						
January	1,171	1,014	.0280	.4633	.0184	.1321
February	1,406	1,274	.0342	.0800	.1120	.1313
March	1,619	1,388	.0373	.0786	.0241	.1213
April	1,508	1,071	.0447	.0671	.0185	.1453
May	1,521	537	.0837	.0833	.0169	.2342
June	1,341	123	.2661	.1268	.0173	.7474
July	1,247	60	.3813	.4192	.0237	1.4246*
August	1,262	351	.0706	.8770	.0621	.3345
September	1,419	1,061	.0365	.2086	.1663	.1379
October	1,558	791	.0595	.0849	.0553	.1560
November	1,222	138	.2288	.0815	.0165	.6185
December	1,053	77	.2630	.3293	.0149	1.1677

* Denotes months when the company may have underadvertised.

time series, spectral analysis, or linear regression models also found that the optimal lag structure is two or three months. (See Jagpal et al., pp. 411–12.) Thus it appears that linear models correctly identify the lag structure; however, they do not provide plausible estimates of advertising productivity.

> **Key Point** *Empirical evidence suggests that in many cases the dynamic carry-over effect of advertising is relatively short (less than three months). In such cases managers do not need to treat advertising as an investment for budgeting decisions. The translog advertising–sales model is an empirically tractable and analytically appealing specification that allows for a flexible pattern of dynamic carryover effects and variable returns to advertising without imposing arbitrary restrictions on the marginal productivities and elasticities.*

Measuring Dynamic Effects: The Simultaneity Problem. The previous analyses have implicitly assumed that single-equation advertising–sales models are appropriate. In other words, firms set advertising policy exogenously. In practice, except for controlled advertising experiments (which are rare), firms often set advertising policy endogenously after evaluating market conditions. Many firms follow advertising budgeting rules where advertising policy is based on projected future sales or some estimate of competitors' advertising budgets. What is the impact of the endogeneity of advertising?

Single-Equation Methods. Single-equation methods will yield incorrect estimates of advertising productivity even in large samples[82] (i.e., the estimates are inconsistent). To illustrate this problem, consider a simple scenario. Suppose the firm increases real advertising by x percent every month and the market is growing by x percent every month because of market growth factors unrelated to advertising. Then advertising will appear to be productive if a single-equation model is used, even if advertising is totally unproductive!

A Simultaneous Equation Approach. To deal with this problem of endogeneity we must use a simultaneous equation methodology and specify separate advertising and sales equations. Granger proposed the following definitions of causality in multiple time-series models. In the context of advertising–sales models let $MSFE_1(S)$ denote the prediction error—known as the mean-squared forecast error (MSFE)—in predicting current sales using only the previous sales history of the product. Let $MSFE_2(S)$ denote the mean-squared forecast error of predicting current sales using knowledge of the previous sales history of the product and knowledge of previous advertising. Then advertising "Granger-causes" sales if knowledge of previous advertising improves prediction accuracy [i.e., $MSFE_2(S) < MSFE_1(S)$]. A similar definition applies when sales "Granger-causes" advertising (e.g., via a budgeting rule). In this case, knowledge of previous sales improves predictive accuracy in the advertising equation. Feedback occurs if advertising "Granger-causes" sales and vice versa. Note that these definitions exclude current levels of these variables as regressors in the advertising and sales models.

Suppose that in the sales equation the inclusion of current advertising as a regressor improves predictive accuracy [i.e., $MSFE_2(S)$ is reduced]. This scenario is known as instantaneous causality and leads to a fundamental difficulty. The structural parameters of the system of advertising and sales equations are not uniquely identified. In particular, an orthogonal transformation can always be found such that the structural equations become recursive (see Granger 1969, p. 427). We shall return to this issue later.

Note that the Granger definitions of causality are very general and do not require the use of linear predictors. Furthermore, causality is defined solely in terms of the predictability of the advertising and sales series. Hence, as in other correlation/regression procedures, spurious causality patterns can be found if relevant variables are omitted from the definition of the universe. In particular, the bivariate time-series model will be incorrect if advertising and sales depend on a third variable. For example, sales could fluctuate cyclically and depend on such general macroeconomic factors as GNP. In addition, the firm could increase advertising during boom conditions and decrease advertising during recessions, possibly for cash-flow reasons.

In order to implement the Granger approach, we need to specify the lag structures in the advertising and sales equations, respectively. Granger and Newbold (1977, pp. 244–55) provide such a methodology.[83]

Simultaneous Equation Methods: Empirical Evidence. Jagpal and Hui (1980) used the Granger–Newbold methodology to analyze the well-known Lydia Pinkham data. They found that feedback was present in the annual data model. Consequently single-equation estimation is inappropriate (i.e., advertising is endogenous). The results for the annual data model also showed that instantaneous causality was present. Thus, on purely statistical grounds, it is impossible to tell whether advertising causes sales, sales cause advertising, or vice versa. In contrast to the annual data model, the results for the monthly data model showed that there is no feedback from sales to advertising. However, there is instantaneous causality. Jagpal and Hui argue that, despite instantaneous causality in the monthly data model, advertising is exogenous. The reason is that current monthly sales cannot cause current monthly advertising because of data collection lags within the firm and market frictions that prevent the firm from making instantaneous adjustments in advertising policy. Hence single-equation methods can be used in the monthly data model. Jagpal and Hui suggest that shorter data intervals be used so that the apparent instantaneous causality resulting from temporal data aggregation is removed.

One weakness of the Jagpal–Hui model and other subsequent multiple time-series advertising–sales models (see Aaker, Carman, and Jacobson 1982) is that the models are linear. Future research should estimate general nonlinear models, recognizing that the Granger definitions of causality do not require linear predictors.

Key Point   *Single-equation advertising–sales models can be used only if advertising is exogenous. The assumption of exogeneity should be tested using the multiple time-series methodology and the Granger definitions of causality. Empirical evidence suggests that advertising is endogenous when the data are highly temporally aggregated. Single-equation models can be used if the sampling interval is short (one month or less). In such cases, researchers should use the translog specification, which allows for general patterns of carryover effect, marginal productivities, and elasticities. (See Jagpal, Sudit, and Vinod 1982.)*

The Effect of Competition

The previous analyses implicitly assumed that the firm is a monopolist. In practice, however, the firm's sales depend on the advertising decisions made by its rivals. One common method of incorporating competition is to estimate market share models rather than sales models. Consider a duopoly. Let MS_1 and MS_2 denote the market shares of Firms 1 and 2, respectively, in a given time period. Let A_1 and A_2, respectively, denote the advertising budgets of Firms 1 and 2. Then the relative advertising shares are $a_1 = A_1/(A_1 + A_2)$ and $a_2 = A_2/(A_1 + A_2)$. Suppose the market shares follow the current-effects model $MS_1 = \alpha_1 + \beta_1 \ln a_1 + u_1$ and $MS_2 = \alpha_2 + \beta_2 \ln a_2 + u_2$, where the αs and βs are parameters and u_1 and u_2 are disturbance terms. Note that in this formulation we assume diminishing returns to advertising share.

Suppose the researcher estimates the two equations separately to obtain $\widehat{MS_1} = \hat{\alpha}_1 + \hat{\beta}_1 \ln a_1$ and $\widehat{MS_2} = \hat{\alpha}_2 + \hat{\beta}_2 \ln a_2$, where the carets denote estimates. Logically, market shares must sum to unity (i.e., $\widehat{MS_1} + \widehat{MS_2} = 1$). Hence logically consistent empirical models require that $\hat{\alpha}_1 + \hat{\alpha}_2 = 1$, $\hat{\beta}_1 = 0$, and $\hat{\beta}_2 = 0$. The main point is that the two market share equations are not independent and form what is known as a singular-equation system. This singularity problem generalizes to oligopoly market share models where there are several firms and advertising has dynamic carryover effects.

How can one correctly estimate market share models? If the industry comprises n firms, we can arbitrarily eliminate one firm and estimate the remaining $(n - 1)$ market share equations. Thus in our example we would estimate MS_1 or MS_2 but not both. This remedy is ad hoc because the results depend on which equation is eliminated. A superior approach is to estimate the whole system of equations subject to the "adding-up" constraints on the parameters imposed by logical consistency (see Berndt 1991, pp. 472–74).

Note that the previous analysis assumed that advertising decisions in an oligopoly are exogenous. However, advertising is a key competitive tool in differentiated markets; that is, advertising is endogenous. Consequently, in the context of market-share models, we need to estimate a system of market-share and advertising-share equations using the multiple time-series methodology and explicitly recognizing that market shares and advertising shares, respectively, sum to unity. I am not aware of any empirical studies that implement this method.

> **Key Point**   *Market-share models must be logically consistent and explicitly recognize that advertising is endogenous in oligopoly models. Researchers should use the multiple time-series methodology, subject to the parametric constraints required by logically consistent market-share models.*

6.8 THE ADVERTISING TIMING DECISION: PULSING

The Managerial Issue

An important managerial issue is whether advertising expenditures should be evenly distributed over a given time period or concentrated in limited bursts. The latter policy is known as *pulsing* or *flighting*. Many patterns of spending are subsumed under pulsing. For example, the firm can adopt a cyclic advertising policy by spending $100 in period 1, zero dollars in period 2, $150 in period 3, zero dollars in period 4, and so on. This policy is an example of alternating pulsation (see Simon 1982). Alternatively, the firm could spend $100 in period 1, $200 in period 2, zero dollars in period 3, $150 in period 4, $160 in period 5, zero dollars in period 6, and so on. This policy is an example of repeat pulsation. Numerous other scenarios are possible.

Let us begin by asking a basic question: Why use a pulsing strategy? The necessary condition is that advertising has a dynamic carryover effect.[84] The rationale is intuitive. If a current-effects model is correct, there are no temporal interdependencies. Consequently, the optimal advertising policy can be chosen period by period (i.e., pulsing is inappropriate).

The Advertising–Sales Relationship

Suppose advertising has dynamic carryover effects. The empirical question is: What is the form of the advertising–sales equation? Considerable empirical and theoretical guidance are available. We summarize below the lucid discussion in Simon (1982, pp. 352–55).

Extensive empirical evidence shows that when advertising is decreased, sales decrease gradually to a new equilibrium level. Standard econometric models can account for this phenomenon. However, when advertising increases, the typical effect is a sharp immediate increase in sales followed by a decline to an equilibrium level somewhere between the peak and the initial level of sales, *even if the increase in advertising is maintained in future periods*. Conventional econometric models cannot account for this result. As Simon emphasizes, the fundamental difficulty is that the functional form of the advertising–sales relationship differs depending on whether the stimulus (i.e., advertising) is decreased or increased.

From a theoretical perspective, adaptation-level theory (Helson 1964) implies that a stimulus such as advertising has two distinct effects: the effect of the absolute stimulus level (i.e., current advertising) and the effect of a stimulus differential (i.e., the deviation of current advertising from some reference or anchor value). In particular, these differential stimuli are likely to induce an initial response that levels off gradually but not completely. The leveling off can be due to perceptual, cognitive, or habitual adaptations, or to a combination of two or more of these factors.

The Simon Model

Consider the general advertising–sales model $S_t = f(A_t, S_{t-1}, A^*)$, where S denotes sales, A advertising, A^* is the anchor value of advertising, and t denotes time. This specification allows for a general pattern of carryover effects. In addition, the model allows for distinct effects due to the level of the stimulus (A_t) and the stimulus differentials that depend on A_t and A^*. Before proposing a general nonlinear model, we discuss Simon's theoretical and empirical results.

Simon theoretically analyzes and tests the model $S_t = a + \lambda S_{t-1} + b \ln A_t + c \max\{0, \Delta A_t\} + u_t$, where a, λ, b, and $c > 0$ are parameters, u_t is a disturbance term, and $\Delta A_t = A_t - A_{t-1}$. In this model, A_{t-1} is the anchor value of advertising and λ measures customer holdover. If advertising in period t is lower than advertising in period $t - 1$ (i.e., $\Delta A_t \leq 0$), the sales equation is $S_t = a + \lambda S_{t-1} + b \ln A_t + u_t$. However, if advertising increases in period t (i.e., $\Delta A_t > 0$), the sales model is $S_t = a + \lambda S_{t-1} + b \ln A_t + c(\Delta A_t) + u_t$. Note that the major advantage of Simon's model is that, in contrast to standard econometric models, the functional form of the advertising–sales relationship differs depending on the stimulus differential ΔA_t.

Simon reports excellent goodness-of-fit results for the brands tested. In particular, the parameter c, which measures the effect of the stimulus differential ΔA_t, is highly significant for two of the three brands tested ($p < 0.05$). Simon's results show that alternating pulsation (i.e., the pattern advertise, do not advertise, advertise, do not advertise) is superior to repeat pulsation (i.e., the pattern advertise, advertise, do not advertise). The budgeting implications are twofold. First, a constant advertising pattern always leads to underadvertising. Second, and more interestingly, both pulsation strategies require the firm to accept losses in pulsation periods. These losses can be considerable in the initial periods when pulsation begins.

A General Nonlinear Model

Simon's model is appealing but makes two simplifying assumptions. First, the marginal productivity of current advertising is strictly declining (i.e., there are no threshold effects). Although much empirical evidence supports this formulation (see Hanssens, Parsons, and Schultz, 1990, pp. 178–79 for a review), some authors and practitioners argue that the relationship between advertising and sales is S-shaped. Mahajan and Muller (1986, p. 94) even assert that pulsing strategies can be optimal if and only if the advertising–sales curve is S-shaped.[85] They further assert that because of data aggregation, S-shaped curves cannot be empirically observed! (See Mahajan and Muller 1986, p. 102.) In particular, they argue that the effect of pulsing is to linearize the region where threshold effects occur (i.e., the convex part of the response function). The second assumption in Simon's model is that the anchoring effect [i.e., the effect of ΔA_t] is linearly separable from the effects of current advertising.

We now propose a simple method that addresses these limitations. Let the general nonlinear advertising–sales model be $S_t = f(S_{t-1}, A_t, \Delta A_t)$. In order to allow for S-shaped or concave functions, general patterns of carryover effects, marginal productivities, and elasticities, use the translog functional form. Recall that the translog model is very general because it is a quadratic approximation to any continuous function. To allow for differential stimuli effects, use a switching regime specification that allows for different functional forms when $\Delta A_t \leq 0$ and $\Delta A_t > 0$.[86] As discussed previously, the data period should be sufficiently short to avoid data-intervalling bias and the simultaneity problem. Simon (1982, p. 357) provides empirical evidence that data aggregation washes out the effect of the differential stimulus ΔA_t. In particular, Simon argues that the data interval should be one month or less. Before estimating the model, the data should be deseasonalized using standard methods such as the Box–Jenkins methodology. See Jagpal and Hui (1980) for an application. Finally, if the observed data do not display sufficient variability, econometric modeling (including the proposed model) is infeasible; consequently, the manager needs to conduct experiments to determine whether pulsing is appropriate.

Model Extensions

Despite the importance of the pulsing problem in advertising, empirical research in this area is scarce. Many important research areas remain open (see Simon 1982, p. 362). Pulsing studies must allow for competitive effects. Strictly, the methodology we have proposed is only appropriate if the firm is a monopolist or competitive policies are exogenously determined. An important issue is whether the lengths of the pulse and nonpulse periods should change over time. From a behavioral perspective, we need to develop better measures of the anchor value of advertising; using the previous period's advertising may be restrictive. In addition, we need to determine how the anchor values adjust to continuous change as a result of pulsation. Finally, optimization studies on advertising timing should allow for differential production costs, changes in inventory costs, and advertising setup costs because the firm incurs an incremental transaction cost each time it chooses a pulsing strategy. Previous studies (Simon 1982 and Mahajan and Muller 1986) assume constant marginal production cost and hence implicitly assume that pulsing has no marginal effects on advertising or inventory costs.

> **Key Point**   *Behavioral theory and empirical evidence suggest that the functional form of the advertising–sales relationship differs depending on whether advertising is decreased or increased. Conventional econometric models do not provide this property and can therefore lead to inefficient advertising timing decisions. Simon (1982) proposes a model that allows for both asymmetric adjustment rates and asymmetric behavioral processes. However, Simon's model assumes strictly diminishing returns to advertising and an additively separable form for the anchoring effect of advertising. The model can be generalized using a switching regime translog model that allows for S-shaped or concave sales functions and a flexible pattern of carryover effects, productivities, and elasticities. This model does not require the anchoring effect of advertising to be separable in the advertising–sales model. Research is necessary to determine how anchor values are formed and change dynamically as a result of competitive behavior, especially the pulsing policies of competing firms.*

6.9 A MULTIPRODUCT ADVERTISING GOODWILL MODEL UNDER UNCERTAINTY

As discussed previously, economic models focus heavily on advertising goodwill. (See Section 6.4.) The empirical literature, however, is extremely sparse. The fundamental problem is that goodwill is unobserved. We now propose a model that allows the firm to measure the effects of advertising goodwill in a multiproduct, multiperiod setting.

Although single-product goodwill models are inherently underidentified,[87] multiproduct goodwill models can be estimated provided the firm follows a policy of *umbrella advertising* (see Jagpal 1982). Two cases are possible. First, firms can use generic slogans in their advertising. For example, General Electric claims to "Bring good things to life" and Xerox positions itself as "The Document Company." Such advertising leads to goodwill for the firm which, in turn, increases sales of the firm's product line. Second, firms can advertise to improve their corporate image.

Single-Period Model

Consider a current-effects advertising model (see Jagpal 1982c). Let X_1 denote the level of advertising for medium 1, X_2 the level of advertising for medium 2, and so on. (See Figure 6.9.) Let G denote the unobserved and stochastic advertising goodwill. Then $G = f(X_1, \ldots, X_n, \zeta)$ where f is a function and ζ is the disturbance term. Let S_i denote the sales for product i. The effect of goodwill on sales is given by $S_i = h_i(G, \varepsilon_i)$, where the h_is are deterministic functions and the ε_is are disturbances. The empirical problem is to estimate the relationships between media spending and goodwill (i.e., the f equation) and between goodwill and sales (i.e., the h_i equations). This recursive model is a special case of the MIMIC (multiple indicator multiple cause) model and can be estimated using the structural equation methodology.[88]

One problem in estimating this advertising goodwill model is that multicollinearity can be significant (especially for highly nonlinear specifications). Jagpal (1982c) develops a ridge estimator to deal with the problem. He estimates a nonlinear (translog) advertising

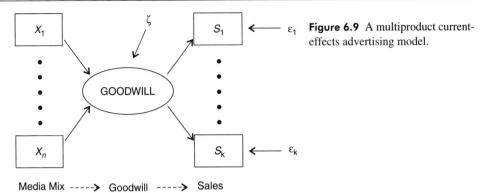

Figure 6.9 A multiproduct current-effects advertising model.

goodwill model for a firm in the banking industry. The results show that the ridge estimator outperforms the standard structural equation estimator; in particular, the ridge estimator gives meaningful and stable estimates of the marginal productivities and elasticities of different media.

Multiperiod Model

Suppose now that advertising goodwill has a carryover effect. Then we can extend the basic model (Jagpal 1982c) in a straightforward manner.

Let G_{t-1} denote the unobserved and uncertain advertising goodwill in period $t - 1$ and G_t the advertising goodwill in period t. Then, as Nerlove and Arrow (1962) and others have argued, it is reasonable to expect that goodwill decreases over time because of consumer forgetting and other effects unless the firm advertises in period t (i.e., $G_t < G_{t-1}$). Figure 6.10 shows a simple dynamic model that allows for advertising decay. Note that, in general, the error terms in G_t and G_{t-1} are correlated to allow for omitted variables (i.e., other variables besides advertising affect goodwill). Similarly the error terms for each

Figure 6.10 A dynamic multiproduct advertising model.

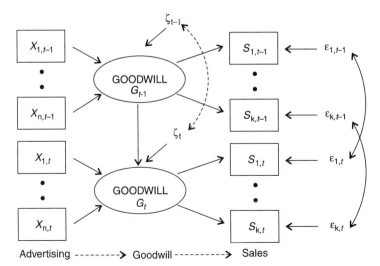

sales equation are correlated over time. Consider the translog specification of the dynamic model depicted in Figure 6.10. This model is identified and can be estimated using the structural equation methodology.[89] More elaborate multiproduct goodwill models can be constructed to allow for customer holdover or customer inertia from previous periods in a straightforward manner.[90]

> **Key Point** *Multiproduct advertising goodwill models can be estimated provided the firm uses product umbrella or corporate image advertising. These models explicitly allow for stochastic and unobserved goodwill. The methodology can be extended to test dynamic multiproduct models which allow goodwill to decay over time and incorporate lagged sales effects to reflect consumer holdover from the past or consumer inertia.*

6.10 CONCLUDING REMARKS

This chapter examines the firm's advertising decision in a stochastic and competitive environment. We have focused heavily on the multiproduct firm and proposed analytical models and empirical procedures for measuring advertising effectiveness in an uncertain environment. In addition, we have paid special attention to the problem of coordinating price and advertising policy in a dynamic stochastic consideration. Most of our analysis focuses on the monopolist; additional research is necessary to develop multiperiod game-theoretic models (and appropriate empirical methods) that simultaneously allow for uncertainty and strategic interdependence among firms.

We have analyzed the firm's advertising decision at a high level of aggregation. From a managerial viewpoint, such analyses must be supplemented by disaggregate analysis in order to maximize performance. In particular, we must develop analytical methods for allocating the firm's advertising budget using two dimensions (time and media) and choosing the optimal advertising message. Chapter 7 examines these issues.

NOTES

1. The dominant brand in an oligopolistic market may sometimes find it profitable to expand primary demand if its market share is sufficiently large. However, even in this case, the firm will prefer brand-specific advertising to stimulate secondary demand.

2. Advertising threshold effects are likely to vary across products, segments, and individuals. Factors influencing these thresholds include: the degree of task involvement (i.e., the importance of the purchase decision), the amount and frequency of purchase, and the form of message delivery (e.g., a humorous advertisement can be effective even if the advertising frequency is relatively low). An alternative behavioral viewpoint is that advertising works subliminally: In particular, an advertising message need not be stored in the consumer's long-term memory to be effective. For example, a consumer may not consciously remember the brand's logo after seeing an ad. However, when the consumer sees the brand logo in a store, a subliminal association is triggered and can result in purchase. To the extent that advertising is subliminal, the argument for a threshold effect becomes less compelling. In particular, if subliminal advertising is significant, advertising becomes less effective as a barrier to entry.

3. Let A denote the advertising budget in dollars and S the sales volume. The advertising–sales relationship in Figure 6.1 is defined by $\ln S = 9.62737 - 1000/A$ for $100 \leq A \leq 500$ and $S = 500 + 250 \ln A$ for $A > 500$. Note that the curve is discontinuous at $A = 500$. The marginal physical productivity of advertising $(\partial S/\partial A)$ is strictly positive throughout. The marginal return to advertising is increasing if $A < 500$ and decreasing if $A > 500$. Specifically

$$\frac{\partial^2 S}{\partial A^2} = \frac{1000}{A^3}(1000/A - 2)S > 0, \qquad \text{if } A < 500 \text{ and}$$

$$\frac{\partial^2 S}{\partial A^2} = -250/A^2 < 0, \qquad \text{if } A > 500.$$

4. Let $q = f(p, A)$, where q denotes demand, p is price, and A is advertising. Let the cost function be $C = C(q)$. Then the profit function is $\Pi = pf(p, A) - C(f(p, A)) - A$. Hence $\Pi_{AA} = (p - C_q)f_{AA} - C_{qq}f_A^2 < 0$ by the second-order conditions, where the subscripts denote the appropriate derivatives. Now $C_{qq} = 0$ if marginal cost is constant and $p - C_q > 0$ by the first-order conditions. Hence $\Pi_{AA} < 0$ implies that the marginal returns to advertising are diminishing $(f_{AA} < 0)$.

5. The simple additively separable form for the demand curve was chosen for analytical tractability. No loss in realism is involved. Recall that if the variable cost per unit is constant, the "optimal" advertising policy conditional on a given price implies that the marginal return to advertising is diminishing at optimality (see note 4). In our example the profit function is strictly concave if $p > 5.5$. Specifically $\Pi_{pp} < 0$ and $\Pi_{AA} < 0$ throughout and $\Pi_{pp}\Pi_{AA} - \Pi_{Ap}^2 > 0$ if $p > 5.5$.

6. As in note 4, the firm's profit is defined by $\Pi = pf(p, A) - C(f(p, A)) - A$. The first-order conditions are $\Pi_A = (p - C_q)f_A - 1 = 0$ and $\Pi_p = (p - C_q)f_p + f = 0$, where the subscripts denote derivatives. Hence $f_A/f_p = -1/f$. Now the advertising elasticity is $\varepsilon_A = f_A(A/f)$ and the price elasticity is $|\varepsilon_p| = -f_p(p/f)$. Making the appropriate substitutions, we obtain $\varepsilon_A/|\varepsilon_p| = A/pf$, which is the Dorfman–Steiner Theorem.

7. Let the sales volume be $q = f(p, A)$ and the cost function be $C = C(q)$ where $q_p < 0, q_A > 0$, $C_q > 0$, and subscripts denote derivatives. Then the profit is $\Pi = pf(p, A) - C(q) - A$. The first-order conditions are $\Pi_p = (p - C_q)f_p + f = 0$ and $\Pi_A = (p - C_q)f_A - 1 = 0$. Let the absolute value of the price elasticity be $|\varepsilon_p| = -f_p(p/f)$. Then $\Pi_{Ap} = (1/f_p)(f^2/p)\,\partial|\varepsilon_p|/\partial A$ using the first-order conditions. That is $\text{sgn}(\Pi_{Ap}) = -\text{sgn}(\partial|\varepsilon_p|/\partial A)$.

   Consider any shift parameter δ. Then $\partial p/\partial\delta = (-\Pi_{p\delta}\Pi_{AA} + \Pi_{A\delta}\Pi_{Ap})/D$ and $\partial A/\partial\delta = (-\Pi_{A\delta}\Pi_{pp} + \Pi_{p\delta}\Pi_{Ap})/D$, where $D = \Pi_{pp}\Pi_{AA} - \Pi_{Ap}^2 > 0$ by the second-order conditions. Now $\Pi_{p\delta}$ and $\Pi_{A\delta}$ depend on the cost structure and $\text{sgn}(\Pi_{Ap}) = \text{sgn}(\partial|\varepsilon_p|/\partial A)$. Hence the result.

8. Let $q' = f(p, A) + \delta A$ be the new demand curve, where $\delta > 0$. Then $\partial A/\partial\delta = -\Pi_{pp}/D > 0$ because $\Pi_{pp} < 0$ by the second-order conditions.

9. By assumption $C_{qq} = 0$. Hence $\partial p/\partial\delta = \Pi_{Ap}/D$. However, $\Pi_{Ap} = (f^2\,\partial|\varepsilon_p|/\partial A)(1/pf_p)$. Hence $\text{sgn}(\partial p/\partial\delta) = -\text{sgn}(\partial|\varepsilon_p|/\partial A)$.

10. In this case $C_{qq} > 0$. Hence $\partial p/\partial\delta = \Pi_{Ap}/D$, where $\Pi_{Ap} = (f^2\,\partial|\varepsilon_p|/\partial A)(1/pf_p) - f_A C_{qq}f_p$. A sufficient condition for $\Pi_{Ap} > 0$ is $\partial|\varepsilon_p|/\partial A < 0$. If $\partial|\varepsilon_p|/\partial A > 0$, the sign of Π_{Ap} is inherently indeterminate.

11. Horowitz (1970) and Leland (1972) develop monopoly models under uncertainty using general

cost functions. However, Horowitz does not consider price and Leland does not include advertising as a decision variable. Our focus here is the joint price–advertising decision. Consequently we assume constant marginal costs (see Dehez and Jacquemin 1975 and Brick and Jagpal 1981).

12. Consider a simple awareness model in which consumers are homogeneous. Let p denote the probability of purchase for any individual and N the number of individuals reached with an advertising budget A. In general $p = p(A)$, where $\partial p/\partial A \geq 0$ and $N = N(A)$, where $\partial N/\partial A > 0$. Suppose there is no word-of-mouth activity. Then the expected demand is $\bar{q} = Np$. Hence $\partial \bar{q}/\partial A = N \partial p/\partial A + p\, \partial N/\partial A > 0$ (i.e., an increase in advertising leads to a higher average sales volume). The variance of sales is $\sigma^2(q) = Np(1-p)$. Hence $\partial \sigma^2(q)/\partial A = p(1-p)\, \partial N/\partial A + N(1-2p)\, \partial p/\partial A$. The first term is strictly positive, and the second term is negative only in the highly unlikely case where $p > 1/2$. Thus $\partial \sigma^2(q)/\partial A > 0$ (i.e., an increase in advertising makes demand more uncertain).

13. The general sales function is $q = f(p, A) + g(p, A)u$, where $f \neq 0$ and $g \neq 1$. The variance of q conditional on any price–advertising policy (p, A) is given by $\sigma^2(q) = g^2(p, A)\sigma^2(u)$. Hence $\partial \sigma^2(q)/\partial p = 2g\sigma^2(u)\partial g/\partial p$ and $\partial \sigma^2(q)/\partial A = 2g\sigma^2(u)\partial g/\partial A$. However, the signs of $\partial g/\partial p$ and $\partial g/\partial A$ are unconstrained. Hence the effects of price and advertising on demand uncertainty can be nonmonotonic and asymmetric.

14. Let π denote the firm's random profit and $U(\pi)$ the firm's utility function. Let $E(\pi) = \bar{\pi}$. Expanding $U(\pi)$ around $\bar{\pi}$ using the Taylor series, we have $U(\pi) = U(\bar{\pi}) + U'(\bar{\pi})(\pi - \bar{\pi}) + \frac{U''(\bar{\pi})}{2!}(\pi - \bar{\pi}) + R$, where the primes denote derivatives and R is the remainder. Hence for sufficiently small uncertainties $EU(\pi) \cong U(\bar{\pi})$. Thus the risk-averse firm behaves like a risk-neutral firm. In practice, demand uncertainty for new products is likely to be large. Hence risk neutrality is not a good approximation when the decision maker is risk-averse.

15. There are several ways in which the manager's compensation can depend on product-line performance. Suppose the manager is paid a base wage w and a fraction μ of gross profits. (Chapter 8 discusses the design of optimal compensation plans.) Let π denote the firm's random gross profits before paying the manager. The linear sharing rule implies that the manager's income is $y = w + \mu\pi$. Let $U(y)$ denote the risk-averse manager's utility function. Then the manager chooses price–advertising policy to maximize $EU(y)$. Alternatively, suppose senior management sets a target profit $\hat{\pi}$ for the manager. If $\pi > \hat{\pi}$, the manager earns a bonus of $\mu(\pi - \hat{\pi})$ in addition to the base wage w. If $\pi < \hat{\pi}$, the manager "pays back" an amount $\mu(\pi - \hat{\pi})$. One way to interpret "paying back" is that the manager does not get promoted or loses the opportunity to be transferred to a more prestigious product line in the future. Given this scenario, the manager's income is $z = w + \mu(\pi - \hat{\pi}) = (w - \mu\hat{\pi}) + \mu\pi$.

Clearly, the firm's particular choices of fixed wage w, bonus rate μ, and target profit $\hat{\pi}$ will affect the manager's choice of price–advertising policy. However, the comparative statics results we discuss—the effects of uncertainty and the degree of risk aversion—will be unaffected regardless of whether π, y, or z is the argument in the utility function. (We assume that the probability of bankruptcy is zero.)

16. Fama (1980) shows that managers will maximize stock value if the managerial labor market is competitive and information is symmetric. In general the product manager knows more about his product than the stock market. Furthermore, for competitive reasons, the manager may not share product information with the stock market. This information asymmetry can lead to an agency problem (i.e., the manager may choose suboptimal policies). The crux of the problem

is the design of the compensation plan. We shall discuss these issues in Chapters 8 and 9. For now simply assume that the firm has chosen the "correct" compensation plan (i.e., the manager chooses policy to maximize stock value).

17. The "certainty" demand function is $\bar{q} = f(p, A) + g(p, A)\bar{u}$, where $E(u) = \bar{u}$. Thus for any price–advertising policy, the expected demand is equal for the certainty and uncertainty cases.

18. In the exogenous uncertainty case, the random demand is $q = f(p, A) + u$ and the random profit $\pi = (p - c)[f(p, A) + u] - A - F$, where F denotes fixed cost. Hence $\bar{\pi} = E(\pi) = (p - c)f(p, A) - A - F$. The locus of price–advertising combinations satisfying $\bar{\pi}_p = 0$ is given by $dp/dA|\bar{\pi}_p = 0 = -\bar{\pi}_{Ap}/\bar{\pi}_{pp}$, where subscripts denote derivatives. Now $\bar{\pi}_{pp} < 0$ by the concavity of $\bar{\pi}$. Hence $\bar{\pi}_p = 0$ is upward (downward) sloping if $\bar{\pi}_{Ap}$ is positive (negative). Similarly, $dp/dA|\bar{\pi}_A = 0 = -\bar{\pi}_{AA}/\bar{\pi}_{Ap}$. However $\bar{\pi}_{AA} < 0$ by concavity. Hence $\bar{\pi}_A = 0$ is upward (downward) sloping if $\bar{\pi}_p = 0$ is upward (downward) sloping. Furthermore $dp/dA|\bar{\pi}_p - dp/dA|\bar{\pi}_A = \left(\bar{\pi}_{AA}\bar{\pi}_{pp} - \bar{\pi}_{Ap}^2\right)/\bar{\pi}_{Ap}\bar{\pi}_{pp}$. Hence the $\bar{\pi}_p = 0$ curve is flatter than the $\bar{\pi}_A = 0$ curve using the concavity of π (see Figures 6.3a and 6.3b).

In order to interpret $\bar{\pi}_{Ap}$, let ε_p denote the price elasticity of demand under certainty [i.e., $\varepsilon_p = -(\partial\bar{q}/\partial p)(p/\bar{q})$, where $\bar{q} = f(p, A) + g(p, A)\bar{u}$ in general].

Differentiating ε_p and using the first-order conditions, we can show that $\partial\varepsilon_p/\partial A = -[p/(p - c)\bar{q}]\bar{\pi}_{Ap}$. Hence $\text{sgn}(\partial\varepsilon_p/\partial A) = -\text{sgn}(\bar{\pi}_{Ap})$.

19. See note 18.

20. The first-order conditions for the certainty model are $\bar{\pi}_p = (p - c)(\partial f/\partial p) + f = 0$ and $\bar{\pi}_A = (p - c) \partial f/\partial A - 1 = 0$. The first-order conditions for the expected utility model are $Z_p = E\{U'[(p - c) \partial f/\partial p + f + u]\} = 0$ and $Z_A = E\{U'[(p - c) \partial f/\partial A - 1]\} = 0$. However, $(p - c) \partial f/\partial A - 1 = 0$ is nonstochastic. Hence the $\bar{\pi}_A = 0$ and $Z_A = 0$ curves coincide. Let (p, A) denote any pair satisfying $\bar{\pi}_p = 0$. Evaluating Z_p at this point, we have $Z_p = \text{Cov}(U', u) < 0$ by risk aversion. Hence p must be decreased to satisfy $Z_p = 0$. That is, the $Z_p = 0$ curve always lies below $\bar{\pi}_p = 0$ (see Figures 6.3a and 6.3b).

21. For the multiplicative uncertainty model, expected utility is defined by $Z = EU[(p - c)g(p, A)u - A - F]$, where $\partial g/\partial A > 0$ and $u > 0$. Hence $Z_A = E\{U'[(p - c)(\partial g/\partial A)\bar{u} - 1]\} + (p - c)(\partial g/\partial A) \text{Cov}(U', u)$, where $E(u) = \bar{u}$. However, $\bar{\pi}_A = [(p - c)(\partial g/\partial A)\bar{u} - 1]$. Let $(\hat{p}, \hat{A})$ be any pair satisfying $\bar{\pi}_A = 0$. Evaluating Z_A at this point, we get $Z_A = (\hat{p} - c)(\partial g/\partial A) \text{Cov}(U', u)$. However, $\partial g/\partial A > 0$ and $\text{Cov}(U', u) < 0$ by risk aversion. Hence $Z_A < 0$. But Z is concave in A. Thus the $Z_A = 0$ curve lies below $\bar{\pi}_A = 0$.

22. In the multiplicative uncertainty model, $\bar{q} = g(p, A)\bar{u}$ and $\sigma(q) = g(p, A)\sigma(u)$, where $\sigma(u)$ denotes the standard deviation of u. Hence $\bar{q}/\sigma(q) = \bar{u}/\sigma(u)$, which does not depend on price or advertising.

23. Consider two firms a and b with utility functions U_a and U_b, respectively. Let w be any arbitrary wealth level. Then firm a is globally more risk averse than firm b if $-U_a''(w)/U_a'(w) > -U_b''(w)/U_b'(w)$, where the primes denote derivatives. (See Pratt 1964.) Let firm a be globally more risk-averse than firm b. Consider the multiplicative uncertainty model. The first-order conditions for firm i are $Z_p^i = E\{U_i'[g + (p - c) \partial g/\partial p]\} = 0$ and $Z_A^i = E\{U_i'[(p - c)(\partial g/\partial A)u - 1]\} = 0$, where $i = a, b$. Let $Z_p^i = 0$ and $Z_A^i = 0$, respectively, denote the loci of the price–advertising policies for firm i that satisfy the first-order conditions.

The $Z_p^a = 0$ and $Z_p^b = 0$ curves coincide. In order to determine the relative locations of the $Z_A^a = 0$ and $Z_A^b = 0$ curves, consider any (p, A) pair satisfying $Z_A^a = 0$. Let u_0 be the value of u for which $\partial \pi / \partial A = 0$ and π_0 denote the corresponding (nonstochastic) profit.

Dividing the first-order conditions for each firm by $U'(\pi_0)$, we obtain $[Z_A^b / U_b'(\pi_0) - Z_A^a / U_a'(\pi_0)] = E\{[U_b'(\pi)/U_b'(\pi_0) - U_a'(\pi)/U_a'(\pi_0)] \, \partial \pi / \partial A\}$. Suppose $u > u_0$. Then $\partial \pi / \partial A > 0$. Furthermore $u > u_0$ implies $\pi > \pi_0$. Hence $[U_b'(\pi)/U_b'(\pi_0) - U_a'(\pi)/U_a'(\pi_0)] > 0$ [see Pratt 1964, Eq. (20)].

Let (p, A) denote any pair satisfying $Z_A^a = 0$. Evaluating Z_A^b at this point, we have $Z_A^b > 0$. But Z^b is concave in A. Hence if p is held fixed, A must be increased to satisfy $Z_A^b = 0$. Thus the $Z_A^b = 0$ curve lies above $Z_A^a = 0$. Consequently an increase in risk aversion is analogous to the introduction of uncertainty.

Similar proofs apply for the exogenous and generalized uncertainty cases (see Jagpal 1982b).

24. Let the demand be $q = f(p, A) + u$, where $E(u) = 0$. Suppose advertising increases and price decreases. Then the expected revenue increases. However, the ratio of advertising to expected revenue is ambiguous. A similar ambiguity arises if both advertising and price decrease when uncertainty is introduced.

25. Consider the generalized uncertainty case where $q = f(p, A) + g(p, A)u$, $\bar{q} = E(q)$, $\pi = (p - c)[\bar{q} + g(u - \bar{u})] - A - F$, and $Z = EU(\pi)$. Define the price elasticity under certainty as $|\varepsilon_p| = -(\partial \bar{q}/\partial p)(p/\bar{q})$ and the advertising elasticity $\varepsilon_A = (\partial \bar{q}/\partial A)(A/\bar{q})$. Using the first-order conditions, we can show that $[\varepsilon_A/|\varepsilon_p|] = (A/p\bar{q})Q/M$, where $Q = [-(\partial g/\partial A) \, \text{Cov}(U', u)/E(U') + 1/(p - c)]$ and $M = \{[g/(p - c) + \partial g/\partial p] \, \text{Cov}(U', u)/[E(U')\bar{q}] + 1/(p - c)\}$. This result generalizes the Dorfman–Steiner Theorem to the uncertainty case.

Consider the exogenous uncertainty specification ($g \equiv 1$). Then $(A/p\bar{q}) = (\varepsilon_A/|\varepsilon_p|)\{\text{Cov}(U', u)/[\bar{q}E(U')] + 1\}$. However, $\text{Cov}(U', u) < 0$ by risk aversion. Hence $(A/p\bar{q}) < (\varepsilon_A/|\varepsilon_p|)$. Suppose f has constant price and advertising elasticities. Then the firm chooses a lower ratio of advertising to expected revenue under uncertainty.

In the multiplicative uncertainty case, we obtain $(A/p\bar{q}) = \varepsilon_A/(|\varepsilon_p|\{1 - \partial g/\partial A \, \text{Cov}(U', u)/[E(U')(p - c)]\})$. However, $\partial g/\partial A > 0$. Hence $(A/p\bar{q}) < (\varepsilon_A/|\varepsilon_p|)$, as in the exogenous uncertainty model. This inequality does not hold for the generalized uncertainty case, where $\partial g/\partial A$ and $\partial g/\partial p$ have arbitrary signs.

26. See note 25.

27. The CAPM assumes that (a) investors are risk averse and seek to maximize their end-of-period wealth; (b) returns from risky assets are normally distributed; (c) investors have homogeneous expectations; and (d) capital markets are perfectly competitive. Although these assumptions are somewhat less general than those of the expected utility model, they can be relaxed to varying extents without changing the basic properties of the model (see Rubinstein 1974). An important property of the CAPM, shown by Rubinstein, is that all investors in the firm can maximize their expected utilities provided their utility functions belong to the linear risk tolerance (HARA) class and there are no production externalities. Furthermore, as discussed later, the CAPM leads to well-defined results for the multiproduct firm because the effect of risk is linearly separable.

28. Let R_m denote the random rate of return on the market portfolio (i.e., the value-weighted return of all securities). Then the market price of risk is $a = [E(R_m) - r]/\sigma^2(R_m)$, where r denotes the risk-free interest rate and $\sigma^2(R_m)$ the variance of R_m.

29. Consider the generalized uncertainty specification $q = f(p, A) + g(p, A)u$. Then the random profit is $\pi = (p - c)(f + gu) - A - F$ and $\sigma^2(\pi) = (p - c)^2 g^2 \sigma^2(u)$.

30. Consider the generalized uncertainty specification $q = f(p, A) + g(p, A)u$. Define the certainty-equivalent demand $\hat{q} = f + g[E(u) - a \operatorname{Cov}(u, R_m)]$. Then the firm's stock value is $V = [(p - c)\hat{q} - A - F](1 + r)^{-1}$. Define the risk-adjusted price elasticity $|\hat{\varepsilon}_p| = -(\partial\hat{q}/\partial p)(p/\hat{q})$ and the risk-adjusted advertising elasticity $\varepsilon_A = (\partial\hat{q}/\partial A)(A/\hat{q})$. Using the first-order conditions we get $\partial|\hat{\varepsilon}_p|/\partial A = [-p(1 + r)/\hat{q}(p - c)] V_{pA}$, where subscripts denote derivatives.

    Hence $\operatorname{sgn}(V_{pA}) = -\operatorname{sgn}(\partial|\hat{\varepsilon}_p|/\partial A)$. Thus V_{pA} has a clear economic meaning regardless of the type of uncertainty. In contrast, for the expected utility model, Z_{pA} has a clear economic meaning only in the cases where uncertainty is exogenous or multiplicative. See Jagpal (1982b) for details.

31. Nerlove and Arrow (1962) recognized that their model is unrealistic because it leads to advertising policies which have "jumps." In particular, they suggest that the firm will make more gradual adjustments to advertising policy if the cost function for additions to goodwill is nonlinear (Nerlove and Arrow 1962, p. 130, Footnote 3). Gould (1970) develops such a model.

32. Consider the deterministic case where $q = f(G, p, A)$, $\partial q/\partial G > 0$, $\partial q/\partial p < 0$, and $\partial q/\partial A > 0$. We assume that the profit function is strictly concave in G, p, and A. Hence returns to goodwill and advertising are strictly diminishing (i.e., $\partial^2 q/\partial G^2 < 0$ and $\partial^2 q/\partial A^2 < 0$). However, cross-derivatives of the sort $\partial^2 q/\partial G \partial A$ have unrestricted signs to allow for general types of interaction among the marketing mix variables (e.g., $\partial^2 q/\partial G \partial A > 0$ implies that advertising reinforces the buying habits of existing customers). In the stochastic model $\partial g/\partial p$, $\partial g/\partial G$, and $\partial g/\partial A$ have arbitrary signs in general. Thus price, goodwill, and advertising can have different effects on demand variability.

33. In contrast to the Nerlove–Arrow (1962) model, our model includes current advertising in the current profit function. Consequently the current-value Hamiltonian is nonlinear in advertising. Thus the optimal policy does not have a jump at time 0 (i.e., the adjustment path to optimality is smooth).

34. This assumption is probably reasonable for the multiperiod CAPM and the multiperiod expected utility model, provided ownership and control are not separated. However, brand managers are likely to have finite horizons. Fama (1980) shows that, in a world of symmetric information and competitive labor markets, the manager will maximize the firm's stock price. By doing so, the manager maximizes the net present value of his future earnings potential. Brands, unlike stocks, are not traded in the marketplace. Firms do not typically make publicly available detailed information on the profitabilities of individual brands. Consequently the labor market cannot be fully informed about the brand manager's performance. Thus the brand manager may have a short planning horizon and focus on maximizing market share or some other publicly available measure of performance.

35. The firm's instantaneous profit at time t is $\pi(t) = (p - c)(f + gu) - A - F$. Let ρ denote the risk-free interest rate and $U(\pi(t))$ the firm's instantaneous utility. Then the firm maximizes $\int_0^\infty EU(\pi(t))e^{-\rho t} \, dt$ subject to $\dot{G} = A - \delta G$, $G(0) = G_0$, and the boundary condition

$\lim_{t \to \infty}(\lambda e^{-\rho t}) = 0$, where λ denotes the shadow price of advertising goodwill at time t measured in terms of expected utility. We assume that u has an arbitrary distribution but is independently and identically distributed (i.i.d.) over time.

36. Let π_t denote the firm's instantaneous random profit at time t and $E(\pi_t) = \bar{\pi}_t$. Then the instantaneous certainty equivalent $\hat{\pi}_t$ is defined by $\hat{\pi}_t = \bar{\pi}_t - a \operatorname{Cov}(\pi_t, R_t)$, where a denotes the market price of risk, R_t is the instantaneous rate of return of the market portfolio at time t, and Cov is the covariance operator. Let ρ denote the risk-free interest rate. Then the firm's stock value at time 0 is simply the net present value of the stream of certainty equivalents discounted at the risk-free rate. That is, the firm's stock value at time 0 is $V = \int_0^\infty [\bar{\pi}_t - a \operatorname{Cov}(\pi_t, R_t)]e^{-\rho t}\, dt$. See Constantinides (1978, pp. 604–5) for a detailed discussion of the assumptions necessary to justify this multiperiod CAPM model. Constantinides (1980) discusses more general CAPM models that allow the distribution of (π_t, R_t) to be nonstationary. We do not discuss these extensions despite their obvious managerial importance. Note, in particular, that the distribution of u_t in the demand function is likely to be nonstationary over the product life cycle (e.g., suppose the firm resegments the market over time and the cyclicality of demand varies by segment).

37. For the exogenous uncertainty specification, the demand function at time t is $f(G_t, p_t, A_t) + u_t$. Drop the t subscripts for convenience. Let $|\varepsilon_p|$ denote the price elasticity of expected demand and ε_A the short-run advertising elasticity. Let H denote the current-value Hamiltonian. Solving the first-order conditions $\partial H/\partial p = 0$ and $\partial H/\partial A = 0$ simultaneously, we obtain

$$\frac{A}{pf} = \frac{\varepsilon_A}{|\varepsilon_p|} \frac{[1 + \operatorname{Cov}(U', u)/E(U')f]}{[1 - \lambda/E(U')]}$$

where U denotes the utility function and λ denotes the implicit price of goodwill. Now $\operatorname{Cov}(U', u) < 0$ by risk aversion. If $\lambda = 0$, advertising has no long-run effects. Hence the ratio of advertising to expected revenue decreases with risk aversion and increases with the long-run effect of advertising λ.

By analogy to the certainty case, define $\varepsilon_A/[1 - \lambda/E(U')]$ as the long-run advertising elasticity. Similarly, define the risk-adjusted price elasticity as $|\varepsilon_p|/[1 + \operatorname{Cov}(U', u)/E(U')f]$. Note that the long-run advertising elasticity is larger than the short-run advertising elasticity for $\lambda > 0$ and does not depend on the firm's risk aversion. In contrast, the risk-adjusted price elasticity increases with risk aversion.

38. Pontryagin's principle implies that the optimal control satisfies the differential equation $\dot{\lambda} = \rho\lambda - \partial H/\partial G$, where ρ denotes the risk-free interest rate and H is the current-value Hamiltonian. For the exogenous uncertainty specification we obtain $\dot{\lambda} = (\rho + \delta)\lambda - (p - c)(\partial f/\partial G)E(U')$. Using $\partial H/\partial p = 0$ and manipulating the results, we get

$$\frac{G\lambda}{pf} = \frac{\varepsilon_G E(U')[1 + \operatorname{Cov}(U', u)/f E(U')]}{|\varepsilon_p|(\rho + \delta - \dot{\lambda}/\lambda)}$$

where $\varepsilon_G = (\partial f/\partial G)(G/f)$ denotes the goodwill elasticity and $G\lambda$ denotes the value of goodwill. Hence the goodwill–sales ratio decreases with risk aversion [$\operatorname{Cov}(U', u) < 0$].

39. In the multiplicative uncertainty case, expected demand is $g(p, G, A)\bar{u}$. Proceeding as in the exogenous uncertainty case, we obtain

$$\frac{A}{pg\bar{u}} = \frac{\varepsilon_A}{|\varepsilon_p|} \frac{[E(U') + \text{Cov}(U', u)/\bar{u}]}{(-\lambda + EU')}$$

$$\frac{G\lambda}{pg\bar{u}} = \frac{\varepsilon_G}{|\varepsilon_p|} \frac{[E(U') + \text{Cov}(U', u)/\bar{u}]}{(\rho + \delta - \dot{\lambda}/\lambda)}$$

where $\varepsilon_G = (\partial g/\partial G)(G/\partial g)$, $\varepsilon_p = (\partial g/\partial p)(p/g)$, and $\varepsilon_A = (\partial g/\partial A)(A/g)$. As in the exogenous uncertainty case, define the long-run advertising elasticity as $\varepsilon_A/(-\lambda + EU')$, the goodwill elasticity as $\varepsilon_G/(\rho + \delta - \dot{\lambda}/\lambda)$, and the risk-adjusted price elasticity as $|\varepsilon_p|/[E(U') + \text{Cov}(U', u)/\bar{u}]$. Note that only the risk-adjusted price elasticity depends on the firm's risk aversion.

40. In the generalized uncertainty specification, let $\bar{\phi} = f(p, G, A) + g(p, G, A)\bar{u}$. Proceeding as in the additive and multiplicative uncertainty cases, we obtain

$$\frac{A}{p\bar{\phi}} = \frac{\varepsilon_A}{|\varepsilon_p|} \frac{[(1/\bar{\phi})(g + (p - c)\,\partial g/\partial p)\,\text{Cov}(U', u) + E(U')]}{[-\lambda + E(U') - (p - c)\,\partial g/\partial A\,\text{Cov}(U', u)]}$$

where $\varepsilon_A = (\partial\bar{\phi}/\partial A)(A/\bar{\phi})$ and $\varepsilon_p = (\partial\bar{\phi}/\partial p)(p/\bar{\phi})$. Note that the advertising–sales ratio depends on $\partial g/\partial p$, $\partial g/\partial A$, and risk aversion [i.e., $\text{Cov}(U', u) < 0$].

By analogy to the certainty case define $\varepsilon_A/[-\lambda + E(U') - (p - c)\,\partial g/\partial A\,\text{Cov}(U', u)]$ as the long-run advertising elasticity. Recall that $\text{Cov}(U', u) < 0$ by risk aversion. Hence if $\partial g/\partial A > 0$, the long-run advertising elasticity and the advertising–sales ratio tend to fall. Similarly, if $\partial g/\partial A < 0$, the advertising–sales ratio tends to increase. Define $|\varepsilon_p|/[(1/\bar{\phi})(g + (p - c)\,\partial g/\partial p)\,\text{Cov}(U', u) + EU']$ as the risk-adjusted price elasticity of demand. Suppose higher prices reduce the variability of profits [i.e., $g + (p - c)\,\partial g/\partial p < 0$]. Then the firm tends to raise prices and the advertising–sales ratio increases.

41. The optimal goodwill–sales ratio in the generalized uncertainty case is defined by

$$\frac{G\lambda}{p\bar{\phi}} = \left(\frac{\varepsilon_G}{|\varepsilon_p|}\right) \frac{\left\{\left[\left(g + \partial g/\partial p(p - c)\right)\right]\text{Cov}(U', u)/\bar{\phi} + E(U')\right\}}{\left[\left(\rho + \delta - \dot{\lambda}/\lambda\right) - (p - c)(\partial g/\partial G)\,\text{Cov}(U', u)/\lambda\right]}$$

where $\varepsilon_G = (\partial\bar{\phi}/\partial G)(G/\bar{\phi})$. Define the risk-adjusted goodwill elasticity as $\varepsilon_G/[(\rho + \delta - \dot{\lambda}/\lambda) - (p - c)(\partial g/\partial G)\,\text{Cov}(U', u)/\lambda]$. In contrast to the exogenous and multiplicative uncertainty cases, the risk-adjusted goodwill elasticity depends on the firm's risk aversion. If $\partial g/\partial G > 0$, the goodwill elasticity and the goodwill–sales ratio fall.

42. See notes 40 and 41.

43. As shown in note 41, the goodwill–sales ratio is inversely related to the firm's marginal opportunity cost of investing in goodwill [$\rho + \delta$]. The intuition is that if the firm invests a dollar now and spends it on advertising later, it makes ρ and saves δ. Consequently, an increase in the goodwill depreciation rate is tantamount to an increase in the firm's cost of capital. Note that an increase in the proportional rate at which the shadow price of goodwill changes over time ($\dot{\lambda}/\lambda$) is analogous to a decrease in the firm's opportunity cost of investing in goodwill ($\rho + \delta$).

44. Let $\hat{q} = f + g[\bar{u} - a\,\text{Cov}(u, R)]$ denote the certainty-equivalent demand at time t. Proceeding

as in the case of the expected utility model, we obtain the advertising–sales ratio $A/p\hat{q} = \hat{\varepsilon}_A/|\hat{\varepsilon}_p|(1 - \lambda)$, where $\hat{\varepsilon}_A = (\partial\hat{q}/\partial A)(A/\hat{q})$ and $\hat{\varepsilon}_p = (\partial\hat{q}/\partial p)(p/\hat{q})$ denote the risk-adjusted advertising and price elasticities, respectively. Let $\bar{q}$ denote expected demand. Then $A/p\bar{q} = [\hat{\varepsilon}_A/|\hat{\varepsilon}_p|(1 - \lambda)](\hat{q}/\bar{q})$. However, $\hat{q} < \bar{q}$. Hence uncertainty tends to reduce the advertising–sales ratio.

Similarly, the goodwill–sales ratio is

$$\frac{G\lambda}{p\bar{q}} = \frac{\hat{\varepsilon}_G}{|\hat{\varepsilon}_p|}\left(\frac{1}{\rho + \delta - \dot{\lambda}/\lambda}\right)\left(\frac{\hat{q}}{\bar{q}}\right).$$

Hence uncertainty tends to reduce the goodwill–sales ratio. The Nerlove–Arrow certainty model is a special case $(\dot{\lambda} = 0, \hat{q} = \bar{q})$.

Note that the concavity of V implies that $\partial^2\hat{q}/\partial A^2 < 0$ and $\partial^2\hat{q}/\partial G^2 < 0$ for all A and G. These conditions are always satisfied in the exogenous and multiplicative uncertainty specifications if $\partial^2\bar{q}/\partial A^2 < 0$ and $\partial^2\bar{q}/\partial G^2 < 0$. In the generalized uncertainty case, stronger conditions are necessary to ensure concavity. Specifically $\partial^2\bar{q}/\partial A^2 < 0$ does not imply $\partial^2\hat{q}/\partial A^2 < 0$ and $\partial^2\bar{q}/\partial G^2 < 0$ does not imply $\partial^2\hat{q}/\partial G^2 < 0$.

45. Let the firm's price and advertising at time t be p and A, respectively. Then the firm's problem is to solve $\text{Max}_{p\geq0, A\geq0}\left\{V = \int_0^\infty e^{-\rho t}[\bar{\pi} - a\,\text{Cov}(\pi, R)]\,dt\right\}$ subject to $\dot{G} = A - \delta G$ and $G(0) = G_0$, where $\bar{\pi} = E\{(p - c)[f(p, A) + g(p, A)u] - A - F\}$.

Solving by Pontryagin's maximum principle, form the current-value Hamiltonian $H = [\bar{\pi} - a\,\text{Cov}(\pi, R)] + \lambda(A - \delta G)$, where λ is the current-value adjoint variable. Let $\hat{\pi} = \bar{\pi} - a\,\text{Cov}(\pi, R)$ denote the instantaneous certainty equivalent of profit. Assume that $\hat{\pi}$ is strictly concave in p, A, and G. Then λ satisfies the differential equation $\dot{\lambda} = \rho\lambda - \partial H/\partial G = (\rho + \delta)\lambda - \partial\hat{\pi}/\partial G$ and the boundary condition $\lim_{t\to\infty}\lambda e^{-\rho t} = 0$. In addition, $\partial H/\partial p = \partial H/\partial A = 0$ at optimality. We assume that H is strictly concave in p, A, and G.

The adjoint variable λ is the shadow price of goodwill at time t. Thus the current-value Hamiltonian H can be interpreted as the instantaneous certainty equivalent of profit including the value $\lambda\dot{G}$ of the new goodwill created by advertising. Furthermore, the marginal opportunity cost of investment in goodwill $\lambda(\rho+\delta)$ equals the sum of the capital gain $\dot{\lambda}$ and the marginal gain from increased goodwill measured in terms of the certainty equivalent. Now $\partial H/\partial p = \partial\hat{\pi}/\partial p = 0$ and $\partial H/\partial A = \partial\hat{\pi}/\partial A + \lambda = 0$. Let $W_p = 0$ and $H_p = 0$, respectively, denote the loci of points satisfying $\partial\hat{\pi}/\partial p = 0$ and $\partial H/\partial p = 0$ at $t = 0$. Clearly $W_p = 0$ and $H_p = 0$ coincide. Let $W_A = 0$ and $H_A = 0$, respectively, denote the loci of points satisfying $\partial\hat{\pi}/\partial A = 0$ and $\partial H/\partial A = 0$. Let (p, A) be any pair satisfying $W_A = 0$. Evaluating H_A at this point, we have $H_A = \lambda > 0$. Hence $H_A = 0$ is to the right of $W_A = 0$ (see Figures 6.5a and 6.5b).

As discussed for the single-period CAPM, Figures 6.5a and 6.5b, respectively, correspond to the cases $\partial|\hat{\varepsilon}_p|/\partial A > (<)0$, where $|\hat{\varepsilon}_p|$ is the price elasticity of the certainty-equivalent demand $\hat{q} = f + g[\bar{u} - a\,\text{Cov}(u, R)]$.

46. In the multiplicative uncertainty model, $q = g(p, A)u$. Hence $(\partial q/\partial p)(p/q) = (\partial g/\partial p)(p/g)$, which is nonstochastic.

47. For the multiplicative uncertainty model, the expected utility is $Z = EU[(p - c)gu - A - F]$. Let the price elasticity of demand be $|\varepsilon_p| = -(\partial g/\partial p)(p/g)$. Then $Z_{Ap} = $

$-[(p - c)gE(U'u)/p](\partial/|\varepsilon_p|/\partial A)$ using the first-order conditions. Hence $\text{sgn}(Z_{Ap}) = -\text{sgn}(\partial|\varepsilon_p|/\partial A)$.

48. Let Z denote expected utility in the exogenous uncertainty model. Let the price elasticity of expected demand be $|\varepsilon_p| = (-\partial f/\partial p)(p/f)$. Then $Z_{Ap}\{p/[f(p - c)E(U')]\} = -(\partial|\varepsilon_p|/\partial A) - [p(\partial f/\partial A)\,\text{Cov}(U', u)]/[f^2(p - c)E(U')]$ using the first-order conditions. However, $\text{Cov}(U', u) < 0$ by risk aversion. Hence $(\partial|\varepsilon_p|/\partial A) < 0$ is a sufficient condition for $Z_{Ap} > 0$.

49. Let $(Z_{1t}, \ldots, Z_{kt})$ denote the vector of exogenous factors at time t. Then the instantaneously optimal advertising–sales and goodwill–sales ratios depend on $(Z_{1t}, \ldots, Z_{kt})$. As Nerlove and Arrow (1962, Theorem 3) point out, an interesting problem can now arise: The best policy may be to keep goodwill G_t below the instantaneously optimal level for some finite period of time because of anticipated future decreases in G^*.

50. Divide time into infinitesimal discrete periods each of duration dt. Let the appropriate time periods be labeled 1, 2, etc. We know that $A_1^m < A_1^O$ and $p_1^m < p_1^O$ if $\partial|\hat{\varepsilon}_p|/\partial A < 0$. The instantaneous certainty equivalent of profit in period 2 is $E_2 = (p_2 - c)[\phi_1(p_2, A_2) + \phi_2(G_1) - a\,\text{Cov}(u_2, R_2)] - A_2$, where $G_1 = A_1 + (1 - \delta)\bar{G}$, $\bar{G}$ denotes the goodwill at time 0, and δ the proportional decay rate for goodwill.

Let (p_2^*, A_2^*) denote the optimal policy in period 2. Recall that ϕ_2 is increasing in G_1. Then $\partial p_2^*/\partial G_1 > 0$ and $\partial A_2^*/\partial G_1 > 0$ if $\partial|\hat{\varepsilon}_p|/\partial A < 0$. However, $G_1^m < G_1^O$. Hence $p_2^m < p_2^O$ and $A_2^m < A_2^O$. But now $G_2^m - G_2^O = (A_2^m - A_2^O) + (1 - \delta)(A_1^m - A_1^O) < 0$. Proceeding as before, we see that $p_t^m < p_t^O$ and $A_t^m < A_t^O$ for all t.

Suppose $\partial|\hat{\varepsilon}_p|/\partial A > 0$. Following the previous approach, we can show that $p_2^m < p_2^O$ and $A_2^m > A_2^O$. However, the sign of $G_2^m - G_2^O$ is now ambiguous. Hence the results are indeterminate.

51. See previous note.

52. Consider the multiplicative uncertainty model. We know that $A_1^m < A_1^O$ and $p_1^m < p_1^O$. The instantaneous certainty equivalent of profit in period 2 is $E_2 = (p_2 - c)[\phi_1(p_1, p_2) + \phi_2(G_1)][\bar{u}_2 - a\,\text{Cov}(u_2, R_2)] - A_2$. Then $\partial p_2^*/\partial G_1 > 0$ and $\partial A_2^*/\partial G_1 > 0$ if $\partial|\hat{\varepsilon}_p|/\partial A < 0$. The rest of the proof is identical to that for the exogenous uncertainty specification (see note 50).

53. For the generalized uncertainty case, demand is defined by $D = [\phi_1(p, A) + \phi_2(G)] + [\phi_3(p, A) + \phi_4(G)]u$, where the signs of $\partial\phi_3/\partial p$, $\partial\phi_3/\partial A$, and $\partial\phi_4/\partial G$ are unrestricted. Proceeding as in the exogenous and multiplicative uncertainty cases, we can show that $p_t^m < p_t^O$ and $A_t^m < A_t^O$ for all t.

54. Let w denote the firm's wealth, U the firm's utility function, and $r(w)$ the Arrow–Pratt coefficient of absolute risk aversion. Then $r(w) = -U''(w)/U'(w)$ and measures the risk premium the firm is prepared to pay to avoid risk. Most economists including Arrow believe that $r(w)$ decreases with wealth.

55. Consider the exogenous uncertainty specification of the multiperiod expected utility model. We know that $A_1^m < A_1^O$ and $p_1^m < p_1^O$ if $\partial|\varepsilon_p|/\partial A < 0$, where $|\varepsilon_p|$ denotes the price elasticity of expected demand. The instantaneous expected utility of profit in period 2 is $M_2 = EU\{(p_2 - c)[\phi_1(p_2, A_2) + \phi_2(G_1) + u_2] - A_2\}$. Hence $\partial^2 M_2/\partial A_2\,\partial G_1 = (\partial\phi_2/\partial G_1)(p_2 - c)E(U'')[(p_2 - c)\,\partial\phi_1/\partial A_2 - 1] = 0$ using the first-order conditions. Similarly $\partial^2 M_2/\partial p_2\,\partial G_1 = $

$(\partial\phi_2/\partial G_1)(E(U')+E\{U''[(p_2-c)(\partial\phi_1/\partial p_2)+\phi_1+\phi_2+u_2]\})$. For any choice of (p_2, A_2), let $u_2 = u_2^*$ denote the level of u_2 for which $(p_2-c)\,\partial\phi_1/\partial p_2+\phi_1+\phi_2+u_2 = 0$ and $w_2 = w_2^*$ the corresponding wealth level. Suppose $u_2 > u_2^*$ and $w_2 > w_2^*$. By the hypothesis of decreasing absolute risk aversion $-U''(w_2)/U'(w_2) < -U''(w_2^*)/U'(w_2^*)$. Now $u_2 > u_2^*$ implies that $-U'(w_2)[(p_2-c)\,\partial\phi_1/\partial p_2+\phi_1+\phi_2+u_2] < 0$. Hence $U''(w_2)[(p_2-c)\,\partial\phi_1/\partial p_2+\phi_1+\phi_2+u_2] > [U''(w_2^*)/U'(w_2^*)]\,U'(w_2)[(p_2-c)\,\partial\phi_1/\partial p_2+\phi_1+\phi_2+u_2]$.

Similarly, we can show that this inequality holds if $u_2 < u_2^*$. Taking expectations of both sides, we have $E\{U''[(p_2-c)\,\partial\phi_1/\partial p_2+\phi_1+\phi_2+u_2]\} > 0$ using the first-order conditions. Hence $\partial^2 M_2/\partial A_2\,\partial G_1 > 0$. Now $\partial\phi_2/\partial G_1 > 0$ and $\partial|\varepsilon_p|/\partial A < 0$ is sufficient for $\partial^2 M_2/\partial A_2\,\partial p_2 > 0$. Hence $\partial p_2^*/\partial G_1 > 0$ and $\partial A_2^*/\partial G_1 > 0$. These results imply that $p_t^m < p_t^O$ and $A_t^m < A_t^O$ for all t.

In the multiplicative uncertainty case, $\partial^2 M_2/\partial p_2\,\partial G_1 = (\partial\phi_2/\partial G_1)E(U'u) > 0$ using the first-order conditions. However, $\partial^2 M_2/\partial A_2\,\partial G_1$ is ambiguous even if absolute risk aversion decreases in wealth. Hence the results are inherently indeterminate.

56. Define the expected demand for brand 1 as $\bar{s}_1 = \alpha_1(A_1, A_2) + \beta_1(A_1, A_2)\bar{u}_1$, where $\bar{u}_1 = E(u_1)$. Then Brands 1 and 2 are substitutes if $\partial^2\bar{s}_1/\partial A_1\,\partial A_2 < 0$ and complements if $\partial^2\bar{s}_1/\partial A_1\,\partial A_2 > 0$. Similar definitions apply for $\bar{s}_2$. These marginal effects need not be symmetric (i.e., $\partial^2\bar{s}_1/\partial A_1\,\partial A_2$ and $\partial^2\bar{s}_2/\partial A_1\,\partial A_2$ could have opposite signs). Hence the definitions of substitutes and complements are somewhat ambiguous. For convenience, we shall assume that $\partial^2\bar{s}_1/\partial A_1\,\partial A_2$ and $\partial^2\bar{s}_2/\partial A_1\,\partial A_2$ have the same signs. However, this condition is not necessary.

57. See previous note.

58. The assumption of constant marginal cost was necessary to analyze the joint price–advertising decision in the one-product model. The additional assumption of fixed prices is necessary to analyze a multibrand model of advertising under uncertainty (see Jagpal 1982a).

Nguyen (1987) develops a multiproduct model of advertising under uncertainty. Nguyen's model allows for increasing costs. However, the demand function is linear in advertising and uncertainty is exogenous. Thus the products are independent (all cross-derivatives in the demand function are zero), there are constant returns to advertising, and advertising policy has no effect on the variabilities of demand. Nguyen also assumes a quadratic utility function. This specification is restrictive because it implies that the firm's absolute risk aversion increases with wealth and that uncertainty is "small." Note that one needs to impose considerable structure on stochastic multiproduct models in order to obtain analytically tractable solutions.

59. The firm's stock value is $V = (1+r)^{-1}\left\{\sum_{i=1}^{2}(m_i\{\alpha_i + \beta_i[\bar{u}_i - a\,\text{Cov}(u_i, R)]\} - A_i) + F\right\}$ where $m_i = p_i - c_i$ denotes the unit profit margin of brand i, $\alpha_i = \alpha_i(A_1, A_2)$ and $\beta_i = \beta_i(A_1, A_2)$. We assume that V is strictly concave in A_1 and A_2.

60. Let $\bar{s}_1 = \beta_1\bar{u}_1$ and $\bar{s}_2 = \beta_2\bar{u}_2$, respectively, denote the demands for brands 1 and 2 under certainty. Let $\bar{\pi} = m_1\beta_1\bar{u}_1 + m_2\beta_2\bar{u}_2 - A_1 - A_2$ denote the corresponding product-line profit. Then the optimal advertising policy $(\bar{A}_1, \bar{A}_2)$ under certainty satisfies $\partial\bar{\pi}/\partial A_i = 0$.

The firm's stock value under uncertainty is defined by $V = \{\bar{\pi} - a[m_1\beta_1\,\text{Cov}(u_1, R) + m_2\beta_2\,\text{Cov}(u_2, R)]\}(1+r)^{-1}$. Thus the optimal advertising policy (A_1^*, A_2^*) satisfies $\partial V/\partial A_i = 0$.

Let $\left(\hat{A}_1, \hat{A}_2\right)$ be any pair satisfying $\partial \bar{\pi}/\partial A_1 = 0$. Evaluating $\partial V/\partial A_1$ at this point, we have $\partial V/\partial A_1 = \{-a[m_1(\partial \beta_1/\partial A_1) \operatorname{Cov}(u_1, R) + m_2(\partial \beta_2/\partial A_1) \operatorname{Cov}(u_2, R)]\}(1+r)^{-1}$. However, $\partial \beta_1/\partial A_1 > 0$ and $\partial \beta_2/\partial A_1 > 0$ because the brands are complementary. Furthermore, $\operatorname{Cov}(u_i, R) > 0$ in general. Hence $\partial V/\partial A_1 < 0$ by the concavity of V. That is, A_1 must be reduced, holding $\hat{A}_2$ fixed, to satisfy $\partial V/\partial A_1 = 0$. Let $\left(\hat{A}_1, \hat{A}_2\right)$ be any pair satisfying $\partial \bar{\pi}/\partial A_2 = 0$. Proceeding as before, we see that A_2 must be reduced, holding $\hat{A}_1$ fixed, to satisfy $\partial V/\partial A_2 = 0$.

Let $\sigma(s_i)$ denote the standard deviation of demand for brand i. For the multiplicative uncertainty specification, $k_i = \partial \sigma(s_i)/\partial A_i = (\partial \beta_i/\partial A_i)\sigma(u_i) > 0$. Suppose the advertising interactions are positive (i.e., $\partial k_i/\partial A_j > 0$ for $i \neq j$). Then $\partial^2 \bar{\pi}/\partial A_1 \, \partial A_2 > 0$.

These results imply that $A_1^* < \bar{A}_1$ and $A_2^* < \bar{A}_2$. If $\partial^2 \bar{\pi}/\partial A_1 \, \partial A_2 < 0$, we can only rule out the case where $A_1^* > \bar{A}_1$ and $A_2^* > \bar{A}_2$. From the form of $\partial V/\partial A_1$ above, it is clear that the results are inherently indeterminate if the two brands are substitutes (i.e., $\partial \beta_1/\partial A_2 < 0$).

61. Suppose the demand for Brand 1 becomes more uncertain. We define an increase in risk using the notion of mean-preserving spread (see Sandmo 1971 and others). Thus the demand for Brand 1 is $s_1 = \xi \beta_1(A_1, A_2)u_1 + \theta$, where ξ and θ are parameters such that $d\theta/d\xi = -\beta_1 \bar{u}_1$.

62. The demand function for Brand 1 is $s_1 = \xi \beta_1 u_1 + \theta$, where ξ and θ are parameters such that $d\theta/d\xi = -\beta_1 \bar{u}_1$. The firm's stock value is $V = \{m_1\theta + m_1\xi\beta_1[\bar{u}_1 - a \operatorname{Cov}(u_1, R)] + m_2\beta_2[\bar{u}_2 - a \operatorname{Cov}(u_2, R)] - A_1 - A_2\}(1+r)^{-1}$. Differentiating V and evaluating at $\xi = 1$, $\theta = 0$, we obtain $V_{1\xi} = -[am_1 \operatorname{Cov}(u_1, R)(\partial \beta_1/\partial A_1)](1+r)^{-1}$ and $V_{2\xi} = -[am_1 \operatorname{Cov}(u_1, R)(\partial \beta_1/\partial A_2)](1+r)^{-1}$, where the subscripts denote derivatives.

Suppose the brands are complementary ($\partial \beta_1/\partial A_2 > 0$). Then $\partial A_i/\partial \xi < 0$ if $V_{12} > 0$. Suppose the brands are substitutes ($\partial \beta_1/\partial A_2 < 0$) and $V_{12} < 0$. Then $\partial A_1/\partial \xi < 0$ and $\partial A_2/\partial \xi > 0$. Note that for the multiplicative uncertainty specification V_{12} has the same sign as the advertising interaction effect [i.e., $\partial^2 g_i/\partial A_1 \, \partial A_2 > (<)0$ implies $V_{12} > (<)0$].

63. Consider the multiplicative uncertainty specification. The certainty product-line profit is $\bar{\pi} = m_1\beta_1(A_1, A_2)\bar{u}_1 + m_2\beta_2(A_1, A_2)\bar{u}_2 - A_1 - A_2$. Using the expected utility model, the decision maker maximizes $Z = EU(\pi) = EU[\bar{\pi} + m_1\beta_1(u_1 - \bar{u}_1) + m_2\beta_2(u_2 - \bar{u}_2)]$. Let $(\hat{A}_1, \hat{A}_2)$ be any pair satisfying $\partial \bar{\pi}/\partial A_1 = 0$. Evaluating $\partial Z/\partial A_1$ at this point, we get $\partial Z/\partial A_1 = m_1(\partial \beta_1/\partial A_1) \operatorname{Cov}(U', u_1) + m_2(\partial \beta_2/\partial A_1) \operatorname{Cov}(U', u_2)$. However, U' depends on u_1 and u_2. Hence the signs of $\operatorname{Cov}(U', u_1)$ and $\operatorname{Cov}(U', u_2)$ are unknown. Consequently the global effect of uncertainty is indeterminate.

In order to determine the marginal effect of uncertainty, let the demand for Brand 1 be $\xi \beta_1 u_1 + \theta$, where $\partial \theta/\partial \xi = -\beta_1 \bar{u}$. Then $Z_{1\xi}$ and $Z_{2\xi}$ contain such terms as $\operatorname{Cov}(U', u_1)$ and $\operatorname{Cov}(U', u_2)$, which are inherently indeterminate.

Finally, it is difficult to examine the effect of parameter shifts in the expected utility model because Z_{12} does not have a clear economic meaning. Subject to this caveat, we can perform limited comparative statics experiments for parameter shifts not involving changes in riskiness or the degree of risk aversion (see Jagpal 1982a).

64. Consider the multiplicative uncertainty expected utility model. Let U_1 and U_2, respectively, denote the utility functions for firms 1 and 2. Colluding firms choose product-line advertising policy (A_1^c, A_2^c) to maximize $U^c = EU_1(\pi_1) + EU_2(\pi_2)$, where $\pi_i = m_i g_i(A_1, A_2) - A_i$. Now

$$\frac{\partial U^c}{\partial A_1} = E\left\{ U_1'\left[m_1\left(\frac{\partial g_1}{\partial A_1}\right)\bar{u}_1 - 1\right]\right\} + m_1\left(\frac{\partial g_1}{\partial A_1}\right)\text{Cov}\left(U_1', u_1\right)$$

$$+ E\left\{ U_2'\left[m_2\left(\frac{\partial g_2}{\partial A_1}\right)\bar{u}_2\right]\right\} + m_2\left(\frac{\partial g_2}{\partial A_1}\right)\text{Cov}\left(U_2', u_2\right)$$

Under certainty the colluding firms choose product-line advertising policy $\left(\bar{A}_1^c, \bar{A}_2^c\right)$ to maximize $\bar{\pi}^c = \bar{\pi}_1 + \bar{\pi}_2$. Hence $\partial\bar{\pi}^c/\partial A_1 = m_1(\partial g_1/\partial A_1)\bar{u}_1 - 1 + m_2(\partial g_2/\partial A_1)\bar{u}_2$. Comparing $\partial U^c/\partial A_1$ and $\partial\bar{\pi}^c/\partial A_1$ we see that the global effect of uncertainty is indeterminate.

Suppose both firms have identical utility functions (e.g., the firms are of approximately equal size). Let U denote the common utility function. Now $\partial U^c/\partial A_i$ simplifies to $\partial U^c/\partial A_i = \partial\bar{\pi}^c/\partial A_i + m_1(\partial g_1/\partial A_i)\,\text{Cov}(U', u_1) + m_2(\partial g_2/\partial A_i)\,\text{Cov}(U', u_2)$, where $\text{Cov}(U', u_i) < 0$ by risk aversion. Hence $A_1^c < \bar{A}_1^c$ and $A_2^c < \bar{A}_2^c$ if the products are complementary (i.e., the colluding firms reduce advertising for each product when uncertainty is introduced globally). If the products are substitutes, the global effect of introducing uncertainty is inherently indeterminate.

Suppose the colluding firms maximize their combined stock value. Proceeding as above, we can show that the colluding firms reduce advertising for each product when uncertainty is globally introduced, provided the products are complementary (e.g., the firms are partners in a strategic alliance involving the two brands).

65. Our graphical presentation is descriptively unrealistic because we are dealing with a simultaneous-move game. That is, each firm must choose its advertising policy before observing its rival's advertising decision. Consequently we only observe the point where the firms' reaction curves intersect (i.e., the Nash equilibrium).

66. A Nash equilibrium does not always exist. We assume that V^1 is strictly concave in A_1 and V^2 is strictly concave in A_2. These assumptions are sufficient for a Nash equilibrium. Note that for the multiplicative uncertainty case, the concavity of V^i implies that the expected marginal productivity of Brand i is strictly diminishing: a strong assumption.

67. The graphical representations in Figures 6.6a and 6.6b is based on the mathematical properties of a stable Nash equilibrium. Let V^1 and V^2, respectively, denote the stock prices of Firms 1 and 2. Let r^1 and r^2, respectively, denote the reaction functions for Firms 1 and 2. Then the slope of Firm i's reaction function is $dr^i/dA_j = -V_{ij}^i/V_{ii}^i$, where the subscripts denote derivatives. A sufficient condition for the Nash equilibrium to be asymptotically stable is $|dr^1/dA_2\|dr^2/dA_1| < 1$ or $V_{11}^1 V_{22}^2 - V_{12}^1 V_{21}^2 > 0$ in an open neighborhood of the Nash equilibrium. See Fudenberg and Tirole (1992, pp. 23–25), Dixit (1986), and Moulin (1986) for further discussion of the Nash stability conditions.

68. For the multiplicative uncertainty specification the expected demand for Brand i is $\bar{s}_i = g_i(A_1, A_2)\bar{u}_i$. Hence the brands are substitutes if $\partial g_i/\partial A_j < 0$ for $i \neq j$. Firm i's stock value is defined by $V^i = \{m_i g_i(A_1, A_2)[\bar{u}_i - a\,\text{Cov}(u_i, R)] - A_i\}(1 + r)^{-1}$. Now the brands are strategic substitutes if $V_{12}^i < 0$ for all i [i.e., $\partial^2 g_i/\partial A_1\,\partial A_2 < 0$]. Thus Brands 1 and 2 may not be strategic substitutes even though they are substitutes.

69. Let $\bar{\pi}^i$ denote the firm's profit under certainty. Then Firm i's stock value under uncertainty is $V^i = [\bar{\pi}^i - am_i g_i(A_1, A_2)\,\text{Cov}(u_i, R)](1 + r)^{-1}$. Firm i's reaction function under uncertainty

is given by $V_i^i = [\bar{\pi}_i^i - am_i(\partial g_i/\partial A_i) \, \text{Cov}(u_i, R)](1 + r)^{-1}$, where the subscripts denote derivatives. Let $(\hat{A}_1, \hat{A}_2)$ be any pair satisfying $\bar{\pi}_1^1 = 0$. Then $V_1^1 < 0$ at this point. Hence, keeping $\hat{A}_2$ fixed, A_1 must be reduced to satisfy $V_1^1 = 0$. Thus $V_1^1 = 0$ lies to the left of $\bar{\pi}_1^1 = 0$ in the (A_1, A_2) plane. By a similar proof we can show that $V_2^2 = 0$ is always below $\bar{\pi}_2^2 = 0$. See Figures 6.6a and 6.6b.

70. Let $\bar{V}^i$ and $\hat{V}^i$, respectively, denote firm i's stock prices under certainty and uncertainty. Let $\bar{A}^i$ and $\hat{A}^i$ denote the corresponding advertising policies. Then $\hat{V}^i - \bar{V}^i = \left\{ \left(\bar{A}_i - \hat{A}_i \right) - m_i \alpha_i \left[g_i \left(\bar{A}_i, \bar{A}_2 \right) - g_1 \left(\hat{A}_1, \hat{A}_2 \right) \right] \right\} (1 + r)^{-1}$, where $\alpha_i = [\bar{u}_i - a \, \text{Cov}(u_i, R)] > 0$. Suppose the brands are strategic complements. Then the second term is negative because $\bar{A}_1 > \hat{A}_1$ and $\bar{A}_2 > \hat{A}_2$. Hence the global effect of uncertainty on stock prices is indeterminate. Similarly, the results for strategic substitutes are also ambiguous.

71. As an aside, note that when uncertainty is globally introduced, the combined stock value of colluding firms always decreases. However, the effects on the individual stock prices are ambiguous.

72. Let $\left(\hat{A}_1, \hat{A}_2 \right)$ denote the Nash solution under uncertainty. Now $D = V_{11}^1 V_{22}^2 - V_{12}^1 V_{21}^2 > 0$ using the Nash stability conditions. For convenience treat $\alpha = \text{Cov}(u_1, R)$ as the shift parameter. [The results will be unchanged if we use the mean-preserving spread approach and set $s_1' = \xi g_1(A_1, A_2) u_1 + \theta$, where $d\theta/d\xi = -g_1 \bar{u}_1$.] Then $d\hat{A}_1/d\alpha = am_1(\partial g_1/\partial A_1) V_{22}^2 D(1+r)^{-1} < 0$ and $d\hat{A}_2/d\alpha = -am_1 m_2(\partial g_1 \, \partial A_1) \left(\partial^2 \hat{q}_2/\partial A_1 \, \partial A_2 \right) D(1 + r)^{-1}$ where $\hat{q}_2 = g_2[\bar{u}_2 - a \, \text{Cov}(u_2, R)]$ denotes the certainty-equivalent demand for Brand 2. Hence $\text{sgn} \left(d\hat{A}_2/d\alpha \right) = -\text{sgn}(\partial^2 g_2/\partial A_1 \, \partial A_2)$. Recall that $\partial^2 g_2/\partial A_1 \, \partial A_2 > (<)0$ if the products are strategic complements (strategic substitutes). Let $\hat{V}^1$ denote the stock price for brand 1 at the Nash equilibrium. Then $d\hat{V}^1/d\alpha = \hat{V}_2^1 \left(d\hat{A}_2/d\alpha \right) + \hat{V}_\alpha^1$, where the first term is an indirect effect due to Firm 2's reaction and the second term is the direct effect of Firm 1's actions. Now $\hat{V}_\alpha^1 = -am_1 g_1(1 + r)^{-1} < 0$ as in the case of the monopolist. Hence $d\hat{V}^1/d\alpha$ is < 0 if the products are strategic substitutes and is indeterminate when the products are strategic complements.

Similarly, $d\hat{V}^2/d\alpha = \left\{ m_1 m_2 (\partial g_1/\partial A_1)(\partial g_2/\partial A_1) a[\bar{u}_2 - a \, \text{Cov}(u_2, R)] V_{22}^2 \right\} D(1 + r)^{-1}$ < 0 always by the second-order conditions. Thus Firm 2's stock price increases.

Let M_1 denote the volume-based market share for brand 1. Then

$$\frac{dE(M_1)}{d\alpha} = E \left\{ \frac{u_1 u_2 \left[g_2 \left(\frac{\partial g_1}{\partial A_1} \frac{\partial \hat{A}_1}{\partial \alpha} + \frac{\partial g_1}{\partial A_2} \frac{\partial \hat{A}_2}{\partial \alpha} \right) - g_1 \left(\frac{\partial g_2}{\partial A_1} \frac{\partial \hat{A}_1}{\partial \alpha} + \frac{\partial g_2}{\partial A_2} \frac{\partial \hat{A}_2}{\partial \alpha} \right) \right]}{Q^2} \right\} \text{ where}$$

$Q = g_1 \left(\hat{A}_1, \hat{A}_2 \right) u_1 + g_2 \left(\hat{A}_1, \hat{A}_2 \right) u_2$. Now $u_i > 0$ in the multiplicative uncertainty case. Hence $dE(M_1)/d\alpha < 0$ if the brands are strategic substitutes. Let R_1 denote the revenue-based market share for brand 1 [i.e., $R_1 = p_1 g_1 u_1/(p_1 g_1 u_1 + p_2 g_2 u_2)$, where p_i denotes the price of brand i]. Replacing g_i above by $p_i g_i$, we see that $dE(R_1)/d\alpha < 0$. The effects on market shares (volume-based or revenue-based) are indeterminate when the products are strategic complements.

73. Let $y = \alpha + \beta x + u$, where α and β are parameters and u is the disturbance term. Suppose $y^m = y + v$, where $E(v) = 0$ and y^m is the measured value of y.

    Let $\text{Cov}(u, v) = 0$, where Cov denotes covariance. Suppose we estimate the model $y^m = a + bx + e$, where e is the disturbance term. Then the least-squares estimate $\hat{b}$ is unbiased [i.e., $E\left(\hat{b}\right) = \beta$]. However, the estimate is unstable because of the measurement error v. Suppose $x^m = x + w$, where $E(w) = 0$. Then the regression of x^m on y^m leads to meaningless results.

74. Given linear response curves, we can obtain a finite solution in two ways. One method is to introduce uncertainty and assume risk aversion [i.e., the firm's profit Π is uncertain and $U''(\Pi) < 0$, where the primes denote derivatives]. A second method is to formulate a multiproduct advertising model where the decision maker allocates a fixed advertising budget across the product line. Neither method is theoretically appealing.

75. Let $m = 1, \ldots, M$ index months and $w = 1, \ldots, W$ weeks. Then the correct weekly model (Model 1) is $S_{mw} = \alpha + \beta A_{mw} + u_{mw}$, where α and β are parameters, A denotes advertising, S denotes sales, and u_{mw} is the stochastic disturbance term. Let u_{mw} be i.i.d. and $\sigma^2(u_{mw}) = V$. Suppose we aggregate the data by week. Then the monthly model (Model 2) is $S_{m.} = W\alpha + \beta A_{m.} + u_{m.}$, where $S_{m.}$ denotes sales in month m, $A_{m.}$ denotes advertising in month m, $u_{m.}$ is the disturbance term, and $\sigma^2(u_{m.}) = WV$. Let $\hat{\beta}_1$ and $\hat{\beta}_2$ denote the least-squares estimates from models 1 and 2, respectively. Clearly, $E\left(\hat{\beta}_1\right) = \beta$ and $E\left(\hat{\beta}_2\right) = \beta$ (i.e., both estimates are unbiased).

    Let the population R^2 values for models 1 and 2 be R_1^2 and R_2^2, respectively. Then $R_1^2 = \beta^2\sigma^2(A_{mw})/\left[\beta^2\sigma^2(A_{mw}) + V\right]$ and $R_2^2 = \beta^2\sigma^2(A_{m.})/\left[\beta^2\sigma^2(A_{m.}) + WV\right]$. Differentiating, we obtain $\partial R_2^2/\partial W = -V\beta^2\sigma^2(A_{m.})/\left(\beta^2\sigma^2(A_{m.}) + WV\right)^2 < 0$ and $\partial^2 R_2^2/\partial W^2 = 2V^2\beta^2\sigma^2(A_{m.})/\left(\beta^2\sigma^2(A_{m.}) + WV\right)^3 > 0$. That is, data aggregation reduces model fit. However, this effect dampens as W increases.

    Comparing the fits of models 1 and 2, we obtain $R_2^2 - R_1^2 = \beta^2 V[\sigma^2(A_{m.}) - W\sigma^2(A_{mw})]/ZN$, where $Z = \beta^2\sigma^2(A_{m.}) + WV > 0$ and $N = \beta^2\sigma^2(A_{mw}) + V > 0$. Hence $R_2^2 < R_1^2$ if $\sigma^2(A_{m.}) < W\sigma^2(A_{mw})$. Let $\hat{\beta}_1$ and $\hat{\beta}_2$ denote the estimates for models 1 and 2, respectively. Then for large samples $\sigma^2\left(\hat{\beta}_1\right) = V/\sigma^2(A_{mw})$ and $\sigma^2\left(\hat{\beta}_2\right) = WV/\sigma^2(A_{m.})$. Hence $\sigma^2\left(\hat{\beta}_2\right) > \sigma^2\left(\hat{\beta}_1\right)$ if $\sigma^2(A_{m.}) < W\sigma^2(A_{mw})$.

    Further simplifications do not appear possible. For example, suppose the weekly advertising data are symmetrically distributed for any given month. Let $\bar{A} = \Sigma_{m,w}A_{mw}/MW$ and $\bar{A}_m = \Sigma_w A_{mw}/W = A_{m.}/W$. Recall that $\bar{A} = \Sigma_m\bar{A}_m/M$. The assumption of symmetry implies that $W(\bar{A}_m - \bar{A})^2 < (A_{m1} - \bar{A})^2 + \cdots + (A_{mW} - \bar{A})^2$ for all m. Summing across all m and dividing by MW, we obtain $\Sigma_m(\bar{A}_m - \bar{A})^2/M < \Sigma_{m,w}(A_{mw} - \bar{A})^2/MW$.

    Now $\bar{A}_m = A_{m.}/W$. Hence $\sigma^2(\bar{A}_m) = \sigma^2(A_{m.})/W^2$. Thus $\sigma^2(A_{m.})/W^2 < \sigma^2(A_{mw})$ and the sign of $R_2^2 - R_1^2$ is indeterminate.

76. Our analysis assumes that the monthly budget of \$6,400 is evenly distributed throughout the month. Different results will be obtained if we change this assumption. However, only the degree of suboptimality will change.

77. Let q denote output and $x_1, \ldots, x_n$ the amounts of inputs $1, \ldots, n$, respectively. Let the stochastic production frontier be $q = f(x_1, \ldots, x_n) + u + v$, where the stochastic term $u \leq 0$ denotes errors due to production inefficiency and v is the usual disturbance term. See Forsund, Lovell,

and Schmidt (1980) for a review of econometric methods to estimate stochastic production frontiers and Kalita, Jagpal, and Lehmann (1991) for an application of the methodology in the context of a price-quality equilibrium model.

78. The assumption of homoscedasticity is not central to the argument. If the price effect is heteroscedastic, the productivity estimates will be unbiased. However, the t-statistics will be biased (e.g., the manager will make incorrect inferences about advertising productivity).

79. Consider the more general case where price and advertising are not perfectly correlated. Suppose the true model is $S = \alpha + \beta \ln A - \gamma(p) + u$, where α and $\beta (> 0)$ are parameters, $\gamma(p)$ is a function such that $\partial \gamma / \partial p > 0$, $E(u) = 0$, $\text{Cov}(p, u) = 0$, and $\text{Cov}(A, u) = 0$. Assume that the researcher estimates the model $S = \alpha_1 + \beta_1 \ln A + v$, where α_1 and β_1 are parameters and v is the disturbance term. Let $\hat{\beta}_1$ denote the least-squares estimate of β_1. Then for large samples $\text{plim}\left(\hat{\beta}_1\right) = \beta - \text{Cov}[\ln A, \gamma(p)]/\sigma^2(\ln A)$. Suppose p and A are negatively correlated. Then $\text{Cov}[\ln A, \gamma(p)] < 0$ because $\ln A$ and $\gamma(p)$ are strictly increasing in their respective arguments. Hence $\text{plim}\left(\hat{\beta}_1\right) - \beta > 0$. That is, the marginal productivities of advertising are systematically overstated. If p and A are positively correlated, $\text{plim}\left(\hat{\beta}_1\right) - \beta < 0$. These results hold for more general functional forms provided expected sales do not diminish as advertising increases (i.e., there is no wearout effect).

    Suppose sales depend on other variables besides price and advertising. Alternatively suppose advertising has dynamic carryover effects. Then omitting price leads to inconsistent estimates of advertising effects. However, the direction of the bias is indeterminate.

80. Another possibility is to use the raw variables themselves in the second-order Taylor expansion instead of their logarithms as in the translog model. The choice of type of quadratic functional form should be made on empirical grounds. Care should be exercised in comparing model fits because the scales of the dependent variable differ across models (i.e., the dependent variable in the translog specification is ln sales and not sales). Other flexible functional forms are discussed in Fuss, McFadden, and Mundlak (1978) and Guilkey, Lovell, and Sickles (1983). Guilkey et al. conclude that the translog form provides a good approximation to reality, provided reality is not too complex. In general, however, the choice among alternative functional forms remains an open question.

81. Strictly one cannot conclude that threshold effects are absent because the minimum advertising–sales ratio for any month during the observation period was 3.09 percent (see Table 6.4). However, the data suggest that if threshold effects exist, they are minimal.

82. Suppose the advertising–sales model is identified (i.e., the parameters of the advertising and sales equations can be recovered given data). Let S denote sales, A advertising, $Z_1, \ldots, Z_k$ the levels of exogenous variables and t time. Let the structural model be $S_t = \phi(A_t) + \mu(Z_{1t}, \ldots, Z_{kt}) + u_t$ where ϕ and μ are deterministic functions and u_t is a stochastic disturbance term. Then A_t and u_t are necessarily correlated when feedback is present. Consequently, single-equation methods will always yield inconsistent estimates of ϕ and μ. Thus the productivity of advertising is mismeasured.

83. Testing for causality using the original advertising (A) and sales (S) data is difficult because the original series are generally nonstationary and autocorrelated. For example, sales growth rates vary over the product life cycle, current sales can depend on previous sales because of consumer loyalty or habitual buying, and advertising budgets can vary seasonally or cyclically.

For statistical purposes, it is necessary to transform the A and S series into nonautocorrelated series called innovations (u and v, respectively). This procedure is called prewhitening, and the appropriate transformations are called prewhitening filters. Pierce and Haugh (1977, pp. 269–70) have shown that a wide class of filters is causality-preserving (e.g., detrending, seasonal differencing, and Box–Cox transforms). Hence we can conduct causality tests using the innovations (u and v) instead of the original advertising and sales series.

The general system of dynamic regression equations can be expressed as (see Granger and Newbold, 1977, p. 244): $u_t = V_1(B)v_t + [\theta_1(B)/\phi_1(B)]\varepsilon_{1t}$ and $v_t = V_2(B)u_t + [\theta_2(B)/\phi_2(B)]\varepsilon_{2t}$, where ε_{1t} and ε_{2t} are mutually uncorrelated white noise residuals and V, θ and ϕ are polynomials in B, the backshift operator [for example, $B^k(v_t) = v_{t-k}$, where k is a positive integer].

The empirical problem is twofold. First, estimate the innovations $\hat{u}_t$ and $\hat{v}_t$. In general separate prewhitening filters must be used for the advertising and sales series (see Haugh 1976 for a proof). Second, estimate the Vs, θs, and ϕs using the estimated innovations $\hat{u}_t$ and $\hat{v}_t$. See Granger and Newbold (1977, pp. 244–55) for details. As discussed in the text, the dynamic regression equations can only be identified if instantaneous causality is absent. Jagpal and Hui (1980) provide a detailed discussion of instantaneous causality in advertising–sales models.

84. Sasieni (1971) develops a continuous-time model in which advertising has a carryover effect. Sasieni's main result is interesting: No cyclic advertising policy can be optimal in the long run. At first glance this result appears to be counterintuitive and to conflict with observed behavior. However, the anomaly occurs because Sasieni allows "chattering" control. That is, the firm can alternate between the states "advertise" and "do not advertise" an infinite number of times during any given time period. Obviously such chattering policies are impossible. Consequently, pulsing may provide the closest solution to the theoretical optimum.

85. The Simon (1982) and Mahajan and Muller (MM; 1986) models are fundamentally different. Simon's model emphasizes the inherent asymmetry in the effects of a decrease or an increase in advertising on the functional form of the advertising–sales equation. The Mahajan and Muller model does not allow such asymmetric effects. In contrast to Simon, MM assumes a fixed planning period (T) and a fixed advertising budget. MM also makes the questionable assumption that total awareness is a good proxy for long-term profit. (MM measures total awareness as the sum of the awareness generated during the planning period T and future awareness, assuming that the firm stops advertising at time T.) Simon models the sales response function directly. Consequently in Simon's model there is no ambiguity about the effect of pulsing on long-term profit (i.e., net present value).

86. The appropriate switching regime translog model is

$$
\begin{aligned}
\ln\, S_t = {} & \alpha_0 + \alpha_1 \ln\, A_t + \alpha_2 D\, \ln(\Delta A_t) + \alpha_3 \ln\, S_{t-1} + \alpha_{11}(\ln\, A_t)^2 + \alpha_{22} D(\ln\, \Delta A_t)^2 \\
& + \alpha_{33}(\ln\, S_{t-1})^2 + \alpha_{12} D(\ln\, A_t)(\ln\, \Delta A_t) + \alpha_{13}(\ln\, A_t)(\ln\, S_{t-1}) \\
& + \alpha_{23} D(\ln\, \Delta A_t)(\ln\, S_{t-1}) + u_t
\end{aligned}
$$

where the αs are parameters, u_t is the disturbance term, and D is a dummy variable such that $D = 0$ if $A_t \le A_{t-1}$ and $D = 1$ if $A_t > A_{t-1}$. Note that if $\Delta A_t < 0$, $\ln(\Delta A_t)$ is undefined. However, this is not problematic: Simply set all terms involving ΔA_t to zero. Thus, if $A_t \le A_{t-1}$, the translog model is

$$\ln S_t = \alpha_0 + \alpha_1 \ln A_t + \alpha_3 \ln S_{t-1} + \alpha_{11}(\ln A_t)^2 + \alpha_{33}(\ln S_{t-1})^2$$
$$+ \alpha_{13}(\ln A_t)(\ln S_{t-1}) + u_t$$

which is a quadratic approximation in logarithms to any continuous function $S_t = \phi_1(S_{t-1}, A_t)$. If $A_t > A_{t-1}$, the model is

$$\ln S_t = \alpha_0 + \alpha_1 \ln A_t + \alpha_2 \ln(\Delta A_t) + \alpha_3 \ln S_{t-1} + \alpha_{11}(\ln A_t)^2 + \alpha_{22}(\ln \Delta A_t)^2$$
$$+ \alpha_{33}(\ln S_{t-1})^2 + \alpha_{12}(\ln A_t)(\ln \Delta A_t) + \alpha_{13}(\ln A_t)(\ln S_{t-1})$$
$$+ \alpha_{23}(\ln \Delta A_t)(\ln S_{t-1}) + u_t$$

which is a quadratic approximation in logarithms to any continuous function $S_t = \phi_2(S_{t-1}, A_t, \Delta A_t)$. To allow for heteroscedasticity in the switching regime model, replace u_t by Du_t.

Note that the translog model allows for general patterns of carryover effect. (Contrast Simon's partial adjustment model, where $\partial S_t / \partial S_{t-1} = \lambda$, a fixed parameter.) The effect of the differential stimulus ΔA_t is not linearized. The marginal productivites and elasticities of advertising are very flexible and depend on the pattern of advertising spending. See Jagpal, Sudit, and Vinod (1982) for a detailed discussion. Standard statistical methods can be used to test the theory of differential stimulus effects (i.e., $\alpha_2 = \alpha_{22} = \alpha_{12} = \alpha_{23} = 0$).

Finally instead of using the absolute stimulus differential, we can use the relative stimulus differential $\Delta A_t = (A_t - A_{t-1})/A_{t-1}$ or allow for threshold effects (i.e., the sales function switches if ΔA_t exceeds some threshold effect). Two interesting research questions are whether A_{t-1} is a reasonable proxy for the anchor value of advertising and how pulsing affects the process of forming anchor values.

87. Consider a current-effects advertising model with two media. Let X_1 and X_2 denote the real advertising expenditures in media 1 and 2, respectively. Let G denote the unobserved advertising goodwill and S sales. For simplicity consider the linear system $G = \gamma_0 + \gamma_1 X_1 + \gamma_2 X_2 + \zeta$ and $S = \beta_0 + \beta_1 G + \varepsilon$, where the γs are parameters and ζ and ε are disturbances satisfying $\text{Cov}(G, \varepsilon) = 0, \text{Cov}(X_1, \zeta) = 0$, and $\text{Cov}(X_2, \zeta) = 0$. The only useful equations available for identification are $\text{Cov}(S, X_1) = \beta_1 \gamma_1 \sigma_{11} + \beta_1 \gamma_2 \sigma_{12}$ and $\text{Cov}(S, X_2) = \beta_2 \gamma_1 \sigma_{21} + \beta_2 \gamma_2 \sigma_{22}$, where σ_{ij} denotes the covariance of X_i and X_j. Recall that only the σ_{ij}s are observable. Hence the structural model is inherently indeterminate (i.e., the βs and γs cannot be identified).

88. In general, the advertising goodwill model in Figure 6.9 is identified provided the firm uses two or more media and has at least two product lines. For simplicity consider a two-media translog model with two products. Let X_1 and X_2 denote the real advertising expenditures in media 1 and 2, respectively. Let S_1 and S_2, respectively, denote the sales of products 1 and 2 and G the stochastic unobserved goodwill. Let $x_1 = \ln X_1, x_2 = \ln X_2, s_1 = \ln S_1, s_2 = \ln S_2$, and $g = \ln G$. (Note that the logarithmic transformation requires that the advertising goodwill G is ratio-scaled. This assumption is reasonable for most interpretations of G such as reach, percentage of the population aware of the firm, and so on.)

Then the structural model is $g = \gamma_0 + \gamma_1 x_1 + \gamma_2 x_2 + \gamma_{11} x_1^2 + \gamma_{22} x_2^2 + \gamma_{12} x_1 x_2 + \zeta, s_1 = \phi_1 + \beta_1 g + \varepsilon_1$, and $s_2 = \phi_2 + \beta_2 g + \varepsilon_2$, where the γs, ϕs, and βs are parameters and ε_1 and ε_2 are stochastic disturbances such that $\text{Cov}(x_i, \varepsilon_j) = 0, \text{Cov}(x_i, \zeta) = 0$ for all i and j, and $\text{Cov}(\varepsilon_1, \varepsilon_2) = 0$. For identification set $\beta_1 = 1$ (say). This parameterization simply sets the scales of g and s_1 to be equal and does not imply a conceptual restriction. (Recall that G, S_1, and S_2 are all ratio-scaled.)

Then we have the following equations $c_1 = Q\gamma$, where $c_1 = ($Cov$(s_1, x_1),$ Cov$(s_1, x_2),$ Cov$(s_1, x_1^2),$ Cov$(s_1, x_2^2),$ Cov$(s_1, x_1x_2))'$, $\gamma = (\gamma_1, \gamma_2, \gamma_{11}, \gamma_{22}, \gamma_{12})'$, and

$$Q = \begin{bmatrix} \sigma^2(x_1) & \text{Cov}(x_1, x_2) & \text{Cov}(x_1, x_1^2) & \text{Cov}(x_1, x_2^2) & \text{Cov}(x_1, x_1x_2) \\ \text{Cov}(x_2, x_1) & \sigma^2(x_2) & \text{Cov}(x_2, x_1^2) & \text{Cov}(x_2, x_2^2) & \text{Cov}(x_2, x_1x_2) \\ \text{Cov}(x_1^2, x_1) & \text{Cov}(x_1^2, x_2) & \sigma^2(x_1^2) & \text{Cov}(x_1^2, x_2^2) & \text{Cov}(x_1^2, x_1x_2) \\ \text{Cov}(x_2^2, x_1) & \text{Cov}(x_2^2, x_2) & \text{Cov}(x_2^2, x_1^2) & \sigma^2(x_2^2) & \text{Cov}(x_2^2, x_1x_2) \\ \text{Cov}(x_1x_2, x_1) & \text{Cov}(x_1x_2, x_2) & \text{Cov}(x_1x_2, x_1^2) & \text{Cov}(x_1x_2, x_2^2) & \sigma^2(x_1x_2) \end{bmatrix}$$

where $\sigma^2(\cdot)$ denotes the variance operator. Recall that c_1 and Q are observable. Hence $\gamma = Q^{-1}c_1$. Let $c_2 = ($Cov$(s_2, x_1),$ Cov$(s_2, x_2),$ Cov$(s_2, x_1^2),$ Cov$(s_2, x_2^2),$ Cov$(s_2, x_1x_2))'$. Proceeding as before, we obtain $c_2 = \beta_2 Q\gamma$. Hence β_2 is identified.

To identify $\sigma^2(\zeta)$ consider Cov$(s_1, s_2) = \beta_2\sigma^2(g)$. Let $g = \gamma_0 + z + \zeta$, where $z = \gamma_1x_1 + \gamma_2x_2 + \gamma_{11}x_1^2 + \gamma_{22}x_2^2 + \gamma_{12}x_1x_2$. Then $\sigma^2(g) = \sigma^2(z) + \sigma^2(\zeta)$. Hence Cov$(s_1, s_2) = \beta_2[\sigma^2(z) + \sigma^2(\zeta)]$. However, β_2 is known, Cov(s_1, s_2) is observable, and $\sigma^2(z)$ is a function of known parameters (i.e., the γs and σ_{ij}s). Hence $\sigma^2(z)$ is identified. Finally $\sigma^2(\varepsilon_1)$ and $\sigma^2(\varepsilon_2)$ are identified using $\sigma^2(s_1) = \sigma^2(g) + \sigma^2(\varepsilon_1)$ and $\sigma^2(s_2) = \beta_2^2\sigma^2(g) + \sigma^2(\varepsilon_2)$.

Note that the advertising goodwill model is very general and implies that the reduced-form structural equations have the translog functional form. In particular,

$$\ln S_1 = (\phi_1 + \gamma_0) + \gamma_1 \ln X_1 + \gamma_2 \ln X_2 + \gamma_{11}(\ln X_1)^2 + \gamma_{22}(\ln X_2)^2$$
$$+ \gamma_{12}(\ln X_1)(\ln X_2) + (\zeta + \varepsilon_1)$$

$$\ln S_2 = (\phi_2 + \beta_2\gamma_0) + \beta_2[\gamma_1(\ln X_1)] + \beta_2[\gamma_2(\ln X_2)] + \beta_2\left[\gamma_{11}(\ln X_1)^2\right] + \beta_2\left[\gamma_{22}(\ln X_2)^2\right]$$
$$+ \beta_2\gamma_{12}(\ln X_1)(\ln X_2) + (\zeta + \varepsilon_2)$$

However, *the model implies that the reduced-form parameters are structurally related in both sales equations.* (Compare coefficients for a given regressor across equations.)

In order to test the goodwill model, consider the null model that the media mix affects sales directly rather than through the intervening goodwill construct. In this case the reduced-form parameters are unconstrained across the sales equations. Note that the advertising goodwill model is a special case of the null model. Consequently we can test the goodwill model using standard likelihood-ratio statistics. In practice, the translog model suffers from multicollinearity. Hence although the likelihood-ratio tests for overall model fit may not be adversely affected, the structural parameters are unstable. Jagpal (1982c) develops a ridge estimator to deal with this problem.

89. In general, the dynamic model shown in Figure 6.10 is identified provided the firm uses at least two media and has two or more product lines. Consider a two-media, two-product model. Using the same notation as in note 88 and introducing a subscript for time, we can write the translog structural model shown in Figure 6.10 as:

$$g_{t-1} = \gamma_0 + \gamma_1x_{1,t-1} + \gamma_2x_{2,t-1} + \gamma_{11}x_{1,t-1}^2 + \gamma_{22}x_{2,t-1}^2 + \gamma_{12}x_{1,t-1}x_{2,t-1} + \zeta_{t-1} \qquad (1)$$

$$s_{1,t-1} = \phi_1 + \beta_1 g_{t-1} + \varepsilon_{1,t-1} \tag{2}$$

$$s_{2,t-1} = \phi_2 + \beta_2 g_{t-1} + \varepsilon_{2,t-1} \tag{3}$$

$$g_t = \gamma_0 + \gamma_1 x_{1t} + \gamma_2 x_{2t} + \gamma_{11} x_{1t}^2 + \gamma_{22} x_{2t}^2 + \gamma_{12} x_{1t} + \mu g_{t-1} + \zeta_t \tag{4}$$

$$s_{1t} = \phi_1 + \beta_1 g_t + \varepsilon_{1t} \tag{5}$$

$$s_{2t} = \phi_2 + \beta_2 g_t + \varepsilon_{2t} \tag{6}$$

where the γs, ϕs, βs and μ are parameters. Note in particular that $\mathrm{Cov}(\zeta_{t-1}, \zeta_t) \neq 0$, $\mathrm{Cov}(\varepsilon_{1,t-1}, \varepsilon_{1t}) \neq 0$ and $\mathrm{Cov}(\varepsilon_{2,t-1}, \varepsilon_{2t}) \neq 0$.

Set $\beta_1 = 1$ for identification (see note 16). Then the γs (except for γ_0), $\sigma^2(\zeta_{t-1})$, $\sigma^2(\varepsilon_{1,t-1})$, $\sigma^2(\varepsilon_{2,t-1})$, and $\sigma^2(g_{t-1})$ are identified using Eqs. (1), (2), and (3).

In order to identify μ consider

$$\mathrm{Cov}(g_t, x_{1,t-1}) = \gamma_1 \, \mathrm{Cov}(x_{1t}, x_{1,t-1}) + \gamma_2 \, \mathrm{Cov}(x_{2t}, x_{1,t-1}) + \gamma_{11} \, \mathrm{Cov}\left(x_{1t}^2, x_{1,t-1}\right)$$
$$+ \gamma_{22} \, \mathrm{Cov}\left(x_{2t}^2, x_{1,t-1}\right) + \gamma_{12} \, \mathrm{Cov}(x_{1t}, x_{1,t-1}) + \mu \, \mathrm{Cov}(g_{t-1}, x_{1,t-1}).$$

Recall that $\mathrm{Cov}(g_{t-1}, x_{1,t-1})$ is a function of known parameters. Hence μ is identified. From Eq. (6) $\mathrm{Cov}(s_{2t}, x_{1t}) = \beta_2 \, \mathrm{Cov}(g_t, x_{1t})$. However, $\mathrm{Cov}(g_t, x_{1t})$ is a function of known parameters. Hence β_2 is identified. Using Eqs. (5) and (6), we have $\mathrm{Cov}(s_{1t}, s_{2t}) = \beta_2 \sigma^2(g_t)$. Hence $\sigma^2(g_t)$ is known. In Eq. (4) let $r_1 = \gamma_1 x_{1t} + \gamma_2 x_{2t} + \gamma_{11} x_{1t}^2 + \gamma_{22} x_{2t}^2 + \gamma_{12} x_{1t} x_{2t} + \mu g_{t-1}$. Then $\sigma^2(g_t) = \sigma^2(r_1) + \sigma^2(\zeta_t)$. However, $\sigma^2(r_1)$ is a function of known parameters. Hence $\sigma^2(\zeta_t)$ is identified. In order to identify $\mathrm{Cov}(\zeta_t, \zeta_{t-1})$, let $r_2 = \gamma_1 x_{1,t-1} + \gamma_2 x_{2,t-1} + \gamma_{11} x_{1,t-1}^2 + \gamma_{22} x_{2,t-1}^2 + \gamma_{12}(x_{1,t-1})(x_{2,t-1})$ in Eq. (1). Using Eqs. (2) and (6), we obtain $\mathrm{Cov}(s_{1,t-1}, s_{2t}) = \beta_2 \, \mathrm{Cov}(g_{t-1}, g_t)$ recalling that $\mathrm{Cov}(\varepsilon_{1,t-1}, \varepsilon_{2t}) = 0$. Hence $\mathrm{Cov}(g_t, g_{t-1})$ is known. However, from Eqs. (1) and (4) $\mathrm{Cov}(g_{t-1}, g_t) = \mathrm{Cov}(r_1, r_2) + \mathrm{Cov}(\zeta_{t-1}, \zeta_t)$. Now $\mathrm{Cov}(r_1, r_2)$ is a function of known parameters. Hence $\mathrm{Cov}(\zeta_{t-1}, \zeta_t)$ is identified. Using Eqs. (2) and (5), we have $\mathrm{Cov}(s_{1,t-1}, s_{1t}) = \mathrm{Cov}(g_{t-1}, g_t) + \mathrm{Cov}(\varepsilon_{1,t-1}, \varepsilon_{1t})$; hence $\mathrm{Cov}(\varepsilon_{1,t-1}, \varepsilon_{1t})$ is identified. Similarly $\mathrm{Cov}(\varepsilon_{2,t-1}, \varepsilon_{2t})$ is identified using Eqs. (3) and (6).

Note that we have examined the identifiability of a distributed lag model. More elaborate dynamic models can be constructed to allow for customer inertia or customer holdover. For example, we could include $s_{1,t-2}$ in Eq. (2), $s_{2,t-2}$ in Eq. (3), $s_{1,t-1}$ in Eq. (5), and $s_{2,t-1}$ in Eq. (6). Proof of identifiability is straightforward but tedious.

90. See previous note.

Media Planning in a Dynamic and Uncertain Environment

This chapter focuses on the firm's choice of media message and media allocation plans. We shall pay particular attention to uncertainty and dynamic considerations. In particular, we analyze whether firms should purchase future advertising at a guaranteed price, purchase advertising at the uncertain future spot rate, or hedge by purchasing some advertising at a guaranteed rate and additional advertising (if necessary) at the uncertain future price. As in the rest of the book, we shall consider both the expected utility and the value maximization frameworks.

7.1 THE MEDIA MESSAGE DECISION

The Role of Perceptions

Choosing the advertising message is a key marketing decision: The best media mix models will fail if the advertising message does not match the target segment. The first step for the brand manager is to identify a target segment(s) and determine consumers' perceptions of the brand and its competitors. These competing products can belong to different product categories (e.g., a mouthwash brand can compete against a toothpaste brand). This perceptual analysis can be performed using confirmatory factor analysis or confirmatory multidimensional scaling. Chapter 4 discusses these empirical methods in detail.

Suppose consumers evaluate a detergent along two perceptual dimensions: gentleness and effectiveness.[1] Consider two brands A and B. Suppose the market consists of three segments labeled 1, 2, and 3, respectively. Assume for simplicity that consumers' perceptions are deterministic. In Figure 7.1, Segment i's perceptions for Brand A's gentleness and perception are given by the point Z_A^i. Segment i's perceptions for Brand B are given by

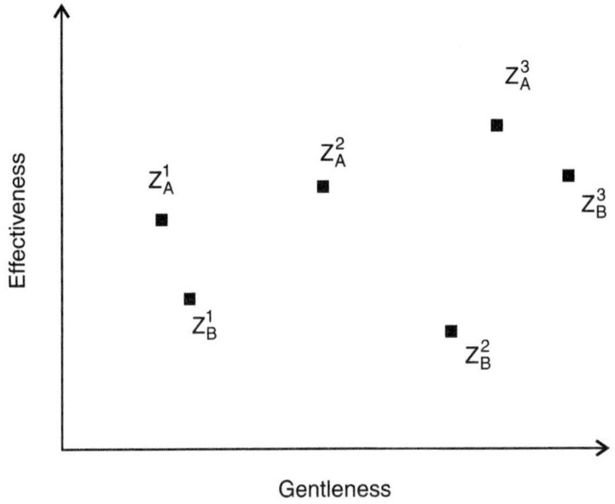

Figure 7.1 A perceptual map for detergents.

Z_B^i. [Assume that Z_A^i and Z_B^i represent the averaged perceptions of Segment i for Brands A and B, respectively. Thus, Z_A^i and Z_B^i represent the centroids for Brands A and B for the ith segment where $i = 1, 3$.]

What are the advertising implications of the perceptual map? Assume that all prices are equal. Let us analyze the problem from the perspective of the brand manager of Brand A. Segment 1 perceives Brands A and B to be similar. (In general a weighted distance measure should be used because the consumer places different importances on the product benefits. Furthermore, because the perceptions are likely to be correlated, the standard Euclidean distance measure is not appropriate.) Consequently, individuals in Segment 1 are likely to switch frequently between Brands A and B. Segment 2, in contrast, perceives Brands A and B to be highly dissimilar. Suppose Segment 2 values gentleness highly. Then Segment 2 will tend to purchase Brand B; that is, consumers in this segment will rarely switch between Brands A and B. Segment 3, like Segment 2, also perceives Brands A and B to be dissimilar but values effectiveness very highly. Consequently Segment 3 tends to purchase Brand A.

Given this scenario, it is inefficient for the brand manager to target Segments 2 and 3. A more reasonable strategy for the brand manager of Brand A is to attempt to change Segment 1's perceptions provided the gross profit potential of Segment 1 is sufficiently high. One useful approach is to compare Brands A and B directly. This strategy is known as comparative advertising. If Brand A has a low market share, Brand A's advertising should identify Brand B by name. This strategy will arouse consumers' attention and hence provide the necessary precondition for attitude change. If Brand A is the market leader, the advertising should not identify Brand B by name. For example, the ad could state: "We compared Brand A to a well-known national brand." This strategy will avoid giving Brand B free publicity or legitimizing Brand B to the consumer.

Message Content and Message Length

The immediate question is: How aggressive should the delivery of the ad message be? Obviously the comparative advertising strategy will not work if the comparison is too timid. Alternatively, if the comparison is too strident, the advertising loses credibility and advertising effectiveness falls. Hence the ad message should be aggressive but not excessively harsh. Empirical studies support this view.

An interesting question is whether the comparative advertising should focus on comparing brands along the dimensions of gentleness, effectiveness, or both. The answer depends on whether effectiveness and gentleness are correlated. Suppose effectiveness and gentleness are uncorrelated. Then the firm can attempt to change one perceptual dimension at a time. If Segment 1 is primarily concerned with gentleness, a short 15-second television commercial that focuses on comparing gentleness across brands may be efficient. Suppose gentleness and effectiveness are negatively correlated (a likely scenario). Then Brand A's advertising message must be detailed and emphasize that Brand A is both gentler and more effective than Brand B. Consequently, a 30-second television commercial may be substantially more effective than a 15-second television commercial. If "more is better" and the perceptual dimensions are positively correlated (as can happen in some cases), advertising efficiency increases because an advertising message that focuses on one perceptual dimension will change the individual's perceptions along several dimensions simultaneously. We say that advertising has a halo effect. Hence 15-second television commercials may be more efficient than 30-second television commercials.

Published empirical studies that compare the effectiveness of 15- and 30-second commercials are rare, despite the managerial importance of this issue. Patzer (1991) found that 30-second television commercials achieve greater brand recall and more favorable attitude change than 15-second television commercials. However, Patzer aggregated data across individuals and brands in different product categories, used only one exposure per brand, and measured recall and attitude immediately after individuals were exposed to advertising.

Additional research is necessary to determine the effects of product type (e.g., durable or nondurable), product life cycle, product familiarity, program length (e.g., 60 minutes or 2 hours), program type (e.g., news or situation comedy), and multiple exposures. Furthermore, such research should perform disaggregate analysis by segment as discussed. The issue of multiple exposures is particularly important because the cost structure of television advertising is nonlinear: two 15-second television commercials can cost considerably more than one 30-second television commercial. See Patzer (1991, p. 18) for details.

> **Key Point**   *The brand manager should determine the perceptual maps for each segment on a brand-by-brand basis. Comparative advertising may be an efficient strategy if the firm targets segments that perceive competing brands to be highly similar.*

Choice of Media

The manager must simultaneously consider the choice of media message and media because the effectiveness of an advertising message is likely to vary across media. In our detergent example, television is probably the most effective way of demonstrating that Brand A is gentler or more effective than Brand B. Furthermore, the firm may find it desirable to use different media or ad messages sequentially. For example, the optimal message strategy for a technical product may be to use television advertising initially to create awareness and then use magazine advertising to provide detailed technical product information.

The firm may also find it desirable to run a long television ad for a new product, especially if the product is superior along several dimensions. When Proctor and Gamble introduced Bounce—a new fabric softener—Bounce ran 60-second television commercials. The fundamental advertising task was to re-educate consumers that the place to add softener was the drier and not the washer. Each commercial mentioned each of the three benefits (i.e., softness, lack of cling in clothing after drying, and freshness) four times. Because of Bounce's demonstrable benefits and frequent reminders during the same ad message, the commercial was extremely successful (see Preimer 1989, pp. 112–13). Note that Proctor and Gamble could have reached the same number of individuals at a substantially lower cost if it had used 30-second commercials. However, these 30-second commercials would have been much less effective.

Strategic Considerations

The firm must consider several additional strategic factors; in particular, the firm may find it difficult to reach the target segment selectively. Suppose Brand A plans to target Segment 1 using a comparative advertising approach; however, Segments 1, 2, and 3 have similar demographic/psychographic profiles (see Figure 7.1). Then, contrary to the firm's plan, the comparative advertising message will reach all three segments. Suppose Segment 3 provides a substantial fraction of Brand A's market share and profit. Then Segment 3 may be confused by the comparative advertising and some members may even switch to Brand B. The severity of this problem depends on Segment 2's relative market share and how close Z_A^2 and Z_B^2 are (see Figure 7.1).

Another key strategic factor is how important Brand B is to its parent company. Suppose Brand B contributes significantly to its parent's product-line profitability. Then Brand B is likely to retaliate. One possibility is for Brand B to run its own comparative advertising against Brand A. Both brands are likely to suffer under this scenario. Under the best conditions, the effects of comparative advertising will cancel out and the market shares of Brands A and B will remain unaffected. Given that both A and B are advertising heavily, profits for Brands A and B will fall. Under the worst conditions, Brands A and B will lose market share as consumers switch to other brands. Consequently, their profits will fall even further.

The previous analysis assumed that Brand B's parent confronts Brand A directly. In reality, most firms have several product lines. Brand B's parent could therefore attack Brand

---

Key Point *The firm should use a strategic perspective when choosing an advertising message. Depending on the task of advertising (e.g., to develop awareness or provide learning), the firm may decide to use short or long commercials. The optimal message strategy may require the firm to use several media and media messages sequentially to move consumers up the "hierarchy of effects" (e.g., awareness, comprehension, and attitude change). Comparative advertising is appealing because it allows the firm to combine the media message with market segmentation. However, the benefits from comparative advertising can be eroded or eliminated when the firm allows for competitive retaliation.*

A's parent in a completely different market where Brand A's parent is weak. This form of retaliation could inflict serious financial damage on Brand A's parent.

The Role of Consumers' Information-Processing Strategies

The previous analysis implicitly assumed that consumers process information in a detailed way. In our example, consumers first form perceptions of the gentleness and effectiveness of a given detergent and then form preferences conditional on these perceptions. We say that consumers follow a *central information-processing strategy*. An alternative theory argues that in many cases, especially for low-involvement products, consumers do not process information in detail. Specifically, individuals do not form explicit perceptions for each perceptual dimension. Instead, they form overall impressions of the brand and are responsive to non-product-related cues (e.g., whether the endorser in the ad is a celebrity). We say that consumers follow a *peripheral information-processing strategy*. See, for example, the elaboration likelihood model (ELM; Petty and Cacioppo 1981 and Petty, Cacioppo, and Schumann 1983).

What are the media message implications of the ELM? First, consumers are heterogeneous. Conceivably, even for a given product category, some consumers process information centrally, whereas others process information peripherally. For example, heavy users could follow the former strategy and light users the latter. Hence the firm should form segments on the basis of the degree of heterogeneity in consumer information-processing strategies. Chapter 4 discusses empirical methods for market segmentation. Second, attitude change stability depends on consumers' information-processing strategies. Attitude change will be more stable for consumers who process information centrally. Consequently such consumers will be less sensitive to future advertising by competitors. Hence from a strategic perspective the firm may achieve higher profits in the long run by focusing on segments that process information centrally rather than peripherally.

Key Point *The firm should vary its message strategy depending on how consumers process information. Consumer segments which process information centrally are attractive because their attitude change is stable. Firms that target such segments may find it necessary to invest more heavily in developing ad copy, run longer commercials, and accept lower short-term profits. Consumer segments that process information peripherally are sensitive to competitive advertising because their attitudes are less stable. Firms that target such segments are likely to invest less in developing ad copy, run shorter commercials, and use celebrities to endorse the product.*

Measuring the Effectiveness of the Message

One important question remains. Suppose the firm has decided on a particular ad message. There are many ways to execute the message. Suppose the brand manager of a toothpaste product has decided that the advertising message should focus on decay prevention. One possible message format—Plan A—is to show an individual from the target segment (e.g., a housewife in the 20–30-year age group) endorsing the brand for its decay prevention. An alternative message format—Plan B—is to show a dentist endorsing the firm's brand because of its effectiveness in decay prevention. Which approach is better?

Suppose the brand manager has developed specific versions of Plans A and B. Then the brand manager can use standard experimental methods to determine which media message plan is superior. Bagozzi (1986, pp. 394–98) provides a succinct review of commercial methods for measuring ad effectiveness. The key managerial decisions are twofold: the choice of target segment and the measure of advertising effectiveness.

The brand manager can use several measures of advertising effectiveness including unaided recall, aided recall, the percentage of individuals who recall the ad message correctly, and attitude change. The choice depends on the firm's market segmentation policy and consumers' information-processing strategies for the product at hand. For example, aided recall may be an appropriate measure for consumers who process information peripherally. A brand-specific information measure may be more useful for consumers who process information centrally.

Regardless of which measure of advertising message effectiveness is used, a crucial choice is the time period between an individual's exposure to the ad and the measure of response (e.g., recall). Some ad messages are effective in the short run (e.g., a period of two days). Other messages may be less effective in the short run but work well in the long run (e.g., the ad is low key but memorable). The appropriate time period depends on the length of the consumer's purchase cycle and the firm's policy. For example, a firm that is planning to run a special limited-time promotion will choose a short time period. A firm that sells a durable may prefer to use a longer time period.

> **Key Point**   *Measuring the effectiveness of a media message strategy requires considerable managerial judgment. The correct choice of criterion depends on consumers' information-processing strategies, consumers' product purchase cycles, the firm's segmentation policy, and the phase of the product in its life cycle. The manager must pay particular attention to the choice of the time period that elapses between ad exposure and measurement.*

Coordinating Strategy and Product Design

The previous analysis assumed that the firm can change the consumer's perceptions without changing the product design. This approach is feasible in two cases. First, the consumer can only verify the brand's attributes (more precisely, the brand's benefits) after purchasing the product. In this case, the firm may be successful in inducing brand trial by changing consumers' perceptions but not necessarily in achieving repeat purchase. Second, suppose that the consumer cannot verify the brand's attributes even after purchase. Fragrance products are a classic example. In these cases, the firm may be able to induce both trial and repeat behavior by changing consumers' perceptions without modifying the product design.

In general, the firm cannot change consumers' perceptions drastically without modifying the product design. Hence a key strategic decision is how to coordinate product design and advertising message strategy. Specifically, the firm needs to determine the relationships between the *observable* product attributes and the *unobserved* perceptions for different segments. Furthermore, the firm needs to perform a cost–benefit analysis comparing new product development (including packaging) and developing new advertising message policy. Chapter 4 proposes empirical methods for performing this type of analysis.

Advertising Frequency

Firms commonly run the same ad several times in a given radio or television time slot (e.g., a 60-minute national news program). At first glance, this policy appears wasteful. However, this conclusion is incorrect. Consider television. Typically only a small fraction of the potential audience is actually exposed to a given ad insertion (see Preimer 1989, pp. 28–29). Suppose the firm runs one ad insertion during a 60-minute television show. Suppose that 30 percent of the potential television audience will be exposed to any given ad. Assume for simplicity that the "trials" are independent. Suppose the firm runs the ad three times during the 60-minute time slot. Then the exposure rate jumps to 65.7 percent [i.e., $1 - (0.7)^3$]. Thus the effective audience is more than doubled: a huge difference!

Dynamic Considerations

Another issue is whether the firm should change its message over time. One theory argues that advertising has a wearout effect (e.g., consumers get bored as a result of repeated exposures to the same ads). Consequently, the firm should change its ads periodically and, if necessary, even the product design. Mechanical adherence to this rule is potentially dangerous. Suppose the advertising target is to achieve a 40 percent awareness rate in a particular segment during a given period. If the advertising is successful, diminishing returns will set in towards the end of the period. The implication is simple: Wearout occurs because advertising is effective and has achieved its goal! Consequently, the correct managerial inference is that new advertising goals are necessary. The firm will commit a strategic blunder by simply developing new ads in response to wearout.

More generally, one can argue that the firm should change its advertising message over time as the brand progresses though the brand life cycle or the firm resegments the market. Such policies are strategic and potentially risky. Frequent changes in ad message create consumer confusion and can be dysfunctional. Burger King—a fast-food chain—has achieved mixed success by switching its advertising theme 18 times in 20 years. (See *The New York Times*, September 1, 1994.) Furthermore, the firm can alienate existing customers and loyal customers in particular, by making sudden or dramatic changes in the advertising message. The opportunity cost to the firm can be considerable. The potential gains from attracting new customers are not equivalent to the losses from customers who switch to other brands. The loss of one loyal customer leads to a large and guaranteed loss in long-term profit. (Recall that the firm is risk-averse.) However, the probability of gaining a new trier is uncertain. Furthermore, there is no guarantee that a new trier will become a repeat buyer. Hence changing the media message can be risky. These effects will be mitigated to the extent that the firm can reach a new target segment selectively without overlapping the existing segment. Such a policy may not always be feasible and, in any case, does require that the new segment and the existing segment have distinct demographic or psychographic profiles.

Message Coordination across Media

An important issue is how to coordinate the media message across media. Consider a new brand of toothpaste. Should the initial advertising use 30-second television commercials to create awareness and subsequent ad insertions use 15-second television commercials to remind consumers?

One approach is to use a differential weighting scheme. Suppose an individual is exposed to a 15-second television commercial. The manager could assign this exposure a low effectiveness weight (possibly zero) if the individual has not been previously exposed to a 30-second television commercial. On the other hand, the manager could assign a high effectiveness weight to the exposure if the individual has been previously exposed to a 30-second commercial and only needs to be reminded. The problem with such weighting schemes is that they are ad hoc and can easily become ex-post methods for rationalizing managerial decisions to favor particular media.

The Multiproduct Firm

Note that our discussion has focused on the effect of advertising for only one brand. In reality, firms often use the same ad message to simultaneously advertise several brands. For example, the ad message for a computer firm might read: "Brand X represents the state-of-the-art technology in personal computers. We also offer a very sophisticated line of ancillary products including printers, etc." Extant methods for measuring media message effectiveness do not consider such multibrand effects. Furthermore, they do not allow for competitive reaction.

Many firms use image advertising to increase goodwill. For example, the firm can use image advertising to signal the stock market that its product will perform well in the future (see Schonfeld and Boyd 1982). Alternatively, the firm can use image advertising to enhance its reputation and hence increase product-line sales. For example, General Electric uses the slogan "GE brings good things to life." At present, managers tend to use judgment in determining the product-line effects of image advertising. Chapter 6, Section 6.9, proposes objective empirical methods for measuring these effects.

If the brand does not provide any distinctive benefits, the firm can pursue alternative message strategies to achieve brand differentiation. For example, a "me-too" detergent might trumpet the slogan "No other detergent cleans better than Brand X." This approach provides two advantages for the firm. At a minimum, Brand X gets into the consumer's consideration set (i.e., the set of brands that the consumer will consider for purchase). Thus, even if consumers think that all detergents are alike, Brand X gains market share. More important, the firm may succeed in making Brand X the consumer's reference brand for brand comparisons. If so, Brand X's gain in market share will increase further.

Another approach for the firm is to capitalize on consumers' ignorance. For example, the firm can announce that Brand X has a particular feature. In reality, all brands have this feature. However, the consumer (segment) does not know this fact. Consequently, Brand X gains market share.

7.2 THE MEDIA-MIX DECISION

In Chapter 6 we focused on the firm's total level of advertising spending. However, in order to maximize performance, the brand manager needs to optimally allocate the advertising budget across media types (e.g., television and magazines) and media vehicles (e.g., particular television programs and specific magazines). We now examine the firm's media allocation decision; in particular, we shall focus on dynamic effects.

Reach or Frequency?

Suppose the brand manager has been assigned an advertising budget of $100,000 for the coming month. The brand manager's first decision is to choose a target segment. For example, is the purpose of advertising to relaunch an existing brand, increase the retention rate of existing customers, or increase the customer switching rate from competitors' products? This decision is crucial and requires considerable managerial judgment supported where possible by marketing research.

Suppose the brand manager decides that the appropriate target segment comprises former buyers of the brand who have switched to competitive Brand A. Market research shows that this segment has the following demographic profile: single, female, belongs to the 25–40-year age group, and earns between $20,000 and $30,000 per year. The second step for the brand manager is to identify a set of media vehicles for which the audience profile matches that of the target segment. The third step is to choose an optimal media plan from this set of media vehicles.

We begin with a simple scenario. Suppose the brand manager has decided that television is the appropriate medium (e.g., the advertising format should focus on visual effects and color). The brand manager has two choices.

One option is to spend the entire advertising budget ($100,000) on a single advertising insertion to be run during a national prime-time television program. Suppose the brand manager expects 200,000 members of the target segment to be exposed to the advertising. We say that this media plan has a reach of 200,000.

A second option is to advertise during an off-peak time period. In particular, the brand manager can buy four advertising insertions at $25,000 each. Suppose the brand manager expects each advertising insertion to reach 40,000 members of the target segment. Assume unrealistically that each advertising insertion reaches the same members of the target segment. (This assumption will be relaxed.) Thus, using the second option, the brand manager can purchase 160,000 advertising messages (impressions). Which plan is better?

The first media plan provides more advertising messages (200,000) than the second (160,000). Hence the simple answer is that the first media plan is superior. However, choosing the first media plan could be an expensive mistake. Suppose the brand belongs to a low-involvement product category (e.g., shampoo). Then one advertising exposure per customer may be insufficient to get the advertising message across. Recall that consumers have a perceptual threshold (i.e., the marginal productivity of advertising is zero unless the advertising frequency exceeds a minimum level). Thus the first option could waste the entire advertising budget.

The second plan, in contrast, reaches a considerably smaller number of segment members (40,000) than the first (200,000). However, the second plan reaches each segment member four times during the period. The first plan reaches each segment member only once during the same time period. Thus the second plan is more likely to penetrate the consumer's perceptual barriers, allow the consumer to learn about the brand, and store the information in long-term memory. Hence the second option is superior.

Consider a third option. Suppose the brand manager can advertise during a bargain time slot (i.e., purchase five spots for $100,000; these advertisements will be aired at 2 a.m.). This media plan reaches 35,000 prospective customers. The question is: Should the firm reach 40,000 potential customers with a frequency of four (i.e., choose the second option) or 35,000 potential customers with a frequency of five (i.e., choose the third option)?

One theory maintains that there is an optimal frequency for a given product purchase cycle. Krugman (1972), for example, proposes that three exposures are optimal. Despite its popularity among some practitioners, such rules are ambiguous. They do not distinguish exposures according to the lengths of the messages used in particular media. For example, are three exposures to a 15-second television commercial equivalent to three exposures to a 30-second television commercial? These rules do not discuss the appropriate spacing of advertising insertions over the consumer's product purchase cycle. Suppose the consumer's product purchase cycle is one month. Are three ad exposures in the two days prior to purchase more effective than three ads spaced out evenly over the month? Finally, these rules do not distinguish the effectiveness of exposures across media. For example, are three television exposures equivalent to two television exposures followed by a magazine ad that provides detailed product information?

An alternative theory hypothesizes that high frequency may be necessary to induce consumer learning. Yet another theory argues that excessive frequency can actually reduce sales because consumers begin to counterargue, derogate the source of the advertising, and become more sensitive to competitive advertising. There is no uniform empirical support for any of these theories.

Let us suppose that there is an optimal frequency of advertising; in particular, the consumer's purchase cycle for the product is one month and the optimal advertising frequency is three per month. Then, assuming that excessive advertising is not harmful, the preferred media plan is to reach 40,000 potential consumers with a frequency of four rather than 35,000 potential customers with a frequency of five. If excessive advertising is harmful, all three media options are inefficient.

The previous analysis assumed that each ad insertion reaches the same potential customers. In reality, the audiences for the different ad insertions will not overlap perfectly. How can the brand manager determine the reach of a given advertising schedule for a particular medium (i.e., the number of individuals who are exposed at least once to the advertising)? Reach increases monotonically with the number of ad insertions. As the number of ads increases, it becomes increasingly difficult for the firm to contact individuals who have not been previously exposed to advertising. Hence the rate at which reach increases slows down as the number of ad insertions increases.

Measuring Reach

The brand manager can use two methods to measure reach. First, he can use published reach tables. This approach provides gross industry averages and is seriously misleading. Second, the brand manager can obtain explicit reach estimates for the brand using historical data. This approach is not as straightforward as it appears to be.

Suppose the firm has previously advertised in four consecutive issues of a weekly magazine. In order to compute reach, the firm needs to know the number of individuals who read all possible combinations of the four ad insertions (i.e., one issue only, all pairs of issues, all triples of issues, and all four issues). Such detailed information is unavailable. Furthermore, this enumerative method is purely descriptive and provides no guidance in making long-term reach projections. For example, suppose the reach for the four-issue schedule is 150,000. What is the potential reach of a six-issue schedule? The brand manager cannot answer this question without estimating a reach model.

Several reach models are available (see Rust 1986, pp. 8–13, for a concise review). All these models are parsimonious in their data requirements and use only the reach of a one-insertion schedule and the reach of a two-insertion schedule to estimate the reach of an n-insertion schedule ($n > 2$) for a given medium. The Agostini (1962) and Metheringham (1964) beta binomial models appear to be the best choices.[2] One weakness of these models is that they do require two-insertion reach figures for each medium. Such data are available for national media including television but may not be available for small local media vehicles. In these cases, the firm may be forced to use published reach tables or a crude binomial model that uses only the one-insertion reach figure for each medium.[3]

Reach Models

Suppose reach is a reasonable criterion (e.g., the purpose of advertising is to inform consumers about a forthcoming sale for the product) and can be accurately measured. For a given advertising budget (say, $100,000) the brand manager can purchase four weekly insertions in magazine A (one insertion per issue) or six weekly insertions in magazine B (one insertion per issue). Suppose the reach for the magazine A plan is 500,000 and the reach for the magazine B plan is 600,000. Is the magazine B plan better? Not necessarily.

The magazine B plan spreads the advertising insertions over a longer time period than the magazine A plan. Consequently, consumers who are exposed to the magazine B plan are more likely to forget the advertising message than consumers who are exposed to the magazine A plan. This forgetting effect is likely to be particularly important for low-involvement products. Suppose consumers consider magazine A to be a more credible source for the product advertising than magazine B. Then a reach of 500,000 in magazine A could be more effective than a reach of 600,000 in magazine B.

Even if reach were comparable across media, the most the brand manager could do would be to choose an efficient media plan (i.e., a plan that maximizes the reach from spending the predetermined advertising budget of $100,000). The brand manager needs to determine *both* the advertising budget and the media plan. Suppose the brand manager can purchase five weekly insertions in magazine A (one insertion per issue) for $120,000 or four weekly insertions in magazine A (one insertion per issue) for $100,000. The reach for the five-insertion plan is 650,000 and the reach for the four-insertion plan is 500,000. Should the firm spend an additional $20,000 to obtain an incremental reach of 150,000?

The answer depends on the relationship between reach and sales (and hence profit). This relationship is typically unknown. Hence the firm cannot objectively determine the optimal advertising plan. The best that the firm can do is to choose an efficient media schedule (i.e., a media plan that maximizes the reach for a predetermined advertising budget).

The brand manager needs to consider several additional practical caveats. Current methods provide inflated measures of reach, often measuring potential and not actual reach (see Preimer 1989, pp. 28–29). The severity of measurement error for reach varies across media. For example, estimates of television reach tend to be significantly inflated and are much less reliable than reach estimates for magazines. Consequently, the firm is likely to overadvertise in television and to choose inefficient media schedules.

How useful is reach as a measure of advertising effectiveness for a given medium? The fundamental difficulty is that reach implies that only the first advertising exposure matters. That is, beyond the first exposure the marginal productivity of advertising for a given individual is zero. This assumption is highly restrictive. A better approach for the brand manager is to analyze the exposure distribution for each medium for a given advertising plan (i.e., determine the proportions of the target segment that are exposed to zero, one, two, . . . , or more insertions).

Exposure Distribution Models: The Single-Medium Case

One popular method for estimating the exposure distribution for a given medium is the beta binomial distribution (Metheringham 1964). The beta binomial model allows consumers to have heterogeneous media habits: Exposure probabilities vary across individuals according to the beta binomial distribution. However, the beta binomial model requires that each individual has an equal probability of exposure to each ad insertion. Once the brand manager has estimated the parameters of the beta binomial distribution using historical data, he can estimate the exposure distribution (and hence reach) for any number of ad insertions in the medium.

The beta binomial model seems to fit cross-sectional data fairly well but tends to overestimate reach and odd-numbered frequencies (see Schreiber 1969 and Chandon 1976). However, in spite of the generally high degree of statistical fit achieved, the beta binomial model may not be appropriate. The assumption that a given individual has equal probabilities of exposure to all ad insertions is unrealistic, particularly for television and radio (see Metheringham 1964). In addition, the beta binomial model can lead to technical difficulties. The reach estimates can be meaningless; in particular, the beta binomial model can imply that reach decreases when the number of insertions increases.

Our analysis so far has focused on cross-sectional measures of advertising effectiveness. How accurate are long-term projections that are based on a cross-sectional estimate of the exposure distribution for a given medium? Published research in this area is scarce. Sabavala and Morrison (1981, p. 638) note in this regard that the beta binomial model tends to underestimate reach and to overestimate high frequencies. Hence the brand manager who fits a beta binomial distribution and then uses the reach criterion is likely to underadvertise. The brand manager who fits a beta binomial distribution and focuses on frequency will overadvertise.

Why are the long-term projections for the beta binomial model subject to error even though the cross-sectional results provide a good fit? The fundamental problem is that an individual's probabilities of exposure to ad insertions vary over time; we say that media habits are nonstationary. Two cases should be distinguished. First, the aggregate exposure distribution for a given medium may be stable even though individual exposure probabilities change over time (see Schreiber 1974). Second, both the aggregate exposure distribution and the individual probabilities can change over time.

Sabavala and Morrison (1981) propose the geometric beta binomial distribution to deal with the case where consumers change their media habits over time but the aggregate exposure distribution is stationary. Their model includes the beta binomial model as a special case and makes two additional assumptions: (1) The individual exposure probabilities have a beta binomial distribution and change randomly over time, and (2) individuals have a common propensity to change their media habits over time. Their main finding is that including the geometric propensity-to-change parameter in the beta binomial model improves the overall model fit considerably, although some of the discrepancies of the actual and expected values can be quite large. Two useful extensions of the Sabavala–Morrison (1981) model are: (1) allowing the individual exposure probabilities at any time to depend on previous exposure probabilities. This dependence can be positive (e.g., individuals are committed to the media vehicle) or negative (e.g., individuals seek media variety), and (2) extending the model to deal with multiple media vehicles.

The second case—nonstationarity of the aggregate exposure distribution over time— does not appear to have been addressed in the literature. Thus current media exposure models are only appropriate for short-term decision making or advertising products that have reached equilibrium in the product life cycle. One research avenue is to extend the Sabavala–Morrison (1981) model by making the beta binomial parameters time dependent or functions of behavioral variables.

Suppose the brand manager has decided to evaluate media plans on the basis of their respective exposure distributions. Two insertions in separate issues of a given magazine (plan A) cost \$50,000, and four insertions in separate issues of the same magazine (plan B) cost \$100,000.

Suppose the brand manager has determined the expected exposure distributions for both plans. The estimates are:

# Issues Read	Two Insertions (Plan A)	Four Insertions (Plan B)
0	700,000	500,000
1	150,000	125,000
2	150,000	125,000
3		110,000
4		140,000
	1,000,000	1,000,000

How should the brand manager choose between plans A and B? The fundamental difficulty is that the advertising effectiveness of a given plan depends on the entire exposure distribution generated by that plan and not merely on reach or some other frequency-based number (e.g., the proportion of individuals who will be exposed to at least three ads during the period). Theory provides limited guidance in combining reach and frequency infor- mation. Thus considerable managerial judgment is necessary. As Sabavala and Morrison

(1981, p. 639) note: "The choice depends upon the advertiser's objectives, the nature and newness of the product or service being advertised, and the amount and complexity of the information being communicated."

Exposure Distribution Models: The Multiple-Medium Case

The previous analysis assumed that the firm uses one medium only. Most firms advertise simultaneously in several media (e.g., television and magazines). Suppose initially that the firm advertises once in each of several media vehicles. Furthermore, the brand manager has decided to measure advertising effectiveness using the combined reach of the media schedule. As discussed previously, this method makes two strong behavioral assumptions: The value of reach does not vary across media vehicles (e.g., one television exposure has the same impact as one magazine exposure), and multiple exposures to a given individual provide no additional value (e.g., magazine readership does not enhance the value of television exposure).

One way for the brand manager to measure reach is to use the single-medium beta binomial model and treat the media vehicles as if they were different insertions of the same vehicle. This method is reasonable in many cases but tends to overestimate reach (see Chandon 1976). Furthermore, the method works badly if the exposure probabilities vary significantly across media. A second approach is to use the Hofmans method (1966), which is an extension of the Agostini method (1962).[4] The Hofmans method is more accurate than the beta binomial model but also overestimates reach (see Chandon 1976). Note that both the beta binomial and the Hofmans methods tend to overestimate reach. Hence the brand manager is likely to overadvertise.

Reach and Frequency Models

Suppose advertising effectiveness depends on both reach and frequency (i.e., the exposure distribution across multiple media). Then, as in the single-medium case, the brand manager must use judgment in comparing different media plans.

In general, the firm uses several media simultaneously and makes multiple insertions in each medium. Hence the brand manager needs to determine the exposure distribution across multiple media vehicles. Suppose all the media vehicles are magazines. In this case, pairwise audience duplication data are typically available. Hence the brand manager can use several methods. One method is the compound Dirichlet multinomial distribution (DMD) model which is the multivariate extension of the beta binomial model[5] (see Chandon 1976 and Leckenby and Kishi 1982). Other methods include the Kwerel geometric distribution (KGD) model, the Hofmans geometric distribution (HGD) model (see Leckenby and Kishi 1982, Appendices A and B), and the log-linear model (see Danaher 1988, 1989).

Leckenby and Kishi (1982) compare the DMD, KGD, HGD, and beta binomial (BBD) models using magazine data. They find that, in general, the HGD model performs better than the BBD, DMD, and KGD models on the criterion of the number of close estimations across exposure levels. However, the "best" model depends on vehicle size (e.g., all models perform badly for large or medium vehicle sizes), gross audience size, and the pattern of duplication. As Leckenby and Kishi (1982) caution, their results may not be general because their study limited the number of insertions to two and the number of magazines to four.

Recently Danaher (1988, 1989) proposed the log-linear model to estimate exposure distribution for magazines. He finds that a parsimonious model with no interactions outperforms the HGD model: the best performer in the Leckenby–Kishi (1982) study.[6]

Suppose the media schedule consists of television insertions. In this case, audience duplication information is generally unavailable. Hence the brand manager needs to make a choice. One approach is to estimate the exposure distribution without using audience duplication data. For example, the brand manager can estimate the beta binomial distribution without using duplication data (see Rust and Klompmaker 1981 and Leckenby and Rice 1985). This method may be inappropriate if the audience exposure probabilities vary significantly across media. A second approach is to proceed sequentially: First estimate audience duplications and then fit a model that uses duplication data to estimate the exposure distribution. Rust (1986, p. 36) suggests that this approach may be superior. However, empirical evidence is scarce.

Suppose the media schedule is mixed and includes magazine and television insertions. In this case, partial audience duplication information is available. Rust and Leone (1984) develop a mixed-media Dirichlet multinomial distribution (MMDMD) model that estimates media duplications using a variant of the Goodhardt–Ehrenberg (1969) method.[7] Their study examined a large number of mixed magazine–television schedules, each of which contained 10 insertions. Furthermore, and important from a marketing viewpoint, Rust and Leone distinguished segments on the basis of demographics and product usage. In all cases the MMDMD model outperformed the HGD model (the best performer in the Leckenby–Kishi 1982 study).

How should the brand manager proceed once he or she has determined the audience exposure distributions across media? As discussed, historical data analysis provides limited guidance unless the decision maker considers only marginal charges in the media mix schedule. Suppose this is indeed the case. The manager must now choose a model that addresses the following problems. First, he needs to determine the disaggregate audience exposure distribution for each consumer segment for a given media vehicle. Second, the manager must determine the relationship between the audience exposure distribution and effectiveness (preferably sales) for each segment. Third, the model should explicitly allow for seasonality and consumer forgetting. Fourth, the model should allow for quantity discounts in the purchase of advertising insertions.

Little and Lodish (1969) develop a general media-mix model MEDIAC that addresses these problems. Interestingly, MEDIAC still remains the state-of-the-art in media-mix models. MEDIAC allows the user to specify subjective parameters for such model parameters as the rate of consumer forgetting. In addition, the user can assign subjective effectiveness weights for exposures to different media (e.g., the user can assign a weight of five to a magazine exposure and a weight of one to a television exposure).

Despite the generality of its model structure, MEDIAC has several limitations. The fundamental difficulty in all media-mix models including MEDIAC is how to estimate accurately audience duplication across media: a key model input.[8] MEDIAC implicitly assumes that firms have homogeneous attitudes to risk and are risk-neutral. Suppose media schedule A provides higher expected profits than media schedule B. However, media schedule A leads to a higher variability in profit than media schedule B. MEDIAC will always choose media schedule A. A risk-averse firm, however, could prefer media plan

B depending on its risk–return tradeoff. In principle, this difficulty can be handled by changing the objective function in MEDIAC. However, this extension is nontrivial because the new objective function will be highly sensitive to the unstable estimates of the audience exposure distributions.[9] As Little and Lodish (1969) recognize, MEDIAC is a monopoly model (i.e., the model does not incorporate competitive advertising). Finally, current media-mix models—including MEDIAC—assume that we can capture heterogeneity by forming segments a priori. In general, the "segment" could contain several populations that cannot be specified a priori for theoretical or empirical reasons. In such cases, the data belong to a mixture. Hence standard media models (including MEDIAC) will be inappropriate. (See Chapter 4 for a discussion of mixture models.)

7.3 UNCERTAINTY IN ADVERTISING RATES

In the previous analysis we have implicitly assumed that advertising rates are known. However, advertising rates are not constant over time. Network television advertising rates, in particular, fluctuate considerably (Preimer 1989, p. 179). Thus the advertiser has several choices: Commit to buying a given number of advertising insertions for the next period at a guaranteed rate (say $100,000 per insertion), wait and buy ad insertions at the uncertain spot market price next period, or hedge by precommitting to buying a fixed number of advertising insertions at the guaranteed rate and buying additional insertions at the uncertain spot rate next period. We now propose a model for analyzing this problem; in order to add realism, we shall consider the case where the firm controls both price and advertising.

Assume that advertising is paid for during the period when the advertising is run. We shall consider two demand scenarios: A current-effects advertising model and a dynamic carryover advertising model. As in previous chapters, we shall examine two objective functions: maximizing expected utility and maximizing stock value. For simplicity we begin with the case where the firm does not hedge.

Current-Effects Advertising Model

Begin with a current-effects advertising model in which both price and advertising are control variables and demand is uncertain. Consider a two-period monopoly model. Let the demand in period t be $\varphi_t = f_t(p_t, A_t) + g_t(p_t, A_t)u_t$, where p_t is the price in period t, A_t is the number of ad insertions run in period t, f_t and g_t are deterministic functions, and u_t is a stochastic disturbance term. This generalized uncertainty formulation allows both price and advertising to affect the variability of demand in a flexible (i.e., nonmonotonic) manner.

The advertising rate in period 1 is known. Consider two advertising rate scenarios for period 2. In scenario A, the firm can buy ad insertions in advance at a guaranteed price of $100,000 per ad insertion. In scenario B, the firm can wait and buy the ads in period 2 at the uncertain spot rate. Suppose the firm expects the average advertising rate in period 2 to be $100,000. Should the firm precommit or wait?

Consider the expected utility model. Recall that a risk-averse firm always prefers a certain amount of $x to a gamble that promises $x on average. Consequently, the expected utility–maximizing firm is always worse off when advertising-rate uncertainty is introduced.[10] Thus the firm will buy advertising insertions for period 2 in advance at the guaranteed rate. In our example, a necessary condition for the firm to wait is that the expected advertising rate in period 2 is lower than the guaranteed rate[11] ($100,000).

Consider the value-maximizing firm and assume that the CAPM holds. Recall that the CAPM defines the firm's value as the net present value of the certainty equivalent of the firm's current and future profits. Thus we can analyze the effect of advertising-rate uncertainty by focusing on the certainty equivalent of advertising rates in period 2. The key issue is: How do advertising rates fluctuate with general economic conditions? Although empirical evidence is unavailable, we expect advertising rates to change in the same direction as the economy (i.e., $\text{Cov}(w_2, R_2) > 0$), where w_2 denotes the uncertain advertising rate in period 2, R_2 the random return on the market portfolio in period 2, and Cov is the covariance operator. By assumption $E(w_2) = 100,000$. Thus the certainty-equivalent advertising rate in period 2 is $\hat{w}_2 = E(w_2) - a\,\text{Cov}(w_2, R_2) < 100,000$. Hence, in contrast to the expected utility model, the value-maximizing firm gains when advertising-rate uncertainty is introduced![12]

Why does advertising-rate uncertainty have different effects in the expected utility and the value-maximization models? The expected utility model does not allow the decision maker to diversify. Consequently, all fluctuations in profit make the decision maker worse off regardless of the source of uncertainty. The CAPM allows stockholders to diversify and values the firm based on the certainty equivalents of profits. For period 2, let $\hat{R}_2$ denote the certainty-equivalent revenue, $\hat{C}_2$ the certainty-equivalent cost, and $\hat{\pi}_2$ the certainty-equivalent profit. Let $\hat{\pi}_2 = \hat{R}_2 - \hat{C}_2$. Now demand uncertainty reduces $\hat{R}_2$ and $\hat{\pi}_2$. Hence the firm is worse off as in the expected utility model. However, cost uncertainty reduces $\hat{C}_2$. But now $\hat{\pi}_2$ increases. Thus, in contrast to the expected utility model, the CAPM implies that the firm is better off when costs are uncertain.

> ***Key Point*** *Demand or cost uncertainty always makes the decision maker in the expected utility model worse off. In contrast, the CAPM implies that demand and cost uncertainty have asymmetric effects on the firm's stock value. In particular, the advertiser gains when future advertising rates are uncertain. A necessary condition for the expected utility–maximizer to accept advertising-rate uncertainty is that the expected future advertising rate is lower than the guaranteed future rate. The value-maximizing firm accepts advertising-rate uncertainty even if it expects the future advertising rates to be higher than the guaranteed rate, provided advertising rates are sufficiently correlated to the performance of the overall economy.*

Suppose the advertiser decides not to precommit and to wait for the advertising-rate uncertainty in period 2 to be resolved. What is the effect on the advertiser's planned price and advertising policies[13] in period 2 (i.e., the global effect of uncertainty)? For the expected utility model, the results are inherently indeterminate even if demand is deterministic.[14] The results for the CAPM are well-defined.[15] The firm plans to advertise more in period 2 regardless of the particular form of demand uncertainty. The reason is that the introduction of advertising-rate uncertainty is equivalent to a decline in future advertising rates. (Recall that advertising-rate uncertainty always reduces the certainty equivalent of future advertising rates.) The effect on the firm's price plan depends on how advertising affects the price elasticity of the certainty-equivalent demand. Suppose higher advertising makes the market less price sensitive. Then the firm will plan to raise price in period 2 to reinforce the effect of the increase in advertising. If higher advertising makes the market more price sensitive, the firm will plan to reduce price in period 2.

What do these results imply about the market demand for advertising in different periods? Suppose advertisers have homogeneous expectations about future advertising rates. When advertising-rate uncertainty is globally introduced, all value-maximizing firms will plan to advertise more in period 2. This "bunching up" of demand will cause advertising rates in period 2 to shoot up, resulting in an advertising-rate cycle.[16]

The previous analysis focused on the global effect of advertising-rate uncertainty (i.e., a comparison of the certainty and uncertainty scenarios). We now examine the marginal effect of advertising-rate uncertainty. Consider two scenarios. In Scenario 1 the firm expects the advertising rate in period 2 to have an average value of $100,000 per insertion with a standard deviation of $20,000 (say). In Scenario 2, the firm expects the same advertising rate as in scenario 1 ($100,000). However, the advertising rate is more uncertain (e.g., the standard deviation is $22,000). How should the firm revise its price and advertising plans for period 2?

Begin with the expected utility model. In this case the results are determinate only if demand is deterministic and the utility function is quadratic.[17] Recall that profit uncertainty now depends exclusively on advertising-rate uncertainty and increases when advertising rates become more uncertain. That is, for any given price–advertising decision the firm's expected profit is unchanged, but the variability of profit increases. Hence the firm plans to advertise less in period 2 and increase (decrease) price in period 2 depending on whether lower advertising decreases (increases) price elasticity.

As discussed previously, the CAPM results for the global introduction of advertising-rate uncertainty are well defined regardless of whether demand is stochastic. The effect of a marginal increase in advertising-rate uncertainty is analogous to that of the global effect of introducing advertising-rate uncertainty.[18] The firm plans to advertise more in period 2 because the certainty-equivalent advertising rate falls. The firm plans to increase (reduce) price in period 2 if the price elasticity of the certainty-equivalent demand decreases (increases) when advertising increases.

Key Point   *The value-maximizing firm and the expected utility–maximizing firm react differently when future advertising rates become more uncertain. The value-maximizing firm plans to advertise more in period 2 regardless of whether demand is stochastic. In contrast, the expected utility–maximizing firm plans to advertise less in period 2 if demand is deterministic and the utility function is quadratic (i.e., uncertainty is "small").*

Dynamic Advertising Model

The previous analysis assumed that advertising does not have any carryover effects. In reality, advertising in period 1 can affect the demand in period 2 for a variety of reasons including consumer loyalty and consumer inertia. Thus the firm's decisions in periods 1 and 2 are interdependent. For analytical tractability, we focus on the advertising decision, holding price fixed. Furthermore, we only examine the CAPM because the expected utility model is intractable.

Let the demand in period 1 be $\varphi_1 = f_1(A_1) + g_1(A_1)u_1$ and the demand in period 2 be $\varphi_2 = f_2(A_1, A_2) + g_2(A_1, A_2)u_2$, where u_1 and u_2 are independent disturbance terms. What is the global effect of introducing advertising-rate uncertainty?[19] As in the current-effects advertising model, the certainty-equivalent advertising rate in period 2 falls. Hence the firm always plans to advertise more in period 2 when future advertising rates are uncertain, regardless of the precise form of demand uncertainty (e.g., the phase of the product life cycle). The effect on advertising in period 1 depends on the precise effect of advertising in period 1 on the marginal productivity of advertising in period 2. Suppose an advertising goodwill model is appropriate and uncertainty is additive or multiplicative.[20] Then higher advertising in period 1 reduces the marginal effectiveness of advertising in period 2. Hence the firm advertises less in period 1 when the future advertising rate is uncertain. Similarly, we can show that the marginal effect of an increase in advertising-rate uncertainty is analogous to the global effect of introducing advertising-rate uncertainty.

> **Key Point**   *If advertising has a dynamic carryover effect, the value-maximizing firm plans to increase its future advertising when advertising-rate uncertainty is introduced. Hence the market demand for advertising in period 2 increases. The effect on the firm's current advertising depends on whether current advertising increases or decreases the marginal productivity of future advertising and the precise form of demand uncertainty. If an advertising goodwill model is appropriate for most firms and demand uncertainty is additive or multiplicative, market demand for current advertising falls. Thus, if advertising has a dynamic carryover effect, advertising rates will fluctuate more than if advertising affects current demand only.*

The previous analyses assumed that the advertiser has only two choices: Either precommit to buying a given number of ad insertions in the future at a guaranteed price or buy advertising in the future at the uncertain spot rate for advertising. We now consider a third possibility: The firm can choose a hedging strategy (i.e., purchase a fixed number of ad insertions at the guaranteed rate and purchase other ad insertions at the uncertain future advertising rate). Does hedging make the firm better off?

Suppose the firm prefers the waiting strategy to the precommitment strategy. Consider the value-maximizing firm. Recall that in the CAPM we can compare different advertising policies purely on the basis of the certainty equivalents of cost. Let $A_2 > 0$ denote any arbitrary number of ad insertions in period 2, C_1 the corresponding guaranteed advertising cost for the precommitment strategy, and $\hat{C}_2$ the certainty equivalent of advertising costs for the waiting strategy. Then the gain in period 2 from choosing the waiting strategy is $C_1 - \hat{C}_2 > 0$.

Consider a hedging strategy where the firm precommits to purchasing φA_2 ad insertions in period 2 at the guaranteed rate and plans to purchase $(1 - \varphi)A_2$ ad insertions in period 2 at the spot rate where $0 < \varphi < 1$. The certainty-equivalent cost in period 2 of this hedging strategy is $\varphi C_1 + (1 - \varphi)\hat{C}_2$. Thus the firm chooses the hedging policy if $\varphi C_1 + (1 - \varphi)\hat{C}_2 < \hat{C}_2$. However, this condition implies that $C_1 - \hat{C}_2 < 0$, which is impossible. Hence the value-maximizing firm will never choose an advertising hedging policy.

Will the expected utility–maximizing firm hedge? Recall that a necessary condition for the firm to choose a waiting strategy is that the expected future advertising rate is lower than the guaranteed advertising rate. Suppose demand uncertainty and advertising-rate uncertainty are independent. Then a hedging strategy decreases the expected profit in period 2 but simultaneously decreases the variability of profit.[21] Hence, in contrast to the value-maximizing firm, the expected utility–maximizing firm could be better off by choosing an advertising hedging policy.

> **Key Point**   *Value-maximizing firms never choose an advertising hedging policy. Consequently the market demand for advertising and advertising rates fluctuate considerably over time. The expected utility–maximizing firm may choose an advertising hedging strategy depending on the magnitudes of demand and advertising-rate uncertainty and the decision maker's risk attitude. Hence the effect of advertising-rate uncertainty on the market demand for advertising and advertising rates over time cannot be determined a priori.*

Suppose advertising has a carryover effect and that a goodwill model is appropriate. An important managerial issue is: How does the goodwill depreciation rate affect the firm's decision to choose a precommitment or waiting strategy? Recall that the goodwill depreciation rate depends on the quality of the firm's advertising message and competitive behavior (e.g., advertising policy). Furthermore, goodwill is likely to depreciate rapidly for low-involvement, frequently purchased products for which the consumer's attitude and post-advertising attitude change are unstable.

For the CAPM, the goodwill depreciation rate affects the certainty equivalent of revenue but has no effect on the certainty equivalent of costs. Hence the goodwill depreciation rate has no effect on the firm's decision to precommit or wait. Consequently firms in different industries will react similarly to advertising-rate uncertainty, provided they have common beliefs about the future advertising rate structure.

For the expected utility model, the goodwill depreciation rate affects the distribution of cash flows and hence the gain from waiting. However, the results are only determinate in special cases. Suppose the firm's absolute risk aversion is constant (i.e., the firm's willingness to gamble is unaffected by the firm's wealth), and demand and the future advertising rate are normally distributed.[22] Then the gain from waiting depends upon the correlation between demand uncertainty and advertising-rate uncertainty and the precise effect of goodwill on demand uncertainty. Suppose demand uncertainty is independent of advertising-rate uncertainty. Then the gain from waiting is unaffected by the goodwill depreciation rate. Suppose demand uncertainty is positively correlated to advertising-rate uncertainty. If demand uncertainty is additive (i.e., goodwill does not affect demand variability), the gain from waiting is unaffected by the goodwill depreciation rate. If demand uncertainty is multiplicative (e.g., the product is in the early stage of the life cycle), the gain from waiting decreases when the goodwill depreciation rate increases. Thus, for a given set of beliefs about future advertising rates, firms that market low-involvement products are more likely to precommit to a guaranteed rate strategy than firms that market high-involvement products. If higher goodwill reduces demand uncertainty, the results are the reverse of those for the multiplicative uncertainty formulation.

> **Key Point**   *The CAPM implies that the goodwill depreciation rate has no effect on the gain from waiting. Consequently firms in all industries will react similarly when advertising rates are uncertain. The expected utility model implies that, in general, the goodwill depreciation rate affects the gain from waiting. Consequently firms in different industries will react differently when advertising rates are uncertain, even if they share the same beliefs about future advertising rates. Furthermore, the firm's reaction depends upon which phase of the product life cycle the firm's product is in (i.e., the precise form of demand uncertainty).*

Our model should be extended in several ways. First, we considered only network television. Future models should allow the firm to choose media portfolios (e.g., network television and local television) over time depending on the anticipated advertising rate structure. Second, we focused on a monopoly model. In an oligopolistic framework, the firm's decision to precommit or wait will depend heavily on the anticipated competitive reactions. Hence game-theoretic models incorporating different sets of behavioral assumptions are necessary. Third, and important, we did not consider supply adjustments by the advertising rate industry (i.e., the number of advertising insertions which are presold and the number of advertising insertions made available at the spot rate). A full analysis should consider supply and demand adjustments simultaneously.

7.4 CONCLUDING REMARKS

This chapter focuses on the firm's media message and media allocation decisions. We analyze the state of the art and propose an analytical model for determining the advertiser's optimal advertising purchasing strategy when advertising rates are uncertain.

Many interesting research opportunities remain open in this area. Standard measures of advertising effectiveness (e.g., reach, frequency, or consumers' exposure distributions to different media) do not allow for competitive or multiproduct effects. Research is necessary to explicate the relationship between behavioral measures of advertising effectiveness and sales (profits) while allowing for unobservable heterogeneity (e.g., different segments use different information-processing strategies), audience duplication, and nonstationarities in consumers' viewing habits.

In this chapter we have implicitly assumed that the only marketing instruments available to the firm are price and advertising. In many industries, however, personal selling is a strategic marketing tool. Chapter 8 focuses on personal selling. As in the rest of the book, we shall pay particular attention to uncertainty and multiproduct and dynamic effects.

NOTES

1. We assume that gentleness and effectiveness are measurable on at least an interval scale. Hence the distance between points can be measured using a generalized Euclidean metric.

2. Suppose the firm runs three ad insertions in a given medium. Let R_3 denote the reach of this schedule and N_i the number of individuals who are exposed to the ith insertion. Then $R_3 = N_1 + N_2 + N_3 - [(N_1 \cap N_2) + (N_1 \cap N_3) + (N_2 \cap N_3)] + (N_1 \cap N_2 \cap N_3)$. Note that pairwise

audience duplications (e.g., $N_1 \cap N_2$) are not sufficient to measure R_3. In particular, we need to know the number of individuals who are exposed to all three ad insertions ($N_1 \cap N_2 \cap N_3$).

Suppose the firm runs $n > 3$ insertions in the medium. Then the reach R_n depends on all single-insertion reach values (N_i), all pairwise audience duplications ($N_i \cap N_j$, where $i \neq j$), and so on up to all n-tuple audience duplications ($N_i \cap N_j \cap \ldots \cap N_n$). Consequently exact measures of reach are impossible.

Most models estimate $R_n (n > 2)$ using data on R_1 and R_2 only. Agostini (1962) estimates reach using the formula $R_n = R_{n-1} + (1 - R_{n-1})(a/nb)$, where $a = R_1$ and $b = (1/\ln 2)$ $\ln[R_1(1-R_1)/(R_2-R_1)]$. Metheringham (1964) uses the beta binomial model to obtain $R_n = 1 - [(b+n-1)(b+n-2) \ldots b/(a+b+n-1) \ldots (a+b)]$, where $a = (R_1 R_2 - R_1^2)/(2R_1 - R_1^2 - R_2)$ and $b = a(1 - R_1)/R_1$. One weakness of the beta binomial model is that the reach estimates are meaningless if $a < 0$ and $b < 0$.

3. Let p denote the proportion of the segment exposed to one insertion of the media vehicle. Let R_n be the reach for n insertions. Then the binomial model implies that $R_n = 1 - (1 - p)^n$. This method seriously overestimates reach.

4. Let p_i denote the fraction of the population that is exposed to one insertion in medium i. Then the Hofmans formula measures reach as $R = (\Sigma p_i)^2 / (\Sigma p_i + \Sigma k_{ij} \, p_{ij})$, where $k_{ij} = (p_i + p_j)/(p_i + p_j - p_{ij})$ and p_{ij} is the duplication between media i and j.

5. Suppose the media schedule consists of one ad insertion in each of two media (1 and 2, respectively). For any given individual let p_1 and p_2, respectively, denote the probabilities of exclusive exposure to media 1 and 2, respectively ($p_1 \neq p_2$), p_{12} the probability of exposure to both media, and p_0 the probability of nonexposure. The Dirichlet model assumes (p_0, p_1, p_2, p_{12}) has a Dirichlet distribution across the population. This specification captures heterogeneity across individuals and media in a flexible way. Any given individual has different exposure probabilities to different media. At the aggregate level, the marginal exposure distributions for each medium follow (different) beta binomial distributions. The Dirichlet model can be easily extended to three or more vehicles provided there is only one insertion in each vehicle.

   Suppose the advertising schedule consists of two insertions in each of two media. Then the Dirichlet model holds provided for any given individual the outcomes of each multimedia insertion are independent: an obvious departure from realism. The Dirichlet model can be extended to the multimedia case provided the number of insertions in different media are equal. This requirement limits the practical usefulness of the Dirichlet model. One method for dealing with unequal insertions across media is to use dummy (i.e., pseudo) insertions for the media that are used less frequently and adjust the results statistically (see Rust and Leone 1984 for a mixed-media application).

6. The log-linear method proposed in Danaher (1988) is computationally demanding. Danaher (1989) develops an algorithm for estimating the log-linear model without using an iterated proportional fitting method provided there are no interactions.

7. Goodhardt and Ehrenberg (1969) estimate television duplications using the equation $p_{ij} = kp_i \, p_j$, where p_i and p_j, respectively, denote the audience proportions for media i and j, respectively, p_{ij} is the duplicated audience, and k is a constant. Goodhardt and Ehrenberg use one k for television programs on the same channel ("self-pairs") and a different k for television programs on different channels ("cross-pairs"). In their mixed-media model, Rust and Leone (1984) define

the duplicated audience of a television program i and a magazine m as $\hat{r}_{im} = k_{jm}\, r_i\, r_m$, where r_i is the audience proportion for television program i, r_m is the audience proportion for magazine m, and k_{jm} is the estimated duplication constant corresponding to magazine m and television program type j, which includes the specific television program i. As Rust (1986, p. 20) notes, $\hat{r}_{im}$ is an imperfect measure because it treats all television programs belonging to a given program type as if they were identical.

8. Following Little and Lodish (1969), let y_{it} be the exposure level of a particular individual in segment i at time t. The key functions in MEDIAC are $r(y_{it})$, where r denotes a nonlinear function of y_{it} and $n_i w_{it} E\{r(y_{it})\}$, where n_i denotes the number of people in segment i and w_{it} is the sales potential of a person in segment i in time period t. Suppose all segment members are identical (i.e., w_{it} is constant). Now the central problem is the estimation of $E\{r(y_{it})\}$. Little and Lodish use a quadratic approximation based on $E(y_{it})$, $E(y_{it}^2)$, and the functional form of r. (More precisely, MEDIAC assumes that $E(y_{it})$ and $E(y_{it}^2)$ are sufficient statistics: that is, the higher-order moments of y_{it} are functions of the first two moments.) Now the estimates of $E(y_{it}^2)$ are based on estimates of pairwise audience duplication and are likely to be unstable. Consequently the objective function in MEDIAC—which depends heavily on the estimate of $E\{r(y_{it})\}$—is also unstable. Suppose consumers within a segment are heterogeneous (i.e., w_{it} is random). Then the objective function depends on $E\{w_{it}\, r(y_{it})\}$, which is a complicated function unless w_{it} and $r(y_{it})$ are independent. If w_{it} and $r(y_{it})$ are not independent, Little and Lodish suggest that the researcher divide the market segment a priori into more homogeneous subgroups. However, the practical feasibility of this approach appears to be unknown.

9. Consider a simple mean-variance model where the objective function depends on $E\{r(y_{it})\}$ and $\sigma^2\{r(y_{it})\}$, where σ^2 denotes the variance operator. Recall that in the simplest case [i.e., a quadratic approximation of $r(y_{it})$], $E\{r(y_{it})\}$ depends on the first two moments of y_{it}. Now $\sigma^2\{r(y_{it})\}$ depends on such terms as $E(y_{it}^4)$. Hence the estimates of $\sigma^2\{r(y_{it})\}$ are likely to be more unstable than the estimates of $E\{r(y_{it})\}$ even if w_{it} is constant (i.e., consumers in a given segment are homogeneous).

10. Let π_1 and π_2, respectively, denote the firm's profits in periods 1 and 2. Let $E(\pi_i) = \bar{\pi}_i$. Let $U(\pi_i)$ denote the appropriate utilities. Now $\pi_1 = \bar{\pi}_1 + g_1(p_1, A_1)(p_1 - c)(u_1 - \bar{u}_1)$, where $\bar{u}_1 = E(u_1)$, c denotes the constant unit cost, and $\bar{\pi}_1 = f_1 + g_1\bar{u}_1 - w_1 A_1$, where w_1 denotes the nonstochastic advertising rate in period 1 and A_1 the number of ad insertions.

Similarly $\pi_2 = \bar{\pi}_2 + g_2(p_2, A_2)(p_2 - c)(u_2 - \bar{u}_2) - (w_2 - \bar{w}_2)A_2$, where $\bar{u}_2 = E(u_2)$, w_2 is the stochastic advertising rate in period 2, $\bar{w}_2 = E(w_2)$, and $\bar{\pi}_2 = f_2 + g_2\bar{u}_2 - \bar{w}_2 A_2$.

The firm chooses policy to maximize $Z = EU(\pi_1) + EU(\pi_2)/(1 + r)$, where r denotes the risk-free interest rate. Recall that U is concave by risk aversion. Hence $EU(\pi_i) < U(\bar{\pi}_i)$ using Jensen's inequality. Thus the firm is worse off when uncertainty is globally introduced (i.e., demand uncertainty, advertising-rate uncertainty, or both).

11. As shown in the previous note, $EU(\pi_2) < U(\bar{\pi}_2)$. Hence the firm chooses the risky advertising rate plan only if $w_2 - \bar{w}_2$ is a sufficiently large positive quantity.

12. Let $\hat{\varphi}_i = f_i(p_i, A_i) + g_i(p_i, A_i)[\bar{u}_i - a\,\mathrm{Cov}(u_i, R_i)]$ denote the certainty-equivalent demands in period i, where a is the market price of risk and R_i is the random rate of return on the

market portfolio in period i. The firm chooses policy to maximize $N_1 = [\hat{\varphi}_1(p_1 - c) - w_1 A_1] + [\hat{\varphi}_2(p_2 - c) - \hat{w}_2 A_2](1 + r)^{-1}$, where $\hat{w}_2 = \bar{w}_2 - a \operatorname{Cov}(w_2, R_2)$ denotes the certainty-equivalent advertising rate and r is the risk-free interest rate.

Suppose future advertising rates are guaranteed (i.e., $w_2 = \bar{w}_2$). Then the firm maximizes $N_2 = [\hat{\varphi}_1(p_1 - c) - w_1 A_1] + [\hat{\varphi}_2(p_2 - c) - \hat{w}_2 A_2](1 + r)^{-1}$. Subtracting, we get $N_1 - N_2 = a \operatorname{Cov}(w_2, R_2) A_2(1 + r)^{-1} > 0$ for any given policy. Hence the value-maximizing firm gains when advertising rates in period 2 are uncertain.

13. Let w_2^r denote the actual advertising rate realized in period 2. Then the firm will choose a revised policy (p_2^r, A_2^r) based on the nonstochastic w_2^r. Clearly $p_2^r \neq p_2^*$ and $A_2^r \neq A_2^*$, where the * denotes the firm's planned strategy for period 2 before the advertising-rate uncertainty is resolved.

14. Because we are considering a current-effects model and advertising-rate uncertainty occurs in period 2, it is sufficient to analyze the cash flows in period 2. We know that the utility-maximizing firm will accept advertising-rate uncertainty only if $\bar{w}_2 - w_2^* < 0$, where $\bar{w}_2 = E(w_2)$ and w_2^* is the guaranteed advertising rate. Assume that $\bar{w}_2 - w_2^* < 0$.

Let (p_2^*, A_2^*) denote the firm's planned policy for period 2 if the advertising rate in period 2 is guaranteed at $\bar{w}_2$. Note that the firm is committed to A_2^* and will not change p_2^* at the end of period 1 because advertising does not have a carryover effect. Let (p_2^{**}, A_2^{**}) denote the firm's planned policy for period 2 if the advertising rate in period 2 is uncertain. We seek to compare p_2^* and p_2^{**} and A_2^* and A_2^{**}, respectively.

Let

$$Z_1 = \frac{EU[(p_2 - c)\bar{\varphi}_2 - w_2^* A_2 + g_2(p_2 - c)(u_2 - \bar{u}_2)]}{(1 + r)}$$

where $\bar{\varphi}_2 = f_2(p_2, A_2) + g_2(p_2, A_2)\bar{u}_2$ denotes the expected demand in period 2. Let

$$Z_2 = \frac{EU[(p_2 - c)\bar{\varphi}_2 - w_2^* A_2 + g_2(p_2 - c)(u_2 - \bar{u}_2) - (w_2 - \bar{w}_2)A_2 - (\bar{w}_2 - w_2^*)A_2]}{(1 + r)}$$

Thus (p_2^*, A_2^*) solves $\partial Z_1 / \partial p_2 = 0$ and $\partial Z_1 / \partial A_2 = 0$ and (p_2^{**}, A_2^{**}) solves $\partial Z_2 / \partial p_2 = 0$ and $\partial Z_2 / \partial A_2 = 0$. Now the global effect of uncertainty is inherently indeterminate if both demand and advertising rates are uncertain, even for the simplest types of uncertainty.

Suppose demand is deterministic but advertising rates are uncertain. Then

$$Z_1 = \frac{EU[(p_2 - c)\bar{\varphi}_2 - w_2^* A_2]}{(1 + r)}$$

$$Z_2 = \frac{EU[(p_2 - c)\bar{\varphi}_2 - w_2^* A_2 - (w_2 - \bar{w}_2)A_2 - (\bar{w}_2 - w_2^*)A_2]}{(1 + r)}$$

Now $\partial Z_1 / \partial p_2 = 0$ and $\partial Z_2 / \partial p_2 = 0$ imply that $[\bar{\varphi}_2 + (\partial \bar{\varphi}_2 / \partial p_2)(p_2 - c)] = 0$. Hence any pair (p_2^1, A_2^1) satisfying $\partial Z_1 / \partial p_2 = 0$ also satisfies $\partial Z_2 / \partial p_2 = 0$. Similarly,

$$\frac{\partial Z_1}{\partial A_2} = \frac{EU'[(p_2 - c)\,\partial \bar{\varphi}_2 / \partial A_2 - w_2^*]}{(1 + r)}$$

$$\frac{\partial Z_2}{\partial A_2} = \frac{EU'[(p_2 - c)\,\partial \bar{\varphi}_2 / \partial A_2 - w_2^* - (w_2 - \bar{w}_2) - (\bar{w}_2 - w_2^*)]}{(1 + r)}$$

Let (p_2^2, A_2^2) be any pair satisfying $\partial Z_1/\partial A_2 = 0$. Evaluating $\partial Z_2/\partial A_2$ at this point, we get

$$\frac{\partial Z_2}{\partial A_2} = \frac{-[\text{Cov}(U', w_2) + (\bar{w}_2 - w_2^*)EU']}{(1+r)}$$

However, $\text{Cov}(U', w_2) > 0$ by risk aversion and $\bar{w}_2 - w_2^* < 0$. Hence the risk-reduction effect and the mean-enhancing effect work in opposite directions. Consequently, the global effect of advertising-rate uncertainty is inherently indeterminate even if demand is deterministic.

15. Let the optimal policies under certainty and uncertainty, respectively, be (p_2^*, A_2^*) and (p_2^{**}, A_2^{**}). Let V_1 be the certainty-equivalent profit in period 2 given the guaranteed advertising rate w_2^*. Let V_2 be the certainty-equivalent profit in period 2 given the uncertain advertising rate w_2. Let the certainty-equivalent advertising rate for w_2 be $\hat{w}_2 = \bar{w}_2 - a \text{ Cov}(w_2, R_2)$. As discussed in note 14, $\hat{w}_2 < w_2^*$ for the firm to prefer the uncertain advertising rate. Now $V_2 = V_1 + A_2[w_2^* - \hat{w}_2]$, where $V_1 = (p_2 - c)\hat{\varphi}_2 - w_2^* A_2$ and the certainty-equivalent demand is $\hat{\varphi}_2 = f_2(p_2, A_2) + g_2(p_2, A_2)[\bar{u}_2 - a \text{ Cov}(u_2, R_2)]$.

Now $\partial V_2/\partial p_2 = \partial V_1/\partial p_2$. Hence any pair (p_2^1, A_2^1) satisfying $\partial V_1/\partial p_2 = 0$ satisfies $\partial V_2/\partial p_2 = 0$. Similarly $\partial V_2/\partial A_2 = \partial V_1/\partial A_2 + (w_2^* - \hat{w}_2)$. Let (p_2^2, A_2^2) be any pair satisfying $\partial V_1/\partial A_2 = 0$. Then, holding p_2^2 fixed, A_2^2 must be increased to satisfy $\partial V_2/\partial A_2 = 0$ because V_2 is concave in A_2.

These results imply that $A_2^{**} > A_2^*$. Furthermore, $p_2^{**} > (<)p_2^*$ if $\partial^2 V_1/\partial p_2 \partial A_2 > (<)0$. As discussed previously, $\text{sgn}(\partial^2 V_1/\partial p_2 \partial A_2) = -\text{sgn}(\partial|\hat{\varepsilon}_{p_2}|/\partial A_2)$, where $\hat{\varepsilon}_{p_2}$ denotes the price elasticity of the certainty-equivalent demand in period 2 [i.e., $\hat{\varepsilon}_{p_2} = (\partial\hat{\varphi}_2/\partial p_2)(p_2/\hat{\varphi}_2)$]. Hence $p_2^{**} > (<)p_2^*$ if $(\partial|\hat{\varepsilon}_{p_2}|/\partial A_2) < (>)0$.

16. This analysis is incomplete because we focus exclusively on demand adjustments. A complete analysis should consider supply adjustments as well (i.e., the advertising industry will change the supply of media insertions in period 2 when advertising-rate uncertainty is introduced).

17. The assumption of a quadratic utility function is only reasonable if the profit uncertainty is "small." Hence the analysis applies strictly to firms whose products are in the maturity phase (i.e., demand is deterministic) and for which advertising is a small component of total costs.

Let $w_2' = \gamma w_2 + \theta$ denote the new advertising rate. Using the mean-preserving spread approach, let $d\theta/d\gamma = -\bar{w}_2$ (i.e., the mean advertising rate is $\bar{w}_2$; as γ increases, the advertising rate becomes more uncertain). Let $Z = EU(\pi_1) + EU(\pi_2)(1+r)^{-1}$ denote the sum of the discounted expected utilities. Differentiating and using the first-order conditions, we have $\partial^2 Z/\partial p_2 \partial\gamma = 0$. Similarly, evaluating $\partial^2 Z/\partial A_2 \partial\gamma$ at $\gamma = 1, \theta = 0$, we obtain

$$\frac{\partial^2 Z}{\partial A_2 \partial\gamma} = -A_2 E\left[U''(w_2 - \bar{w}_2)\left((p_2 - c)\partial\varphi_2/\partial A_2 - w_2\right)\right] - \text{Cov}(U', w_2)$$

where φ_2 is the nonstochastic demand. Now the first term is indeterminate in general. Suppose the utility function is quadratic (i.e., U'' is a negative constant). Then

$$\frac{\partial^2 Z}{\partial A_2 \partial\gamma} = -A_2 U'' E\left\{(w_2 - \bar{w}_2)\left[(p_2 - c)\partial\varphi_2/\partial A_2 - w_2\right]\right\} - \text{Cov}(U', w_2)$$

Now $\text{Cov}(U', w_2) > 0$ by risk aversion and

$$E\left[(w_2 - \bar{w}_2)\left((p_2 - c)\frac{\partial \varphi_2}{\partial A_2} - w_2\right)\right] = \text{Cov}\left[w_2, \left((p_2 - c)\frac{\partial \varphi_2}{\partial A_2} - w_2\right)\right] < 0$$

Hence $\partial^2 Z/\partial A_2\, \partial \gamma < 0$. Consequently $\partial A_2/\partial \gamma < 0$ and $\text{sgn}(\partial p_2/\partial \gamma) = -\text{sgn}(\partial^2 Z/\partial A_2\, \partial p_2)$.

Now $Z = EU[(p_2 - c)\varphi_2(p_2, A_2) - w_2 A_2]$, where w_2 is stochastic. Differentiating and using the first-order conditions, we obtain $\partial_2 Z/\partial A_2\, \partial p_2 = -(EU')[\varphi_2(p_2 - c)/p_2][\partial|\varepsilon_{p_2}|/\partial A_2]$, where $\varepsilon_{p_2} = (\partial \varphi_2/\partial p_2)(p_2/\varphi_2)$ denotes the price elasticity of demand. Hence $\partial A_2/\partial \gamma < 0$ and $\text{sgn}(\partial p_2/\partial \gamma) = \text{sgn}(\partial|\varepsilon_{p_2}|/\partial A_2)$.

18. Let $w_2' = \gamma w_2 + \theta$, where $d\theta/d\gamma = -\bar{w}_2$. The certainty-equivalent profit in period 2 is $\hat{\pi}_2 = (p_2 - c)\hat{\varphi}_2 - (\gamma \bar{w}_2 + \theta)A_2 + aA_2\,\text{Cov}(\gamma w_2 + \theta, R_2)$, where $\hat{\varphi}_2 = f_2(p_2, A_2) + g_2(p_2, A_2)[\bar{u}_2 - a\,\text{Cov}(u_2, R_2)]$. Differentiating $\hat{\pi}_2$ and evaluating at $\gamma = 1, \theta = 0$, we obtain $\partial^2 \hat{\pi}_2/\partial A_1\, \partial \gamma = 0$ and $\partial^2 \hat{\pi}_2/\partial A_2\, \partial \gamma = a\,\text{Cov}(w_2, R_2) > 0$. Hence $\partial A_2/\partial \gamma > 0$ and $\text{sgn}(\partial p_2/\partial \gamma) = -\text{sgn}(\partial|\hat{\varepsilon}_{p_2}|/\partial A_2)$, where $\hat{\varepsilon}_{p_2}$ denotes the price elasticity of the certainty-equivalent demand in period 2.

19. Let the demand in period 1 be $\varphi_1 = f_1(A_1) + g_1(A_1)u_1$ and the demand in period 2 be $\varphi_2 = f_2(A_1, A_2) + g_2(A_1, A_2)u_2$, where u_1 and u_2 are i.i.d.

    Suppose the guaranteed future advertising rate in period 2 is $\bar{w}_2 = E(w_2)$, where w_2 is random. Then the certainty-equivalent profit in period 1 is $\hat{\pi}_1 = \bar{\pi}_1 - amg_1(A_1)\,\text{Cov}((u_1, R_1)$ and the certainty-equivalent profit in period 2 is $\hat{\pi}_2 = \bar{\pi}_2 - amg_2(A_1, A_2)\,\text{Cov}(u_2, R_2)$, where $\bar{\pi}_1 = m\bar{\varphi}_1 - w_1 A_1, \bar{\pi}_2 = m\bar{\varphi}_2 - \bar{w}_2 A_2$, and m is the unit profit margin.

    Suppose w_2 is random. Then the certainty-equivalent profit in period 1 is $\hat{\hat{\pi}}_1 = \hat{\pi}_1$. The certainty-equivalent profit in period 2 is $\hat{\hat{\pi}}_2 = \hat{\pi}_2 + aA_2\text{Cov}(w_2, R_2)(1 + r)^{-1}$. Hence given advertising-rate certainty, the firm maximizes $Q_1 = \hat{\pi}_1 + \hat{\pi}_2/(1 + r)$, where r is the risk-free interest rate. Under uncertainty the firm maximizes $Q_2 = \hat{\hat{\pi}}_1 + \hat{\hat{\pi}}_2/(1 + r)$.

    Let (A_1^*, A_2^*) denote the optimal policy given no advertising-rate uncertainty and $(A_1^{**} A_2^{**})$ the optimal policy given advertising-rate uncertainty. Now $\partial Q_2/\partial A_1 = \partial Q_1/\partial A_1$. Furthermore $\partial Q_2/\partial A_2 = \partial Q_1/\partial A_2 + a\,\text{Cov}(w_2, R_2)(1+r)^{-1}$. Let (A_1, A_2) be any pair satisfying $\partial Q_1/\partial A_2 = 0$. Then, holding A_1 fixed, A_2 must be increased to satisfy $\partial Q_2/\partial A_2 = 0$ because Q_2 is concave in A_2. These results imply that $A_2^{**} > A_2^*$. Furthermore, $A_1^{**} > (<)A_1^*$ depending on whether $\partial_2\hat{\varphi}_2/\partial A_1\, \partial A_2 > (<)0$, where $\hat{\varphi}_2 = f_2(A_1, A_2) + g_2(A_1, A_2)[\bar{u}_2 - a\,\text{Cov}(u_2, R_2)]$ is the certainty-equivalent demand in period 2.

20. Let the goodwill at the beginning of time 1 be G_0. Then the demand in period 1 is $\varphi_1 = f_1(A_1 + G_0) + g_1(A_1 + G_0)u_1$. Let δ be the goodwill depreciation rate ($0 < \delta < 1$). Then the demand in period 2 is $\varphi_2 = f_2[A_2 + (1 - \delta)(A_1 + G_0)] + g_2[A_2 + (1 - \delta)(A_1 + G_0)]u_2$. The certainty-equivalent demand in period 2 is $\hat{\varphi}_2 = f_2[A_2 + (1-\delta)(A_1+G_0)] + g_2[A_2 + (1-\delta)(A_1 + G_0)][\bar{u}_2 - a\,\text{Cov}(u_2, R_2)]$. Let $G = A_2 + (1 - \delta)(A_1 + G_0)$. Suppose uncertainty is additive (i.e., $g_2 \equiv 1$). Then $\partial^2 \hat{\varphi}_2/\partial A_1\, \partial A_2 = (\partial^2 f_2/\partial G^2)(1 - \delta) < 0$. Suppose uncertainty is multiplicative (i.e., $f_2 \equiv 0$). Then $\partial^2 \hat{\varphi}_2/\partial A_1\, \partial A_2 = (\partial^2 g_2/\partial G^2)(1 - \delta)[\bar{u}_2 - a\,\text{Cov}(u_2, R_2)] < 0$. Hence $A_2^{**} > A_2^*$ and $A_1^{**} < A_1^*$.

21. Consider a current-effects advertising model. Let the demand in period 2 be $f_2(p_2, A_2) + g_2(p_2, A_2)u_2$, where $E(u_2) = \bar{u}_2$. Let w_2 be the random advertising rate in period 2 and w_2^* the guaranteed advertising rate per insertion. Let $A_2 > 0$ be any arbitrary number of ad insertions in period 2. Suppose the firm prefers a waiting strategy to a precommitment strategy [i.e.,

$w_2^* > E(w_2) = \bar{w}_2$]. The firm's profit in period 2 given a waiting strategy is $\pi_2^W = (p_2 - c)(f_2 + g_2 u_2) - w_2 A_2$. Suppose the firm hedges and purchases φA_2 ad insertions at a guaranteed rate of w_2^* per ad insertion and $(1 - \varphi) A_2$ ad insertions at the spot rate w_2, where $0 < \varphi < 1$. Then the firm's profit in period 2 given a hedging strategy is $\pi_2^H = (p_2 - c)(f_2 + g_2 u_2) - [\varphi A_2 w_2^* + (1 - \varphi) A_2 w_2]$. Let $\bar{\pi}_2^H$ and $\bar{\pi}_2^W$, respectively, denote the expected profits in period 2 given the hedging and waiting strategies. Then $\bar{\pi}_2^H - \bar{\pi}_2^W = \varphi A_2 (\bar{w}_2 - w_2^*) < 0$. Let $\sigma^2(\pi_2^H)$ and $\sigma^2(\pi_2^W)$, respectively, denote the profit variances in period 2 for the hedging and waiting strategies. Then $\sigma^2(\pi_2^H) - \sigma^2(\pi_2^W) = [(1 - \varphi)^2 - 1] A_2^2 \sigma^2(w_2) + 2\varphi(p_2 - c) g_2 A_2 \, \mathrm{Cov}(u_2, w_2)$. Suppose $\mathrm{Cov}(u_2, w_2) = 0$. Then $\sigma^2(\pi_2^H) < \sigma^2(\pi_2^W)$. Hence hedging simultaneously reduces the expected profit and the variability of profit in period 2. Thus the expected utility–maximizing firm could prefer hedging to the waiting policy. If $\mathrm{Cov}(u_2, w_2) > 0$ is sufficiently large, the firm may prefer the waiting policy.

22. Let the demands in periods 1 and 2, respectively, be $\varphi_1 = f_1(A_1 + G_0) + g_1(A_1 + G_0) u_1$ and $\varphi_2 = f_2[A_2 + (1 - \delta)(A_1 + G_0)] + g_2[A_2 + (1 - \delta)(A_1 + G_0)] u_2$, where G_0 is the initial goodwill at the start of period 1 and δ is the goodwill depreciation rate. Then the profit in period 1 is $\pi_1 = m(f_1 + g_1 u_1) - w_1 A_1$. The profit in period 2 if the firm chooses a precommitment policy is $\pi_2^P = m(f_2 + g_2 u_2) - w_2^* A_2$, where w_2^* is the guaranteed advertising rate per insertion. The profit in period 2 if the firm chooses a waiting policy is $\pi_2^W = m(f_2 + g_2 u_2) - w_2 A_2$, where w_2 is the random advertising rate.

Consider any arbitrary utility function. Let $EU(\pi_2^P)$ and $EU(\pi_2^W)$, respectively, denote the firm's expected utilities in period 2 given the precommitment and waiting strategies. Let $M = [EU(\pi_2^W) - EU(\pi_2^P)](1 + r)^{-1}$ denote the gain from waiting. Suppose demand uncertainty is additive (i.e., demand in period 2 is $f_2 + u_2$). Then $\partial M / \partial \delta = [m(\partial f_2 / \partial G_2)(A_1 + G_0)][E(U^P)' - E(U^W)'](1 + r)^{-1}$, where $G_2 = A_2 + (1 - \delta)(A_1 + G_0)$. Now $\delta f_2 / \partial G_2 > 0$. However, the sign of $E(U^P)' - E(U^W)'$ is unknown. Hence the effect of a change in the goodwill depreciation rate is indeterminate.

Suppose the firm has an exponential utility function and (u_2, w_2) has a bivariate normal distribution. Then maximizing $EU(\pi_i)$ is equivalent to maximizing $\bar{\pi}_i - \beta/2\sigma^2(\pi_i)$, where $\bar{\pi}_i = E(\pi_i)$ and β is the firm's constant coefficient of absolute risk aversion. Given the firm's precommitment policy, the firm's discounted expected utility is $Z^P = [\bar{\pi}_1 - (\beta/2)\sigma^2(\pi_1)] + [\bar{\pi}_2^P - (\beta/2)\sigma^2(\pi_2^P)](1 + r)^{-1}$. The firm's expected utility for the waiting policy is $Z^W = [\bar{\pi}_1 - (\beta/2)\sigma^2(\pi_1)] + [\bar{\pi}_2^W - (\beta/2)\sigma^2(\pi_2^W)](1 + r)^{-1}$. For any policy (A_1, A_2) the gain from waiting is $Z^W - Z^P = A_2(w_2^* - \bar{w}_2)(1 + r)^{-1} - (\beta/2)(1 + r)^{-1}[A_2^2 \sigma^2(w_2) - 2mg_2 A_2 \, \mathrm{Cov}(u_2, w_2)]$. Let $G_2 = A_2 + (1 - \delta)(A_1 + G_0)$. Then $\partial(Z^W - Z^P)/\partial \delta = -(1 + r)^{-1} \beta m A_2 \, \mathrm{Cov}(u_2, w_2)(\partial g_2 / \partial G_2)(A_1 + G_0)$. Suppose $\mathrm{Cov}(u_2, w_2) > 0$. Then $\mathrm{sgn}[\partial(Z^W - Z^P)/\partial \delta] = -\mathrm{sgn}(\partial g_2 / \partial G_2)$. Suppose uncertainty is additive (i.e., $g_2 \equiv 1$). Then the gain from waiting is independent of the goodwill depreciation rate. If uncertainty is multiplicative, $\partial(Z^W - Z^P)/\partial \delta < 0$. If higher goodwill reduces the variability of demand (i.e., $\partial g_2 / \partial G_2 < 0$), $\partial(Z^W - Z^P)/\partial \delta > 0$.

The Personal Selling Decision in a Dynamic and Uncertain Environment

Personal selling is one of the most important components of the marketing mix. According to one estimate (Dalrymple and Cron 1992, p. 7, Table 1.1) U.S. firms spent $127 billion on personal selling but only $95 billion on advertising. Furthermore, the U.S. sales sector employed 7 to 8 million people.

This chapter will deal with basic issues in sales force management. Although we shall use the phrase *sales force* throughout, our results apply to other employees in the firm (e.g., managers). We shall deal with the design of the compensation plan in a firm that employs multiple salespersons and that produces multiple products. We shall focus on the problems stemming from uncertainty and discuss the implications for planning and control in both nonhierarchical and multilevel hierarchical organizations (e.g., firms in which a national sales manager supervises district sales managers who, in turn, supervise sales agents in their respective geographical territories). We shall identify those cases where the firm should decentralize decision making and discuss how employees at different levels in the organization (e.g., district managers and sales agents) should be compensated when decentralization occurs. We shall deal with the firm's training investment decision, the personnel selection problem, and sales force turnover, paying particular attention to uncertainty and distinguishing cases where the training is firm-specific and where the sales agent's new skills are portable (i.e., the agent can quit the firm after the training program and find alternative employment elsewhere). We shall discuss the particular difficulties that the firm faces in coordinating the compensation decision with other elements of the marketing mix (e.g., the design of compensation plans when the salesperson has some degree of control over price). Finally, we shall propose methods for measuring agents' ability (which is unobservable to the firm) both cross-sectionally and dynamically using market-level sales data and/or test scores. Although we focus on measuring the ability and performance of sales agents, the methods we propose are general; in particular, the methodology can be used to evaluate the abilities and performances of divisional managers and even the Chief Executive Officers of multidivisional firms.

8.1 THE CERTAINTY CASE

We shall first consider a firm that has one salesperson ("agent") and produces only one product. Suppose that the agent has no control over price and can produce a sales revenue of $5,000 during an eight-hour workday. Furthermore, the firm knows the agent's reservation income (i.e., market value) of $500 per day. Assume that the product is sold in a competitive market; in particular, the selling price of the product is $100 per unit and the firm's variable cost of production is $60 per unit.

The One Agent, One Product Case

How should the firm pay the agent? One option is to pay the agent a piece rate of $10.00 per unit sold (or, equivalently, 10 percent of sales revenue). If the agent shirks, he or she will not earn the reservation income—hence there is no incentive problem. An alternative approach for the firm is to offer the agent the following contract: a sum of $500 if a sales quota of $5,000 is met, and nothing if the quota is underfulfilled (a "forcing" contract). Here again the agent has no incentive to shirk; if he does so, he will not earn his reservation income. The reader can easily construct alternative compensation plans that lead to the equivalent result. In short, under certainty several contracts can be found that lead to the same result. That is, we do not have a well-defined theory of compensation. Note, in particular, that the firm can pay the agent based on either sales or profit.

Model Extensions

This model can be extended in several ways. Consider the following scenarios. Suppose the agent sells multiple products for the firm; in particular, these products can be complementary or substitutes. Assume that sales effort has dynamic carryover effects (e.g., successful sales visits lead to customer retention in the future). Alternatively, the firm employs several agents or uses a sales team. For each of these scenarios (or combinations thereof) the previous results remain unchanged.[1]

> **Key Point**   *The firm does not need to use an incentive-based contract when the relationship between sales and effort is deterministic. This result holds regardless of the firm's organizational structure (e.g., whether the firm uses team selling or agents sell multiple products).*

8.2 THE UNCERTAINTY CASE: BASIC MODEL

We now extend the previous model by incorporating uncertainty. Consider a simple scenario in which there is only one agent who sells one product. Suppose that the agent can produce an expected sales revenue of $5,000 during an eight-hour workday (i.e., sales could be either higher or lower than this figure). The agent's reservation income, the product price, and the variable cost per unit are identical to those in the certainty example. Assume that both the agent and the firm share the same beliefs about sales and that the firm knows the agent's risk attitude.

Risk Aversion

To determine the compensation contract, we need to introduce the concept of risk aversion; in particular, we shall use the result that in order to be induced to bear uncertainty a risk-averse agent must be paid an expected income that exceeds his reservation income.[2] A risk-neutral agent, in contrast, is indifferent among all contracts which pay the same expected income, regardless of the variability of that income. The same definitions apply for the firm.

Suppose both the firm and the agent are risk-neutral (i.e., neither party is concerned about income volatility). We shall assume initially that the agent's effort is observable by the firm (e.g., the firm determines the agent's sales call policy) and that sales effort does not have a dynamic carryover effect. One possibility is for the firm to pay the agent a guaranteed wage of $500 per day. This contract is feasible because the agent's effort is observable and the agent cannot shirk. The firm could offer the agent a pure commission plan which pays a 10 percent commission rate on sales revenue; alternatively, the firm could offer the agent a combination wage–commission plan (e.g., a fixed wage of $250 and a 5 percent commission on sales revenue). All these contracts are equally preferred by both players. Thus as in the certainty case, many contracts lead to identical results.

Suppose that the firm is risk-neutral and the agent is risk-averse. If the firm pays the agent a guaranteed wage of $500 per day, the firm will earn an expected income of $1,500. Suppose the firm offers the agent a risk-sharing plan (i.e., a plan in which some portion of the agent's income is uncertain). Then regardless of which specific plan the firm offers the risk-averse agent, he will require an expected income which exceeds $500. The firm's expected income, however, after paying the agent will now be less than $1,500. Hence the optimal policy is for the firm to pay the agent a guaranteed wage of $500.

> **Key Point**   *If the firm is risk-neutral but the agent is risk-averse, the firm will "insure" the agent by paying him a fixed wage.*

Suppose the agent is risk-neutral and the firm is risk-averse. Now the optimal policy is for the agent to "buy" the firm for a fixed sum of money. (This anomalous result is not surprising: In the previous analysis replace "firm" by "agent" and "agent" by "firm." Large firms often act as agents by purchasing patents from inventors and providing the "selling effort" for marketing the proprietary technology.)

Suppose both the firm and the agent are risk-averse; their precise risk attitudes, however, are unknown. Then the optimal contract requires risk sharing between the firm and the agent.[3] At this level of generality we can only conclude that both the agent the firm earn more when gross profit is higher (see Raiffa, 1968, pp. 200–1).

> **Key Point**   *In general both the firm and the agent are risk-averse. Hence the optimal compensation contract requires risk sharing. That is, a pure wage plan cannot be optimal.*

For managerial insight, we shall focus on two risk-aversion scenarios: (1) Both the firm and the agent have exponential utility functions; and (2) both the firm and the agent have logarithmic utility functions. The reader can analyze alternative scenarios.[4] Recall that for an exponential utility function, the individual's willingness to pay a premium to avoid a fair gamble does not depend on the individual's wealth level. For the logarithmic utility function, the premium decreases when wealth increases.

The Exponential Utility Model

Consider the exponential utility case first. The optimal contract is shown by AB in Figure 8.1a. Note that the contract consists of a fixed wage (OA) and a linear profit-sharing rule.[5] In practice, many firms will be unwilling to use a profit-based compensation rule because they do not want to share cost and profit information with their employees. This problem is easy to resolve because the firm knows the production cost structure and hence the relationship between gross profits and sales. Thus the firm can choose an equivalent sales-based compensation plan.

   The Role of the Cost Structure.   Four cases are of interest. First, suppose marginal cost is constant for feasible sales volumes (as in our previous examples). Then the optimal contract can be written as a fixed wage plus a linear commission on sales revenue. See Figure 8.2a. Second, suppose marginal cost decreases with volume. In this case the optimal contract is a wage–commission plan in which the commission rate increases with sales revenue (i.e., the commission rate structure is progressive).[6] See Figure 8.2b. Third, suppose marginal cost increases with volume. Then the commission rate decreases with sales revenue (i.e.,

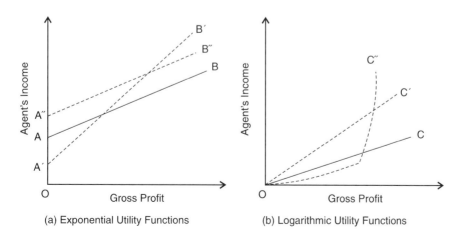

Figure 8.1 The optimum compensation plan for different risk attitudes.

the commission rate structure is regressive). See Figure 8.2c. Fourth, suppose marginal cost decreases initially as volume increases but increases thereafter (i.e., the marginal cost curve is U-shaped). The commission structure is now progressive until marginal cost reaches its minimum value and regressive thereafter. See Figure 8.2d.

> ***Key Point*** *The firm does not want to share profit information with the agent. Consequently, the firm can pay the agent on the basis of sales because the firm knows the cost structure. In particular, the firm will use a nonlinear compensation plan (based on sales revenue) when marginal cost varies with volume.*

A Slab Compensation System. In practice the firm can operationalize these contracts using a suitable slab system. For example, if marginal cost decreases with volume, the firm might offer a progressive commission structure with a commission rate of 5 percent on sales between $0 and $3,000, a commission rate of 7 percent on sales between $3,000

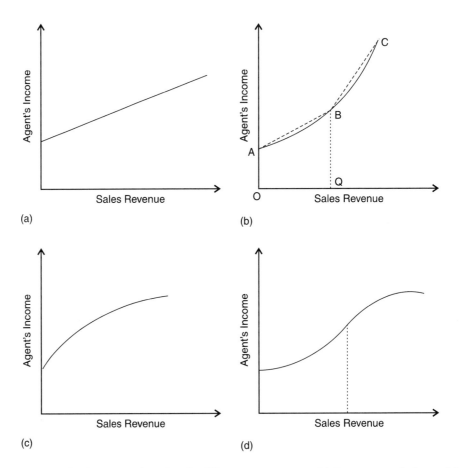

Figure 8.2 Optimal compensation plans for different cost structures. (a) Constant marginal cost. (b) Decreasing marginal cost. (c) Increasing marginal cost. (d) U-shaped marginal cost curve.

and $4,000, and so on (see Figure 8.2b). By using a suitable number of slabs, the firm can approximate the optimal contract to any desired level of accuracy. In practice the firm will have to trade off accuracy and simplicity (i.e., too many slabs may confuse the agent). Note that a progressive two-slab commission structure is equivalent to a combination wage–commission–bonus plan with a linear commission rate on total sales and a linear bonus scheme in which the agent is paid a bonus for exceeding the sales quota (see the broken line ABC in Figure 8.2b, where OQ denotes the quota).

> ***Key Point*** *For practical reasons the firm should use a slab system to operationalize a progressive or regressive compensation plan. By using a sufficiently large number of slabs the firm can approximate the optimal (smooth) contract.*

The Logarithmic Utility Case

Suppose both the firm and the agent have logarithmic utility functions. Then there is no fixed wage: The optimal contract is a simple commission structure in which the agent is paid a fixed commission rate based on profit (see OC in Figure 8.1b).[7] As discussed above, the firm can easily transform this profit-based compensation plan into one based on sales. For example, if marginal cost increases with volume, the commission structure based on sales is regressive.

Unobservable Effort

The previous analysis made a simplifying assumption: The agent's effort is observable. In many cases the agent controls the sales call policy and allocates his or her time across products and clients; furthermore the firm cannot costlessly observe the agent's effort. How does unobservability of effort affect the optimal compensation plan?

First, suppose that the relationship between sales effort and sales is deterministic. In this case the firm can use realized sales to determine precisely the agent's effort, and there is no need for the firm to monitor the agent. Consequently the certainty results hold: In our example, the firm offers the agent a forcing contract in which the agent gets paid $500 if he or she meets the sales quota of $5,000 and nothing otherwise.

Second, suppose that the relationship between sales effort and sales is uncertain. Now the firm cannot use realized sales to infer the agent's effort precisely. Consider the case of a risk-neutral firm and a risk-averse agent. As discussed in the observable effort case, the ideal policy would be for the firm to absorb all the risk and pay the agent a guaranteed wage of $500. The difficulty is that because effort is now unobservable the agent will shirk. (The agent is guaranteed a wage of $500 regardless of the sales outcome and "leisure" has positive utility.) Consequently the firm cannot use a fixed-wage plan; a risk-sharing arrangement is necessary in which some portion of the agent's income is uncertain. This contract can assume several forms (e.g., a pure commission plan, a mixed wage–commission plan, or a wage–bonus plan).[8] Regardless of which contract is used, the risk-averse agent in our example must earn an expected income exceeding $500. Consequently the risk-neutral firm earns lower expected profits (less than $1,500) as a result of the unobservability of effort. Thus there is an incentive problem; that is, the risk-sharing contract is "second-best." This problem—the need to use second-best contracts as a result of the unobservability of effort—is known as the moral hazard problem.[9] Jagpal (1983a,b) discusses this issue in detail in the general context of the multiproduct firm which employs many agents.

> **Key Point**   *Suppose both the firm and the agent are risk-averse and the firm cannot observe the agent's effort. Then a "second-best" contract is necessary because the agent always has an incentive to shirk.*

8.3 THE UNCERTAINTY MODEL: SINGLE-PERIOD EXTENSIONS

We can use the basic results in Section 2 to analyze several real-world scenarios. For example, what is the optimal contract if the agent desires a minimum guaranteed income (e.g., an amount sufficient to cover the mortgage payment on his or her house)?

A Quota Model: The "Draw" System

Consider the exponential utility case (see Figure 8.3). The optimal contract in the absence of a minimum income requirement is shown by AB. Suppose the agent requires a minimum income of OC. Then the optimal contract is given by the broken line CDE.[10] This contract is equivalent to a wage–quota plan in which the agent is paid a fixed wage OC until he or she reaches the quota OQ and a bonus if he or she exceeds the quota. Note that the firm insures the agent when sales revenue is less than OP. Furthermore, DE and AB are parallel; that is, the bonus rate given this plan equals the commission rate in a contract in which the firm does not provide any income guarantees. Suppose the agent's minimum income requirement increases from OC to OF. Then the quota increases from OQ to OR; the bonus rate, however, is unchanged (GH is parallel to DE).

These results explain why firms provide new agents with different temporary minimum income guarantees during a transition period after which they use the optimal risk-sharing plan (e.g., pay the agent according to the contract FGH for the first three months, CDE for months 4 through 6 inclusive, and AB thereafter).

The wage–commission and wage–bonus contracts are related to contracts based on the draw: a practice where the firm provides the agent an advance against uncertain future earnings. Suppose the draw is AC (see Figure 8.3). If the draw is recoverable, when the sales revenue is less than OP (say ON), the agent returns the shortfall in commission (JK) to the firm. If the sales revenue exceeds OP (say OS), the agent obtains a commission (ML) in addition to the draw AC. This contract based on a recoverable draw is equivalent to a wage–commission contract with no income constraints (AB); the only advantage of the former is that the draw allows the agent to smooth out his cash flows over the contract period. If the draw AC is nonrecoverable, the agent does not return money to the firm when there is a shortfall in sales revenue. As discussed in the previous paragraph, the optimal contract is now given by the broken line CDE; in particular, the agent only earns commission if the sales revenue exceeds OQ.

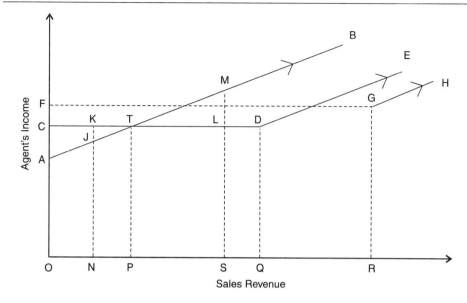

Figure 8.3 The effect of a minimum income requirement on the compensation plan.

> **Key Point** *Firms can use recoverable or nonrecoverable draws to help smooth out the agent's income.*

A Price Delegation Model

The previous discussion assumed that price is fixed. We now consider the observable effort case where the firm has some degree of market power (i.e., the firm has control over price). Suppose there is no demand uncertainty. Then the firm can delegate the pricing decision to the agent and offer him a simple forcing contract based on meeting a sales revenue quota.[11]

Suppose demand is uncertain and, in particular, that only the agent can correctly observe market conditions ("states"). For convenience suppose there are two states: "bad" and "good." In Figure 8.4, let AB represent the demand curve for the bad state, A′B′ the corresponding demand curve for the good state, and MC the marginal cost curve. Then the optimal price that maximizes the gross profit for the good condition is OP′ and the optimal price for the bad condition is OP.

Because the optimal price depends on which state is realized, it is suboptimal for the firm to fix the price prior to allowing the agent to observe the market condition. The firm should delegate the pricing decision to the agent and offer the agent a contract that leads the agent to maximize the gross profit for each market condition. The firm can achieve this result by offering the agent a contract in which the agent's income increases with gross profit; the precise form of this contract depends on the risk attitudes of the agent and the

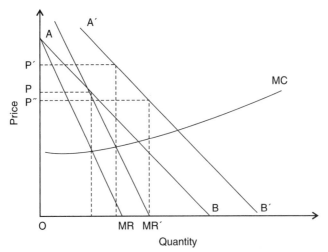

Figure 8.4 Optimal pricing when the agent has price-setting authority.

firm and the cost structure.[12] Note that the agent will always underprice in a given state if his compensation is based on sales revenue. For example, when the good state occurs, the agent will choose a price of OP″ instead of the optimal price OP′.

Key Point *Suppose demand is uncertain and only the agent can observe market conditions (states). Then the firm should delegate the pricing decision to the agent and compensate him on the basis of gross profits and not sales revenue. If the firm pays the agent on the basis of sales revenue, the agent will always underprice regardless of which market condition occurs.*

The Role of Selling Expenses

An interesting question is whether the firm and the agent should share selling expenses (e.g., travel and lodging costs). First, consider the case where the agent has no discretion over selling expenses. Then the effect of selling expenses on the optimal contract depends crucially on the precise risk attitudes of the agent and of the firm.

Suppose both the firm and the agent have exponential utility functions.[13] Because the optimal risk-sharing rule is linear, the firm can choose two equivalent contracts: Pay the agent a lower wage and a fixed share of the standard contribution margin (i.e., sales revenue less production costs) or a higher wage and the same fixed share of net profits (i.e., sales revenue less production costs less selling expenses). In either case, the firm fully absorbs all the selling expenses.

Second, suppose the agent has no discretion over selling expenses and that both the firm and the agent have logarithmic utility functions.[14] Recall that in this case the optimal wage is zero and the agent is paid a fixed fraction of net profits. Consequently the firm and the agent share the selling expenses in a fixed proportion, depending on the agent's reservation income and the distribution of cash flows.

> ***Key Point*** *Suppose selling expenses are fixed. Then the firm absorbs all the selling expenses if the firm and the agent have exponential utilities (their risk attitudes can differ). In contrast, if both the firm and the agent have logarithmic utilities, they will share the selling expenses in a fixed proportion.*

Some selling expenses (e.g., entertainment) are not fixed and affect demand. Assume initially that price is fixed. One alternative is for the firm to choose the level of selling expenses a priori. This centralized policy is suboptimal in general because the agent can observe market conditions and should be allowed to adjust the selling expenses accordingly (e.g., the agent can entertain the client at a superior restaurant if he thinks that this decision will increase the probability of a sale). Consequently, the firm will delegate the selling expense decision to the agent and pay him on the basis of profits (net of selling expenses) and not on the basis of contribution margin. If the firm pays the agent on the basis of the contribution margin, the agent will always exceed the optimal selling expense.[15] This result holds regardless of the precise forms of the firm's and the agent's utility functions and whether the firm has delegated both pricing and selling expense authority to the agent.

> ***Key Point*** *Suppose the agent can observe market conditions and adjust policy if necessary depending on which market condition (state) is realized. Then the firm should allow the agent to determine the level of selling expenses. In particular, the firm should pay the agent on the basis of net profits (after deducting selling expenses).*

Nonselling Activities

In many cases the firm requires the agent to spend time on nonselling activities (e.g., market analysis, recruiting, quality control, and attending trade shows). What is the effect of these activities on the optimal contract?

Suppose both the firm and the agent have exponential utility functions.[16] Then only the fixed wage will change: In particular, the linear commission rate remains unchanged. For example, in Figure 8.1a the contracts AB and A″B″, respectively, correspond to low and high nonselling activity.

If the firm and the agent have logarithmic utilities, the commission rate for the high nonselling activity case is increased; the fixed wage, however, is zero. In Figure 8.1b, the linear commission structures OC and OC′, respectively, correspond to the low and high nonselling activities. (Note that the horizontal axis now measures profit net of selling expenses.)

> ***Key Point*** *The compensation contract varies depending on the extent to which the firm requires the agent to perform nonselling activities. In the exponential utility case the agent's wage rate changes but the commission rate remains unchanged. In contrast, in the logarithmic utility case, the profit-sharing rate increases when the agent spends more time on nonselling activities.*

8.4 THE HIERARCHY PROBLEM IN A MULTIPRODUCT FIRM

The previous analyses made the simplifying assumption that there are only two levels in the firm's organizational structure: The owner deals directly with the agent. In practice many firms are structured hierarchically and have multiple levels. Consider a three-level hierarchy that consists of the owner, district sales managers, and sales agents (see Figure 8.5). Each district sales manager supervises several sales agents in his district and, in addition, sells to key customer accounts. Each sales agent in a given district is assigned an exclusive geographical territory (i.e., sales agents do not compete with one another) and sells several products. For convenience, we shall use the words *group* and *players* to refer collectively to the owner, the district sales managers, and the sales agents; we shall use the word *employees* to refer collectively to the district sales managers and the sales agents.

The Fixed-Price Case

Suppose initially that all prices are fixed. We shall consider two scenarios.

Marketing Plan Does Not Affect Demand Uncertainty

Assume that the variability of demand for any product in a given territory or district does not depend on the marketing plan (i.e., the allocation of the district manager's supervisory effort to different sales agents, and the sales call policies of the district manager and of the sales agents). In this case the players will always agree on the optimal marketing plan.[17] Consequently the owner acts as a centralized decision maker. Furthermore, the optimal marketing plan does not depend on market conditions ("states"); hence there is no need for the owner to delegate decision-making authority even if the employees can observe market conditions (states) before choosing their sales call policies. Given the centrally determined policy, optimal risk sharing can be achieved as in the simple two-level case (where the owner directly supervises the sales agent) given knowledge of the precise risk attitudes of the players.

Key Point   The owner acts as a centralized decision maker if the marketing plan does not affect demand uncertainty. This result does not depend on the particular utility functions of the firm and its agents.

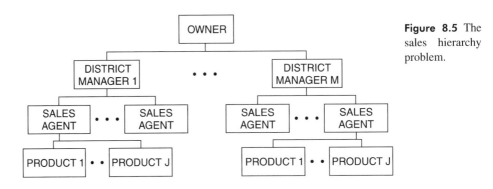

Figure 8.5 The sales hierarchy problem.

Marketing Plan Affects Demand Uncertainty

Suppose that the variability of demand depends on the marketing plan[18] (e.g., increased selling time spent on key accounts by the district manager stabilizes sales to those accounts). In contrast to the previous scenario, the players will only agree on the marketing plan if a group utility function exists (e.g., all players have exponential or logarithmic utility functions). Given this condition, the optimal strategy is for the owner to act as a centralized decision maker.

Key Point   *Suppose the firm's marketing policy affects demand uncertainty. Then the owner will act as a centralized decision maker provided a group utility function exists.*

The Resolution of Uncertainty

Suppose the employees cannot observe market conditions before choosing their sales call policies. Then the owner does not delegate decision-making authority. If, however, the employees can observe market conditions before they need to choose their sales call policies, a two-step approach is necessary.

   Assume that a group utility function exists. In the first step, the owner chooses the marketing plan using the group utility function; thereafter, the district managers expend their supervisory effort according to this centrally-determined plan. The employees then observe market conditions in their respective districts or territories. In the second step, the owner delegates decision-making authority and allows the employees to adjust their sales call policies once demand uncertainty has been resolved. Because each employee's compensation increases with the firm's gross profits, the employees will choose the optimal revised marketing plan (i.e., all employees will maximize the firm's gross profits for any particular market realization). The precise risk-sharing formula depends on the group utility function. For example, if all players have exponential utility functions, each employee gets a wage and a fixed proportion of the firm's gross profits.

Key Point   *Suppose employees have the opportunity to choose their sales call policies after demand uncertainty has been resolved. Assume that a group utility function exists. Then the owner should choose the marketing plan using the group utility function and delegate sales call policy to its employees.*

The Price Delegation Case

We now consider the general case where the firm has some degree of market power; that is, the marketing plan consists of prices, supervisory effort allocation plans, and sales call policies. Now even for the simplest specification (i.e., the variability of sales volume does not depend on the marketing plan) the players will only agree on policy if a group utility function exists.[19] In this case, if all decisions are made prior to the resolution of uncertainty, the owner acts as a centralized decision maker, chooses the marketing plan for each territory and district, and does not delegate decision-making power. If, however, the employees can observe market conditions prior to choosing their sales call policies, the owner delegates sales call policy and pricing authority to these employees. As in the simpler scenario where prices are fixed, all employees choose the optimal revised marketing plan because their compensation is tied to the firm's gross profit.

8.5 MODEL EXTENSIONS: MULTIPERIOD EFFECTS

Our discussion so far has assumed that sales effort does not have carryover effects. In many cases, however, personal selling can have a significant effect on the future behavior of consumers. In this section we focus on the observable effort case under uncertainty where both the firm and the agent are risk-averse and sales effort has dynamic carryover effects (e.g., customers in the current period will make repeat purchases in future periods).

For simplicity we shall consider the single-product firm. Begin with the simple case where price is fixed and the firm can precisely determine the future demand once it knows the sales level in the current period; the only problem is that sales in the current period are uncertain. One possibility is for the firm to offer the agent a single-period contract in which the agent is paid solely on the basis of current gross profits. This policy is *myopic* because, although both the firm and the agent share risk in the current period, the firm bears all the risk in subsequent periods. Consequently, in general it is desirable for the firm to offer a contract in which the agent shares both current and future payoffs.

Recall that we have assumed that the conditional relationship between current and future demand is known with certainty. (This assumption will be relaxed later.) Now, because the precise relationship between future and current profits is known, the firm can develop an optimal contract that is based on current profits. In particular, the optimal contract depends on how the firm and the agent value future income (i.e., their respective discount rates).

Key Point   *Suppose personal selling has dynamic effects; in particular, the firm knows the relationship between current and future sales with certainty. (Note that current sales are uncertain.) Then the compensation contract should induce the agent to share the risk of future profits with the firm. However, because the conditional relationship between current sales and future demand is known with certainty, there is no need to explicitly include future sales in the contract.*

Case 1: Common Discount Rates

We first consider the case where both the firm and the agent have a common discount rate.

The Exponential Utility Case

Suppose both the firm and the agent have exponential utility functions and marginal production cost and price are fixed. In Figure 8.1, let AB denote the myopic contract, which is based on current profits. Now, because the future pattern of profits is precisely known for any realization of sales in the current period, it is possible to write a contract that is based on current profit.

Several scenarios are possible. Consider Scenario 1, where profits depend linearly on current profits. For example, the repeat purchase rate is 80 percent (i.e., 80 percent of current customers will remain as customers in the next period, 64 percent will remain in the subsequent period, and so on). Then the firm will offer the agent a one-period contract with a linear profit-sharing plan.[20] In order to induce the agent to share the risk of future profits, the firm will offer the agent a higher commission on current sales than the myopic contract; the agent's fixed wage, however, is lower (see A′B′ in Figure 8.1a). The profit-sharing rate (i.e., the slope of A′B′) increases with the repeat purchase rate and decreases with the discount rate. When the discount rate is high, future profits become less important to the firm and the agent. Consequently the loss from using a myopic single-period contract is reduced.

Suppose current customers increase their purchase amounts in subsequent periods or engage in positive word-of-mouth activity (Scenario 2). Then the optimal contract based on current sales is likely to be progressive.[21]

***

Key Point   *Suppose the firm knows the relationship between current and future sales with certainty. Assume that the firm and the agent have exponential utility functions. Then the firm reduces the agent's fixed wage and increases the commission rate on current sales. The optimal compensation plan for a product depends on the product's stage in the life cycle and industry characteristics. For example, in the introductory stage personal selling can lead to positive word-of-mouth activity or increased purchases by current customers. Hence the commission structure should be progressive even if there are no economies of scale.*

***

The Logarithmic Utility Case

Suppose both the agent and the firm have logarithmic utility functions. Then the myopic single-period contract is optimal provided the relationship between current and future sales is linear (Scenario 1). This result is not surprising because optimal risk sharing does not require the firm to pay the agent a fixed wage; in addition, long-term profit is an exact multiple of the single-period profit.[22] Suppose future sales is an increasing function of current sales (Scenario 2). Then, as in the exponential utility model, the optimal contract requires a progressive commission structure (see OC″ in Figure 8.1b).

Case 2: Unequal Discount Rates

We now consider the case where the agent and the firm have different discount rates. In the exponential utility case, the agent's fixed wage depends on both the agent's and the firm's discount rates.[23] Because the agent and the firm share the uncertain future gross profits according to a fixed linear rule, the agent's share of current gross profits depends only on the agent's discount rate. In the logarithmic utility case, the results for Scenarios 1 and 2 remain unchanged from those for the common discount rate case.

Model Extensions

These results can be extended to the case where the agent sells to different market segments (e.g., mature and growth) and the dynamic carryover effects differ by segment. Suppose the agent and the firm have a common discount rate. Then the optimal commission rate varies by segment; if marginal cost is constant, the firm chooses a fixed commission rate for sales in the mature segment and a progressive commission rate in the growth segment.[24]

8.6 SATISFACTION-BASED COMPENSATION CONTRACTS

The Basic Model

Section 8.5 assumed that future sales can be precisely determined given knowledge of current sales. In many cases, current sales may not be sufficient to predict future sales; that is, we must consider additional variables in order to predict future sales. For example, customer satisfaction in the current period can affect both the customer retention rate and the future quantity purchased by current customers. (Witness the growing use of customer satisfaction in total quality management programs and the increasing emphasis on relationship marketing.) Consequently the optimal contract should be based on both sales and satisfaction.

For simplicity we shall focus on a single product, two-period model and assume that the unit cost of production is constant. We shall consider the exponential utility case and assume that both the firm and the sales agent have a common discount rate. The interested reader can use our approach to analyze the logarithmic utility case. Initially we shall assume (unrealistically) that satisfaction can be measured without error. This assumption will be relaxed later.

Case 1: Satisfaction Only Affects the Retention Rate

Suppose that customer satisfaction affects only the customer retention rate (e.g., the product market is highly competitive or the product is in the mature stage of the product life cycle). Then the optimal contract consists of three parts: a fixed wage, a linear commission rate on current sales volume, and a commission on current sales volume weighted by a *satisfaction multiplier*. The precise form of the satisfaction multiplier depends on how satisfaction affects the customer retention rate.

Several scenarios are possible.[25] Suppose there are decreasing returns to satisfaction (i.e., as satisfaction increases, the retention rate increases at a decreasing rate). Then the satisfaction multiplier is regressive (see AB in Figure 8.6). If there are increasing returns to satisfaction, the satisfaction multiplier is progressive. Suppose that satisfaction has a threshold effect (e.g., the retention rate is positive only if satisfaction exceeds a certain level x). Then the satisfaction multiplier is zero for satisfaction levels lower than x and positive when satisfaction exceeds x (see OFG in Figure 8.6). Suppose that customers expect a certain level of sales effectiveness by the sales agent (i.e., the reference level of satisfaction is y). If satisfaction is less than y, the customer retention rate falls sharply; if satisfaction exceeds y, the retention rate increases slowly. Now the satisfaction multiplier is progressive when satisfaction is less than y and regressive when satisfaction exceeds y (see CDE in Figure 8.6, where OH denotes the reference level of satisfaction).

Figure 8.6 Satisfaction multipliers for different scenarios. OH = y (reference satisfaction level); OF = x (threshold satisfaction level).

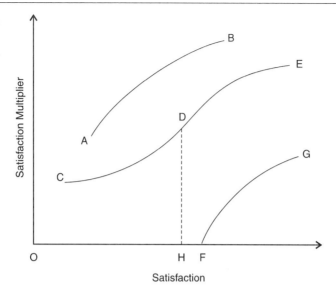

Case 2: Satisfaction Affects Both the Retention Rate and Purchase Quantity

Consider the general model where satisfaction affects both the customer retention rate and the quantity purchased by repeat customers (e.g., the product is in the early stages of the product life cycle). The optimal contract now consists of four parts: a fixed wage, a linear commission on current sales volume, a satisfaction-weighted commission on current sales volume (which can be progressive or regressive, as discussed in the previous paragraph), and a satisfaction bonus that is based purely on the satisfaction level.[26] More complex scenarios can be analyzed similarly.

Satisfaction-based compensation contracts of the sort discussed above appear to be gaining in popularity. See Mott (1994) for a readable account of current managerial practices.

> **Key Point** *In general future demand depends on both current demand and consumer satisfaction in the current period. Hence, in addition to a fixed wage and a commission on current sales, compensation contracts should include additional components which are based on a satisfaction multiplier. The number and structure of these components depend on the phase of the product in the life cycle and the extent to which future demand is sensitive to consumer satisfaction. Hence the firm may need to offer different compensation structures for different products (i.e., the number and importance of the different components of the compensation package should vary across products).*

Model Refinements: The Effect of Measurement Error

We now consider the more general case where satisfaction is measured with error (e.g., the firm uses data from a customer satisfaction survey). For the moment we shall focus on the effect of measurement error on the compensation contract. In Section 8.10 we shall consider the important empirical issue of designing an appropriate instrument to measure customer satisfaction. We shall distinguish several scenarios and focus on the effect of measurement error on the uncertain components of the agent's income (i.e., commissions and bonuses). The interested reader can use our approach to examine the effect of measurement error on other components of the compensation package.

Case 1: The Use of Unbiased Estimates of Satisfaction

Suppose that on average the firm can correctly measure satisfaction (i.e., the measure is unbiased). Although intuition might suggest that both the agent's expected commission income and the volatility of that income will increase, this conclusion is not always correct. The result depends on the precise relationship between satisfaction and the retention rate, the magnitude of the measurement error, and whether satisfaction affects the future quantities purchased by repeat buyers.

Satisfaction Affects the Retention Rate. Consider the simple model where satisfaction affects only the retention rate.[27] Suppose the error in measuring satisfaction is small. Then although the agent's commission income becomes more volatile, the agent's expected commission income does not change. If the measurement error is large, the effect on the agent's income depends on the precise form of the satisfaction multiplier. Suppose the satisfaction multiplier is linear. Then the previous result holds. If there are increasing returns to satisfaction, both the agent's expected commission income and the volatility of that income increase. If there are decreasing returns to satisfaction (e.g., the product is in the mature stage of the life cycle), the agent's expected commission income decreases, but the effect on the volatility of that income is ambiguous. If customer satisfaction depends on a reference level of customer service, the effect of measurement error on the agent's expected commission income and the volatility of that income are ambiguous.

Satisfaction Affects Both the Customer Retention Rate and Quantity Purchased Suppose that, on average, the firm can correctly measure satisfaction and that satisfaction affects both the customer retention rate and the amounts purchased by repeat buyers.[28] Recall that for this scenario the agent's uncertain income includes three components: a commission based on current sales volume, a satisfaction-weighted commission based on current sales volume, and a bonus based solely on satisfaction. We shall refer to this uncertain income as the *commission–bonus income.* Suppose that the relationship between satisfaction and the retention rate is linear or there are increasing returns to satisfaction. Then the intuition expressed previously holds: Regardless of the magnitude of the error in measuring satisfaction, both the expected commission–bonus income and the variability of that income increase.

Key Point Satisfaction measures should be used in compensation contracts even if the measures are imprecise. The effects of measurement error on the optimal compensation contract are complex and vary depending on the phase of the product in the life cycle.

Case 2: The Use of Biased Estimates of Satisfaction

The assumption that the firm can obtain an unbiased measure of satisfaction is strong; in reality the firm may be forced to use an unreliable measure of satisfaction that is on average either over- or understated. (Psychometric scales are rarely perfectly reliable.)

Suppose that satisfaction is overstated in either the pure retention model[29] or the more general model in which satisfaction also affects the quantity purchased by repeat buyers.[29a] In addition, the relationship between satisfaction and the retention rate is either linear or increasing. Then, regardless of the magnitude of the error in measuring satisfaction, the agent earns a higher expected commission (bonus–commission) income and faces higher income volatility.

Suppose satisfaction is understated. Then we can determine the effect on the agent's commission income when satisfaction affects only the retention rate. When the error is small, the agent's expected commission income decreases. When the error is large, the agent's expected commission income decreases if there are decreasing returns to satisfaction (e.g., the product is in the mature stage of the life cycle). The effect of measurement error (small or large) on the volatility of the agent's commission income is ambiguous.

Case 3: The Effect of Construct Validity

The previous discussion assumed that the measured satisfaction reflects customer satisfaction with the sales agent's performance. The measured satisfaction may, however, reflect satisfaction with the sales agent, the product, or both. Suppose the measured satisfaction[30] at the end of the current period has some relationship to future sales, however imperfect. Then optimal risk sharing requires that the compensation plan be based on measured satisfaction. Measurement error, however, will bias the firm's estimates of the sales agent's ability and consequently distorts future contracts. In Section 8.10 we shall discuss empirical methods for dealing with this problem by separating the effects of customer satisfaction with the agent and the product.

8.7 SALES FORCE SELECTION

We now consider the important practical problem of selecting the sales force. According to one estimate (Posner 1977), the out-of-pocket costs associated with recruiting and selection range from 20 to 80 percent of a salesperson's annual salary. Suppose 100 candidates have applied for a sales position in a given firm and have submitted applications including information regarding their education, work experience, and general background. The firm must determine which candidates to interview and in which sequence. The problem is that the applicants' abilities are unobservable to the firm.

An Intuitive Model

We shall assume that several individuals in the firm ("judges") evaluate the candidates. Suppose each judge scores each candidate's ability using a scale ranging from 1 to 10 (see Figure 8.7). A simple approach for the firm is to average the rating scores across judges,

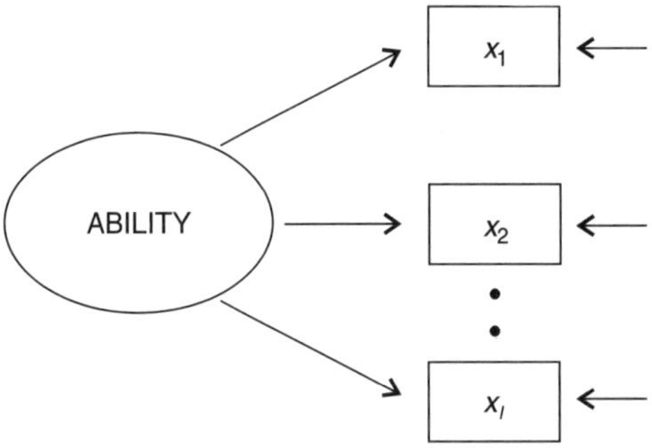

Figure 8.7 Measuring ability using judges' ratings. x_i is judge i's rating score ($i = 1, \ldots I$).

rank the candidates accordingly, and interview those candidates whose averaged scores exceed a specified threshold level. This intuitive approach has several limitations.

Averaging assumes that all judges use the rating scale similarly and are equally accurate in their assessment of the candidate's ability. In practice, judges are likely to use different anchor points (e.g., the score "5" has a different meaning for each judge) and are not equally reliable. The use of a threshold level ignores the variability in ratings across judges and fails to consider the firm's attitude to risk. For example, suppose there are three judges and that in a world of certainty the firm would hire an applicant whose rating score is "7" or higher. Consider two scenarios in which the average ratings across judges are equal. In Scenario 1 each judge assigns a rating score of 7 to a given candidate; in Scenario 2 the judges assign the candidate ratings of 4, 7, and 10, respectively. Now the risk-neutral firm will interview the candidate under both scenarios; in contrast, the risk-averse firm will only interview the candidate under Scenario 1.

A Confirmatory Factor Model

The limitations of the intuitive model can be avoided by applying confirmatory factor analysis to the ratings data.[31]

The Risk-Neutral Case

We shall assume initially that the firm is risk-neutral. Consider the example in Table 8.1, where three judges (labeled A, B, and C) have each assigned rating scores to 100 candidates (labeled 1 through 100) using a scale from 1 to 10. For convenience we shall focus on candidates 1, 22, 35, and 42. Suppose the firm applies confirmatory factor analysis to the data and determines that the weights (known as "factor score regression weights") to be applied to the ratings of judges A, B, and C, respectively, are 0.3, 0.5, and 0.4. Then candidate 22 obtains the highest score (known as a "factor score") of 8.5, and candidate 1 obtains the lowest score of 6.5.

Suppose that under certainty the firm would hire applicants who are rated "7" or higher. Then the risk-neutral firm should eliminate candidate 1, interview candidate 22 first, and then interview either candidate 35 or candidate 42, each of whom received a factor score of 7.[32]

Note that incorrect rankings will be obtained if we apply equal weights to the judges' rating scores; for example, candidate 35 will be ranked below candidate 42. Furthermore, the

Table 8-1 Confirmatory Factor Analysis of Ratings Data

Candidate	Judge A	Judge B	Judge C	Candidate's Rating
1	4	5	7	6.5
•				
•				
22	9	6	7	8.5
•				
•				
35	10	4	5	7.0
•				
•				
42	7	7	7	7.0
•	•	•	•	•
•	•	•	•	•
100				

Note: The factor score regression weights for judges A, B, and C are 0.3, 0.5, and 0.4 respectively. Thus candidate 22's rating $= 0.3(9) + 0.5(6) + 0.4(7) = 8.5$.

selection procedure is biased if the firm uses the ratings of any one judge alone. For example, if the firm relies on judge B alone, it will incorrectly eliminate candidates 22 and 35.

The Risk-Aversion Case

Suppose the firm is risk-averse. Assume as before that in a world of certainty the firm would hire candidates who are rated "7" or higher. In contrast to the risk-neutral case the risk-averse firm cannot rank candidates based solely on the factor scores and must consider the variability of ratings across judges.[33] For example, even though both candidates 22 and 35 obtain a factor score of 7, the risk-averse firm will eliminate candidate 35.

> **Key Point**   *The firm should use a confirmatory factor approach to analyze judges' evaluations of candidates. This approach allows the firm to rank candidates meaningfully while explicitly correcting for the fact that judges idiosyncratically interpret the rating scales and rate candidates with different degrees of accuracy. The firm cannot rank candidates purely on the basis of the factor scores; the firm's risk attitude is of particular importance.*

Model Extensions

The standard confirmatory factor analysis model can be extended in several ways. The firm can include additional explanatory variables (e.g., the candidate's socioeconomic and demographic background, previous training, and job experience) that determine the agent's ability.[34] In addition, if historical data are available, the firm can choose its interview plan based on the empirically measured relationship between ability and performance.[35]

8.8 SALES FORCE TRAINING

Many firms conduct periodic training programs to increase the sales agent's ability after the agent has been hired; recruiting is expensive, and it is often more economical to train sales agents who are already in place. For example, the average training costs per sales trainee in the printing and textile and apparel industries, respectively, are $30,000 and $26,000. (See the *Dartnell Sales Manager's Handbook*, 1989, p. 858, for a detailed table showing sales training costs by industry.) Training costs are likely to become increasingly important as the rate of new product introduction increases and product life cycles shorten.

We shall focus on the case where the effect of training on sales is uncertain and first consider the case where the firm has already decided how much to spend on training. In particular, we shall distinguish between training that is firm-specific (i.e., the firm teaches the agent to "do things its way") and training that develops portable skills (e.g., the agent can apply his new knowledge to sell products for other firms in the industry). Later we shall discuss the general problem of choosing the optimal level of training for different scenarios. To focus on essentials we shall consider the one-product firm and assume that the unit cost of production is constant.

Firm-Specific Training: Exogenously Fixed Training Expenditure

Consider the case where the firm has already chosen the expenditure on a firm-specific training program. Then for any given market condition (i.e., state of nature) the agent can sell more after completing the training program. Because the improvement in the sales agent's selling ability is not portable, the agent's reservation income is not affected.

The Deterministic Case

Assume that both the firm and the agent have exponential utilities. Other utility functions can be examined using the same approach.

The Effect on the Compensation Contract. The increase in sales after training is either deterministic or uncertain. Regardless of which scenario is true, the firm and the agent share the training cost; specifically the more risk-averse player (typically the agent) pays a smaller share.[36] The firm does not need to pay the agent on the basis of profit (net of the training cost); in particular, the firm can incorporate the agent's share of the training cost into the agent's fixed wage and continue to pay the agent a commission on sales. Because of the linear sharing rule, the commission rate on sales will remain unchanged. Consequently, given the improvement in productivity after the training program, the agent's expected commission income will always increase.

> ***Key Point*** *If the firm and the agent have exponential utility functions, they will share the training cost, regardless of whether the improvement in productivity is deterministic or stochastic.*

The Effect on the Agent's Income. The effects on the agent's fixed wage and the variability of the agent's income depend on whether the increase in sales after the training program is deterministic or uncertain. Several scenarios are possible.

Suppose the effect of the training program on sales is deterministic. Then the fixed wage is reduced because the training program increases gross profit by a constant amount for every market condition.[37] The variability of the agent's income does not change because the commission rate is unchanged and the training program has no effect on the volatility of gross profit. The effect on the agent's expected income, however, cannot be determined without more specific information. If sales are normally distributed, the agent trades off expected income and the variance of income.[38] Consequently the training program has no effect on the agent's expected income.

The Stochastic Case

Suppose the effect of the firm-specific training program on the sales agent's productivity (henceforth *the training effect*) is uncertain. As in the deterministic case, the firm and the agent share the training cost, the firm continues to compensate the agent on the basis of sales and not profit, and the commission rate on sales is unchanged.[39] Consequently, because of the improvement in productivity, the agent always earns a higher expected commission income after completing the training program. In contrast to the deterministic case, the effects on the variability of the agent's income and the agent's fixed wage depend on the type of training program (discussed in the next paragraph) and the stage of the product life cycle.

Consider the variability of the agent's income. The firm will use different types of training program depending on the phase of the product life cycle. If the product is new, the firm is likely to pursue an aggressive policy (i.e., training helps the agent to sell more when market conditions are good). If the product is in the maturity phase, the firm is likely to pursue a defensive policy (i.e., training helps the agent to sell more when market conditions are bad).

Suppose the training program is either neutral (i.e., the training effect is independent of sales) or aggressive. Then gross profit becomes more volatile after the training program. Consequently because of the linear sharing rule, the agent's income becomes more volatile. If the training program is defensive, gross profit could become less volatile. In this case the variability of the agent's income decreases.

More information is necessary to determine the effect of the training program on the agent's expected income and fixed wage. Suppose sales and the training effect are normally distributed.

If the training program is neutral or aggressive (e.g., the product is new), the variability of the agent's income increases. Consequently the agent's expected income increases. The effect on the agent's fixed wage is less well defined. As in the deterministic case, the increase in expected sales after training tends to reduce the fixed wage.[40] The training program, however, makes gross profits more volatile and this effect tends to increase the fixed wage. Hence, in contrast to the deterministic case, the firm may have to increase the agent's fixed wage after the training program.

If the training program is defensive (e.g., the product is in the maturity phase of the life cycle), sales could become less volatile. In this case both the agent's expected income and fixed wage will be reduced.

Model Extensions

Other types of utility function (e.g., logarithmic) can be analyzed using a similar approach.[41]

> ***Key Point***   *The effect of the training program on the agent's income and the volatility of income depend on whether the improvement in productivity is deterministic or stochastic. These effects vary with the firm's market segmentation policy and the phase of the product in the life cycle.*

Firm-Specific Training: An Optimal Approach

We now consider the more general case where the firm chooses both the level of firm-specific training and the optimal compensation contract.

Deterministic Training Effect

Suppose the training effect is deterministic or, alternatively, training does not affect the variability of the training effect. This specification allows the training effect to be neutral, aggressive, or defensive. Because the only effect of training is to increase the average gross profit, the firm can proceed sequentially.[42] First, choose the level of firm-specific training. This decision does not depend on the magnitudes of the uncertainties, the risk aversions of the firm and the agent, and the type of training program (e.g., whether training helps the agent to sell more when market conditions are good). Second, choose the optimal contract for this level of training (see previous discussion).

> ***Key Point***   *If the improvement in productivity after the training program is deterministic, the firm can proceed sequentially by first choosing the optimal level of training expenditure and then choosing the optimal compensation contract conditional on the chosen level of training expenditure.*

Stochastic Training Effect

Suppose training affects the variability of the training effect. Then regardless of whether the training effect is neutral, aggressive, or defensive, the firm cannot proceed sequentially.[43] That is, both the optimal training expenditure and the commission rate depend on the risk aversions of the firm and the agent and the precise form in which training affects the variability of the training effect. Suppose the training program is either neutral or aggressive and sales and the training effect are normally distributed. Then the optimal training expenditure under uncertainty is higher (lower) than in the certainty case provided higher training decreases (increases) the variability of the training effect.[44]

> ***Key Point***   *If the improvement of productivity after the training program is uncertain, the firm cannot proceed sequentially by separating out the training expenditure decision and the choice of the optimal compensation contract.*

In practice the firm may find it necessary to use a transition compensation strategy if the training program requires a significant change in the compensation plan (e.g., a large reduction in the agent's fixed wage). For example, the firm may offer the agent a guarantee that during the transition period after the training program his income will not fall below a certain level (e.g., 90 percent of last year's income). See Dahm (1994, pp. 176–92) for a detailed discussion of alternative transition strategies.

> **Key Point**   *The firm should use a transition compensation strategy if it plans to introduce a major change in the compensation plan.*

Portable Training

Our previous analysis assumed that all training is firm-specific. Many training programs, however, help the agent to develop skills which are portable (e.g., an IBM sales agent who goes through an IBM training program learns how to sell computers in general and not just IBM computers). Consequently, in contrast to a firm-specific training program, the agent's reservation income increases after the agent has been through a training program.

We shall examine a two-period model where training occurs in the first period. Consider two scenarios. In the first scenario all training is firm-specific (i.e., the agent's reservation income does not change after training). In the second scenario training is portable (i.e., the agent's reservation income increases after training). To avoid trivial solutions, we shall assume that when training is portable, the increase in the agent's reservation income exceeds the agent's search cost in finding another job. For each scenario the firm chooses the optimal level of training expenditure in the first period and the optimal compensation contracts for both periods.

The Expected Utility Model

Suppose the firm and the agent have exponential utilities. Consider the general case where the training program affects the variability of sales; in addition, the training program can be neutral, aggressive, or defensive (e.g., higher training helps the agent to sell more when market conditions are bad). Assume that sales and the training effect are normally distributed. In Figure 8.8, BDE shows the net present value of the firm's profit for different training expenditures when training is firm-specific. ACF shows the corresponding net present value when training is portable. Note that for any training expenditure the vertical distance between the BDE and ACF curves (e.g., BA) represents the discounted value of the increase in the agent's reservation income (net of search costs). In particular, these distances increase as training expenditure increases (i.e., ACF is flatter than BDE for any training expenditure). Hence, regardless of the particular form of uncertainty, the firm always spends less on training when training is portable.[45]

> **Key Point**   *If cash flows are normally distributed, the firm always spends less on training when training is portable.*

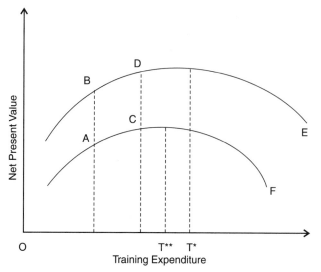

Figure 8.8 The effect of portable skills on training expenditure. OT* is the training expenditure when skills are firm-specific; OT**, the training expenditure when skills are portable.

We now compare the optimal compensation contracts when the training is firm-specific and portable. Suppose the variability of the training effect does not depend on the training expenditure.[46] Then for any given period the difference in the fixed wages for the firm-specific and portable training cases depends only on the mean training effect. As discussed in the previous paragraph, the mean training effect is higher for the firm-specific training case. Consequently, for the portable training scenario the fixed wages in both periods are always higher regardless of whether the training program is neutral, aggressive, or defensive.

> **Key Point**   *If the variability of the training effect does not depend on the training expenditure, the agent's fixed wage is higher when training is portable. This result holds regardless of the firm's market segmentation policy or the phase of the product in the life cycle.*

Suppose the variability of the training effect depends on the training expenditure.[47] Then for any given period the difference in the fixed wages for the firm-specific and portable training cases depends on whether the training program is neutral, aggressive, or defensive and whether higher training expenditure makes the training effect more or less volatile. Suppose the training program is neutral or aggressive and higher training makes the training effect less volatile. Then the mean training effect is reinforced by the uncertainty. Consequently portable training leads to a higher fixed wage in each period.

> **Key Point**   *If the volatility of the training effect depends on the training expenditure, the optimal policy for the firm may be to pay the agent a lower wage when training is portable compared to the case where training is firm-specific.*

Logarithmic Utility Model

Suppose both the firm and the agent have logarithmic utilities. Recall that in this case the agent's fixed wage is zero and the commission structure for both periods is linear. Consequently the results are better defined than in the exponential utility case. Specifically the firm always spends more on training in the firm-specific training case, regardless of the distributions of sales and the training effect and whether the training effect is neutral, aggressive, or defensive.[48]

Arbitrary Utility Functions

The previous results for the exponential and logarithmic utility cases stem from the fact that the optimal sharing rule is linear. For other classes of utility function, the optimal sharing rule may be nonlinear. Consequently we can no longer compare the marginal effects of training on the firm's net present value in the firm-specific and portable training scenarios (i.e., in Figure 8.8 curve ACF may not be flatter than curve BDE for all levels of training).[49] Hence it is possible that the firm will spend less on training when the training effect is firm-specific and stochastic. Furthermore, the firm may even lower the fixed wage when training develops portable skills.

8.9 THE SALES FORCE TURNOVER PROBLEM

Sales force turnover is expensive: When an agent quits, the firm loses profits on lost sales and incurs search costs to find and train a new agent. The firm may also incur additional costs resulting from a loss in customer goodwill and proprietary information. According to a study of five hundred salespeople and sales managers in the United States and Canada, sales force turnover can cost up to $200,000 per agent (*Learning International* 1989).

The previous results (see Section 8.8) on firm-specific and portable training are useful in analyzing the sales force turnover problem. Consider a two-period model in which the firm can choose either of two strategies. The firm can train agents in the first period and retain them in the second period, recognizing that the agents' reservation incomes have increased as a result of training (Strategy 1). Alternatively, the firm can follow a turnover policy by training agents in each period, achieving improved productivity in that period, and allowing the agents to leave at the end of the period (Strategy 2). We shall assume that the firm and the agent have exponential utility functions.

Exogenous Uncertainty

Suppose training expenditure does not affect the variability of demand. Then the firm's choice between the two strategies depends on the average effect of training on demand, the discount rate, the search cost to the firm of finding new workers, and the search cost to the agent of finding a new job. Because training affects only the average demand and the sharing rule is linear, the firm's choice between the two strategies does not depend on the risk aversions of the firm and of the agent.[50] Furthermore, the firm is more likely to prefer the turnover strategy if the discount rate is higher (i.e., the present value of future profits from the retention strategy is reduced) and the search costs to the firm and the agent are higher.

> **Key Point** *Firms with a high cost of capital obtain reduced benefits from a retention strategy. Consequently, the sales force turnover rate will vary across industries and across firms in a given industry provided firms have heterogeneous costs of capital.*

Generalized Uncertainty

Suppose training expenditure affects the variability of demand. Then the firm's choice of strategy depends in addition on how training expenditure affects the variability of demand, and on whether the training effect is neutral, aggressive, or defensive.[51] Consequently, the firm's choice depends on the risk attitudes of the firm and of the agent and the phase of the product life cycle. Regardless of how training affects the variability of demand, the firm is more likely to pursue the retention strategy when the firm and the agent are highly risk-averse, training increases the variability of demand, and the training effect is neutral or aggressive (e.g., the product is in the early stages of the product life cycle and training helps the agent to sell more when market conditions are good).

> **Key Point** *If training affects the volatility of demand, the sales force turnover rate will depend on the firm's segmentation policies and the phase of the product in the life cycle.*

Model Extensions

The previous analysis focuses on one firm only. The model can be extended to deal with industry equilibrium, recognizing that all firms will readjust their training programs when agents switch jobs.[52]

8.10 MEASURING ABILITY AND REWARDING PERFORMANCE

As discussed previously, the agent's ability is often unobservable to the firm. The firm can use three methods to measure the agent's ability. The first uses market-level sales data. The second uses survey data from customers to estimate a surrogate measure of the agent's ability (e.g., customer satisfaction). The third uses test scores from a training program. We discuss these in turn and propose empirical methods for measuring ability for each scenario.

Measuring Ability Using Market-Level Data

The firm's sales depend on the firm's marketing mix (e.g., the sales call policy), uncontrollable variables (e.g., economic conditions and the marketing mix of competitors), the sales agent's ability, and chance (i.e., a random effect). The firm seeks to determine the effectiveness of its marketing mix and measure the ability of its sales agents so that it can

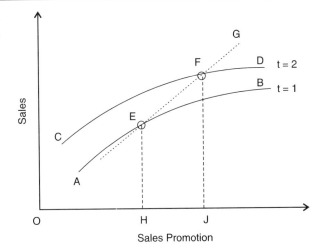

Figure 8.9 Measuring the effect of sales promotion when the agent's ability changes.

improve its marketing decisions and reward productive sales agents. The problem is that the sales agents' abilities are unobservable to the firm, vary across agents, and change over time as agents become more experienced.

The One Product, One Agent Case

We begin with a simple scenario in which a single-product firm employs one sales agent and the agent's effort is fixed and observable. Assume that the agent's ability increases with experience over time. For convenience we shall assume that sales promotion is the only variable in the marketing mix. In Figure 8.9, AB represents the average sales volumes for different sales promotion expenditures in period 1 and CD represents the corresponding average sales volumes for period 2. Suppose the firm chooses promotional outlays of OH and OJ, respectively, in periods 1 and 2. Then by not allowing for the change in the agent's ability over time, the firm will overstate the effect of sales promotion (see EFG) and overspend on sales promotion. Furthermore, the firm will be unable to measure the agent's ability.[53]

> **Key Point**   *Suppose the firm employs one agent and sells only one product. Then the firm cannot measure the ability of the agent even if it has time-series data on performance.*

The One Product, Many Agent Case

Now consider a scenario in which a single-product firm employs many sales agents and the agents' effort is fixed and observable. Assume that each agent is assigned his own exclusive sales territory and sales data are available for one time period only. For simplicity assume that each agent's sales (s) consist of three parts: the effect of the marketing mix and uncontrollable variables in that territory (A), the effect of the agent's unobserved ability (B), and a random effect (C) with an average value of zero.

Suppose the firm performs a regression of the marketing mix and uncontrollable variables on sales using these cross-sectional data. Then in contrast to the single-agent scenario, the firm can correctly estimate A and use these results to predict sales ($\hat{s}$) for each agent.[54] Define the difference between actual sales and predicted sales ($\hat{s}$) for each agent as that agent's residual. Now this residual is the sum of two effects: B and C. The effect of C, however, is on average zero. Hence the firm can use the residuals to rank the agents according to their ability (agents with positive residuals are more productive than the average agent). This procedure, however, is not efficient. For example, suppose the relationship between the marketing mix and sales is not strong (i.e., the random effect C has a high variance). Then the estimated abilities—which include the effect C—will be highly imprecise. Consequently agents will be rewarded or penalized largely on the basis of chance.

These policy implications remain unchanged if the firm uses the discrepancy between the agent's sales and the agent's sales quota for a given period to infer the agent's ability.[55]

> ***Key Point*** *Suppose the firm has cross-sectional data on the performance of its sales agents. Then, on average, the firm can correctly rank the agents according to ability. However, these estimates will be imprecise.*

The Many Product, Many Agent Case

Consider a scenario where the firm employs many agents, each of whom sells three or more products. (The condition that each agent sells at least three products is necessary to make the model identifiable.)

Suppose cross-sectional sales data are available by agent and by product type. Now in contrast to the single-product case, the firm can achieve greater precision by separating out the effects of ability and chance because additional information is available.[56] In particular the firm can eliminate the random effects (C) and correctly rank agents according to their ability. (The statistical technique we propose is a hybrid model that combines regression analysis and confirmatory factor analysis to estimate the unobservable heterogeneity in agents' abilities.)

Table 8.2, column 1, shows some hypothetical results. In the first period ($t = 1$) agent 3 has the highest ability and agent 1 the lowest (the negative score shows that agent 1 is below average in ability). The firm can use these estimates to reward agents, negotiate new

Table 8-2 Hypothetical Factor Scores for Sales Agents

		Time period				
		t = 1	**t = 2**	**t = 3**	**• • •**	**t = T**
	1	-3	•	2	•	•
Sales	2	1	•	-2	•	•
agents	3	5	•	4	•	•
	•	•	•	•	•	•
	•	•	•	•	•	•
	•	•	•	•	•	•
	I					

compensation contracts, reallocate agents to different territories, and decide which agents should be trained.

> **Key Point**   *Suppose the firm employs many agents and each agent sells at least three products. Then the firm can analyze cross-sectional data to separate the effects of ability and random fluctuations. Consequently, the estimates of ability are more precise than in the case where each agent sells only one product. The firm can therefore use these estimates for strategic planning, resource allocation, and adjusting reward structures.*

Suppose the firm employs many agents, each of whom sells three or more products and time-series sales data are available by agent and by product type. Then the firm can extend the previous statistical methodology (i.e., a combination of regression and confirmatory factor analysis) to analyze the pooled cross-sectional, time-series data. In particular, the firm can compare sales agents' abilities at a given point in time and track changes in any given sales agent's ability over time.[57]

Consider the hypothetical results shown in Table 8.2. The cross-sectional results show that agents 1 and 2, respectively, have the lowest abilities in the first and third periods. The time-series results show that the ability of agent 1 has increased the most during the second and third periods. The managerial implications are clearly stronger than in the previous scenario, where only cross-sectional data are available.

> **Key Point**   *If pooled cross-sectional and time-series data are available, the firm can use a dynamic hybrid regression/confirmatory factor analysis model to make cross-sectional and dynamic comparisons of agents' abilities. This information allows the firm to perform dynamic strategic planning, measure unobservable (and changing) heterogeneity among the sales force, and update compensation contracts based on objective measures of productivity.*

Model Extensions

The previous methodology can be extended in several ways. The firm can analyze segment-level data (e.g., sales can be divided by industry type or consumer type) for each product. The results will help the firm to improve resource allocation by determining which segments are most sensitive to sales effort. If segments are unobservable, the firm can use the structural equation mixture methodology proposed by Jedidi, Jagpal, and DeSarbo (1997a,b) to identify sales agents of similar (e.g., high and low) ability.[58] Thus the firm can use the fundamental approach of marketing (market segmentation) to form homogeneous segments of sales agents, customize the reward structure to each segment (much in the same way that firms perform market segmentation among consumers), determine which agents should attend a training program, and so on.

Note that although we have focused on measuring the abilities of sales agents, our methodology can be used to measure the abilities of sales managers, division managers, and even the Chief Executive Officers of multidivisional firms.[59]

> **Key Point** *The mixed regression/confirmatory factor analysis model can be used to analyze pooled cross-sectional/time-series data and identify unobserved heterogeneity among sales agents. In particular, the methodology allows us to measure and compare the abilities of senior managers in multiproduct (multidivisional) firms, both cross-sectionally and dynamically.*

Measuring Ability Using Customer Satisfaction

The previous analysis focused on using market-level data to infer an agent's ability. An alternative approach is to use a behavioral measure (e.g., customer satisfaction) as a proxy of future performance. Suppose the firm decides to use customer satisfaction as a surrogate measure of the agent's unobserved ability. The problem is that customer satisfaction is also unobservable and proxy measures of satisfaction contain error. The firm must therefore obtain data from customers using a survey instrument that contains several questions measuring customer satisfaction (e.g., satisfaction with the frequency of contact by the sales agent, the agent's knowledge of the product, and the agent's ability to provide comparisons with competing products).

Note that using any one measure as a proxy of satisfaction will lead to measurement error and incorrect inferences. Consequently the firm should use several (at least three) measures of satisfaction and estimate a confirmatory factor model with one factor. For sufficiently large samples this methodology allows us to eliminate measurement error and obtain correct estimates of customer satisfaction.[60]

Construct Validity

One potential difficulty with the one-factor confirmatory model is that certain questions may reflect the customer's satisfaction with both the agent and the product (e.g., satisfaction with the quality of technical assistance provided). In such cases the one-factor estimates of customer satisfaction will be meaningless, and an alternative approach (described below) is necessary.[61]

In general, for both diagnostics and control the firm should measure customer satisfaction at two levels: satisfaction with the agent and the product. In contrast to sales, both dimensions of satisfaction are leading indicators of performance (i.e., a drop in satisfaction precedes a decline in sales); in addition, measures of customer satisfaction with the agent are necessary to allow the firm to distinguish agents based on their productivity.

Suppose the survey instrument contains several questions that measure satisfaction with the agent and with the product (see Figure 8.10). In particular, some questions measure only one dimension, whereas others measure both dimensions (see the dotted lines). Then the firm can use the standard confirmatory factor model (with two correlated factors since satisfaction with the product and with the agent are likely to be positively correlated) to estimate any given customer's satisfaction with the product and with the agent.[62]

The firm can use these estimates as inputs to a satisfaction-based compensation contract for the current period (see Section 8.6), rank agents according to ability, update its beliefs about an agent's ability, and negotiate future compensation contracts with different agents. The firm can also use these estimates of customer satisfaction with the product to track

Figure 8.10 A confirmatory factor model for measuring customer satisfaction.

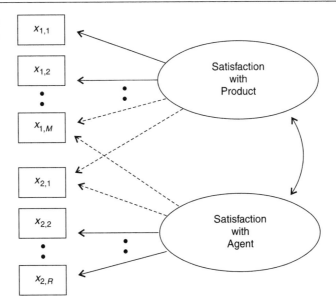

changes in consumer behavior and change the marketing mix if necessary. Perhaps most important, the firm can customize employment contracts and hence escape from a pooling equilibrium in which it is forced to offer heterogeneous agents identical contracts.

Model Extensions

We can extend the model in several ways to deal with additional sources of heterogeneity. If the firm can define consumer segments (e.g., light and heavy users) a priori, the firm can estimate the satisfaction model at the disaggregated segment level. If a priori segmentation is infeasible and the sample size is large, the firm can use the mixture structural equation methodology (Jedidi, Jagpal, and DeSarbo 1997a,b) to identify unobserved segments and obtain segment-specific estimates of the two dimensions of satisfaction. If pooled cross-sectional time-series data on satisfaction are available, the firm can "fine tune" its performance measurement and reward structures.

Measuring Ability after a Training Program

The previous analyses focused on using either market-level data or customer satisfaction surveys to infer an agent's ability. Another approach is to use objective test or subjective rating scores to infer ability.

Suppose the firm administers several tests to a group of sales agents before they join a training program. Then, as discussed previously in the context of judges' ratings, the firm can rank the agents according to ability before they join the training program. (In Figure 8.7, replace "judges" by "tests.") If the firm also administers these tests to the agents after they have completed the training program, it can use the structural equation method to determine whether the mean ability of the group has increased as a result of training. The firm can also determine which sales agents have increased their ability the most.[63]

The previous discussion assumes that ability is unidimensional. The method can, however, be extended to allow the training program to affect two dimensions of ability: firm-specific and portable skills.[64]

8.11 MODEL EXTENSIONS AND REFINEMENTS

The Impact of Financial Markets

The previous analysis (Sections 8.1–8.10) implicitly assumed that the firm is either owned by one individual or, alternatively, that the owners of the firms can be treated as if they are equivalent to one individual (i.e., they agree on a group utility function that represents their idiosyncratic risk attitudes). In particular, we have assumed that the owners of the firm do not have any diversification opportunities outside the firm. We now relax these assumptions and consider the case of a firm that is owned by many stockholders, each of whom holds a diversified portfolio of investments across all firms in the economy; in particular, we focus on the case where the objective of the firm is to maximize stock value.[65]

The One Product, One Agent Case

For simplicity consider the case of a single-product firm that employs one agent. Assume that unit production costs are constant over feasible sales levels, the agent is risk-averse, and the agent's effort is observable. (Complications are introduced when the agent's effort is unobservable. Jagpal 1983a,b develops a model to address this problem.)

Now the firm's gross profits before paying the agent is the sum of three parts: the average gross profit (A), an uncertain component (B) that fluctuates with general economic conditions, and an uncertain component (C) that is idiosyncratic to the firm and therefore purely random. The key point is that by choosing a diversified portfolio across firms, stockholders can eliminate the idiosyncratic risk C.

Two scenarios are possible. First, suppose B is zero. Then stockholders can eliminate all risk by diversifying even if C is highly volatile; that is, the firm behaves as if it is risk-neutral. Consequently, in contrast to the expected utility model, risk sharing is unnecessary and the optimal strategy for the firm is to pay the agent a flat wage. Second, suppose the industry in which the firm operates is highly cyclical (i.e., B is volatile). Now, by diversifying across firms the stockholders can reduce but not eliminate the effect of B on the stock price. Consequently, the optimal strategy for the firm is to share risk with the agent and offer the agent a mixed compensation plan that contains a fixed wage and an uncertain component (e.g., a commission or a bonus).

Consider two agents (1 and 2, respectively) who have the same reservation income; the only difference is that Agent 2 works in a more cyclical industry than Agent 1. Optimal risk sharing suggests that Agent 2 should be paid a lower wage than Agent 1; Agent 2, however, will be paid a higher share of gross profits (i.e., he will earn a higher expected income than Agent 1 but face higher volatility in income). This intuitive result is correct, regardless of the agents' specific degrees of risk aversion.[66]

> **Key Point** In a stock market model the owners of the firm can diversify to reduce risk; in particular, only systematic risk is relevant. Consequently, in contrast to the expected utility model, we are able to obtain testable implications using market-level data. In particular, the stock market model implies that agents in highly cyclical industries earn lower fixed wages than those in less cyclical industries (holding productivity constant).

Market Segmentation

The basic model can be extended to capture heterogeneity more fully. In practice, the degree of cyclicality (B) varies across market segments. For example, a computer manufacturer may face higher market risk when it markets a given computer model to the manufacturing sector rather than to the individual household market. Consequently the firm should offer the agent a higher commission rate for sales to the manufacturing sector.

Multiproduct, Multiagent Models

The basic stock market model can be extended to the case where the firm employs multiple agents and sells multiple products.[67] Jagpal (1983a,b) develops a general multifactor model in which there are several sources of systematic risk. His model is consistent with Sharpe's multibeta capital asset pricing model (1977) and the arbitrage pricing model (Ross 1976) and allows for general patterns of stochastic interdependence among the firms' products (e.g., when an agent allocates more selling time to a given product sales to other products are also affected). In addition, Jagpal analyzes the multiproduct, multiagent case where the agent's effort is unobservable.[68]

Compensating Advertising Agencies: The Multiproduct Case

One special case of interest is the compensation of advertising agencies by multiproduct firms. Consider two scenarios.

First, suppose sales of each product line are uncertain but there are no synergies (i.e., cost interdependencies or cross-product marketing mix effects across product lines). In particular, assume that the sales of different product lines fluctuate with general economic conditions and are therefore correlated. Then the stock market values each product line separately regardless of the stochastic interdependencies in demand. Consequently, if the firm decides to employ different advertising agencies for each product line, it does not need to determine simultaneously the compensation contracts for these agencies.[69]

Second, suppose sales of each product line are uncertain but there are synergies (e.g., a significant number of customers purchase several product lines made by the firm). Now the stock market values the firm's product lines jointly, taking into account these synergistic effects. Consequently, if the firm employs several advertising agencies, it must simultaneously determine the compensation contracts for those agencies. Given these additional transaction costs, the firm may decide to employ only one advertising agency.

Finally, as discussed in the context of multilevel hierarchies (see Figure 8.5), the firm should compensate advertising agencies on the basis of gross profits and not sales revenue if it delegates significant decision-making power to the agencies. This result applies to all firms, regardless of whether the firm uses the expected utility or value maximization model.

> **Key Point**   *The stock market valuation model has important implications for the compensation of advertising agencies by the multiproduct firm and whether the firm should employ a "portfolio" of advertising agencies to reduce risk.*

The Effect of Asymmetric Information

In our analysis of compensation contracts, we implicitly assumed that the firm knows the ability of the agent and the agent's risk attitude; in addition, the firm and the agent share the same knowledge of the market (i.e., both players agree on the shape of the stochastic relationship between effort and sales). We now discuss the implications of relaxing these assumptions.

Consider the one product, one agent case. Assume initially that the firm knows that the agent is risk-neutral; the only problem is that the firm does not know the agent's productivity. Now the firm can discover the agent's beliefs about his productivity by offering him a choice of contracts. For example, suppose the firm offers the agent a choice between two contracts. Contract D offers the agent a fixed wage of $500 per week and a commission rate of 3 percent on sales revenue. Contract E offers the agent a higher fixed wage of $600 per week but a lower commission rate of 2 percent on sales revenue. If the agent prefers D, his choice implies that he expects to produce a sales revenue exceeding $10,000; if he prefers E, his choice implies that he expects to produce a sales revenue of less than $10,000. Consequently the firm can sort agents according to ability (assuming that the agent's beliefs about his productivity are not unrealistic).

Suppose that the agent is risk-averse and the firm does not know the agent's precise attitude to risk. Now even for the simplest scenarios the firm cannot infer the agent's productivity from his choice between contracts D and E.[70]

> **Key Point**   *When information is asymmetric, the firm can use a "revealed preference" approach to segment agents according to their (self-estimated) productivities provided the firm knows the agents' risk attitudes. To implement this approach the firm can use proxy variables (e.g., age) to distinguish agents a priori according to their risk attitude.*

8.12 CONCLUDING REMARKS

This chapter has focused on developing analytical and empirical methods for choosing employment contracts when demand is uncertain and personal selling has dynamic carryover effects. We have paid particular attention to the problems caused by unobservable heterogeneity in a firm that employs multiple agents and sells multiple products. We have developed methods for measuring ability using objective market-level data. In particular, we propose a hybrid regression/confirmatory factor model for analyzing pooled cross-sectional, time-series data and determining how agents' unobservable abilities vary both cross-sectionally and dynamically. We have developed models for determining the optimal level of expenditure on training sales agents, while explicitly recognizing the turnover problem.

One important future research area is to extend the models to allow for supply adjustments (we have focused on partial equilibrium analysis). In addition, empirical research is necessary to test the robustness of the statistical methods we propose.

Finally, up to this point we have paid little attention to strategic considerations (e.g., the firm's choice of an optimal product portfolio in an uncertain environment). In addition, we have not considered the particular problems of multinational firms, which face additional sources of uncertainty (e.g., the risk of currency fluctuations and determining the currency in which the performance of country managers should be measured). Chapter 9 addresses these issues.

NOTES

1. Suppose one agent sells one product and sales effort has dynamic carryover effects. Under certainty the future gross profit in any given period is an exact function of current profit. Hence the optimal compensation plan is a forcing contract based on a profit or sales quota for the current period.

   Suppose the firm uses a sales team consisting of I agents who are assigned to J sales accounts (projects). Let t_{ij} denote the time ("effort") spent by agent i on account j, $t_{i.}$ the total time spent by individual i, y_i agent i's reservation income, p_j the price paid by account j, and p the price vector. To allow for general demand and cost interdependencies, let $s_j = f_j(p, t_{ij}, \ldots, t_{Ij})$ denote the sales function for account j and $C(s_1, \ldots, s_J)$ the total cost function. Then the gross profit is $\pi = \sum_{j=1}^{J} p_j f_j(p, t_{1j}, \ldots, t_{Ij}) - C(f_1, \ldots, f_J)$. Let t_{ij}^* denote the time allocation plan that maximizes π for given values of $t_{i.}$ and f_j^* denote the corresponding sales levels. Then the firm offers the team a simple forcing contract based on sales quotas for each account (f_j^*). If the team meets all these quotas, each agent i is paid y_i; if any quota is not satisfied, no agent is paid. Because the problem is deterministic, the firm does not need to supervise the team; in addition, team members do not need to monitor each other.

   This model of teams includes as a special case the single-agent, multiple-product problem. [Set $i = 1$ and define the sales accounts as products.]

2. Let $u_1 = u_1(\pi_1)$ denote the agent's utility function, where π_1 denotes the agent's payoff. Risk aversion implies that u_1 is concave in π_1 [i.e., $u_1''(\pi_1) < 0$, where the primes denote derivatives]. By Jensen's inequality, $Eu_1(\pi_1) < u_1(\bar{\pi}_1)$, where $\bar{\pi}_1$ is the expected payoff.

3. Suppose the agent and the firm are risk-averse and the agent's effort is fixed. Let π_k denote the gross profit corresponding to state $a_k(k = 1, \ldots, K)$, π_{k1} the agent's share, and π_{k2} the firm's share (i.e., $\pi_{k1} + \pi_{k2} = \pi_k$). Let $u_1(\pi_{k1})$ and $u_2(\pi_{k2})$, respectively, denote the agent's and the firm's utility functions which are scaled so that $u_1(0) = u_2(0) = 0$. Then optimal risk sharing (i.e., Pareto optimality) requires one to maximize $\lambda_1 u_1(\pi_{k1}) + \lambda_2 u_2(\pi_{k2})$ subject to $\lambda_1 + \lambda_2 = 1$ and $(\pi_{k1}) + (\pi_{k2}) = \pi_k$ for all k. See Raiffa (1968, pp. 200–1). Note in particular that the optimum risk-sharing plan is independent of the probabilities of the states a_k.

4. Use the approach in note 3 to analyze specified utility functions for the firm and the agent. See Wilson (1968) for an extensive discussion of optimal risk-sharing rules.

5. Let the agent's exponential utility function be $u_1(\pi_{k1}) = 1 - e^{-\pi_{k1}/c_1}$ and the firm's exponential utility function be $u_2(\pi_{k2}) = 1 - e^{-\pi_{k2}/c_2}$, where c_1 and c_2 are positive constants. Then the optimal risk-sharing plan (see note 3) is the linear rule

$$\pi_{k1} = \left(\frac{c_1}{c_1 + c_2}\right)\pi_k - \left(\frac{c_1 c_2}{c_1 + c_2}\right)\ln\left(\frac{\lambda_2 c_1}{\lambda_1 c_2}\right)$$

$$\pi_{k2} = \left(\frac{c_2}{c_1 + c_2}\right)\pi_k - \left(\frac{c_1 c_2}{c_1 + c_2}\right)\ln\left(\frac{\lambda_1 c_2}{\lambda_2 c_1}\right)$$

where the agent's commission rate on gross profit is $[c_1/(c_1 + c_2)]$ and the agent's fixed wage ("side payment") is $-[c_1 c_2/(c_1 + c_2)]\ln(\lambda_2 c_1/\lambda_1 c_2)$. See Raiffa (1968, p. 202) for the derivation.

Note that the side payments sum to zero. The Arrow–Pratt absolute risk aversion coefficients for the agent and the firm, respectively, are $1/c_1$ and $1/c_2$; in general, we expect the firm to be more risk averse than the agent ($c_1 < c_2$). The values of λ_1 and λ_2 are obtained by using the profit-sharing rule to solve $Eu_1(\pi_{k1}) = \bar{u}_1$, where $\bar{u}_1$ denotes the utility of the agent's reservation income (i.e., market value). Note that the agent's fixed wage depends on the agent's reservation income, the risk attitudes of the firm and of the agent, and the probabilities of the states. The profit-sharing rule, however, depends only on the risk attitudes of the agent and the firm.

6. Suppose the agent and the firm have exponential utility functions with parameters c_1 and c_2, respectively.

Let s_k denote the sales volume in state k, $C(s_k)$ the cost function, and p the unit price. Then the gross profit is $\pi_k = ps_k - C(s_k)$ and the agent's share is

$$\pi_{k1} = \frac{c_1}{c_1 + c_2}[ps_k - C(s_k)] - \frac{c_1 c_2}{c_1 + c_2}\ln\frac{\lambda_2 c_1}{\lambda_1 c_2}$$

Suppose the number of states is infinite. Dropping the k subscript and differentiating, we have

$$\frac{\partial^2 \pi_1}{\partial s^2} = \frac{-c_1}{c_1 + c_2}\frac{\partial^2 C}{\partial s^2}$$

Hence $\text{sgn}(\partial^2 \pi_1/\partial s^2) = -\text{sgn}(\partial^2 C/\partial s^2)$. If the cost structure is nonlinear and the firm uses a revenue-based compensation plan, the agent cannot infer production costs. The agent can only infer that marginal costs are decreasing (increasing) if the revenue-based compensation plan is progressive (regressive). If the cost structure is linear, however, the agent can precisely determine the firm's marginal cost if he knows the firm's risk attitude (i.e., c_2). Specifically, the agent's revenue-based commission rate is $[c_1/(c_1 + c_2)][(p - \omega)/p]$, where ω denotes the constant marginal cost of production.

These results are based on the mild condition that price exceeds marginal cost at all feasible sales level (i.e., $\partial \pi_1/\partial s > 0$). They also depend on the assumption that input prices are fixed (i.e., costs are stochastic only because sales are uncertain).

7. Suppose both the agent and the firm have the logarithmic utility function $u(\pi) = \ln \pi$, where π denotes the payoff. Let π_k denote the gross profit in state k and π_{k1} and π_{k2} the respective shares of the agent and the firm. Then optimal risk sharing requires $\pi_{k1} = \lambda_1 \pi_k$ and $\pi_{k2} = \lambda_2 \pi_k$, where λ_1 and λ_2 are chosen such that $Eu(\pi_{k1}) = \bar{u}_1$, where $\bar{u}_1$ denotes the utility of the agent's reservation income. (See note 3.) Note that the optimal contract is a pure commission plan (i.e., the fixed wage is zero).

8. The optimal contract depends heavily on the risk attitudes of the agent and the firm, the precise

form of the stochastic relationship between effort and sales, and the probability distribution of the states. See Holmström (1979, pp. 79–80) for a discussion. In particular, the utility functions must be bounded for an optimal contract to be feasible. This restriction is reasonable since the agent's wealth puts a lower bound and the firm's wealth (augmented by its payoff from the contract) puts an upper bound on the agent's share. Mirrlees (1974) presents an example where the utility function is unbounded and no optimal solution exists.

9. We considered the extreme case where the agent is paid a fixed wage. In any risk-sharing plan, however, the gross payoff is suboptimal because the risk-averse agent will always shirk to some degree when effort is unobservable (see Holmström 1979, Proposition 1). This problem of shirking disappears in the special case where the agent is risk-neutral, regardless of whether the firm is risk-neutral or risk-averse. See Shavell 1979, Proposition 4. The risk-neutral agent is unconcerned about the volatility of his income and is therefore willing to insure the firm fully against the risk of variation in the "net return" (i.e., the gross payoff minus the "cost" of his effort). Suppose the agent pays the firm a fixed fee and keeps the residual payoff. Then the agent will maximize the expected net return (i.e., choose the optimal effort) because he bears the cost of his effort and is risk-neutral. Hence the first-best contract can be achieved.

The moral hazard problem disappears if the agent can be sufficiently penalized when the gross payoff is too low. In this case a nondifferentiable sharing rule exists that gives the firm and the agent the same expected utility as a first-best solution (see Holmström 1979, pp. 77–78). This situation is highly unlikely in the sales force context.

10. Suppose the agent's minimum income requirement is $\hat{y}$. Consider the case where both the agent and the firm have exponential utilities with parameters c_1 and c_2, respectively. Then (see note 6) optimal risk sharing requires us to maximize $W = \lambda_1(1 - e^{-\pi_{k1}/c_1}) + \lambda_2(1 - e^{-\pi_{k2}/c_2})$ subject to the constraints $\pi_{k1} + \pi_{k2} = \pi_k$, $\pi_{k1} \geq \hat{y}$, and $\lambda_1 + \lambda_2 = 1$ for all states k.

Solving this problem, we obtain the wage–bonus plan $\pi_{k1} = \hat{y}$ if

$$\pi_k < \hat{y}\left(1 + \frac{c_2}{c_1}\right) + c_2 \ln\left(\frac{\lambda_2 c_1}{\lambda_1 c_2}\right)$$

$$\pi_{k1} = \frac{c_1}{c_1 + c_2}\pi_k - \left(\frac{c_1 c_2}{c_1 c_2}\right)\ln\left(\frac{\lambda_2 c_1}{\lambda_1 c_2}\right)$$

otherwise. Note that the profit-sharing rate $[c_1/(c_1 + c_2)]$ is the same as that in the case where the agent does not have a minimum income constraint. The bonus is used for optimal risk sharing and not as a motivational tool. The only effect of increasing the agent's minimum income requirement $(\hat{y})$ is to increase the quota.

One can derive similar wage–bonus plans for other utility functions (e.g., logarithmic).

11. Let $s = f(p, \hat{e})$ denote the deterministic sales function, where p is price and $\hat{e}$ is the agent's contractually determined effort. Let $C(s)$ denote the cost function. Then the firm's gross profit is $\pi = pf(p, \hat{e}) - C[f(p, \hat{e})]$. Let p^* maximize π for any given $\hat{e}$ and π^* denote the corresponding value of π. Then the firm can set price at p^* and offer the agent several equivalent forcing contracts. For example, the firm can pay the agent his reservation income for effort $\hat{e}$ if he meets a sales volume quota of $f(p^*, \hat{e})$ and nothing otherwise. Equivalently, the firm can pay the agent his reservation income if he meets a sales revenue quota of $p^* f(p^*, \hat{e})$ and nothing otherwise. Because the sales function is deterministic, the agent will not shirk (i.e., the firm does not need to monitor the agent's effort).

12. Suppose there are K states. Let $\hat{\pi}_k$ denote the gross profit for state $k(k = 1, \ldots, K)$ if the firm follows a centralized pricing strategy and sets price before observing the state. Let $\hat{\pi}_{1k}$ and $\hat{\pi}_{2k}$ denote, respectively, the agent's and the firm's shares of $\hat{\pi}_k$ for the best contract given centralized pricing. Let π_k^* denote the maximum gross profit for state k if price can be set after observing the state. Then $\pi_k^* = \hat{\pi}_k + a_k$, where $a_k \geq 0$ for all k and $a_k > 0$ for at least one k.

Consider any policy A that maximizes π_k^* for all k. Then it is feasible for the firm to pay the agent $\hat{\pi}_{1k}$ and to keep $\hat{\pi}_{2k} + a_k$. Hence the firm should delegate price-setting authority to the agent and choose a contract based on gross profit.

Suppose the firm delegates price-setting authority to the agent and pays him on the basis of sales revenue. Let $\hat{\hat{\pi}}_k$ denote the gross profit for the best such contract and $\hat{\hat{\pi}}_{1k}$ and $\hat{\hat{\pi}}_{2k}$, respectively, denote the corresponding shares of the agent and of the firm. Then $\pi_k^* = \hat{\hat{\pi}}_k + b_k$, where $b_k > 0$. If the firm chooses policy A, it can pay the agent $\hat{\hat{\pi}}_{1k}$ and keep $\hat{\hat{\pi}}_{2k} + b_k$ for all k. Hence a contract based on sales revenue cannot be optimal.

These results do not depend on the precise forms of the utility functions or on the probability distribution of profits.

13. Let $\bar{E}$ denote the fixed selling expenses. Then the gross profit for state k is $\pi_k = ps_k - C(s_k) - \bar{E}$, where p denotes price, s is sales, and C is the cost function. If the agent and the firm have exponential utility functions with parameters c_1 and c_2, respectively, the agent's income for state k is

$$\pi_{k1} = \frac{c_1}{c_1 + c_2}[ps_k - C(s_k) - \bar{E}] + w$$

where w is the fixed wage. Hence $\partial w/\partial \bar{E} = c_1/(c_1 + c_2) > 0$; that is, π_{k1} does not vary with $\bar{E}$. (Recall that the firm pays the agent his reservation income.)

A simpler and equivalent contract is

$$\pi_{k1} = \frac{c_1}{c_1 + c_2}[ps_k - C(s_k)] + w'$$

where $ps_k - C(s_k)$ denotes the contribution margin and w' is the fixed wage. Hence $\partial w'/\partial \bar{E} = 0$. In both contracts the firm absorbs all the selling expenses.

14. When both the agent and the firm have logarithmic utility functions, the agent's share for any state k is $\pi_{k1} = \lambda_1[ps_k - C(s_k) - \bar{E}]$. Hence the agent and the firm share the fixed selling expenses in the ratio $\lambda_1 : \lambda_2$. In particular, the agent's share of gross profit increases when sales expenses go up $(\partial \lambda_1/\partial \bar{E} = \lambda_1 E\{1/[ps_k - C(s_k) - \bar{E}]\} > 0)$.

Equivalently, the firm can choose the contract $\pi_{k1} = \lambda_1[ps_k - C(s_k)] - \lambda_1 \bar{E}$, where the agent pays a franchise fee $(\lambda_1 \bar{E})$ and obtains a share λ_1 of the gross contribution margin. When sales expenses increase, both the franchise fee and the agent's share λ_1 increase.

For both contracts let y_1 denote the agent's income and $\sigma^2(y_1)$ the variance of the agent's income. Then $\partial \sigma^2(y_1)/\partial \bar{E} = 2\lambda_1(\partial \lambda_1/\partial E)\sigma^2[ps_k - C(s_k)] > 0$ and $\partial E(y_1)/\partial \bar{E} = \lambda_1[E(\pi_k) E(1/\pi_k) - 1] > 0$ using Jensen's inequality. These results are distribution-free.

15. This result can be derived using the approach in note 14.

16. Let the profit for state k when the agent spends time a on nonselling activities be $\pi_k' =$

$\pi_k - \theta(a)$, where $\partial\theta/\partial a > 0$. In the exponential utility case, the agent's share is $\pi_{k1} = [c_1/(c_1 + c_2)] [\pi_k - \theta(a)] + w$. Hence $\partial w/\partial a = [c_1/(c_1 + c_2)] \partial\theta/\partial a$; that is, for every state k the agent's income is unchanged. In the logarithmic utility case $\pi_{k1} = \lambda_1[\pi_k - \theta(a)]$ and $\partial\lambda_1/\partial a = \lambda_1(\partial\theta/\partial a)E\{1/[\pi_k - \theta(a)]\} > 0$. Consequently when the time on nonselling activities increases, the agent's expected income and the variance of the agent's income increase.

17. Consider a three-level hierarchy consisting of the owner, district sales managers (indexed by m), and sales agents (indexed by i). Suppose all effort levels are contractually fixed, each sales agent is assigned an exclusive sales territory and sells J products (indexed by j), all prices p_j are fixed, and the unit cost of production ω_j for each product j is constant. Let $z_i^{(m)}$ denote the time spent by manager m on "supervising" agent i, and $t_j^{(m)}$ the time spent by manager m on selling product j. Let $t_{ij}^{(m)}$ denote the time spent on product j by sales agent i in district m.

Suppose the sales volumes for sales agent i are $s_{ij}^{(m)} = \varphi_{ij}^{(m)}(p_1, \ldots, p_J; t_{i1}^{(m)}, \ldots, t_{iJ}^{(m)}; z_i^{(m)}) + g_{ij}^{(m)}$, where $g_{ij}^{(m)}$ is stochastic. In addition, the sales volumes generated by district manager m are $q_j^{(m)} = \alpha_j^{(m)}(p_1, \ldots, p_J; t_1^{(m)}, \ldots, t_J^{(m)}) + v_j^{(m)}$, where $v_j^{(m)}$ is stochastic. Then the gross profit is $\Pi = \sum_{m=1}^{M} \pi^{(m)}$, where $\pi^{(m)} = \sum_{i=1}^{A_m} \sum_{j=1}^{J}[(p_j - \omega_j)(\varphi_{ij}^{(m)} + \alpha_j^{(m)})] + \sum_{i=1}^{A_m} \sum_{j=1}^{J}[(p_j - \omega_j)(g_{ij}^{(m)} + v_j^{(m)})] = A + B$, where A_m denotes the number of agents in district m.

Suppose each district manager's income increases with his district's profits. Then centralized decision making by the district manager is optimal because B does not depend on the decision variables (i.e., supervisory effort and the sales call plan). In particular, it is not necessary for district managers to delegate authority to sales agents because the optimum sales call plans do not depend on the realized values of $g_{ij}^{(m)}$.

These results do not depend on the precise utility functions of the firm, the district managers, and the sales agents. Consequently the contract can focus on optimal risk sharing.

18. The previous results depend heavily on the assumption that the $s_{ij}^{(m)}$ are additively separable in the $g_{ij}^{(m)}$ and the $q_j^{(m)}$ are additively separable in the $v_j^{(m)}$ (i.e., the volatility of demand does not depend on the control variables). In general

$$\pi^{(m)} = \sum_{i=1}^{A_m} \sum_{j=1}^{J} \{(p_j - \omega_j)[\varphi_{ij}^{(m)}(p_1, \ldots, p_J; t_{i1}^{(m)}, \ldots, t_{iJ}^{(m)}, z_i^{(m)}, g_{ij}^{(m)}) $$
$$+ \alpha_j^{(m)}(p_1, \ldots, p_J; t_1^{(m)}, \ldots, t_J^{(m)}; v_j^{(m)})]\}$$

Now the results are tractable if a group utility function exists.

Consider the exponential utility case where $\hat{\beta}$ is the sum of the exponential utility parameters for all the players. Let $\Pi = \sum_{m=1}^{M} \pi^{(m)}$ denote gross profit and $U(\Pi) = 1 - e^{\Pi/\hat{\beta}}$ denote the group utility function.

Suppose all decisions must be made prior to the resolution of uncertainty. Then the optimal policy is for the owner to choose the supervisory efforts ($z_i^{(m)*}$) and sales call policies ($t_j^{(m)*}$, and $t_{ij}^{(m)*}$) to maximize $EU(\Pi)$. Let Π_k^* denote the value of Π for any state k, given this choice of policy. For player r let w_r denote the fixed wage and β_r the parameter in the exponential utility function. Then player r receives $w_r + (\beta_r/\hat{\beta})\Pi_k^*$, where $\sum_r w_r = 0$.

Suppose the district managers and the sales agents can observe market conditions (i.e., the realized values $\hat{g}_{ij}^{(m)}$ and $\hat{v}_j^{(m)}$) prior to choosing their sales call policies. Then the first step is for the owner to choose the marketing plan $(z_i^{(m)*}, t_j^{(m)*}, t_{ij}^{(m)})$ that maximizes $EU(\Pi)$. Now supervisory effort occurs before uncertainty is resolved. Let $\hat{z}^{(m)} = \bar{z}^{(m)} - \sum_{i=1}^{A_m} z_i^{(m)*}$ denote district manager m's available time for personal selling after supervision, where $\bar{z}^{(m)}$ denotes manager m's contractually fixed effort. The second step is for the owner to delegate sales call policy to the district managers and the sales agents. For any realization $\hat{g}_{ij}^{(m)}$ and $\hat{v}_j^{(m)}$ we have

$$\hat{\pi}^{(m)} = \sum_{i=1}^{A_m} \sum_{j=1}^{J} \{(p_j - \omega_j)[\varphi_{ij}^{(m)}(p_1, \ldots, p_J; t_{i1}^{(m)}, \ldots, t_{iJ}^{(m)}, z_i^{(m)*}, \hat{g}_{ij}^{(m)})$$
$$+ \alpha_j^{(m)}(p_1, \ldots, p_J; t_1^{(m)}, \ldots, t_J^{(m)}, \hat{v}_j^{(m)})]\}$$

Because each player's income increases with gross profit, the district manager and sales agents will choose policies $(\hat{t}_{ij}^{(m)}, \hat{t}_j^{(m)})$ that maximize $\hat{\pi}^{(m)}$, where $\sum_{j=1}^{J} \hat{t}_j^{(m)} = \hat{z}^{(m)}$. Optimal risk sharing requires that player r receive $\hat{w}_r + (\beta_r/\hat{\beta})\hat{\Pi}^*$, where $\hat{\Pi}^* = \sum_{m=1}^{M} \hat{\pi}^{(m)*}$ and $\hat{\pi}^{(m)*}$ denotes district m's profits for the policy $(\hat{t}_{ij}^{(m)}, \hat{t}_j^{(m)}, z_i^{(m)*})$.

19. Suppose price is an additional control variable. Now even for the simplest form of uncertainty [i.e., $s_{ij}^{(m)} = \varphi_{ij}^{(m)}(\cdot) + g_{ij}^{(m)}$ and $q_j^{(m)} = \alpha_j^{(m)}(\cdot) + v_j^{(m)}$], the results are only determinate if a group utility function exists.

Suppose all decisions (i.e., price, supervisory effort, and sales call policy) must be made prior to the resolution of uncertainty. Then the owner acts as a centralized decision maker and chooses the marketing plan $(p_j^{(m)*}, t_j^{(m)*}, t_{ij}^{(m)*}, z_i^{(m)*})$ that maximizes $EU(\Pi)$, where U denotes the group utility function.

Suppose price and sales call policy can be chosen after uncertainty is resolved [i.e., $\hat{g}_{ij}^{(m)}$ and $\hat{v}_j^{(m)}$ are known]. Then in the first step the owner chooses the marketing plan $(p_j^{(m)*}, t_j^{(m)*}, t_{ij}^{(m)*}, z_i^{(m)*})$ that maximizes $EU(\Pi)$. In the second step the owner delegates price and sales call policy to the district managers and the sales agents. Given $z_i^{(m)*}$ and the realizations $\hat{g}_{ij}^{(m)}$ and $\hat{v}_j^{(m)}$, the district managers and the sales agents choose the revised plan $(\hat{p}_j^{(m)}, \hat{t}_j^{(m)}, \hat{t}_{ij}^{(m)})$ that maximizes $\hat{\pi}^{(m)}$. In the exponential utility case player r's income is $\hat{w}_r + (\beta_r/\hat{\beta})\sum_{m=1}^{M} \hat{\pi}^{(m)*}$, where $\hat{w}_r$ denotes the fixed wage, $\hat{\beta}$ is the group utility parameter, β_r is player r's utility parameter, and $\hat{\pi}^{(m)*}$ denotes district m's profits for the policy $(\hat{p}_j^{(m)}, \hat{t}_j^{(m)}, \hat{t}_{ij}^{(m)}, z_i^{(m)*})$.

20. Suppose all payoffs for a given period t occur at the end of that period. Let the gross profit for any period t ($t = 1, \ldots, T$) be $\varphi_t(\pi_k^{(1)})$, where $\varphi_1(\pi_k^{(1)}) = \pi_k^{(1)}$ is the gross profit in period 1 when state k occurs. Suppose both the agent and the firm have time-additive utility functions U_1 and U_2, respectively. For any period t and state k let the agent's share be $\pi_{1k}^{(t)}$ and the firm's share be $\pi_{2k}^{(t)}$.

Suppose both the agent and the firm have a common discount rate d. Then the Pareto optimal risk-sharing rule requires that for any state k the $\pi_{1k}^{(t)}$ and $\pi_{2k}^{(t)}$ are chosen to maximize $\lambda_1 U_1 + \lambda_2 U_2$ subject to $\pi_{1k}^{(t)} + \pi_{2k}^{(t)} = \varphi_t(\pi_k^{(1)})$ for $t = 1, \ldots, T$ and $\lambda_1 + \lambda_2 = 1$, where

$$U_i = \sum_{t=1}^{T} \frac{u_i(\pi_{ik}^{(t)})}{(1+d)^t}$$

Suppose the agent and the firm have exponential utility functions with parameters c_1 and c_2, respectively. Then the optimal contract is

$$\pi_{1k}^{(t)} = \frac{c_1}{c_1 + c_2} \varphi_t(\pi_k^{(1)}) - \frac{c_1 c_2}{c_1 + c_2} \ln\left(\frac{\lambda_2 c_1}{\lambda_1 c_2}\right)$$

for all t. This multiperiod contract is equivalent to the single-period contract

$$\hat{\pi}_{1k}^{(1)} = \frac{c_1}{c_1 + c_2} \sum_{t=1}^{T} \frac{\varphi_t(\pi_k^{(1)})}{(1+d)^{t-1}} + \hat{w}$$

where the fixed wage

$$\hat{w} = -\frac{c_1 c_2}{c_1 + c_2} \ln\left(\frac{\lambda_2 c_1}{\lambda_1 c_2}\right) \sum_{t=1}^{T} \frac{1}{(1+d)^{t-1}}$$

and all payments are made at the end of period 1. Now the myopic single-period contract has the form

$$\hat{\hat{\pi}}_{1k}^{(1)} = \left(\frac{c_1}{c_1 + c_2}\right) \varphi_1(\pi_k^{(1)}) + \hat{\hat{w}}$$

where $\hat{\hat{w}}$ denotes the fixed wage. Hence $\hat{w} < \hat{\hat{w}}$.

Suppose the number of states is infinite and price exceeds marginal cost for all states. Differentiating and dropping the subscripts k, we have $\partial \hat{\pi}_1^{(1)} / \partial \pi^{(1)} > \partial \hat{\hat{\pi}}_1^{(1)} / \partial \pi^{(1)}$ (i.e., for any state the agent's share increases faster under the optimal contract than under the myopic contract).

Consider the special case where the product price p and the marginal cost ω are constant. Suppose the market is mature and the customer retention rate decays exponentially over time; specifically $s_k^{(t)} = \alpha^{t-1} s_k$, where s_k denotes sales for state k and $0 < \alpha < 1$. Then the optimal single-period contract for an infinite horizon is the linear rule $\hat{\pi}_{1k}^{(1)} = \hat{\beta} s_k^{(1)} + \hat{w}$, where

$$\hat{\beta} = \left(\frac{c_1}{c_1 + c_2}\right)(p - c)\left(\frac{1}{1 - \alpha/(1+d)}\right),$$

$$\alpha/(1+d) < 1, \quad \text{and} \quad \left(\frac{1}{1 - \alpha/(1+d)}\right) s_k^{(1)}$$

denotes "long-term sales." The myopic single-period contract, however, is $\hat{\hat{\pi}}_{1k}^{(1)} = \hat{\hat{\beta}} s_k^{(1)} + \hat{\hat{w}}$, where $\hat{\hat{\beta}} = [c_1/(c_1 + c_2)](p - \omega)$. Hence $\hat{\beta} > \hat{\hat{\beta}}$. Note that the agent's share $\hat{\beta}$ increases with the customer retention rate α; α, in turn, depends on industry characteristics and varies over the product life cycle. In addition, $\hat{\beta}$ decreases with the discount rate; that is, the loss from using the myopic single-period contract decreases when the discount rate is higher.

21. Suppose $s_k^{(t)}$ is convex in $s_k^{(1)}$ for $t > 1$ (e.g., word-of-mouth activity in period 1 has a significant effect on future sales). Then the optimal single-period contract is a fixed wage plus a progressive commission structure based on current sales revenue. See note 20.

22. Suppose both the agent and the firm have logarithmic utility functions. Following the approach in note 20, we can show that the optimal multiperiod contract is $\pi_{1k}^{(t)} = \lambda_1 \varphi_t(\pi_k^{(1)})$; the equivalent single-period contract is

$$\hat{\pi}_{1k}^{(1)} = \lambda_1 \sum_{t=1}^{T} \frac{\varphi_t(\pi_k^{(1)})}{(1+d)^{t-1}} = \lambda_1 A$$

where d is the discount rate.

Suppose price and marginal cost are constants and $s_k^{(t)} = \alpha^{t-1} s_k^{(1)}$, where $0 < \alpha < 1$ and s_k denotes sales for state k. Then A is an exact multiple of $\pi_k^{(1)}$. Consequently the myopic single-period contract is optimal. If A is convex in $\pi_k^{(1)}$ (e.g., the word-of-mouth or diffusion effect is strong), the optimal single-period contract is progressive in current sales revenue (see OC″ in Figure 8.1b).

These results hold for all other classes of utility function that lead to a linear sharing rule with no side payments (i.e., pure commission contracts). For example, $u_1(x) = u_2(x) = \sqrt{x}$, where x denotes the one-period payoff.

23. Suppose the agent's discount rate (d_1) differs from the firm's discount rate (d_2). Then the effect on the optimal contract (denoted below by "*") depends on the precise forms of the utility functions. In the exponential utility case, the agent's fixed wage depends on both d_1 and d_2; the agent's share of gross profit, however, depends on d_1 only. In particular,

$$\pi_{1k}^{(1)*} = \frac{c_1}{c_1 + c_2} \sum_{t=1}^{T} \frac{\varphi_t(\pi_k^{(1)})}{(1+d_1)^{t-1}} + w^*, \qquad \text{where}$$

$$w^* = -\left(\frac{c_1 c_2}{c_1 + c_2}\right) \ln\left(\frac{\lambda_2\, c_1(1+d_1)}{\lambda_1\, c_2(1+d_2)}\right) \sum_{t=1}^{T} \frac{1}{(1+d_1)^{t-1}}$$

In the logarithmic utility case, the profit-sharing rate depends in general on d_1 and d_2. In particular,

$$\pi_{1k}^{(1)*} = \lambda_1' \sum_{t=1}^{T} \frac{\varphi_t(\pi_k^{(1)})}{(1+d_1)^{t-1}}, \text{ where } \lambda_1' = \frac{\lambda_1(1+d_2)}{1+\lambda_1 d_2 + \lambda_2 d_1}$$

In the special case $\pi_k^{(t)} = \alpha \pi_k^{(t-1)}$, where $0 < \alpha < 1$ and price and marginal cost are constant, $\pi_{1k}^{(1)*} = \theta \pi_k^{(1)}$, where θ is a positive constant. Hence the "myopic" single-period contract is optimal. In general the profit-sharing rate is progressive if φ_t is convex [$t > 1$] regardless of the particular values of d_1 and d_2.

24. Suppose that there are M segments and that the carryover effects differ by segment. The gross profit depends on how the agent's contractually fixed effort is allocated across segments (i.e., which lottery is chosen). Hence the optimal contract requires the correct choice of lottery and risk-sharing rule.

Suppose the agent and the firm have time-additive exponential utility functions with parameters c_1 and c_2, respectively, and have a common discount rate. Let u_* denote the group exponential utility function with parameter $c_* = c_1 + c_2$. For any time allocation plan let $\Pi_k^{(t)}$ denote the gross profit for period t when state k occurs in period t. Then the optimal strategy is to allocate the agent's effort across segments to maximize $\sum_{t=1}^{T} u_*(\Pi_k^{(t)})/(1+d)^t$. See Raiffa (1968, pp. 208–10) for a proof in the one-period case. Let Π_{mk}^* ($m = 1, \ldots, M$) denote the net present value of gross profit in segment m for state k when the optimal time allocation plan is chosen. Then Pareto-optimal risk sharing requires that the agent's income in period 1 is $\hat{\pi}_{1k}^{(1)} = [c_1/(c_1+c_2)] \sum_{m=1}^{M} \Pi_{mk}^* + \hat{w}$, where $\hat{w}$ is the fixed wage.

Suppose marginal cost is constant and there are two segments: mature (indexed "1") and growth (indexed "2"). Then Π_{1k}^* is linear in segment 1's sales for period 1 and Π_{2k}^* is convex in segment 2's sales for period 1. Hence the optimal contract consists of a fixed wage, a constant commission rate on segment 1 sales, and a progressive commission rate on segment 2 sales.

If the firm and the agent have logarithmic utility functions, $\hat{\pi}_{1k}^{(1)} = \lambda \sum_{m=1}^{M} \Pi_{mk}^{**}$, where "**" denotes the gross profit when the optimal time allocation plan is chosen. Hence for the scenario discussed in the exponential utility case, the optimal contract is a pure commission plan with a constant commission rate on Segment 1 sales and a progressive commission rate on Segment 2 sales.

These results depend heavily on the existence of a group utility function (i.e., the agent and the firm agree on the best time allocation plan). Group utility functions, however, do not always exist; see Raiffa (1968, pp. 211–13) for an example and Raiffa (1968, pp. 233–37) for a lucid discussion of the opposing Group Bayesian and Paretian views.

25. Let s_i denote sales volume in period i ($i = 1, 2$) and S_1 denote customer satisfaction measured at the end of period 1. Suppose $s_2 = \varphi(S_1)s_1$, where $\varphi(S_1) < 1$ is the customer retention rate and $\partial \varphi(S_1)/\partial S_1 \geq 0$. For exponential utilities the agent's income at the end of period 1 is

$$ y_1 = w_1 + \left(\frac{c_1}{c_1 + c_2} \right) (p - c) \left(s_1 + \frac{\varphi(S_1)s_1}{1 + \delta} \right) $$

where c_1 and c_2, respectively denote the agent's and the firm's risk parameters, p is the fixed price, ω is the constant unit cost of production, d is the discount rate, and w_1 is the agent's fixed wage.

Let $\alpha = [c_1/(c_1+c_2)](p-\omega)$ and $\beta = \varphi(S_1)/(1+d)$. Then $y_1 = w_1 + \alpha s_1 + \alpha \beta s_1 = w_1 + A + B$. Thus the agent's contract consists of three parts: (1) a fixed wage; (2) a linear commission rate (α) on sales volume in period 1, and (3) a satisfaction multiplier (β) applied to the total commissions on sales in period 1 (αs_1). Note that $A > B$ and the satisfaction multiplier varies inversely with the discount rate.

Suppose $\varphi(S_1)$ is strictly concave in S_1. Then the satisfaction multiplier is regressive (see AB in Figure 8.6).

Suppose there is a threshold level of satisfaction S_1^T; in particular $s_2 = rs_1$ if $S_1 \leq S_1^T$ and $s_2 = [r + \mu(S_1)]s_1$ if $S_1 > S_1^T$, where r is the base customer retention rate and $\partial \mu/\partial S_1 \geq 0$. Then

$$ y_1 = w_1 + \left(\frac{c_1}{c_1 + c_2} \right) (p - \omega) \left(1 + \frac{r}{(1+d)} \right) s_1 \text{ if } S_1 \leq S_1^T $$

$$ y_1 = w_1 + \left(\frac{c_1}{c_1 + c_2} \right) (p - \omega) \left(1 + \frac{r}{(1+d)} \right) s_1 $$

$$ + \left(\frac{c_1}{c_1 + c_2} \right) (p - \omega) \left(\frac{\mu(S_1)}{(1+d)} \right) s_1 \text{ if } S_1 > S_1^T $$

Thus the satisfaction multiplier only applies when satisfaction exceeds the threshold level (see OFG in Figure 8.6). Suppose customers expect a certain level of satisfaction and that the effect on the retention rate depends asymmetrically on the difference between realized satisfaction and expected satisfaction (OH in Figure 8.6). Then $\varphi(S)$ is S-shaped. Hence the satisfaction multiplier function is convex (concave) in satisfaction if realized satisfaction is less than (greater than) the reference level. See CDE in Figure 8.6.

26. Suppose customer satisfaction affects both the retention rate and the future quantity purchased by repeat buyers. Let $s_2' = \varphi(S_1)(s_1 + aS_1)$, where $\partial\varphi/\partial S_1 \geq 0$ and $a > 0$. Then the agent's income at the end of period 1 is $y_1 = w_1 + A + B + C$, where w_1 is the fixed wage, A is the commission income on sales in period 1, B is the satisfaction-weighted commission income on sales in period 1, and C is a bonus based purely on satisfaction. In particular

$$A = \left(\frac{c_1}{c_1 + c_2}\right)(p - \omega)s_1$$

$$B = \left(\frac{c_1(p - \omega)}{(c_1 + c_2)(1 + d)}\right)s_1\varphi(S_1)$$

$$C = \left(\frac{ac_1(p - \omega)}{(c_1 + c_2)(1 + d)}\right)S_1\varphi(S_1)$$

Note that $\partial C/\partial S_1 > 0$ but $\partial^2 C/\partial S_1^2$ is ambiguous (i.e., without empirical information we cannot determine whether the satisfaction-based bonus structure is progressive or regressive).

27. Suppose satisfaction only affects the retention rate. Let $S_1' = S_1 + \theta$ denote measured satisfaction where $E(\theta) = 0$ and θ is independent of S_1. If $\theta \equiv 0$, the agent's commission income is $z_1 = q_1s_1 + q_2\varphi(S_1)s_1$, where $q_1 = c_1(p - \omega)/(c_1 + c_2)$ and $q_2 = c_1(p - \omega)/[(c_1 + c_2)(1 + d)]$, where d is the discount rate.

Suppose θ is small. Then the agent's commission income is $z_1' \cong q_1s_1 + q_2[\varphi(S_1) + (\partial\varphi/\partial S_1)\theta]s_1$. Let σ^2 denote the variance operator. Then $E(z_1') - E(z_1) = E[q_2(\partial\varphi/\partial S_1)s_1 \theta] = 0$ always, regardless of the precise form of φ. Similarly $\sigma^2(z_1') - \sigma^2(z_1) = q_2^2\sigma^2[(\partial\varphi/\partial S_1)s_1 \theta] > 0$.

Suppose θ is large and

$$\varphi(S_1') \cong \varphi(S_1) + \frac{\partial\varphi}{\partial S_1}\theta + \frac{\partial^2\theta}{\partial S_1^2}\left(\frac{\theta^2}{2}\right)$$

Then

$$E(z_1') - E(z_1) = \frac{q_2}{2}E\left(\frac{\partial^2\varphi}{\partial S_1^2}s_1 \theta^2\right)$$

Hence $E(z_1') = E(z_1)$ if φ is linear in S_1 and $E(z_1') > (<)E(z_1)$ if φ is convex (concave) in S_1. This result also holds if satisfaction only affects the customer retention rate after a threshold level has been reached. If there is a reference level of satisfaction, $\partial^2\varphi/\partial S_1^2 > (<)0$ if $S_1 < (>)\hat{S}_1$, where $\hat{S}_1$ denotes the reference point. Hence $E(z_1') - E(z_1)$ is ambiguous.

Similarly

$$\sigma^2(z_1') - \sigma^2(z_1) = q_2^2\sigma^2\left(\frac{\partial\varphi}{\partial S_1}s_1\theta\right) + \frac{q_2^2}{4}\sigma^2\left(\frac{\partial^2\varphi}{\partial S_1^2}s_1 \theta^2\right) + q_1q_2E(\theta^2)\,\text{Cov}\left(s_1, \frac{\partial^2\varphi}{\partial S_1^2}s_1\right)$$

$$+ q_2^2 E(\theta^2) \, \text{Cov}\left(s_1 \varphi(S_1), \frac{\partial^2 \varphi}{\partial S_1^2} s_1\right) + q_2^2 \, E(\theta^3) \, \text{Cov}\left(\frac{\partial \varphi}{\partial S_1} s_1, \frac{\partial^2 \varphi}{\partial S_1^2} s_1\right)$$

If φ is linear in $S_1, \sigma^2(z_1') > \sigma^2(z_1)$. In the nonlinear case, distributional assumptions are necessary. Suppose $s_1 = \eta(S_1) + \varepsilon$, where $E(\varepsilon) = 0, \partial \eta(S_1)/\partial S_1 > 0$, and S_1, ε, and θ are pairwise independent. Assume that θ has a symmetric distribution [i.e., $E(\theta^a) = 0$ if a is odd]. Then $\sigma^2(z_1') > \sigma^2(z_1)$ if $\partial^3 \varphi/\partial S_1^3 \geq 0$ and $\partial^2 \varphi/\partial S_1^2 > 0$. The proof is straightforward.

28. Suppose satisfaction at the end of period 1 affects both the retention rate in period 2 and the amount purchased by repeat buyers. Let $s_2 = \varphi(S_1)(s_1 + aS_1)$, where $a > 0$ and measured satisfaction $S_1' = S_1 + \theta$, where $E(\theta) = 0$.

For small θ, $E(z_1') - E(z_1) = aq_2 E(\partial \varphi/\partial S_1) E(\theta^2) > 0$. In general $\sigma^2(z_1') - \sigma^2(z_1)$ is a complicated expression even if φ is linear in S_1. Suppose $s_1 = \eta(S_1) + \varepsilon$, where $E(\varepsilon) = 0, \partial \eta(S_1)/\partial S_1 > 0$, and S_1, θ, and ε are pairwise independent. Assume that θ has a symmetric distribution. Then $\sigma^2(z_1') > \sigma^2(z_1)$ if $\partial^2 \varphi/\partial S_1^2 \geq 0$.

Suppose θ is large and

$$\varphi(S_1') \cong \varphi(S_1) + \left(\frac{\partial \varphi}{\partial S}\right)\theta + \frac{\partial^2 \varphi}{\partial S_1^2}\left(\frac{\theta^2}{2}\right)$$

Then

$$E(z_1') - E(z_1) = q_2\left[aE\left(\frac{\partial \varphi}{\partial S_1}\right)E(\theta^2) + \frac{1}{2}E\left(\frac{\partial^2 \varphi}{\partial S_1^2}s_1\right)E(\theta^2) + \frac{a}{2}E\left(\frac{\partial^2 \varphi}{\partial S_1^2}S_1\right)E(\theta^2)\right.$$
$$\left. + \frac{a}{2}E\left(\frac{\partial^2 \varphi}{\partial S_1^2}\right)E(\theta^3)\right]$$

Hence $E(z_1') > E(z_1)$ if $\partial^2 \varphi/\partial S_1^2 \geq 0$ and θ has a symmetric distribution. Suppose $s_1 = \eta(S_1) + \varepsilon$, as discussed above, and $\partial^3 \varphi/\partial S_1^3 \geq 0$. Then $\sigma^2(z_1') > \sigma^2(z_1)$.

29. Consider the model $s_2 = \varphi(S_1)s_1$, where satisfaction only affects the retention rate. Suppose $S_1' = \lambda_1 S_1 + \theta$, where $E(\lambda_1) \neq 1$ and $E(\theta) = 0$. Let Z_1' denote the agent's commission income when S_1' is used in the contract and z_1' denotes the corresponding commission income when an unbiased measure of satisfaction is available ($\lambda_1 = 1$).

For small θ, $E(Z_1') - E(z_1') \cong q_2(\lambda - 1)E[(\partial \varphi/\partial S_1)S_1 s_1] > (<)0$ if $\lambda > (<)1$. Suppose $\partial \eta/\partial S_1 > 0$ and $s_1 = \eta(S_1) + \varepsilon$, where ε, S_1, and θ are pairwise independent. Then

$$\sigma^2(Z_1') - \sigma^2(z_1') = q_2^2(\lambda - 1)^2\sigma^2\left(\frac{\partial \varphi}{\partial S_1}S_1 s_1\right)$$
$$+ 2q_1 q_2(\lambda - 1)\left[\text{Cov}\left(\eta(S_1), \frac{\partial \varphi}{\partial S_1}S_1 \eta(S_1)\right) + E\left(\frac{\partial \varphi}{\partial S_1}S_1\right)E(\varepsilon^2)\right]$$
$$+ 2q_2^2(\lambda - 1)\left[\text{Cov}\left(\varphi(S_1)\eta(S_1), \frac{\partial \varphi}{\partial S_1}S_1 \eta(S_1)\right) + E\left(\varphi(S_1)\frac{\partial \varphi}{\partial S_1}S_1\right)E(\varepsilon^2)\right]$$

Then $\sigma^2(Z_1') > \sigma^2(z_1')$ if $\lambda > 1$ and $\partial^2 \varphi/\partial S_1^2 \geq 0$. This result is distribution-free.

For large θ,

$$\varphi(S_1') \cong \varphi(S_1) + \frac{\partial \varphi}{\partial S_1}[(\lambda - 1)S_1 + \theta] + \frac{1}{2}\frac{\partial^2 \varphi}{\partial S_1^2}[(\lambda - 1)S_1 + \theta]^2$$

Hence

$$E(Z_1') - E(z_1') = q_2(\lambda - 1)E\left(\frac{\partial \varphi}{\partial S_1}\ S_1 s_1\right) + \frac{1}{2}q_2(\lambda - 1)^2 E\left(\frac{\partial^2 \varphi}{\partial S_1^2}\ S_1^2 s_1\right)$$

Consequently $E(Z_1') > E(z_1')$ if $\lambda > 1$ and $\partial^2 \varphi/\partial S_1^2 > 0$ and $E(Z_1') < E(z_1')$ if $\lambda < 1$ and $\partial^2 \varphi/\partial S_1^2 < 0$. This result is distribution-free.

As in the case where θ is small, the sign of $\sigma^2(Z_1') - \sigma^2(z_1')$ is only determinate if $\lambda > 1$ (i.e., the bias is positive). Suppose $s_1 = \eta(S_1) + \varepsilon$, as discussed above, and θ has a symmetric distribution. Then $\sigma^2(Z_1') > \sigma^2(z_1')$ if $\partial^2 \varphi/\partial S_1^2 \geq 0$ and $\partial^3 \varphi/\partial S_1^3 \geq 0$.

29a. Consider the model $s_2 = \varphi(S_1)(s_1 + aS_1)$, where satisfaction affects both the customer retention rate φ and the quantity purchased by repeat buyers ($a > 0$). Suppose the measured satisfaction is $S_1' = \lambda S_1 + \theta$, where $\lambda \neq 1$, $E(\theta) = 0$, and S_1 is independent of θ.

Let Z_1' denote the agent's commission income when S_1' is used in the contract and z_1' the corresponding commission income when $\lambda = 1$ (i.e., the measure of satisfaction is unbiased).

For small θ,

$$E(Z_1') - E(z_1') = q_2(\lambda - 1)\left[aE[\varphi(S_1)S_1] + E\left(\frac{\partial \varphi}{\partial S_1}\ S_1 s_1\right) + aE\left(\frac{\partial \varphi}{\partial S_1}\ S_1^2\right)\right]$$

$$+ q_2\ a(\lambda - 1)^2 E\left(\frac{\partial \varphi}{\partial S_1}\ S_1^2\right) > 0$$

if $\lambda > 1$, regardless of the distribution of θ.

For large θ,

$$\varphi(S_1') \cong \varphi(S_1) + \frac{\partial \varphi}{\partial S_1}[(\lambda - 1)S_1 + \theta] + \frac{1}{2}\frac{\partial^2 \varphi}{\partial S_1^2}[(\lambda - 1)S_1 + \theta]^2$$

Hence

$$\begin{aligned} E(Z_1') - E(z_1') = q_2\Big[& a(\lambda - 1)E[\varphi(S_1)S_1] + (\lambda - 1)E\left(\frac{\partial \varphi}{\partial S_1}\ S_1 s_1\right) \\ & + a(\lambda - 1)E\left(\frac{\partial \varphi}{\partial S_1}\ S_1^2\right) + a(\lambda - 1)^2 E\left(\frac{\partial \varphi}{\partial S_1}\ S_1^2\right) \\ & + \frac{1}{2}(\lambda - 1)^2 E\left(\frac{\partial^2 \varphi}{\partial S_1^2}\ S_1^2 s_1\right) + \frac{1}{2}a(\lambda - 1)^2 E\left(\frac{\partial^2 \varphi}{\partial S_1^2}\ S_1^3\right) \\ & + \frac{1}{2}a(\lambda - 1)^3 E\left(\frac{\partial^2 \varphi}{\partial S_1^2}\ S_1^3\right) + a(\lambda - 1)E\left(\frac{\partial^2 \varphi}{\partial S_1^2}\ S_1\theta^2\right) \\ & + \frac{1}{2}a(\lambda - 1)E\left(\frac{\partial^2 \varphi}{\partial S_1^2}\ \theta^2 S_1\right)\Big] > 0 \end{aligned}$$

if $\lambda > 1$ and $\partial^2 \varphi / \partial S_1^2 \geq 0$ regardless of the distribution of θ.

We can only determine the sign of $\sigma^2(Z_1') - \sigma^2(z_1')$ if $\lambda > 1$ (i.e., the bias is positive). Let $s_1 = \eta(S_1) + \varepsilon$, where $\partial \eta / \partial S_1 > 0$, $E(\varepsilon) = 0$, and θ, ε, and S_1 are pairwise independent. Suppose θ is small. Then $\sigma^2(Z_1') > \sigma^2(z_1')$ if $\partial^2 \varphi / \partial S_1^2 \geq 0$ and θ has a symmetric distribution. If θ is large, $\sigma^2(Z_1') > \sigma^2(z_1')$ if we add the condition $\partial^3 \varphi / \partial S_1^3 \geq 0$.

30. For period 1 let S_1 denote satisfaction with the agent and S_1^P satisfaction with the product. Then sales in period 2 are $s_2 = \varphi(s_1, S_1, S_1^P)$, where s_1 denotes sales in period 1. Suppose the agent and the firm have exponential utilities. Then optimal risk sharing requires that the agent's income at the end of period 1 is

$$ y_1 = w_1 + \left(\frac{c_1}{c_1 + c_2} \right) (p - \omega) \left(s_1 + \frac{\varphi(s_1, S_1, S_1^P)}{1 + d} \right) $$

where w_1 denotes the agent's fixed wage and d is the common discount rate.

Suppose that only customer satisfaction with the product in the current period has an effect on future sales [i.e., $s_2 = \varphi_1(s_1, S_1^P)$] and that the measured satisfaction $S_1^M = S_1^P$. Then the optimal contract is

$$ y_1 = w_1 + \left(\frac{c_1}{c_1 + c_2} \right) (p - \omega) \left(s_1 + \frac{\varphi(s_1, S_1^M)}{1 + d} \right) $$

Note that optimal risk sharing depends on customer satisfaction with the product even though the agent has no control over this outcome. The firm, however, will choose suboptimal contracts in the future if it uses S_1^M as a measure of the agent's ability.

In general $s_2 = \varphi(s_1, S_1, S_1^P)$, where both S_1 and S_1^P are unobserved. Hence empirical methods (discussed later) are necessary for estimating S_1 and S_1^P.

31. Let ξ denote the candidate's unobserved ability and x the judge's rating score. Let j index the candidates and i the judges. Then $x_{ij} = v_i + \lambda_i \xi_j + \delta_{ij} (i = 1, \ldots, I; j = 1, \ldots, J)$, where v_i varies over i (i.e., the judges use different anchor points), λ_i varies over i (i.e., the judges have different reliabilities), and $i \geq 3$ for identifiability. Let $\sum_{xx}$ denote the population covariance matrix of the xs and $\sum_{\delta\delta}$ the diagonal population covariance matrix of the δs. Set $\sigma^2(\xi) = 1$ for identification. Let $x_j = (x_{ij})$ denote the vector of rating scores for candidate j, $\hat{\sum}_{xx}$ the fitted covariance matrix of the xs , and $\hat{\Lambda}$ the estimated vector of factor loadings.

Now the factor scores ξ_j are inherently indeterminate because the number of latent variables and measurement errors $(I + 1)$ exceeds the number of observables (I). Consequently several methods are available for factor score estimation (see McDonald and Burr 1967; Lawley and Maxwell 1971; and Saris, de Pijper, and Mulder 1978). For example, Lawley and Maxwell's method (1971, p. 109) gives the factor score estimates $\hat{\xi}_j = \hat{\Lambda}' \hat{\sum}_{xx}^{-1} x_j$, where the elements of $\hat{\Lambda}' \hat{\sum}_{xx}^{-1}$ are the estimated factor score regression weights. Note that these weights depend on the accuracies (i.e., the λs) and the degree of congruence among the judges (i.e., $\hat{\sum}_{xx}$). Furthermore, the factor score regression weights do not in general sum to unity and are unequal. One potential difficulty is that the different estimators need not rank the $\hat{\xi}_j$ identically; in practice, however, the $\hat{\xi}_j$ estimates are often highly correlated across methods.

32. Consider the Lawley–Maxwell estimator (see previous note). Then the estimated factor score for

candidate j is $\hat{\xi}_j = \hat{\Lambda}' \hat{\sum}_{xx}^{-1} x_j = \sum_{i=1}^{I} \hat{w}_i \, x_{ij}$, where the $\hat{w}$s denote the estimated factor score regression weights and the x_{ij}s denote judge is rating of candidate j. We know that the $\hat{w}_i$s are consistent estimators of the true weights w_i. For a large sample consider the distribution of $\hat{\xi}_j$ conditional on the rating scores x_j. Suppose ξ^* is the threshold level of ability under certainty. Then the risk-neutral firm will use $\hat{\xi}_j$ to rank the candidates and will only interview those candidates for whom $\hat{\xi}_j > \xi^*$. The firm can refine the personnel selection procedure if it knows the relationship between the agent's ability (ξ) and performance (η). Suppose there are diminishing returns to ability (i.e., η is concave in ξ). Let η^* denote the threshold level of performance under certainty and ξ^* denote the corresponding threshold level of ability. Let ξ^{**} denote the threshold level of ability under uncertainty. Then $\xi^{**} > \xi^*$ using Jensen's inequality. Hence the risk-neutral firm uses $\hat{\xi}_j$ to rank the candidates as before but only interviews candidates for whom $\hat{\xi}_j > \xi^{**}$.

33. Suppose the firm is risk-averse. Now the firm cannot rank the candidates using $\hat{\xi}_j$ even in the simple case where the ability–performance relationship is known. In particular, the firm must analyze the third- and higher-order moments of $\hat{\xi}_j | x_j$ and specify its utility function before making the personnel selection decision. For example, suppose x_j has a multivariate normal distribution. Then $\hat{\Lambda}$ has an asymptotic normal distribution; the distribution of $\hat{\sum}_{xx}^{-1}$, however, is unknown. Thus $\hat{\xi}_j | x_j$ cannot be normally distributed. Hence the firm must use numerical methods to analyze the higher-order moments of $\hat{\xi}_j | x_j$.

34. Let z_{bj} denote the jth candidate's score on background variable $b(b = 1, \ldots, B; j = 1, \ldots, J)$. Then the ability model has the MIMIC form $\xi_j = \gamma_0 + \sum_{b=1}^{B} \gamma_b z_{bj} + \zeta_j, x_{ij} = v_i + \lambda_i \xi_j + \delta_{ij}$, where the γs are parameters, ζ_j is a stochastic disturbance term, and $i = 1, \ldots, I$ indexes the judges. For notational convenience we shall continue to refer to ability as ξ even though ability is endogenous in the MIMIC model.

   Set $\lambda_1 = 1$ for identification. Then $\hat{\xi}_j = \sum_{i=1}^{I} \hat{w}_i x_{ij} + \sum_{b=1}^{B} \hat{a}_b z_{bj}$, where the w_is and $\hat{a}_b$s denote factor score regression weights. In the special case $i = 1$ the model reduces to $x_{ij} = (v_1 + \gamma_0) + \sum_{b=1}^{B} \gamma_b z_{bj} + (\zeta_j + \delta_{ij})$. Hence $\sigma^2(\zeta_j)$ and $\sigma^2(\delta_{1j})$ are not identified (i.e., the structural and measurement errors cannot be separated).

35. Let η denote the agent's unobserved performance and f index the indicators y, which measure performance ($f = 1, \ldots, F$). Then the augmented model is

$$\xi_j = \gamma_0 + \sum_{b=1}^{B} \gamma_b z_{bj} + \zeta_j$$

$$x_{ij} = v_i + \lambda_i \zeta_j + \delta_{ij}$$

$$\eta_j = \alpha + \beta \xi_j + u_j$$

$$y_{fj} = \theta_f + \mu_f \eta_j + \varepsilon_{fj}$$

where $\alpha, \beta, \theta_f, \mu_f$ are parameters and u_j and ε_{fj} are stochastic disturbances. Set $\lambda_1 = 1$ and $\mu_1 = 1$ for identification. Then $\hat{\xi}_j = \sum_{i=1}^{I} \hat{w}_i x_{ij} + \sum_{b=1}^{B} \hat{a}_b z_{bj} + \sum_{f=1}^{F} \hat{d}_f y_{fj}$, where the $\hat{w}_i, \hat{a}_b$, and $\hat{d}_f$ denote the factor score regression weights.

   Suppose the ability–performance relationship is nonlinear, e.g., $\eta_j = \alpha + \beta_1 \xi_j + \beta_2 \xi_j^2 + u_j$. Now, in contrast to the linear model, it is necessary to make distributional assumptions to establish identifiability. Suppose ξ_j and the disturbances have a multivariate normal distribution. Then the system of equations is identified and one can estimate the model using a generalized least-squares approach (e.g., McDonald's COSAN procedure, which is described in Fraser 1980). See Kenny and Judd (1984, pp. 201–2) for a simple description of how to set up the measurement model for nonlinear terms (e.g., ξ_j^2).

36. Consider the exponential utility case. Let s_1 denote the uncertain sales when the firm does not use a training program, p denote price, and ω the constant unit production cost. Let y_1 and y_1', respectively, denote the agent's income when the firm does not use a training program and when the firm uses a predetermined firm-specific training expenditure of $\bar{T}$. Let $\varphi(\bar{T})$ denote the increase in sales after the training program. Then $y_1 = w_1 + [c_1/(c_1 + c_2)](p - \omega)s_1$ and $y_1' = w_1' + [c_1/(c_1 + c_2)](p - \omega)[s_1 + \varphi(\bar{T}) - \bar{T}]$, where w_1 and w_1' denote the agent's fixed wages for the two scenarios. Because the training program is firm-specific, the agent's reservation income does not change. Hence $w_1' < w_1$. Note that the agent and the firm share the training cost in the ratio $c_1 : c_2$ (i.e., the more risk-averse player pays a smaller proportion of the training cost). This result holds even if the effect of training is stochastic. Furthermore $y_1' = w_1'' + [c_1/(c_1 + c_2)](p - \omega)[s_1 + \varphi(\bar{T})]$, where $w_1'' = w_1' - [c_1/(c_1 + c_2)](p - \omega)\bar{T} < w_1'$. Hence there is no need for the firm to include training cost explicitly in the contract; specifically, the firm can continue to pay the agent a commission based on sales after the agent has completed the training program.

37. See previous note.

38. If s_1 is normally distributed, the agent's expected utility after the training program is

$$Eu_1(y_1') \cong E(y_1') - \left(\frac{1}{2c_1}\right)\left(\frac{c_1}{c_1 + c_2}\right)^2 (p - \omega)^2 \sigma^2(s_1) = \bar{u}_1$$

where $\bar{u}_1$ denotes the agent's constant certainty-equivalent income. Hence $E(y_1') = E(y_1)$.

39. Let the increase in sales volume after the agent has been trained be $\varphi_1(\bar{T}) + \varphi_2(\bar{T})h_1$, where $\bar{T}$ is predetermined and h_1 is stochastic. Let $\pi = (p - \omega)s_1$ denote the gross profit before the agent attends the training program and $\pi' = (p - \omega)[s_1 + \varphi_1(\bar{T}) + \varphi_2(\bar{T})h_1]$ the gross profit after the agent has been trained. Then the agent's income before the training program is $y_1 = w_1 + m$, where the commission income is $m = [c_1/(c_1 + c_2)](p - \omega)s_1$ and the agent's post-training income is $y_1'' = w_1'' + m''$, where $m'' = [c_1/(c_1 + c_2)](p - \omega)[s_1 + \varphi_1(\bar{T}) + \varphi_2(\bar{T})h_1]$ and the fixed wage w_1'' is adjusted for the training cost. Then $E(m'') > E(m)$, regardless of the distributions of s_1 and h_1.

Let σ^2 and Cov, respectively, denote the variance and covariance operators. Then

$$\sigma^2(y_1) = \left(\frac{c_1}{c_1 + c_2}\right)^2 (p - \omega)^2 \sigma^2(s_1)$$

$$\sigma^2(y_1'') = \left(\frac{c_1}{c_1 + c_2}\right)^2 (p - \omega)^2[\sigma^2(s_1) + \sigma_2^2(\bar{T})\sigma^2(h_1) + 2\varphi_2(\bar{T})\,\text{Cov}(s_1, h_1)]$$

Recall that the agent's post-training reservation income is unchanged.

Suppose s_1 and h_1 are normally distributed. If $\text{Cov}(s_1, h_1) \geq 0$, $\sigma^2(y_1'') > \sigma^2(y_1)$. Hence $E(y_1'') > E(y_1)$. Furthermore $w_1'' - w_1 = A + B$, where

$$A = \frac{-c_1}{c_1 + c_2}[\varphi_1(\bar{T}) + \varphi_2(\bar{T})E(h_1)] < 0$$

$$B = \frac{1}{2c_1}\left(\frac{c_1}{c_1+c_2}\right)^2 (p-\omega)^2 [\varphi_2^2(\bar{T})\sigma^2(h_1) + 2\varphi_2(\bar{T})\,\mathrm{Cov}(s_1, h_1)] > 0,$$

if $\mathrm{Cov}(s_1, h_1) \geq 0$

Note that the mean training effect A tends to reduce the agent's fixed wage. In contrast the increase in the variability of gross profit, $(p-\omega)^2[\varphi_2^2(\bar{T})\sigma^2(h_1) + 2\varphi_2(\bar{T})\,\mathrm{Cov}(s_1, h_1)]$, tends to increase the agent's fixed wage.

Suppose the training program is aggressive (i.e., training helps the agent to sell more when market conditions are good). Then $\mathrm{Cov}(s_1, h_1) > 0$ and it is likely that B will swamp A (i.e., $w_1'' > w_1$).

40. This partial equilibrium analysis implicitly assumes that the firm faces an infinitely elastic supply of agents with reservation utility $\bar{u}_1$. In general the supply curve of agents of a given ability is upward sloping. Consequently $\bar{u}_1$ increases when firms increase their firm-specific training outlays. Thus there is upward pressure on the fixed wage rate.

41. Suppose both the agent and the firm have logarithmic utilities. Then the agent's income before the training program is $y_1 = \lambda_1(p-\omega)s_1$, where $0 < \lambda_1 < 1$ (see note 7). After the training program the agent's income is $y_1' = \lambda_1'(p-\omega)[s_1 + \varphi_1(\bar{T}) + \varphi_2(\bar{T})h - \bar{T}]$, where h is in general stochastic and $0 < \lambda_1' < 1$. Hence the commission rate always declines after the training program ($\lambda_1' < \lambda_1$). Suppose the training effect is deterministic or defensive [i.e., $\mathrm{Cov}(s_1, h_1) < 0$ and is sufficiently large]. Then the variance of the agent's income falls after the training program [$\sigma^2(y_1') < \sigma^2(y_1)$]. Regardless of the scenario, the effect of the training program on the agent's expected income is indeterminate. Note that in contrast to the exponential utility model, the form of the contract depends on whether the firm pays commission on the basis of gross profit or sales. In the latter case the agent pays the firm a fee of $\lambda_1'(p-\omega)\bar{T}$.

42. Suppose the firm and the agent are risk-averse. Let T denote the outlay on firm-specific training. Then the gross profit after training is $\pi(T) = (p-\omega)[s_1 + \varphi(T) + h - T]$, where h is stochastic. Let $\hat{T}$ maximize $\varphi(T) - T$ and $\hat{\hat{T}}$ denote any other value of T. Let $\hat{f}(\pi(\hat{T}))$ and $\hat{\hat{f}}(\pi(\hat{\hat{T}}))$, respectively, denote the firm's shares when $T = \hat{T}$ and $T = \hat{\hat{T}}$.

Suppose $T = \hat{\hat{T}}$. Then the firm's share is $\hat{\hat{f}}(\pi(\hat{\hat{T}}))$ and the agent's share is $\pi(\hat{\hat{T}}) - \hat{\hat{f}}(\pi(\hat{\hat{T}}))$, where the firm chooses $\hat{\hat{f}}$ to provide the agent his reservation income.

Suppose $T = \hat{T}$. Now $\pi(\hat{T}) - \pi(\hat{\hat{T}}) = R > 0$. Hence for any state the firm can obtain $\hat{\hat{f}}(\pi(\hat{\hat{T}})) + R$ and pay the agent $\pi(\hat{\hat{T}}) - \hat{\hat{f}}(\pi(\hat{\hat{T}}))$. Consequently $\hat{\hat{T}}$ cannot be optimal. Thus the firm proceeds in two steps: First choose T^* to maximize $\varphi(T) - T$ and then choose the optimal contract based on the risk aversions of the firm and the agent.

43. The separation result of the previous note does not hold if the training effect has the general form $\varphi(T, h)$. In this case the sign of $\varphi(\hat{T}) - \varphi(\hat{\hat{T}})$ is state-dependent. Hence T^* depends on the risk aversions of the players.

44. Suppose the agent and the firm, respectively, have exponential utilities with parameters c_1 and c_2. Let sales after the training program be $s_1 + \varphi_1(T) + \varphi_2(T)h_1$, where T denotes firm-specific training, $\varphi_2(T) \neq 1$, s_1 and h_1 and are normally distributed, and $\mathrm{Cov}(s_1, h_1) \neq 0$ in general. Then the firm chooses T^* to maximize its certainty-equivalent income

$$M = (p - \omega)[E(s_1) + \varphi_1(T) + \varphi_2(T)E(h_1) - T] - \bar{u}_1 - \frac{(p - \omega)^2}{2(c_1 + c_2)}$$

$$[\sigma^2(s_1) + \varphi_2^2(T)\sigma^2(h_1) + 2\varphi_2(T)\,\mathrm{Cov}(s_1, h_1)]$$

where $\bar{u}_1$ denotes the agent's certainty-equivalent income. Hence T^* depends on the risk aversions of the players (c_1 and c_2).

Let $\bar{T}^*$ be the optimal firm-specific training in the quasicertainty case, where after-training sales are $s_1 + \varphi_1(T) + \varphi_2(T)E(h_1)$. Suppose $\mathrm{Cov}(s_1, h_1) \geq 0$ (i.e., the training effect is independent of sales or training helps the agent to sell more when market conditions are good). Then $T^* > (<) \bar{T}^*$ if $\partial\varphi_2(T)/\partial T < (>)0$. Other comparative static results can be determined similarly.

45. Consider a two-period model in which the firm trains the agent in period 1. Suppose the agent and the firm, respectively, have time-additive exponential utility functions with parameters c_1 and c_2; in addition, the common discount rate is d. If the training is firm-specific, the agent's certainty-equivalent income is $\bar{u}_1$ for both periods. If the training is portable, the agent's certainty-equivalent incomes for periods 1 and 2, respectively, are $\bar{u}_1$ and $\bar{u}_1 + \mu(T) - n$, where $\mu(T) > 0$ is the increase in the agent's reservation income after training, $n > 0$ is the agent's search cost in finding another job, and $\mu(T) - n > 0$ to avoid a trivial solution. Let sales in period i be $s_i + \varphi_1(T) + \varphi_2(T)h_i$, where h_i is stochastic ($i = 1, 2$) and the vector stochastic process (s_i, h_i) has a bivariate normal distribution and is covariance stationary, i.e., $\sigma^2(s_1) = \sigma^2(s_2)$ and $\mathrm{Cov}(s_1, h_1) = \mathrm{Cov}(s_2, h_2)$.

    If training is firm-specific, the firm chooses T^* to maximize the net present value, M_1, of its certainty-equivalent incomes, where

$$M_1 = \sum_{i=1}^{2} \left(\frac{Q_i}{(1 + d)^{i-1}} \right) - T - \bar{u}_1 \left(1 + \frac{1}{1 + d} \right), \qquad \text{where}$$

$$Q_1 = \Bigg((p - \omega)[E(s_i) + \varphi_1(T) + \varphi_2(T)E(h_i)] - \frac{(p - \omega)^2}{2(c_1 + c_2)}[\sigma^2(s_i) + \varphi_2^2(T)\sigma^2(h_i) + \dots$$

$$+ 2\varphi_2(T)\,\mathrm{Cov}(s_i, h_i)] \Bigg)$$

   If training is portable, the firm chooses T^{**} to maximize the net present value $M_2 = M_1 - (1 + d)^{-1}[\mu(T) + n]$. Now $\partial M_2/\partial T < 0$ when $T = T^*$ because $\partial\mu(T)/\partial T > 0$; furthermore, M_2 is concave in T. Hence $T^{**} < T^*$ (i.e., the firm spends less on training when the agent's skills are portable).

46. Suppose the training effect is $\varphi(T) + h_i$, where h_i is stochastic. Let $w_{1,i}^*$ and $w_{1,i}^{**}$, respectively, denote the agent's fixed wages in period i ($i = 1, 2$) in the firm-specific and portable training cases where commissions are based on gross profits (i.e., the agent's share of the training cost is absorbed into the fixed wage). Let $y_{1,i}^*$ and $y_{1,i}^{**}$, respectively, denote the agent's incomes in period i for the firm-specific and portable training scenarios. Recall that in the firm-specific training case, the agent's reservation income ($\bar{u}_1$) is constant for both periods. If the training is portable, the agent's reservation income in the second period $[\bar{u}_1 + \mu(T^{**}) - n]$ is higher than in the first. Assume that (h_i, s_i) has a bivariate normal distribution and is covariance stationary.

Then $w_{1,i}^{**} - w_{1,i}^* = [c_1/(c_1 + c_2)](p - \omega)[\varphi(T^*) - \varphi(T^{**})] > 0$. That is, portability leads to a higher fixed wage in the first period after allowing for different outlays by the firm on training in the firm-specific and portable training cases. Similarly

$$w_{1,2}^{**} - w_{1,2}^* = [\mu(T^{**}) - n] + \frac{c_1}{c_1 + c_2}(p - \omega)[\varphi(T^*) - \varphi(T^{**})] > 0$$

The variance of sales does not depend on training. Hence $\sigma^2(y_{1,i}^*) = \sigma^2(y_{1,i}^{**})$, $E(y_{1,1}^*) = E(y_{1,1}^{**})$, and $E(y_{1,2}^{**}) > E(y_{1,2}^*)$.

Note that these results do not depend on the sign of $\text{Cov}(s_1, h_1)$, i.e., whether the training program is neutral, aggressive, or defensive.

47. Suppose the training effect is $\varphi_1(T) + \varphi_2(T)h_1$, where $\varphi_2(T) \neq 1$ and the sign of $\partial\varphi_2(T)/\partial T$ is not specified. Then

$$\sigma^2(y_{1,i}^*) - \sigma^2(y_{1,i}^{*,*}) = \left(\frac{c_1}{c_1 + c_2}\right)^2 (p - \omega)^2[\varphi_2(T^*) - \varphi_2(T^{**})]$$
$$\{2\,\text{Cov}(s_i, h_i) + \sigma^2(h_i)[\varphi_2(T^*) + \varphi_2(T^{**})]\} > (<)0$$

if $\text{Cov}(s_i, h_i) \geq 0$ and $\partial\varphi_2(T)/\partial T > (<)0$, recalling that $T^* > T^{**}$. Hence $E(y_{1,i}^*) > (<)E(y_{1,i}^{**})$ if $\text{Cov}(s_i, h_i) \geq 0$ and $\partial\varphi_2(T)/\partial T > (<)0$.

Similarly

$$w_{1,1}^{**} - w_{1,1}^* = \frac{1}{2c_1}\left(\frac{c_1}{c_1 + c_2}\right)^2 (p - \omega)^2[\varphi_2(T^{**}) - \varphi_2(T^*)]$$
$$\{2\,\text{Cov}(s_1, h_1) + \sigma^2(h_1)[\varphi_2(T^{**}) + \varphi_2(T^*)]\}$$
$$+ \left(\frac{c_1}{c_1 + c_2}\right)(Z^* - Z^{**})(p - \omega)$$

where $Z^* = \varphi_1(T^*) + \varphi_2(T^*)E(h_1)$, $Z^{**} = \varphi_1(T^{**}) + \varphi_2(T^{**})E(h_1)$, and $Z^* - Z^{**} > 0$, recalling that $T^* > T^{**}$. Hence $w_{1,1}^{**} - w_{1,1}^* > 0$ if $\text{Cov}(s_1, h_1) \geq 0$ and $\partial\varphi_2(T)/\partial T < 0$ and indeterminate otherwise. Furthermore

$$w_{1,2}^{**} - w_{1,2}^* = [\mu(T^{**}) - n] + \frac{1}{2c_1}\left(\frac{c_1}{c_1 + c_2}\right)^2 (p - \omega)^2[\varphi_2(T^{**}) - \varphi_2(T^*)]$$
$$\{2\,\text{Cov}(s_2, h_2) + \sigma^2(h_2)[\varphi_2(T^{**}) + \varphi_2(T^*)]\}$$
$$+ \left(\frac{c_1}{c_1 + c_2}\right)(Z^* - Z^{**})(p - \varphi) > 0$$

if $\text{Cov}(s_2, h_2) \geq 0$ and $\partial\varphi_2(T)/\partial T < 0$.

48. Suppose the agent and the firm have time-additive logarithmic utility functions and a common discount rate d. Let U_2^f and U_2^p, respectively, denote the firm's utility functions for the firm-specific and portable training scenarios. Then for the firm-specific training case the firm chooses T^* to maximize

$$E(U_2^f) = E \, \log\{\lambda_2(p - \omega)[s_1 + \varphi(T, h_1) - T]\}$$
$$+ (1 + d)^{-1} E \, \log\{\lambda_2^f(p - \omega)[s_2 + \varphi(T, h_2)]\}$$

where $\lambda_2 = \lambda_2(\bar{u}_1, T)$ and $\lambda_2^f = \lambda_2^f(\bar{u}, T)$, respectively, denote the firm's shares of the net profits in periods 1 and 2, and $\bar{u}_1$ denotes the agent's reservation incomes in both periods. In the portable training case, the firm chooses T^{**} to maximize

$$E(U_2^p) = E \, \log\{\lambda_2(p - \omega)[s_1 + \varphi(T, h_1) - T]\}$$
$$+ (1 + d)^{-1} E \, \log\{\lambda_2^p(p - \omega)[s_2 + \varphi(T, h_2)]\}$$

where $\lambda_2 = \lambda_2(\bar{u}_1, T)$ and $\lambda_2^p = \lambda_2^p(\bar{u}_1', T)$, where the agent's reservation income in period 2 is $\bar{u}_1' = \bar{u}_1 + \mu(T) - n$ and $\mu(T) - n > 0$. If $T = T^*$,

$$\frac{\partial E(U_2^p)}{\partial T} = (1 + d)^{-1} \left(\frac{1}{\lambda_2^p} \right) \left[\left(\frac{\partial \lambda_2^p}{\partial \bar{u}_1'} \right) \left(\frac{\partial \mu(T)}{\partial T} \right) + \frac{\partial \lambda_2^p}{\partial T} \right] < 0$$

But $E(U_2^p)$ is concave in T. Hence $T^{**} < T^*$. This result is distribution-free and applies for any functions $\varphi(T, h_i)$. Contrast the exponential utility case where we assumed normality and considered the linearly separable case $\varphi(T, h_i) = \varphi_1(T) + \varphi_2(T)h_i$.

The effect of portable training on the compensation contract is inherently indeterminate. For example, suppose $\varphi(T, h_i) = \varphi_1(T) + h_i$. Because the sharing rule is linear, we need to determine the sign of

$$q_1 = [s_1 + \varphi_1(T^*) + h_1 - T^*] - [s_1 + \varphi_1(T^{**}) + h_1 - T^{**}]$$
$$= [\varphi_1(T^*) - \varphi_1(T^{**})] + (T^{**} - T^*) = A + B$$

However, $A > 0$ and $B < 0$. Hence the sign of q_1 is ambiguous.

49. Suppose the agent and the firm have any arbitrary risk-averse time-additive utility functions. Then the profit-sharing rules for the second period differ for the firm-specific and portable training cases. Let $E(U_2^f)$ and $E(U_2^p)$, respectively, denote the appropriate discounted expected utilities for the firm. Then $\partial E(U_2^p)/\partial T - \partial E(U_2^f)/\partial T$ is inherently indeterminate even in the simplest case where the training effect in period i is $\varphi_1(T) + h_i$.

50. Consider a two-period model in which the firm can choose either of two strategies. First, the firm can train agents in the first period and retain them in the second period, recognizing that the agents' reservation incomes have increased as a result of training (Strategy 1). Second, the firm can follow a turnover policy by training agents in each period and allowing them to leave at the end of the period (Strategy 2).

Assume that the agent and the firm have time-additive exponential utilities with different risk aversions (c_1 and c_2, respectively) and a common discount rate d. For period 2 let the search cost to the agent of discovering alternative employment be n_1 and the search cost to the firm of finding a new agent be n_2. Let $\mu(T)$ be the increase in the agent's certainty-equivalent income in period 2, given a training outlay T by the firm in period 1.

Suppose the training expenditure does not affect the variability of demand. Let demand in period i be $s_i + \varphi_1(T) + h_i$, where (s_i, h_i) has a bivariate normal distribution where $\text{Cov}(s_i, h_i) \neq 0$ in general. Assume without loss of generality that the profit margins per unit for both periods are unity.

Let $T^{(i)}$ denote the optimal training expenditure for Strategy i $(i = 1, 2)$. Then we can show that the firm prefers the turnover strategy if $\{[\varphi(T^{(1)}) - T^{(1)}] - [\varphi(T^{(2)}) - T^{(2)}]\}(2 + d) + [\mu(T^{(2)}) - n_1] > n_2 + T^{(2)}$. Note that Strategy 2 is more likely to be preferred if d is large; furthermore, the risk aversions of the players (c_1 and c_2) and the signs of $\text{Cov}(s_i, h_i)$ do not affect the firm's choice among strategies.

This result generalizes to the multiperiod case.

51. Suppose training affects the variability of demand [i.e., the demand in period i is $s_i + \varphi_1(T) + \varphi_2(T)h_i$, where $\varphi_2(T) \neq 1$]. Then the firm's choice of strategy will depend on the risk aversion parameters (c_1 and c_2), the sign of $\partial\varphi_2(T)/\partial T$ and the sign of $\text{Cov}(s_i, h_i)$, i.e., whether the training program is neutral, aggressive, or defensive.

Specifically, the firm prefers the turnover policy if

$$\{[\bar{\varphi}(T^{(1)}) - T^{(1)}] - [\bar{\varphi}(T^{(2)}) - T^{(2)}]\}(2 + d) + [\mu(T^{(2)}) - n_1] - B(1 + d)\{2\,\text{Cov}(s_1, h_1)$$
$$+ \sigma^2(h_1)[\varphi_2(T^{(1)}) + \varphi_2(T^{(2)})]\} - B\{2\,\text{Cov}(s_2, h_2) + \sigma^2(h_2)[\varphi_2(T^{(1)}) + \varphi_2(T^{(2)})]\}$$
$$> n_2 + T^{(2)}$$

where $B = [1/2(c_1 + c_2)][\varphi_2(T^{(1)}) - \varphi_2(T^{(2)})]$ and the $\bar{\varphi}(\cdot)$s denote expected demand. This condition is less likely to be satisfied if the training effect is neutral or aggressive [i.e., $\text{Cov}(s_i, h_i) \geq 0$], highly uncertain [i.e., $\sigma^2(h_i)$ is large], or $c_1 + c_2$ is small (i.e., the firm and the agent are highly risk-averse).

52. Suppose the firm (indexed by "2") pursues a turnover strategy. Then industry equilibrium requires that in period 2 other firms (indexed by "3") should be indifferent between hiring an agent who has been trained by firm 2 in period 1 and hiring other agents in the marketplace. Let firm 3's sales in period 2 be $b_2 + \alpha(T^{(2)}) + m_2$, where m_2 is stochastic, $\text{Cov}(b_2, m_2) \neq 0$, and $T^{(2)}$ denotes firm 2's training outlay in period 1. Assume without loss of generality that the unit profit margins are unity for both firms and that the search costs and risk aversions are equal for both firms (i.e., $n_2 = n_3$ and $c_2 = c_3$). Then we can show that

$$\alpha(T^{(2)}) = [\mu(T^{(2)}) - n_1] + n_2 + \frac{1}{2(c_1 + c_2)}[2\,\text{Cov}(b_2, m_2) + \sigma^2(m_2)]$$

Now $\alpha - \mu$ is not concave in $T^{(2)}$ even though α and μ are. Hence such expressions as $\partial(T^{(2)})/\partial n_i$ are indeterminate.

53. Let s denote sales and t index time $(t = 1, \ldots, T)$. Then the agent's sales in period t are $s_t = f(X_t) + g'_t$, where X denotes a vector of regressors (i.e., the marketing mix and uncontrollable variables), f is a deterministic function, and the disturbance $g'_t = \alpha\xi_t + g_t$, where ξ denotes the agent's unobserved ability (which changes over time), $\text{Cov}(\xi_t, g_t) = 0$, and $E(g_t) = 0$. Now $E(g'_t)$ varies with t. Hence the regression estimate $\hat{f}$ is inconsistent and the estimated residuals cannot be used to infer the agent's ability.

54. Let i index sales agents $(i = 1, \ldots, I)$, ξ_i denote agent is unobserved ability, and X_i

the vector of regressors for sales territory i. Then the cross-sectional sales model is $s_i = f(X_i) + \alpha E(\xi_i) + \{\alpha\xi_i - E(\xi_i)] + g_i\}$, where $\alpha > 0$, g_i is stochastic, and $E[\cdot] = 0$. Hence the regression estimates $\hat{f}$ are unbiased. Let the estimated residuals for agents i and i', respectively, be $\hat{r}_i$ and $\hat{r}_{i'}$. Taking probability limits we get $\text{plim}(\hat{r}_i - \hat{r}_{i'}) = \alpha(\xi_i - \xi_{i'}) + (g_i - g_{i'})$. Hence the firm will, on average, correctly rank sales agents by ability; the noise term $(g_i - g_{i'})$ reduces precision.

55. Let the sales model for agent i in period t be $s_{it} = f(X_{it}) + \alpha\xi_{it} + g_{it}$, where f is a function, α a parameter, X_{it} denotes the vector of marketing mix variables in territory i, ξ_{it} is agent is ability, and $E(g_{it}) = 0$. Assume for simplicity that f and α are known. For all i let $\hat{X}_{it}$ and $\hat{\xi}_{it}$, respectively, denote the firm's anticipated values of the marketing mix variables in territory i and agent is ability at the beginning of period t. Then agent is sales quota for period t is $\hat{s}_{it} = f(\hat{X}_{it}) + \alpha\hat{\xi}_{it}$.

Suppose the realized values $X_{it}^* = \hat{X}_{it}$. Then the sales discrepancy from the quota is $d_{it} = \alpha(\xi_{it} - \hat{\xi}_{it}) + g_{it}$, where ξ_{it} denotes agent is true ability and $E(d_{it}) = \alpha(\xi_{it} - \hat{\xi}_{it})$. Hence the firm will on average correctly revise its beliefs about agents' abilities; the disturbances g_{it}, however, reduce precision.

Suppose the realized values $X_{it}^* \neq \hat{X}_{it}$. Then the sales discrepancy from the original quota is $d_{it} = [f(X_{it}^*) - f(\hat{X}_{it})] + \alpha(\xi_{it} - \hat{\xi}_{it}) + g_{it}$, which is meaningless for inferring the agent's ability. Define the revised quota $s_{it}^* = f(X_{it}^*) + \alpha\hat{\xi}_{it}$ and the new sales discrepancy $d_{it}^* = s_{it} - s_{it}^* = \alpha(\xi_{it} - \hat{\xi}_{it}) + g_{it}$. Now $E(d_{it}^*) = \alpha(\xi_{it} - \hat{\xi}_{it})$. Hence the firm can use d_{it}^* to revise its beliefs about agent is ability; as in the previous case, however, g_{it} reduces precision.

56. Let i index sales agents and j index products ($i = 1, \ldots, I$; $j = 1, \ldots, J$, where $J \geq 3$). Then the cross-sectional sales model is $s_{ij} = f_j(X_i^j) + \alpha_j\xi_i + g_{ij}$, where X^j denotes the vector of regressors for product j (including the appropriate time allocations across products), the functions f_j measure the effect of X^j, the α_js are parameters, $\text{Cov}(\xi_i, g_{ij}) = 0$ for all i and j, and $\text{Cov}(g_{ij}, g_{ij'}) = 0$ for all i, $j \neq j'$.

We can show that this mixed regression/factor model is identified, using the result that a one-factor model with three or more indicators is identified. The firm can estimate the model using either a limited-information approach (i.e., first regress s_{ij} on X_i^j and then use the residuals for each product to estimate a one-factor model) or a full-information maximum likelihood method, which specifies the distributions of the random variables and estimates the model in one step. Once the model estimates are available, the firm can use the estimated factor scores to rank the agents according to their ability. See note 31 and references cited therein for details.

57. Let i index sales agents ($i = 1, \ldots, I$), j index products ($j = 1, \ldots, J$), and t index time ($t = 1, \ldots, T$). Then the general dynamic sales model is $s_{ijt} = f_{jt}(X_{it}^j) + \alpha_j\xi_{it} + g_{ijt}$, where the f_{jt} are time-dependent functions, the α_js are parameters, and the following conditions hold for all i, j, t : $E(g_{ijt}) = 0$, $\text{Cov}(\xi_{it}, g_{ijt}) = 0$, $\text{Cov}(g_{ijt}, g_{ij't}) = 0$ for $j \neq j'$, and $\text{Cov}(g_{ijt}, g_{ijt'}) \neq 0$ for $t \neq t'$. Without loss of generality set $E(\xi_t) = 0$ for all t and let $\hat{\xi}_{it}$ denote the estimated factor scores for all i, t. For any given period t, the firm can use the $\hat{\xi}_{it}$ values to rank agents by ability. For any given time interval (a periods), the firm can use $\hat{\xi}_{i,t+a} - \hat{\xi}_{it}$ to determine which agents have improved their ability the most.

In general, the firm's marketing policy varies over the business cycle. Hence, in order to avoid specification error dynamic sales models should include market risk as a regressor. One can generalize the model in a straightforward manner by allowing ability to be endogenous or introducing lagged sales terms.

58. The firm can use the cross-sectional or dynamic mixed regression/factor models to compare, respectively, the abilities of district sales managers at any point of time or to track changes in the managers' ability over time (replace "sales agent" by "district sales manager"). Measuring the ability of divisional managers is more difficult because product lines vary by division. Consequently the firm cannot compare ability using cross-sectional data. If, however, each division sells at least three product lines and time-series product-level sales or profit data are available by division, the dynamic model is identified. Hence the firm can use the estimated factor scores to compare the abilities of divisional managers at any given time and to track changes in the ability of divisional managers over time. Using the same approach, one can compare the abilities (cross-sectionally and over time) of the CEOs of different companies provided each company contains at least three divisions and time-series performance data are available by division for each corporation.

59. The previous discussion (see notes 53–58) assumed that the sales agents belong to one population. Suppose in contrast that the agents belong to K unknown segments based on ability, where K is finite.

   Assume that the f_j and f_{jt} functions are linear and that the vectors of random variables have multivariate normal distributions. Then we can show that the mixture regression/factor model is identified, using the standard approach for establishing the identifiability of structural equation models and the result that mixtures of multivariate normal distributions are identified (see Yakowitz and Spragins, 1968, p. 211). Hence the firm can use limited-information or full-information methods to estimate the f_j and f_{jt} functions and to segment agents according to ability.

   If f_j and f_{jt} are arbitrary nonlinear functions, it is difficult to prove mixture identifiability. (See Titterington, Smith, and Makov, 1985, pp. 35–42, for a succinct discussion.) In these cases the firm should perform simulation studies for particular nonlinear specifications of f_j and f_{jt} to test for identifiability before estimating the mixture model.

60. Let S denote customer satisfaction with the agent and x_{2r} the indicators of S, where $x_{2r} = v_r^{(2)} + \lambda_{2r} S + \delta_{2r}$ $(r = 1, \ldots, R)$, the vs are intercepts, the λs are factor loadings, and the δs are measurement errors such that $\text{Cov}(\delta_{2a}, \delta_{2b}) = 0$ for $a \neq b$. This confirmatory model is identified for $R \geq 3$. Set $E(S) = 0$. Then the firm can use the estimated factor scores $\hat{S}$ as proxies of the agents' abilities.

61. Suppose $R > 3$ in the one-factor model described in note 60. Assume that $x_{24} = v_4^{(2)} + \lambda_{24} S + \alpha S^P + \delta_{24}$, where S^P denotes satisfaction with the product, $\alpha \neq 0$, and $\text{Cov}(S, S^P) \neq 0$. Then the model is misspecified. Consequently the parameter estimates are inconsistent, and the estimated factor scores are meaningless.

62. Assume first that any question measures satisfaction with the product or the agent but not both. Let x_{1m} and x_{2r}, respectively, denote the indicators of customer satisfaction with the product (S^P) and of customer satisfaction with the agent (S), where S^P and S are unobservable. Then the confirmatory factor model is

$$x_{1m} = v_m^{(1)} + \lambda_{1m} S^P + \delta_{1m} (m = 1, \ldots, M),$$

$$x_{2r} = v_r^{(2)} + \lambda_{2r} S + \delta_{2r} (r = 1, \ldots, R)$$

where the vs are intercepts, the λs are factor loadings, $\mathrm{Cov}(S^P, S) \neq 0$, and the δs are measurement errors such that $\mathrm{Cov}(\delta_{1m}, \delta_{2r}) = 0$ for all (m, r) pairs. This model is identified if $M \geq 2$ and $R \geq 2$. Set $E(S^P) = E(S) = 0$.

Then the firm can analyze the pooled data across sales agents and customers and use the set of estimated factor scores $\hat{S}$ for each sales agent as a proxy of that agent's ability. In addition, the firm can use the set of estimated factor scores $\hat{S}^P$ to identify dissatisfied customers and take corrective action if necessary.

Suppose some questions measure both satisfaction with the product and with the agent. Now it is necessary to establish model identifiability on a case-by-case basis. For example, if $M = R = 3$, the model is identified if x_{13} and x_{23} measure both dimensions of satisfaction. Hence the firm can estimate $\hat{S}$ and $\hat{S}^P$.

63. Let the superscripts 1 and 2, respectively, index the pre- and post-training values for the manifest and latent variables (alternatively, the manifest variables can represent the judges' ratings of ability for the first and second periods). Let a index test scores, i the sales agents, x denote the test scores, and ξ the agent's ability.

Then the confirmatory factor model is $x_{a1}^{(m)} = v_a + \lambda_a \xi_i^{(m)} + \delta_{ai}^{(m)} (a = 1, \ldots, A; m = 1, 2)$, where the vs are intercepts, the λs factor loadings, and the δs denote measurement errors, where $\mathrm{Cov}(\delta_{ai}^{(1)}, \delta_{ai}^{(2)}) \neq 0$ in general because the measurements are repeated over time. This model is identified if $A \geq 3$. Set $E(\xi^{(1)}) = 0$. Then the firm can measure the mean training effect and use the factor scores $\hat{\xi}_i^{(m)}$ to compare agents cross-sectionally and dynamically.

Note that the standard multisample method is inappropriate because $\mathrm{Cov}(\delta_{ai}^{(1)}, \delta_{ai}^{(2)}) \neq 0$. If the standard method is used, the parameter estimates will be consistent; the significance tests, however, will be incorrect.

64. Let the subscripts 1 and 2, respectively, index firm-specific and portable ability. Then the confirmatory factor model is

$$x_{ai}^{(m)} = v_a + \lambda_a \xi_{1i}^{(m)} + \delta_{ai}^{(m)} (a = 1, \ldots, A_1; m = 1, 2)$$
$$x_{ai}^{(m)} = v_a + \lambda_a \xi_{2i}^{(m)} + \delta_{ai}^{(m)} (a = A_1 + 1, \ldots, A_1 + A_2; m = 1, 2)$$

where A_1 and A_2, respectively, denote the number of test scores for firm-specific and portable ability and $\mathrm{Cov}(\delta_{ai}^{(1)}, \delta_{ai}^{(2)}) \neq 0$ in general for all a. This model is identified if $A_1 \geq 2$ and $A_2 \geq 0$. Set $E(\xi_1) = E(\xi_2) = 0$. Then the firm can measure the mean training effects for both dimensions of ability. In addition, the firm can use the estimated factor scores $\hat{\xi}_{1i}^{(m)}$ and $\hat{\xi}_{2i}^{(m)}$ to make cross-sectional and dynamic comparisons among agents.

As in the simpler case where ability is unidimensional, the standard multisample approach is inappropriate. If some tests measure both dimensions of ability, one must establish identifiability on a case-by-case basis before estimating the model.

65. See Fama (1980) for a multiperiod model in which the firm's stockholders delegate decision making to the manager (agent). Fama shows that, given certain assumptions (e.g., a competitive labor market and symmetric information for stockholders and managers), a compensation plan exists such that the agent acting in his own self-interest will choose policy to maximize the firm's stock value.

66. Let the random demand be $q = E(q) + \theta_1 + \theta_2$, where θ_1 and θ_2 are stochastic terms such that $E(\theta_1) = E(\theta_2) = 0$, $\text{Cov}(\theta_1, R_m) \neq 0$, and $\text{Cov}(\theta_2, R_m) = 0$, where R_m denotes the random return on the market portfolio. Let p denote price, ω the constant marginal cost of production, F the fixed cost, R the risk-free interest rate, and a_m the market price of risk (i.e., a parameter that measures the collective risk aversion of the stock market as a whole). Let $U(y)$ denote the agent's utility function, $\bar{u}$ the agent's reservation utility, and $y = w + \alpha\pi$ the agent's income, where w is the agent's fixed wage, α the fixed profit-sharing rate, and π the gross contribution margin.

Suppose the capital asset pricing model holds. The firm chooses w and α to maximize its stock value $V = \{-F - w + (1 - \alpha)(p - \omega)[E(q) - a_m \text{Cov}(\theta_1, R_m)]\}(1 + R)^{-1}$ subject to $EU(w + \alpha\{(p - \omega)[E(q) + \theta_1 + \theta_2]\}) \geq \bar{u}$.

Suppose $(\theta_1, \theta_2, R_m)$ has a multivariate normal distribution. Then the parameter $\text{Cov}(\theta_1, R_m)$ measures market risk (cyclicality). Let μ denote the Lagrangian multiplier and $H > 0$ the bordered Hessian determinant.

Then

$$\frac{\partial w}{\partial \text{Cov}(\theta_1, R_m)} = \frac{-a_m(p - \omega)^2 EU' E(U'q)}{H(1 + R)} < 0$$

because $q \geq 0$. Similarly

$$\frac{\partial \alpha}{\partial \text{Cov}(\theta_1, R_m)} = \frac{(p - \omega)a_m E^2(U')}{H(1 + R)} > 0$$

Let $\bar{y} = w + \alpha E(q)$ denote the agent's expected income. Differentiating and simplifying, we get

$$\frac{\partial \bar{y}}{\partial \text{Cov}(\theta_1, R_m)} = \frac{-a_m(p - \omega)^2 EU' \text{Cov}(U', q)}{H(1 + R)} > 0$$

because $\text{Cov}(U', q) < 0$ by risk aversion.

Let σ^2 denote the variance operator. Then

$$\frac{\partial \sigma^2(y)}{\partial \text{Cov}(\theta_1, R_m)} = 2\alpha \left(\frac{\partial \alpha}{\partial \text{Cov}(\theta_1, R_m)} \right) \sigma^2(q) > 0$$

If $w < 0$ the firm charges the agent a franchise fee. When market risk increases, the franchise fee increases, but the franchisee's profit-sharing rate also goes up.

Other comparative statics results can be obtained similarly (see Jagpal 1983a).

67. Suppose the agent's effort is observable. Consider the multiproduct firm that sells J products and employs I agents, each of whom is assigned an exclusive territory. Let j index products, i agents, and F denote fixed cost. For all j let ω_j denote the constant marginal cost of product j. For all i and j let p_{ij} and q_{ij}, respectively, denote the appropriate prices and demand levels, where $\bar{q}_{ij} = E(q_{ij})$. For all i let t_i^* denote the contractually fixed efforts and t_{ij}^* the time allocation plans, where $\sum_j t_{ij} = t_i^*$.

Let $q_{ij} = \bar{q}_{ij}(p_{i1}, \ldots, p_{iJ}; t_{i1}, \ldots, t_{iJ}) + \varphi_{ij}(p_{i1}, \ldots, p_{iJ}; t_{i1}, \ldots, t_{iJ})\theta_{1ij} +$

$\mu_{ij}(p_{i1}, \ldots, p_{iJ}; t_{i1}, \ldots, t_{iJ})\theta_{2ij} = \bar{q}_{ij} + A_{ij} + B_{ij}$, where θ_{1ij} and θ_{2ij} are stochastic terms such that $E(\theta_{1ij}) = E(\theta_{2ij}) = 0$ for all i and j, and the φ_{ij}s and μ_{ij}s are functions. This specification is general because the products can be complements or substitutes (i.e., $\partial^2 \bar{q}_{ij}/\partial t_{im}\, \partial t_{in} \neq 0$ for any i and $\partial^2 \bar{q}_{ij}/\partial p_{im}\, \partial p_{in}$ for $m \neq n$) and the market risk depends on the marketing mix (e.g., for $\partial^2 \varphi_{ij}/\partial t_{im}\, \partial t_{in} \neq 0$ for $m \neq n$). Note that the firm's idiosyncratic risk does not affect the firm's stock value (i.e., $\mathrm{Cov}(B_{ij}, R_m) = 0$ for all i and j, where R_m denotes the random return on the market portfolio).

Let w_i and α_{ij}, respectively, denote the appropriate fixed wages and linear profit-sharing rates for all i and j. Assume that all control variables must be chosen prior to the resolution of uncertainty.

Then the firm chooses the compensation, pricing, and time allocation plans (i.e., the w_is, α_{ij}s, p_{ij}s, and t_{ij}s) to maximize its stock value

$$V = \left(-F - \sum_i w_i + \sum_i \sum_j \{(p_{ij} - \omega_j)(1 - \alpha_{ij})[\bar{q}_{ij} - a_m \varphi_{ij} \, \mathrm{Cov}(\theta_{1ij}, R_m)]\} \right)$$
$$(1 + R)^{-1}$$

subject to $EU_i[w_i + \sum_j (1 - \alpha_{ij})(p_{ij} - \omega_j)q_{ij}] \geq \bar{u}_i (i = 1, \ldots, I)$, where the U_is and $\bar{u}_i$s, respectively, denote the utility functions and reservation utilities for agent i $(i = 1, \ldots, I)$.

Now $V = -F/(1 + R) + \sum_i V_i$, where the value added by agent i is

$$V_i = \left(-w_i + \sum_j \{(p_{ij} - \omega_j)(1 - \alpha_{ij})[\bar{q}_{ij} - a_m \varphi_{ij} \, \mathrm{Cov}(\theta_{1ij}, R_m)]\} \right) (1 + R)^{-1}$$

Hence the firm chooses policy to maximize $\sum_i V_i$ subject to $EU_i \geq \bar{u}_i (i = 1, \ldots, I)$. That is, the multiproduct multiagent problem simplifies to a set of independent single-agent problems.

Consider any agent, say the kth. Suppose $\mathrm{Cov}(\theta_{1kj}, R_m) = 0$ for all j. Then the firm behaves as if it were risk-neutral vis-à-vis agent k (i.e., stockholders can eliminate market risk by diversification). Hence the optimal strategy for the firm is to pay the kth agent a flat wage (i.e., $\alpha_{kj} = 0$ for all j).

Suppose agent ks effort is unobservable and $\mathrm{Cov}(\theta_{1kj}, R_m) = 0$ for all j. Then agent k will shirk if the firm chooses the "first-best" contract (i.e., a fixed wage). Thus, as in the expected utility model, the value-maximizing firm will choose a "second-best" solution in which agent k shares risk (e.g., the firm offers the agent a contract with a fixed wage that is lower than the optimal fixed wage and positive commissions on sales).

We can extend the model to deal with decentralized decision making (see Figure 8.5) and cases where the agent can choose a subset of control variables (e.g., the time allocation plans) after the uncertainty is resolved. Jagpal (1983a,b) discusses the multiproduct multiagent problem in detail and considers a general multifactor model in which market risk has several components.

68. Consider a multiple-agent, multiple product sales model. Let i index products, j index agents, and t_{ij} denote the selling time allocated to product i by agent $j (i = 1, I; j = 1, J)$. Let $\tilde{Z}_n$ denote the nth systematic risk factor $(n = 1, N)$ and $\tilde{Z}_{n+1}$ a firm-specific risk factor. Then $\mathrm{Cov}(\tilde{Z}_n, \tilde{Z}_{N+1}) = 0$ for all n.

Suppose each agent is assigned an exclusive territory. Then the demand for the ith product in agent js territory is

$$\tilde{q}_{ij} = \varphi_{i0j}(t_{1j}, \ldots, t_{Ij}) + \varphi_{i1j}(\tilde{Z}_1, t_{1j}, \ldots, t_{Ij}) + \cdots + \varphi_{iNj}(\tilde{Z}_N, t_{1j}, \ldots, t_{Ij})$$
$$+ \varphi_{i,N+1,j}(\tilde{Z}_{N+1}, t_{1j}, \ldots, t_{Ij})$$

for all i, j. This formulation of demand leads to a profit function that is consistent with Sharpe's multibeta capital asset pricing model (1977) and with Ross's arbitrage pricing theory (1976), assuming constant costs for each product. Note that the φs need not be separable in their arguments and, in general, $\partial^2\varphi(\cdot)/\partial t_{aj}\ \partial t_{bj} \neq 0$ for $a \neq b$ to allow for general patterns of stochastic substitution and complementarity. Jagpal (1983a,b) analyzes this general model structure for both the observable and unobservable effort cases.

69. Suppose the firm assigns product line M_i to advertising agency $i(i = 1, \ldots, I)$. Let Z_i denote the vector of marketing mix decisions (e.g., product prices and advertising outlays) for product line M_i.

Suppose the product lines are independent (i.e., for all $i \neq i'$ the elements of Z_i have no effect on the demands for $M_{i'}$); within a product line, however, the marketing mix variables have joint effects (e.g., the products can be substitutes or complements). Let each product line M_i contain J_i distinct products. Let $\hat{\pi}(M_i)$ denote the certainty equivalent of future gross profits for product line M_i.

Then the firm's certainty-equivalent gross profit before paying the advertising agencies is $\hat{\Pi} = \sum_i \hat{\pi}(M_i)$, where

$$\hat{\pi}(M_i) = \left(\sum_{j=1}^{J_i}(p_{ij} - \omega_{ij})[\bar{q}_{ij}(Z_i) - a_m\varphi_{1ij}(Z_i)\operatorname{Cov}(\theta_{1ij}, R_m)] \right)(1 + R)^{-1}$$

Hence the firm can choose the marketing mix and advertising agency compensation plan for each product line separately.

This separability condition does not hold if the product lines are interdependent [i.e., for at least one pair (i, i'), $\hat{\pi}(M_i)$ depends on $Z_{i'}$, where $i \neq i'$].

70. Consider a simple case where the firm and the agent agree that the demand conditional on the agent's effort is normally distributed. Let $E(s)$ and $\sigma^2(s)$, respectively denote the expected sales revenue and the variance of the sales revenue. Suppose the firm knows that the agent has an exponential utility function; the firm, however, does not know the agent's Arrow–Pratt risk-aversion parameter r. If the agent prefers contract D to contract E, the firm can only conclude that $0.01 E(s) - (r/2)\sigma^2(s)[(0.03)^2 - (0.02)^2] > 100$. Hence the firm cannot infer the agent's beliefs $[E(s)$ and $\sigma^2(s)]$ or risk attitude (r). Because of this ambiguity, the multiagent firm cannot use the agent's choices among contracts to infer the agents' beliefs about their productivities.

Choosing Domestic and International Marketing Strategy in an Uncertain Environment

This chapter discusses some fundamental issues in choosing domestic and international marketing strategy under uncertainty. We shall focus on the firm's product portfolio decision and choice of performance measures; in particular, we shall evaluate the theoretical and empirical validity of several popular managerial propositions.

9.1 DOMESTIC MARKETING STRATEGY

The firm's fundamental strategic decision is to choose an appropriate product mix (portfolio). Marketing theory strongly suggests that the firm should not conduct the analysis at the product level; instead, the firm should conduct a disaggregate analysis and examine different segments for each product. For example, an automobile parts manufacturer should distinguish between two segments: original equipment manufacturers (OEM) and the replacement part market.

Financial theory suggests that sales to different segments are likely to have different degrees of cyclicality (i.e., sensitivity to general market conditions). Thus in our example the firm should expect different returns from the OEM and replacement part markets. Experience shows that different segments have different growth rates and sensitivities to the marketing mix (e.g., price). In many cases the firm cannot meaningfully define segments on a product-by-product basis (e.g., the same set of consumers may purchase several products in the firm's product line).

Suppose that the firm markets one product line and addresses several market segments. Assume that product quality varies by segment, the production process for each quality level is independent, demand is uncertain, and there are no cross-segment marketing mix effects. (These assumptions will be relaxed later.) Then the profits for each segment will be correlated because all segments belong to the same product category and are affected similarly (though not to the same degree) by general economic conditions.

We now evaluate several managerial propositions.

Proposition 1: *The firm should serve several market segments to reduce financial risk.*

Consider the theory that the firm should diversify in order to reduce risk (e.g., the firm should serve a large number of market segments instead of a few). This argument is correct for a firm that is owned by one individual; more investment opportunities are better than fewer, provided the returns on these investments are not perfectly correlated (see Markowitz 1952).

Suppose the firm is owned by many individuals (i.e., stockholders), each of whom has the opportunity to diversify outside the firm. We shall distinguish two scenarios. First, assume that the firm diversifies into a segment that is new to the firm but not new to the marketplace (i.e., the firm targets a segment that is currently served by other firms in the industry). Second, assume that the firm creates a segment that is new to the marketplace.

For both scenarios the cash flow for each segment only depends on the firm's strategy for that segment (i.e., the production process for each segment is different and there are no cross-product marketing mix effects). Hence the stock market values each segment's profitability separately even though the cash flows are correlated across segments.[1]

In the first scenario, prior to the firm's decision to diversify stockholders already have the opportunity to purchase shares in firms that serve the "new" segment. Consequently the firm does not reduce shareholder risk by diversifying. Suppose the product market is competitive (i.e., the prices of all products of the same quality are identical). Then the only way in which the firm can increase its stock value is by improving the expected cash flow from the new segment (e.g., by introducing a more efficient production process to reduce costs).

In the second scenario, the firm offers stockholders a genuinely new investment opportunity (i.e., one which offers a different risk–return combination from existing products offered by extant firms). Consequently diversification can add value (e.g., the new segment offers a somewhat lower expected return than existing segments but reduces market risk considerably because demand is considerably less sensitive to general market conditions). Thus for both scenarios the stock market evaluates each market segment separately: The risk-reduction argument for diversification is irrelevant.[2]

Proposition 2: *The firm should serve several market segments to reduce the risk from sudden changes in demand and production technology.*

This argument is fundamentally different from that presented in Proposition 1 because the firm has the opportunity to make sequential decisions. For example, the firm can either enter a new market segment immediately or postpone the decision until more information is available about the degree of competition in or the growth rate of that segment. Similarly, suppose the firm has already selected a target segment. The strategic decision facing the firm is whether to build a large manufacturing plant immediately to take advantage of experience-curve effects or to build a smaller plant now and add plant capacity later if demand is strong and new production technology becomes available.

For convenience we shall focus on the firm that is owned by many stockholders; the arguments, however, apply equally to the firm which is owned by one individual.

Recall that, by assumption, the market segments are independent (i.e., there are no cost or marketing mix interdependencies). One approach is for the firm to determine the net present value (NPV) of the stream of uncertain cash flows for each segment ("project") separately using a different but fixed discount rate to reflect that segment's market risk.

(Roughly speaking, the discount rate is higher for more cyclical segments.) This approach is incorrect because it implicitly assumes that the firm cannot revise its decisions once uncertainty is resolved (i.e., flexibility in decision making does not add economic value).

As our examples illustrate, adaptive decision making is the sine qua non of strategic planning. The correct economic value of a project is the sum of the value of the "option" provided by decision-making flexibility and the standard NPV computed using the method described above. (See Brealey and Myers 1996, pp. 588–609 for a lucid discussion of real options and numerical examples.) Thus a project whose NPV is negative may be an attractive choice when the firm factors in the economic advantage of future flexibility in decision making. Similarly even if a project has a positive NPV, the optimal policy may be to wait (i.e., the option of waiting has a significant positive value).

In sum, the essence of the proposition is correct: The firm should use the options approach to evaluate explicitly the impact of sudden changes in demand and cost on market value. This principle does not, however, imply that the firm gains from serving a large number of segments.

For example, suppose the firm is considering two strategies: A and B. In Strategy A the firm focuses on a small number of new market segments with limited expected growth potential but can abandon its investment without significant economic loss if market demand is low (e.g., investment consists primarily of plant and equipment that can be adapted at low cost to produce other product lines if the new products fail). In Strategy B the firm focuses on a larger number of market segments that have a higher expected growth potential; the salvage value of investment, however, is low (e.g., investment consists primarily of advertising and developing new specialized distribution channels). One can easily construct scenarios where the firm prefers Strategy A to Strategy B.[3]

Proposition 3: *Research shows that market share and profitability are highly correlated. Hence corporate strategy should focus on building market share rapidly in the targeted segments.*

Empirical studies on market share and profitability typically fail to recognize that the data do not include information on firms that have failed in the marketplace (i.e., there is a sample selection bias). Because the data comprise only successful firms, the observed correlation between market share and profitability may be spurious (i.e., we can only conclude tautologically that a firm is successful because it is successful).

This proposition implicitly relies on two theoretical arguments. First, the "pioneering" firm obtains a strategic demand advantage over late entrants ("followers") because consumers have high switching costs (i.e., the probability of repeat purchase given trial is high). For big-ticket consumer durables consumers may be highly risk-averse; for low-priced products the consumer may behave as if he is risk-averse because of inertia (i.e., the implicit cost of change is high). The pioneer's brand may become the reference brand ("exemplar") against which consumers compare followers' brands. Because consumers are risk-averse, followers are at a strategic disadvantage. For complex industrial products, the purchasing firm may prefer to stay with the pioneer because changing suppliers is likely to lead to a high cost of retraining employees. Second, the pioneering firm can reduce its future costs by building volume to take advantage of experience-curve effects in production or marketing (e.g., advertising or distribution).

Suppose these assumptions hold. The proposition relies heavily on the argument that the firm should sacrifice short-term profits in exchange for higher long-term profits. This argument does not, however, imply that the firm should attempt to maximize market share (see Chapter 1, Section 1.2). If the opportunity cost of capital (i.e., the discount rate for the project) is sufficiently high, building market share beyond a point may actually reduce the firm's value because long-term profits are worth less.

More important, the proposition relies heavily on the assumption that both cost and demand conditions are static. The experience-curve argument essentially assumes that there is no technology spillover (i.e., followers cannot learn from the pioneer), that technology is static, and that there is no uncertainty regarding the magnitudes of the experience-curve effect. The demand argument assumes that the pioneer knows the market segments a priori and can accurately predict the evolution of these segments over time.

These assumptions do not hold in general. As shown in Chapter 1 (Section 1.6), the simultaneous presence of cost and demand uncertainty leads to additional complications. Contrary to the proposition, when demand conditions are turbulent, the prudent strategy for the firm may be to "exercise an option" to wait until new market data are available. Similarly, if new technology is in the offing, the optimal strategy could be to wait because the strategic gains from the experience-curve effect may not materialize. Even if new technology is not imminent, the risk-averse firm may find that the benefits from the experience curve are too uncertain to justify investment.

In summary, the proposition is too simplistic. As discussed in Proposition 2, the economic value of a given strategy is the sum of the net present value of the cash flows from that strategy and the value of the firm's marketing options (e.g., waiting for uncertainty to be resolved). Building market share rapidly may therefore be suboptimal.

Proposition 4: *The firm should use a different rate of return for each product when allocating resources across product lines.*

Suppose the firm is owned by many stockholders. Consider a pasta manufacturer who markets both generic and branded pasta products. Assume that each type of product has a different degree of sensitivity to fluctuations in general economic conditions. Suppose the demand for branded pasta is more sensitive to economic conditions than the demand for generics. Then the market risk (i.e., the risk borne by shareholders after they have diversified across all firms in the economy) of branded pasta is higher than that for generic pasta. Consequently the pasta manufacturer should require a higher rate of return from investing in branded pasta. If the firm applies the same cost of capital to branded and generic pastas, it is likely to overinvest in its branded pasta line and to underinvest in generic pastas.

Thus the proposition should be modified to read, "The firm should allocate resources using a different required rate of return for each *product–market* combination."

Proposition 5: *Firms should make high-quality products to maximize their performance.*

Let us consider this argument theoretically and empirically. Suppose initially that there are no barriers to entry or exit; that is, firms can enter or exit an industry costlessly. Consumers, however, have imperfect information; in particular, one segment is "informed" or "expert" (i.e., this group of consumers can evaluate product attributes with certainty), and the other segment is "uninformed" or "novice" (i.e., this group of consumers does not have high confidence in evaluating the product attributes or benefits).

Given this scenario, and the fact that high-quality products generally cost more to produce, the high-quality firm will attempt to distinguish itself from low-quality firms by signaling (e.g., charging an excessively high price or even dissipating resources by engaging in uninformative advertising!). Of course, this signaling strategy can only work if low-quality firms find it economically wasteful to mimic the signaling policies of the high-quality firms (e.g., a low-quality firm cannot afford to sink money into uninformative advertising).

For simplicity we shall assume that the high-quality firm uses only one signal: price.[4] We shall present a model due to Wolinsky (1983). This model is behaviorally rich because it allows consumers to have heterogeneous and uncertain perceptions, search among brands (i.e., update their perceptions), and evaluate product attributes before making a purchase decision. Wolinsky shows that prices can serve as signals that exactly differentiate the available quality levels. Figure 9.1 represents Wolinsky's fundamental result (Proposition 1 in his paper). DC shows the price–quality equilibrium if all consumers are perfectly informed (i.e., for each quality level there is only one price that equals the marginal cost of production). Because consumers are imperfectly informed, high-quality firms will signal to uninformed consumers by pricing higher than the standard competitive equilibrium price (e.g., a firm that produces a product of quality OC will choose a price of CE instead of CD). The strength of the price signal (the ratio of DE to DC in our example) depends on the proportions of informed and uninformed consumers. Thus price signaling should be prevalent in informationally "noisy" markets and should diminish over time as products progress through the product life cycle.

Now the standard approach in estimating the price–quality frontier is to perform a hedonic regression (i.e., a regression where price is the dependent variable and the various objective dimensions of quality are regressors). Recall that the error terms in a standard regression model can be either positive or negative. Wolinsky's model, however, implies that the regression residuals are strictly non-negative (see DE in Figure 9.1).

To deal with this problem, Kalita, Jagpal, and Lehmann (1991) use a methodology developed in the stochastic production function literature. They test a model where the equilibrium price is the sum of three effects: *A, B,* and *C. A* represents the deterministic effect of the various dimensions of quality (as in the standard hedonic regression model),

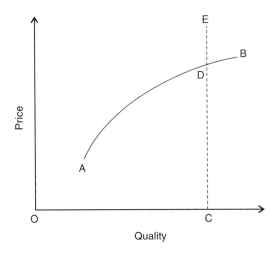

Figure 9.1 A price signaling equilibrium. ADB is the competitive equilibrium frontier; DE, the price signal for quality OC; and DE/DC, the strength of the price signal for quality OC.

B is a random non-negative term (as Wolinsky's model requires), and C is the standard regression error term that captures the effect of omitted variables and misspecifications in the functional form of Λ. Note that the hedonic regression model is a special case of the model (i.e., $B = 0$). Consequently empirical testing is straightforward.[5]

Kalita, Jagpal, and Lehmann (1991) analyze a large data set collected from the annual issues of *Consumer Reports*. The results show that the signaling effect (B) is highly significant for many durable and nondurable products. Markets for nondurables, however, appear to be more inefficient than those for durables. For example, the average strength of the price signal in the VCR industry is 3.3 percent (i.e., the average brand in this industry charges a price that is 3.3 percent higher than the full-information price for the quality provided), whereas the average strength of the price signal in the toilet paper industry is 17.9 percent. These results suggest that markets for frequently purchased nondurable products are inefficient (i.e., the fraction of uninformed consumers is high even though the products are in the mature phase of the product life cycle).

Does the Kalita et al. study show that firms that produce high-quality products are more profitable? No. Wolinsky's model assumes competitive equilibrium. That is firms can enter or exit the industry costlessly. Consequently no firm can earn excess profits. The main insight from Wolinsky's model is that in a world of imperfectly informed consumers firms that charge prices in excess of marginal costs are not necessarily monopolists.

Many empirical results, however, find that quality and profitability are highly correlated (see, for example, the PIMS studies described in Buzzell and Gale 1987, pp. 103–34). We argue that, even allowing for the inferential problems resulting from ambiguous measurements (e.g., the use of accounting measures of profitability and the allocation of joint costs across product lines in a multiproduct firm), the observed quality–profitability relationship is spurious. Excess returns (after controlling for market risk) can occur if and only if there are barriers to entry, market imperfections, or strategic advantages to the high-quality firm (e.g., a strong patent that is difficult to imitate).

We conclude that this proposition leads to a mechanical and potentially harmful approach to strategic planning. Standard signaling models assume unrealistically that the firm cannot identify the uninformed and informed segments. Consequently firms cannot choose customized marketing policies for each segment. Standard signaling models do not capture the behavior of oligopolies because they do not allow for barriers to entry or exit (e.g., advertising is an irreversible investment). Hence we cannot conclude that the observed correlation between profitability and quality is causal.

What practical advice can we offer the marketing manager? Given the absence of a well-developed theory of oligopolistic equilibrium in informationally imperfect markets, we suggest that the manager proceed heuristically using the following sequential procedure.

Use market research to identify and measure the sizes of different consumer segments (e.g., informed and uninformed). Behavioral theory is particularly relevant; in particular, "quality" should be defined in terms of subjective consumer benefits (which are unobserved and uncertain) and not objective measures. Chapter 4, Section 4.6 proposes empirical techniques. Determine the relationship between the objective product attributes (including price as a signal of quality) and consumers' subjective perceptions. Determine the most cost-efficient way of providing a given set of perceived consumer benefits to each segment. (This problem is nontrivial because consumers' perceptions are uncertain.) For each segment estimate a choice model to determine the effect of the firm's marketing decisions and, in particular, price on demand. (As discussed previously, standard signaling models assume that the firm cannot distinguish among types of consumers and consequently pursues an undifferentiated marketing strategy.) Perform sensitivity analysis to predict the effect of competitive reaction (e.g., a price cut by a firm that produces a low-quality product) on the demand for the firm's products and hence the firm's profitability. Use these results to develop a multibrand strategy to maximize performance (after allowing for cannibalization) within the given product category. We shall explain this methodology in detail elsewhere.

Financial theory is particularly relevant when the firm chooses a multibrand strategy. In particular, the demands for some product qualities may be more sensitive to general economic conditions than others (e.g., the demand for high-quality products is more cyclical than the demand for low-quality products). Hence the required rate of return varies by quality level. More important, the firm's strategic options will vary depending on the initial level of product quality chosen by the firm. For example, specialized equipment may be necessary to produce high-quality products (i.e., the salvage value may be low). Similarly, a new set of strategic options may be available to the firm in the future if it introduces a high-quality product and the product is successful (e.g., the firm can sequentially enter the lower-quality segments using the "brand equity" from its previous success in the high-quality segment).

In summary, the proposition is a simplistic guide to strategic planning. The firm should choose product quality on a case-by-case basis using an options-valuation approach and the sequential methodology outlined above.

Proposition 6: *Firms that develop innovative new products should preannounce these products prior to market introduction.*

Preannouncing new products means providing product-related information to the public (e.g., consumers, the stock market, and competitors) well before introducing the product in the marketplace. Thus preannouncing new products is a strategic decision (i.e., the firm gives up its strategic option to wait before choosing marketing policy).

We first examine theoretical arguments. Consider a durable-goods manufacturer whose stock is publicly traded. Suppose the firm preannounces a new product (i.e., the firm publicly releases such new product information as a description of the new product's functionalities or the planned date on which the product will be introduced into the marketplace). Given this information consumers may decide to postpone purchase until the firm introduces the new product or model; in addition, the firm's competitors have the opportunity to develop preemptive strategies. Thus the preannouncement reduces and may even eliminate the value of the firm's marketing options (i.e., the firm sacrifices flexibility in choosing future marketing policy).

Given this loss in strategic value, why should the manufacturer preannounce its new product? Recall that the economic value of an investment is the sum of two parts: the net present value of the incremental cash flows discounted at a project-specific interest rate and the net present value of the option resulting from the opportunity to revise decisions in the future. Thus the preannouncing firm can only gain if the net present value of the firm's incremental cash flows increases. That is, the stock market revises upward its expectations of the firm's future cash flows, perceives that the firm's market risk (i.e., the sensitivity of the firm's cash flows to fluctuations in general economic conditions) has fallen, or both.

Investors will increase their expectations of the firm's future cash flows if they view the firm's preannouncement as a signal of the firm's commitment to the industry. Investors may conclude that the preannouncement will increase the firm's future cash flows by deterring new competitors from entering the industry. These effects on the anticipated cash flows will be especially strong if the manufacturer announces that it will commit considerable project-specific resources to the new product (e.g., the manufacturer announces that it will develop a new specialized distribution channel to market the new product). Investors will conclude that the firm's market risk has fallen if the preannouncement contains information that the firm has made a strategic change to focus on a less risky market segment than those served by its current product line.

Does empirical evidence support the proposition? Koku, Jagpal, and Viswanath (1997) examined the effect of new product preannouncements on stock price using the standard event-study methodology (Fama, Fisher, Jensen, and Roll 1969). They analyzed a sample of 332 preannouncements made during the 1980–1989 period by firms whose stock was traded on either the New York Stock Exchange or the American Stock Exchange. The results show that, on average, preannouncements have a significant positive effect on the preannouncing firm's stock price; the firm's market risk, however, is not affected. That is, the market revises upward the expected cash flows of the preannouncing firm; in particular, the effect of this gain swamps the loss in value that occurs because the firm foregoes the option of flexibility in choosing future marketing policy. This cash-flow effect of preannouncements, however, is industry-specific. Preannouncements have the largest effect on stock price in the manufacturing industry (Standard Industrial Code 390). This result is not surprising: Capital investments in the manufacturing sector are powerful entry-deterrence strategies because these outlays are often lumpy and irreversible (Klein and Leffler 1981). Consequently preannouncements in the manufacturing sector lead to a substantial upward revision of the preannouncing firm's expected cash flows by the stock market.

In sum, preannouncements are only effective if the increase in the net present value of the firm (resulting from the stock market's upward revision of the firm's anticipated future cash flows) exceeds the loss in the value of the firm's future marketing options. These effects are likely to be industry-specific. If entry and exit into the industry are costless and customer switching costs are low, the increase in the net present value of the firm's anticipated cash flows following a preannouncement will be small. If the discount rate is high (e.g., the demand for the new product is likely to be highly sensitive to general economic conditions), the loss in the value of the firm's marketing options following a preannouncement will be reduced. Thus the gain from new product preannouncements depends on industry structure (e.g., barriers to entry and exit, customer switching costs, and market risk) and not whether the product is innovative per se.

Proposition 7: *Managers should evaluate marketing strategy using the theory of financial options.*

There are basic similarities between evaluating marketing strategies and financial options. The option of abandoning a project (e.g., conducting a test market and not introducing the product nationally if the product does poorly) is analogous to a put option. The option of launching new products in the future (e.g., the opportunity to target a niche segment first and broaden the market focus if the product succeeds) is analogous to a call option.

There are, however, several important differences between financial and marketing options. A financial option typically has an expiration date (e.g., the firm may offer the manager an option to purchase up to 5,000 shares of the firm's stock at a guaranteed price at any time during a contractually specified period). Marketing options, in contrast, do not have a finite expiration date because the firm is an ongoing concern. Standard financial option pricing models typically assume that the relevant cash flows are either normally or lognormally distributed; in addition, the decision maker cannot influence the distribution of the cash flows.[6] The normal and the lognormal distributions may not capture the cash flows from new products; more important, the firm's marketing policies are explicitly chosen to influence the distribution of the firm's cash flows. The firm's marketing options can include the opportunity to target new markets in the future; thus stockholders may be unable to construct portfolios of existing stocks and a risk-free asset that can replicate the payoff of the marketing option. (This condition is necessary in financial options pricing models to preclude arbitrage opportunities.) Consequently it may be difficult to choose the appropriate risk-adjusted discount rate to value marketing options.[7]

We argue that these differences are important but not fundamental. The main result of financial option theory applies to marketing strategy. That is, the economic value of a project is the sum of two parts: The net present value of the incremental cash flows (after allowing for joint costs, cannibalization, and complementarity) and the net present value of the options contained in the project. Even though standard financial options theory (e.g., the Black–Scholes 1973 model) may be incorrect for evaluating marketing strategies, the marketing manager can still use a decision-tree approach to determine the value of marketing options (see Hull and White 1988 and Hull 1993). The manager should, however, recognize that marketing options often involve different market segments from those initially targeted. Consequently it is incorrect to apply the same discount rate to the initial and followup projects. For example, if future segments have lower market risk (i.e., demand in these segments is less sensitive to general economic conditions) than the initial segment targeted, the firm should use a lower discount rate to compute the value of the marketing option and a higher discount rate to compute the net present value of the project.

Proposition 8: *The stock market will correctly evaluate a firm's strategic options.*

As discussed in Proposition 7, the marketing manager should use an options framework to evaluate marketing strategies. The problem is that except for preannouncements (see Proposition 6) the firm will not reveal its strategic options to the public. Given this informational asymmetry, will the manager choose marketing strategy to maximize the true economic value of the firm? In addition, will the firm's current stock price correctly measure the firm's long-term profitability?

Suppose the marketing manager is considering two strategies: either continue to target an existing market segment and focus on cost reduction (i.e., pursue a *cost-cutting* strategy) or perform product and market research to develop a new product line for new market segments (i.e., pursue a *market-development* strategy). Assume that the cost-cutting strategy yields a positive net present value (A). The market-development strategy yields a negative net present value (B) and a positive option value (C); in particular this strategy is economically superior to the cost-cutting strategy (i.e., $B + C$ is greater than A). The firm is willing to announce the cost-cutting strategy to the marketplace but, for strategic reasons, is unwilling to preannounce the market-development strategy. Will the manager make the correct choice?

Not necessarily. Suppose the manager's compensation is based on the firm's short-term profits or short-term stock performance, where the short term is 12 months (say). Assume that the uncertainty in the market-development strategy will be resolved during the next 24 months. Then in the short run the stock market will assume that the option embedded in the market-development strategy has no economic value (i.e., $C = 0$). Consequently the firm's short-term stock price will increase if the manager chooses the cost-cutting strategy and decrease if the manager chooses the market-development policy (i.e., the stock price does not reflect true economic value). Hence there is an incentive problem.

Given the inherent informational asymmetry between the firm and the stock market, what can the firm do to make sure that the manager maximizes economic value and the stock market values the firm's marketing options? The firm must compensate the manager, at least in part, on the basis of the future stock price. For example, the firm can offer the manager an option to purchase a specified number of its shares for a guaranteed "exercise" price (at or above the current share price when the option is awarded) during a specified period exceeding 24 months. If the stock price appreciates and the manager exercises his option, he receives the difference between the market price of the stock and the exercise price.

This deferred compensation policy will encourage the manager to choose the strategy that maximizes economic value provided the manager's planning horizon is sufficiently long (in our example at least 24 months) and the manager's discount rate for future earnings is not excessively high. (For managers who live only in the present, the net present value of future income is zero.)

If the manager accepts a deferred compensation plan and chooses the market-development strategy, the stock market will interpret the manager's decision as a signal that the firm has viable marketing options in the future (i.e., the stock market will assign a positive value to C). If this signal is sufficiently strong (i.e., C swamps B), the firm's short-term stock price will rise; because of the informational asymmetry, however, the firm's short-term stock price may not reflect the true economic value of the firm.

We conclude that in general the stock market will not correctly value the firm's strategic options. Furthermore, the manager will not maximize economic value for the firm's stockholders if managerial turnover is high and the managerial labor market uses the manager's short-term performance to infer his ability. These efficiency and incentive problems will be mitigated if shareholders offer managers long-term employment contracts with a deferred compensation plan.[8]

Our discussion so far has assumed that all cost and demand interdependencies across the firm's product lines are purely stochastic (i.e., the firm's marketing decisions for any given product line only affect that product line's profitability). Furthermore, we have implicitly assumed that the firm's organizational structure is fixed (e.g., the firm always buys raw materials from external suppliers). We now relax these conditions.

Proposition 9: *Mergers and acquisitions add economic value to shareholders.*

We shall distinguish several forms of market expansion: vertical integration (e.g., a manufacturer integrates backward when it purchases a raw material supplier and forward if it purchases or establishes a distribution outlet for selling its product), horizontal mergers (i.e., two firms in the same industry merge), conglomerate mergers (i.e., firms in unrelated industries merge), and mergers that lead to economies of scope (e.g., the merger leads to cost savings, sharing of marketing skills and market information, or a reduction in financial risk).

Consider a manufacturer who vertically integrates. No value is added if the industry into which the manufacturer integrates (in our example the raw material or distribution industries) is competitive; value is increased, however, if those industries have market power (e.g., the raw material or distribution industries are controlled by a small number of oligopolists).

Consider an oligopolistic industry. When two firms merge horizontally, their combined market share increases. Consequently the firms can legally "collude" and increase their joint profits. This result is independent of whether or not there are any economies of scope (e.g., the merged firm can reduce the sales force by eliminating duplication).

Do conglomerate mergers add economic value? Consider the argument that conglomerates reduce stockholder risk because the firm is more diversified and therefore less sensitive to unanticipated economic shocks. This argument is specious (see Proposition 1): Stockholders can diversify more efficiently than the firm. There is, however, one source of gain for the conglomerate's stockholders: The merger reduces the probability of financial distress because the cash flows of unrelated firms are not perfectly correlated. Consequently the conglomerate can increase borrowing and the firm can benefit from the increased tax shield.[9]

Suppose a merger leads to economies of scope (commonly referred to as "synergies" in the strategy literature) or new strategic options. As discussed in Proposition 8, management is likely to reveal information about several types of economies of scope (e.g., cost reduction to reduce duplication of resources) to the marketplace; for strategic reasons, however, management will not reveal its private information about other sources of economies of scope (e.g., new marketing options resulting from the merger). Consequently the short-term stock price of the merged firm may not reflect true economic value.

Christian and Jagpal (1988a,b) examined the effect of economies of scope on the merged firm's long-term performance by analyzing data collected from senior managers who were closely involved in mergers in the United States in the 1970s.[10] (The authors followed a census approach and contacted all firms reported in the 1981 *Federal Trade Commission Statistical Report on Mergers and Acquisitions.*) They used a structured questionnaire to collect data from two key informants in each firm, one of whom was with the acquiring firm at the time of the merger and the other of whom was with the acquired firm. Each respondent answered three sets of questions measuring his beliefs about postmerger opportunities and the magnitudes of the economies of scope, distinguishing among three levels of aggregation: the firm level, the "principal business" unit level (i.e., the financial reporting unit in which the acquired firm or the greatest percentage of it was placed), and the "other business" unit level.

Christian and Jagpal (1988a) used multigroup confirmatory factor analysis to analyze the three data sets simultaneously in order to explicitly allow for measurement error in the managers' responses, establish construct validity, and obtain consistent estimates of the unobserved dimensions of the economies of scope (e.g., financial and production synergy) for each level. In contrast to the standard event-study methodology, which measures short-term effects, Christian and Jagpal (1988b) used the growth rates of profitability and sales of the acquiring firm over a three-year period following the merger as proxies of long-term performance (Source: *Value Line* financial tapes).

The results show that, on average, mergers lead to limited economies of scope. At the firm level, there is no relationship between long-term performance and economies of scope. In contrast, at the principal business unit level, economies of scope lead to an improvement in long-run profitability. On average only the transfer of marketing skills (i.e., improved market segmentation, product positioning, and marketing tactics) increases the principal business unit's long-run performance; the other dimensions of the economies of scope (e.g., financial and administrative synergy) are not significant.

We conclude that horizontal mergers and vertical integration in imperfect markets add economic value; conglomerate mergers do not. If the merger leads to a sharing of marketing skills across the acquiring and acquired firms and provides new marketing opportunities (i.e., strategic options), long-term economic value can be added. This gain, however, appears to occur at the principal business unit level and not at the level of the firm.[11]

Proposition 10: *Strategic alliances and joint ventures add economic value to shareholders in the partnering firms.*

Strategic alliances and joint ventures are double-edged swords. The partnering firms gain by sharing complementary technologies or skills; in addition, they reduce financial risk by pooling resources. This policy, however, may result in firms foregoing strategic options in the future. For example, consider a manufacturer who enters into a strategic alliance with a distributor to enter a new market. Over time the distributor will obtain strategic market information and can become a rival, thereby eliminating the manufacturer's future marketing options.

Koku, Jagpal, and Viswanath (1996) used the event-study methodology to analyze the effect of announcements of strategic alliances on the stock prices of the partners. They analyzed 16 strategic alliances involving 33 Fortune 500 firms reported in the *Predicast S & F Index* during the 1980–1989 period. The results show that although in most cases (25 out of 33 firms) the strategic alliances did not have a significant impact on stock prices, industry-specific effects were important. For example, in 1982 when Columbia Pictures and RCA announced a joint project to make video cassettes and video discs (in the largest video agreement to date in the United States), the stock price of Columbia Pictures fell sharply, whereas the stock price of RCA was not significantly affected. In 1985 when John Deere and Avco announced a joint project to develop a turbocharged rotary engine, Avco's stock price fell sharply; John Deere's stock price did not change. In 1986 when Inland Steel, Bethlehem Steel, and Armco announced a strategic alliance to develop jointly a direct sheet-casting process to reduce costs, the stock price of Inland Steel fell sharply but the stock prices of Bethlehem Steel and Armco were unaffected. Only 2 of the 33 firms in the sample (International Harvester and American Home Products in different strategic alliances) experienced significant increases in stock value following the announcement.

We conclude that strategic alliances do not, in general, have a significant effect on the short-term stock prices of the partnering firms. In the short run the stock market appears to penalize firms that choose strategic alliances in areas that are not consistent with the stock market's perception of the firms' "core competencies." Except in rare cases, the short-term stock prices of the partnering firms do not increase following the announcement of the strategic alliance.

These results do not imply that the proposition is false: Empirical research is necessary to test whether strategic alliances increase the stock prices of the partnering firms in the long run (i.e., the stock market may be unable to value the partners' strategic options at the time when the strategic alliance is announced).

Proposition 11: *The information superhighway will lead to the demise of market segmentation and will increase consumer welfare.*

As detailed databases become increasingly available, multiproduct firms will obtain a strategic advantage; for example, by determining consumers' cross-product purchases, they will be able to introduce customized "one-on-one" marketing policies and sell different product bundles to individual consumers. The transaction costs to consumers of determining product quality and price will be substantially reduced. (For example, consumers will be able to "surf" the Internet. Some consumers may even derive positive utility from surfing and discovering the best buys!) In some industries barriers to entry will be reduced because new firms will become increasingly able to target customers given the relatively low investment required to advertise on the information superhighway.

Can we conclude that the growth of the information superhighway will lead to informed consumers, a reduction of barriers to entry and exit, and a competitive equilibrium (i.e., the law of one price)? Marketing theory suggests that in many cases including the purchase of frequently purchased nondurables, consumers have heterogeneous perceptions (i.e., not all consumers are informed). For empirical evidence see the discussion of the Kalita, Jagpal, and Lehmann (1991) study in Proposition 5. In addition, especially in less developed countries and in the poorer segments of developed countries, a large number of consumers will not have access to the information superhighway. Consequently these consumers will still face high transaction costs in determining product quality and finding the lowest-priced vendor for a particular brand.

We conclude that the information superhighway may not lead to an increase in consumer welfare. Analyzing large databases to perform one-on-one marketing requires sophisticated mathematical modeling; large oligopolies will clearly have a strategic advantage over other competitors given the scarcity of such analytical skills in the marketplace. Because of the increased market power of oligopolists who straddle several industries (e.g., strategic alliances among firms in different industries to market product bundles or cross-coupon to selected consumers), we do not expect prices to fall despite the reduction in transaction costs to consumers who use the information superhighway.

A segmented equilibrium is likely to result in which the poorer segments pay higher prices and incur higher search costs than the richer segments. Consequently, especially in less developed countries (where the inequality in income is already significant), we expect a widening gap among the "haves" and the "have-nots." One can only conjecture what this phenomenon will do to future economic growth rates.

Proposition 12: *The manager should be careful in choosing marketing strategy based on statistical models.*

The marketing manager must make decisions based on *estimated* parameter values (which may be subjectively or statistically chosen) because the true values are unknown. Choosing the average or most likely values of a parameter can lead to serious policy errors even if the manager does not allow for competitive reaction.

Consider the following example. Suppose the manager chooses a price of $10 per unit for a given product. Suppose there are three equally likely levels of demand: 50, 100, or 150 units (i.e., the average demand is 100 units). Assume that the unit costs, respectively, for these demand levels are 5, 4, and 5 and the firm is risk-neutral. Then the expected profit given a price of $10 per unit is $533.33. The expected profit corresponding to the average demand, however, is $600, a serious overestimate.

Analytical modeling in this area is scarce. The problem of parameter uncertainty is particularly important in a game-theory setting because a firm does not know either its own parameters or those of its rivals accurately. An important issue therefore is what behavioral mode firms should follow. For example, should firms play a Nash game or should one firm attempt to be the market leader, and if so, which firm?

Choi and Jagpal (1995) examine the effect of parameter uncertainty in a duopoly pricing model where both firms attempt to maximize their respective expected utilities and have different degrees of risk aversion. They show that parameter uncertainty has important implications for marketing strategy; in particular, the results differ considerably from those in the standard case, where all players know their own parameters and those of their rivals with certainty. For example, the potential gains to the market leader from Stackelberg price leadership are likely to be eroded when both the leader and the follower face parameter uncertainty. That is, the prudent strategy may be to wait for other firms to move first rather than to attempt to glean a "first-mover" advantage by becoming the price leader.

We suggest that the manager choose marketing policy by explicitly allowing for competitive reaction and considering parameter uncertainty. In practice, the manager may be unable to specify fully the joint distribution of the parameters; consequently he should examine the profitability of each marketing strategy for different scenarios instead of using the set of average or best-estimate values for the parameters.[12]

9.2 INTERNATIONAL MARKETING STRATEGY

Our previous discussion focused on firms that operate in one country. Many firms invest or operate in several countries; this phenomenon is widespread and increasing. According to a United Nations (1993) study, the number of multinational corporations was as high as 35,000 with control over 170,000 affiliate companies. The largest 100 multinationals, excluding those in banking and finance, accounted for $3,100 billion of worldwide assets in 1990; of this total $1,200 billion was outside the home country of the multinational concerned.

We now discuss some managerial propositions dealing with the special problems faced by multinationals.

Proposition 13: *Multinational marketing theory is inherently different from domestic marketing theory.*

Consider some stylized facts. Across countries consumer preferences differ (e.g., the French prefer stronger coffee than North Americans do), logos and product names have different meanings, incomes vary, and channels of distribution differ. Does it follow that multinational marketing theory is inherently different from domestic theory? We disagree.

Although the marketing manager must certainly be highly sensitive to differences among consumers in different countries, he can apply the standard theory of consumer behavior (e.g., conjoint analysis and choice modeling). For example, consider a U.S. multinational that manufactures a consumer durable product and sells the product in both the United States and France. Suppose consumers in France typically proceed sequentially by first choosing the store (e.g., a department store) and then the brand. In contrast, most consumers in the United States typically choose the brand first and then the store. If the multinational manager in France analyzes data from French consumers using the standard nested logit choice model, the results will clearly show that American and French consumers use different decision processes. (See Chapter 3, Section 3.4 for a discussion of the nested logit model.)

Obviously it would be a serious strategic mistake to assume a priori that French consumers follow the same decision process as U.S. consumers.

Proposition 14: *Multinational firms have a strategic advantage over domestic firms.*

The value of any project, international or domestic, depends on the expected cash flow from that project and the appropriate risk-adjusted discount rate. Most multinationals are oligopolists and enjoy an expected cash-flow advantage over domestic firms for several reasons including superior technology, brand equity, and patent ownership. Whether multinationals also have a lower cost of capital (i.e., the project-specific risk-adjusted discount rate) than domestic firms is an open question.

Consider two extreme theories of international capital markets.

First, suppose the world is a collection of independent domestic economies (i.e., the capital asset pricing model applies separately to each country and barriers prevent the free flow of capital across countries). Then the multinational firm will have an additional cost-of-capital advantage over domestic firms because it expands the set of investment opportunities to its stockholders, allowing them to reduce risk by diversifying across countries. Suppose the world market is segmented and the economies of less developed countries are not strongly related to those of industrialized countries. Then the gain (via a reduced cost of capital) to stockholders of a multinational based in an industrialized country will be maximized if the multinational enters less developed countries.[13]

Second, suppose the world financial markets are completely integrated and the international capital asset pricing model holds (i.e., capital is mobile across national boundaries and the economies of different countries fluctuate together based on world economic conditions). Then stockholders can freely diversify across countries and hold a world portfolio; consequently the multinational does not help its stockholders to reduce risk[14] (i.e., the multinational does not have a cost-of-capital advantage over domestic firms).

In practice, international capital markets are imperfect because of government controls and investor psychology (e.g., the reluctance of many U.S. investors to invest abroad). If there are economies of scale in global scanning to detect departures from international equilibria (e.g., interest rates in a particular country at a given time may be excessively low), multinationals may have a cost-of-capital advantage over domestic firms.

In summary, multinationals have an advantage over domestic firms in terms of expected cash flows and may have an additional advantage from a lower cost of capital.[15]

Proposition 15: *The multinational firm can apply the standard theory of the firm to maximize performance.*

As discussed in Proposition 14, international capital markets are imperfect. Furthermore, compared to their local rivals, multinationals face additional coordination and transaction costs because of logistics, governmental regulations, and the like. Multinationals deal with these problems by choosing an appropriate organizational structure (e.g., product-based, country-based, or a combination matrix approach) and delegating financial and marketing decision making. We shall focus on the country-manager structure in which the country manager is responsible for the firm's product line in a given country. We shall also assume that the firm is owned by stockholders; in particular, the multinational seeks to maximize the performance of the parent.

The multinational must choose corporate strategy flexibly after valuing its marketing options in different countries. (The argument parallels the discussion in Proposition 2.) International markets are typically highly uncertain; hence *ceteris paribus* marketing options are highly valuable (the economic value of an option increases with volatility). To the extent that multinationals have a cost-of-capital advantage over domestic firms, the economic value of these marketing options will be increased.

The multinational must therefore choose a deferred compensation plan to encourage the country manager to evaluate marketing options and choose strategy to maximize the long-term performance of the parent (see Proposition 8). The problem is that, unlike high-ranking multinational executives, the country manager is only responsible for a limited portion of the parent's investments; consequently deferred stock option plans based on the parent's stock are less valuable to him.

We can use two approaches to deal with this incentive problem.

First, suppose that the parent sets up an independent foreign subsidiary and delegates both financial and marketing decision-making authority to the country manager. Now the economic value of the foreign subsidiary to the parent company is the sum of three parts (all valuations should be in the currency of the parent's home base): the net present value of the after-tax operating cash flow (A), the net present value of the tax shield provided by debt raised in the foreign country (B), and the value of the subsidiary's marketing options (C).[16]

The country manager's strategic decisions impact all three components of economic value to the parent. The country manager's marketing and financing decisions are inter-dependent (e.g., the subsidiary's debt level affects the pricing decision and hence the subsidiary's operating cash flows); in addition, the riskiness of each component differs (for example, operating cash flows are risky, whereas the tax shield from debt is certain. Hence the discount rate for the former is higher than that for the latter).

Consequently, the country manager's compensation should be based on three compo-nents: The first is based on the subsidiary's current after-tax operating cash flow, the second on the value of the tax shield provided by the subsidiary's debt, and the third on a deferred stock option plan to purchase up to a specified number of the subsidiary's shares during a given time period. The profit-sharing rates should reflect the appropriate degrees of risk for each component (e.g., net after-tax operating cash flows are more risky than the tax shield from debt), and the time period during which the country manager can exercise his stock option should be at least as long as the period during which the subsidiary can exercise its marketing options (this period may vary from country to country). See discussion of Proposition 8.

Standard accounting measures of profitability should be adjusted to measure economic profit (e.g., cannibalization effects that occur if one subsidiary impacts the economic performance of another) and cash flows over which the manager has no control (e.g., interest-rate subsidies by the host country and funds-flow adjustments and group hedging decisions that are coordinated by the parent company) should be excluded from the country manager's compensation plan.[17]

An interesting issue is whether the country manager should be paid in local currency given that the multinational seeks to maximize performance measured in the home currency of the parent. We argue that, for strategic planning purposes, the parent should measure the subsidiary's net economic value by projecting cash flows (A, B, and C, respectively) in local currency terms, adjust these values for the expected rate of local inflation using different discount rates for each component to reflect their differential riskiness, and then convert these values to home currency flows by using future exchange rates, allowing for home taxes and anticipated inflation in the home country. For administrative simplicity and efficiency, we argue that the country manager should be compensated in local currency.[18]

Suppose the parent chooses financial policy on a centralized basis (e.g., the parent chooses the debt policies of all subsidiaries or provides subsidiaries with debt financing) but delegates marketing decision making to country managers. Then the tax shield component

(*B*) of the parent's value is outside the country manager's control. Consequently, the country manager's compensation should be based only on the net after-tax operating cash flow of the subsidiary and a deferred compensation plan based on the subsidiary's future net after-tax operating cash flow, where the time period for the deferred plan should exceed the anticipated period during which the subsidiary can exercise its marketing options.

In conclusion, multinationals cannot apply the standard theory of the firm directly (e.g., offer country managers deferred compensation plans based on ownership of the parent's stock) to maximize the parent's performance. We expect the future supply of efficient global managers to be limited; in addition, the volatility of demand across countries is likely to increase (i.e., marketing options will become increasingly valuable). Consequently, multinationals must reward country managers on the basis of long-term performance in order to reduce managerial turnover and maximize the parent's performance.

Proposition 16: *Multinational firms should pursue global strategies.*

We begin with the simple case where the parent and the country manager share the same information.

Suppose the parent owns independent production facilities in each country and cost and demand conditions are homogeneous across countries. Then the firm should pursue a global strategy (i.e., choose the same marketing policy in each country).[19] If demand is heterogeneous across countries but there are strong experience effects or economies of scale in production and advertising ("cost economies"), global strategies will be efficient provided the cost economies are sufficiently strong to swamp the demand differences across countries. If demand heterogeneity is significant but there are substantial cost economies, the multinational may prefer to use a partially global strategy in which it chooses a common product quality for all countries but uses customized marketing policies (e.g., price and advertising strategies) for each country. An additional reason for choosing a partially global strategy is that the multinational's product may be in different phases of the product life cycle in different countries; in such cases a global strategy is likely to be a strategic mistake.

When deciding on the appropriateness of a global strategy, the multinational must recognize that the economic value of different marketing options in a given country is likely to depend heavily on the marketing strategies it pursues in that country. The value of these options in less developed countries is likely to exceed substantially those from investments in the parent country, where the market is often saturated; this value is enhanced to the extent that multinationals enjoy a cost-of-capital advantage over local firms. To the extent that these international differences are significant, a global strategy is likely to be suboptimal.

Consider the more likely case where country managers and the parent do not share the same information. Then the difficulties stemming from a global strategy will be exacerbated because of incentive problems.

We therefore argue that strictly global strategies can be dysfunctional despite the obvious benefits from reduced coordination costs; in particular, multinationals should pursue country-specific policies and delegate at least partial marketing responsibility to the country manager. For this strategy to work, however, the multinational must compensate country managers using a deferred compensation plan based on the long-term performance of the subsidiary (see Proposition 15 for a discussion).

NOTES

1. Let i index market segments, R_m denote the random return on the market portfolio, a_m the market price of risk, r the risk-free interest rate, and Z_i the vector of marketing policies for the ith segment ($i = 1, \ldots, I$). Then the random profit for the ith segment is $\pi_i = \alpha_i(Z_i, W_i) + \beta_i(Z_i, W_i)u_i + v_i$, where W_i denotes a vector of exogenous variables, α_i and β_i are known deterministic functions, $\text{Cov}(u_i, R_m) \neq 0$ in general, and v_i denotes firm-specific risk [i.e., $\text{Cov}(v_i, R_m) = 0$].

   Suppose the capital asset pricing model holds (i.e., the firm is owned by stockholders who can diversify risk by holding a portfolio of assets). Then the certainty-equivalent profit from segment i is

   $$V_i = \frac{\alpha_i(Z_i, W_i) + \beta_i(Z_i, W_i)[E(u_i) - a_m \text{Cov}(u_i, R_m)]}{(1 + r)}, \qquad i = 1, \ldots, I$$

   and the value of the firm is $V = \sum_{i=1}^{I} V_i$. Note that the V_is do not depend on the Z_js (for all $j \neq i$). Hence the firm can choose the marketing policy for each segment independently even though the profits are correlated across segments [i.e., $\text{Cov}(\pi_i, \pi_j) \neq 0$ for $i \neq j$].

   Suppose the owner(s) of the firm cannot diversify risk. Let U denote the appropriate utility function. Then the firm chooses the marketing policies $(Z_1, \ldots, Z_I)$ to maximize $EU(\sum \Pi_i)$. Consequently the firm must in general coordinate its marketing policies across segments. In two cases, however, the firm can choose the marketing policy for each segment separately even though profits are correlated across segments: (a) the firm is risk-neutral (formally this is a special case of the CAPM where $a_m = 0$), and (b) the firm's marketing policies do not affect the variabilities of the cash flows [i.e., $\pi_i = E(\pi_i) + a_i$, where the random terms a_i do not depend on the Z_is].

2. Suppose the firm introduces a product that is inherently new (i.e., the product provides a new set of consumer benefits). Then the firm must subjectively estimate the required risk-adjusted return on the new product.

3. Our analysis implicitly assumes that the firm is an oligopolist. If the firm operates in competitive markets, future unanticipated industry-wide shocks in demand and technology will not provide any option value because firms can enter or exit the industry without cost.

4. Wolinsky's competitive model (1983) assumes that fixed production costs are small relative to the size of the market and that the marginal cost of making products of a given quality is constant. Consequently, price is a sufficient signal and the separating equilibrium is "essentially unique" (Wolinsky 1983, p. 655). In most price signaling models, however, multiple separating equilibria exist (see, for example Bagwell and Riordan 1991); the standard approach is to select among equilibria using the "intuitive criterion" (see Cho and Kreps 1987).

   Firms typically choose among several signals including price, advertising, and product warranties. See Bagwell and Riordan (1991, pp. 224–26) for a succinct review of the signaling literature and Milgrom and Roberts (1986) for a multiperiod monopoly model in which the firm can use both price and advertising signals. In general, modeling is complicated when firms can use multiple signals; the difficulty arises because we may not be able to order firms completely by their incremental signaling costs (i.e., the rankings vary depending on the type of signal). In such cases, a separating equilibrium exists provided (roughly speaking) the relationship between the vector of marginal signaling costs and the value of the firm's product is decreasing and quasiconvex (see Engers 1987, Theorem 2).

We conclude that signaling theory is a promising approach for helping to resolve the debate whether firms that produce high-quality products earn positive risk-adjusted profits. Research is necessary to develop econometric methods to test signaling models in which firms use multiple signals; in addition, we need to develop theoretical models of imperfect competition that endogenize the firm's quality (i.e., product design) decision.

5. For any product category let i index brands, p denote price, and $x = (x_1, x_2, \ldots, x_k)$ the quality vector. Kalita, Jagpal, and Lehmann (1991) estimated the price-signaling model $p_i = f(x_{1i}, \ldots, x_{ki}) + u_i + v_i$, where $u_i \geq 0$ and v_i are independent stochastic disturbances. Kalita et al. used the maximum likelihood method to estimate the model for a large number of product categories using two distributional specifications for u_i (half-normal and exponential); the results were similar. Note that the hedonic regression model is nested in the signaling model ($u_i \equiv 0$). Hence Kalita et al. were able to use the standard log-likelihood approach to test whether the signaling effect u_i is significant.

6. The basic assumptions of the Black–Scholes (1973) options model are that (a) returns are normally distributed, (b) returns during separate times periods are not correlated, (c) returns have the same mean and standard deviation (risk) over any two time periods of equal length, and (d) traders are able to adjust their portfolios continuously without transaction costs. (See Duffie 1989, pp. 299–307 for a succinct discussion and Cox and Rubinstein 1985 for a detailed presentation.) As will be discussed in note 7, assumption (c) is problematic for marketing applications.

7. The fundamental difficulty in valuing marketing ("real") options is that the firm's marketing decisions impact the firm's cash flows. Our presentation draws on Dixit and Pindyck (1994, pp. 106–21) and uses their notation. Let u denote the firm's marketing decisions, x a vector of states describing the firm's current status, t time, and $\pi(x, u, t)$ the firm's instantaneous profit. For simplicity assume that x and u are scalars; generalization to the vector case is straightforward.

Most economic models use a continuous-time approach and assume that x evolves according to the Ito process $dx = a(x, u, t) + b(x, u, t) \, dz$, where a and b are known deterministic functions and dz is the increment of a standard Wiener process. That is, in continuous time $dz = \varepsilon_t \sqrt{dt}$, where ε_t is a normally distributed random variable with mean zero and standard deviation 1 and $\text{Cov}(\varepsilon_t, \varepsilon_{t+s}) = 0$ for $t \neq s$. Note that the firm's marketing policies affect both the firm's expected profit and the volatility of profit [i.e., the vector $\partial b(x, u, t)/\partial u$ depends on u]. Furthermore, the standard financial options model is a special case [$a \equiv 0$, $b \equiv 1$]. See Dixit and Pindyck (1994, pp. 112–14) for a discussion of the technical difficulties in modeling discrete jumps, e.g., the sudden arrival of a new competitor in the marketplace.

Two approaches are standard in valuing the continuous profit stream $\pi(x, u, t)$ and choosing optimal policy given flexibility. First, suppose the owners of the firm cannot diversify risk. Let U denote the appropriate utility function and ρ the subjectively chosen discount rate (usually assumed to be constant). Then policy is chosen to maximize $\int EU(x, u, t)e^{-\rho t} \, dt$ over a planning horizon. Second, suppose the firm is owned by stockholders and information is symmetric (i.e., investors know the firm's strategic marketing options). Then the stock market will correctly value the firm provided markets are complete (i.e., investors can replicate the risk and return characteristics of the firm's marketing options at all times by constructing suitable portfolios of existing traded assets including stocks, futures contracts, and risk-free assets). This assumption (also known as "spanning") can be problematic in valuing such strategic marketing options as the opportunity to introduce novel products into the marketplace. Note that introducing products with new attributes or a different combination of existing attributes does not violate the spanning conditions provided the set of consumer benefits remains unchanged; most new products are of this type. Only novel products that provide new consumer benefits will violate spanning.

8. This view is empirically supported by Brickley, Bhagat, and Lease (1985), who found that, on average, stockholders gained a 2 percent return when firms adopted long-term executive incentive plans.

9. This theory was proposed by Lewellen (1971) and has led to considerable debate in the finance literature (see Higgins and Schall 1975 and Galai and Masulis 1976).

10. Of the 223 mergers and acquisitions listed in the Federal Trade Commission report (1981), premerger financial data were only available for 156. In order to avoid data contamination due to multiple mergers, Christian and Jagpal (1988a,b) excluded those firms that had made another merger within five years of the identified merger. This reduced the sampling frame to 66 mergers; of these, 34 firms responded for a 52 percent response rate. Christian and Jagpal tested for self-selection bias; the results show that the sample was representative both in terms of the relative sizes of the merging firm and industry composition.

   In contrast to Christian and Jagpal, merger studies do not model expectations or the sources for takeover gains because of measurement error. We argue that confirmatory factor analysis (and more generally structural equation modeling) is a powerful tool for modeling these effects in merger studies. Applications of structural equation modeling in finance are rare (see, for example, Titman and Wessels 1988).

11. There is considerable debate whether mergers generate positive gains. See Brealey and Myers (1996, pp. 913–48, and in particular pp. 943–44) for a review of the mergers and acquisition literature. In contrast to the standard methodology in finance, Christian and Jagpal (1988b) attempt to distinguish the sources of takeover gains (for example, synergies from vertical integration or complementary marketing skills) and determine at what organizational level (corporate, divisional, or business unit) these gains occur.

12. In general, the firm must simultaneously consider parameter estimation and the choice of marketing policy. Consider the simple demand model $q = \beta_0 - \beta_1 p + \beta_2 A + u$, where q denotes demand, p is price, A is advertising, the β_is are unknown parameters, $E(u) = 0$, $\text{Cov}(p, u) = 0$, $\text{Cov}(A, u) = 0$, and u is a homoscedastic and serially uncorrelated disturbance term. Suppose the unit production cost, c, is constant. Then the firm's random profit is $\pi = (p - c)(\beta_0 - \beta_1 p + \beta_2 A + u)$. Let $\hat{\beta}_i (i = 0, 1, 2)$ denote the ordinary least squares (OLS) estimates and $\hat{\pi} = (p - c)(\hat{\beta}_0 - \hat{\beta}_1 p + \hat{\beta}_2 A)$, the corresponding profit for any marketing policy (p, A).

   Consider two scenarios. First, suppose the firm is risk-neutral. Then $E(\hat{\pi}) = E(\pi) = \bar{\pi}$ for any marketing policy because $E(\hat{\beta}_i) = \beta_i$ for all i. Hence the OLS estimator is optimal.

   Second, suppose the firm is risk-averse. Let $U(\pi)$ denote the firm's utility function, where $U''(\pi) < 0$ and the primes denote derivatives. Expanding $U(\pi)$ around $\bar{\pi}$ using a Taylor series, we have $U(\pi) = U(\bar{\pi}) + U'(\bar{\pi})(\pi - \bar{\pi}) + [U''(\pi)/2](\pi - \bar{\pi})^2 + R$. Assume that $R \simeq 0$. For all i let $\hat{\hat{\beta}}_i$ denote any arbitrary estimator of β_i, $\hat{\hat{\pi}}$ the corresponding point estimate of profit, $\sigma^2(\hat{\hat{\beta}}_i)$ the appropriate variances, and Cov the covariance operator.

   Then $U(\hat{\hat{\pi}}) = U(\bar{\pi}) + U'(\bar{\pi})(\hat{\hat{\pi}} - \bar{\pi}) + [U''(\bar{\pi})/2]\hat{\hat{Z}}$, where

$$\hat{Z} = (p-c)^2 [\sigma^2(\hat{\bar{\beta}}_0) + \sigma^2(\hat{\bar{\beta}}_1)p^2 + \sigma^2(\hat{\bar{\beta}}_2)A^2$$
$$- 2\text{Cov}(\hat{\bar{\beta}}_0, \hat{\bar{\beta}}_1)p + 2\,\text{Cov}(\hat{\bar{\beta}}_0, \hat{\bar{\beta}}_2)A - 2\,\text{Cov}(\hat{\bar{\beta}}_1, \hat{\bar{\beta}}_2)pA]$$

In particular, for the OLS estimator $U(\hat{\pi}) = U(\bar{\pi}) + U'(\bar{\pi})(\hat{\pi} - \bar{\pi}) + [U''(\bar{\pi})/2]\hat{Z}$, where

$$\hat{Z} = (p-c)^2 [\sigma^2(\hat{\beta}_0) + \sigma^2(\hat{\beta}_1)p^2 + \sigma^2(\hat{\beta}_2)A^2$$
$$- 2\,\text{Cov}(\hat{\beta}_0, \hat{\beta}_1)p + 2\,\text{Cov}(\hat{\beta}_0, \hat{\beta}_2)A - 2\,\text{Cov}(\hat{\beta}_1, \hat{\beta}_2)pA]$$

Taking expectations and subtracting, we have

$$EU(\hat{\bar{\pi}}) - EU(\hat{\pi}) = U'(\bar{\pi})[E(\hat{\bar{\pi}} - \bar{\pi}) - E(\hat{\pi} - \bar{\pi})] + \frac{U''(\bar{\pi})}{2}[E(\hat{\bar{Z}}) - E(\hat{Z})]$$

In practice, price and advertising are often highly correlated (e.g., the firm historically advertises heavily when it reduces price). Because of this multicollinearity problem, the OLS estimates are unstable [i.e., $E(\hat{\pi}) - \bar{\pi} = 0$, but the values of $\sigma^2(\hat{\beta}_i)$ are large for some i].

Recall that $U''(\pi) < 0$ for the risk-averse firm. Hence the firm may prefer to choose marketing policy using an estimator that provides more stable estimates than OLS [i.e., $E(\hat{Z}) > E(\hat{\bar{Z}})$] even though this estimator provides a biased estimate of expected profit [$E(\hat{\bar{\pi}} - \bar{\pi}) \neq 0$]; that is, the risk-averse firm chooses the statistical estimator and marketing policy based on the optimal tradeoff between parameter bias and parameter stability.

We argue that, because multicollinearity is endemic in marketing data and firms are risk-averse, the decision maker should use Bayesian methods (e.g., ridge and Stein-like estimators) instead of OLS to estimate model parameters and choose marketing policy. Standard statistical packages can be used to perform the analysis. See Judge, Hill, Griffiths, Lütkepohl, and Lee (1985, pp. 912–30) for a succinct but readable technical discussion of the statistical theory.

13. Note that this argument is based solely on the cost of capital and does not consider the expected cash flows from investments in different countries. Furthermore, the argument should not be pushed too far. For example, the major element in the systematic risk in any extractive industry (say copper) depends on worldwide demand, which in turn depends on the world economy. Consequently a multinational that sets up a copper-mining project abroad will not help its stockholders to reduce risk by diversifying across countries.

14. An empirical study on the international capital asset pricing model by Morgan Stanley Capital International (reported in Buckley 1996, pp. 402–3) finds that on average the international capital market is becoming increasingly integrated. There are, however, interesting outliers (for example, Australia, Hong Kong, and Singapore).

15. Suppose U.S. multinationals (say) have a cost-of-capital advantage. Then after correcting for size effects (U.S. multinationals are generally large), movements in the stock prices of U.S. multinationals should be more closely related to a world market index than to a U.S. market index. Furthermore, this correlation should be higher for those U.S. multinationals that have extensive international operations. The empirical evidence is conflicting (see Buckley 1996, pp. 397–99, for a review).

16. Our method combines the approach of Myers (1974) and the theory of real options. For the parent, the economic value added by the subsidiary is the combined value of the subsidiary's marketing options (C) and the subsidiary's adjusted present value (APV), which is the sum of the subsidiary's base-case net present value under all-equity financing (A) and the net present value of the subsidiary's tax shield due to debt (B). For any given country the discount rate used to compute A will exceed that used to compute B because equity income is more risky.

In designing country managers' compensation plans, the multinational must consider several factors. First, for any country, the country manager's decisions affect all three components of value (A, B, and C) to the parent; in particular, the marketing and financing decisions are interdependent. For example, in a single-period setting the country manager will coordinate debt and price policy; in a multiperiod setting he will adjust the subsidiary's future debt level based on past profitability. (Higher operating cash flows enhance the subsidiary's future "debt capacity." To the extent that the subsidiary's cash flows enhance the overall debt capacity of the multinational by stabilizing world cash flows, there will be an additional gain to the parent company. This effect is likely to be small unless the subsidiary accounts for a substantial proportion of the multinational's world investments.) Second, because of international capital market imperfections, the discount rates for equity and debt vary across countries. Third, tax rates and the economic value of marketing options also vary across countries.

Consequently the multinational should customize the country managers' compensation plans. For example, suppose that market risk is higher in industrialized countries (e.g., France) than in less developed countries (e.g., Thailand); marketing options, however, are more valuable in the latter. Then *ceteris paribus* compared to the Thailand country manager a higher proportion of the French country manager's expected income should be based on the French subsidiary's after-tax operating cash flow (component A) and a smaller proportion on deferred compensation based on the value of the French subsidiary's marketing options (component C).

In measuring economic value the multinational must measure the true economic profit to the parent; furthermore, the multinational must reward and measure the performance of country managers solely on the basis of those cash flows that those country managers control. These adjustments include cannibalization (one subsidiary increases its performance at the expense of another), netting (subsidiaries cancel out amounts owed with amounts due and settle for the difference), matching (a more general approach than netting because it involves third parties), leading and lagging (techniques that involve making an advance payment or delaying payments on amounts due and denominated in foreign currency), pricing policy (increasing prices to allow for expected changes in exchange rates), and asset and liability management (manipulating financial or marketing decisions to balance the currency of payments with the currency of inflows). In particular, items over which the country manager has no control (e.g., interest-rate subsidies to the parent by the host country) should be excluded from the compensation plan and performance measurement. See any standard text on multinational finance for details (for example, Buckley 1996, pp. 202–12).

As in the theory of the multidivisional domestic firm, transfer pricing poses particular difficulties for the multinational. Suppose, for tax or quota reasons, the parent inflates the transfer price paid by the subsidiary. Then the country manager will charge an excessively high price unless the multinational uses the correct transfer price (e.g., the arm's-length market price) to measure and reward performance.

17. If the parent chooses financial policy on a centralized basis, the present value of the tax shield from debt is not under the country manager's control. The parent's financing decision will, however, affect the country manager's marketing policy and hence the subsidiary's after-tax operating cash flow. Hence the parent should compensate the country manager only on the basis of the subsidiary's after-tax operating cash flow (A) and a deferred compensation plan that reflects the value of the subsidiary's strategic marketing options (C). In contrast to the case where the parent delegates both equity and debt financing decisions, the country manager's deferred compensation plan should be based on some long-term measure of the economic profit of the subsidiary and not on a stock option plan (unless the subsidiary accounts for a substantial proportion of the multinational's total investment).

18. Equilibrium theory suggests that currency fluctuations involve minimal systematic risk. Hence the multinational can separately analyze the project (nondiversifiable) risk of a subsidiary and the effects of inflation and currency fluctuations on stockholder wealth. International equilibrium theory argues that for any pair of countries the expected difference in inflation rates equals the expected change in the spot exchange rate (purchasing power parity), which in turn equals the difference in the nominal risk-free interest rates (the international Fisher effect). The purchasing power parity theory is only an approximation; furthermore, the empirical evidence is ambiguous whether the international Fisher effect holds even in the long run. Hence temporary disequilibria may occur. (See Buckley 1996, pp. 126–28, for a review of the empirical literature on foreign exchange market efficiency.) Consequently, the multinational may prefer to use its own expectations of differential inflation rates and foreign exchange fluctuations for international capital budgeting, designing the compensation plans of country managers, and measuring the performance of subsidiaries.

19. This approach abstracts from differential tax rates and competitive structures across countries, multiperiod issues (e.g., the product may be in the introduction phase of the brand life cycle in one country and in the maturity phase in another), transfer pricing problems due to tax or quota considerations, and differences in market risk across countries.

Conclusion

I hope I have persuaded the reader that the rigorous methodology developed in economics can be fruitfully applied in marketing. Particular care is necessary, however, to address the special problems that marketers face. These include the treatment of heterogeneity at different levels (for example, among consumers and retailers) and measurement error (an endemic problem in survey data), decision making in the presence of demand and cost uncertainty, and the need to choose policy in a multiproduct setting (generally referred to as "formulating strategy").

Managers must recognize that the standard assumption of perfect markets is a reasonable approximation in finance; the product market (the so-called "real" sector), however, is imperfect. Notwithstanding this fact, modern capital asset pricing theory is highly relevant for strategic decision making and, in particular, for choosing the appropriate reward structure at different levels in the firm's organizational structure.

New theories and empirical methods are necessary in marketing; it is not sufficient directly to "borrow" theories and statistical procedures developed in other disciplines. This book extends and integrates concepts gleaned from such fields as statistics, psychology, finance, and economics to develop theoretical and empirical models that are of particular relevance to the marketing manager. For example, we propose analytical and empirical methods for integrating the product design process and optimizing marketing decisions (standard techniques allow the manager to integrate product design and price but not advertising), designing compensation plans for the multilevel firm that is organized as a hierarchy, designing compensation plans that recognize that sales effort has dynamic and uncertain effects, choosing price and advertising policy in a dynamic environment under uncertainty, and determining the firm's optimal expenditure on sales training programs.

An important area that deserves increasing attention is how the firm should compensate managers both domestically and internationally (in the case of multinational firms), explicitly recognizing that the economic value of flexibility in decision making will become increasingly important as markets and technological change become more turbulent. As discussed in Chapter 9, standard managerial compensation contracts are inefficient because they do not factor in the economic value of the firm's future options (for example, a project which provides a negative net present value may be optimal if the economic value of future flexibility in decision making is sufficiently large).

Much remains to be done in the area of designing managerial contracts; in particular, we need to develop integrated models that use the insights from options theory (especially real options theory), agency theory, and game theory and more fully reflect marketing reality (for example, the facts that systematic market risk varies by market segment and that there may be an optimal sequence in which the firm should target market segments).

Finally, future research should focus on developing stochastic multiperiod game-theoretic models to understand the problems of choosing domestic and international strategy better. In order to more fully capture institutional reality, strategic marketing models should use multiperiod asset pricing models to explicate the relationship between the firm's marketing policy and the firm's performance measured by stock price and dynamic changes in stock price.

Aaker, David A., James M. Carman, and Robert Jacobson (1982), "Modeling Advertising–Sales Relationships Involving Feedback: A Time Series Analysis of Six Cereal Brands," *Journal of Marketing Research* **19**, February, 116–25.

Abel, Andrew B. (1990), "Consumption and Investment," in Benjamin Friedman and F. Hahn, Eds., *Handbook of Monetary Economics*, New York: North-Holland, pp. 726–78.

Agostini, Jean-Michael (1962), "Analysis of Magazine Accumulative Audience," *Journal of Advertising Research*, October, 24–27.

Akaike, H. (1974), "A New Look at Statistical Model Identification," *IEEE Transactions in Automatic Control* **AC**-19, 716–23.

Albright, S. Christian, and Wayne Winston (1979), "Markov Models of Advertising and Pricing Decisions," *Operations Research* **27**(4), July–August, 668–81.

Allais, M. (1988), "The General Theory of Random Choices in Relation to the Invariant Cardinal Utility Function and the Specific Probability Function," in Munier, B., Ed., *Risk, Decision and Rationality*, Dordrecht: Reidel, pp. 233–89.

Amemiya, Takeshi (1985), *Advanced Econometrics*, Cambridge, Massachusetts: Harvard University Press.

Anderson, Simon P., Andre de Palma, and Jacques-Francois Thisse (1992), *Discrete Choice Theory of Product Differentiation*, Cambridge, Massachusetts: MIT Press.

Bagozzi, Richard P. (1986), *Principles of Marketing Management*, Chicago, Illinois: Scientific Research Associates, Inc.

Bagwell, Kyle, and Michael H. Riordan (1991), "High and Declining Prices Signal Product Quality," *American Economic Review* **81**(1), 224–39.

Ben-Akiva, Moshe, and Steven R. Lerman (1985), *Discrete Choice Analysis: Theory and Application to Predict Travel Demand*, Cambridge, Massachusetts: MIT Press.

Berndt, Ernst R. (1991), *The Practice of Econometrics*, Reading, Massachusetts: Addison-Wesley.

Black, Fisher, and Myron Scholes (1973), "The Pricing of Options and Corporate Liabilities," *Journal of Political Economy* **81**, May–June, 637–54.

Bock, Hans-Herman (1996), "Probability Models and Hypotheses Testing in Partitioning Cluster Analysis," in P. Arabie, L.J. Hubert, and G. De Soete, Eds., *Clustering and Classification*, River Edge, New Jersey: World Scientific, pp. 377–453.

Bozdogan, H. (1987), "Model Selection and Akaike's Information Criterion (AIC): The General Theory and its Analytical Extension," *Psychometrika* **52**, 345–70.

Bozdogan, H. (1994), "Mixture-Model Cluster Analysis and Choosing the Number of Clusters Using a New Informational Complexity ICOMP, AIC, and MDL Model-Selection Criteria," in H. Bozdogan, S. L. Sclove, A. K. Gupta, D. Haughton, G. Kitagawa, T. Ozaki, and K. Tanabe, Eds., *Multivariate Statistical Modeling*, Dordrecht: Kluwer, Vol. II, pp. 69–113.

Brealey, Richard A., and Stewart C. Myers (1988), *Principles of Corporate Finance*, third edition. New York: McGraw-Hill.

Brealey, Richard A., and Stewart C. Myers (1996), *Principles of Corporate Finance*, fifth edition. New York: McGraw-Hill.

Brick, Ivan, and Harsharanjeet S. Jagpal (1981), "Monopoly Price–Advertising Decision-Making under Uncertainty," *Journal of Industrial Economics*, March, 279–85.

Brick, Ivan, and Harsharanjeet S. Jagpal (1984), "Utility Theory, Value Maximization and the Quality Decision under Uncertainty," *International Economic Review*, June, 369–77.

Brickley, James, Sanjai Bhagat, and Ronald C. Lease (1985), "The Impact of Long-Term Managerial Compensation Plans on Shareholder Wealth," *Journal of Accounting and Economics* **7**, April, 151–74.

Browne, Michael W., and Richard Cudeck (1989), "Single Sample Cross-Validation Indices for Covariance Structures," *Multivariate Behavioral Research* **24**, 445–55.

Browne, Michael W., and Richard Cudeck (1993), "Alternative Ways of Assessing Model Fit," in K. A. Bollen and J. S. Long, Eds., *Testing Structural Equation Models*, Newbury Park, California: Sage Publications, pp. 136–62.

Buckley, Adrian (1996), *Multinational Finance*, third edition. New York: Prentice Hall.

Bulow, J., J. Geanakoplos, and P. Klemperer (1985), "Multimarket Oligopoly: Strategic Substitutes and Complements," *Journal of Political Economy* **93**, 488–511.

Buzzell, Robert D., and Bradley T. Gale (1987), *The PIMS Principles: Linking Strategy to Performance*, New York: The Free Press.

Chandon, Jean-Luc (1976), "A Comparative Study of Media Exposure Models," Unpublished Doctoral Dissertation, Evanston, Illinois: Northwestern University.

Chandrashekaran, Rajesh, and Harsharanjeet S. Jagpal (1995a), "Measuring Internal Reference Prices: Some Preliminary Results," *Pricing Strategy and Practice: An International Journal*, **3**(4), 29–35.

Chandrashekaran, Rajesh, and Harsharanjeet S. Jagpal (1995b), "The Role of Involvement in the Formation and Use of Internal Reference Prices," Working Paper, Rutgers University.

Cho, In-Koo and David M. Kreps (1987), "Signaling Games and Stable Equilibria," *Quarterly Journal of Economics* **102**, May, 179–221.

Choi, S. Chan, and Harsharanjeet S. Jagpal (1995), "Duopoly Pricing under Risk Aversion and Parameter Uncertainty," Working Paper, Rutgers University.

Christian, Thomas A., and Harsharanjeet S. Jagpal (1988a), "Merger-Related Synergy: Its Meaning and Operationalization," Working Paper, Rutgers University.

Christian, Thomas A., and Harsharanjeet S. Jagpal (1988b), "Merger-Related Synergy: More Fiction than Fact," Working Paper, Rutgers University.

Clarke, Darral G. (1976), "Econometric Measurement of the Duration of Advertising Effects on Sales," *Journal of Marketing Research* **13**(4), November, 345–57.

Clarke, Frank H., Masako N. Darrough, and John M. Heineke (1982), "Optimal Pricing Policy in the Presence of Experience Effects," *Journal of Business* **55**(4), 517–30.

Constantinides, George M. (1978), "Market Risk Adjustment in Project Valuation," *Journal of Finance* **33**(2), May, 603–16.

Constantinides, George M. (1980), "Admissible Uncertainty in the Intertemporal Asset Pricing Model," *Journal of Financial Economics* **8**, 71–86.

Cox, J., and M. Rubinstein (1985), *Options Markets*, Englewood Cliffs, New Jersey: Prentice Hall.

Daganzo, Carlos (1979), *Multinomial Probit: The Theory and its Application to Demand Forecasting*, New York: Academic Press.

Dahm, Joanne M. (1994), "Implementing a New Sales Compensation Plan," in William Keenan, Jr., Ed., *Commissions Bonuses & Beyond*, Chicago, Illinois: Probus Publishing, pp. 175–92.

Dalrymple, Douglas J., and William L. Cron (1992), *Sales Management*, New York: Wiley.

Danaher, Peter J. (1988), "A Log-Linear Model for Predicting Magazine Audiences," *Journal of Marketing Research* **25**, November, 356–62.

Danaher, Peter J. (1989), "An Approximate Log-Linear Model for Predicting Magazine Audiences," *Journal of Marketing Research*, November, 473–79.

The Dartnell Sales Manager's Handbook (1989), Chicago, Illinois: Dartnell Corporation.

Dehez, P., and A. Jacquemin (1975), "A Note on Advertising Policy under Uncertainty and Dynamic Conditions," *Journal of Industrial Economics*, September, 73–78.

Dixit, Avinash K. (1986), "Comparative Statics for Oligopoly," *International Economic Review* **27**(1), 107–22.

Dixit, Avinash K., and Robert S. Pindyck (1994), *Investment under Uncertainty*, Princeton, New Jersey: Princeton University Press.

Duffie, Darrell (1989), *Futures Markets*, Englewood Cliffs, New Jersey: Prentice Hall.

Elrod, Terry and Michael P. Keane (1995), "A Factor-Analytic Probit Model for Representing the Market Structure in Panel Data," *Journal of Marketing Research*, February, 1–16.

Engers, Maxim (1987), "Signaling with Many Signals," *Econometrica* **55**(3), May, 663–74.

Eskin, G. J., and P. H. Baron (1977), "Effects of Price and Advertising in Test-Market Experiments," *Journal of Marketing Research*, November, 499–508.

Fama, E. F. (1980), "Agency Problems and the Theory of the Firm," *Journal of Political Economy* **80**, 288–307.

Fama, E. F., Lawrence Fisher, Michael Jensen, and Richard Roll (1969), "The Adjustment of Stock Prices to New Information," *International Economic Review* **10**, 1–21.

Federal Trade Commission (1981), *Statistical Report on Mergers and Acquisitions*, Washington, D.C.: Federal Trade Commission.

Forsund, Firn R., C. A. Knox Lovell, and Peter Schmidt (1980), "A Survey of Frontier Production Functions and of Their Relationship to Efficiency Measurement," *Journal of Econometrics* **13**, 5–25.

Fraser, C. (1980), *COSAN User's Guide*, Toronto: The Ontario Institute for Studies in Education.

Fudenberg, Drew, and Jean Tirole (1992), *Game Theory*, Cambridge, Massachusetts: MIT Press.

Fuss, Melvyn, Daniel McFadden, and Yair Mundlak (1978), "A Survey of Functional Forms in the Economic Analysis of Production," Chapter II.1 in Melvyn A. Fuss and Daniel McFadden, Eds., *Production Economics: A Dual Approach to Theory and Applications*, Amsterdam: North-Holland Press, pp. 219–68.

Galai, D. and R. W. Masulis (1976), "The Option Pricing Model and the Risk Factor of Stock," *Journal of Financial Economics* **3**, January–March, 53–81.

Gilboa, I. (1987), "Expected Utility with Purely Subjective Non-additive Probabilities," *Journal of Mathematical Economics* **16**(1), 65–88.

Glaister, Stephen (1974), "Advertising Policy and Returns to Scale in Markets Where Information Is Passed between Individuals," *Economica* **41**, May, 139–56.

Goodhardt, G. J., and A. S. C. Ehrenberg (1969), "The Duplication of Viewing between and within Channels," *Journal of Marketing Research* **6**, May, 169–78.

Gould, J. P. (1970), "Diffusion Processes and Optimal Advertising Policy," in E. S. Phelps et al., *Microeconomic Foundations of Employment and Inflation Theory*, New York: Norton Press, pp. 338–68.

Granger, C. W. J. (1969), "Investigating Causal Relations by Econometric Models and Cross-Spectral Methods," *Econometrica* **37**, May, 424–38.

Granger, C. W. J., and P. Newbold (1977), *Forecasting Economic Time Series*, New York: Academic Press.

Grant, S., A. Kajii, and B. Polak (1992), "Many Good Risks: An Interpretation of Multivariate

Risk and Risk Aversion without the Independence Axiom," *Journal of Economic Theory* **56**(2), 338–51.

Green, J. and B. Jullien (1988), "Ordinal Independence in Nonlinear Utility Theory," *Journal of Risk and Uncertainty* **1**(4), 355–88.

Green, Paul E., and V. Srinivasan (1978), "Conjoint Analysis in Consumer Research: Issues and Outlook," *Journal of Consumer Research* **5**, September, 102–23.

Green, Paul E., and V. Srinivasan (1990), "Conjoint Analysis in Marketing Research: New Developments and Directions," *Journal of Marketing* **55**(4), October, 3–19.

Guilkey, David, C. A. Knox Lovell, and Robin C. Sickles (1983), "A Comparison of the Performance of Three Flexible Functional Forms," *International Economic Review* **24**(3), October, 591–616.

Gul, F. (1991), "A Theory of Disappointment Aversion," *Econometrica* **59**(3), 667–86.

Hanssens, Dominique M., Leonard J. Parsons, and Randall L. Schultz (1990), *Market Response Models: Econometric and Time Series Analysis*, Boston, Massachusetts: Kluwer Academic Publishers.

Haugh, L. D. (1976), "Checking the Independence of Two Covariance-Stationary Time Series: A Univariate Residual Cross-Correlation Approach," *Journal of the American Statistical Association* **71**, June, 378–85.

Hausman, J. A. and D. McFadden (1984), "Specification Tests for the Multinomial Logit Model," *Econometrica* **52**, 1219–40.

Helson, Harry (1964), *Adaptation-Level Theory*, New York: Harper and Row.

Higgins, R. C., and L. D. Schall (1975), "Corporate Bankruptcy and Conglomerate Merger," *Journal of Finance* **30**, March, 93–114.

Hofmans, Pierre (1966), "Measuring the Cumulative Net Coverage of Any Combination of Media," *Journal of Marketing Research*, August, 269–78.

Holmström, Bengt (1979), "Moral Hazard and Observability," *The Bell Journal of Economics* **10**(1), Spring, 74–91.

Horowitz, Ira (1970), "A Note on Advertising and Uncertainty," *Journal of Industrial Economics* **18**, 151–60.

Hull, J. C. (1993), *Options, Futures and Other Derivative Securities*, second edition, Englewood Cliffs, New Jersey: Prentice Hall.

Hull, J. C., and A. White (1988), "The Use of the Control Variate Technique in Option Pricing," *Journal of Financial and Quantitative Analysis* **23**, 237–51.

Jagpal, Harsharanjeet S. (1982a), "Theory of Advertising in the Multiproduct Firm under Uncertainty," Working Paper, Rutgers University.

Jagpal, Harsharanjeet S. (1982b), "Static and Dynamic Advertising Policy under Uncertainty," Working Paper, Rutgers University.

Jagpal, Harsharanjeet S. (1982c), "Multicollinearity in Structural Equation Models with Unobservable Variables," *Journal of Marketing Research*, November, 431–39.

Jagpal, Harsharanjeet S. (1983a), "Optimal Sales Force Compensation Policy under Uncertainty: Part I," Working Paper, Rutgers University.

Jagpal, Harsharanjeet S. (1983b), "Optimal Sales Force Compensation Policy under Uncertainty: Part II," Working Paper, Rutgers University.

Jagpal, Harsharanjeet S. (1984), "The Theory of the Monopolist Facing Uncertain Input and Output Markets," Working Paper, Rutgers University.

Jagpal, Harsharanjeet S. (1986), "Simulation Studies Testing the Robustness of Structural Equation Preference Models," Rutgers University. (With contribution by Sonia Tewari.)

Jagpal, Harsharanjeet S. (1988), "A General Structural Equation Model for Estimating Preferences," Paper presented at TIMS-ORSA Conference, New York.

Jagpal, Harsharanjeet S. (1994), "Utility-Theoretic and Stock Market Duopoly Models of Advertising under Uncertainty," Working Paper, Rutgers University.

Jagpal, Harsharanjeet S., and Ivan E. Brick (1982), "The Marketing Mix Decision under Uncertainty," *Marketing Science*, Winter, 79–92.

Jagpal, Harsharanjeet S., and Baldwin S. Hui (1980), "Measuring the Advertising–Sales Relationship: A Multivariate Time Series Approach," in J. Leigh and C. Martin, Eds., *Current Issues and Research in Advertising*, Ann Arbor, Michigan: University of Michigan, Division of Research, pp. 211–28.

Jagpal, Harsharanjeet S., Kamel Jedidi, and Aradhana Krishna (1996), "A New Method for Identifying Latent Segments Using Product Bundling," Working Paper, Rutgers University.

Jagpal, Harsharanjeet S., Ephraim S. Sudit, and Hrishikesh D. Vinod (1982), "Measuring Dynamic Marketing Mix Interactions Using Translog Functions," *Journal of Business* **55**(3), 401–15.

Jedidi, Kamel, Harsharanjeet S. Jagpal, and Wayne S. DeSarbo (1997a), "STEMM: A General Latent Class Structural Equation Methodology," *Journal of Classification* **14**, 23–50.

Jedidi, Kamel, Harsharanjeet S. Jagpal, and Wayne S. DeSarbo (1997b), "Finite Mixture Structural Equation Models for Response-Based Segmentation and Unobserved Heterogeneity," *Marketing Science* **16**(1), 39–59.

Jedidi, Kamel, Harsharanjeet S. Jagpal, and W. S. DeSarbo (1992), "Latent Class Structural Equation Models for Marketing Research," Working Paper, Columbia University.

Jedidi, Kamel, Rajeev Kohli, and W.S. DeSarbo (1996), "Consideration Sets in Conjoint Analysis: A Method for Estimation and Market Share Simulation," Working Paper, Columbia University.

Jöreskog, Karl G. (1971), "Simultaneous Factor Analysis in Several Populations," *Psychometrika* **36**, 409–26.

Jöreskog, Karl G., and Dag Sörbom (1993), *LISREL 8*, New Jersey: Lawrence Erlbaum Associates.

Judge, George G. J., R. C. Hill, W. E. Griffiths, H. Lütkepohl, and T. C. Lee (1982), *Introduction to the Theory and Practice of Econometrics*, New York: Wiley.

Judge, George G. J., W. E. Griffiths, R. C. Hill, H. Lütkepohl, and T. C. Lee (1985), *The Theory and Practice of Econometrics*, New York: Wiley.

Kahneman, David, and Amos Tversky (1979), "Prospect Theory: An Analysis of Decision under Risk," *Econometrica* **47**, March, 263–91.

Kalish, Shlomo (1983), "Monopolistic Pricing with Dynamic Demand and Production Cost," *Marketing Science* **2**, March, 135–59.

Kalita, Jukti K., Harsharanjeet S. Jagpal, and Donald R. Lehmann (1991), "Price Signaling and Product Market Equilibrium: A New Empirical Methodology," Working Paper, Columbia University.

Kamakura, Wagner A., and Gary J. Russell (1989), "A Probabilistic Choice Model for Market Segmentation and Elasticity Structure," *Journal of Marketing Research* **26**, November, 379–90.

Kenny, David A., and C. M. Judd (1984), "Estimating the Nonlinear and Interactive Effects of Latent Variables," *Psychological Bulletin* **96**(1), 201–10.

Kirk, R. E. (1982), *Experimental Design*, second edition, Pacific Grove, California: Brooks/Cole.

Klein, B., and K. B. Leffler (1981), "The Role of Market Forces in Assuming Contractual Performance," *Journal of Political Economy* **89**, August, 615–41.

Kohli, Rajeev, and Vijay Mahajan (1991), "A Reservation-Price Model for Optimal Pricing of Multiattribute Products in Conjoint Analysis," *Journal of Marketing Research* **28**, August, 347–54.

Koku, Paul S., Harsharanjeet S. Jagpal, and P. V. Viswanath (1996), "The Impact of New Product Development Alliances on Stock Prices," Working Paper, Rutgers University.

Koku, Paul S., Harsharanjeet S. Jagpal, and P. V. Viswanath (1997), "The Effect of New Product

Announcements and Preannouncements on Stock Price," *Journal of Market Focused Management*, **2**(2), 183–99.

Kon, Yoshinori (1983), "Capital Input Choice under Uncertainty: A Putty-Clay Technology Case," *International Economic Review* **24**(1), 183–97.

Krugman, Herbert E. (1972), "Why Three Exposures May Be Enough," *Journal of Advertising Research* **12**, December, 11–14.

Lancaster, Kelvin J. (1966), "A New Approach to Consumer Theory," *Journal of Political Economy* **74**, 132–57.

Lawley, D. N., and A. E. Maxwell (1971), *Factor Analysis As a Statistical Method*, London, England: Butterworths.

Learning International (1989), "What Does Sales Force Turnover Cost You?" Stamford, Connecticut: Learning International.

Leckenby, John D., and Shizue Kishi (1982), "Performance of Four Exposure Distribution Models," *Journal of Advertising Research*, April/May, 35–44.

Leckenby, John D., and Marshall D. Rice (1985), "A Beta Binomial Network Exposure Model Using Limited Data," *Journal of Advertising* **3**, 25–31.

Leland, Hayne E. (1972), "Theory of the Firm Facing Uncertain Demand," *American Economic Review* **62**, June, 278–91.

Lewellen, W. G. (1971), "A Pure Financial Rationale for the Conglomerate Merger," *Journal of Finance* **26**, May, 521–37.

Lintner, John (1965), "The Valuation of Risk Assets and the Selection of Risky Investments in Stock Portfolios and Capital Budgets," *Review of Economics and Statistics* **47**, February, 13–37.

Little, John D. C. (1979), "Aggregate Advertising Models: The State of the Art," *Operations Research* **27**(4), July–August, 629–67.

Little, John D. C. and Leonard M. Lodish (1969), "A Media Planning Calculus," *Operations Research*, January–February, 1–35.

Luce, D. (1959), *Individual Choice Behavior: A Theoretical Analysis*, New York: Wiley.

Luce, R. and John W. Tukey (1964), "Simultaneous Conjoint Measurement: A New Type of Fundamental Measurement," *Journal of Mathematical Psychology* **1**, 1–27.

Machina, M. (1982), " 'Expected Utility' Analysis without the Independence Axiom," *Econometrica* **50**(2), 277–323.

Machina, M. (1983), "Generalised Expected Utility Analysis and the Nature of Observed Violations of the Independence Axiom," in B. Stigum and F. Wenstop, Eds., *Foundations of Utility and Risk with Applications*, Dordrecht, Holland: Reidel.

Machina, M. (1984), "Temporal Risk and the Nature of Induced Preferences," *Journal of Economic Theory* **33**, 199–231.

Mahajan, Vijay, and Eitan Muller (1986), "Advertising Pulsing Policies for Generating Awareness for New Products," *Marketing Science* **5**(2), Spring, 89–106.

Majd, Saman, and Robert S. Pindyck (1989), "The Learning Curve and Optimal Production under Uncertainty," *Rand Journal of Economics* **20**(3), 331–43.

Markowitz, Harry M. (1952), "Portfolio Selection," *Journal of Finance* **7**, March, 77–91.

Markowitz, Harry M. (1959), *Portfolio Selection: Efficient Diversification of Investments*, New York: Wiley.

McDonald, Roderick P., and E.J.A. Burr (1967), "A Comparison of Four Methods of Constructing Factor Scores," *Psychometrika* **32**, 381–401.

McFadden, Daniel (1978), "Modeling the Choice of Residential Location," in A. Karlquist et al., Eds., *Spatial Interaction Theory and Residential Location*, Amsterdam: North Holland, pp. 75–96.

McFadden, Daniel (1987), "Regression Based Specification Tests for the Multinomial Logit Model," *Journal of Econometrics* **34**, 63–82.

McFadden, Daniel (1989), "A Method of Simulated Moments of Discrete Response Variables without Numerical Integration," *Econometrica* **57**, 995–1026.

Metheringham, Richard A. (1964), "Measuring the Net Cumulative Coverage of a Print Campaign," *Journal of Advertising Research*, December, 23–28.

Milgrom, Paul, and John Roberts (1992), *Economics, Organization and Management*, Englewood Cliffs, New Jersey: Prentice Hall.

Milligan, Glenn W. (1980), "An Examination of the Effect of Six Types of Error Perturbation on Fifteen Clustering Algorithms," *Psychometrika* **45**, 325–42.

Milligan, Glenn W. (1996), "Clustering Validation: Results and Implications for Applied Analysis," in P. Arabie, L. J. Hubert, and G. De Soete, Eds., *Clustering and Classification*, River Edge, New Jersey: World Scientific, pp. 341–75.

Milligan, Glenn W., and M. C. Cooper (1988), "A Study of Variable Standardization," *Journal of Classification* **5**, 181–204.

Mirrlees, James (1974), "Notes on Welfare Economics, Information, and Uncertainty," in M. Balch, D. McFadden, and S. Wu, Eds., *Essays on Economic Behavior under Uncertainty*, Amsterdam: North Holland, pp. 243–57.

Miyamoto, J. M. (1988), "Generic Utility Theory: Measurement Foundations and Applications in Multiattribute Utility Theory," *Journal of Mathematical Psychology* **32**, 357–404.

Mossin, Jan (1966), "Equilibrium in a Capital Asset Market," *Econometrica* **34**, October, 768–83.

Mott, Thomas R. (1994), "Rewarding for Customer Satisfaction: It Just Might Be a Good Idea," in William Keenan, Jr., Ed., *Commissions Bonuses & Beyond*, Chicago, Illinois: Probus Publishing, pp. 97–113.

Moulin, Hervé (1986), *Game Theory for the Social Sciences*, New York: New York University Press.

Myers, Stewart C. (1974), "Interactions of Corporate Financing and Investment Decisions—Implications for Capital Budgeting," *Journal of Finance* **29**, March, 1–25.

Nerlove, Marc, and Kenneth J. Arrow (1962), "Optimal Advertising Policy under Dynamic Conditions," *Economica* **29**, 129–42.

Nguyen, D. (1987), "Advertising, Random Sales Response and Brand Competition: Some Theoretical and Econometric Implications," *Journal of Business* **60**(2), 259–79.

Ozga, S. (1960), "Imperfect Markets Through Lack of Knowledge," *Quarterly Journal of Economics* **74**, 29–52.

Patzer, Gordon L. (1991), "Multiple Dimensions of Performance for 30-Second and 15-Second Commercials," *Journal of Advertising Research*, August–September, 18–23.

Petty, Richard E., and John T. Cacioppo (1981), *Attitudes and Persuasion: Classic and Contemporary Approaches*, Iowa: William C. Brown.

Petty, Richard E., John T. Cacioppo, and David Schumann (1983), "Central and Peripheral Routes to Advertising Effectiveness: The Moderating Role of Involvement," *Journal of Consumer Research* **10**, September, 135–146.

Pierce, D. A., and L. D. Haugh (1977), "Causality in Temporal Systems: Characteristics and a Survey," *Journal of Econometrics* **5**, 265–93.

Pindyck, Robert S. (1985), "The Measurement of Monopoly Power in Dynamic Markets," *Journal of Law and Economics* **28**, April, 193–222.

Pindyck, Robert S. (1991), "Irreversibility, Uncertainty, and Investment," *Journal of Economic Literature* **29**, September, 1110–48.

Pindyck, Robert S. (1993), "Investments of Uncertain Cost," *Journal of Financial Economics* **34**, August, 53–76.

Posner, Barry (1977), "Improving the Selection Process: A Neglected Part of the Manager's Job," *Santa Clara Business Review* **8**, Summer, 71.

Pratt, John (1964), "Risk Aversion in the Small and in the Large," *Econometrica* **32**, 122–36.

Priemer, August B. (1989), *Effective Media Planning*, Massachusetts: Lexington Books, D. C. Heath and Company.

Quiggin, John (1982), "A Theory of Anticipated Utility," *Journal of Economic Behavior and Organisation* **3**(4), 323–43.

Quiggin, J. (1989), "Stochastic Dominance in Regret Theory," *Review of Economic Studies* **57**(2), 503–11.

Quiggin, J. (1993), *Generalized Expected Utility Theory: The Rank-Dependent Model*, Boston: Kluwer Academic Publishers.

Raiffa, Howard (1968), *Decision Analysis: Introductory Lectures on Choices under Uncertainty*, New York: Random House.

Ramsay, J. O. (1982a), *MULTISCALE II: Four Programs for Multidimensional Scaling by the Method of Maximum Likelihood*, Chicago: National Educational Resources.

Ramsay, J. O. (1982b), "Some Statistical Approaches to Multidimensional Scaling Data" (with discussion), *The Journal of the Royal Statistical Society, Series A* **145**, 285–312.

Richard, Scott F. (1975), "Multivariate Risk Aversion, Utility Independence and Separable Utility Functions," *Management Science* **22**(1), 12–21.

Ross, Stephen A. (1976), "The Arbitrage Theory of Capital Asset Pricing," *Journal of Economic Theory* **13**, December, 341–60.

Rubinstein, Mark (1974), "An Aggregation Theorem for Securities Markets," *Journal of Financial Economics* **1**, 225–44.

Rust, Roland T. (1986), *Advertising Media Models*, Massachusetts: Lexington Books, D. C. Heath and Company.

Rust, Roland T., and Jay E. Klompmaker (1981), "Improving the Estimation Procedure for the Beta Binomial TV Exposure Model," *Journal of Marketing Research*, November, 442–48.

Rust, Roland T., and Robert P. Leone (1984), "The Mixed-Media Dirichlet Multinomial Distribution: A Model for Evaluating Television–Magazine Advertising Schedules," *Journal of Marketing Research*, February, 89–99.

Sabavala, Darius A., and Morrison, Donald G. (1981), "A Nonstationary Model of Binary Choice Applied to Media Exposure," *Management Science* **27**(6), June, 637–57.

Sandmo, A. (1971), "On the Theory of the Competitive Firm under Uncertainty," *American Economic Review* **61**(1), March, 65–73.

Saris, W. E., W. M. de Pijper, and J. Mulder (1978), "Optimal Procedures for Estimation of Factor Scores," *Sociological Methods and Research* **7**, 85–106.

Sasieni, Maurice W. (1971), "Optimal Advertising Expenditure," *Management Science* **18**, December, B64–72.

Schmeidler, D. (1989), "Subjective Probability and Expected Utility Without Additivity," *Econometrica* **57**, 571–87.

Schmidt, P. (1976), "On Statistical Estimation of Parametric Frontier Production Functions," *Review of Economics and Statistics* **63**, 238–39.

Schonfeld, Eugene P., and John H. Boyd (1982), "The Financial Payoff in Corporate Advertising," *Journal of Advertising Research*, February–March, 45–55.

Schreiber, Robert J. (1969), "The Metheringham Method for Media Mix: An Evaluation," *Journal of Advertising Research* **9**, June, 54–56.

Schreiber, Robert J. (1974), "Instability in Media Exposure Habits," *Journal of Advertising Research* **14**(2), 13–17.

Schwarz, G. (1978), "Estimating the Dimensions of a Model," *Annals of Statistics* **6**, 461–64.

Segal, U. (1989), "Anticipated Utility: A Measure Representation Approach," *Annals of Operations Research* **19**, 359–74.

Sethi, Suresh P. (1977), "Dynamic Optimal Control Models in Advertising: A Survey," *SIAM Review* **19**, 685–725.

Sethi, Suresh P. (1979), "A Note on the Nerlove–Arrow Model under Uncertainty," *Operations Research* **27**(4), July–August, 839–42.

Sharpe, William F. (1964), "Capital Asset Prices: A Theory of Market Equilibrium under Conditions of Risk," *Journal of Finance* **19**, September, 425–42.

Sharpe, William F. (1977), "The Capital Asset Pricing Model: A 'Multi-Beta' Interpretation," in H. Levy and M. Sarnat, Eds., *Financial Decision Making under Uncertainty*, New York: Academic Press.

Shavell, Steven (1979), "Risk Sharing and Incentives in the Principal and Agent Relationship," *The Bell Journal of Economics* **10**(1), Spring, 55–73.

Silberberg, Eugene (1990), *The Structure of Economics: A Mathematical Analysis*, second edition, New York: McGraw-Hill.

Simon, Hermann (1982), "ADPULS: An Advertising Model with Wearout and Pulsation," *Journal of Marketing Research*, August, 352–63.

Sörbom, Dag (1974), "A General Method for Studying Differences in Factor Means and Factor Structures between Groups," *British Journal of Mathematical and Statistical Psychology* **27**, 229–39.

Swamy, P. A. V. B. (1970), "Efficient Inference in a Random Coefficient Regression Model," *Econometrica* **38**, 311–23.

Tapiero, Charles S. (1978), "Optimal Advertising and Goodwill under Uncertainty," *Operations Research* **26**(3), May–June, 450–63.

Thaler, R. (1985), "Mental Accounting and Consumer Choice," *Marketing Science* **4**, Summer, 199–214.

Tirole, Jean (1989), *The Theory of Industrial Organization*, Cambridge, Massachusetts: MIT Press.

Titman, Sheridan, and Roberto Wessels (1988), "The Determinants of Capital Structure Choice," *Journal of Finance* **43**(1), March, 1–19.

Titterington, D. M., A. M. F. Smith, and U. E. Makov (1985), *Statistical Analysis of Finite Mixture Distributions*, New York: Wiley.

Tversky, Amos (1972a), "Choice by Elimination," *Journal of Mathematical Psychology* **9**, 341–67.

Tversky, Amos (1972b), "Elimination by Aspects: A Theory of Choice," *Psychological Review* **79**, 281–99.

United Nations (1993), *World Investment Report of the Transnational Corporations and Management Decisions of the United States, Geneva*.

Vidale, H. L. and H. B. Wolfe (1957), "An Operations Research Study of Sales Response to Advertising," *Operations Research* **5**, 370–81.

Wakker, P., and Tversky, A. (1991), An Axiomatization of Cumulative Prospect Theory, Nijmegen, The Netherlands.

Wilson, Robert (1968), "The Theory of Syndicates," *Econometrica* **36**, January, 119–32.

Winsberg, Suzanne, and J. Douglas Carroll (1989), "A Quasi-Nonmetric Method for Multidimensional Scaling via an Extended Euclidean Model," *Psychometrika* **54**(2), 217–29.

Wolinsky, A. (1983), "Prices as Signals of Product Quality," *Review of Economic Studies* **50**, 647–58.

Yakowitz, S. J., and J. D. Spragins (1968), "On the Identifiability of Finite Mixtures," *Annals of Mathematical Statistics* **39**, 209–14.

Yellott, J. I. (1977), "The Relationship between Luce's Choice Axiom, Thurstone's Theory of Comparative Judgment, and the Double Exponential Distribution," *Journal of Mathematical Psychology* **5**, 109–44.

Zielske, Hubert A. (1959), "The Remembering and Forgetting of Advertising," *Journal of Marketing* **23**, January, 239–43.

SUBJECT INDEX